SURVEYS OF
AFRICAN ECONOMIES

SURVEYS OF AFRICAN ECONOMIES

VOLUME 1: CAMEROON, CENTRAL AFRICAN REPUBLIC, CHAD, CONGO (BRAZZA-VILLE), AND GABON. 1968.

VOLUME 2: KENYA, TANZANIA, UGANDA, AND SOMALIA. 1969.

VOLUME 3: DAHOMEY, IVORY COAST, MAURITANIA, NIGER, SENEGAL, TOGO, AND UPPER VOLTA. 1970.

SURVEYS OF
AFRICAN ECONOMIES

VOLUME 3: DAHOMEY, IVORY COAST, MAURITANIA,
NIGER, SENEGAL, TOGO, AND UPPER VOLTA

INTERNATIONAL MONETARY FUND
WASHINGTON, D. C.
1970

Preface

This third volume of the *Surveys of African Economies* is devoted to seven countries in Western Africa, namely, Dahomey, Ivory Coast, Mauritania, Niger, Senegal, Togo, and Upper Volta. The materials contained in this volume are based mainly on published sources, supplemented by data gathered by Fund missions from the Central Bank and national authorities, who have authorized their publication.

Since the seven countries share common interests and institutions, much of the information about them lends itself to a general analysis of these countries as a whole. Hence, in addition to an introduction, Chapters 2 through 6 deal with regional economic cooperation, development planning, money and banking, balance of payments, and exchange controls in the seven West African countries. Chapters 7 through 13 analyze recent economic developments in each of these countries.

The names of privately owned enterprises and organizations have not been translated into English in the text. Most government agencies that perform public functions, however, such as port authorities, ministries, and the Central Bank, as well as international agencies, are referred to in English. A listing of all these bodies, in both English and French, is given in the index. Abbreviations are used for a few organizations that are referred to frequently (for example, EEC for the European Economic Community, and CCCE for the French Caisse Centrale de Coopération Economique). These will also be found in the index, along with their full names. The metric system of weights and measures used in these countries has been used in this volume. Temperatures have been expressed in Fahrenheit. English equivalents are provided occasionally in parentheses; a full list of conversion factors is to be found on p. xxxvii.

This volume has been prepared under the direction of Mr. U Tun Wai, Senior Advisor in the African Department. The economists of the African Department who prepared the general chapters are Messrs. Pierre E. Berthe and Jean-Claude Eude (Balance of Payments), Moncef Guen (Regional Economic Cooperation), Gregory N. T. Hung (Development Planning), and Joseph E. Pegues (Introduction, and Money and Banking). Mr. J. H. C. de Looper, Advisor in the Exchange and Trade Relations Department, prepared the chapter on the Exchange System and the material on commercial policy in the chapter on Balance of Payments. Other staff members who made major contributions to the country chapters are Messrs. Naguib M. Abu-zobaa, George A. T. Donely, Paul A. Gibeault, Joachim W. Kratz, Manfred Reichardt, and Gyorgy Szapary, economists in the African Department, and Mrs. Maria O. Tyler, economist in the Exchange and Trade Relations Department. The volume has been edited by Mrs. Geniana R. Edwards and Miss O. Mary Price, and the maps have been prepared by Mr. Sergio Erazo, draftsman in the Graphics Section.

May 26, 1970

MAMOUDOU TOURÉ
Director, African Department
International Monetary Fund

CONTENTS

Page

Page

8 Ivory Coast (*continued*)

Tables (*continued*)

9 Mauritania *(continued)*

Tables *(continued)*

Page

Conversion Factors and Symbols Used in Volume 3

Exchange Rates

Unless indicated, conversions in this volume have been calculated at the rate before August 10, 1969.

Before August 10, 1969

246.853 CFA francs = 1.00 U.S. dollar
50 CFA francs = 1.00 French franc
4.93706 French francs = 1.00 U.S. dollar

August 10, 1969 and thereafter

277.710 CFA francs = 1.00 U.S. dollar
50 CFA francs = 1.00 French franc
5.55419 French francs = 1.00 U.S. dollar

Weights and Measures

1 meter = 3.28084 feet
1 kilometer = 0.621371 mile
1 square kilometer = 0.386102 square mile
1 hectare = 2.471054 acres
1 kilogram = 2.204623 pounds
1 metric ton = 2,204.6 pounds = 1.10231 short tons = 0.984207 long ton
Temperatures are given in Fahrenheit

In the Tables

A long dash (—) indicates zero or less than half the unit shown, or that the item does not exist
Dots (. . .) indicate that the data are not available

In the Tables and Text

A slash between years (1968/69) indicates a single fiscal or crop year
A short dash between years (1968–69) indicates a period of two or more years, though not necessarily calendar years
The word "billion" means 1,000 million

CHAPTER 1

Introduction

This volume discusses the economies of Dahomey, Ivory Coast, Mauritania, Niger, Senegal, Togo, and Upper Volta. Together, these countries cover a partly contiguous area of about 3.3 million square kilometers in the westernmost bulge of the African continent (see map on opposite page). Niger, which is about twice the size of France, is the largest of these countries and occupies nearly 1.2 million square kilometers, and Togo, the smallest, less than 0.06 million. The terrain ranges from the desert land of Mauritania and Niger through the savanna regions of Senegal and Upper Volta to the tropical rain forests of Ivory Coast, Togo, and Dahomey. Although Upper Volta and Niger are landlocked, the other five countries border the Atlantic Ocean.

The total population of the seven West African countries is estimated at 23 million. In 1969, none of these countries had more than 5.5 million inhabitants, ranging from about 1 million in Mauritania to 5.3 million in Upper Volta. Ivory Coast and Senegal are the most economically advanced countries in the region and have the highest level of urbanization. In Senegal, 27 per cent of the population lives in towns of more than 10,000 inhabitants, and in Ivory Coast 19 per cent, compared with an average of slightly more than 10 per cent for the area as a whole. Dakar, the capital and largest city in Senegal, has a population of about 600,000 and Abidjan (Ivory Coast), 500,000, compared with 80,000 in Niamey (Niger) and 100,000 in Ouagadougou (Upper Volta). In all seven countries, the per capita gross national product is less than US$200.

All these countries except Togo were part of the French West African Federation (Afrique Occidentale Française, or AOF) before their independence in 1959–60. Togo, on the other hand, was a United Nations Trust Territory under French administration. After becoming independent, they maintained special economic and financial relations with France and continued their association with the European Economic Community (EEC). Moreover, economic cooperation between the seven African states was developed, especially on an institutional basis. At present, these countries are members of the West African Monetary Union (Union Monétaire Ouest Africaine, or UMOA) and share a central bank, the Banque Centrale des Etats de l'Afrique de l'Ouest (BCEAO), which issues a common currency, the CFA franc; and some of them jointly participate in regional groups such as the Conseil de l'Entente and the West African Customs Union (Union Douanière des Etats de l'Afrique de l'Ouest, or UDEAO).

.   .   .   .   .   .

Although the economies of the seven countries are linked by a number of common institutional arrangements, progress toward full economic integration is hampered by inadequate transportation throughout the area. The present transport network (railways and main roads) generally extends from the hinterland to the coast (see first map after text). Therefore, the principal land communication links between the UMOA and neighboring countries are generally perpendicular to the coast. The transport system is such that facilities exist mainly within each subgroup of countries—Senegal-Mali-Mauritania, Ivory Coast-Upper Volta, and Togo-Dahomey-Niger. The transport network was originally designed primarily to serve overseas trade. Since the trade was essentially seaborne, this network increased the importance of ports (Dakar, Abidjan, and, to a lesser extent, Cotonou) and resulted in substantial transit trade within each subgroup of countries. Thus, the present pattern of land communications allows for little interstate traffic and does not serve the purpose of increasing intra-union trade or even, because of the lack of secondary and feeder roads, to expand domestic trade within each country. Moreover, some communication lines do not link the landlocked countries to the nearest outlet to the sea (e.g., Ghana for Upper Volta).

Before independence and within the framework of the former French West African Federation, Dakar was the center of the area's administrative and economic activity. Although strictly comparable national accounts data are not available, it appears that since independence the rate of real growth in gross domestic product (GDP) has nonetheless been greater in Ivory Coast, averaging some 6–8 per cent annually, than in Senegal or in the other UMOA countries.

The economies of the UMOA countries, mainly agricultural, are largely dependent on the production of one or two cash crops for export. According to available estimates, the share of agriculture, forestry, and fishing in GDP ranges from about 30 per cent in Ivory Coast to about 60 per cent in Niger. Manufacturing in the region is estimated to account for 6 per cent of over-all production. The major commodities produced for export are coffee and cocoa (mainly in Ivory Coast and on a much smaller scale in Togo), palm products (in Dahomey), bananas (mainly in Ivory Coast), and cotton and groundnut products (in almost all of the seven countries, but mainly Senegal and Niger). Since 1960, there has been an upward trend in both production and exports of these commodities. Their relative share in total export trade, however, has declined as a result of a rise in the export of timber products from Ivory Coast and minerals from Senegal, Togo, and Mauritania. The most important minerals produced in the area are iron ore, phosphates, and manganese. Among mineral exports, iron ore, exclusively from Mauritania and exported for the first time in 1963, has shown the most spectacular growth; iron ore exports rose from CFAF 10.6 billion in 1964, the first full year of production, to CFAF 17.5 billion in 1969. Production and export of other minerals also increased in this period, mainly because of expansion in Togo's exports of phosphates. Despite the rise in mineral exports, agricultural and forestry products still account for the largest share of exports from the UMOA countries.

All the UMOA countries have endeavored to diversify and broaden the base of their economies within the framework of development plans. In view of the predominance of agricultural activities throughout the area, the countries have generally emphasized two goals in formulating their development plans: (1) increased production of agricultural commodities for local consumption and export and (2) development of the secondary sectors (industry, mining, energy, and construction). Planned investments in these and related areas have been substantial and largely concentrated in the public sector, which is generally responsible for undertaking infrastructure projects and for development of the traditional agricultural sector. Private sector investments have been devoted primarily to mining, manufacturing, and processing industries.

.   .   .   .

In financing public sector investments, these countries have so far relied primarily on foreign aid and the mobilization of domestic savings through an improvement in the fiscal performance of the central governments and in the operations of publicly owned enterprises or financial institutions. While Mauritania and Niger have depended greatly on foreign aid to finance planned investments, Togo and Ivory Coast have been the most successful in mobilizing domestic resources. A number of factors account for the greater success of Togo and Ivory Coast in the mobilization of domestic savings. One has been the steady increase in foreign-controlled economic activity, which has broadened the revenue base. Another, no less important, has been the ability of their governments to restrain nonessential current expenditures so as to generate budgetary surpluses and in consequence release a larger share of revenue for investment. Senegal also has drawn on the accumulated foreign exchange reserves of its Treasury to finance public sector investments. Although other countries have attempted to mobilize domestic savings, the need for larger current budget expenditures in these countries has limited the contribution of public sector savings to their investment efforts.

The impact of planning on economic activity in the UMOA area has varied from one country to the other as they embarked on planning at different levels of economic development. This factor precludes a close comparison of their economic performance in postindependence years. Suffice it to say that, given the available resources, Ivory Coast seems to have made the greatest progress with a minimum of financial strain. In Mauritania, discovery and exploitation of minerals has also contributed substantially to economic development. Despite a comparatively high level of planned investments, Senegal has achieved little improvement in its economy, remaining heavily dependent on the earnings from the export of groundnuts, which have steadily declined in price on the world market. Many Senegalese industries, originally created to serve all of French West Africa, have found themselves with an excess capacity and accordingly have had to adjust their operations to a much smaller market. Although Upper Volta is poorly endowed with natural resources, the Government has tried through planning to stimulate economic growth, which, since independence, has barely kept pace with increases in the population. The broad objective of the Government's development effort is to encourage the productive sectors of the economy and to limit expansion in current budget expenditures that would follow enlarged social services.

Development expenditure and increasing outlays for current operations have resulted in persistent budgetary deficits in the UMOA area and a consequent strain on the government treasuries. The degree of strain, however, has varied from one country to the other; Dahomey and Upper Volta have incurred the largest deficits in relation to government revenue. The over-all budgetary deficits in UMOA countries have been financed mainly by foreign loans and grants and in some countries by the use of treasury reserve funds and other savings of the public sector. Although government revenue in the UMOA area has risen rapidly, the rate of increase in total expenditure has been higher.

The increase in ordinary budget expenditure has been necessitated by new services relating to representation abroad, defense expenditures, postal service, and telecommunications—expenditures previously borne by France. Expenditure has also risen with expansion in administrative machinery, higher wages and salaries, and the need to subsidize new public and semipublic enterprises.

The largest share of ordinary budget revenue in the UMOA countries comes from tax receipts; nontax revenue, such as receipts derived from government property and charges for services rendered by the government, account on average for about 8 per cent of government revenue. Indirect taxes, mainly import and export taxes, constitute the major source of government tax receipts. These taxes yield about three to four times the revenue collected from direct taxes, partly because of the importance of foreign trade, which can be taxed with relative ease, and partly because of the administrative difficulties in assessing and collecting direct taxes in economies characterized by a small monetized sector (where goods are exchanged for cash in lieu of barter), low per capita income, and the lack of adequate fiscal administrative machinery.

The tax burden, judged either by the ratio of tax revenue to GDP or by per capita tax receipts, differs throughout the area, owing in part to differences in the size of the monetized sector and the relative importance of foreign trade. The ratio of tax revenue to GDP is highest in Senegal and lowest in Togo.

In recent years, efforts have been made to redress the deteriorating fiscal situation in Dahomey and Upper Volta, the two countries which have encountered the most serious budgetary problems. Measures taken by the Government of Upper Volta since 1966 have proved effective and have achieved their immediate objectives. Chronic budget deficits have been eliminated, and most of the recorded payments arrears have been liquidated. Measures taken by Dahomey have only moderately improved its fiscal performance.

. . . .

The fundamental features of the monetary arrangements between UMOA countries are the guarantee of the parity and of convertibility of the CFA franc into French francs by the French Treasury and the prudent policies to be pursued by the BCEAO's Executive Board. Convertibility of the CFA franc is assured through the mechanism of an operations account maintained by BCEAO with the French Treasury. BCEAO keeps its foreign exchange reserves on deposit in the operations account and has unlimited overdraft facilities. The Central Bank, however, has not incurred a debit balance on its operations account with the French Treasury. In fact, except for a decline in 1963 and

1964, the level of gross foreign reserves generally increased in the 1960's. Pooling of foreign reserves provides member countries in balance of payments difficulties with an immediate source of financing which reduces the need for abrupt changes in monetary and fiscal policies and the need for reliance on import and exchange restrictions.

In line with the area's development effort, the combined money supply of the UMOA countries has expanded at a steady pace since the creation of the present Central Bank in 1962. The bases for the increase in money supply have been the steady rise in the BCEAO's foreign assets and an expansion in both credit to the government and private sector. The rise in the BCEAO's foreign reserves resulted mainly from a substantial inflow of foreign aid and, for some of the countries concerned, the satisfactory performance of exports related partly to the preferential markets in France and other EEC countries. These developments, combined with the relatively liberal system of trade and exchange controls, have ensured adequate supplies of imported goods, which have helped to maintain the stability of prices and wages. Prices have risen only moderately in the last several years, and the upward adjustments of wages have been no larger than the increases in the cost of living associated with the higher prices of imported goods and the increase of import duties.

In the 1960's, Ivory Coast, Togo, and Upper Volta were the principal contributors to the rise in external reserves of the BCEAO area. Since 1962, the official reserves of these countries have increased by an average of about CFAF 2.7 billion annually. This rise, however, has been offset by a decline in the reserves of the other countries with the consequence that the total official reserves of the UMOA have risen by an average of only CFAF 0.6 billion annually.

Owing mainly to developments in Ivory Coast and Senegal, which together account for about 80 per cent of private sector credit, total private sector credit in the BCEAO area has increased at a compound rate of about 6 per cent annually since 1963. In almost all BCEAO countries, private sector credit follows a distinct seasonal pattern, coinciding with the financing of the main agricultural crops. However, since agricultural seasons differ from one country to another, the peaks and troughs partly offset each other, making the amplitude of seasonal variations for the area as a whole smaller than that in some of the member countries.

The principal instrument of credit policy in the BCEAO area is rediscount ceilings. Use of this device has been facilitated by the reliance of commercial and development banks on central bank rediscounts to finance their credit operations. Judicious use of the rediscount ceiling as an instrument of credit control by BCEAO, together with moral suasion, has been beneficial to the UMOA economies. To meet the eligibility requirements for use of BCEAO's rediscount facilities, enterprises have endeavored to rationalize their operations. Moreover, as a consequence of encouraging branches or subsidiaries of foreign concerns to exploit foreign sources of financing before resorting to the use of credit financed by BCEAO rediscounts, there has been some additional inflow of foreign capital.

Commercial banking activity has developed along similar lines in each BCEAO country since independence. The commercial banks in all seven countries engage almost exclusively in short-term credit operations, mainly to finance foreign trade. Medium-term and long-term credit is of little significance and is normally extended only if the debtor complies with the Central Bank's requirements for rediscounting.

In addition to the commercial banks, development banks have been established in all BCEAO countries in the years following the attainment of independence. Usually, the national government is the main shareholder in the capital of these banks. Other shareholders include the Caisse Centrale de Coopération Economique (CCCE), a French agency; the Central Bank; and foreign banking institutions. Though the activities of the development banks in all the countries have grown steadily in recent years, the sectoral distribution of their credits has been rather uneven; the greater proportion of credit extended by them has been used to finance housing construction and the marketing of crops, particularly in Senegal and Niger.

During 1964 and 1965, all BCEAO countries enacted new commercial banking legislation, replacing preindependence regulations, which had consisted of legislation similar to that in France, and an intrabank agreement regulating interest rates. Based on guidelines set up by BCEAO, the new legislation is practically uniform throughout the UMOA area. In addition to a number of formal provisions regarding the banking profession, the new legislation fixes solvency ratios to be maintained by the banks and sets limitations on mixed banking. Moreover, the legislation established a new schedule of interest rates to be charged by the banks on credit for various purposes. In contrast to previous provisions under the intrabank agreement, the new interest rates are related primarily to the nature of the project being financed, instead of to the creditworthiness of the borrowing enterprise. The new rates are generally lowest for projects of primary importance to economic development.

.   .   .   .

The preferential arrangements for French imports in the BCEAO countries were initially maintained after these countries became independent but were gradually extended to the other EEC countries in accordance with the EEC's association arrangements. However, some imports from all sources, including France and other EEC countries, have become subject to restrictions imposed for protective reasons. One of the goals of the association of the BCEAO countries with EEC is to encourage the expansion of trade by the establishment of free trade area arrangements.

Under the first Yaoundé Convention of Association of African and Malagasy States with EEC, effective on June 1, 1964, all EEC members eventually received equal tariff treatment in the BCEAO countries, since imports from the EEC countries became exempt from customs duties (though not from fiscal taxes) in countries where such duties were applied. Moreover, quantitative restrictions on imports from EEC countries other than France were gradually removed. Customs duties levied by the EEC countries on imports from the CFA countries were reduced while a common external tariff applicable to imports from third countries was being established.

The Convention provided for a gradual elimination of French support prices for commodities imported from the CFA countries except for bananas. Therefore, French price support for groundnut products, the last commodities to receive this support from France, was terminated at the end of 1967. In order to facilitate the abolition of these French price supports, the first Yaoundé Convention provided for financial aid to agricultural production and diversification in associated countries for the duration of the Convention (i.e., until May 31, 1969). EEC aid to agricultural production consisted of programs for increasing productivity and for paying price subsidies on certain crops, mainly groundnuts and cotton. The price subsidies declined progressively until they were eliminated in mid-1969. Starting in 1967, the EEC's price support to agricultural exports of the CFA countries was extended by a new stabilization scheme applicable to exports of oil and oilseeds and aiming at cushioning the effects of major declines in world prices on export receipts of associated countries.

A second Yaoundé Convention, signed on July 29, 1969, will enter into force after ratification by all parties concerned. It is to have a duration of five years but is to expire no later than January 31, 1975. The structure of the new Convention is basically the same as that of its predecessor; however, its content has been changed, in part substantially, on specific points. Some of the changes incorporated into the second Yaoundé Convention are as follows: (1) the EEC's common external tariff has been lowered for a number of tropical products (coffee from 9.6 per cent to 7.0 per cent, cocoa from 5.4 per cent to 4.0 per cent, and palm oil from 9 per cent to 6 per cent); (2) aid to production in the form of price support has been abandoned; (3) a new form of aid, intended to cope with exceptional situations, permits ad hoc intervention, case by case, especially if a fall in world prices should seriously jeopardize the economy of an associated country; (4) wider freedom has been given to associated trade areas and economic cooperation agreements have been widened; (5) the Community has indicated readiness to waive application of the most-favored-nation clause when regional cooperation between the associated states and other African countries is involved; and (6) the right of associated states to protect local industries, in particular new industries, has been increased. EEC grants and loans to the 18 associated African states, including the UMOA countries, and Madagascar will be increased from US$730 million to US$918 million, or by 26 per cent. Although grants, totaling US$748 million, still constitute the larger share of EEC assistance to associated states, loans to these countries will be increased to US$170 million, or by 54 per cent.

Exchange regulations in the UMOA countries are patterned on those of France and are adjusted by their governments to local conditions and requirements. Generally speaking, while imports from the franc area and from EEC countries have been liberalized, imports from other countries are subject to licensing within the framework of an annual import program. Normally, however, licenses for such imports are issued liberally. In line with changes in the exchange regulations in France and other operations account countries, the UMOA exchange system was further liberalized on July 1, 1967, when exchange control was abolished and special capital controls were introduced. In mid-1968, the UMOA countries re-established temporary exchange controls but abolished them again by the end of September 1968. Following similar action taken by France, the UMOA countries in November 1968 reinstated controls on current and capital payments to countries other than France, Monaco, and countries maintaining an operations account with the French Treasury. Generally, however, these controls did not restrict current payments other than those in respect of travel.

.   .   .   .

Prospects for continued economic growth in the UMOA area appear to be favorable. The somewhat more favorable prospects of Ivory Coast are due mainly to the substantial expansion and diversification of its agricultural exports and, during the early years of independence, to the establishment of processing and manufacturing industries, with the aid of considerable foreign investment and the inflow of manpower from abroad. This early development, reinforced by the relative stability and pragmatic policies followed by the authorities in monetary and fiscal matters, provided a firm basis for sustained economic growth. While development in the other six countries has been less pronounced, indications are that, with the resolution of certain structural and financial problems, the future holds promise for them as well. Continued evolution of the present monetary arrangements and the relatively liberal and basically uniform system governing trade and payments are likely to produce additional advantages for the area in the future. These advantages, together with an intensification of regional economic cooperation which has already begun, even with countries outside UMOA, will go a long way toward facilitating economic development in the area.

CHAPTER 2

Regional Economic Cooperation

EARLY COOPERATION

BEFORE INDEPENDENCE

Before 1960 the territories forming the French West African Federation (Afrique Occidentale Française, or AOF),[1] established in 1895, had achieved a remarkable degree of integration.[2] AOF had constituted a customs union providing free movement of goods and services between the territories; it had also adopted a common external tariff.[3] Since 1904, AOF had maintained a general budget in addition to the territorial budgets. The Banque de l'Afrique Occidentale, a commercial bank, was the common bank of issue until 1955, when the right of issue was transferred to a new, publicly owned institution, the Institut d'Emission de l'Afrique Occidentale Française et du Togo. On April 4, 1959 the name of this institution was changed to the Banque Centrale des Etats de l'Afrique de l'Ouest (BCEAO). Attainment of independence in 1960 jeopardized the integration previously achieved. Conscious of the unifying factors such as language, education, and transportation that still linked them, the former AOF members, except for Guinea, decided to set up a number of common arrangements and institutions to promote mutual economic cooperation.

FORMER WEST AFRICAN CUSTOMS UNION [4]

One of the arrangements considered to be the most promising for economic cooperation was a customs union. On June 9,. 1959, Dahomey, Ivory Coast, Mali, Mauritania, Niger, Senegal, and Upper Volta signed a convention establishing the first West African Customs Union (Union Douanière entre les Etats de l'Afrique Occidentale, or UDAO), intended to maintain the customs union regime in effect before independence and to harmonize import taxation among member countries. Although the French Community provided for the absence of customs duties and quantitative restrictions on goods in trade between its member countries, it did not call for the elimination of other duties and taxes.

The two-tier tariff comprising both customs and fiscal duties was an important feature of the UDAO tariff structure. Customs duties were levied for fiscal as well as protective purposes but were not applicable to imports from France. They also varied between goods imported from countries receiving most-favored-nation treatment (goods subject to the minimum tariff) and goods imported from other countries (goods subject to the general tariff, usually three times as high as the minimum tariff). The general tariff was applied to only a few countries, including Japan and Portugal. The revenue nature of fiscal duties was more clear cut since the duties do not differentiate as to the origin of imports (thus, they were applied also to imports from France). In addition, there usually were certain surcharges (e.g., statistical tax, and examination,

---

[1] Dahomey, Guinea, Ivory Coast, Mali, Mauritania, Niger, Senegal, and Upper Volta. Togo was administered by France under UN trusteeship.

[2] Cf. Roland Julienne, "The Experience of Integration in French-Speaking Africa," in *African Integration and Disintegration,* Arthur Hazlewood, ed. (New York, 1967), Chapter 9.

[3] Togo, however, owing to its special status, had applied fiscal duties to imports from Federation territories; Togo's single-column tariff does not provide for customs duties.

[4] Mali is included in this chapter as it is a member of the West African Customs Union.

sealing, and warehouse fees) and a turnover tax on import transactions. This last tax, which varied from one country to another, was levied on the c.i.f. value of imports plus all import taxes (customs, fiscal, and others), including the turnover tax itself.

Member countries differ as to the composition of duties and taxes on imports. For example, Ivory Coast does not levy a statistical tax but levies a special import duty, in addition to customs and fiscal duties. Upper Volta levies a temporary development tax of 10 per cent of the c.i.f. value of imports and a stamp duty of 3 per cent of the c.i.f. value of imports. Dahomey levied a stamp duty of 3 per cent of total duties and taxes on imports before the tariff reform on June 1, 1967 which consolidated all import levies.

Principal Objectives

Many essential characteristics of a customs union were present in the objectives of the UDAO convention, particularly absence of tariff and nontariff barriers between the partners, establishment of a common external tariff, and harmonization of tax legislation in member countries.

(1) The 1959 convention stipulated that UDAO members should not levy customs or fiscal duties on trade with other members (Article 1). This provision should be considered against the background that duties and taxes on imports have been by far the largest single source of government revenue in these countries, partly because foreign trade can be taxed more easily than other sectors and partly because direct taxes are difficult to collect in economies with relatively limited monetized sectors and weak fiscal machinery. Between 1964 and 1966, proceeds from duties and taxes on imports accounted for about 60 per cent of total tax receipts in Dahomey, Ivory Coast, and Upper Volta; 45 per cent in Senegal; 40 per cent in Mali; 34 per cent in Niger; and 33 per cent in Mauritania (Table 1). In the same period, the ratio of revenue from duties and taxes on imports to the value of total imports was estimated at 47 per cent in Upper Volta; 39 per cent in Dahomey; 35 per cent in Ivory Coast, Mali, and Senegal; 28 per cent in Niger; and 27 per cent in Mauritania.

(2) The establishment of a common external tariff extended to both customs and fiscal duties levied by the member countries. Imports from

TABLE 1. UDEAO COUNTRIES: RELATIVE IMPORTANCE OF RECEIPTS FROM
IMPORT DUTIES [1] AND TAXES,[2] 1964–66

| | Import Duties[1] and Taxes[2] as a Per Cent of | | | | | |
| | Tax receipts | | | Imports | | |
	1964	1965	1966	1964	1965	1966
Dahomey	60.4	66.0	57.9	37.0	38.6	40.3
Ivory Coast	59.7	62.0	63.4	34.0	34.5	37.3
Mali	51.0	35.6	37.6	36.3	29.1	41.4
Mauritania	41.2	30.2	29.5	36.8	21.3	22.8
Niger	27.1	36.3	38.7	30.6	26.1	26.4
Senegal	47.2	46.2	44.1	37.8	35.7	35.0
Upper Volta	60.5	63.8	. . .	45.8	50.0	. . .

Source: Data provided by UDEAO countries.

[1] Fiscal and customs duties.

[2] Import turnover tax, and statistical and other surcharges on imports.

nonmember countries were made subject to a common customs tariff.
Fiscal duties in effect on March 31, 1959 and applied to imports from
nonmember countries were to be maintained, and all parties to the convention were to agree on any modification or introduction of new
duties. This provision precluded any member from changing the level or
structure of its import taxes without prior concurrence of all other partners (Article 1).

(3) The UDAO convention provided for a Committee of Experts to
study the harmonization of the laws and regulations on internal taxes,
in order to prevent illicit trade between the member countries (Article 3). This Committee was also entrusted with undertaking studies on
other matters designed to facilitate the implementation of the convention, particularly problems of double taxation and tax evasion. Measures dealing with such problems could be embodied in multilateral or
bilateral agreements to be worked out by the interested parties. The
convention did not specifically call for coordination of investment policies or for the adoption of similar investment regulations; but this
objective was partly implied in the expected harmonization of the fiscal
systems.

Functions

Procedure for revenue transfers.—The 1959 convention stated that
receipts from import and export taxation should be distributed in a
manner so as to give each country its appropriate share (Article 2).

Joint commissions were to be set up in two or several member states for determining the distribution of receipts on the basis of customs declarations, investigations among traders, and other relevant elements of estimation. Disbursement of receipts was to be made quarterly.

Arrangements were worked out between member countries for a system of sharing proceeds from duties and taxes on imports. Senegal and Mauritania had an arrangement whereby such proceeds were distributed on the basis of 91.38 per cent for the former and 8.62 per cent for the latter. Similar arrangements existed between Ivory Coast and Upper Volta and between Dahomey and Niger.

However, the sharing procedure adopted by the UDAO countries proved to be complex and time consuming. First, the 1959 convention did not settle the problem of origin of goods or define the goods originating within the UDAO area. Second, goods originating in nonmember countries were subject to taxation and reimbursement each time they crossed country boundaries within the UDAO area. Third, various regulations infringed upon the importers' freedom to choose points of entry and forced them to fractionate their imports according to countries of final destination.

Common institutions.—The UDAO convention provided for the establishment of several common institutions with a view to settling problems arising from the implementation of the customs union (Articles 2–6). Apart from the joint commissions which were to determine the distribution of revenue from import and export duties and taxes and apart from the Committee of Experts which was to study fiscal harmonization, the convention established a Customs Union Committee vested with decisionmaking powers (Article 5). It was composed of one representative from each member state, and its decisions were binding on all parties. The Customs Union Committee was to make decisions on important matters, such as the distribution of revenue collected from import and export duties and taxes and the proposals for fiscal harmonization submitted by the Committee of Experts. Disputes arising from implementation of the customs union could be brought before the Court of Arbitration of the French Community (Article 6).

Problems of Implementation

UDAO failed to achieve a full customs union mainly for two reasons: (1) its goals were overambitious under the prevailing circumstances and (2) the procedures and unifying machinery were complicated and weak.

Except for the establishment of a common customs tariff in all UDAO countries, none of the goals of the 1959 convention was achieved. According to the 1959 convention, the customs union was expected to be realized immediately, not through evolutionary steps. Furthermore, it was foreseen that a common external tariff could be created consisting not only of customs duties but also of fiscal duties and other related taxes. However, differentiated structure of fiscal duties and other related taxes continued to be maintained. The 1959 convention made it difficult for any member to increase tax receipts from its major revenue source, import taxes, to obtain the revenue needed to match the fast growth of government expenditures in the post-independence era. Actually, in the early years of independence, each member country did modify its fiscal duties in accordance with its own financial needs. The base of fiscal duties was broadened, rates were raised, and excise taxes were increased. Besides, products originating in member countries were subjected to fiscal duties, beginning in 1962 (Decree 53/UD/62 of the Customs Union Committee).

No progress was made in fiscal harmonization. The 1959 convention did not provide for adequate consultation between its member states. The single body vested with collective decisionmaking, the Customs Union Committee, seemed to be too supranational and powerful to allow for a flexible and realistic approach. Unlike the Equatorial Customs Union established in the same year,[5] UDAO did not call for varied and permanent institutions such as a general secretariat, an executive committee, and a council of heads of state or of ministers.

In the absence of adequate permanent institutions, UDAO members could find no way to simplify the procedure of revenue distribution, set up common customs services for collection of import and export taxes, and resolve problems which were not covered by the 1959 convention. For example, the convention did not address itself to the problem of regionally balanced development. In May 1959 a Solidarity Fund was created to transfer to certain countries part of government revenue

_____

[5] See *Surveys of African Economies*, Vol. 1, 1969, pp. 8–13.

raised in other more advanced countries, but this fund was established within the Entente Council outside the framework of the customs union.[6] Each member state was to pay one tenth of its government receipts to the Solidarity Fund; one fifth of the total was to be held in a reserve, and the rest was to be distributed among member states in inverse proportion to their contribution.

Finally, the convention did not settle the problem of origin of imported goods and did not introduce the system of the single tax operating in the Equatorial Customs Union. In the face of these disappointing results, UDAO member countries met in Paris in 1966 to seek a better solution.

FORMATION OF THE PRESENT WEST AFRICAN CUSTOMS UNION

The result of the Paris meeting in 1966 was the signing of a new convention, establishing, with effect from December 15, 1966, the present West African Customs Union (Union Douanière des Etats de l'Afrique de l'Ouest, or UDEAO). While the Central African countries transformed their customs union into a broader economic union in 1966, the West African countries transformed their customs union into a much looser customs grouping.

ESSENTIAL CHANGES INTRODUCED BY UDEAO

Scope

The UDEAO convention does not provide for a complete customs union (Article 1). Taking into consideration the evolution of tariff legislation in each country, it maintains the common customs duty and calls only for a further harmonization of legislation on other import and export taxation (Article 2). It excludes any tariff concessions below the minimum tariff on goods imported from countries outside UDEAO

---

[6] Togo became a member of the Entente Council (Conseil de l'Entente) on June 8, 1966 but did not join UDAO or its successor. Three UDAO member countries (Mali, Mauritania, and Senegal) are not members of the Entente Council.

(Article 3), but allows for concessions between the minimum and the general tariff (Article 4). It provides a definition of origin of imported goods: products grown, extracted, or manufactured in a member country are to be considered as originating in the UDEAO area (Article 5). Operations of simple conditioning, preservation, or assembly are not considered as manufacturing; however, the criteria differentiating these operations from actual manufacturing were not specified.

Organization

The 1966 convention established a number of permanent institutions consisting of a Council of Ministers, a Committee of Experts, and a General Secretariat (Articles 9–12).

The Council of Ministers, the only decisionmaking body of UDEAO, consists of the Finance Ministers (or another cabinet member appointed by each member state) of member countries. Its decisions require a majority, the determination of which is left to the Council itself. These decisions are binding on all member countries and come into effect within a maximum period of four months from the date of notification by the General Secretariat to each member state. The Council holds an annual meeting in ordinary session successively in each member state, and may meet in extraordinary sessions on the request of its chairman. The Council is chaired by the representative of the member state where the meeting is held.

The Committee of Experts, composed of delegates representing member states, holds ordinary meetings semiannually, but may hold extraordinary meetings on the request of the Secretary-General, who acts as chairman. Acting in an advisory capacity, the Committee submits proposals or recommendations at the request of the Secretary-General. It may set up internal commissions in order to draft proposals or study matters conducive to the achievement of UDEAO's objectives.

Under the direction of the Council of Ministers, the Secretary-General, based in Ouagadougou (Upper Volta), conducts the current operations of UDEAO. He establishes permanent liaison with member states, undertakes the study of a common external tariff and of the problems of fiscal harmonization, prepares the meetings of the Council of Ministers and the Committee of Experts, and supervises the implementation of the Council's decisions. The Secretary-General is appointed by the Council for a period of three years, and his term may be renewed.

UDEAO CUSTOMS ARRANGEMENTS

Customs duties, as well as fiscal duties and other taxes levied on imports, are shown in Table 2.

Trade Within the UDEAO Area

Commodities grown, extracted, or manufactured within the UDEAO area are exempted from customs duty, but are subject to fiscal duties and other taxes, which in total shall not exceed 50 per cent of the aggregate of the most favorable treatment accorded to similar goods imported from third countries (Article 6). A higher rate amounting to 70 per cent is authorized to protect an industry that may be less competitive than a new, similar industry in another member country. Goods simply assembled in another member country and for which spare parts are imported from outside the UDEAO area enjoy the same favorable treatment only up to a fixed quota to be agreed upon by both trading member countries. The provisions of the 1966 convention applicable to intra-union trade do not supersede pre-existing bilateral arrangements among member countries that had special trade relationships before the convention entered into effect. The agreements between Ivory Coast and Upper Volta, signed on March 19, 1963, and between Senegal and Upper Volta, signed on September 7, 1965, remain operative. Since these agreements provide for the same favorable treatment as that accorded under UDEAO, they are compatible with its provisions. No restrictions shall be imposed on the mobility of goods originating in the UDEAO area (Article 7); nevertheless, in order to correct possible imbalances in its economy, a member state may resort to quantitative restrictions provided it promptly informs the Council of these measures.

Trade with Countries Outside UDEAO

The convention stipulates that goods originating in third countries and transferred from one member country to another shall be subject to the full rates applicable according to their origin, and the importer shall be reimbursed for the duties and taxes he had paid in the transit coun-

REGIONAL ECONOMIC COOPERATION

TABLE 2. UDEAO COUNTRIES: CUSTOMS DUTIES, FISCAL DUTIES, AND OTHER TAXES LEVIED ON IMPORTS, 1967

Importing countries	Customs Duties on Imports from				Fiscal Duties and Other Taxes on Imports from [1]			
	UDEAO	EEC	Other associated countries [2]	Third countries	UDEAO	EEC	Other associated countries [2]	Third countries
Dahomey	—	—	—	External tariff [3]	50 per cent of the total applicable to similar goods imported from third countries accorded the most favorable treatment; 70 per cent, if there is an industry less competitive than a similar industry in another member country.	Full rates	Full rates	Full rates
Ivory Coast	—	—	—					
Mali [4]	—	—	—					
Mauritania	—	—	—					
Niger	—	—	—					
Senegal	—	—	— [5]					
Upper Volta	—	—	—					

Source: EEC Commission, Direction Générale du Développement de l'Outre-Mer, *Notes Documentaires*, June 1967.

[1] Fiscal import duty and import turnover tax, except in Ivory Coast, which replaced this latter tax by a special import duty at a rate of 10 per cent and a value-added tax. Mali, in addition to the fiscal duty and import turnover tax, levies a special import tax. On June 1, 1967, Dahomey consolidated the fiscal duty, turnover tax, and statistical fee into a single fiscal import tax. All UDEAO countries except Ivory Coast levy statistical fees as well as other taxes.

[2] Cameroon, the People's Republic of the Congo, Gabon, the Central African Republic, Chad, the Malagasy Republic, Togo, Somalia, Burundi, the Democratic Republic of Congo, and Rwanda. Associated countries which are also members of the franc area are accorded an exemption from the customs duty. Imports from other associated countries are subject to the minimum tariff.

[3] Some UDEAO member countries have signed agreements granting third countries a reduction in the minimum tariff (agreements between Ivory Coast and Israel, Ivory Coast and Tunisia, and Niger and Tunisia).

[4] Imports from countries accorded the most-favored-nation treatment are exempted from the customs duty.

[5] Franc area countries are exempted from the customs duty; other associated countries are subject to the minimum tariff.

try (Article 8). Thus, rates of customs and fiscal duties and other taxes are to be differentiated according to the origin of imports. The current regime applicable to foreign trade with countries outside UDEAO is as follows:

(1) In general, imports are subject to the common customs duty comprising a minimum and a general duty. Intermediate duties may be negotiated with third countries. Fiscal duties and other taxes are permitted to vary from one member country to another until the expected fiscal harmonization is achieved.

(2) Imports from European Economic Community (EEC) member countries (including France and its overseas territories) are exempted from the customs duty as a result of the Yaoundé Convention of Association, but they are subject to fiscal duties and other taxes. However, some imports from Togo into Dahomey are subject to the minimum duty because until 1968 the Togolese tariff was generally lower and imports from other countries to Dahomey entered sometimes through Togo. Also, some UDEAO countries levy customs duties on goods of Moroccan or Tunisian origin.

(3) Imports from other non-franc area countries associated with EEC, in practice, receive varying treatment, depending on the country of entry. Dahomey, Ivory Coast, and Niger do not levy customs duties; Upper Volta applies the minimum customs duty; and Mali, Mauritania, and Senegal have apparently not taken any position on this matter, probably because there is almost no trade between UDEAO countries and other associated countries outside the franc area.

Thus, the UDEAO arrangements fall short of organizing a customs union. While the Central African Customs and Economic Union (Union Douanière et Economique de l'Afrique Centrale, or UDEAC) has a common external tariff (customs and fiscal duties and other surcharges combined), the UDEAO tariff varies from one member country to another when allowance is made for elements in the tariff other than the customs duty. These comprise not only fiscal duties but a large variety of other taxes levied on imports; the other taxes are subject to repeated modifications, as are the standard values (*valeurs mercuriales*) on which some import taxes are calculated. Since its establishment, UDEAO has made little progress toward harmonization of fiscal policies. Despite the provision in the 1966 convention for the institutional machinery which was lacking in the 1959 convention, the General Secretariat has apparently been understaffed, owing to insufficient financial resources, and has not been able to carry out its tasks fully. At its annual meeting in September 1968, the Council of Ministers of UDEAO doubled the budget of the General Secretariat to enable it to increase its staff and particularly to acquire qualified personnel.

Furthermore, although the convention provides that member states may set up an economic union between themselves and may grant each other more substantial advantages than those set forth in the convention (Article 13), there has been no movement toward this goal.

OTHER COOPERATIVE ARRANGEMENTS

UDEAO arrangements constitute only one facet of economic cooperation in French-speaking West Africa.

STRONG LINKS WITH EUROPE

The countries in this region remain closely linked to France as to trade and financial arrangements. The bulk of their foreign trade is with France, and their annual import programs for non-EEC non-franc area countries are determined by a mixed committee composed of France and the countries concerned. In addition, these countries, together with other African countries and the Malagasy Republic, have been associated with EEC under the first and second Yaoundé Conventions since June 1, 1964; before that date, they were associated under the terms of the Treaty of Rome and an annexed implementing treaty. This association encourages the expansion of trade with the European Common Market through the gradual establishment of a free trade area. Moreover, EEC provides the associated African countries with development aid, particularly for agriculture as well as for diversification and price subsidies to facilitate the marketing of their exports at world market prices as the French price support programs for African exports are being phased out.

WEST AFRICAN MONETARY UNION

In French-speaking West Africa, particularly the countries of the West African Monetary Union (Union Monétaire Ouest Africaine, or

UMOA),[7] the gains from the customs union are enhanced by the existing monetary arrangements. These seven countries are all members of the franc area, and on May 12, 1962 they concluded a joint cooperation agreement with France. Under this agreement, France guarantees the convertibility of the CFA franc into the French franc, and the West African countries keep their external reserves in an operations account, maintained by their common Central Bank (BCEAO) with the French Treasury. (For details, see Chapter 4, below.) Mali did not ratify the treaty establishing UMOA and did not join in the cooperation agreement. However, after the 1967 devaluation of the Mali franc and negotiations with France, Mali established an operations account, with effect from March 29, 1968, and its agreements with France provide that it may eventually join UMOA.

Thus, the UMOA countries need not be burdened by problems of balance of payments in intra-union trade; surplus countries can avoid inflationary policies and deficit countries can avoid deflationary policies. To the extent that it is not depleted, the pool of foreign exchange reserves can provide balance of payments assistance to UMOA member countries.

OTHER INSTITUTIONAL TIES

The UDEAO countries except Mali also belong to the Organisation Commune Africaine et Malgache (OCAM),[8] established June 27, 1966 to coordinate development programs and other economic and political activities of its member states. It also represents members' interests in relation to international agreements, particularly in connection with their association with the EEC. The OCAM countries have undertaken to organize their mutual trade in sugar and beef. Under the International Coffee Agreement, these countries have a global export quota which is suballocated to member countries by OCAM.

In 1966 the five Entente countries transformed the Solidarity Fund into a Guarantee Fund (Fonds d'Entraide et de Garantie des Emprunts du Conseil de l'Entente). The main objective of the Solidarity Fund, an

---

[7] Dahomey, Ivory Coast, Mauritania, Niger, Senegal, Togo, and Upper Volta.
[8] During 1969 this became the Organisation Commune Africaine, Malgache, et Mauricienne, but the earlier organization is referred to throughout this volume.

autonomous multinational public institution, is to encourage the flow of foreign private and public capital to member countries. It guarantees the repayment of principal and interest on foreign loans received in the member countries by the governments or by public, semipublic, or private enterprises operating in the Entente countries for financing sound projects in agriculture, industry, tourism, and commerce or for financing infrastructure investments. The Guarantee Fund has an Executive Board composed of the heads of state of member countries. An Administrative Secretary manages the Guarantee Fund's current operations under the supervision of a Management Committee, which derives its authority from the Executive Board; this Committee is composed of two representatives from each member country. Decisions of the Executive Board and of the Management Committee require the consent of all members.

The resources of the Guarantee Fund consist of (1) annual contributions of member countries determined each five-year period by its Executive Board, (2) subsidies and grants, and (3) investment returns and commissions on its guarantee operations. The Guarantee Fund began operations in late 1966 with an initial pool of resources of CFAF 1.3 billion. This pool was subscribed by member countries as follows: Ivory Coast CFAF 1 billion, Dahomey CFAF 84 million, Niger CFAF 84 million, Togo CFAF 48 million, and Upper Volta CFAF 84 million. The resources are deposited with a private bank in Paris, the Banque Internationale pour l'Afrique Occidentale.

The Guarantee Fund operates in three different ways. Essentially, it guarantees repayment to foreign creditors on loans secured by member governments and on government-approved loans secured by public or private institutions or enterprises. There is a ceiling on the amount of such guarantees, since the Guarantee Fund cannot commit more than ten times its nominal resources in the sum total of all guarantee operations or more than 15 per cent of its total guaranteeing capacity on a single project. Furthermore, the Guarantee Fund assists in obtaining foreign financing of preinvestment studies involving several or all Entente countries. It also investigates possibilities of foreign financing for certain projects at the request of member governments. Finally, it helps in coordinating the study and implementation of industrial projects of interest to several member countries. During its first year of operations, the Fund's activities may be summarized as follows: (1) it secured from abroad CFAF 182.8 million for financing preinvestment studies; (2) it investigated possibilities for financing certain projects, mainly in telecommunications, amounting to about CFAF 175.5 million; (3) it studied projects including production and marketing of meat, development of agricultural resources, and promotion of trade with English-speaking neighboring countries; and (4) it contributed to the industrial coordination among member states of a number of projects (e.g., a cement plant for Dahomey and Togo, a textile printing mill in Niger, a groundnut oil factory and a kenaf plant in Dahomey, and a sugar factory in Upper Volta). Ivory Coast, the main contributor to the Guarantee Fund, has pledged not to request any guarantee for its borrowings from abroad for five years, thus allowing other member countries to make a larger use of the Fund's resources. It is envisaged that when these resources increase substantially, the Guarantee Fund will broaden its operations; for example, it will participate in the share capital of enterprises, finance infrastructure projects, grant investment incentives, subsidize part of interest charges on foreign loans, and cover the local currency costs of projects financed by foreign aid.

In addition, the UDEAO countries except Mali cooperate within larger commodity agreements (groundnuts and cocoa) and own jointly with Equatorial African countries a common airline, Air Afrique; some of them participate in the joint development of the Sénégal and Niger Rivers. The Organization of Senegal River States (Guinea, Mali, Mauritania, and Senegal), which succeeded the four-state committee set up in 1965 to study common irrigation projects in the river basin, aims at coordinating industrial, agricultural, health, and educational policies of member countries. In August 1968 the four countries drafted a multilateral trade agreement and announced plans to set up a multilateral payments system.

In April 1968, under the auspices of the UN Economic Commission for Africa (ECA), a conference of West African heads of state was held in Monrovia. Members of the conference signed a Protocol for the establishment of a West African Economic Community, following preparatory meetings in Accra and Dakar in 1967. Out of 14 countries, 9 have agreed upon the Articles of Association: The Gambia, Ghana, Guinea, Liberia, Mali, Mauritania, Nigeria, Senegal, and Upper Volta.

Recently, negotiations among Dahomey, Ghana, and Togo led to an agreement under which Ghana will supply Dahomey and Togo with electricity from the Akosombo power station on the Volta. Many committees set up by ECA are working on the promotion of cooperation in various projects, including industrial development and transport projects in the West African subregion.

IMPACT OF THE CUSTOMS UNION

In French-speaking West Africa the setting up of an immediate and complete customs union in 1959 constituted in principle an advanced state of economic integration. Taking into account not only the absence of trade barriers between member countries, the equalization of tariffs on trade with third countries, and the harmonization of fiscal policies which the UDAO convention called for but also the relatively free movement of labor and capital among the CFA franc countries, UDAO came close to being an economic union, which would in fact have been no more than a continuation of the AOF arrangements. Yet, judged by almost any test of economic integration, the countries concerned moved away from the goals of the 1959 customs union. And as regards the 1966 convention, this should be considered a free trade area arrangement rather than a customs union, which is a much looser form of integration.

TRADE CREATION AND TRADE DIVERSION

The traditional theory of a customs union deals mainly with welfare gains and losses arising from the removal of trade barriers and its consequences on the pattern of production, consumption, and trade under somewhat static assumptions and with relevance mainly to the conditions and problems of developed countries. The central argument of this theory is that beyond the primary trade expansion resulting from freer trade among the participating countries, the net effects of a customs union on welfare should be assessed by striking a balance between the "trade creation" and the "trade diversion" generated by the customs union.[9] Where a union leads a member country to switch from high-

---

[9] Jacob Viner, *The Customs Union Issue*, Carnegie Endowment for International Peace (New York and London, 1950), pp. 41–81.

cost domestic production to imports from low-cost countries within the union, bringing about a more efficient use of resources, there is trade creation. On the other hand, where a union leads a member country to switch from low-cost sources outside the union to high-cost supplies from other member countries, resulting in a misallocation and waste of resources, there is trade diversion.

Trade-creation effects are likely to outweigh trade-diversion effects and lead to a net increase in welfare where four conditions are fulfilled. (1) The economies to be integrated are "actually very competitive or similar but potentially very complementary or dissimilar." [10] The member countries are very competitive because they have developed some high-cost domestic production by protection. After the union is established, under competition, each member country will specialize in those commodities for which it has a comparative advantage in view of its factor endowments. Under conditions of elastic supply and demand, intra-union trade tends to increase and low-cost sources within the union tend to displace high-cost sources; the member countries will thus complement each other. (2) The proportion of foreign trade of each member is low in relation to domestic trade; intra-union trade supplied from lower-cost sources within the union will increase to the detriment of domestic high-cost production. (3) The initial rates of duty on trade between the partner countries are high; after union, these high tariffs which were important obstacles to trade are reduced or removed among member countries. (4) The scope for economies of scale within the union is wide, allowing industries with potential large-scale production to undercut similar industries.

Since most of these conditions are not fulfilled in the UDEAO countries, traditional theory leaves them with little basis for economic integration. They rely on subsistence farming and the export of a narrow range of competing cash crops (groundnuts, cotton, coffee, and oil palm products). Industrialization is still nascent, little coordinated, and only slightly geared to import substitution, making it premature to judge whether, in the foreseeable future, they will be complementary. Moreover, the proportion of foreign trade to national income is high at

[10] James E. Meade, *The Theory of Customs Unions* (Amsterdam, 1955), p. 107; see also his *Problems of Economic Union* (Chicago, 1953).

least for the monetized sector. Finally, since these countries had already formed a common customs territory, the customs union could not be expected to contribute much to a reduction in fiscal barriers among them.

WIDENING THE MARKET

Recent literature on customs unions, however, is concerned primarily with the dynamics of economic growth and emphasizes the positive effects of the creation of regional markets on the development pace of member countries.[11] In this process, the leading factor is the widening of the market. Although the size of the customs union is of crucial importance in determining the potential of the regional market, noneconomic factors may play a decisive role in influencing the formation of the union and in consequence its size.

Creation of a regional market may enhance opportunities for profitable foreign and domestic investment, mobilize unemployed resources, broaden the export base, and accelerate the rate of economic growth. Taking into account the desire of most West African countries to industrialize rapidly, it seems to be far more beneficial, in terms of efficient and sustained growth, to industrialize in an orderly and coordinated fashion at the regional level than to duplicate, within the individual small markets, industrial ventures which could be overburdened by financial difficulties.

Initially, the removal of trade barriers within a group of countries may have little effect on the agricultural sector: the available exportable surplus of foodstuffs is generally negligible, and cash crops have their traditional outlets, often in the former metropolitan country. The impact on the manufacturing sector, however, should be important. Widening of the market encourages some of the existing plants, particularly those producing consumer goods, to increase capacity close to optimal levels, bringing about more efficient use of resources. New plants may be established, and hitherto unemployed resources are mobilized. Rising incomes, in turn, stimulate aggregate demand and induce further changes in the productive structure. Investment opportunities

---

[11] For example, the relevance of conventional theory is discussed by Arthur Hazlewood, "Problems of Integration Among African States," in *African Integration and Disintegration* (New York, 1967), Chapter 1, pp. 3–25.

for both domestic and foreign entrepreneurs further improve as new outlets open up and investment patterns change through the use or introduction of new processes and new distribution methods. The combination of internal and external economies is likely to lower unit costs, enhance the profitability of existing firms, and further raise the expectations of prospective investors. A regionally integrated market may lead some firms, particularly foreign firms, to establish plants with large potential for economies of scale. Depending on the size of the newly expanded market, import-substitution industries may become profitable and develop into leading sectors of the economies. Moreover, the switch from overseas imports to regionally produced goods—albeit still costly— is likely to be less costly than the switch to domestically produced goods. Industries (for the manufacture of intermediate goods, for example) which would not be possible or would be possible only at high costs, had the market not been enlarged, may be set up as per capita income rises.

In the UDEAO area, only the beginnings of a regionally integrated market have been made. Import taxes are still levied on intra-union trade in the form of fiscal duties. The share of recorded intra-union trade in over-all UDEAO trade is small and is even declining. Since exports still consist essentially of primary products whose traditional outlets are in Europe, it is difficult to expand intra-union trade despite the existence of the customs union. However, if market-oriented food production is expanded—within the framework of the modernization and diversification of agriculture—and larger import-substitution industries are established within the area, the proper implementation of the customs union might increase intra-union trade considerably. Commodities having immediate prospects for increased intra-union trade include maize, rice, wheat, barley, salt, fish, cigarettes, cotton fabrics, cement, domestic utensils, and footwear.

During most of the period the UDAO convention was in effect (1959–66), recorded intra-union trade data, though approximate and for one country incomplete, indicate a declining trend in this trade (Table 3). Trade between UDAO member countries declined from CFAF 8.2 billion, or 7 per cent of their total imports, in 1961 to CFAF 6.0 billion, or 5 per cent of their total imports, in 1965. The major trading countries have been Ivory Coast and Senegal because of their relative economic size; however, the intraflow of goods is usually

TABLE 3. UDEAO COUNTRIES: INTRA-UNION TRADE, 1961-65 [1]

(*In billions of CFA francs*)

	1961	1962	1963	1964	1965
Imports					
Dahomey	0.7	0.8	0.8	0.6	0.4
Ivory Coast	3.8	2.3	2.2	2.5	2.1
Mali	1.0	0.9	0.9	0.8	0.6
Mauritania	—	—	. . . [2]	. . . [2]	—
Niger	0.8	1.1	0.5	0.6	0.3
Senegal	1.4	1.9	0.9 [2]	1.2 [2]	1.9
Upper Volta	0.5	1.4	0.9	1.0	0.5
Total imports	8.2	8.5	6.2	6.7	6.0
Exports					
Dahomey	0.3	0.9	0.1	0.1	0.1
Ivory Coast	2.9	3.3	1.4	1.9	2.7
Mali	—	0.1	0.8	0.7	0.6
Mauritania	—	—	. . . [2]	. . . [2]	—
Niger	0.1	0.1	0.3	0.3	0.3
Senegal	4.8	3.6	2.8 [2]	2.5 [2]	0.4
Upper Volta	0.1	0.5	0.7	1.0	1.9
Total exports	8.2	8.5	6.2	6.7	6.0

Sources: BCEAO, *Notes d'Information et Statistiques,* No. 93, April 1963; No. 100, November 1963; No. 131, July 1966; and No. 147, January 1968.

[1] Because of rounding, figures do not add to all totals in this table or some of the following tables. Also, the figures in this table and the following tables may differ somewhat from those in tables for individual countries, as the latter are from other sources.

[2] Data for Senegal include Mauritania's trade, which could not be estimated separately.

the highest within subgroups of contiguous countries using the same transport system: Senegal-Mali-Mauritania, Ivory Coast-Upper Volta, and Dahomey-Niger. Commodities chiefly traded include foodstuffs and beverages (mainly cereals, dried fish, vegetables, sugar, salt, kolanuts, beer, and soft drinks) and manufactured products (mainly textiles, shoes, utensils, and building materials).

However, when account is taken of some border and coastal trade, intra-union trade is much larger than that recorded by the customs. For example, in 1961, whereas recorded trade among member countries totaled CFAF 8.2 billion, on the basis of information on the coastal trade in and out of Dakar, intra-union trade was estimated at CFAF 10.6 billion, or 10 per cent of total imports (Table 4). Allowance

TABLE 4.   UDEAO COUNTRIES: INTRA-UNION TRADE,
INCLUDING COASTAL TRADE, 1961

(In millions of CFA francs)

Exports from	Exports to							
	Dahomey	Ivory Coast	Mali	Mauritania	Niger	Senegal	Upper Volta	Total
Dahomey	—	160	5	—	60	160	—	385
Ivory Coast	460	—	900	5	250	1,450	240	3,305
Mali	—	875	—	10	45	—	135	1,065
Mauritania	—	10	10	—	—	70	—	90
Niger	40	—	140	—	—	10	5	195
Senegal	260	3,265	25	1,115	460	—	275	5,400
Upper Volta	15	20	50	—	—	60	—	145
Total	775	4,330	1,130	1,130	815	1,750	655	10,585

Source: BCEAO, *Notes d'Information et Statistiques,* No. 93, April 1963.

for the usually substantial border trade would make the estimated exchange of goods still larger. Border trade is important in West Africa, and although it deprives governments of potential revenue, it is not considered, prima facie, as illegitimate trading. Traditionally, landlocked countries have exported their live animals, dried fish, cereals, and root crops to the coastal countries in return for manufactured consumer goods. Since ethnic groups live on both sides of the frontiers and since the nearest market center is sometimes in the neighboring country, the flow of goods across state boundaries is normally considerable. In any case, the importance of border trade bears no relationship to the customs union, since this trade would have taken place with or without it. In short, the relatively low level of recorded intra-union trade and its decline between 1961 and 1965 suggest that the customs union did not contribute to the creation of an integrated regional market.

Furthermore, the impact of the customs union on the industrialization process in the UDEAO region appears to be insignificant. Already, many existing plants operate at levels below capacity, particularly in food processing industries, where rates of capacity utilization were as low as 39 per cent and even 16 per cent in Senegal in 1965/66 (Table 5). The degree of protection provided to infant industries competing with overseas imports may need to be reviewed.

TABLE 5. UDEAO COUNTRIES: CAPACITY AND UTILIZATION IN MANUFACTURING, 1965/66

(Capacity in thousands of metric tons, except as noted; capacity use in per cent)

	Dahomey			Ivory Coast			Mali			Mauritania			Niger			Senegal			Upper Volta		
	Number of plants	Capacity	Capacity use	Number of plants	Capacity	Capacity use	Number of plants	Capacity	Capacity use	Number of plants	Capacity	Capacity use	Number of plants	Capacity	Capacity use	Number of plants	Capacity	Capacity use	Number of plants	Capacity	Capacity use
Agriculture and food processing industries																					
Flour mills	—	—	—	1	50	97	—	—	—	—	—	—	—	—	—	2	200.0	39	—	—	—
Biscuit bakeries	—	—	—	—	—	—	—	—	—	—	—	—	—	—	—	4	15.0	75	—	—	—
Pastry mills	—	—	—	—	—	—	—	—	—	—	—	—	—	—	—	—	0.6	16	—	—	—
Sugar plants	—	—	—	—	—	—	1	4.0	...	—	—	—	—	—	—	2	58.0	65	—	—	—
Breweries	1	35	85	2	310[1]	41	—	—	—	—	—	—	—	—	—	1	140.0[1]	66	1	100[1]	70
Soft drink units	—	—	—	2	270	81	1	20.0[1]	50	—	—	—	11	20[1]	45	2	138.0[1]	67	2	50[1]	38
Cigarette factories	—	—	—	1	1.7	...	1	0.6	...	—	—	—	—	—	—	1	1.3	100	1	0.2[1]	...
Building industries																					
Cement plants	—	—	—	2[2]	300	73	—	—	—	—	—	—	1	50	48	1	220.0	89	—	—	—
Brickyards	—	—	—	1	10	80	1	11.0	11	—	—	—	1	12	...	2	16.0	42	1	15	...
Textile industries																					
Spinning mills	—	—	—	1	3.6	100	1	0.8	...	—	—	—	—	—	—	3	3.2	...	—	—	—
Weaving mills	—	—	—	1	1.9	...	1	1.2	...	—	—	—	—	—	—	1	9.0[3]	86	—	—	—
Dyeing plants	—	—	—	1	0.3	...	1	0.3	...	—	—	—	—	—	—	1	24.0[3]	...	—	—	—
Shoe factories	—	—	—	3	7.1[4]	49	1	0.6[4]	...	—	—	—	1	0.4	69	3	6.3[4]	60	1	0.9	35
Chemical industries																					
Liquid air units	1	0.5[5]	...	1	2.7[5]	...	1	0.3[5]	...	1	1.0[5]	...	—	—	—	1	1.3[5]	34	—	—	—
Paint factories	—	—	—	2	3.3	67	—	—	—	—	—	—	—	—	—	2	2.7	39	—	—	—
Soap factories	2	3.0	53	2	40.0	41	2	7.2	69	—	—	—	1	3.4	35	2	16.6	98	1	3.6	53
Match factories	—	—	—	1	...	...	1	45.0[6]	...	—	—	—	—	—	—	—	...	...	1	3.0	...
Insecticide plants	—	—	—	2	1.0[7]	56	—	—	—	—	—	—	—	—	—	2	1.0[7]	...	—	—	—

Source: Tableau des Industries de Consommation Locale en Afrique Noire (Situation et Projets), Bulletin de l'Afrique Noire, No. 506 (Paris), May 1, 1968.

1 Thousands of hectoliters. 2 Clinker units. 3 Millions of meters. 4 Millions of pairs. 5 Millions of cubic meters. 6 Millions of match boxes. 7 Millions of liters.

COMPLEMENTARITY OF MEMBER COUNTRIES

Another important factor in the integration process is the planned complementarity to be achieved among the partner countries. If industries are to be efficient, not only must they be assured of access to a wider market but also they must be specialized on the basis of factor endowments and availability of raw materials. Given the scarcity of resources, these resources should be utilized so as to maximize comparative advantages. Duplication of productive units could be avoided through harmonization of industrial development within the area and reconciliation of national development plans. Without complementarity, intra-union trade would remain negligible, as governments would invoke safeguard clauses or take fiscal measures to protect industries from their competitors in other member countries. Foreign aid could also play an important role in shaping investment patterns to promote a greater degree of complementarity. According to an EEC study on the industrialization of the African Associated Countries, a number of import-substitution plants could be set up in the UDEAO countries as a first major step in promoting the area's industrialization (Table 6). This study takes into account the level of development of the countries concerned, the problems of localization of the plants in the light of available raw materials, and transport facilities to the major consumer centers and is based on the assumption of an integrated market for the area of the Associated Countries. The study includes mainly light industries which are designed to meet the anticipated needs of these countries in the first half of the 1970's.

Another problem is whether, and to what extent, a measure of competition can be reconciled with the objective of complementarity. Competition is not a widely accepted principle among developing countries, and too many competitive undertakings contradict the basic foundation of a union, namely, the complementarity of its members. Nevertheless, as industrialization and agricultural diversification proceed, some degree of competition is beneficial. Competition would provide the best means of testing the efficiency of choices of industries, their locations, and, more generally, the rationality of the guidelines of the planned complementarity. A balance has to be found between competition and regional planning on the basis of the market size. If the regional market is now or will be large enough to absorb the output of more than one industrial unit (e.g., in West Africa, for some food products such as margarine, milk products, canned fish, sugar, fertilizers, cement, and tires), competition may be beneficial.

POLARIZATION OR DIFFUSION OF DEVELOPMENT

A choice is also to be made between the polarization and the diffusion of development within a union encompassing heterogeneous countries with substantial inequalities in development levels as in West Africa. By intensifying investments in a few locations, the polarization effect would accentuate disparities between member countries and aggravate economic dualism within the union. Certain offsetting measures could be taken to achieve a development that is as geographically balanced as possible. Investment locations, allocations of plants, and intersectoral links could be commonly agreed upon. Encouragement in the form of tax inducements and the provision of overhead facilities could be granted to attract investments in the less advanced countries. Governments of the less advanced countries could participate in the share capital of enterprises located outside their territories as a possible compensation. However, the UDEAO countries did not set up a mechanism for channeling investment expenditures (e.g., through a regional development bank), and did not devise a procedure for a reallocation of government revenue to the less advanced and landlocked countries among them.

OBSTACLES TO INTEGRATION

The obstacles to economic integration in French-speaking West Africa are numerous. Despite the common features and institutional links of these countries, they are far from forming a homogeneous area. Geographically and ethnically, French-speaking West Africa exhibits a great degree of diversity. Aside from the problems arising from the nation-building process as such, serious economic problems stand in the way of integration and explain much of the slow progress achieved in regional integration.

DISPARITIES IN DEVELOPMENT LEVELS

Ivory Coast and Senegal, the most advanced countries in the area, have the highest gross domestic product (GDP) per capita; the land-

TABLE 6. UDEAO COUNTRIES AND TOGO: INVESTMENT PROJECTS IN THE MANUFACTURING SECTOR

Commodities to be Manufactured	Location of Plants	Annual Capacity [1]	Investments	Operating Costs [2]	Annual Foreign Exchange Savings	Value Added	Profitability [3] Profits/ investment	Profits/ turnover
				—————Million CFA francs—————			——Per cent——	
Margarine	Senegal	1,000	106	119	−28	63	45.3	28.3
Milk products	Upper Volta	1.8 [4]	50	67	13	25	31.1	21.5
Canned fish	{ Togo or Dahomey	400	85	88	23	31	5.7	5.2
	{ Togo or Dahomey	800	137	157	55	65	19.0	14.0
Glucose	Togo	1,200	38	29	9	14	9.0	8.5
Sugar	{ Senegal	20,000	2,000–3,000	...	...	...	...	...
	{ Ivory Coast	20,000	2,000–3,000	...	...	...	...	...
	{ Dahomey	20,000	2,000–3,000	...	...	...	...	...
Jute and other hard fiber materials	{ Mali	3,000–3,500	500–800	...	...	...	...	...
	{ Niger	3,000–3,500	500–800	...	...	...	...	...
Fish products	{ Ivory Coast	150	185	161	67	95	31.9	26.8
	{ Ivory Coast	300	340	298	144	193	41.8	32.3
Hides and skins	{ Niger	35,000 [5]	155	117	30	51	12.3	13.2
	{ Niger	100,000 [6]						
Tires, car and truck	Ivory Coast	4,600	3,300	1,492	−48	770	9.5	17.4

Tires, cycle	Ivory Coast	7,500[7]	506	254	40	132	11.9	19.3
	Ivory Coast	2[7]	1,004	573	180	332	18.9	24.8
Fertilizers	Senegal	120,000	506	..	..	..	..	..
	Ivory Coast	62,000	1,004	..	..	..	..	..
Detergents	Togo or Dahomey	1,000	160	188	−10	34	5.0	4.1
Bottles	Senegal or Ivory Coast	7,500[7]	532	221	−7	124	7.0	14.3
Ceramic products	Senegal or Ivory Coast	8,700	800	259	147	252	19.0	30.6
Cement	Senegal	100,000	1,260	382	8	320	15.7	51.8
	Mali	50,000	1,390	430	20	290	7.9	20.4
	Togo	100,000	2,010	589	−248	340	6.0	20.6
	Ivory Coast	300,000	2,280	813	144	450	6.5	18.1
Steel elements	Ivory Coast	35,000	1,533	1,113	119	447	14.8	16.1
Screws	Senegal	440	106	44	−15	33	15.1	21.0
Agricultural tools	Ivory Coast	900	255	136	19	81	5.1	8.7
Utensils	Ivory Coast	1,625	440	327	38	141	7.5	9.2
Oil lamps	Ivory Coast	300	290	108	28	75	6.5	15.0
Refrigerators	Ivory Coast	..	218	206	18	74	16.5	15.2
Batteries for cars	Togo	675	132	98	49	100	58.0	44.0
Batteries	Senegal or Ivory Coast	2,400	295	498	18	178	11.9	6.6
Spare parts for cars	Senegal or Ivory Coast	..	150	..	..	..	..	..
and trucks	Togo or Dahomey	..	500	..	..	..	..	..

Source: "Possibilités d'Industrialisation des Etats Africains et Malgache Associés à la CEE," reproduced in BCEAO, *Notes d'Information et Statistiques*, No. 146, December 1967.

1 Metric tons, except as noted.
2 Including amortization but excluding fiscal and financial charges.
3 Profits represent the difference between sales and operating costs.
4 Million liters.
5 Goats.
6 Head of cattle.
7 Units.

locked countries have the lowest. According to an EEC study, per capita GDP in the monetized sector was estimated to average CFAF 19,500 for the region as a whole, but it was estimated at CFAF 47,000 in Ivory Coast and CFAF 36,000 in Senegal and at only CFAF 5,500 in Upper Volta.[12] Of the 470,000 industrial wage earners in the area as a whole, Ivory Coast and Senegal together had 304,000, or 65 per cent. Abidjan and Dakar together accounted for about 44 per cent of the manufacturing units established in the area and for 60 per cent of the electrical power generated and consumed for industrial use. With the exception of Mauritania, where mining is a major economic activity, the ratio of output in the secondary sector (mining, manufacturing, construction, handicraft, and power) to GDP was highest in Ivory Coast and Senegal (16 per cent). These two countries together accounted for 75 per cent of the total foreign trade of the UDEAO countries in 1965–67. Coexistence of more and less developed economies within a regionally integrated market is likely to seriously challenge integration in the UDEAO region and, for that matter, throughout Africa. As industrialization expands, more and more plants may be concentrated in a few centers for reasons of both external and internal economies.

Trade diversion, in the meantime, may become substantial and detrimental to the balance of advantages among partner countries. In short, this coexistence can lead to subsidization of the more advanced economies by the less advanced ones; the latter would tend to subsidize the former by purchasing its higher priced manufactures rather than similar imports from overseas while continuing to export its primary commodities at world market prices.[13] Subsidization of the more advanced countries by the less advanced will be the more aggravated, the faster the polarization effect operates. Moreover, the less advanced countries will find themselves obliged to forgo a part of their revenue from customs

---

[12] "Possibilités d'Industrialisation des Etats Africains et Malgache Associés à la CEE," reproduced in BCEAO, *Notes d'Information et Statistiques*, No. 146, December 1967, p. 10.

[13] A.J. Brown, "Economic Separatism Versus a Common Market in Developing Countries," *Yorkshire Bulletin of Economic and Social Research*, Vol. 13 (1961), pp. 31–40 and 89–96, and Andrew M. Kamarck, *The Economics of African Development* (New York and London, 1967), pp. 148–65.

and fiscal duties, which are by far the most important sources of budget receipts.

EARLY STAGE OF INDUSTRIALIZATION

The UDEAO region as a whole is in an early stage of industrialization. Dakar emerged as an important industrial center immediately after World War II, when several manufacturing plants were set up in Dakar to serve the whole of French-speaking West Africa. Since 1959, however, with the West African Federation splitting into independent states, industrial expansion has slowed down in Senegal, and the industrial importance of Abidjan has increased. In the mid-1960's, output per capita in the secondary sector was estimated at CFAF 7,100 in Ivory Coast and CFAF 6,400 in Senegal. Manufacturing production in Ivory Coast, which rose by an average of about 25 per cent annually between 1960 and 1966, catered largely to domestic needs but also partly supplied the markets of neighboring Upper Volta, Mali, Dahomey, and Niger.

Besides some industries processing export crops, the main thrust was in the import-substitution industries for the production of consumer goods, particularly foodstuffs and textiles. The emphasis on import substitution may be due to the existence of an actual demand for the imported goods and to the small size of the respective domestic markets which prevented the establishment of other types of industries. Some progress is also being made in promoting export-processing plants since the bulk of present exports remains unprocessed.

Despite the impressive progress made in Ivory Coast, the region as a whole has undergone little industrialization, mainly because of the narrowness of individual domestic markets. It has been said that some of the countries of the region would offer a market no larger than that of a medium-sized West European town.[14] Thus, the early stage of industrialization in the UDEAO region limits the scope of intra-union trade. Until economic diversification and expansion of per capita income reach a certain level, the present pattern and direction of trade are likely to continue.

---

[14] H. Bourguinat, "Les Groupements Economiques Régionaux des Pays en Voie de Développement: Pour une Ré-évaluation," *Notes d'Information et Statistiques,* No. 151, May 1968.

PATTERN AND DIRECTION OF TRADE

Another important obstacle to integration is to be found in the pattern and direction of the area's foreign trade. This trade is not diversified enough to allow for an increase in mutual exchange of goods and is outwardly oriented.

The predominance of subsistence farming and, simultaneously, the rapid expansion in cash crops, the outlets of which are traditionally assured in overseas markets, have resulted in the concentration of exports on a few primary commodities (in Niger, Upper Volta, and Mauritania, mainly on a single commodity) and a heavy reliance on imports of foodstuffs and consumer durable goods.

As shown by EEC trade statistics, the main export items of the area consist of groundnuts and groundnut oil, coffee, cocoa, tropical woods, palm products, livestock on the hoof, and, as far as mineral products are concerned, iron ore and phosphates (Table 7). Some of these commodities are processed before export (fats and woods), but the bulk is exported unprocessed. In the past, most of the agricultural products received higher prices in the French market than those prevailing in the world markets. These price support programs gave financial advantages to the African countries and stimulated their exports. Although the price-supported exports were not competitive in the world markets, French support was gradually terminated; instead, EEC aid to productivity and diversification was extended to bring about the adjustment of export prices to world market conditions. The diversification process succeeded in increasing the importance of new cash crops such as cotton in Niger, Dahomey, and Mali and of staples such as rice, but it is still early for its full impact on production patterns to be felt; meanwhile these countries remain dependent on the export of a few items. During 1961–66, iron ore represented more than 90 per cent of Mauritania's total exports by value, groundnuts and phosphates 85 per cent of Senegal's exports, groundnuts and livestock more than 80 per cent of Niger's exports, and livestock about 50 per cent of Upper Volta's exports.

Among imports, the commodity distribution shows the overriding importance of consumer goods—foodstuffs and manufactured goods

TABLE 7.   UDEAO COUNTRIES: CONCENTRATION OF EXPORTS, 1961–66

(Value in billions of CFA francs)

	1961	1962	1963	1964	1965	1966
Dahomey						
Total exports	3.7	2.7	3.1	3.2	3.4	2.6
Major exports						
Palm products	1.9	1.6	2.1	2.4	2.3	1.3
Cotton (ginned)	0.2	—	0.1	0.1	0.2	0.3
Groundnuts	0.6	0.2	0.3	0.2	0.1	0.1
Major exports as a per cent of total exports	73	67	81	84	76	65
Ivory Coast						
Total exports	43.6	45.0	56.9	74.6	68.4	76.7
Major exports						
Coffee	20.1	18.7	24.4	31.7	25.9	30.3
Cocoa	9.8	10.5	11.3	14.5	10.9	13.1
Tropical woods	7.8	8.3	11.4	16.0	15.0	14.9
Bananas	2.1	2.8	3.5	3.2	2.7	2.8
Major exports as a per cent of total exports	91	90	89	88	80	80
Mali						
Total exports	3.5	2.5	2.6	4.1	3.9	3.2
Major exports						
Groundnuts	1.3	1.0	1.0	0.8	0.5	0.3
Cotton	0.3	0.2	0.3	0.3	0.6	0.8
Cattle	0.3	0.2	0.3	0.7	1.1	0.7
Major exports as a per cent of total exports	54	56	62	44	56	56
Mauritania						
Total exports	0.5	0.7	4.0	11.3	14.2	17.0
Major export: Iron ore	—	—	2.7	10.6	13.3	15.8
Major export as a per cent of total exports	—	—	68	94	94	93
Niger						
Total exports	3.8	4.8	5.3	5.3	6.3	8.6
Major exports						
Groundnuts	3.0	2.9	3.6	3.8	3.4	6.2
Livestock on the hoof	0.4	1.1	1.0	0.6	1.0	0.9
Major exports as a per cent of total exports	89	83	87	83	70	83
Senegal						
Total exports	30.7	30.7	27.3	30.3	31.7	36.8
Major exports						
Groundnuts and groundnut oil	25.4	24.8	20.2	23.5	24.9	28.6
Phosphates	1.0	1.4	1.3	2.4	2.7	2.6
Major exports as a per cent of total exports	86	85	79	85	87	85
Upper Volta						
Total exports	0.9	1.9	3.1	3.3	3.7	4.0
Major export: Livestock on the hoof	0.5	0.9	1.0	1.5	1.9	2.0
Major export as a per cent of total exports	56	47	32	45	51	50

Source: EEC, *Foreign Trade Statistics.*

(Table 8). Between 1961 and 1966, this group of commodities
accounted for an average of 66 per cent of total imports of the region.
Foodstuffs, beverages, and tobacco averaged 23 per cent of total
imports. Although imports of capital goods increased at about the same
annual rate as total imports (7 per cent), they averaged 25 per cent of
the region's total imports during the period. The importance of con-

TABLE 8. UDEAO COUNTRIES: COMMODITY DISTRIBUTION OF IMPORTS, 1961–66

(*In billions of CFA francs*)

	1961	1962	1963	1964	1965	1966
Foodstuffs, beverages, and tobacco						
Dahomey	1.2	1.7	1.8	1.9	1.9	2.0
Ivory Coast	6.4	6.4	6.9	10.0	10.3	12.6
Mali	1.7	2.2	1.8	1.5	2.1	1.9
Mauritania	0.4	0.5	0.4	0.3	0.3	0.4
Niger	1.1	1.5	1.0	1.0	1.2	1.4
Senegal	12.2	12.1	13.0	15.8	14.8	13.8
Upper Volta	1.3	1.8	2.2	2.5	2.2	2.5
Total	24.3	26.2	27.1	33.0	32.8	34.6
Raw materials and fuels						
Dahomey	0.7	0.7	0.7	0.6	0.6	0.5
Ivory Coast	2.8	2.4	3.2	4.1	4.2	4.8
Mali	0.8	0.9	1.0	1.0	1.0	1.2
Mauritania	0.4	0.4	0.3	0.3	0.2	0.3
Niger	0.5	0.6	1.0	1.2	1.0	1.5
Senegal	2.7	2.8	2.8	2.7	6.3	4.5
Upper Volta	0.6	1.0	1.6	1.5	2.6	1.6
Total	8.5	8.8	10.6	11.4	15.9	14.4
Capital goods						
Dahomey	1.5	1.3	1.5	1.2	1.4	1.5
Ivory Coast	10.8	9.2	12.1	18.4	16.4	17.3
Mali	1.6	4.2	1.9	2.5	2.4	1.4
Mauritania	3.0	3.1	4.9	2.3	3.3	2.9
Niger	0.8	3.1	2.8	4.5	5.5	6.5
Senegal	6.4	6.5	6.7	6.7	5.8	6.0
Upper Volta	1.7	1.9	1.6	1.8	1.2	1.6
Total	25.8	29.3	31.5	37.4	36.0	37.2
Other manufactured goods						
Dahomey	2.9	2.9	4.2	4.1	4.5	4.2
Ivory Coast	18.1	16.4	19.6	27.9	27.3	28.6
Mali	4.7	4.1	3.8	4.0	5.0	4.5
Mauritania	3.9	4.9	1.9	0.9	2.3	2.1
Niger	2.3	1.6	1.7	1.6	1.6	1.6
Senegal	17.0	16.8	16.1	17.1	15.7	15.0
Upper Volta	3.5	3.9	3.8	4.0	3.0	3.5
Total	52.4	50.6	51.1	59.6	59.4	59.5
Grand Total	111.0	114.9	120.3	141.4	144.1	145.7

Source: EEC, *Foreign Trade Statistics.*

sumer goods imports suggests room for import substitution within the UDEAO region and for expansion of intra-union trade in foodstuffs and manufactured consumer goods if their production within the region is developed.

Most of the foreign trade of the UDEAO countries is with EEC, particularly the former metropolitan country, France. According to EEC foreign trade statistics, the proportion of foreign trade of the UDEAO countries with EEC averaged 68 per cent during 1962–66. The proportion of imports from France, however, declined from 69 per cent in 1961 to 49 per cent in 1966 and that of exports declined from 71 per cent to 53 per cent. The major trading countries of UDEAO, Ivory Coast and Senegal, accounted for roughly 80 per cent of total UDEAO trade with France.

TRANSPORTATION PROBLEMS

Transportation difficulties and, particularly, high transport costs make it difficult for the exports of the inland countries to compete with those of coastal countries. The former are compelled to reduce producer prices below those prevailing in the coastal countries and thus lower rural incomes. At the same time, the higher prices they must pay for imported commodities, compared with prices in the coastal countries, tend to raise their real cost of living. Thus the main consequences of the lack of an adequate integrated transport network in this part of West Africa are, on the one hand, to hinder the intra-union trade and, on the other, to widen the gap in incomes between inland and coastal countries.

CONCLUSIONS

Regional cooperation among French-speaking West African countries is based on the desire of these countries to continue under new arrangements the economic integration achieved in the pre-independence era. These efforts in regional collaboration are also part of a larger framework characterized by strong links with France and EEC. The monetary union arrangements, which include most UDEAO countries, also enhance the integration process. However, less progress has been made in the solution of some problems, particularly the setting up of a customs union and a regional investment policy. In spite of the ambitious goals contained in the UDAO convention of 1959, its contribution to the growth of trade within the area and to the establishment of a regionally integrated market has been practically negligible.

The UDEAO convention of 1966 falls short of organizing a customs union, since member countries have certain variable elements in their tariff structure for imports. It amounts essentially to a free trade area arrangement. Under prevailing circumstances, this arrangement appears to be realistically designed to achieve the maximum permissible degree of economic integration while retaining a certain flexibility in fiscal matters. The UDEAO countries rely on subsistence farming and the export of a narrow range of competing cash crops which have traditional outlets outside the region. Their industrialization is still nascent and little coordinated, and their transport network does not facilitate intra-union trade. Moreover, given the present disparities in development levels, the absence of mechanisms for channeling investment expenditures and government revenue into the less advanced and landlocked countries within the region also seriously hampers the integration process. These obstacles explain the slow progress made so far and emphasize some of the difficulties to be overcome in the path toward integration in this part of West Africa.

Common customs arrangements can make an important contribution toward regionally integrated development in the UDEAO area, but they need to be supplemented by other policies, particularly more integrated actions in fiscal, social, and investment matters. The existence of institutions such as the Entente Guarantee Fund, BCEAO, the river basin organizations, and the institutional machinery created by the UDEAO convention may strengthen the efforts of these countries to further their economic integration.

CHAPTER 3

Development Planning

EARLY PLANNING

The first year of the "development decade" (the 1960's) was also the year when the French West African States (AOF)[1] achieved independence. Even before the BCEAO countries[2] became independent, there was some planning effort in the region, but it was centered mainly on the formulation of investment programs for the public sector. Furthermore, these programs were prepared, financed, and executed directly by France.

The first of the early plans, a six-year development program (1947–53), was launched in 1947 to cover the whole AOF territory. A second plan, covering a period of five years (1954–59), followed and terminated the last program prepared and implemented directly by France. The two plans, formulated only for development projects in the public sector, were financed exclusively by the Fonds d'Investissement et de Développement Economique et Social (FIDES), a French public development agency. During 1947–59 a total of CFAF 78.2 billion (equivalent to US$313 million) was invested in Dahomey, Ivory Coast, Mauritania,

Niger, Senegal, Togo, and Upper Volta (Table 1). Senegal had the largest share (33 per cent), Ivory Coast the next largest (28 per cent), and Mauritania the smallest (6 per cent). Nearly CFAF 46 billion, or 58 per cent, was invested in infrastructure; the rest was invested in social and administrative projects.

TABLE 1. BCEAO COUNTRIES: INVESTMENTS FINANCED BY FIDES,
BEFORE INDEPENDENCE, 1947–59

(*Amount in billions of CFA francs*)

	First Plan (1947–53)	Second Plan (1954–59)	Total		Investment in Infrastructure	
			Amount	Per cent of regional total	Amount	Per cent of country total
Dahomey	2.3	2.9	5.2	7	2.6	50
Ivory Coast	9.0	13.0	22.0	28	16.7	76
Mauritania	0.7	4.3	5.0	6	2.5 [1]	50
Niger	1.6	4.4	6.0	8	3.0 [1]	50
Senegal	15.8	10.0	25.8	33	12.0	47
Togo	2.3	2.9	5.2	7	2.6	50
Upper Volta	3.5	5.5	9.0	11	6.3	70
Total or average	35.2	43.0	78.2	100	45.7	58

Source: *Mémento de l'Economie et de la Planification Africaines,* Numéro Spécial du Bulletin de l'Afrique Noire, No. 509 (Paris, 1968), pp. 161, 183, 234, 274, 297, 336, and 381.

[1] Estimated.

As soon as the seven BCEAO countries became independent in 1960, they initiated programs for a smooth transition from colonial to national planning and as soon as possible established national plans designed to ensure orderly progress toward goals of accelerated eco-

---

[1] Afrique Occidentale Française: Dahomey, Guinea, Ivory Coast, Mali, Mauritania, Niger, Senegal, Togo, and Upper Volta.

[2] Dahomey, Ivory Coast, Mauritania, Niger, Senegal, Togo, and Upper Volta, all members of the West African Monetary Union (Union Monétaire Ouest Africaine, or UMOA), having a common central bank, the Banque Centrale des Etats de l'Afrique de l'Ouest.

nomic growth (Table 2).[3] The planning process differed from the public sector programing in being more detailed and comprehensive.

TABLE 2. BCEAO COUNTRIES: DEVELOPMENT PLANS SINCE INDEPENDENCE

	Intermediate Plan	Four-Year Plan	Five-Year Plan	Ten-Year Perspective Plan	Plan Under Preparation
Dahomey	—	1962–65	1966–70	—	—
Ivory Coast	1962–63	1967–70	—	1960–70	1971–75
Mauritania	1960–62	1963–67	—	—	—
Niger	1961–64 [1]	1965–68	—	1965–74	—
Senegal	—	{ 1961–65 [2] 1965–69 [3] }	—	—	—
Togo	—	—	1966–70	—	—
Upper Volta	1963–64	1967–70	1963–67 [4]	—	1971–75

Sources: National plans—Dahomey, *Plan de Développement Economique et Social, 1966–1970* (Porto-Novo); Ivory Coast, Ministère du Plan, *Loi-Plan de Développement Economique Social et Cultural, 1967–1970* (Abidjan); Mauritania, *Plan Quadriennal de Développement Economique et Social, 1963–1966* (Nouakchott); Niger, *Plan Quadriennal, 1965–1968* (Niamey); Senegal, *Deuxième Plan Quadriennal de Développement Economique et Social, 1965–1969* (Dakar); Togo, *Plan de Développement Economique et Social, 1966–1970* (Lomé); and Upper Volta, *Plan Cadre, 1967–1970* (Ouagadougou).

[1] Originally covered 1961–63 but was extended to 1964.
[2] Originally covered 1961–64 but was extended to 1965.
[3] July 1965–June 1969.
[4] Later dropped.

All the countries except Togo started with plans that covered relatively short periods, either in the form of a provisional or intermediate plan, ranging from two years (Ivory Coast, Mauritania, and Upper Volta) to three years (Niger), or in the form of a four-year plan (Dahomey and Senegal). Togo, the last country to embark on development planning, began with a five-year plan. The major objectives of the provisional plans were to undertake certain priority projects (in agriculture, manpower, health, and administration) and to lay the foundation for further planning. In all countries, the intermediate plans covered only investment in the public sector, having no global targets of growth for all sectors of the economy. During the period of intermediate plans, special efforts were also undertaken to strengthen the planning authori-

---

[3] For more details, see Roland Julienne, "L'Afrique à l'Heure des Plans," *Recueil Penant*, No. 701 (April-June 1964), pp. 179–204 (Paris), and Michel Gaud, *Les Premières Expériences de Planification en Afrique Noire* (Paris, 1967).

ties and to improve the statistical basis for subsequent planning, especially for demographic data, agricultural survey, and social research.

CURRENT PLANS

Experience in planning during the early years of independence caused planners to move quickly to formulate a second generation of plans. Thus, four countries which had completed their intermediate plans (Ivory Coast, Mauritania, Niger, and Upper Volta) immediately launched a subsequent five-year plan. Ivory Coast and Niger projected a five-year plan within the framework of a Ten-Year Perspective Plan. Since it is not possible to cover in detail all the plans of these seven countries, the following section deals only with plans that are either being implemented (as of 1969) or are the latest to be completed. These include two Five-Year Plans (Dahomey and Togo) and five Four-Year Plans (Ivory Coast, Mauritania, Niger, Senegal, and Upper Volta), as presented in Table 3. All the plans except that of Mauritania are within the period between 1965 and 1970; Mauritania completed its first Four-Year Plan in mid-1967 and the next plan will cover the period 1970–73.

ORGANIZATION OF THE PLANNING AUTHORITIES

In addition to the executive and legislative branches of government, planning authorities also involve representatives of other groups (e.g., chambers of commerce, trade unions, business firms, and youth and labor organizations). In practice, however, the authority of plan preparation, execution, and control is delegated to a central planning agency. The agency may be established as (1) an Office of Planning (Commissariat au Plan), as in Niger and Togo, where planning is under the direct control of the presidency, (2) a Ministry of Planning (Ministère du Plan), or (3) a Department of Planning within a ministry, e.g., Ministry of Finance in Dahomey.

In the process of planning, several governments have changed the status of the planning authorities with a view to strengthening them; usually the change was made in transferring an office into a department (Dahomey and Togo) or a department into a ministry (Ivory Coast and Senegal).

TABLE 3. BCEAO COUNTRIES: SELECTED ECONOMIC INDICATORS RELATED TO DEVELOPMENT PLANS

(Amount in billions of CFA francs)

	Plan Being Implemented (or Latest Plan)	Number of Years Covered	Estimated Amount of GDP [1]	Projected Growth Rates			Over-All Planned Investment					Average Annual Investment		
				GDP	Population	Per capita income	Public investment		Private investment		Total amount	Amount	As a per cent of GDP	
							Amount	Per cent of total	Amount	Per cent of total			First plan year	Final plan year [2]
				Per cent										
Dahomey	1966–70	5	46.5	4.0	2.8	1.2	25.0	70.3	10.3	29.2	35.3	7.0	15.0	12.4
Ivory Coast	1967–70	4	273.0	7.7	2.9	4.8	116.0	51.7	108.0	48.2	224.0	56.0	20.5	15.2
Mauritania	1963–66	4	31.0	9.2	1.7	7.5	13.6	50.0	14.2	51.1	27.8	7.0	22.6	15.9
Niger	1965–68	4	74.1	5.5	2.5	3.0	33.3	77.0	9.9	23.0	43.2 [3]	10.8	14.6	11.8
Senegal	1965–69	4	191.9	6.0	2.2	3.8	73.0 [4]	61.3	46.0	38.7	119.0	29.7	15.4	12.3
Togo	1966–70	5	53.1	5.0	2.6	2.4	20.0	70.0	8.6	30.1	28.6	5.7	10.7	8.4
Upper Volta	1967–70	4	63.2	4.0	1.8	2.2	27.3	83.0	5.6	17.0	32.9	8.2	13.0	11.0
Total or average				5.8	2.3	3.5	308.2	60.3	202.6	39.7	510.8	17.8	16.8	12.4

Sources: Tables 1 and 2 and data supplied by country authorities.

[1] Estimates of GDP based on the most recent figures available and the growth rates set out in plans.
[2] Estimates based on GDP in first year of plan and GDP growth rates.
[3] Later reduced to CFAF 30 billion.
[4] Originally planned at CFAF 84.2 billion.

GENERAL OBJECTIVES OF THE PLANS

The economies of the BCEAO countries have many common characteristics in structure and problems, and their plans have envisaged fairly similar objectives, although these objectives might be stated in different ways, and often in very broad terms. Generally speaking, all the plans have emphasized the achievement of economic independence and the raising of living standards and welfare for the population over a relatively short period of time (e.g., to double per capita income in 10 to 20 years). In order to do so, the planners have aimed at (1) elimination of regional economic discrepancies, (2) structural changes in the economy, (3) diversification of the agricultural sector, (4) creation of import-substitute industries, (5) orientation and training of technicians, and (6) setting the stage for further growth in the long term.

Specifically, the plans have established targets for growth rates in gross domestic product (GDP) averaging 5.8 per cent annually; this rate implies roughly the doubling of per capita income in 20 years, taking into consideration the average annual growth in population of 2.4 per cent (see Table 3). The GDP's annual growth rate targets, however, ranged from 4 per cent (Dahomey and Upper Volta) to 9.2 per cent (Mauritania). All other things being equal, a country with a lower rate of population growth can increase its per capita GDP more rapidly than a country with a higher rate of population growth. Having the lowest population growth rate among the seven countries, Mauritania projects the highest rate of per capita income increase (7.5 per cent compared with Dahomey's lowest rate of 1.2 per cent).

Since the agricultural sector predominates in the economies of these countries (from 30 per cent of GDP in Ivory Coast to 60 per cent in Niger), the development strategy during the 1960's apparently placed great emphasis on the need for structural changes in the economies. Consequently, all the plans projected much faster growth rates for the secondary sectors (industry, mining, energy, and construction) than for the primary sectors (Table 4). In Senegal the rates were 5.1 per cent for the secondary sector and 3.8 per cent for the primary sector, and in Mauritania 19.1 per cent and 2 per cent. Thus, while all plans recognized the important role of agriculture, they envisaged a decrease in agriculture's share in the GDP by the final year of plan implementation.

TABLE 4. BCEAO COUNTRIES: PROJECTED GROWTH RATES BY SECTORS

(*In per cent*)

	GDP	Primary Sector	Secondary Sector	Tertiary Sector
Dahomey (1966–70)	4	3.8	8.0	3.0
Ivory Coast (1967–70)	7.7	3.8	15.4	8.0
Mauritania (1963–67)	9.2	2.0	19.1	12.0
Niger (1965–68)	5.5	2.4	11.8	8.1
Senegal (1965–69)	6.0	3.8	5.1	3.0
Togo (1966–70)	5.0	3.4	13.0	5.8
Upper Volta (1967–70)	4.0	—	—	—

Sources: Same as Table 2.

The high growth rates projected for the industrial sector appeared to reflect the widely held belief throughout the developing nations that industrial development is the shortest road to economic progress and rapid expansion in the economy.

LEVEL AND STRUCTURE OF INVESTMENT

The largest investments in the seven BCEAO countries were CFAF 224 billion in Ivory Coast for its 1967–70 Plan and CFAF 119 billion in Senegal for its 1965–69 Plan. The smallest investment was CFAF 27.8 billion projected by Mauritania for its 1963–67 Plan.[4] For BCEAO countries as a whole, the plans called for nearly CFAF 511 billion (US$2.0 billion), a level representing an annual average of CFAF 18 billion, or 17 per cent of GDP in the first year of the plans and 12 per cent in the last year. As the plans were implemented, many downward adjustments of investment targets were made to adjust the plans' objectives to the means available in view of the foreign aid disbursed and the countries' trade balances, which are affected by fluctuations of world prices of agricultural products. The following discussion is focused only on the level of investment as originally planned, except for Senegal, where adjustment of public investment was taken into account because of the availability of detailed information on the adjusted figures.

---

[4] The plan was originally scheduled to cover 1963–66.

All the plans contemplated a greater capital outlay by the public sector than by the private sector. The planned share of public investment in total investment ranged from about 50 per cent in Mauritania to 83 per cent in Upper Volta. For the BCEAO countries as a whole, the public sector's investment averaged 60 per cent, and the private sector's 40 per cent (see Table 3). Generally, the major part of public investment was concentrated on infrastructure, especially on roads, water resources, and agriculture, while that of the private sector was devoted to industry (mainly manufacturing and processing) and mining.

The sectoral breakdown of investments of the seven plans is shown in Table 5. On the average, nearly 31 per cent of over-all investments were allocated for the industrial and mining sector, 29 per cent for infrastructure, 20 per cent for agriculture, and the rest for education and other purposes. On an individual basis, Dahomey and Niger provided the largest share of investments for agriculture; Mauritania and Senegal the largest for industry, mining, and commerce; and Ivory Coast, Togo, and Upper Volta the largest for infrastructure. The composition of investment readily shows the planners' choice of priorities, which in turn was based on the structures of their economies.

Dahomey

For agricultural development, Dahomey provided 34 per cent (CFAF 12.1 billion) of its total investment. This choice undoubtedly reflected the Government's desire to deal with structural problems in the Dahomean economy. Agriculture, which accounts for nearly all the country's export earnings, was expected during 1965–70 to contribute almost one half of GDP. Nevertheless, only about 11 per cent of total cultivable land (1 million hectares) is actually under cultivation. Relatively large investment in agriculture during the plan was made with a view to increasing both productivity of land as well as the area under cultivation. Special emphasis was given to the production of oil palm products, cotton, and groundnuts. Major palm development included the Grand Hinvi and Agonvy projects, together representing a total investment of nearly CFAF 4 billion; they are expected to cover a total of 13,000 hectares when completed.

TABLE 5. BCEAO COUNTRIES: SECTORAL DISTRIBUTION OF PLANNED INVESTMENTS [1]

	Research Information and General Studies	Agriculture (Including Livestock and Fishing)	Industries, Mining, and Commerce	Infrastructure	Education, Social, Health, and Urban Affairs	Administration	Other	Total
AMOUNT (billion CFA francs)								
Dahomey	0.2	12.1	9.9	10.3	1.9	0.7	0.2	35.3
Ivory Coast	4.8	34.5	71.2 [2]	82.2	15.0	8.8	7.3 [3]	224.0
Mauritania	1.6	4.3	10.7	3.4	5.7	2.1	—	27.8
Niger	2.1	11.8	8.6	8.8	11.0	0.9	—	43.2 [4]
Senegal	3.9	22.2	47.0 [5]	23.7	21.4	0.8	—	119.0
Togo	—	5.9	3.8	10.3	7.8	0.8	—	28.6
Upper Volta	1.6	9.1	6.0	11.4	4.8	—	—	32.9
Total	14.2	99.9	157.2	150.1	67.6	14.2	7.5	510.8
PER CENT OF TOTAL								
Dahomey	0.6	34.3	28.0	29.2	5.4	1.9	0.6	100.0
Ivory Coast	2.1	15.4	31.8	36.7	6.7	3.9	3.3	100.0
Mauritania	5.7	15.5	38.5	12.2	20.5	7.5	—	100.0
Niger	4.8	27.3	19.8	20.4	25.4	2.3	—	100.0
Senegal	3.3	18.7	39.4	20.0	18.0	0.6	—	100.0
Togo	—	21.0	13.3	36.0	27.3	2.8	—	100.0
Upper Volta	4.9	27.7	18.1	34.6	14.6	—	—	100.0
Average	2.8	20.0	30.7	29.3	13.1	2.7	1.4	100.0

Sources: Same as Table 2.

[1] Under the plans indicated in Table 2; because of uniformity, distribution of investments by sectors in this table differs slightly from that of individual plans, and because of rounding, figures do not add to all totals.
[2] Estimate according to implication of the plan; CFAF 38.0 billion was allocated to industries and mining.
[3] Including participation of the Government in promotion of agricultural diversification and small industries.
[4] Later reduced to CFAF 30 billion.
[5] Of which CFAF 46 billion was private investment.

Ivory Coast

Infrastructure looms very large in Ivory Coast's development effort (37 per cent of total investment). First priority was given to the transport section, of which the San-Pédro port and the Kossou (Bandama) dam represent the leading projects. Port construction is expected to play a vital role in the future exploitation of the highly underdeveloped southwestern region. Located about halfway between Abidjan and the Liberian border, the port will create a second region for urban development and, in addition, will permit exploitation of forest resources not previously tapped because of transportation difficulties; it will also open up new areas for agricultural development and possibly mineral development. Together with related roads and urban development, the port project requires an investment of some CFAF 7.4 billion over the three years 1968–70. The Kossou hydroelectric project, the largest development project to be carried out in Ivory Coast, will include a large dam, power station, and distribution system. The over-all cost of this project is estimated to reach CFAF 26 billion.

Mauritania

Because of lack of rain in almost the whole territory and the scarcity of arable land (amounting to less than 1 per cent of the total area), agricultural activity in Mauritania is only of a subsistence nature. Except for the gum arabic collected, no crops are exported on a significant scale. Thus, in the early 1950's the Government decided to exploit the country's rich deposits of iron ore and copper. Prospect for profitable mining at Fdérik (Fort-Gouraud) was, no doubt, the factor behind the country's choice of priority in its 1963–67 Plan. Over one third of total investment was allocated to mining, divided between iron ore at Zouîrât (Zouerate) and copper at Akjoujt. By the end of 1966, total investment in the Fdérik project by the Mining Company (Société des Mines de Fer de Mauritanie, or MIFERMA) amounted to CFAF 50 billion, of which CFAF 6 billion was spent in 1966; production of iron ore was estimated to reach nearly 8 million tons in 1968, contributing nearly CFAF 17 billion to Mauritania's export receipts. Exploitation of copper near Akjoujt represents another major project in the plan. Total investment in the project, including the paving of the Nouakchott-Akjoujt road, was to reach CFAF 14 billion; production was expected to start in 1970 with an estimated capacity of 50,000 tons of concentrate a year.

Niger

Allocation to agriculture of over 27 per cent of total investment (CFAF 12 billion) indicates Niger's effort to expand its agriculture, which had shown few signs of progress and which accounts for more than one third of its GDP and two thirds of its export receipts. A land-locked country, Niger also has few interior water resources, and irrigation poses a great problem to agricultural production. During implementation of the plan, special emphasis was given to developing of water resources and irrigation and to expanding annual production of groundnuts to 167,000 tons and of cotton to 14,000 tons by 1968.

Senegal

Although public investment was focused on agriculture in Senegal's second plan, private investment was aimed mainly at industry and mining sectors. Over-all investment in the modern sector amounted to CFAF 47 billion, or nearly 40 per cent of total investment. Heavy public investment in agriculture was envisaged in order to implement the Government's agricultural diversification program covering cotton, rice, vegetables, and fruit production and to increase yields of groundnuts and millet. On the other hand, profitability of the highly developed manufacturing sector appears to be attractive to private foreign investment. New investment in this sector includes important projects in chemical industry, petroleum refinery, food industry, and mining industry. Among these projects, the groundnut oil mills involve CFAF 1 billion of new investment. The mining sector appears also to be promising. Under the plan, further exploitation was projected for two large deposits of phosphates: (1) a calcium phosphate deposit at Taïba and (2) an aluminum phosphate deposit at Thiès.

Togo

One of the main objectives of the Togolese plan was to strengthen the country's transport system. Thus, the 1967–70 Plan allocated nearly

36 per cent of total investment (CFAF 10.3 billion) for infrastructure, which included the construction of new roads and the completion of the Lomé port. The Lomé port, which had dominated construction activity in Togo between 1965 and 1968, involved a cost of CFAF 5.4 billion. It replaced the former wharf to handle all Togo's foreign trade.

Upper Volta

A landlocked country, Upper Volta provided CFAF 11.4 billion (35 per cent of total investment) for infrastructure during its 1967–70 Plan with priority given to the improvement of the national road network in order to increase its access to the outside world. The road program included the paving of the Ouagadougou-Pô road, which carries the major part of Upper Volta's trade with Ghana; the Bobo Dioulasso-Faramana road carrying traffic to Mali; and the Ouagadougou-Fada Ngourma road connecting Upper Volta with Niger, Togo, and Dahomey. Investment in roads alone amounted to CFAF 6.7 billion, or over 60 per cent of resources provided for infrastructure.

FINANCING INVESTMENT

Because of the very low level of domestic saving, planners in these seven West African countries relied heavily on foreign resources to finance the plan. On the average, 37 per cent of total financial requirements was expected to come from domestic sources and 63 per cent from external sources (Table 6). Senegal and Ivory Coast, the two countries with the most domestic resources, projected the largest proportion of domestic financing (48 per cent and 40 per cent), while Mauritania and Niger projected the largest proportion of external financing (87 per cent and 78 per cent).

Domestic resources include those of the public and private sectors. In the plans of Mauritania, Niger, and Upper Volta these resources were divided about equally; in those of Ivory Coast and Senegal planned public resources were substantially higher than private resources; only in Dahomey and Togo did the planners envisage domestic private financing in excess of public financing.

Public Sector

Domestic public financing of investment includes mainly savings from the government budget, retained earnings of public enterprises, contri-

TABLE 6. BCEAO COUNTRIES: FINANCING OF PLANNED INVESTMENT
(*Amount in billions of CFA francs*)

Plan Being Implemented (or Latest Plan)	Public Resources					Private Resources					All Resources				
	Domestic		External		Total amount	Domestic		External		Total amount	Domestic		External		Total amount
	Amount	Per cent of country total	Amount	Per cent of country total		Amount	Per cent of country total	Amount	Per cent of country total		Amount	Per cent of country total	Amount	Per cent of country total	
Dahomey 1966–70	5.1	20	20.5	80	25.6	6.1	63	3.6	37	9.7	11.2	32	24.1	68	35.3
Ivory Coast 1967–70	67.5	58	48.5	42	116.0	21.0 [1]	19	87.0 [1]	81	108.0	88.5	40	135.5	60	224.0
Mauritania [2] 1963–66	1.5	11	12.1	89	13.6	1.2	9	13.0	91	14.2	3.7	13	24.1	87	27.8
Niger 1965–68	4.6	14	28.8	86	33.4	4.9	50	4.9	50	9.8	9.5	22	33.7	78	43.2 [3]
Senegal 1965–69	31.4	43	41.6	57	73.0 [4]	26.0	57	20.0	43	46.0	57.4	48	61.6	52	119.0
Togo 1966–70	3.4	17	16.7	83	20.1	6.7	79	1.8	21	8.5	10.1	35	18.5	65	28.6
Upper Volta 1967–70	4.2	15	23.1	85	27.3	4.2	75	1.4	25	5.6	8.4	26	24.5	74	32.9
Total	117.7	40	191.3	60	309.0	70.1	35	131.7	65	201.8	188.8	37	322.0	63	510.8

Sources: Same as Table 2.

[1] The plan does not specify the exact amount of domestic and external private resources. Estimates were made on the implications of the plan (see p. 64 of plan).
[2] Extended to 1967.
[3] Later reduced to CFAF 30 billion.
[4] Originally planned at CFAF 84.2 billion.

butions from local budgets, and domestic borrowing by the government. All the plans emphasized the need to achieve surplus current budgets and to channel these surpluses into development budgets. Ivory Coast planned up to 71 per cent (CFAF 48.6 billion) of total domestic public financing to come from the national budget. The high proportion was envisaged in view of the high ratio of public savings, which accounted for nearly 30 per cent of government revenue during 1960–65. Upper Volta planned some 40 per cent of financial resources to come from the state. The other countries planned smaller proportions of public resources of budgetary nature, ranging from 12 per cent (Togo and Niger) to 29 per cent (Dahomey). The last category of countries appeared to rely more on contributions from the state enterprises, including mainly the Railway Authorities, the Port Administrations, the Office of Agricultural Products, and the Road Funds. Among these enterprises, the Road Funds play an important role in financing public investment in Dahomey and Niger, while the Office of Agricultural Products contributes heavily to Togolese public investment.

In addition to resources from the budget and from public enterprises, many of these governments counted on domestic short-term and long-term borrowing to finance the remaining and often important gap in the financing of public development programs. Short-term borrowing takes the form of Treasury bills and central bank advances, while long-term and medium-term borrowing are undertaken through the issue of bonds, the sale of nonnegotiable savings certificates, and the acceptance of savings deposits by the Post Office and other government savings institutions (*caisses d'épargne*). The Governments of Ivory Coast and Dahomey have established new institutions to mobilize private domestic savings: the National Investment Fund (FNI) and the National Finance Company (SONAFI) in Ivory Coast and the National Investment Fund in Dahomey. The role of Ivory Coast's National Investment Fund is to collect private funds through a compulsory scheme, with the objective of utilizing domestically part of the profits of foreign-owned enterprises which would otherwise have been transferred abroad. The Investment Fund's resources consist of a levy on business income and a levy on income from real estate property, both in the form of compulsory subscriptions to noninterest-bearing certificates with no specific maturity. These certificates are redeemable if the holder makes new productive investments approved by the Investment Company to a multiple of three times the face value of the certificates. They may also be converted into bonds of the National Finance Company provided the holder subscribes an equal amount in cash. The Investment Fund may spend 10 per cent of its resources on research projects of general interest for the country's development and use the remainder for financing development projects.

The National Finance Company is entrusted with the primary objective of mobilizing voluntary domestic savings through sales of long-term bonds to private individuals and enterprises. Another objective envisaged by the Government with the establishment of the Finance Company was to create a basis for a domestic capital market. The bonds issued by the Finance Company mature in 20 years and yield an interest of 6 per cent a year, tax free. In principle, its resources may be used for various investments. In practice, however, they have been utilized mainly for taking over government participations in various enterprises and to promote the creation of new enterprises by capital participation or lending.

Government use of credit from the Central Bank to finance planned investments as well as other operations is subject to statutory limitations. The Central Bank may grant short-term advances to the treasuries of these countries for a period not exceeding 240 days, consecutive or not, a calendar year, and in an amount not exceeding 15 per cent of the government's fiscal receipts of the preceding budgetary year. Upon a justified request of a government, BCEAO may also extend use of these advances until the first working day of the following year. Treasury bills of member countries with a maturity of less than six months may also be rediscounted or accepted as collateral for an advance within the fixed limits.

Except in Ivory Coast, most of the public investment comes from foreign financing. The largest source of foreign financing is grants from EEC through the European Development Fund (EDF) and from France through the Fonds d'Aide et de Coopération (FAC).

The first EDF was established in 1958 by a Convention annexed to the Treaty of Rome, which embodied the principle of association with overseas territories and colonies. The five-year Convention earmarked a total of CFAF 144 billion (US$581 million) for development aid to eco-

nomic and social projects in associated territories, to be administered by
EEC under the financially autonomous EDF. The Convention provided
for gradual disbursements of EEC development aid. The second EDF
covered the five-year period June 1, 1964 to May 30, 1969. In contrast
to the first EDF, which provided for investment subsidies only, the
second EDF includes also grants for economic and social investments,
soft special-term loans, aid to agricultural production and diversification, technical cooperation indicating the financing of general studies,
studies related to EEC-financed investment projects, and professional
training programs, as well as short-term advances to stabilization funds
to alleviate the consequences of world price fluctuations.

By the end of 1968, commitments to the seven BCEAO countries
under the second EDF totaled CFAF 30.2 billion, or 64 per cent of
total funds committed to all the CFA countries. Disbursements started
in 1965 and by the end of 1968 totaled about CFAF 18.6 billion,
including aid for agricultural production and diversification, and technical assistance. Aid from France takes several forms: (1) grants and
soft loans through FAC, (2) technical assistance, (3) subsidies for the
University of Dakar (staff and other expenditures) and scholarships,
(4) soft loans granted by the Caisse Centrale de Coopération Economique (CCCE), and (5) financial advantages in the form of a guaranteed price for groundnut product exports.

Apart from France and EEC, other foreign resources include financial and technical assistance from Germany, the United States, Canada,
Italy, Japan, and international organizations. U.S. aid includes commodity assistance loans under U.S. Public Law 480, donations from
voluntary relief agencies, and technical assistance.

Private Sector

In the private sector the distinction between domestic and foreign
resources is not always very clear. In some plans (Ivory Coast), private
resources of domestic and foreign origins are not separated; in others,
the distinctions are merely rough estimates. It appears clear, however,
that because of a very low level of local saving, investments in the private sector are expected to come mainly from retained earnings and
new capital of foreign enterprises. The division between domestic

resources and private foreign resources in the private sector averages about the same as the distinction in the public sector (see Table 6). On the basis of individual plans, however, financing in the private sector differs from that in the public sector: plans which foresee small domestic public resources envisage larger private domestic financing (Dahomey, Niger, Togo, and Upper Volta).

As investment planning in the private sector of the economy is neither as comprehensive nor as firm as in the public sector, implementation of the plan is somewhat uncertain. In general, the planners recognize that, besides the low level of per capita income and subsequently the low level of savings, it is very difficult to mobilize local savings. Furthermore, a substantial amount of these savings is made in the subsistence sector and never takes a monetary form. It is also believed that private savings in these countries have flowed out of the country because of the financial and monetary arrangement of UMOA and convertibility of the CFA franc to the French franc. This observation may be seen in the balance of payments of these countries: the private capital outflows have been large in recent years.

In order to increase domestic savings, the governments of these countries have created new public institutions such as the National Investment Fund and the National Finance Company, as well as the National Development Banks. The Development Banks were set up in order to mobilize domestic resources to support national development programs. Normally, these Banks extend credit—short-term, medium-term, and long-term—for the development of agriculture, industry, commerce, and handicraft activities by private and public enterprises and by cooperative societies; these Banks also take minority participations in private and public investment enterprises. In order to encourage foreign private capital, each country has adopted an investment code giving general guarantees and tax exemptions for new investment. These guarantees assure foreigners who invest capital against discrimination as to legal treatment, taxation, and social contributions; they are allowed to transfer abroad a substantial part of their earnings from investments which have been regarded as contributing to economic development. Tax advantages are given to two groups of enterprises, priority enterprises and enterprises with a special government convention.

ACHIEVEMENTS UNDER PLANS

By the end of 1969, three four-year plans were completed (Mauritania, Niger, and Senegal) and another four plans were heading toward their final years of implementation. Unfortunately, information is not available in the form of comprehensive evaluation or adequate progress reports on development plans to permit a meaningful comparison of targets and achievements. This section attempts only to briefly survey the main results based on fragmentary information embodied in the national plans' performance reports and incomplete accounts on national income, capital formations, and balance of payments of the seven countries. These data, subject to a large margin of errors, can only be taken as illustrative of the results of the plans. As far as possible, an attempt has been made to appraise the performance of the plans in five aspects: (1) plan formulation and review, (2) actual rates of economic growth, (3) levels of actual investment, and (4) disbursements of foreign resources.

Plan Reviews

A common deficiency in the planning process in the West African countries is the lack of a system of follow-up and operational control of the execution of the plan. None of the seven countries has an efficient and integrated reporting system to centralize all information on the progress of development projects for frequent inspections and appraisals. As a result, the value of the plans as stable guides diminishes toward the end of implementation.

In the public sector, however, some review occurs at periodic intervals. These reviews have resulted in reports regarding the performance of the plan on a yearly basis. There is, however, an average gap of from one to two years between the reporting year and the completion of the reports. Periodic reports on major public projects often accompany the annual budget presentation to the national assemblies.

In one country (Niger), the planning authority features a system of continuous programing, according to which each year a four-year investment program is prepared for the public sector within the over-all Four-Year Plan. Such a program is based on reports of actual public expenditures and on disbursement of foreign assistance during the previous year. Nevertheless, many reports do not arrive on time or provide sufficient details. Furthermore, some reports by the planning authorities on individual projects are inconsistent with those of other government agencies responsible for carrying out these projects. For example, in Senegal—the country which has adopted more advanced planning techniques than others—records of realized public development expenditures kept by the Ministry of Planning are only figures of commitments of funds, while actual disbursements of development funds through the capital budget, by public agencies, and from some extrabudgetary foreign assistance sources are recorded in accounts kept at the Ministry of Finance which cannot be fully reconciled with the projections contained in the development plan.

Also, reporting commonly lags considerably after actual happenings. Factors such as crop failures, declines in export prices, declining rate of foreign assistance, and other shortfalls are only ascertained long after they have occurred. The result is that there is not enough time to take policy measures to correct these shortfalls while they still can be corrected. It is encouraging, however, to note that the governments of the seven countries are now increasingly aware of the need to improve the process of planning and are seeking additional technical assistance from abroad in project preparation, as well as plan implementation.

Economic Growth and Investment

Despite the weakness of reporting systems and the lack of information to appraise the development efforts, it is possible to draw some conclusions. Annual growth rates assumed under the plans of the countries differ greatly; these rates ranged from 4.0 per cent (Dahomey and Upper Volta) to 9.2 per cent (Mauritania), averaging 5.7 per cent for the region as a whole (Table 7). In setting the target growth rates, the planners had adopted a realistic view taking into account the past rates of increase in GDP. Except in Dahomey and Senegal, all the plans projected a growth rate lower than the average rate during the previous years. On the other hand, it must be pointed out that figures on GDP are subject to a large margin of error; it is also difficult to compare GDP growth rates of one country to that of another because of differences in methods of computation as well as coverage. For example, the

TABLE 7. BCEAO COUNTRIES: PAST TRENDS, PLAN TARGETS,
AND ACTUAL RESULTS OF GDP GROWTH RATES

	Past Trends		Plan Target Rates (Annual Average)	Actual Results	
	Period	Annual average		Period	Annual average
	←——— Per cent ———→				Per cent
Dahomey	1963–65	2.6	4.0	1966–68	3.6 [1]
Ivory Coast	1960–65	8.0	7.7	1966–67	5.0
Mauritania	1960–63	21.0	9.2	1963–66	14.0
Niger	1960–64	8.0	5.5	1965–66	6.3
Senegal	1961–64	4.3	6.0	1965–66	4.7
Togo	1963–64	10.0	5.0	1965–66	5.6 [1]
Upper Volta	1959–64	6.0	4.0	1966–67	2.0

Sources: Dahomey, data supplied by Dahomean authorities; Ivory Coast, Ministère du Plan, *Les Comptes de la Nation—Principaux Résultats, 1966–67*; Mauritania, *Notes d'Information*, February 1963, and *Memento*, 1968; Niger, Commissariat Générale au Plan, Service de la Statistique, *Comptes Economiques, 1963–66*;
Senegal, Ministère du Plan, *Situation Economique du Sénégal en 1967*; and Upper
Volta, Ministère du Développement et du Tourisme, *Les Comptes Economiques
de la Nation en 1964*, and *Rapport sur l'Execution de la Première Année du Plan
Cadre 1967–70*.

[1] Estimated.

distinction between the subsistence sector and the monetary sector is
often imprecise. In some countries (Mauritania and Togo), the high
growth rates are believed to result partly from the improvement of statistical coverage.

With these reservations, the available data indicate that (except for
Upper Volta and, to a lesser extent, Dahomey) annual growth rates
realized by these countries during the beginning years of the plan either
exceeded the planned targets (Mauritania, Niger, and Togo) or, though
below the targets, exceeded 4.5 per cent (Ivory Coast and Senegal).
They ranged from 2 per cent (Upper Volta) to 14 per cent (Mauritania).

Another important indication of plan results is the size of actual
investment realized during the plans based on the national accounts
(Table 8). Except in Togo, all plans anticipated an average annual
capital formation either equal to past trends (Dahomey) or higher
(other countries). Compared with the plans' targets, the actual investments realized by the area as a whole appear to be satisfactory with the
exception of Upper Volta, where estimated actual investment amounted
to only about 46 per cent of target.

TABLE 8. BCEAO COUNTRIES: PAST TRENDS, PLAN TARGETS,
AND ACTUAL RESULTS OF INVESTMENTS

(*In billions of CFA francs*)

	Past Trends		Plan Target Rates (Annual Average)	Actual Results		
					Annual average	
	Period	Annual average		Period	Amount	Per cent of target
Dahomey	1963–65	7.0	7.0	1966–68	7.9	112.9
Ivory Coast	1960–65	30.0	56.0	1966–67	49.0	87.5
Mauritania	1960–63	. . .	7.0	1963–66	8.3	118.6
Niger	1960–64	8.0	10.8	1965–66	9.3	86.1
Senegal	1961–64	18.2	29.7	1965–66	21.4	72.1
Togo	1963–64	6.3	5.7	1965–66	9.5	166.7
Upper Volta	1964–65	4.2	8.2	1966–67	3.8	46.3

Sources: Same as Table 7.

The rate of actual investment obtained by these countries during the
early phase of their plans are crucial elements in determining the rates
of growth and the success of the plans.

Dahomey.—Total investment in Dahomey during 1966–68 averaged
nearly CFAF 8 billion annually, or 14 per cent higher than the planned
target; the average annual GDP growth rate was estimated at 3.6 per
cent, or slightly lower than the planned rate. Although none of the major
industrial projects included in the Dahomean plan (a cement factory,
textile mills, a brickyard, and a groundnut oil factory) was established
during 1966–68, a cotton ginning mill at Parakou that was to be started
in 1969 was, in fact, built in 1966, owing to the rapid progress in cotton
production. A kenaf factory, which was not included in the plan, was
also started in 1967 and completed in 1968.

Ivory Coast.—In Ivory Coast, actual annual investment during
1966–67 averaged CFAF 49 billion against a planned level of CFAF 56
billion, or about 13 per cent below target. The average annual GDP
growth rate during this period was therefore 5 per cent, against 7.7 per
cent as planned. A high degree of realization was achieved in the San-
Pédro project, timber development, and the agricultural diversification
program (oil palms, cotton, rubber, and rice).

Mauritania.—With the relatively high level of investment realized
(CFAF 8.3 billion annually), compared with the target of CFAF 7 billion, Mauritania experienced the highest GDP annual growth rate

among the seven countries, averaging 14 per cent during 1963–66. The unusually rapid growth rate, compared with the target of 9.2 per cent, was due to rapid expansion of the mining investment by the Mining Company (MIFERMA). From 1962 to 1966 the modern sector, consisting primarily of the Mining Company's iron ore mines in the northwest and the fishing industry of Nouadhibou (Port-Etienne), registered a rate of economic growth of nearly 70 per cent, whereas the traditional sectors showed a growth rate of about 30 per cent between 1962 and 1964.

Niger.—The rate of investment during 1965–66 in Niger, CFAF 9.3 billion annually, was 14 per cent lower than the target; but its GDP growth rate was slightly higher than planned. Substantial progress was recorded in transportation and water resources. A large portion of the main east-west axis road (Niamey-Zinder) was paved and secondary roads were expanded. Also, exploitation of an important uranium deposit was undertaken at Arlit in the Sahara Desert.

Senegal.—An average annual investment of CFAF 21.4 billion recorded in Senegal during 1965–66 fell below the CFAF 29.7 billion envisaged. The annual GDP growth rate during this period (4.7 per cent) also was lower than expected (6 per cent). Satisfactory progress was made in acceleration of agricultural diversification and improvement in productivity.

Togo.—In Togo the average annual investment during 1966–69 was substantially higher than the planned level of CFAF 5.7 billion, and GDP grew at an estimated rate of 7 per cent a year during the same period, or two percentage points higher than planned. The sectors which expanded fast were industry and transport, as the Dadja textile complex was greatly extended and the port of Lomé was completed. Activity in the commercial sector also expanded rapidly.

Upper Volta.—The average annual investment of CFAF 3.8 billion achieved in Upper Volta in 1966–67 was about half of the average implied in its plan. The GDP growth rate during this period was estimated to be 2 per cent annually, or less than half of the planned rate. It appears, therefore, that achievement in Upper Volta, which had the least ambitious plan, was also the least encouraging among the seven countries. Lack of progress in the economy was due to slow development in the agricultural sector. However, progress was made in infrastructure with the extension of the railway up to Kaya (91 kilometers northeast of Ouagadougou) as part of a much larger project consisting of a line linking Ouagadougou with Tambao, and in industry with the establishment in 1968 of the textile mill at Koudougou.

Financing

It was perhaps in financing that performance lagged farthest behind objectives. All the plans relied heavily on foreign resources for financing. The important role assigned to foreign resources, especially EEC, in development planning can be seen from the fact that as high as 63 per cent of the financial resources were expected to come from foreign origins (see Table 6).

The volume of these external resources flowing into the region during the plan periods apparently fell far short of expectations (Table 9). Although no quantitative estimate of the actual flow of external resources for each year can be made because of the absence of comprehensive data, some evidence of this conclusion may be found in the foreign aid and the balance of payments figures.

TABLE 9.   BCEAO COUNTRIES: DISBURSEMENT OF EEC AID UNDER THE
SECOND EDF, 1965–68

(*In billions of CFA francs*)

		Annual Average	
	Total [1]	Actual	Planned [2]
Dahomey	1.8	0.5	1.4
Ivory Coast	5.9	1.5	4.1 [3]
Mauritania	1.6	0.4	1.4
Niger	1.2	0.3	2.2 [4]
Senegal	6.7	1.7	3.8
Togo	0.4	0.1	1.4 [5]
Upper Volta	1.0	0.3	2.3
Total	18.6	1.2	4.2

Sources: *Bulletin de l'Afrique Noire,* No. 511, June 12, 1968, and data supplied by EEC.

[1] Including aid for investment, agricultural diversification and production, and technical assistance.

[2] As indicated or implied in national plans.

[3] Including FAC and CCCE.

[4] For 1968 only.

[5] Estimated as 30 per cent of total external resources.

For Ivory Coast, Niger, and Togo, the figures concerning expected EEC aid were not separately shown in the plans, hence they are only estimates based on implications in the plan. For the seven countries as a whole, disbursement totaled CFAF 18.6 billion during 1965–68, an annual average of CFAF 1.2 billion, or about 29 per cent of the amount indicated or implied in the national plans. The large discrepancy between actual and planned disbursements stemmed from the planners' overestimate of available resources, delays in authorizing specific projects, and inadequate administration of projects and the public bidding procedures. Inadequate implementation of various projects not only slowed the carrying out of the plan as a whole through repercussions on other sectors but also tended to deter the whole development process by setting up imbalances within various economic sectors.

DEVELOPMENT PLANS AND ECONOMIC COOPERATION

One important aspect of development planning of the BCEAO countries deserving comment is their intention, either explicitly stated in the plans or implied through various projects having multinational characters, to proceed toward economic cooperation. Careful analysis of the development problems in the region gives the impression that a necessary condition for successful development in most countries was the establishment of a wider market, and that the smaller economic size of these countries was a severe handicap to establishing industries. The BCEAO countries range in population from 1.1 million in Mauritania to 5.3 million in Upper Volta; GDP ranges from CFAF 41 billion in Mauritania to CFAF 269 billion in Ivory Coast (1966). Aware of these obstacles to development, the countries have embarked upon several plans for economic cooperation as a means of overcoming the limitations imposed by the small size of the national markets. The seven countries are members not only of the West African Monetary Union (UMOA) but also of the African Development Bank and, most important of all, the Conseil de l'Entente. The Entente Council, formed in 1959, now comprises Dahomey, Ivory Coast, Niger, Togo, and Upper Volta. The aim of the Council is to coordinate the economic and foreign policies of member countries in the fields of taxation, public administration, labor legislation, public works, and communications. A Guarantee Fund (formerly Solidarity Fund) was set up to guarantee foreign loans for the development projects having multinational character. Taking into account the objectives of the Council, member countries have included regional projects, especially in infrastructure, in their individual plans. In 1963, Senegal and Mauritania joined Guinea and Mali in establishing a committee for the improvement of the Sénégal River Basin. In the same year, Dahomey, Ivory Coast, Niger, and Upper Volta joined Cameroon, Guinea, Chad, Mali, and Nigeria in the common scheme to develop the Niger River. A number of studies have suggested the necessity of joint planning in the field of heavy industries for the West African region. A regional iron and steel plant has been considered since 1963 by these countries in conjunction with others. Other immediate possibilities for cooperation are in the form of chemical industries, pulp and paper mills, and textile industries. The immediate benefit that the planners hoped to derive from the setting up of these industries was the advantage of lower production costs resulting from the economies of larger scale of output. They are now considering the possibility of harmonizing their development plans in the future.

CONCLUSION

By 1970 all the plans made in the first decade of planning in the BCEAO countries will come to an end; many of these countries will be ready to embark upon a "second generation" of plans, taking into account experience obtained from development planning during the 1960's. Already Mauritania, Niger, and Senegal have launched their third plans covering 1970–73, 1968/69–1971/72 and 1969/70–1973/74, respectively, while Ivory Coast is prepared to adopt its fourth plan for 1971–75, and Upper Volta its third plan covering the same period.

In reviewing the success of these plans, one must distinguish between realization in the public and private sectors. In general, the public sector realized most of the projects listed in the plan directives with a reasonable amount of success, while progress in the private sector appeared to be modest.

Major weaknesses of the planning process may be found in the first phase of planning; that is, the preparation and formulation of the plans. Widespread deficiencies in executive procedures in both central and local governments have seriously impeded the preparation of development programs, while shortage of skills and experience have handicapped their implementation. Moreover, during the period of plan execution, all countries experienced difficulties in securing adequate financial resources, particularly those of private origin.

These weaknesses in the planning process and implementation, however, should not obscure the results achieved in the seven BCEAO countries during the 1960's. The annual average growth rate of GDP in all countries except Ivory Coast and Upper Volta exceeded either the target established in the plans or the apparent trend of the early 1960's. Even in Ivory Coast this growth rate averaged 5 per cent. Before independence, there was no systematic effort at comprehensive planning in the countries under review. At best, planning was confined only to the formulation of major public programs. After independence, however, economic planning became the major goal of all the countries. As evidenced in their development plans, these countries are increasingly interested in exploiting their natural resources and human potentialities to the fullest extent; the current plans represent their first attempts to channel their scarce resources so as to change the structure of their mainly single-crop economies. They have attempted to develop the countries from several fronts: agricultural diversification, import substitution, raising the rate of domestic capital formation, setting up new industries, and developing a solid infrastructural base for further development.

The first decade of plans in the seven West African countries surveyed undoubtedly has provided useful experience for further planning. In the African scene, the process of economic planning is new. In their next development plans, planners of these countries will be in a better position not only to prepare comprehensive and realistic development programs but also to proceed from stronger economic bases than they did in the earlier years of planning during the postindependence era. Furthermore, it seems clear that the trend toward planning in a regional framework will become more evident in the new generation of plans.

CHAPTER 4

Money and Banking

MONETARY SYSTEM

On May 12, 1962 a treaty establishing the West African Monetary Union (Union Monétaire Ouest Africaine—UMOA) and providing for a common currency and a common central bank was signed by Dahomey, Ivory Coast, Mali, Mauritania, Niger, Senegal, and Upper Volta. The old BCEAO was dissolved on October 31, 1962 and was replaced by a new central bank of the same name but with enlarged responsibilities and an intergovernmental organization. On the same date the above-mentioned countries concluded with France a cooperation agreement by which France guaranteed the convertibility of the CFA franc, issued by the BCEAO, into French francs, and the members of the UMOA undertook to keep their external reserves in an operations account opened by the new BCEAO at the French Treasury, with which a special relationship was established. The treaty establishing the UMOA and the agreement for cooperation are two separate documents; the treaty providing for a monetary union and a common central bank could continue in force even if the agreement for cooperation were to be abrogated.

Mali did not ratify the treaty or the agreement; on the other hand, Togo (which had participated in the negotiations only as an observer) formally signed both documents on November 27, 1963 and subsequently ratified them. The capital of the BCEAO is set at CFAF 2,800 million and is distributed evenly among the seven members of the UMOA (Dahomey, Ivory Coast, Mauritania, Niger, Senegal, Togo, and Upper Volta).

CENTRAL BANK

Organization

BCEAO, with temporary headquarters in Paris, maintains an agency in the capital of each member country and has established subagencies in some other places within the UMOA territory. Over-all management is entrusted to a Board of Directors in which each member country appoints two directors, from whom one is elected President; and France, under the provisions of the cooperation agreement, appoints seven directors, or the equivalent of half of the total number appointed by the UMOA countries. As a rule, the decisions of the Board are taken by a simple majority, but certain important decisions must be adopted by a two-thirds majority. Amendments of the statues require the unanimous decision of the Board.

In each member country, a five-member National Monetary Committee, appointed by the government and including the two national directors, implements the general credit and rediscount policy decisions taken by the Board of Directors. Day-to-day management of BCEAO is entrusted to a Director-General, appointed for an indefinite term by the Board of Directors. The Director-General attends, either personally or through a delegate, all meetings of the Board and the National Monetary Committees. He represents BCEAO in all its external relations. All BCEAO personnel are appointed and removed from office by the Director-General, although appointment of agency managers requires the prior approval of the government of the country in which the agency is established.

Functions

Issuance of currency.—BCEAO has the sole right to issue the CFA franc in each member country. The rate of the CFA franc, which is fully convertible into French francs, was CFAF 246.853 = US$1 from January 1, 1960 to August 10, 1969. After devaluation of the French franc in mid-1969, the rate became CFAF 277.710 = US$1, but the relationship of the CFA franc to the French franc remained unchanged at CFAF 1 = F 0.02.

Notes and coins issued by BCEAO are legal tender in all member countries and circulate freely within UMOA. Identification of CFA notes by a letter following the serial number enables BCEAO to keep separate accounts for each country's currency in circulation. Coins, which account for roughly 4 per cent of total currency in circulation, are not identified by country. Statistics, based on issuance of each country's notes and withdrawal of notes of other countries, reveal a fairly large intercountry movement of notes, particularly between Mauritania and Senegal, between Dahomey and Togo, and among Ivory Coast, Niger, and Upper Volta.

Depository of external reserves.—External reserves of UMOA are held by BCEAO in French francs in an operations account at the French Treasury. The procedural aspects of the centralization of BCEAO's reserves in the operations account are regulated by a convention between BCEAO and the French Treasury. An amendment to this convention dated June 2, 1967 made it possible for BCEAO to invest part of its exchange reserves in certain types of negotiable bonds, maturing within two years, issued by international organizations of which all BCEAO countries are members. Since this amendment, BCEAO has invested part of its foreign reserves in short-term bonds issued by the International Bank for Reconstruction and Development (World Bank). Transfers between member countries and France are unrestricted.

BCEAO statutes provide for specific measures in case of a continuous and sizable reduction of exchange reserves. These measures are to be applied when the ratio of the average amount of BCEAO's foreign assets to the average amount of its demand liabilities has remained equal to or less than 20 per cent for 30 days, or when the evolution of the economic and financial situation of UMOA gives reason to believe that this ratio may drop to less than 20 per cent. Under these circumstances, the President of BCEAO must convene the Board for the purpose of examining the situation and taking the appropriate decisions. Such decisions may include an increase in the discount rate and a reduction of the rediscount ceilings, advances, and other facilities, as well as a review of exceptional increases in an overdraft granted to the Treasuries.

When the ratio of foreign assets to the average amount of demand liabilities becomes equal to or less than 10 per cent and remains at this level for 30 days, the President of BCEAO notifies members of the Board of Directors and the Chairmen of the National Monetary Committees. The Board of Directors is then convened without delay in order to decide on any possible increase in the discount rate, and to reduce rediscount ceilings, advances, and other facilities, as well as any assistance granted to the Treasuries following a decision of the Board. These measures may not be rescinded as long as the ratio remains equal to or less than 10 per cent for 30 days, unless the Board decides to repeal them by a three-fourths majority.

Under the cooperation agreement with France, BCEAO's discount rate and charges on advances must be increased by 1 percentage point if the operations account for the area as a whole with the French Treasury shows a debit for 60 days. Moreover, under these circumstances, agencies with a debit balance in the external operations account must reduce their ceilings on rediscount, advances, and other facilities by 20 per cent, and those with positive balances of less than 15 per cent of their currency issue in circulation also must reduce their ceilings on these facilities by 10 per cent. In both circumstances, these BCEAO agencies may not grant any new authorizations for medium-term credit. However, the BCEAO Board of Directors, which is immediately convened, may introduce modifications or exceptions to these provisions by a three-fourths majority.

Pursuant to the cooperation agreement concerning the operations account, in the event that the deposits in this account are exhausted, BCEAO may require public and private organizations to surrender their French francs or other foreign currency holdings to BCEAO against CFA francs. BCEAO may restrict this requirement solely to public institutions and banks and, at its discretion, may implement it only in countries whose external transactions through the operations account show a deficit.

The French Treasury pays interest to BCEAO on balances in the operations account at an annual rate at least equal to the rediscount rate of the Bank of France, but never less than 2.5 per cent; in 1966/67 the effective rate was 4.5 per cent, and in 1967/68 it was 5.3 per cent. Conversely, BCEAO pays interest to France on any overdraft balance at an annual rate which increases from 1 per cent for amounts up to F 5 million to 2 per cent for amounts between F 5 million and F 10 million. For greater overdraft balances, the annual rate is the same as the rediscount rate of the Bank of France, but never less than 2.5 per cent. Interest paid by BCEAO on negative balances is deducted from the royalties or dividends to be paid to member countries according to the negative external reserve position of each country. If the imputed share of BCEAO's foreign reserves for any member country becomes negative, the country pays a charge on its debit balance at an annual rate equal to the average rate of interest on BCEAO's foreign investments or borrowings. The reason for this provision is to maintain equity among member countries; as BCEAO's profits are distributed equally among member countries, the net use by a member of the common pool of reserves reduces earnings in foreign exchange holdings and, subsequently, the profits available for distribution.

Credit to banks.—Within the framework of rediscount ceilings which are the principal means of control, BCEAO is authorized to extend both short-term and medium-term credit. Short-term credit is extended in the form of rediscount of short-term paper and temporary advances (*prises en pension*) against private and government paper, as well as direct advances secured by either gold or foreign exchange [1] and securities acceptable to BCEAO. Normally the period for which short-term credit is granted is limited to six months, but it may be extended up to nine months for financing crops and public contracts.

Semiannually, BCEAO's Board of Directors determines the over-all rediscount ceiling for each member country. In this determination, it is guided by the proposals of the National Monetary Committees based on

---

[1] So far advances secured by either gold or foreign exchange have not been provided.

the over-all credit requirements of the economy and the resources likely
to be available to banks. The National Monetary Committee in each
member country then allocates this over-all ceiling between the Treasury (for discount of customs duty bills) and the banks in proportions
reflecting their credit requirements and available resources. The ceiling
assigned to each bank may not exceed half its anticipated short-term
credits. Nevertheless, banks actively participating in the financing of
agricultural activities may go beyond this limit. However, the ceiling
that may be granted should not exceed the cumulative total of 80 per
cent of the probable amount of agricultural credit operations and
50 per cent of other credit operations.

Also semiannually, BCEAO's Board of Directors determines the
over-all medium-term rediscount ceiling for each country by increasing
the outstanding credits by an amount equivalent to investment projects
eligible for such financing. This ceiling is not allocated among the
banks. However, medium-term credit operations of banks are annually
subject to limits established on the basis of their capital, their reserve
funds, and their demand and time deposits after deduction of their fixed
assets. During any given six-month period, only BCEAO's Board of
Directors, on the proposal of the National Monetary Committee, may
modify the over-all short-term and medium-term ceilings previously
fixed, while each Monetary Committee may at its discretion change the
allocation of its short-term over-all rediscount ceilings among the
banks. Medium-term credits are granted by BCEAO for periods not
exceeding five years.

Commercial paper may be rediscounted at the Central Bank only
after the National Monetary Committee is satisfied that the financial situation of the individual borrower conforms to certain minimum requirements. To be eligible for medium-term credit, proposed projects must be
in accordance with the country's development policy and must be profitable enough to ensure amortization of the credit. Moreover, the amount
of credit requested must not exceed 50 per cent of the project's total
cost. For projects having special importance, this ratio may be raised to
65 per cent and for some categories of construction projects to 80 per
cent.

Credit to member governments.—BCEAO may grant the Treasury of
any UMOA country ways-and-means or short-term advances for a

period not exceeding 240 days, consecutive or not, per calendar year, and in an amount not exceeding 10 per cent of the government's fiscal receipts during the preceding budgetary year. Nevertheless, on a justified request of the country, BCEAO's Board of Directors may extend use of these advances until the first working day of the following year. On December 10, 1968, BCEAO statutes were amended to enable the Board of Directors, after reviewing developments in the currency issue and evaluating the effects of its decision on the development of the currency issue, to raise the maximum amount of short-term advances to an amount equal to 15 per cent of fiscal receipts. In this circumstance, the Board of Directors determines the duration of this overdraft, which, however, may not exceed the limits mentioned above. In determining the permissible short-term advances, the amount related to the previous year's fiscal receipts is reduced by the amount of Treasury bills held by BCEAO as well as by the indebtedness of the Treasury vis-à-vis banks availing themselves of the BCEAO rediscount facilities. Moreover, BCEAO may discount Treasury customs duty bills, provided such bills have a maturity of less than four months, have been issued by a solvent debtor, and are guaranteed by a bank. So far, practically all UMOA governments have at one stage or another taken advantage of the BCEAO's ways-and-means advances; however, Dahomey, Niger, and Upper Volta have made more intensive use of this facility as these countries have experienced the most severe fiscal problems.

In addition to short-term advances, Treasury bills of UMOA member countries with a maturity of less than six months may be (1) rediscounted or accepted for temporary advances (*prises en pension*); (2) accepted as collateral for an advance within the limits fixed by the Board of Directors; and (3) bought from or sold to the banks without endorsement, provided that banks do not act as intermediaries for the Treasuries.

The total amount of BCEAO operations on Treasury bills of each of the banks shall not exceed 10 per cent of the average amount of its demand and time deposits during the previous 12 months. For this purpose, deposits placed with banks by the Treasury and the Postal Checking System shall be taken into account only to the extent that they correspond to deposits received from individual or private corporate bodies.

Liquidity Ratio and Reserve Requirements

Banks must permanently maintain a minimum ratio between their liquid and rediscountable assets and their short-term liabilities. This ratio was fixed at 73 per cent for the fiscal year 1968/69 and will increase by 1 percentage point each year until it reaches 75 per cent, starting with 1970/71. Rediscountable credits granted by a bank are included on its liquid assets side, while rediscounted credits are included on both the liquid assets and the current liabilities side. This method of calculation induces the banks to grant rediscountable credits.

BCEAO may impose reserve requirements on banks when requested by a member government, but so far this has not been done.

COMMERCIAL BANKS

Nine commercial banks operate throughout the UMOA countries. Although most of these banks are controlled by foreign interests, local authorities participate to some extent in their share capital (Table 1). Three banks have more than a 10 per cent participation by the government of the country in which they operate: Union Togolaise de Banque (35 per cent), Société Dahoméenne de Banque (31 per cent), and Union Sénégalaise de Banque (22.6 per cent). The provision of short-term credit to finance mainly produce marketing and transformation activity rates highest on the list of services rendered by commercial banks in the UMOA countries. Medium-term and long-term credit are of little significance and are usually extended only if the debtor complies with the central bank requirements for rediscounting.

DEVELOPMENT BANKS

In addition to the commercial banks, development banks have been established in all UMOA countries since they became independent (Table 2). Usually the national government is the main shareholder in the capital of the development banks; shareholders may also include the Caisse Centrale de Coopération Economique (CCCE), BCEAO, and in one country (Ivory Coast) foreign banking institutions and the International Finance Corporation (IFC), an affiliate of the World Bank.

Although the primary function of the development banks is to provide financing and technical assistance for investment projects, they have also been engaged in financing real estate enterprises and in short-term financing of crops, particularly in Senegal and Niger. On average, short-term credit extended by development banks accounts for 40 per cent of their total credit operations, medium-term credit for 18 per cent, and long-term credit for 31 per cent. In financing their credit operations, these banks rely heavily on deposits of public institutions, CCCE loans, and BCEAO rediscount facilities. Development banks have access to BCEAO rediscount facilities only to the extent that funds are not provided by the CCCE and/or the Banque Ivoirienne de Développement Industriel (BIDI) in Ivory Coast.

OTHER FINANCIAL INSTITUTIONS

Besides the commercial and development banks, other financial institutions operate in some UMOA countries. Unlike the commercial and development banks, these institutions were created to provide specific credit services. For example, in Ivory Coast, the Amortization Fund (Caisse Autonome d'Amortissement) acts as a banker to public enterprises; the National Agricultural Credit Fund (Caisse Nationale de Crédit Agricole) was created to make medium-term loans to farmers; and the Crédit de la Côte d'Ivoire finances small industrial ventures, handicraft industries, and private institutions. Except for the Amortization Fund, most of the specialized financial institutions play a minor role in credit operations.

INTEREST RATES

Since the establishment of UMOA, both the BCEAO discount rate and the rate for documentary credit relating to financing of crops have been kept unchanged at 3.5 per cent and 3 per cent, respectively, per annum. Because of the large number of public and semipublic enterprises operating in the UMOA area, BCEAO has refrained from increasing the discount rate so as to keep the cost of borrowing by these enterprises at a minimum. It appears, however, that as a result of this policy and in the light of rising interest rates abroad, there has been a tendency in recent years for banks to rely more on BCEAO rediscount facilities while transferring their own funds abroad to earn a

TABLE 1. BCEAO COUNTRIES: COMMERCIAL BANKS, SEPTEMBER 1969

	Head Office	Countries Having Permanent Offices	Date of Establishment	Amount and Distribution of Capital
Banque Internationale pour l'Afrique Occidentale (BIAO)	Paris	Ivory Coast Dahomey Upper Volta Mauritania Niger Senegal Togo	1965	F 60 million (Compagnie Financière France-Afrique 51% and First National City Bank 49%)
Banque Internationale pour le Commerce et l'Industrie en Côte d'Ivoire	Abidjan	Ivory Coast	1962	CFAF 300 million (Government of Ivory Coast 10% and French banks 90%)
Banque Internationale pour le Commerce et l'Industrie au Sénégal	Dakar	Senegal	1962	CFAF 500 million (Banque Nationale de Paris 41%, Société Financière pour les Pays d'Outre-Mer 51%, and private Senegalese shareholders 8%)
Société Générale de Banques en Côte d'Ivoire	Abidjan	Ivory Coast	1962	CFAF 875 million (Government of Ivory Coast 10%, French banks 60%, German banks 5%, Italian banks 10%, Swiss banks 5%, and U.S. banks 10%)
Société Générale de Banques au Sénégal	Dakar	Senegal	1962	CFAF 500 million (Société Générale 51%, other banks 39%, and private Senegalese interests 10%)

Société Ivoirienne de Banque	Abidjan	Ivory Coast	1962	CFAF 625 million (Government of Ivory Coast 10%, French banks 42%, German banks 16%, Italian banks 16%, and U.S. banks 16%)
Banque Nationale de Paris	Paris	Dahomey Upper Volta Togo	1966	FF 325 million (French commercial banks)
Société Dahoméenne de Banque	Cotonou	Dahomey	1962	CFAF 125 million (Government of Dahomey 31%, Crédit Lyonnais 29%, Banque Dahoméenne de Développement 20%, Banca Commerciale Italiana 10%, and Deutsche Bank 10%)
Société Mauritanienne de Banque	Nouakchott	Mauritania	1967	CFAF 50 million (Government of Mauritania 10%, Société Général 65%, and other interests 25%)
Union Sénégalaise de Banque pour le Commerce et l'Industrie	Dakar	Senegal	1961	CFAF 690 million (Government of Senegal 22.6%, Banque Nationale de Développement du Sénégal 21.8%, Crédit Lyonnais 42.7%, Banca Commerciale Italiana 4.3%, Deutsche Bank 4.3%, and Morgan Guaranty International Banking Corporation 4.3%)
Union Togolaise de Banque	Lomé	Togo	1964	CFAF 130 million (Government of Togo 35%, Crédit Lyonnais 35%, Deutsche Bank 18%, and Banca Commerciale Italiana 12%)

Source: BCEAO, *Annuaire des Banques de l'Union Monétaire Ouest Africaine, 1969.*

TABLE 2. BCEAO COUNTRIES: DEVELOPMENT BANKS, SEPTEMBER 1969

	Date Established	Name of Bank	Amount and Distribution of Capital
Ivory Coast	1965	Banque Ivoirienne de Développement Industriel (BIDI)	CFAF 700 million (Government of Ivory Coast 21%, CCCE 11%, BCEAO 6%, Chase International Corporation 9%, IFC 6%, Banque Française du Commerce Extérieur 5%, and others 42%)
Dahomey	1961	Banque Dahoméenne de Développement (BDD)	CFAF 300 million (Government of Dahomey 55%, CCCE 34%, BCEAO 10%, and others 1%)
Upper Volta	1961	Banque Nationale de Développement de la Haute Volta (BND-HV)	CFAF 355 million (Government of Upper Volta, CCCE, and BCEAO)
Mauritania	1961	Banque Mauritanienne de Développement (BMD)	CFAF 200 million (Government of Mauritania 58%, CCCE 34%, and BCEAO 8%)
Niger	1962	Banque de Développement de la République du Niger (BDRN)	CFAF 480 million (Government of Niger 55%, BCEAO 10%, CCCE 10%, and others 25%)
Senegal	1964	Banque Nationale de Développement du Sénégal (BNDS)	CFAF 1,360 million (Government of Senegal 56%, CCCE 28%, BCEAO 7%, Caisse des Dépôts et Consignations 5%, and Caisse de Compensation 4%)
Togo	1967	Banque Togolaise de Développement (BTD)	CFAF 300 million (Government of Togo 60%, CCCE 20%, BCEAO 10%, and others 10%)

Source: BCEAO, *Annuaire des Banques de l'Union Monétaire Ouest Africaine, 1969.*

higher rate of return. While the rates charged by BCEAO remained unchanged, the structure of interest rates charged by banks was revised in May 1966. Before that date, banks charged uniform interest rates determined in relation to the customer's creditworthiness; consequently, interest rates for small customers tended to be relatively high. The new interest rate structure aims at discontinuing this practice by relating interest rates to the nature of the operation financed. All rates on credit operations are computed on the basis of the present official BCEAO discount rate plus specified percentage points. Effective annual interest rates of 4.50–5.25 per cent are charged on short-term credit for financing crops, and on short-term and medium-term credit for productive purposes and for enterprises which received priority status under the Investment Code. Interest rates of 7.0–7.5 per cent are charged on real estate operations not declared to be of social interest. Penalty rates of 8.0–8.5 per cent are charged on all credit operations in excess of individual rediscount limits with BCEAO.

THE TREASURY, POSTAL CHECKING SYSTEM, AND SAVINGS BANKS

Treasury System

In UMOA countries the Treasury acts as the government fiscal agent and as a banker for the public sector. In principle, all public entities, including price stabilization funds, the Postal Checking System, and savings banks, keep the bulk of their liquid resources on deposit with the Treasury. In Ivory Coast, however, part of the public sector savings is invested outside the Treasury with the Amortization Fund; in Niger, many public agencies keep their liquid assets on deposit with the Development Bank. In addition to serving as a depository for public entities, the Treasury also receives deposits from the private sector consisting, in part, of small balances awaiting settlement on account of estates, tax refunds, and indemnities.

The Treasury extends short-term credit in the form of promissory notes (*obligations cautionnées*) accepted in lieu of payments for customs duties. These promissory notes, which the Treasury can discount at the Central Bank, are subject to the latter's short-term global rediscount ceilings. The Treasury may also issue short-term bonds, but so far such operations have been limited.[2]

Postal Checking System and Savings Banks

Checking accounts are managed and operated by the Post Office in each country. The Postal Checking System receives demand deposits from the private and public sectors. It operates the largest deposit network in each country, and deposits its funds with the Treasury and development banks.

The savings banks are financially autonomous public entities. They receive private savings and use the facilities of the Post Office in the different countries.

MONETARY AND CREDIT DEVELOPMENTS

Monetary and credit developments in the BCEAO countries are subject to marked seasonality because of crop-financing requirements. Credit generally rises to a peak during the early part of the year and falls to a low around September. Tables 3 to 5 present monetary data based on years ended September 30 to reflect changes in the underlying monetary situation.

The primary objective of BCEAO's credit policy is to facilitate orderly economic growth in member countries while maintaining an appropriate balance between financial and real resources. Abstracting seasonal variations, BCEAO's credit operations since 1962 have expanded at a steady rate. From September 1962 to September 1964, domestic credit expanded at an average annual rate of nearly 17 per cent to CFAF 65.8 billion (see Table 3). Credit to the private sector rose significantly in all BCEAO countries and was one of the main expansionary factors during this period. On the basis of September data, the total increase in the private sector credit was CFAF 24.2 billion, or 38 per cent; CFAF 9.1 billion, or more than one third, was financed by rediscounts with BCEAO. On a net basis, the Government's position vis-à-vis the banking system exercised a contractionary impact

---

[2] For further details, see Petrus J. Van de Ven and Dirk J. Wolfson, "Problems of Budget Analysis and Treasury Management in French-Speaking Africa," IMF, *Staff Papers*, Vol. XVI (1969), pp. 140–58.

TABLE 3. BCEAO COUNTRIES: MONETARY SURVEY, 1962–69 [1]

(In billions of CFA francs; end of September, except as noted)

	1962	1963	1964	1965	1966	1967 Sept.	1967 Dec.	1968 Mar.	1968 June	1968 Sept.	1968 Dec.	1969 Mar.	1969 June	1969 Sept.
Foreign assets (net)	34.51	31.73	31.09	33.50	39.29	35.63	35.89	38.46	35.27	37.59	40.45	46.80	46.49	47.65
Domestic credit														
Claims on government (net)														
Claims on government	5.31	9.07	8.78	11.52	10.86	10.18	12.78	10.50	10.39	9.77	10.48	8.81	8.99	10.79
Less government deposits	−20.71	−26.61	−30.94	−31.86	−31.75	−27.68	−28.11	−31.06	−29.61	−26.30	−27.64	−30.14	−28.86	−28.59
Total claims on government	−15.41	−17.54	−22.16	−20.33	−20.89	−17.20	−15.33	−20.56	−19.22	−16.53	−17.15	−21.33	−19.87	−17.80
Claims on private sector	63.75	74.11	87.93	94.01	94.48	98.35	106.48	130.69	125.63	116.52	127.83	144.57	134.89	127.36
Total domestic credit	48.34	56.57	65.78	73.68	73.59	81.15	91.15	110.12	106.41	99.99	110.68	123.23	115.02	109.56
Assets = liabilities	82.85	88.30	96.87	107.18	112.88	116.78	127.04	148.58	141.68	137.58	151.13	170.03	161.51	157.21
Money	73.38	79.36	80.33	84.56	91.32	93.56	104.00	122.40	113.42	109.82	120.67	134.95	126.08	117.95
Quasi-money	4.03	3.86	9.63	11.42	9.35	10.12	12.01	14.68	15.75	13.75	17.37	21.66	21.74	23.03
Other items (net)	5.44	5.08	6.92	11.20	12.20	13.10	11.04	11.50	12.50	14.01	13.09	13.42	13.68	16.23

Source: IMF, International Financial Statistics (monthly).

[1] Because of rounding, figures do not add to all totals in this table or the following tables.

TABLE 4. BCEAO COUNTRIES: CONSOLIDATED ASSETS AND LIABILITIES OF THE CENTRAL BANK, 1962–69

(In billions of CFA francs; end of September, except as noted)

	1962	1963	1964	1965	1966	1967		1968				1969		
						Sept.	Dec.	Mar.	June	Sept.	Dec.	Mar.	June	Sept.
Foreign assets	34.56	30.28	31.15	30.69	38.76	40.12	43.44	43.78	41.74	42.12	43.84	44.66	46.14	45.39
Claims on government	0.09	3.12	0.55	2.38	1.72	0.96	3.42	1.09	1.15	0.94	1.98	1.00	0.98	1.41
Claims on banks	16.92	18.28	26.04	25.73	22.00	21.23	26.98	43.36	35.95	26.34	33.29	44.74	32.77	25.92
Short-term	15.09	15.74	23.30	22.52	18.37	16.99	22.14	39.27	31.54	22.28	29.18	40.27	28.32	20.11
Medium-term	1.83	2.54	2.74	3.21	3.63	4.24	4.84	4.09	4.41	4.06	4.11	4.47	4.45	5.81
Assets = liabilities	51.57	51.68	57.74	58.80	62.48	62.31	73.84	88.23	78.84	69.40	79.11	90.40	79.89	72.72
Currency and banks' deposits	40.12	40.17	43.16	45.20	48.06	47.87	59.16	70.52	60.34	54.95	64.48	74.30	62.75	56.71
Currency outside banks	*37.45*	*38.65*	*41.62*	*42.35*	*44.93*	*44.92*	*54.49*	*66.15*	*57.03*	*51.41*	*60.18*	*69.06*	*58.07*	*53.04*
Foreign liabilities	2.05	0.22	1.26	1.40	0.46	0.34	1.07	1.08	0.82	0.67	1.60	0.35	1.21	0.37
Government deposits	7.68	9.49	11.43	9.79	11.52	11.44	10.78	12.91	13.24	10.50	9.13	12.02	11.94	11.46
Other items (net)	1.72	1.80	1.89	2.41	2.45	2.66	2.83	3.72	4.44	3.28	3.90	3.72	3.99	4.15

Source: IMF, *International Financial Statistics* (monthly).

TABLE 5. BCEAO COUNTRIES: CONSOLIDATED ASSETS AND LIABILITIES OF COMMERCIAL AND DEVELOPMENT BANKS, 1962–69

(In billions of CFA francs; end of September, except as noted)

	1962	1963	1964	1965	1966	1967		1968				1969		
						Sept.	Dec.	Mar.	June	Sept.	Dec.	Mar.	June	Sept.
Reserves	2.17	1.29	1.18	2.57	2.71	2.45	4.14	3.53	3.26	3.40	4.72	5.09	4.24	3.31
Foreign assets	2.00 [1]	12.67	17.35	17.95	17.19	9.24	10.66	13.86	14.78	12.92	18.27	22.10	24.59	26.41
Claims on government	0.14	0.30	2.66	4.05	4.51	4.43	4.37	4.38	4.12	4.03	3.60	2.19	2.22	3.98
Claims on private sector	58.82	68.90	82.73	88.44	89.39	93.80	101.63	125.31	120.48	112.29	122.62	139.20	130.18	122.65
Assets = liabilities	**63.13**	**83.16**	**103.92**	**113.01**	**113.80**	**109.92**	**120.80**	**147.08**	**142.64**	**132.64**	**149.21**	**168.58**	**121.23**	**156.35**
Demand deposits	30.49	34.91	33.04	37.01	41.71	43.77	44.50	51.10	51.24	53.60	55.56	60.27	62.14	59.49
Time deposits	4.03	3.86	9.63	11.42	9.35	10.12	12.01	14.68	15.75	13.75	17.37	21.66	21.74	23.03
Foreign liabilities	...	11.00	16.15	13.74	16.21	13.39	17.14	18.10	20.43	16.77	20.06	19.61	23.03	23.47
Government deposits	8.10	11.91	14.30	16.50	15.14	11.39	12.48	12.77	11.22	11.57	13.30	12.75	12.21	12.39
Credit from Central Bank	16.83	18.32	26.05	25.53	22.00	21.23	27.00	42.10	34.10	26.34	33.29	44.74	32.77	25.92
Other items (net)	3.68	3.16	4.75	8.81	9.39	10.01	7.68	8.32	9.90	10.61	9.63	9.25	9.33	12.05
TREASURY CLAIMS ON PRIVATE SECTOR AND SPECIAL DEPOSITS														
Treasury claims on private sector	4.93	5.21	5.21	5.57	5.09	4.55	4.85	5.38	5.15	4.23	5.21	5.37	4.71	4.71
Post Office checking deposits	5.08	5.65	5.57	5.09	4.63	4.79	4.99	5.03	5.12	4.80	4.90	5.62	5.79	5.40
Savings bank deposits	1.38	1.58	1.75	1.97	2.17	2.51	2.58	2.74	2.83	2.85	2.94	3.11	3.17	...

Source: IMF, *International Financial Statistics* (monthly).

1 Net foreign assets.

on money supply. The net liabilities of the area's banking system to governments rose from CFAF 15.4 billion in September 1962 to CFAF 22.2 billion in September 1964, or at an annual average rate of about 20 per cent. Government net borrowing from the banking system increased relatively little in Mauritania, Niger, and Upper Volta and decreased sizably in the four remaining countries. The impact of over-all credit expansion on money supply was further offset by a more than twofold rise in quasi-money liabilities and a reduction of CFAF 3.4 billion in the area's net foreign assets position.

The decline in UMOA's net foreign assets in 1962/63 is attributed primarily to the outflow of capital by private enterprises which was motivated by the intensification of credit restrictions in France. Rather than use their own resources to finance current and capital outlays, private enterprises, especially branches and subsidiaries of the large French companies operating in the area, placed greater reliance on commercial bank borrowing, at the same time transferring funds abroad to be used as financing by affiliates in France. For the same reasons, UMOA commercial banks in financing the demand for private sector credit resorted more to the use of BCEAO's rediscounting facilities than to the use of funds from their parent offices or foreign branches. To reverse this trend and prevent a further decline in the area's net foreign assets by encouraging more intensive use of local financial resources, BCEAO lowered its rediscount ceiling. This measure, together with general moral suasion, appears to have contributed, at least in part, to the improvement in the area's net foreign assets position in 1964/65 and 1965/66.

From September 1964 to September 1966, domestic credit expanded at an average annual rate of 6 per cent, a much slower rate than in the two preceding years. Nevertheless, money supply rose at a faster average annual rate (7 per cent) than in the previous period (5 per cent), owing mainly to a reduction in quasi-monetary liabilities and an increase (CFAF 2.4 billion in 1964/65 and CFAF 5.8 billion in 1965/66) in the banking system's net foreign assets. Net foreign assets rose by CFAF 5.3 billion in Ivory Coast, by CFAF 2.2 billion in Togo, and by CFAF 1.1 billion in Mauritania, reflecting a favorable development in these countries' exports. Although net foreign assets also increased in Upper Volta (by CFAF 1.5 billion), the rise apparently reflected a contraction of business activity and government outlays. In Dahomey, net foreign assets declined slightly (by CFAF 0.3 billion); in Niger and Senegal, they continued to decline though at a reduced rate. In the last three countries the decline seemed partly attributable to transactions of the public sector (i.e., budget deficits in Dahomey and Senegal and mainly bank-financed losses of public institutions in Niger).

After declining slightly in the year ended September 1966, domestic credit extended by the UMOA banking system increased by 10 per cent to CFAF 81.2 billion during the following year. This increase was due essentially to credit expansion in Ivory Coast and Senegal. In both countries the rise reflected an increased use in Treasury deposits with banks to finance government operations. In Ivory Coast, private sector credit to finance a larger coffee crop and rising industrial and commercial activity also increased substantially. Much of this credit was supplied by the Amortization Fund from resources previously held abroad. Repatriation of these resources was one of the main factors leading to the decline in Ivory Coast's net foreign assets position, and consequently in that of the area. The area's net foreign assets declined from CFAF 39.3 billion at the end of September 1966 to CFAF 35.6 billion at the end of the following year, or by 9 per cent. This decline exerted a contractionary impact on money supply, which increased by only 2 per cent in the second year of this period, compared with a gain of 8 per cent in the previous year.

From September 1967 to September 1969, money supply in BCEAO countries rose by about 26 per cent to CFAF 118.0 billion. This expansion resulted from increases in both domestic credit (35 per cent) and the area's net foreign assets (34 per cent). At the same time money rose by CFAF 12.9 billion to CFAF 23.0 billion. As net claims of the banking system on government increased by less than 4 per cent, credit to the private sector, which expanded by 25 per cent, was the principal source of domestic credit expansion. Ivory Coast accounted for the largest share (58 per cent) of the total increase in private sector credit of CFAF 29.0 billion, followed by Senegal (10 per cent) and Mauritania (9 per cent). Togo accounted for 7 per cent and Dahomey for 6 per cent of total private sector credit expansion; Upper Volta and Niger accounted for the remaining 10 per cent. In Mauritania, credit to the private sector more than doubled in the two-year period ended September 1969; this increase was due to the rise in credit associated with a higher level of imports through the Nouakchott wharf of consumer goods traditionally brought into Mauritania through the port of Dakar. Even with this increase, however, the outstanding amount of credit to the private sector in Mauritania represented only about 4 per cent of the combined total for all BCEAO countries at the end of September 1969. The proportion of private sector credit financed by rediscounting at BCEAO was slightly lower than the previous years' average.

CHAPTER 5

Balance of Payments

STRUCTURE AND RECENT DEVELOPMENTS

No official over-all balance of payments data are available for the BCEAO countries, except Ivory Coast. Detailed data are published only on transactions with countries outside the franc area, which represent a minor part of the BCEAO countries' foreign transactions. Therefore, in order to establish an over-all balance of payments of the BCEAO area, transactions with other countries in the franc area are estimated on the basis of customs records on trade, estimates of French aid, and global data relating to nontrade payments made through the BCEAO (Table 1).

During 1960–67 the over-all balance of payments of the BCEAO area was characterized by (1) deficits in 1961 and 1963, a growing surplus in 1964–66, and a deficit again in 1967; (2) substantial and growing net inflow of official unrequited transfers, which exceeded the trade deficit by increasingly larger amounts after 1962; and (3) the movement of other recorded items—including services, private unrequited transfers, and nonmonetary capital—from a small surplus

TABLE 1. BCEAO Countries: Estimated Balance of Payments, 1960–67 [1]

(In billions of CFA francs)

	1960	1961	1962	1963	1964	1965	1966	1967
A. Goods (net) [2]								
Exports	78.9	91.1	92.4	103.2	134.7	134.1	153.8	153.7
Imports	−94.5	−112.3	−114.3	−118.4	−141.0	−142.0	−147.0	−154.7
Trade balance	−15.6	−21.2	−21.9	−15.2	−6.3	−7.9	6.8	−1.0
With franc area	−11.4	−22.9	−12.9	−13.6	−21.5	−18.5	−10.9	−12.4
With other areas	−4.2	1.7	−9.0	−1.6	15.2	10.6	17.7	11.4
B. Official unrequited transfers (net)								
With franc area	…	18.1	20.1	19.3	16.5	19.2	16.4	18.0
With other areas	…	3.5	8.6	9.9	13.1	14.6	17.1	18.1
Total official unrequited transfers	…	21.6	28.7	29.2	29.6	33.8	33.5	36.1
C. Services, private unrequited payments, and nonmonetary capital (net)								
With franc area (net)								
Official transfers [3]	…	25.7	10.7	9.6	12.5	−3.6	−5.7	−3.7
Private transfers [4]	…	−28.5	−19.2	−25.1	−38.2	−29.6	−24.1	…
Total with franc area	…	−2.8	−8.5	−15.5	−25.7	−33.2	−29.8	…
With other areas (net)								
Services	−0.8	0.2	−2.4	−3.3	−3.1	−4.1	−5.2	…
Private unrequited transfers	0.2	0.4	0.7	0.9	0.6	1.7	1.2	…
Nonmonetary capital	2.4	6.4	12.0	6.4	4.1	4.4	−2.5	…
Total with other areas	1.8	7.0	10.3	4.0	1.6	2.0	−6.5	…
Total services, private unrequited payments, and nonmonetary capital	…	4.2	1.8	−11.5	−24.1	−31.2	−36.3	−39.4

D. Recorded balance (A + B + C)	...	4.6	8.6	2.5	-0.8	-5.3	4.0	-4.3
With franc area	...	-7.6	-1.3	-9.8	-30.7	-32.5	-24.3	...
With other areas	...	12.2	9.9	12.3	29.9	27.2	28.3	...
E. Errors and omissions (net)	...	-6.2	-8.0	-5.7	0.9	7.0	4.4	-1.4
F. Over-all balance (D + E)	5.5	-1.6	0.6	-3.2	0.1	1.7	8.4	-5.7
G. Monetary movements (net)								
Central Bank (net)	-1.9	1.7	-4.6	4.6	3.4	-5.7	-4.0	-0.1
Other banks (net)								
Assets	...	...	...	...	-5.8	3.5	-4.3	6.3
Liabilities	...	...	...	...	2.3	0.5	-0.1	-0.5
Total other banks	-3.6	-0.1	4.0	-1.4	-3.5	4.0	-4.4	5.8
Total monetary movements	-5.5	1.6	-0.6	3.2	-0.1	-1.7	-8.4	5.7

Sources: Comité Monétaire de la Zone Franc, *La Zone Franc*; IMF, *International Financial Statistics*; BCEAO, *Rapport d'Activité*; and data supplied by the French authorities.

[1] Positive figures indicate credit; negative figures indicate debit.
[2] Customs data taken from the reports of the Monetary Committee of the franc area. They differ somewhat from customs data shown in Tables 2, 4, and 6, which were taken from other sources and also were adjusted.
[3] Includes pensions paid by the French Government to BCEAO country nationals formerly employed in the French armed forces or in colonial administration. Normally these pensions should be included in private transactions with the franc area.
[4] Includes CCCE loans to semipublic enterprises in 1967.

through 1962 to a rapidly increasing deficit, amounting to CFAF 39 billion in 1967.

An increase in foreign assets first appeared in the over-all balance of payments in 1962, owing to larger foreign grants and the net nonmonetary capital flow. In 1963 and 1964, BCEAO reserves declined; continued improvement in the balance of trade and foreign aid was offset by adverse developments in services and nonmonetary capital. A small surplus reappeared in 1964; the surplus became much larger in 1966 (CFAF 8.4 billion), presumably because of changes in private capital flows and a remarkable improvement in the balance of trade in 1966. In 1967 there was a substantial over-all deficit (CFAF 5.7 billion). In 1968, however, movements in aggregate net foreign assets for the area indicated an over-all surplus of CFAF 4.6 billion and in the first nine months of 1969, one of CFAF 7.0 billion.

Over the period 1960–67, components in the balance of payments in the BCEAO area gradually underwent considerable change. In the early 1960's, there were large trade deficits, roughly matched by receipts of official grants, and small positive balances in some years on account of other recorded transactions, including mainly services and nonmonetary capital. During 1961–63, nonrecorded flows had large negative balances, presumably resulting from private capital outflows in the early years of independence of the countries concerned. In recent years, on the other hand, exports have generally risen faster than imports, reducing the trade deficits and even creating a surplus in 1966 while foreign aid receipts have continued to grow. The large trade surplus in 1966 was due to the marketing of bumper coffee and groundnut crops and increased mineral output. On other recorded transactions, as a whole, however, the deficit, which first appeared in 1963, grew rapidly thereafter. As opposed to substantial deficits in the early 1960's, nonrecorded flows showed surpluses or only small deficits after 1963.

The balance of recorded payments of BCEAO countries with other countries of the franc area was in constant deficit over the 1960's, but particularly during 1964–66, when the deficit averaged CFAF 29.2 billion a year. Substantial negative balances on account of trade and private nontrade transactions largely offset the steady inflow of official grants from France. Allowing for errors and omissions, it may be presumed that unrecorded private transactions with the franc area had the effect of increasing the deficit in the early 1960's and of reducing it in later years. Payments with countries outside the franc area consistently showed a positive balance, particularly during 1964–66, when it averaged CFAF 30.2 billion a year. This improvement was due mainly to substantial trade surpluses (largely from expanding wood and mineral exports to these countries) and greater official grants (largely from the European Economic Community).

Ivory Coast provided the main element of strength in external payments of the BCEAO area. During 1963–66 it had a surplus in its balance of payments, averaging CFAF 4 billion annually. In these years, relatively large surpluses on trade and nonmonetary capital transactions exceeded a large deficit on services and unrequited transfers. In 1967 a deficit of CFAF 6.3 billion appeared, mainly because of a decline in the net inflow of recorded and unrecorded nonmonetary capital. A recorded surplus of CFAF 8.6 billion, however, was registered in 1968, when the trade surplus more than doubled, while the net nonmonetary capital flow improved. Togo also made steady, though smaller, contributions to the area's foreign assets. Throughout 1964–68 it achieved moderate surpluses, averaging about CFAF 1 billion annually, moderate deficits on trade and services being more than offset by surpluses on unrequited transfers and nonmonetary capital.

Senegal is the second most important country of the area in terms of production, but its contribution to the area's foreign reserves was negative during 1963–68, except in 1966, mainly because of substantial deficits on goods and services as well as nonmonetary capital movements. In 1966, a surplus of CFAF 2.3 billion occurred, largely reflecting the rise in exports from a bumper groundnut crop. In 1967, however, a deficit (CFAF 2.1 billion) reappeared and became greater in 1968 (CFAF 3.9 billion). Mauritania and Niger have also had balance of payments deficits in most of the years 1963–68. In Mauritania, rising receipts from mineral exports were matched by larger import expenditures largely on equipment goods destined for the mining industry. In Niger, surpluses on trade and unrequited transfers have generally been offset by deficits on services and nonmonetary capital. The balance of payments situations of Dahomey and Upper Volta tended to improve in 1964–67, when these countries achieved small surpluses, except for Dahomey in 1967.

Throughout 1960–67 the balance of payments of the BCEAO area, as a whole, was not under inflationary pressures. Whereas estimated aggregate gross domestic product (GDP) of the area rose by 28 per cent during 1963–66, domestic credit rose by 21 per cent and money supply by only 15 per cent. Expansion of credit to governments was contained within the limits set by the Central Bank's statutes, and the authorities had recourse to foreign grants or borrowing—mainly from France—in order to finance their outstanding deficits. Although credit to the private sector expanded at a steady rate, it nonetheless remained closely linked to crop financing needs.

FOREIGN TRADE

Despite the deficits in most years, the trade balance of the BCEAO area improved during 1960–67. The trade deficits averaged CFAF 18.5 billion a year through 1963 but only CFAF 7.1 billion in 1964 and 1965. In 1966, there was a surplus of CFAF 6.8 billion and in 1967 only a small deficit of CFAF 1.0 billion (see Table 1). Export receipts nearly doubled over the period, the annual growth rate averaging 13.5 per cent, while imports rose by an average annual rate of 9 per cent. Preliminary data indicate that a trade surplus of a few billion CFA francs was achieved in 1968, mainly on account of increased exports from Ivory Coast and Dahomey.

Exports

Despite significant progress in sales of mineral products since 1963, exports from the BCEAO countries have continued to consist largely of agricultural and forestry products (Table 2). The upward trend in export receipts during 1960–67 resulted from both exploitation of new mineral deposits and expansion of agricultural production by increasing the cultivated area and improving yields. The value of exports, however, has fluctuated substantially (Table 3) with the size of crops, depending on the weather, and changes in world prices. For coffee, world prices have evolved favorably; for groundnuts and palm oil, they have remained fairly stable; and for cocoa and cotton, they fell sharply during 1964–66 but recovered later. On the other hand, the effects of world price fluctuations for a number of agricultural exports

TABLE 2. BCEAO COUNTRIES: EXPORTS BY COMMODITIES, 1960–67

(Value in billions of CFA francs)

	Value								Per Cent of Total	
	1960 [1]	1961	1962	1963	1964	1965	1966	1967	1960	1967
Agricultural and forestry products										
Coffee, raw	19.4	21.7	20.5	30.4	35.4	27.4	32.3	26.4	25	17
Wood	6.3	8.3	9.1	12.5	17.9	18.5	18.6	21.8	8	14
Groundnut products										
Shelled nuts	13.4	14.7	13.3	11.1	12.8	13.2	18.7	12.1	17	8
Oil	10.6	11.6	11.7	9.8	12.5	13.4	14.0	14.4	14	9
Total groundnut products	24.0	26.3	25.0	20.9	25.3	26.6	32.7	26.5	31	17
Cocoa	10.1	11.1	11.7	12.5	16.0	12.6	14.8	16.2	13	11
Cotton, ginned	0.5	0.4	0.3	0.7	0.6	0.8	1.2	2.4	1	2
Oil palm products										
Kernels	3.4	2.0	1.9	2.4	2.7	1.8	1.1	1.0	4	1
Palm and palm-kernel oil	0.7	0.5	0.5	0.5	0.7	1.8	1.2	0.7	1	—
Total oil palm products	4.1	2.5	2.4	2.9	3.4	3.6	2.3	1.7	5	1
Bananas	1.3	2.1	2.8	3.5	3.2	2.8	2.8	3.0	2	2
Total listed products	65.7	72.4	71.8	83.4	101.8	92.3	104.7	98.0	85	64
Mineral products										
Iron ore	—	—	—	2.7	10.7	13.0	15.8	15.4	—	10
Phosphates	0.3	1.3	1.4	2.1	4.1	4.9	6.3	5.6	1	4
Manganese	0.1	0.6	0.5	0.4	0.5	0.7	0.8	0.5	—	—
Total mineral products	0.4	1.9	1.9	5.3	15.3	18.6	22.9	21.5	1	14
All other	10.6	12.4	15.2	11.4	17.4	22.5	26.1	32.7	14	22
Grand Total	76.7	87.7	88.9	100.1	134.5	133.4	153.7	152.2	100	100

Sources: France, Institut National de la Statistique et des Etudes Economiques, *Données Statistiques*, and data supplied by national authorities.

[1] Includes Mali for the first six months of 1960.

TABLE 3. AVERAGE ANNUAL EXPORT PRICES OF MAIN AGRICULTURAL CASH CROPS ON EUROPEAN MARKETS, 1961–68

(In CFA francs per kilogram, c.i.f.)

	1961	1962	1963	1964	1965	1966	1967	1968
Coffee, robusta								
Le Havre (from Ivory Coast)	102	111	154	194	170	192	189	182
Antwerp (from Congo)	89	98	131	192	163	189	183	...
Groundnuts, shelled								
Marseilles (from Senegal)	53	53	53	54	54	54	53	...
London (from Nigeria)	49	43	43	47	52	47	45	41
Cocoa								
Le Havre (from Cameroon)	119	115	139	128	92	132	156	194
London (from Ghana)	124	117	143	131	97	135	162	191
Cotton: Liverpool (from Uganda)	...	183	195	195	172	169	183	205 [1]
Bananas: Hamburg (from Ecuador)	34	34	36	32	35	33	32	32
Palm oil: European ports (from Nigeria)	57	53	55	59	67	58	56	...

Sources: IMF, *International Financial Statistics*; Food and Agriculture Organization, *Monthly Bulletin of Agricultural Economics and Statistics*; International Cotton Advisory Committee, *Cotton—World Statistics*, Washington; *Revue des Principaux Marchés Tropicaux*, Antwerp; and France, Institut National de la Statistique et des Etudes Economiques, *Données Statistiques*.

[1] January-August only.

TABLE 4. BCEAO COUNTRIES: COMMODITY COMPOSITION OF IMPORTS, 1960–67

(Value in billions of CFA francs)

	Value								Per Cent of Total	
	1960 [1]	1961	1962	1963	1964	1965	1966	1967	1960	1967
Consumer goods	52.2	62.7	62.2	64.9	79.6	78.7	81.5	77.7	58	53
Food	*20.6*	*20.8*	*25.1*	*25.8*	*34.1*	*32.5*	*36.1*	*32.6*	*23*	*22*
Energy	5.2	5.6	5.8	6.3	7.0	7.9	8.7	7.7	6	5
Raw materials and semiprocessed goods	13.8	14.8	15.8	18.3	20.9	22.5	24.4	26.7	15	18
Capital goods	19.1	24.3	28.0	28.9	35.1	34.1	34.4	34.2	21	24
Total imports	90.3	107.4	111.8	118.4	142.6	143.2	149.0	146.3	100	100

Sources: France, Institut National de la Statistique et des Etudes Economiques, *Données Statistiques*, and data provided by national authorities.

[1] Includes Mali for the first six months of 1960.

have been alleviated through marketing arrangements with France and price subsidies from EEC.

Since 1931, France had operated import controls for foodstuffs and raw materials that were linked to price support schemes designed for the benefit of the overseas countries of the French franc area, and serving after World War II also to conserve non-franc area currencies. These schemes included (1) the withholding of import licenses for supplies from sources outside the franc area unless prices in France rose above a predetermined level or until the crops of the CFA countries had been disposed of and (2) linking systems (*jumelage*) requiring French manufacturing industries to use both franc area and non-franc area supplies of a particular commodity. Usually, however, price support schemes for the overseas countries of the franc area comprised a guaranteed import quota (*contingent*) for a commodity still subject to import restriction in France and a guaranteed price in excess of the world market price (the difference between the two was referred to as *surprix*); some also involved a tariff preference in the French market. These schemes were of great importance to BCEAO producers, particularly of coffee, groundnuts and groundnut oil, and bananas.

The variety of support mechanisms was large. For some commodities, direct subsidies were given to producers. In addition, the Central Stabilization Fund (Fonds National de Régularisation des Cours des Produits d'Outre-Mer, or FNRCPOM), which obtained its resources from the French Treasury, extended short-term loans to local stabilization funds when market prices fell below the "intervention prices" fixed for certain commodities. Cocoa was one of the few important tropical foodstuffs that never had the benefit of *surprix* arrangements in France, but the Central Stabilization Fund did set an intervention price and made loans to local stabilization funds. Cotton also occupied a special position, since imports from the African countries did not receive either price support in France or tariff or quota protection, but the Fonds de Soutien des Textiles des Territoires d'Outre-Mer (FSTTOM), which obtained its resources mainly from a special tax levied in France on textiles and from the French budget, granted loans and subsidies to regional and local stabilization funds.

The financial advantage derived during the years 1960 through 1966 by the BCEAO countries (exclusive of Mauritania and Upper Volta, for which the benefit was minor and impossible to calculate) is estimated at approximately CFAF 60.9 billion (about US$244 million). This estimate does not include the benefits obtained on minor exports (e.g., pepper, coconuts, and tuna fish), but it does include the subsidies to cotton producers and exporters that were financed by France through stabilization funds. Virtually all of this amount accrued to Senegal (CFAF 28.9 billion) and Ivory Coast (CFAF 25.2 billion). The price support schemes were gradually dismantled during the 1960's (see "Regional distribution of imports and import programs," below).

The first Yaoundé Convention of Association between EEC and 18 African and Malagasy states (including all BCEAO countries) came into force in mid-1964. It provided for the gradual elimination of the preferential treatment granted by France to the exports of the associates in the form of tariff preferences, quantitative restrictions, and guaranteed export prices. As a counterpart, exports from the associates to all EEC countries were to be freed from duty and were granted, vis-à-vis third countries, the protection of the EEC common external tariff, which became fully effective in July 1968. A significant exception to full freedom of market access, however, concerned certain commodities subject to EEC internal market regulations (i.e., rice, manioc, processed fruit with sugar added, and sugar); these commodities were subject, with a certain degree of relief, to the same compensatory levies as similar products from third countries. The advantages granted to exports from the associates also included financial aid to agricultural production and diversification, totaling US$230 million, aimed at helping these countries to achieve the adjustments necessary to market their products at world prices by the end of the Convention in 1969. This aid included price subsidies to certain agricultural exports, which were scheduled to decline progressively over the duration of the Convention.

Pursuant to the 1964–69 Convention of Association, French price support ended in 1963/64 for palm oil, in 1964/65 for coffee and cotton, in 1965/66 for sugar, and in 1968 for groundnut products. Bananas are the only commodity that still receives preferential treatment; imports into France from non-franc area sources continue to be subject to quantitative restrictions, and quotas are usually reserved for the French Antilles, Ivory Coast, Cameroon, the Malagasy Republic, and the Canary Islands.

EEC price subsidies—mainly for groundnut products and cotton— generally started in 1964/65, sometimes concurring with remaining French price guarantees. From July 1967, EEC support to oil and oil-seed exports from its associates was complemented by a special price stabilization scheme aimed at alleviating the effects of major world price declines; this support totaled US$13 million.

The new Convention of Association, signed in July 1969 and to terminate in 1975, does not continue the previous program for aid to agricultural production and diversification. In exceptional circumstances, however, similar grants may be extended on an ad hoc basis, especially if a fall in world prices should seriously threaten the economy of an associated country. The total amount earmarked for such grants is limited to the equivalent of US$60 million. According to the new Convention, the protection granted on EEC markets to certain tropical products from associated countries is to be lessened by lowering the common external tariff (on coffee from 9.6 per cent to 7 per cent, on cocoa from 5.4 per cent to 4 per cent, and on palm oil from 9 per cent to 6 per cent).

Imports

In evaluating the data on import expenditures, it is important to note that throughout the period under review imports from France were unrestricted and that since 1968 the same has been true of imports from other EEC countries (with minor exceptions). Although over-all import expenditures of the BCEAO countries rose in every year throughout 1960–67, the rate of increase varied considerably among countries. In most of these countries, marketed crops generate the greater part of cash income; therefore, the level of import expenditures closely reflects the value of agricultural exports. Variations in imports also arise from other factors, such as the requirements of the new administrations immediately after independence and the availability of foreign financing, on which the major part of capital goods imports depends.

The total recorded value of imports into the BCEAO countries rose by approximately two thirds during 1960–67, from CFAF 94 billion to CFAF 155 billion, or at an average annual growth rate of 9 per cent (see Table 1). This growth was particularly marked in 1961, immediately following independence, and again in 1964, when consumption expenditure rose fast, mainly as a result of bumper cocoa and coffee crops. Imports rose in 1966, a year of good groundnut and coffee crops; again in 1967; and even more steeply (according to preliminary data) to CFAF 168 billion in 1968, mainly because of increased imports into Upper Volta, Senegal, and Ivory Coast.

For the BCEAO countries as a whole, the import structure remained remarkably stable throughout 1960–67. Consumer goods accounted for more than half of total import expenditures and capital goods for roughly one fourth; the remainder consisted mainly of raw materials and semiprocessed goods (Table 4). In spite of the basic similarity of the economies involved, the import structure varies considerably from one country to another, owing to differences in certain elements (e.g., consumption patterns, government spending policies, and the stage and nature of economic development).

Consumer goods predominate among imports into some countries, such as Senegal and Dahomey, reflecting the historical influence of European consumption patterns. On the other hand, equipment predominates among imports into countries where capital-intensive industries (i.e., manufacturing and mining) are being rapidly developed. A striking example is Mauritania, where equipment imports for the iron ore industry accounted for 90 per cent of the total import value during 1963–65. In Ivory Coast, where manufacturing has already reached a comparatively advanced stage of development, imports of raw materials and semifinished products tended to rise faster than those of equipment goods.

Terms of Trade

Lack of systematic data makes it difficult to establish an index of the terms of trade for the BCEAO area. Some conclusions, however, may be drawn from the EEC estimates of the terms of trade between EEC and 14 of the African associated countries (including the seven BCEAO countries). EEC accounts for nearly 70 per cent of the BCEAO area's total trade. According to EEC estimates (Table 5), the indices of the terms of trade fluctuated around an upward trend during 1962–67. For the unit value of imports, the index rose by 8 per cent from 1962 to 1965 and then leveled off. The upward trend of

TABLE 5. INDICES OF TERMS OF TRADE BETWEEN THE EEC AND THE
AFRICAN AND MALAGASY ASSOCIATED COUNTRIES, 1963–67

(1962 = 100)

	1963	1964	1965	1966	1967
African associated countries [1]					
Unit value of exports	102	108	101	106	106 [2]
Unit value of imports	104	106	108	108	107 [2]
Terms of trade	98	102	94	98	99 [2]
Ivory Coast					
Unit value of exports	104	114	98	113	...
Unit value of imports	103	106	105	109	...
Terms of trade	101	108	93	104	...
Togo					
Unit value of exports	104	111	102	118	120
Unit value of imports	98	99	97	101	98
Terms of trade	106	112	105	117	122
Upper Volta					
Unit value of exports	102	109	118	128	...
Unit value of imports	99	110	116	117	...
Terms of trade	103	99	102	109	...

Source: Commission of the European Communities, *Les Echanges Commerciaux entre la CEE et les Etats Africains et Malgache Associés, 1958–1966/67,* Brussels, 1969.

[1] Excluding the Democratic Republic of Congo, Rwanda, Burundi, and Somalia.
[2] Estimated.

import prices is explained by rising prices in the country of origin and increased import duties—as well as higher transportation costs, which represent up to 50 per cent of import costs in landlocked countries. For the unit value of exports, the index also had a basic upward trend, but it fluctuated widely because of marked swings in the world prices for certain agricultural commodities, mainly coffee and cocoa (see Table 3). The favorable trend is mainly explained by developments in the export prices of wood and minerals.

EEC has also estimated separately the terms of trade of three BCEAO area countries: Ivory Coast, Togo, and Upper Volta. For these countries, the trend over 1962–67 generally appeared to be more favorable than in the above-mentioned over-all index of the terms of trade, especially because of the upward trend in the export value indices.

Trade by Countries

Ivory Coast plays a key role in the trade balance of the BCEAO area, not only in absolute value, accounting for nearly half of the area's total trade (imports plus exports) in 1967, but also in its constant and large trade surpluses (Table 6). During 1960–67, Ivory Coast's surpluses averaged CFAF 11.4 billion a year, while there was an average annual deficit in the trade balance of the area excluding Ivory Coast of CFAF 21.6 billion, with export receipts covering only 72 per cent of import expenditures. Exports from Ivory Coast more than doubled during 1960–67, reaching CFAF 80 billion, mainly reflecting the expanded tropical wood sales, which accounted for 27 per cent of the total export value in 1967, compared with 30 per cent for coffee and 17 per cent for cocoa. Its imports also doubled over this period, reaching CFAF 65 billion in 1967. In 1968, according to preliminary figures, Ivory Coast's exports rose further by 31 per cent to CFAF 105 billion, mainly on account of coffee and cocoa bumper crops, while imports totaled CFAF 78 billion, an increase of 20 per cent.

In terms of the absolute value of trade, Senegal ranks second to Ivory Coast. Senegalese exports and imports accounted for 24 per cent of the total area's trade in 1967. However, Senegal's trade balance was constantly negative during 1960–67, the deficit averaging CFAF 7 billion a year. Import expenditure remained stable at about CFAF 40 billion; the export value fluctuated with proceeds from groundnut sales, which usually account for nearly 80 per cent of total export proceeds. After reaching a low level in 1963, export receipts tended to increase, generally narrowing the trade deficit, which amounted to only CFAF 1 billion in 1966 and to CFAF 5 billion in 1967. In 1968, however, Senegal's trade balance again deteriorated, and the deficit approached CFAF 8 billion.

Among the five smaller countries of the BCEAO area, only two showed a favorable trend in trade over the period 1960–67. Since 1964, Mauritania's trade has shown widening surpluses, averaging CFAF 9 billion a year. In 1968 another surplus of about the same amount was recorded, resulting from the rapid increase in iron ore exports. Upper Volta had persistent trade deficits over the period, but these tended to decline, averaging about CFAF 5 billion in 1965–68,

TABLE 6. BCEAO COUNTRIES: FOREIGN TRADE BY COUNTRIES, 1960 AND 1967 [1]

(*Value in billions of CFA francs*)

	1960					1967				
	Exports		Imports		Balance	Exports		Imports		Balance
	Value	Per cent of total	Value	Per cent of total		Value	Per cent of total	Value	Per cent of total	
Dahomey	4.5	6	7.6	8	−3.1	3.7	2	10.7	7	−7.0
Ivory Coast	38.8	49	32.4	34	6.4	80.3	52	65.0	42	15.2
Mauritania						17.2	11	8.6	6	8.6
Niger	3.1	4	3.5	4	−0.4	6.3	4	11.4	7	−5.0
Senegal	27.9 [2]	35 [2]	42.5 [2]	45 [2]	−14.6 [2]	33.9	22	38.8	25	−5.0
Togo	3.6	5	6.4	7	−2.8	7.9	5	11.2	7	−3.2
Upper Volta	1.0	1	2.1	2	−1.1	4.5	3	9.0	6	−4.5
Total	78.9	100	94.5	100	−15.6	153.8	100	154.7	100	−0.9

Sources: Comité Monétaire de la Zone Franc, *La Zone Franc*, 1963–67.

[1] Customs data taken from the reports of the Monetary Committee of the franc area. They differ somewhat from customs data shown on Tables 2, 4, and 7, which were taken from other sources and also were adjusted in certain cases.
[2] Includes Mali and Mauritania.

compared with CFAF 7 billion in the previous three years. Although Togo's export receipts more than doubled during 1960–67, mainly owing to phosphate and cocoa sales, import expenditures followed a parallel trend, leaving a fairly stable trade deficit, which amounted to CFAF 3.2 billion in 1967. In 1968, however, the deficit narrowed to CFAF 2.1 billion. In Niger, export receipts (about 70 per cent from groundnut products) generally grew at a slower rate than import expenditures; consequently the trade deficit grew from small amounts in the early 1960's to an average of CFAF 3 billion in 1964–66 and a record CFAF 5 billion in 1967, followed by a slight improvement in 1968. Dahomean exports, largely palm products, remained at the same level over the period, while imports rose by 41 per cent; the trade deficit more than doubled, reaching CFAF 7 billion in 1967 and 1968.

Direction of Trade

France accounted for roughly half of the BCEAO area's trade in either direction in 1967 (Table 7). The importance of France as a trading partner stems from several factors, including the maintenance of cooperation agreements for comprehensive aid and reciprocal trade preferences, and the dominance of this trade by French firms or their subsidiaries. Nevertheless the French share in the BCEAO area's trade tended to decline with regard to both exports and imports. Among factors behind this tendency were the gradual elimination of the preferential system with France, liberalization of imports from other EEC countries, the declining number of French nationals living in the BCEAO countries, and the rapid expansion in mineral exports finding their main markets in industrial countries other than France. The share of other franc area countries in total trade of the BCEAO countries is minor and showed only minor changes. Since 1960 the trade deficit with the whole franc area, though still substantial, has declined, exceeding CFAF 12 billion in 1967.

Trade with EEC countries other than France expanded considerably over 1960–67 in both directions; these countries took 18 per cent of total exports of the area in 1967 and represented 19 per cent of total imports. The widening role of these countries in the BCEAO area's trade is explained by the special trade and aid relations developed under the Conventions of Association and also by the same factors

TABLE 7. BCEAO COUNTRIES: DIRECTION OF FOREIGN TRADE, 1960 AND 1967 [1]

	France	Franc Area Excluding France	EEC Excluding France	Other Countries	Total
VALUE (*billion CFA francs*)					
Exports [2]					
1960	49.8	3.2	6.9	16.6	76.5
1967	76.2	19.2	30.2	38.4	164.0
Imports [2]					
1960	60.4	8.2	7.8	15.2	91.6
1967	82.4	13.2	29.1	30.1	154.8
Trade balance					
1960	−10.6	−5.0	−0.9	1.4	−15.1
1967	−6.2	6.0	1.1	8.3	9.2
PER CENT OF TOTAL					
Exports					
1960	65	4	9	22	100
1967	46	12	18	23	100
Imports·					
1960	66	9	8	17	100
1967	53	9	19	19	100

Sources: France, Institut National de la Statistique et des Etudes Economiques, *Données Statistiques*, and data supplied by national authorities.

[1] Data differ somewhat from those in Tables 1–4 and 6 because different sources for certain countries had to be used for composition and direction of trade.
[2] Includes Mali for the first six months of 1960.

which caused the French share to decrease. Over 1960–67 the balance of trade of the BCEAO area with EEC countries other than France improved somewhat—showing a small surplus of CFAF 1 billion in 1967—while the balance of trade with other countries, as a whole, improved considerably. Countries outside the franc and EEC areas have slightly increased their share of both imports and exports; increased marketing of mineral products contributed to the expansion in exports, and some liberalization of import restrictions allowed more imports, mainly from the United States, the United Kingdom, and Japan.

Regional Distribution of Imports and Import Programs

In principle, the BCEAO countries did not apply quantitative restrictions to imports of franc area origin. Imports from countries outside the franc area, however, were limited by national import programs (except in Togo). Before independence, these programs were drawn up by the central authorities of the French franc area; subsequently, they were agreed with France in the Joint Committees in which France and the BCEAO country concerned had an equal voice, as provided in the cooperation agreements. The early postwar programs had been determined in the light of general French franc area policy considerations, a principal consideration being that of their impact on the area's dollar pool. Most of these were programs broken down by monetary areas and took into account purchase and licensing commitments under bilateral trade agreements, including bilateral quotas negotiated by France on behalf of individual overseas territories. In France their scope had narrowed over the years as imports, first from countries of the Organization for European Economic Cooperation (OEEC), then from the United States and the rest of the dollar area, and finally from other countries outside the French franc area, were progressively liberalized.

In the former French West African Federation (Afrique Occidentale Française, or AOF), corresponding liberalization lists for OEEC countries and dependent territories, for the United States and Canada, and for countries not included in either group were issued in 1957 and 1959. The lists were confined mainly to raw materials and semimanufactured products. These lists were maintained after independence, but apparently no further commodities were added to them. When the BCEAO countries became members of the International Monetary Fund, the size and composition of their annual import programs were already becoming increasingly liberal, in part because the preferential market access accorded to France was gradually being extended also to the other EEC member states. This equalization of access was to take place in several stages, the time schedule being different for customs duties and quantitative import restrictions. The association arrangements contained no provisions, however, with respect to quota restrictions on imports into the associated states from non-EEC countries, although the latter could not be treated more favorably than EEC members. The import programs covered only nonliberalized goods of non-French franc area origin [1] and initially comprised two types of quotas (normally established in terms of value, not quantity)—one applicable to all EEC countries other than France, and the other to all other countries outside the

---

[1] Some programs, however, have included figures for liberalized imports from non-EEC sources.

French franc area.[2] The latter were called global quotas, although in fact the former were also global rather than single country quotas. Under most programs, the quotas for non-EEC countries could also be used (except for goods subject to a ceiling) to import the commodities concerned from EEC countries, once the corresponding quotas for the latter were exhausted, but the reverse was not permitted. Certain other imports from outside the French franc area were admitted under the liberalization lists mentioned above. There have occasionally been other imports outside the program of commodities of non-franc area origin. Togo, in view of its policy of nondiscrimination, did not issue liberalization lists or establish import programs.

The structure and implementation of most programs were affected by one or more special arrangements. Imports of certain sensitive items could be subject to a ceiling applicable to all countries outside the French franc area or a floor for imports of French origin. Imports of specified other commodities, mainly textiles, could be subject to a ceiling when originating in "low-wage" countries or "countries with abnormal competition," which might include such sources as Hong Kong, India, Pakistan, Portugal, the Republic of China, and Japan.[3] There have also been ceilings on imports from Eastern Europe and mainland China (*pays de l'Est*). Import programs could provide for an aggregate floor for imports of French origin, guaranteeing in effect a minimum amount for such imports. Some import programs included a clause to the effect that capital goods should be purchased in France whenever price and quality were comparable to those of other suppliers. At times, imports of some market organization commodities, notably sugar and wheat, were reserved entirely for the French franc area.

The ceilings and floors in the import programs were established, on an annual basis, in the Joint Committees and generally had the effect of providing French producers with a sheltered market for certain items

---

[2] Ivory Coast's programs include a separate global quota for countries with which trade agreements are in force. Senegal's programs include a "reserve" quota without area designation, which is allocated during the year.

[3] Niger had no special quotas for "low-wage" countries because it preferred to import from the cheapest source. Ivory Coast prohibited certain imports from such countries administratively and also applied the triple customs tariff (general tariff) to them. Togo's policy of nondiscrimination precluded the use of ceilings and floors.

(e.g., dairy products, beverages other than whisky and gin, refrigerators, air-conditioners, radios, automobiles, tractors, jute bags, and some other textiles, particularly cotton piece goods). A ceiling restricted the import of the commodity concerned from outside the French franc area, even when the goods were offered on a transit basis by firms established in the French franc area, to a specified amount or quantity. A floor for a specified commodity implied that in principle imports from sources outside the French franc area would not be licensed until a given amount or quantity of that commodity had been purchased in the French franc area, although in practice this did not necessarily mean that import licenses for other sources were refused until imports from France had reached a predetermined level.

Starting in 1959, the markets of the BCEAO countries have been progressively opened up to imports originating outside the French franc area. This liberalization has occurred primarily through (1) relaxation and eventually elimination of quantitative restrictions on imports from EEC countries other than France, (2) reduction and then elimination of customs duties on commodities originating in those countries, and (3) gradual dismantling of the ceiling and floor systems under which imports of French origin had been guaranteed preferential access. Restrictions on imports from non-EEC countries outside the French franc area have also been relaxed, but at a slower pace. The BCEAO countries accorded all EEC states duty-free entry from December 1, 1964 and liberalized imports of EEC origin on or before June 1, 1968. However, the Yaoundé Convention contained no provisions with respect to quota restrictions on imports of associated countries from third countries, and these remain restricted by import programs. The implementation of the association arrangements has involved the setting up of detailed rules both in the EEC countries and the associated states to establish the origin of imported commodities. Before the process of improving market access is described in more detail, the relevant provisions of that Convention will be summarized.

The first Yaoundé Convention aimed at the expansion of trade by the establishment of free trade areas between the EEC and each of the associated countries, in which the EEC countries on the one hand and the associated countries on the other would not apply any quantitative import restrictions or customs duties against each other while maintaining their own national or EEC regimes with respect to both, vis-à-vis third countries. When the Convention entered into force on June 1, 1964, imports from all EEC countries into the BCEAO countries had to be exempted from customs duties within six months, i.e., by December 1, 1964.[4] Their quantitative restrictions on imports from EEC countries other than France had to be removed gradually, and to be abolished, at the latest, four years after the entry into force of the Convention, i.e., by June 1, 1968.[5] Each associated state, however, could maintain or introduce customs duties to further its own development and protect its infant industries, or for revenue purposes. Moreover, an associated country could maintain existing quantitative restrictions on imports from the EEC or impose new ones under any one of three conditions: (1) if its tariff measures were insufficient to provide the desired protection, (2) if it had balance of payments difficulties, or (3) if any existing regional market organization for agricultural products made quantitative restrictions necessary. The associated states also retained their freedom as to their import tariff vis-à-vis third countries. The EEC countries other than France would progressively reduce their import duties on commodities of BCEAO origin (while abolishing immediately the duty on coffee, cocoa, and certain other tropical products) and dismantle their quantitative restrictions on such commodities, generally in accordance with the Treaty of Rome or the arrangements agreed for its implementation; there was a declaration of intent for commodities covered by the EEC's common agricultural policy, which

---

[4] The associated states undertook to abolish any tariff discrimination between the six within six months of the entry into force of the Convention and gradually (through annual reductions of 15 per cent) to eliminate customs duties and charges with equivalent effect on imports from the Community. They chose to make the tariff treatment identical, not by terminating the preferences accorded to France but by extending these to the other EEC countries.

[5] The six associated countries that on the basis of international agreements in force in 1957 applied an "open-door" policy were allowed an extension of three years for being unable to implement immediately and wholly some provisions of the Convention; Togo was the only BCEAO country among them. When the Togolese waiver expired, discussions were started on the establishment of a two-column customs tariff favorable to the EEC. Also, two exceptions were permitted to the commitment not to give more favorable treatment to non-EEC countries than to EEC member countries: one related to local border trade; the other covered the creation of customs unions or free trade areas, either between associated states or between associated states and nonmember countries.

had not taken effect. It should be noted that well before 1964 virtually all major exports of the BCEAO countries had already been fully liberalized (from all sources) in the EEC countries other than France, one of the principal exceptions being imports of bananas into Italy. The Convention also provided for a gradual elimination of French support schemes for exports of the associated countries; Annex III to the Convention established a timetable for the transition to marketing at world prices. France accordingly abolished all restrictions on imports of coffee on July 3, 1964, and the last major price support scheme but one, that for groundnuts and groundnut products, was terminated at the end of 1967, when France eliminated its quantitative restrictions on imports irrespective of origin; bananas, which were not listed in Annex III, continue to receive preferential treatment.

Protocol No. 2 to the Convention set up a schedule for enlargement of import quotas. Each associated country was to establish for each restricted commodity a basic global import quota available equally to all EEC countries other than France. This quota was to be 175 per cent of that for the year 1959 (as calculated in accordance with Article 11 of the Implementing Convention of March 25, 1957 annexed to the Rome Treaty), but at least equivalent to 15 per cent of total imports of the product during the last year for which statistical information was available. The basic quota had to be increased by 20 per cent for the first year and then annually, in relation to the previous year, by 20 per cent for the second year, by 30 per cent for the third year, and by 40 per cent for the fourth year. However, the protocol also provided that whenever actual imports of a given product had been smaller than the scheduled quotas for two consecutive years, the quota for it must be removed immediately.[6]

The BCEAO countries generally met these quota requirements in drawing up their annual import programs. Also, in practice, they liberalized any commodity fully for the EEC when a given percentage of the relative quota remained unutilized in two successive years or even in any one year. As a result, most imports from EEC countries were fully liberalized well before the Yaoundé deadline. The escape clause permit-

_____
[6] Article 4 of Protocol No. 2 contained an acceleration clause in which each associated state declared its readiness to liberalize imports more rapidly than provided in that protocol, if its economic situation so permitted.

ting the use of quantitative restrictions (nondiscriminatory as between EEC countries) has been used on a limited number of occasions.[7]

The evolution of the import programs of the BCEAO countries reflects the progressively improving market access granted to countries outside the franc area. A comparison of successive import programs for one country is difficult, however, and a comparison of different countries' programs is even more hazardous. First, it is not always certain that they have been implemented as announced. Then, programs did not always run concurrently, some covering the calendar year and others the crop year. Sometimes, an existing program was continued pro rata until the Joint Committee could discuss a new one. Some programs have included EEC quotas for commodities that were already liberalized when imported from the EEC, or included a general quota of which the allocation between EEC and non-EEC sources of supply cannot readily be ascertained (reserve quota, quota for trade agreement countries, or raw materials quota). Nevertheless, adding up the import programs of different countries over a period of years does give an indication of their general evolution.

Table 8, which combines the figures for Ivory Coast and Senegal, is presented with these reservations in mind. It shows that after 1962 EEC quotas increased over 300 per cent up to the moment of full liberalization in mid-1968 despite the progressive elimination of quotas for individual commodities that were liberalized over this period. The program quotas for imports ˙from non-EEC countries outside the French franc area were at least doubled between 1963 ˙and 1968. Similar regular increases, but starting from much smaller absolute amounts, have occurred in the other BCEAO countries (except Togo, which did not operate import programs). During 1964–67 the ratio of

---

[7] The Convention expired on May 31, 1969. On May 29, 1969, transitional measures were agreed which provided the necessary legal basis for the continuation of the principal trade, aid, and other commercial and financial provisions of the first Convention until the coming into force of a new Convention, but not later than June 30, 1970. The second Yaoundé Convention, signed on July 29, 1969, will enter into force after ratification by all signatory countries. It is to have a duration of five years but is to expire not later than January 31, 1975. The new Convention maintains the basic structure and general concepts of the first. It includes provisions, however, to allow the associated states to participate in a generalized system of preferences, and confirms and enhances the right of these countries to protect local industry.

TABLE 8. COMBINED IMPORT PROGRAMS OF IVORY COAST AND SENEGAL, 1963–68

(*In billions of CFA francs*)

	1963	1964	1965	1966	1967	1968
EEC quotas	3.8	6.7	10.6	13.6	17.2	13.5 [1]
Global quotas	10.3	14.0	15.1	18.0	18.6	20.6
Other quotas [2]	0.6	0.4	0.8	1.7	2.2	2.2
Total program	14.7	21.1	26.5	33.3	38.0	36.4

Source: Data supplied by national authorities.

[1] Provisional; imports were fully liberalized in the course of 1968.
[2] Reserve quotas and quotas for trade agreement partners.

import program to actual imports from all sources went up from about 25 per cent to about 40 per cent in Senegal and from about 20 per cent to over 30 per cent in Ivory Coast. In 1968 the import programs were reduced in size with the complete elimination of EEC quotas, although Ivory Coast has maintained indicative quotas. Quotas for non-EEC non-franc area countries also increased, but relaxation of restrictions on imports from such sources has been slower and has not resulted in full liberalization. The relaxation has been implemented both by increases in quotas and by elimination or raising of ceilings for countries outside the French franc area and elimination or lowering of floors for France.[8] Commodities that are being imported more freely as a result of the last two factors include automobiles, refrigerators, air-conditioners, and textiles. Dismantling of ceilings and floors also was gradual. As an intermediate stage, it has involved a shift from ceilings to floors, which in several instances has led to a nondiscriminatory increase in imports from all sources. Togo never adhered to either type of arrangement but, it is understood, has on occasion applied informal ceilings for automobiles and one or two other items.

Ordinarily, import quotas are taken up quickly in countries that apply severe restrictions, particularly under inflationary conditions or when balance of payments pressures lead to fears of an exchange rate adjustment or of further intensification of restrictions. However, because of the different conditions in the BCEAO area during most of the period 1963–68, and particularly in view of the continuing freedom

---

[8] Article 6, Section 4, of the Yaoundé Convention provided that foreign trade plans drawn up by the associated states should not contain or bring about, *de jure* or *de facto*, any direct or indirect discrimination between EEC members.

of importation from the French franc area, it is not surprising that the degree of utilization of the import programs usually has been well under 100 per cent. On the other hand, less than complete utilization does not necessarily indicate that the over-all restrictive effect of the quotas was minor. In virtually each country, and under virtually each program, the degree of utilization of the global quotas has been much higher than that of the EEC quotas.[9]

The BCEAO countries have virtually refrained from reliance on bilateral payments arrangements, and the trade agreements they have entered into are relatively few in number and simple in structure. Most provide reciprocal assurances with respect to market access, but any commodity lists that are attached are usually of the indicative type, stating the types of commodities which the partner countries expect to exchange rather than listing binding licensing or purchase commitments. Hence, bilateral agreements have had little impact on the direction of trade.

The French share in total imports into the BCEAO countries has declined in recent years because of the progressive elimination of preferences accorded to products of French origin and because of certain other factors (e.g., termination of the French franc area "market organizations" for sugar, wheat, and certain other foodstuffs, and reduction in the number of French nationals residing in or posted to the BCEAO area). Annual growth rates for total imports, imports from France, and imports from other EEC countries are compared in Table 9.

OFFICIAL TRANSFER PAYMENTS

From 1961 to 1967, disbursements of foreign official grants to the BCEAO countries rose by 68 per cent to an estimated CFAF 36 billion and averaged CFAF 30 billion a year (Table 10). Of the total disbursed over this period, nearly two thirds came from France and about one fifth from EEC. Other sources of aid included mainly the United States, UN, and Germany.

French grants-in-aid to BCEAO countries, channeled primarily through the Fonds d'Aide et de Coopération (FAC), fluctuated between CFAF 16 billion and CFAF 20 billion annually over the

---

[9] The only noteworthy exception seems to have occurred under Dahomey's program for 1965/66.

TABLE 9.   UDEAO COUNTRIES AND TOGO:
ANNUAL GROWTH RATES OF IMPORTS, 1962–66

(In percentages, based on c.i.f. data)

Importing Country	World	EEC other than France	France	EEC
		Origin of Imports		
Mauritania	−12.8	14.5	−24.0	−19.3
Mali	−0.4	−23.0	−15.6	−17.0
Senegal	1.5	9.1	−5.0	−2.8
Upper Volta	0.9	24.5	0.1	2.8
Niger	17.8	41.7	17.0	20.1
Ivory Coast	15.4	26.6	11.9	14.1
Dahomey	4.0	28.6	−0.4	3.6
Togo	17.0	30.4	15.0	20.8
Average UDEAO countries and Togo	7.6	19.4	2.8	5.4

Source: Commission of the European Communities, *Les Echanges Commerciaux entre la CEE et les Etats Africains et Malgache Associés, 1958–1966/67,* Annex 1, Brussels, 1969.

period. Financial aid averaged CFAF 10 billion annually, including investment grants, financing a large variety of projects, and direct subsidies to ordinary and capital budgets. Technical assistance was also an important aspect of French aid, at an average annual cost of CFAF 7 billion (net of recipient countries' contributions); the number of French technical assistants has approximated 9,000 in recent years.

EEC grants to BCEAO countries, disbursed under the first and second programs of the European Development Fund (EDF, Fonds Européen de Développement, or FED), started on a substantial scale in 1962 and increased rapidly in the following years. In 1966, they reached a peak of CFAF 10.1 billion, or one third of total grants-in-aid received by BCEAO countries in that year. After some decline in 1967, they exceeded CFAF 9 billion in 1968. The first EDF program was established in 1958 by a convention annexed to the Treaty of Rome; this convention earmarked a total of US$581 million (CFAF 143 billion) for development aid to economic and social projects in former colonies and overseas territories of EEC member countries. By the end of 1968, about CFAF 39 billion had been disbursed under the first EDF program in BCEAO countries, mainly on infrastructure projects for transportation, education, and health.

The second EDF program was established by the 1964–69 Convention of Association, which included a US$730 million (CFAF 180 bil-

(In millions of CFA francs)

	1960	1961	1962	1963	1964	1965	1966	1967
Bilateral aid								
France (FAC) [1]								
Investment grants	3,018	7,601	8,290	7,791	6,699	7,734	6,166	7,767
Budget contributions	...	3,250	4,802	4,004	1,784	3,187	1,880	1,650
Technical assistance	...	8,838	8,564	8,942	9,294	9,910	10,403	11,033
Scholarships and training programs	...	600 [2]	658	844	957	793	616	600 [2]
Reverse grants [3]	...	−2,284	−2,260	−2,372	−2,451	−2,628	−2,819	−3,038
Grants to common organizations	8	51	45	43	209	171	177	132
Total France	...	18,056	20,099	19,252	16,492	19,167	16,423	18,144
United States								
AID [4]	284	1,087 [2]	1,294 [2]	1,707	831	999	947	983
Public Law 480 [5]		501	356	555	2,637	1,450	979	1,452
Total United States		1,588	1,650	2,262	3,468	2,449	1,926	2,435
Other countries [6]	2	40	141	400	662	968	3,283	5,315
Total bilateral aid	...	19,648	21,890	21,914	20,622	22,584	21,632	25,762
Multilateral aid								
EEC								
First EDF [7]	14	1,387	5,846	5,631	7,569	6,910	5,810	4,130
Second EDF	—	—	—	—	—	2,868	4,303	4,390
Investment grants	—	—	—	—	—	2	402	737
Aid to production and diversification	—	—	—	—	—	2,671	3,803	3,354
Technical assistance	—	—	—	—	—	195	−98	299
Total EEC	14	1,387	5,846	5,631	7,569	9,778	10,113	8,520
UN	136	509	983	1,097	1,368	1,405	1,769	1,769
Total multilateral aid	150	1,896	6,829	6,728	8,937	11,183	11,882	10,289
Total grants-in-aid	...	21,544	28,719	28,642	29,559	33,767	33,514	36,183

Sources: France, Institut National de la Statistique et des Etudes Economiques, *Données Statistiques*; Organization for Economic Cooperation and Development (OECD), *Geographical Distribution of Financial Flows to Less Developed Countries*; U.S. Agency for International Development, *Operations Report*; and data provided by national authorities, EEC, CCCE, and OECD.

[1] Fonds d'Aide et de Coopération.
[2] Estimated.
[3] Receiving countries' contribution toward the cost of FAC technical assistants.
[4] Agency for International Development, including some loans.
[5] Food deliveries.
[6] Mainly Germany, the United Kingdom, Canada, Sweden, Switzerland, and Italy.
[7] European Development Fund (Fonds Européen de Développement, or FED). All investment grants.

lion) program of aid to associated states. This program provided for several forms of aid, including grants for economic and social investments, soft-term special loans, short-term advances to stabilization funds, and technical cooperation and aid to agricultural production and diversification. Aid to agricultural production, linked to the progressive elimination of the trade preferences by France, included two categories of subsidies—price subsidies and subsidies for structural improvements. The latter are expected to help improve agricultural productivity and lower production costs through provision of advisory personnel, agricultural equipment, fertilizers, insecticides, and draft animals.

By the end of 1968, the second EDF disbursements in BCEAO countries totaled CFAF 18.6 billion, of which CFAF 13.5 billion represented aid to production and diversification (Table 11). Although production aid chiefly benefited Senegal (which received CFAF 6.2 billion, mainly in price subsidies to groundnut exports), aid to diversification was nearly exclusively granted to Ivory Coast (which received CFAF 5.5 billion for oil palm plantations). Senegal also received, in 1968, a CFAF 0.9 billion advance to its groundnut stabilization fund. Special loans have been granted to Ivory Coast and Mauritania in the total amount of CFAF 3.1 billion. Disbursements under the special scheme for the stabilization of export prices of oil and oilseeds were not to start before 1970, totaling an estimated CFAF 2.2 billion in Senegal and Niger.

Under the new Convention of Association signed in July 1969, EEC financial aid through the third EDF program will total US$1 billion (CFAF 247 billion). Aid to production will be granted only in exceptional circumstances, as mentioned above, while larger funds will be devoted to loan operations, which are to total $190 million, or 60 per cent more than in the former Convention.

SERVICES, PRIVATE UNREQUITED TRANSFERS, AND NONMONETARY CAPITAL

Information published by the Monetary Committee of the franc area on nontrade transactions of BCEAO countries makes it possible to show under separate headings the net balances on services, private unrequited transfers, and nonmonetary capital flows only with countries outside the franc area and until 1966 (see Table 1). Information given

TABLE 11. BCEAO COUNTRIES: EEC AID TO PRODUCTION AND DIVERSIFICATION—FIVE-YEAR COMMITMENTS AND PROGRAMS, AND DISBURSEMENTS AS OF DECEMBER 31, 1968

(In millions of CFA francs)

	Ivory Coast	Senegal	Niger	Upper Volta	Togo	Dahomey	Mauritania	Total
Commitments 1964/65–1968/69								
Aid to production [1]								
Price subsidies	—	3,674	530	—	212	273	—	4,689
Subsidies for structural improvements	—	4,579	665	—	670	697	—	6,611
Total aid to production	—	8,253	1,195	—	882	970	—	11,300
Aid to diversification	11,535	3,282	411	1,482	524	390	1,235	18,859
Total commitments [2]	11,535	11,535	1,606	1,482	1,408	1,359	1,235	30,016
Disbursements as of December 31, 1968								
Aid to production								
Price subsidies	—	3,380	389	—	27	96	—	3,892
Subsidies for structural improvements	—	2,813	142	—	116	336	—	3,407
Total aid to production	—	6,193	531	—	143	432	—	7,299
Aid to diversification	5,597	213	15	132	—	26	215	6,198
Total disbursements	5,597	6,406	546	132	143	458	215	13,497

Sources: EEC, Fonds Européen de Développement, *Situation Trimestielle des Projets du 2e FED en Exécution*, December 31, 1968, and data supplied by EEC.

[1] As provided in the five-year programs bilaterally agreed upon between EEC and aid-receiving countries.
[2] As provided for by Protocol No. 5 of the Convention of Association between EEC and the African and Malagasy states.

on nontrade transfers with other franc area countries consists only of global data on payments made through the Central Bank until 1966, classified into official transfers and private transfers.

Transactions with the Franc Area

Official transfers.—The category of official transfers includes all those originating from government or assimilated agencies such as CCCE in France. These transfers are made on account of various transactions (e.g., government expenditures for embassies or other agencies abroad, expenditures of the French armed forces abroad, pensions paid by the French Government to Africans retired from former colonial administrations and from the French armed forces, and transfers on account of aid by the French Government or by French public agencies). In Table 1, official nontrade transfers have been adjusted by excluding the official unrequited transfers shown in Table 10.

The balance on nontrade official transfers with other countries of the franc area deteriorated over 1961–66, with surpluses averaging CFAF 14.6 billion in the early 1960's and deficits of CFAF 3.6 billion in 1965 and CFAF 5.7 billion in 1966. Presumably, this change resulted mainly from a decline in local expenditures of the French Government —following the departure of the colonial administrations and of the French armed forces—and from an increase in expenditures abroad by governments of BCEAO countries, mainly on account of diplomatic representations. In 1967, the balance again showed a deficit, which, however, was reduced to its 1966 level, or to CFAF 3.7 billion.

Private transfers.—Nontrade private transfers with other countries of the franc area related to various private transactions (e.g., services, unrequited transfers, and nonmonetary capital movements). A large deficit on these transactions persisted throughout 1961–66, averaging CFAF 2.8 billion a year; presumably it was due mainly to deficits on the services account.

As for capital movements between the BCEAO area and the franc area, the information available is very incomplete. However, data from Ivory Coast's balance of payments, the only one for which complete estimates are regularly published, indicate small surpluses on official capital throughout 1963–67, averaging CFAF 1.3 billion a year. In 1968 the surplus increased to CFAF 4.8 billion. For private nonmonetary movements, the available information is even scantier. In several BCEAO countries, the years following independence were characterized by a heavy, mostly unrecorded return of French capital because of the political uncertainties and the economic recession, especially in Senegal, which followed independence. The situation, however, seems to have reverted in the mid-1960's. One factor in attracting foreign capital may have been the adoption by all BCEAO countries of various fiscal incentives (mostly tax holidays) to speed up investments, embodied in Investment Codes. From 1962 to 1967 the total number of enterprises in the BCEAO area benefiting from the advantages provided for through Investment Codes rose from 39 to 159. The main beneficiary of the private capital inflow from the franc area was undoubtedly Ivory Coast, which registered large net surpluses on over-all private capital movements during 1963–68, averaging CFAF 4.0 billion a year.

Transactions with Countries Outside the Franc Area

The deficit in service transactions with countries outside the franc area rose rapidly from CFAF 0.8 billion in 1960 to CFAF 5.2 billion in 1966. For private unrequited transfers, on the other hand, there were small surpluses, which also grew steadily to CFAF 1.2 billion in 1966. The net inflow of nonmonetary capital from non-franc area countries, after reaching CFAF 12 billion in 1962, tended to decline and even became negative in 1966, when amortization outlays exceeded new capital inflows. Nonmonetary capital movements mainly concerned EEC countries other than France; their net contribution averaged CFAF 2.1 billion annually during 1962–65 (Table 12), benefiting

TABLE 12. BCEAO COUNTRIES: NET NONMONETARY CAPITAL MOVEMENTS WITH NON-FRANC AREA COUNTRIES, 1960–66

(In billions of CFA francs)

	1960	1961	1962	1963	1964	1965	1966
United States and Canada	0.6	—	1.7	2.0	0.7	0.9	...
EEC countries other than France	0.6	0.4	1.2	2.8	2.3	2.7	...
International organizations	—	3.6	7.0	0.3	—	0.3	...
Others	1.1	2.4	2.1	1.3	1.1	0.5	...
Total	2.3	6.4	12.0	6.4	4.1	4.4	2.5

Source: Comité Monétaire de la Zone Franc, *La Zone Franc*, 1960–66.

TABLE 13. BCEAO COUNTRIES: NET FOREIGN EXCHANGE HOLDINGS, 1962–69 [1]

(In billions of CFA francs; end of period)

	1962	1963	1964	1965	1966	1967	1968 Sept.	1968 Dec.	1969 (Sept.)
Central Bank (net) [2]									
Dahomey	2.47	2.45	2.44	2.51	2.27	1.98	1.92	2.35	2.18
Ivory Coast	8.67	9.79	9.34	14.62	14.92	16.97	16.88	18.21	15.57
Mauritania	1.96	2.32	2.57	2.41	1.92	2.17	2.03	1.84	1.44
Niger	2.31	2.10	1.75	0.73	0.94	0.15	0.89	0.58	1.78
Senegal	17.97	11.83	8.41	8.25	11.27	8.44	4.28	3.64	4.17
Togo	2.12	2.22	2.83	4.32	4.58	5.46	5.65	6.22	6.41
Upper Volta	3.38	3.52	3.30	3.44	4.01	4.50	5.21	5.58	5.95
Total Central Bank	40.49	35.94	32.55	38.28	42.30	42.37	41.45	42.24	45.02
Treasuries and Postal Checking Systems (net)	*0.02*	*0.50*	*−0.78*	*−0.38*	*−0.09*	*0.03*	*...*	*−0.04*	*...*
Other banks (net)									
Holdings (gross)									
Dahomey	−0.69 [3]	0.21	0.11	0.34	0.61	0.41	1.41	0.81	0.58
Ivory Coast	−2.85 [3]	7.15	12.58	8.54	11.37	5.87	7.56	14.59	19.67
Mauritania	1.24 [3]	0.94	0.49	0.69	1.34	0.95	0.35	0.40	0.57
Niger	−0.73 [3]	0.14	0.62	0.38	0.24	0.45	0.27	0.51	0.74
Senegal	−2.81 [3]	2.43	2.70	2.28	1.97	1.95	1.91	1.45	1.82
Togo	−0.51 [3]	0.06	0.57	1.11	1.61	1.48	2.18	1.58	3.98
Upper Volta	0.25 [3]	0.37	0.16	0.25	0.17	0.19	0.68	0.61	0.37
Total holdings	−6.10 [3]	11.30	17.23	13.59	17.31	11.30	14.36	19.95	27.73
Liabilities (gross)									
Dahomey	...	−1.38	−1.41	−1.54	−1.21	−1.29	−1.09	−1.37	−1.17
Ivory Coast	...	−8.31	−9.38	−7.51	−7.23	−8.39	−8.28	−10.44	−9.50
Mauritania	...	−0.16	−0.33	−0.56	−0.42	−0.55	−0.63	−0.68	−0.56
Niger	...	−0.72	−1.70	−1.71	−1.65	−0.90	−1.36	−1.83	−2.25
Senegal	...	−4.11	−2.90	−4.79	−5.20	−4.43	−4.81	−4.25	−8.47
Togo	...	−0.80	−0.96	−1.19	−1.46	−1.11	−1.27	−1.55	−1.67
Upper Volta	...	−1.00	−0.91	−1.08	−0.78	−0.90	−0.81	−1.22	−1.25
Total liabilities	...	−16.48	−17.59	−18.38	−17.95	−17.57	−18.25	−21.34	−24.87
Total other banks	−6.10	−5.18	−0.36	−4.79	−0.64	−6.27	−3.89	−1.39	2.86
Total net holdings	34.39	30.76	32.19	33.49	41.66	36.10	37.56	40.85	47.88

Source: IMF, *International Financial Statistics.*

[1] Positive figures indicate assets; negative figures indicate liabilities.

[2] Aggregate net holdings of the Central Bank do not equal the sum of the shares allocated to each member country because small amounts of the Bank's assets and liabilities are not allocable to any particular UMOA member.

mainly Ivory Coast, Mauritania, and Togo. In the same period, the
United States and Canada contributed an average of CFAF 1.1 billion
on a net basis. Net capital inflow from international institutions was
especially large in 1961 (CFAF 3.6 billion) and in 1962 (CFAF 7.0
billion). Loans to BCEAO countries by the European Investment Bank
(EIB) started on a small scale in 1965. In 1968, EIB granted a large
loan (CFAF 2.7 billion) to Mauritania for copper mining.

FOREIGN EXCHANGE RESERVES

A breakdown of aggregate foreign exchange holdings of BCEAO
countries at the end of the year during 1962–68 and for September 1969
is given in Table 13. Total net foreign assets fluctuated between
CFAF 34 billion and CFAF 31 billion at the end of the years 1962–65,
but they rose by 26 per cent to CFAF 42 billion by the end of 1966.
After a decline in the next year, they rose again to CFAF 41 billion at
the end of 1968 and to CFAF 48 billion by the end of September 1969.
Holdings of the Central Bank generally exceeded these figures because
the net foreign holdings of other banks were negative during 1962–68,
with maximum negative holdings of about CFAF 6 billion. During the
first nine months of 1969, however, the net foreign holdings of other
banks shifted to positive. This development was due almost entirely to
the substantial rise in foreign assets held by the Amortization Fund
(Caisse Autonome d'Amortissement) in Ivory Coast. If the assets of this
institution are excluded, the over-all net reserve position of other banks
remains negative. Treasuries and the Postal Checking Systems of
BCEAO countries also held small foreign balances.

Ivory Coast's share of the net foreign holdings of the BCEAO area
held by the Central Bank doubled in absolute amount over 1962–68,
reaching a peak of CFAF 18 billion at the end of 1968, but declined
to CFAF 16 billion, or to 36 per cent of the Central Bank's total
net foreign assets, at the end of September 1969. Senegal's net contribution declined drastically from CFAF 18 billion, or 44 per cent of total
foreign assets, at the end of 1962 to only CFAF 4 billion, or 9 per cent
of the total, at the end of September 1969. While the shares of Togo
and Upper Volta tended to increase over the period, those of the other
countries (Mauritania, Dahomey, and Niger) remained stable.

For other banks in the BCEAO area, the negative balances on net foreign holdings resulted from the excess of large foreign indebtedness over foreign assets. Gross foreign liabilities of these banks at the end of the year averaged CFAF 18 billion during 1963–67 and rose to CFAF 21 billion at the end of 1968 and to CFAF 25 billion by the end of September 1969. The extent of the foreign indebtedness of commercial banks is explained by their reliance, for the financing of domestic operations, on the facilities provided by foreign banks to which they are closely related either as branches or subsidiaries.

CHAPTER 6

The Exchange System

INITIAL EXCHANGE ARRANGEMENTS

After the seven BCEAO countries [1] became independent in 1960, they remained members of the French franc area, continued to use the French franc as their reserve currency, and initially maintained their principal preferential trade arrangements with France. During 1960–63 each BCEAO country signed an economic, financial, and monetary cooperation agreement with France. The agreements provided for continued membership in the French franc area and application of the area's basic exchange regulations, maintenance of a reciprocal preferential trade relationship with France, and coordination of commercial and financial policy vis-à-vis countries outside the French franc area. However, they left the BCEAO countries free to adapt the basic exchange regulations of the franc area to their specific requirements and also to conclude commercial and financial agreements in their own behalf, although settlements of BCEAO members with countries outside the French franc area would continue to be channeled through the Paris exchange market. For purposes of coordination, each agreement provided for a joint committee in which France and the partner country had equal status (*commission mixte paritaire*).

Membership in the French franc area had three implications for the BCEAO countries that were confirmed by the terms of the cooperation agreements, although not explicitly stated in every agreement: a fixed exchange rate between their own currency and the French franc, unlimited access to French francs, and freedom of transfer between France and these countries. Most of the original cooperation agreements also provided for the use of an operations account. Article 21 of the Ivory Coast agreement states:

> Convertibility between the CFA franc and the French franc is unlimited and is guaranteed by the functioning of an Operations Account opened in the name of the institute of issue on the books of the French Treasury. This Account will be the subject of an appropriate agreement. Transfers of funds between the two States are free.[2]

Article 22 reads:

> The definition and the parity of the monetary unit are maintained. They can only be modified by agreement between all member States of the Monetary Union and the French Republic.

The text of the agreements with Dahomey, Niger, and Upper Volta is identical.[3] Article 11 of the same four agreements provides that France and the partner country

> agree to maintain, for a renewable period of five years, their trade relations within the framework of a reciprocal preferential system based on the following principles: free movement of goods and duty-free entry . . . , privileged access afforded by both parties for the principal products and goods, in particular in the form of quotas and of guaranteed prices, coordination of trade policies vis-à-vis third countries, and protection for the industries of [the African country].

Togo, however, maintained its "open door" policy. The cooperation

---

[1] In 1962, Dahomey, Ivory Coast, Mauritania, Niger, Senegal, and Upper Volta ratified the agreement which established the West African Monetary Union (Union Monétaire Ouest Africaine, or UMOA) and the Banque Centrale des Etats de l'Afrique de l'Ouest (BCEAO); Togo adhered to the agreement in 1963. See also Chapters 2 and 4.

[2] The operations account arrangements between France and the CFA countries represent in fact the continuation in a more formalized manner of preindependence facilities governing the access of the overseas territories to French francs.

[3] Most of the provision of Articles 21 and 22 were repeated in a "multilateral" cooperation agreement of May 12, 1962 between France and the members of UMOA.

agreements also provided for the opening on the books of the French Exchange Stabilization Fund of a "drawing right" account in which the country's receipts and expenditures in non-French franc area currencies were reflected. These accounts were of a purely statistical nature, and the net position did not affect the country's access to the Paris exchange market, i.e., to non-French franc area currencies.

The BCEAO countries joined the International Monetary Fund (IMF) shortly after assuming independence. All chose to avail themselves of Article XIV, Section 2, of the Fund Agreement, which permits the Fund member to maintain existing restrictions on payments and transfers for current international transactions temporarily and to adapt them to changing circumstances. So far, no BCEAO country has accepted the obligations of Article VIII, Sections 2, 3, and 4, and no par value for the CFA franc has yet been established. The first Yaoundé Convention contained provisions regarding exchange restrictions in Articles 35, 36, and 37.

EVOLUTION OF EXCHANGE SYSTEM

The evolution of the exchange systems of the BCEAO countries is summarized below in three stages: developments during 1962–66, when on the whole the exchange systems were simplified, although there were some experiments with exchange taxes and payments agreements; abolition of exchange control in 1967, when a set of new capital controls was introduced; and developments during 1968–69, when exchange control was re-established and the new capital controls were further elaborated.[4]

DEVELOPMENTS DURING 1962–66

At the beginning of the 1962–66 period, the exchange systems of the BCEAO countries were similar in structure since they were all based on uniform exchange control principles that were applied throughout the French franc area. The centralization of reserves was basic; this implied that all purchases and sales of non-franc area currencies were

---

[4] See Chapter 5 for a description of the import system. Additional details on the exchange and trade controls are to be found in the country sections in successive issues of the IMF's *Annual Report on Exchange Restrictions*.

channeled through the Paris exchange market. Some relaxation of
exchange restrictions and simplification of exchange controls had
already taken place before independence, but these changes had not
been as far reaching as in France. Now access to non-franc area currencies was unlimited and individual countries could draw up their own
exchange control regulations. Nevertheless, the exchange systems of the
BCEAO countries showed relatively few structural changes during the
period up to 1967, although their application undoubtedly became
more liberal.

In 1962, current and capital transfers between the BCEAO countries
and between these and other parts of the French franc area were unrestricted and free of exchange control, although some other countries of
the area had recently broken with this principle. All payments and
receipts between the BCEAO countries and countries outside the French
franc area were subject to exchange control, which was administered
by a national Exchange Office under the supervision of the national
Ministry of Finance or Economy. To the extent possible, this exchange
control had to be uniform in all countries concerned in order to prevent
evasion through the countries with the weakest controls. Settlements
with foreign countries had to be made through authorized banks. Transactions in non-franc area currencies took place on the exchange market
in France, and the rates for such currencies were based on the fixed
rate for the French franc and the Paris exchange market rate for the
currency concerned, including a commission. A distinction was made,
along the lines of the French regulations, between resident and nonresident accounts, and corresponding prescription of currency regulations
were applied indicating the channels through which external payments
and receipts must be made and the currencies to be used.

As members of the French franc area, the BCEAO countries made
their settlements with other countries in the French franc area in
French francs or in any other currency of that area. Settlements with
countries outside the French franc area were usually made through
banks in France. If the country concerned maintained a bilateral payments agreement with France, settlements took place in France through
Foreign Accounts in Bilateral Francs related to that country. Otherwise,
settlements were effected in the currency of any non-franc area country
not maintaining a payments agreement with France, provided that it

was quoted on the Paris exchange market, or through French Foreign Accounts in Convertible Francs. As an exception to these rules, certain BCEAO countries which had after independence concluded one or two payments agreements of their own channeled settlements with the partner countries through their own agreement accounts.

Although all payments to and receipts from countries outside the French franc area were subject to exchange control, most inward payments were in fact unrestricted, but virtually all receipts in non-franc area currencies had to be surrendered (i.e., sold on the Paris exchange market). There also were deposit requirements for foreign assets, particularly securities issued outside the franc area. Capital transfers to countries outside the French franc area were usually restricted, while current payments were approved with varying degrees of restrictiveness. For import payments due to those countries, the import title (import license or certificate) enabled the importer to pay in foreign currency or by credit to a Foreign Account in francs on proof that the goods had been shipped, but the import transaction had to be domiciled with an authorized bank and the Exchange Office had to give its visa on the import title; foreign currency could be purchased when the visa had been granted, but not on a spot basis unless a documentary credit was opened.

Payments for most invisibles appearing in a long "list of normal current payments" similar to that employed by the French exchange control authorities were freely permitted upon submission of documentary evidence, with the actual approval authority in a few cases delegated to authorized banks. For other invisibles, individual approval of the national Exchange Office was required. Payments for invisibles related to trade were permitted freely when the underlying trade transaction had been approved. Transfers of income accruing to nonresidents of the franc area (e.g., profits, dividends, and rents) were authorized freely by the Exchange Office. Except in Togo, the treatment of other transfers was along the following lines, with small differences from country to country for specific allocations. There was a basic allowance for each tourist traveling to countries outside the French franc area of CFAF 75,000 (about US$300) annually, with the possibility of an increase up to the equivalent of CFAF 125,000 for extended travel. Allocations for business travel (which could also be financed with funds from EFAC accounts, see below) were granted according to the nature and length of the trip and the status of the applicant. Facilities also existed for the transfer of savings from salaries by persons of non-franc area origin working in the BCEAO countries (up to 20 per cent of salary for those having their family in the country concerned and up to 50 per cent for others) and for transfers for family support (CFAF 20,000 a month to each beneficiary). Payment of educational expenses usually was approved in full, on submission of the relevant bills. Insurance cover had to be taken out either in the French franc area or with non-franc area companies established in the area; with this proviso, it is understood that all types of insurance (including life insurance) were permitted up to any amount. In screening applications for personal payments, the authorities were inclined to take into account the applicant's financial status, since personal capital transfers outside the franc area in principle remained prohibited.

Claims on nonresidents of the French franc area had to be collected when due, and amounts received in non-franc area currencies had to be surrendered within a short period, usually three months. Exporters had to execute a foreign exchange commitment (*engagement de change*) to confirm that they would sell their non-franc area proceeds on the Paris exchange market, and exports to countries outside the French franc area required a license and the visa of the Exchange Office. There were two main exceptions to the surrender requirements. (1) Amounts not exceeding the equivalent of CFAF 5,000 received for services or as income from foreign securities could be retained. (2) More important was the exemption operated along the lines of French practice, through the so-called EFAC system. Export proceeds in non-franc area currencies, unless used to make authorized payments abroad, had to be surrendered within three months, but exporters could retain a part in foreign currency accounts, EFAC (*Exportations-Frais Accessoires*) accounts. The retained proceeds could be used by the exporter himself to pay for imports of raw materials or equipment needed in his business, for representation and advertising expenses, or for business travel outside the French franc area. Permitted retention ratios varied from country to country, but the general pattern was that 12 per cent of export proceeds could be credited to EFAC accounts for firm sales to the United States and Canada, 8 per cent for firm sales to other countries outside the French franc area, and 6 per cent for sales on consignment.

Exchange control was exercised over exports of both BCEAO bank-notes and other French franc area banknotes and over imports of BCEAO currency. Travelers to other UMOA countries could take out any amount in banknotes issued by any bank of issue within the French franc area, including those of BCEAO, but travelers to non-UMOA countries in the French franc area could not take out more than CFAF 75,000 in BCEAO banknotes, although they were free to take in addition any amount in banknotes issued by any other bank of issue within the French franc area. For travel to countries outside the French franc area, there were limits on all types of banknotes issued in the area; travelers to such countries could not take out more than F 750 in French francs, or CFAF 75,000 or CFPF 75,000 in CFA or CFP francs, or the equivalent of CFAF 37,500 in notes in any other French franc area currency. Similarly, travelers coming from UMOA countries could bring in any amount in BCEAO banknotes, but, except in Ivory Coast, travelers coming from other countries were limited to CFAF 75,000 in such banknotes. All travelers, however, could bring in any amount of banknotes issued by any bank of issue of the French franc area other than BCEAO. The limitations on the import and export of BCEAO notes had been introduced in 1962. France cooperated in their enforcement by limiting the exchange of BCEAO notes to CFAF 75,000 per traveler.

Controls over banknotes issued outside the French franc area were simple. Resident travelers could not take out more in foreign banknotes than the amount allocated to them as part of a travel allocation. All travelers could freely bring in any amount of foreign banknotes (and coins other than gold coins), with the exception that in most BCEAO countries the import of Guinean and Malian currency was prohibited at the request of the authorities of Guinea and Mali; residents had to surrender the foreign currency they brought in, but nonresidents were merely required to declare it. Nonresident travelers could take out foreign banknotes and coins up to the amount declared by them on entry. Imports and exports of gold were subject to strict controls.

Outward capital transfers were restricted and many of a personal nature were in principle prohibited, so that individual residents could not purchase non-franc area securities or real estate, but the transfer of inheritances, dowries, and the assets of departing residents was nor-

mally approved, as "normal current payments." Inward direct investment required the prior approval of the Exchange Office and was
usually covered by a special agreement concluded in accordance with
the provisions of a national Investment Code; the procedures normally
involved fully guaranteed transferability of earnings and liquidation
proceeds. Direct investment outside the franc area was approved only
when considered beneficial to the economy. Most borrowing and lending
between residents and nonresidents was controlled.

Thus, the exchange systems of the BCEAO countries already were
liberal in 1962, at least regarding current payments, and the approval
of outward transfers to countries outside the French franc area was
generally given or withheld without discrimination. During 1962–67
there was evidence of an increasingly liberal attitude of the Exchange
Offices in approving applications. Also, the BCEAO countries followed
France in some relatively minor formal relaxation or simplification
measures. Thus, they allowed payments up to CFAF 1 million for
imports from countries outside the French franc area to be made as
soon as the import transaction was domiciled. The period within which
proceeds from exports to countries outside the French franc area had
to be surrendered was lengthened. Exemption from the deposit requirements was granted to securities issued by public or private juridical
persons domiciled outside the French franc area, provided that the
securities were exclusively denominated in French francs and that they
were serviced only in the BCEAO country concerned. Residents were
permitted to sell forward all receipts in non-franc area currencies, and
were enabled to obtain spot or forward cover for all payments to
countries outside the French franc area. Authorized banks could freely
grant credit to nonresidents, in the form of overdrafts on Foreign
Accounts and for periods up to six months. More important measures
were the introduction of exchange taxes, the negotiation of additional
payments agreements, the abolition of the EFAC arrangements, and
the introduction of restrictions for security reasons.

Dahomey, Togo, and Upper Volta introduced exchange taxes on
payments to countries outside the French franc area in order to finance
the expense of running their own Exchange Offices.[5] All three countries

---

[5] Dahomey introduced its tax on December 31, 1962, Togo on January 1,
1965, and Upper Volta on July 1, 1964.

exempted government payments; Togo and Upper Volta also exempted payments related to export transactions. The taxes were small: 0.5 per cent in Dahomey, with a minimum charge of CFAF 100; 0.5 per cent in Togo, on payments in excess of CFAF 10,000; and on a graduated scale in Upper Volta, with an exemption for amounts up to CFAF 10,000, and a range from CFAF 250 on amounts between CFAF 10,001 and CFAF 25,000 to CFAF 3,500 on amounts over CFAF 1 million. These taxes were terminated in 1967, when both exchange control and Exchange Offices were abolished.

In 1962, the BCEAO countries were still utilizing the few remaining French payments agreements; these had been concluded by France on behalf of the entire French franc area. The partner countries were Bulgaria, Czechoslovakia, Eastern Germany, Hungary, and Rumania. France terminated these agreements during 1962–65. Although the cooperation agreements gave the BCEAO countries the right to conclude their own financial and commercial agreements, resort to bilateral payments agreements has been minor. In all, five countries concluded ten such agreements. Ivory Coast and Togo never concluded any, and none have been concluded between BCEAO countries or between BCEAO countries and other French franc area countries (except with Mali, at a time when that country did not have an operations account relationship with the French Treasury). All payments agreements concluded by BCEAO countries have either been terminated or become inoperative. Senegal had concluded a payments agreement with Guinea in 1961 and added one with Mali in 1963. Both agreements were viewed as emergency measures to maintain or restore trade with neighboring countries that were in serious balance of payments difficulties. The agreements are now inoperative; Mali's agreement, though not yet formally abolished, became redundant in 1968, when Mali established an operations account with the French Treasury. Mauritania negotiated payments agreements with Spain (in 1964) and Mali (in 1963), but these were terminated in 1968. Upper Volta signed a payments agreement with Ghana (in 1961), but this appears never to have been put into effect, and a 1968 trade agreement provides for the use of convertible currencies between the two countries. Dahomey entered into four payments agreements, of which the one with Ghana (signed in 1961) was terminated in 1968, while those with Eastern Germany (1964),

Hungary (1965), and the United Arab Republic (1965) are inoperative. Niger concluded a payments agreement with the United Arab Republic in 1963 but terminated it in 1966. Niger in 1964 entered into an arrangement with Mali involving a special account in CFA francs on the books of the BCEAO agency in Niamey, but this was a technical facility rather than a genuine payments agreement and was discontinued in 1968. The abolition of exchange control in 1967, which implied in principle the use of convertible exchange only, was followed by the formal termination of three agreements.

The EFAC arrangements for proceeds from exports to countries outside the French franc area were terminated gradually—in Ivory Coast in 1963; in Senegal, Dahomey,[6] and Mauritania in 1966; and in Niger and Togo when exchange control was abolished on July 1, 1967. In Upper Volta, no EFAC facilities appear to have been in existence since the beginning of the 1960's.

For security reasons, all BCEAO countries have introduced certain restrictions on payments to specified countries outside the French franc area (viz., Israel, Portugal, Rhodesia, and South Africa) and/or financial or commercial transactions with these countries. Financial relations with South Africa and Portugal are prohibited in Senegal and Dahomey. Financial relations with Rhodesia are prohibited in Ivory Coast, Dahomey, Upper Volta, Niger, Senegal, and Togo. Financial relations with Israel, Portugal, and South Africa are prohibited in Mauritania. No attempt is made to list the various prohibitions relating specifically to trade with these countries.

ABOLITION OF EXCHANGE CONTROL IN 1967

Changes in French Legislation

On January 31, 1967, France abolished exchange control and introduced a system of special controls over capital transactions.[7] Before

---

[6] As early as March 7, 1963, Dahomey had extended the use of EFAC balances to any outward payment that was covered by a general or special authorization and had ceased to require the periodic surrender of a part of any unused balances. When Dahomey abolished the EFAC accounts on August 8, 1966, it allowed temporarily the retention by exporters of 10 per cent of their foreign currency proceeds.

[7] Law No. 68–1008 of December 28, 1966 and Decree No. 67–78 of January 27, 1967.

that, the controls still in effect were already essentially capital controls, particularly over direct investment and access to the French capital market. This action restored complete freedom of payments between France and foreign countries for the first time since 1939, making the French franc, which had become convertible on external account in 1958, both internally and externally convertible. All inward and outward movements of funds, whether by residents or nonresidents, by banks or nonbanks, could take place without limit, control, or authorization. Imports and exports of gold became entirely free. Repatriation (collection and surrender) of foreign claims and of receipts in non-French franc area currencies no longer was required, and the remaining deposit requirements for foreign securities were rescinded. The distinction between residents and nonresidents was abolished, as were the system of nonresident accounts, the prescription of currency, and the concept of an authorized bank as a bank through which all exchange transactions were channeled. The exchange control concept of the French franc area —within which payments already were free—ceased to exist, although the concept continued to be used in a broader sense. The concept of "foreign country" (which under previous legislation was equivalent to "country outside the French franc area") was extended to include all countries other than France (i.e., other than continental France; Corsica; the Overseas Departments; and the Overseas Territories, except French Somaliland, shortly thereafter renamed the French Territory of the Afars and the Issas); Monaco was assimilated with France. The new capital controls covered inward and outward direct investment and borrowing abroad, whereas lending abroad was completely free. They were not applicable, however, to countries whose bank of issue at the time was linked with the French Treasury by an operations account,[8] with the exception that all capital issues in France continued to require prior approval in accordance with legislation dating from 1916. Since Algeria, Morocco, and Tunisia did not maintain operations accounts with the French Treasury, the capital controls did apply to these three countries of the French franc area. Simi-

---

[8] The seven BCEAO countries, the five BCEAEC (Banque Centrale des Etats de l'Afrique Equatoriale et du Cameroun) countries, and the Malagasy Republic. On March 30, 1968, Mali (which in February 1967 undertook to join UMOA at a later stage) also became an operations account country.

larly, when France re-established exchange control in May 1968 and again in November 1968, the exchange control measures were not applied to the operations account countries.

Abolition of exchange control in France in 1967 made no change in the regimes applicable in France to trade with countries and territories that benefited from a privileged treatment, including the BCEAO countries.[9] The only change that took place affecting imports and exports was the elimination of certain exchange control requirements for trade transactions with countries outside the French franc area, mainly those of domiciliation of import transactions and of the foreign exchange commitment for exports.

Corresponding Changes in BCEAO Countries

The cooperation agreements and Article 10 of the UMOA Treaty prescribed harmonization of exchange control legislation with France and among the BCEAO countries. On July 1, 1967 the BCEAO countries also abolished exchange control and introduced special capital controls generally applicable only to countries other than France, Monaco, and the operations account countries. However, the BCEAO countries did not follow France in exempting imports and exports of gold from prior authorization because it was feared that gold could become a sterile hoarding instrument. The detailed measures taken varied slightly in content and timing from country to country, and the abolition of exchange control was not complete in all countries, some maintaining one or two bilateral payments agreements, or certain prohibitions or restrictions on settlements with Israel, Portugal, Rhodesia, or South Africa. Also, the BCEAO countries generally maintained their prohibition on the import and domestic circulation or negotiation of Guinean and Malian currency.[10] Dahomey, Togo, and Upper Volta eliminated

---

[9] These were first listed in Article 86 of an Arrêté issued by the Director-General of Customs and Indirect Taxes on January 30, 1967. At present they consist of the operations account countries and Algeria, Cambodia, Guinea, Laos, Morocco, North Viet-Nam, Republic of Viet-Nam, Tunisia, and the New Hebrides. This Arrêté also avoids the expression French franc area.

[10] This prohibition was introduced (rather than maintained) by the new legislation of Dahomey and Togo. In Ivory Coast and Senegal, however, the prohibition was rescinded on July 1, 1967. The importation and domestic negotiation of Malian currency ceased to be prohibited in the BCEAO countries early in 1968, when Mali became an operations account country.

their exchange taxes and Niger and Togo their EFAC arrangements. The limitation on the amount of BCEAO banknotes that travelers could take out to or bring in from countries outside UMOA was abolished; thereafter BCEAO repurchased such banknotes in any amount when tendered by foreign banks.

Although the individual countries did not enact identical legislative measures abolishing exchange controls and introducing special capital controls, the measures generally conformed to the following pattern. With effect from July 1, 1967, a law was enacted which established the principle that financial relations with foreign countries were free and revoked all existing legislation contrary to this principle, but which also provided for the statistical registration of all inward and outward payments, including settlements with France and the operations account countries. This registration would enable the authorities to compile a national balance of payments for the first time; previously, there was no registration of settlements with French franc area countries. An implementing decree issued at the same time established the rules for the application of the new law. The decree defined "foreign countries" and indicated the types of capital transactions with foreign countries (inward and outward direct investment, the issuing, advertising, or offering for sale of foreign securities, and borrowing abroad) that would be subject either to prior declaration or prior approval; France, Monaco, and the operations account countries were exempt from capital controls, except those over foreign securities. The decree also provided that the import and export of gold, with certain exceptions, required prior approval by the Minister of Finance and that the import and export of banknotes and coins issued by BCEAO were free, with the proviso that residents traveling to countries outside the UMOA must declare to the customs any amount in BCEAO notes carried if that amount exceeded CFAF 150,000 (CFAF 250,000 in Togo; initially no such requirement was applied in Ivory Coast).

Another decree set up in the country concerned a Balance of Payments Committee under the authority of the Minister of Finance and gave that Committee the task of periodically compiling a national balance of payments. For this purely statistical purpose, BCEAO was authorized to collect, either directly or through the banks and the Postal Administration, any information necessary to compile the balance of payments. The secrecy of the data received concerning individual firms or persons was guaranteed in the relevant legislation.

The remaining Exchange Offices were closed [11] and a Directorate of External Finance was established in the Ministry of Finance and charged with the execution of the new capital controls and the licensing of imports and exports of gold.

As in France, the collection and surrender of claims, earnings, and proceeds accruing abroad were no longer required. The concept of an authorized bank was discarded, as was the distinction between resident and nonresident accounts. The prescription of currency regulations and the deposit requirements for foreign securities were abolished, the former with minor exceptions relating to the few payments agreements and the prohibition on financial relations with specified countries. The import and export regulations themselves were not affected, although certain exchange control formalities were eliminated, such as the domiciliation of import transactions, the exchange control visa on import licenses and import certificates, and the foreign exchange commitment regarding exports.

New Capital Controls as Typified in Senegal

The new capital controls were virtually identical with those introduced in France; they covered inward and outward direct investment, borrowing abroad, and the issuing, advertising, or offering for sale of foreign securities in the country concerned—but not lending abroad.[12] Most BCEAO countries, however, applied the new regulations also to imports of French securities. Furthermore, some countries subsequently added to the standard controls a regulation making the collection of domestic funds for deposit or investment outside the country subject to

---

[11] Upper Volta had closed its Exchange Office on January 1, 1967 but transferred its functions to a new Exchange Control Department in the Ministry of Finance and Commerce. That Department was abolished on July 1, 1967. In Ivory Coast and Niger also, exchange control had already been entrusted to a different agency: the Department of External Finance and Credit, with a Bureau of Exchange Operations, in Ivory Coast's Ministry of Economy and Financial Affairs, and the Foreign Finance Division in Niger's Ministry of Finance.

[12] Lending by local banks to nonresidents or to nonresident-controlled firms also was freed from restrictions.

prior approval. The general pattern of the new controls, as applied for example in Senegal, is set out below.

Residents and nonresidents could import or export capital freely without a license, through banks or any other channel. Foreign and domestic securities of all types could be imported or exported freely, whether through the intermediary of a bank or not, and transactions between residents and nonresidents in domestic and foreign real estate (except when forming part of a direct investment) were unrestricted. Capital assets abroad of residents were not subject to repatriation and could be freely disposed of, unless these assets formed part of a direct investment. Lending abroad was not subject to authorization or declaration, and banks in Senegal could freely grant overdrafts on nonresident accounts for any period.

Certain controls were maintained over borrowing abroad, over inward and outward direct investment, and over the issue, advertising, or offering for sale of foreign securities in Senegal. These controls, however, related to the transactions themselves, not to payments or receipts; with the exception of those over the sale of foreign securities in Senegal, the control measures did not apply to France and its Overseas Departments and Territories (except the French Territory of the Afars and the Issas), Monaco, and the other operations account countries.

Foreign direct investments in Senegal [13] and Senegalese direct investments abroad [14] required prior declaration to the Minister of Finance unless they took the form of a capital increase resulting from reinvestment of undistributed profits. During a period of two months from receipt of the declaration, the Minister could request the postponement of the projects submitted to him. The liquidation of inward or outward direct investment also was subject to declaration. In addition, both the actual making and the liquidation of direct investments, whether Senegalese investments abroad or foreign investments in Senegal, had to be reported to the Minister of Finance within 20 days following each opera-

---

[13] Including those made by companies in Senegal that were directly or indirectly under foreign control and those made by branches or subsidiaries in Senegal of foreign companies.

[14] Including investments made through the intermediary of foreign companies that were directly or indirectly controlled by persons in Senegal and those made by branches or subsidiaries abroad of companies in Senegal.

tion. Direct investments were defined as investments implying control of a company or enterprise. Mere participation, on the other hand, was not considered as direct investment, provided that it did not exceed 20 per cent in the capital of a company whose shares were quoted on a stock exchange.

The issue, advertising, or offering for sale of foreign securities in Senegal required prior authorization by the Minister of Finance, as did issues by Senegalese companies. Exempt from authorization, however, were operations in connection with (1) loans backed by a guarantee from the Senegalese Government and (2) shares similar to securities whose issue, advertising, or offering for sale in Senegal had previously been authorized.

Borrowing abroad by physical or juridical persons, whether public or private, whose normal residence or registered office was in Senegal, or by branches or subsidiaries in Senegal of juridical persons whose registered office was abroad, required prior authorization by the Minister of Finance. The following borrowings, however, were exempt from this authorization: (1) loans constituting a direct investment, which were subject to prior declaration, as indicated above; (2) loans directly connected with the rendering of services abroad by the persons or firms mentioned above, or with the financing of commercial transactions either between Senegal and countries abroad or between foreign countries, in which these persons or firms took part; (3) loans contracted by banks; and (4) loans other than those mentioned above, when the total amount outstanding of these loans did not exceed CFAF 50 million for any one borrower. However, the contracting of loans referred to under (4) that were free of authorization, and each repayment thereon, had to be notified to the Minister of Finance within 20 days after the transaction or repayment took place, unless the total outstanding amount of all loans contracted abroad by the borrower was CFAF 500,000 or less.

REIMPOSITION OF EXCHANGE CONTROL, 1968–69

On May 29, 1968, France found it necessary to re-establish temporary exchange controls in relations with countries other than Monaco and the operations account countries, and the BCEAO countries took corresponding action in June 1968. The controls, which lasted only a few months and were not applicable to France or the operations account countries, were relatively mild. Repatriation and surrender requirements were reintroduced for proceeds from exports and most other receipts; but the surrender of existing foreign assets was not required, external convertibility was maintained, and no nonresident-owned assets were blocked. The institutions of authorized banks and nonresident accounts were reintroduced. The export of BCEAO bank-notes to foreign countries (i.e., countries other than France, Monaco, and the operations account countries) was restricted. BCEAO bank-notes (as well as French banknotes and those issued by any other insti-tute of issue maintaining an operations account with the French Trea-sury) could no longer be credited to nonresident accounts. Exchange allocations for travel to foreign countries were introduced, but current payments generally remained unrestricted. The new capital controls were not affected.

These exchange controls were lifted in September 1968 when the May control was terminated in France. However, again following similar action taken by France on November 24, 1968, comprehen-sive exchange controls were reintroduced vis-à-vis countries other than France and the operations account countries. First, as an emer-gency measure, the June controls were put into effect again. After con-sultation within UMOA, each country then rescinded these provisional measures and issued a large number of exchange control circulars and other instructions, generally following the issuance of corresponding regulations in France. As in France, the new controls were maintained when the French franc and the CFA franc were devalued in August 1969. A meeting of Ministers of Finance of the French franc area, held on August 10, 1969, reached the conclusion that the parities between the French franc and the CFA franc, the Mali franc, and the Malagasy franc should be maintained at the levels fixed by the cooperation agreements. Hence the parity of the CFA franc was modified to CFAF 277.710 per US$1. On September 25, 1969, another meeting of Ministers of Finance of the French franc area agreed that exchange control had to be maintained for the time being. Meanwhile, the BCEAO countries are harmonizing their exchange control regulations and capital controls.

The 1967 capital controls have remained, although most of the transactions covered have now additionally become subject to exchange control approval, as has lending to foreign countries. The exchange controls themselves, which again are not applied in relations with France, Monaco, or the operations account countries, now have the following principal characteristics.[15] Full surrender requirements are in effect. While outflows of resident-owned capital are restricted, generally the only restriction on current payments is on travel allowances. Standard allocations have been introduced for tourist travel, business travel, family support, savings from salaries, and certain other current transfers, but applications, except in connection with travel, are treated liberally and approved on submission of documentary evidence showing that bona fide current payments are involved; much of the approval authority has been delegated to authorized banks. All import and export transactions relating to foreign countries must be domiciled with an authorized bank when their value exceeds a specified amount. The foreign exchange necessary to make import payments cannot be purchased earlier than eight days before shipment if a documentary credit is opened or eight days before the payment is due if the commodities have already been imported. Forward purchases of foreign currency are limited to import transactions, only certain listed raw materials and foodstuffs qualifying for such cover. The export of BCEAO banknotes is restricted; they are no longer repurchased from monetary authorities and commercial banks in foreign countries, nor can they be credited to nonresident accounts, although they may be brought in in any amount by resident or nonresident travelers. The foreign position of the authorized banks in CFA francs and all other currencies has become subject to limitation. Despite the reintroduction of exchange control and exchange restrictions, existing import liberalization has been maintained, but in some countries the global quotas for imports from non-EEC countries outside the French franc area have not been increased sufficiently in terms of CFA francs to offset the reduction in dollar terms that resulted from the devaluation.

---

[15] The capital controls were further modified and tightened toward the end of 1969. Additional elements of the controls became applicable also to France and the operations account countries. Furthermore, all investment in countries other than France and the operations account countries henceforth required prior authorization by the Minister of Finance.

CHAPTER 7

Dahomey

GENERAL SETTING

Dahomey gained its independence on August 1, 1960. The country embraces an area of 112,600 square kilometers (about 43,000 square miles), or about one fifth the size of France. From a narrow corridor on the Gulf of Guinea, the country stretches northward 670 kilometers (about 415 miles) to the Niger River and its tributary, the Mékrou, which together form the country's boundary with Niger. Most of the northern part of the country is wider than the southern part. Dahomey also borders Upper Volta on the north, Togo on the west, and Nigeria on the east.

Dahomey became a member of the International Monetary Fund (IMF) on July 10, 1963, its current quota is $10,000,000 (April 1970). On the same day it joined the International Bank for Reconstruction and Development (IBRD, or World Bank), current subscription $10,000,000; on September 16, 1963 it joined the International Development Association (IDA), current subscription $500,000. Among other international organizations, it is a member of the United Nations (UN), UN Educational, Scientific, and Cultural Organization (UNESCO), General Agreement on Tariffs and Trade (GATT), UN Economic Commission for Africa (ECA, or Commission Economique pour l'Afrique, CEA), African Development Bank (ADB), Common Organization of African and Malagasy States (Organization Commune Africaine et Malgache, or OCAM). It is also an associate member of the European Economic Community (EEC).

With Ivory Coast, Mali, Mauritania, Senegal, and Upper Volta, it participates in the West African Customs Union (Union Douanière des Etats de l'Afrique de l'Ouest, or UDEAO). With Ivory Coast, Mauritania, Niger, Senegal, Togo, and Upper Volta, it participates in the West African Monetary Union (Union Monétaire Ouest Africaine, or UMOA); in a common central bank, the Banque Centrale des Etats de l'Afrique de l'Ouest (BCEAO); and in a common currency, the CFA franc issued by BCEAO.

The country is predominantly agricultural, growing most of its own food, and most nonfood products are exported. Manufacturing consists mainly of the processing of agricultural products.

Except for Cotonou, the country has no ports. Coastal sand banks limit access to the sea, and there are no natural harbors, river mouths, or islands. Close to the coast is a series of lagoons from the one at Grand-Popo, joined to Lac Ahémé, to the one west of Porto-Novo, into which the Ouémé flows. This river, the longest in the country, is navigable for 200 kilometers. Another river, the Couffo, empties into Lac Ahémé. The Mono, forming part of the southwestern boundary with Togo, is navigable for only 80 kilometers and is subject to torrential floods. The northern rivers, the Mékrou, Alibori, and Sota (tributaries of the Niger) and the Pendjari (tributary of the Volta in Ghana after crossing Togo) are all too rapid and rocky for navigation.

North of the coastal sands is a region of lateritic clay where most of the oil palms are grown. This region is interrupted by a marshy depression extending into Nigeria. Northward most of the country ranges between 50 and 150 meters in elevation except for the Dassa hills in the south and the Chaîne d'Atakora (400–750 meters), which continue from Togo into northwestern Dahomey.

South of Savalou, the climate is equatorial, hot and humid, with a long dry season (December–March) when the hot, dry harmattan winds blow; a heavy rainy season (March–July); a short dry season (July–September); and a short rainy season (September–November). Annual rainfall increases from about 800 millimeters (32 inches) in the south-west to 1,325 millimeters (53 inches) in central Dahomey. In the north there is only one rainy season (May–September), and the harmattan winds blow for the rest of the year. Here, the annual rainfall averages 1,000 millimeters.

The total population, estimated at 2.6 million in 1968, increases at an annual rate of about 2.8 per cent. The few non-Africans are mainly French. Perhaps 15 per cent of the African population are Muslims, mostly in the north. There are a few Christians. The predominant ethnic group is the Fon, which, with the closely related Adja and Aizo, represent over half of the population. Smaller groups include the Yaruba, Bariba, and Fulani.

The official language is French; other languages include Fon and Yaruba in the south and Bariba in the north.

Porto-Novo, the capital, had an estimated population of 70,000 in 1968, and Cotonou 110,000. Other cities and towns include Abomey (25,000), Ouidah (21,000), and Parakou (6,500).

Nearly half of the population is under 15 years of age and about 12 per cent live in urban centers. The primary school attendance rate was slightly over 27 per cent in 1966. The average population density is 23 per square kilometer, but density is highest in the south, where it reaches 121 per square kilometer, compared with only 7 per square kilometer in the northwest. The pressure of population in the three southern provinces (*départements*), substantial migration to urban areas, and the repatriation of Dahomeans employed in neighboring countries before independence, have contributed to unemployment, especially in the largest city, Cotonou.

STRUCTURE OF THE ECONOMY

GROSS DOMESTIC PRODUCT

Official national accounts estimates are available for 1963-65 at current market prices, and estimates have been prepared for 1966-68 at constant 1966 prices on the basis of data provided by the Dahomean authorities but are only provisional, especially for 1968. These official estimates indicate relatively slow growth of the Dahomean economy during 1963-65 (Table 1). The gross domestic product (GDP) rose at an average annual rate of 2.6 per cent at current market prices. Since total population is estimated to have increased by 2.8 per cent a year and prices apparently remained relatively stable during this period, per capita GDP in real terms probably declined. Production of cash crops increased but little throughout this period, and the value added by mining, manufacturing, and services also rose relatively slowly.

In 1966, GDP at market prices is estimated to have risen by 5.7 per cent, partly because of a bumper crop. The estimated value added by mining, manufacturing, construction, and utilities declined by 3 per cent, reflecting mainly a decline in construction activity. The contribution of government wages and salaries went down by 8.8 per cent after the Government introduced certain austerity measures. Provisional estimates indicate a rise in GDP in real terms of about 3 per cent in 1967 and 2 per cent in 1968. In 1967, agricultural production increased only slightly over 1966; production of food crops and of certain export crops (mainly cotton and groundnuts) improved, but the output of palm products declined. On the other hand, the contribution of the secondary sector is estimated to have increased by about 10 per cent with the revival in business conditions; the transportation, trade, and services sector expanded by about 5 per cent. In 1968, exports of major cash crops rose by 21 per cent, resulting in an estimated increase in value added by transportation, trade, and services, of 8 per cent; the over-all growth rate, however, was held down by a drop in the production of food crops, caused by flood damage.

Effective demand, measured by expenditures at current prices, rose by about 4 per cent a year during 1963-65 (Table 2). Private consumption increased from 75 per cent of GDP in 1963 to 78 per cent in 1965, but public consumption remained unchanged at slightly above 19 per cent of GDP. Gross fixed investment, which had reached a peak of 17 per cent of GDP in 1963, declined to 16 per cent in 1964 and 1965 as construction of the port of Cotonou neared completion. Excess demand was absorbed by the increasing deficit on goods and nonfactor services accounts with the rest of the world. The ratio of the resource

TABLE 1. DAHOMEY: GROSS DOMESTIC PRODUCT BY ORIGIN, 1963–68 [1]

(*Amount in billions of CFA francs*)

	1963		1964		1965		1966 [2]		1967 [2]		1968 [2]	
	Amount	Per cent	Amount	Per cent	Amount	Per cent	Amount	Per cent	Amount	Per cent	Amount	Per cent
Agriculture (including livestock, fishing, and forestry)	19.9	47.6	20.2	47.9	21.4	48.6	23.9	51.4	24.0	48.5	22.9	46.8
Mining, manufacturing, construction, and utilities	4.1	9.8	4.5	10.7	4.3	9.8	4.2	9.0	4.6	10.7	4.6	9.4
Transportation, trade, and services	12.4	29.6	12.0	28.4	12.6	28.6	13.2	28.4	13.9	30.0	15.0	30.6
Government	5.4	13.0	5.5	13.0	5.7	13.0	5.2	11.2	5.4	10.8	6.4	13.2
Total GDP	41.8	100.0	42.2	100.0	44.0	100.0	46.5	100.0	47.9	100.0	48.9	100.0

Source: Data provided by the Dahomean authorities.

[1] At current prices during 1963–65 and at 1966 prices during 1966–68.
[2] Provisional estimates.

TABLE 2. DAHOMEY: USE OF GROSS DOMESTIC PRODUCT, 1963–68 [1,2]

	1963	1964	1965	1966	1967 [3]	1968 [3]
	VALUE (*billion CFA francs*)					
Consumption						
Private	31.3	32.4	34.5	37.3	. . .	. . .
Public	8.1	8.3	8.5	8.7	. . .	. . .
Total consumption	39.4	40.7	43.0	46.0	47.5	46.9
Gross fixed investment						
Private	2.7	2.8	4.2	2.0	· . . .	. . .
Public	4.4	4.0	3.0	4.3	. . .	. . .
Total gross fixed investment	7.1	6.8	7.2	6.3	8.6	8.7
Change in stocks	0.2	0.2	0.2	0.2	0.2	0.2
Exports of goods and nonfactor services	3.9	4.7	5.0	6.6	7.1	8.8
Less imports of goods and non-factor services	−8.8	−10.2	−11.4	−12.6	−15.5	−15.7
Total GDP	41.8	42.2	44.0	46.5	47.9	48.9
	PER CENT OF TOTAL VALUE					
Consumption						
Private	74.9	76.8	78.4	80.2	. . .	. . .
Public	19.4	19.7	19.3	18.7	. . .	. . .
Total consumption	94.3	96.4	97.7	98.9	99.2	95.9
Gross fixed investment						
Private	6.5	6.6	9.5	4.3	. . .	. . .
Public	10.5	9.5	6.9	9.2	. . .	. . .
Total gross fixed investment	17.0	16.1	16.4	13.5	18.0	17.8
Change in stocks	0.5	0.5	0.5	0.4	0.4	0.4
Exports of goods and nonfactor services	9.3	11.1	11.4	14.2	14.8	18.0
Less imports of goods and non-factor services	−21.1	−24.2	−26.0	−27.0	−32.4	−32.1
Total GDP	100.0	100.0	100.0	100.0	100.0	100.0

Source: Data provided by the Dahomean authorities.

[1] At current prices during 1963–65 and at 1966 prices during 1966–68.
[2] Because of rounding, figures in this table and some of the following tables do not add to all totals.
[3] Provisional estimates.

gap to GDP increased from 12 per cent in 1963 to nearly 15 per cent in 1965.

Total consumption continued to rise in 1966, mainly because of a further increase in private consumption to 80 per cent of GDP. With implementation of the Government's austerity program, the public consumption ratio to GDP dropped below 19 per cent. However, fixed capital formation decreased even more (by about 13 per cent), owing partly to the completion of certain infrastructural investments and partly to dampened business conditions.

In 1967, total domestic expenditures rose by 7 per cent, reflecting essentially an expansion in fixed capital formation. The ratio of gross fixed investment to GDP increased from less than 14 per cent in 1966 to 18 per cent in 1967 as new projects were undertaken. Total consumption increased more moderately, reflecting the Government's efforts in restraining the growth of disposable incomes through higher taxation. In real terms and on a per capita basis, consumption declined slightly.

In 1968, total domestic expenditures continued to rise, though at a slower pace than in the preceding years. Total consumption, however, declined by more than 1 per cent, and estimated per capita consumption fell from CFAF 19,000 in 1967 to CFAF 18,000 in 1968, or by about 6 per cent, mainly as a result of the improvement in the financial position of the public sector. Indications are that fixed capital formation increased further in 1968.

Table 3 shows the changes in domestic savings and investment. The figures for domestic savings are derived from the figures for gross investment adjusted for the changes in the balance of payments.

The domestic savings ratio to GDP declined from 6 per cent in 1963 to an average of less than 1 per cent in 1966 and 1967. During this period, consumption increased more rapidly than GDP and public savings were negative because of large budget deficits on the current account. Capital formation was increasingly financed from foreign resources, mainly grants provided by FAC (Fonds d'Aide et de Coopération) and EDF (European Development Fund). In 1968, there was a reversal of this trend; the ordinary budget deficit was substantially

TABLE 3.   DAHOMEY: DOMESTIC SAVINGS AND INVESTMENT, 1963–68 [1]

(*In billions of CFA francs*)

	1963	1964	1965	1966	1967	1968
GDP at market prices	41.8	42.2	44.0	46.5	47.9	48.9
Consumption	39.4	40.7	43.0	46.0	47.5	46.9
Domestic savings	2.4	1.5	1.0	0.5	0.4	2.0
Import surplus	4.9	5.5	6.4	6.0	8.4	6.9
Gross investment	7.3	7.0	7.4	6.5	8.8	8.9

Sources: Tables 1 and 2.

[1] Provisional estimates for 1966–68 at 1966 prices.

reduced and the resource gap declined from nearly 18 per cent of GDP in 1967 to 14 per cent. As a result, the ratio of gross domestic savings to GDP rose to about 4 per cent.

The low ratio of savings in Dahomey reflects primarily a lack of public savings—in fact, current public sector consumption is financed partly from foreign grants—and very little private savings and investment outside the traditional sector. Not only the public sector investment but also much of the private sector investment is financed from foreign sources.

During 1963-65, gross investment remained virtually unchanged in absolute terms at about CFAF 7.2 billion. Public sector investment averaged about 54 per cent of gross fixed investment during this period. The bulk of public sector investment has been in undertakings involving long gestation periods, such as the construction of the port of Cotonou, administrative buildings, and oil palm plantations. In 1966, gross investment declined to an all-time low of CFAF 6.5 billion, of which about 65 per cent was made in the public sector. In 1967 and 1968, gross investment recovered significantly in both the public and private sectors. During the two years 1967-68, public sector investment rose as a result of the stepping up of oil palm and cotton planting programs and the establishment of some mixed manufacturing plants, notably the kenaf factory. Private sector investment also increased (mainly in manufacturing and petroleum exploration). Capital formation in the subsistence sector (mainly in traditional housing and land clearance) is estimated at CFAF 2.4 billion in 1968.

AGRICULTURE, FISHING, AND FORESTRY

Agriculture employs over 75 per cent of the working population and accounts for almost all exports. During 1965–67, agriculture contributed nearly one half of GDP even though only 1 million hectares of the total cultivable area of 9 million hectares were estimated to be actually used for agriculture. Most of the cultivable area is in the three southern provinces (*départements*), where only 50 to 60 per cent of the cultivable land is actually under cultivation. Furthermore, yields are relatively low because of deficiencies in cultivation methods, and inadequate extension services, storage facilities, and marketing channels. It is estimated that average yields of major food crops could be substantially increased if modern techniques, including the use of fertilizers, were introduced.

In order to improve agricultural production, the Government has undertaken to develop the cultivation of cash crops with the assistance of certain public bodies and foreign specialized institutions. In part because of these efforts, agricultural production is estimated to have increased in 1966 and 1967, compared with its relative stagnation in previous years. The competitiveness of certain agricultural exports has also improved.

Food Crops

The staple food crops currently grown are corn, cassava, yams, sorghum, millet, and rice. Some products (i.e., groundnuts and palm products) are produced both for local consumption and for export. Although data are not very reliable, indications are that the production of food crops under normal weather conditions is sufficient for domestic needs.

During 1965–67, both area and production of corn and beans increased, whereas the area and production of sorghum remained unchanged (Table 4). Although the area of yams and potatoes declined, production of both crops rose, suggesting improved yields. For millet and rice, however, there was a decrease in both the area under cultivation and production. As export prices were generally favorable,

TABLE 4. DAHOMEY: AREA UNDER CULTIVATION AND PRODUCTION OF PRINCIPAL FOOD CROPS, 1965–67

	Area Under Cultivation			Production		
	1965	1966	1967	1965	1966	1967
	Thousand hectares			*Thousand metric tons*		
Corn	384	369	406	218	203	246
Cassava	136	126	121	933	768	797
Sorghum	109	97	110	59	49	58
Millet	16	17	5	6	6	3
Beans	62	56	84	19	14	27
Yams	61	54	58	540	454	565
Potatoes	11	8	7	38	110	106
Rice	3	2	2	1	2	1

Source: Data provided by the Dahomean authorities.

some unrecorded exports of food crops were made in 1965–67 to neighboring countries.

In 1968, floods reduced the harvest of food crops by 10–20 per cent. Another reason for the decline in production is reported to be the fact that institutions specializing in agricultural development concentrated their efforts on cash crops.

In order to increase food production, the National Rural Development Agency (Société Nationale de Développement Rural, or SONADER) has encouraged farmers in the area under its supervision to organize into cooperatives to grow food crops; over 40 cooperatives were operating in 1968. Under this system, implemented in selected areas, individual farmers receive full returns from their cultivation. The Government has indicated that, beginning in 1969, it will establish Regional Rural Development Centers (Centres d'Action Régionale pour le Développement Rural, or CARDER's) to promote food crop production in the three southern provinces (*départements*), where improved cultivation methods are most urgently needed by the rapidly growing population.

Certain food crops, such as corn, are marketed by a public corporation, the Agricultural Marketing Office (Office de Commercialisation Agricole du Dahomey, or OCAD), but its activities are hampered by a lack of adequate storage facilities.

Export Crops

Dahomey's main agricultural exports are palm products, cotton, groundnuts, sheanuts, copra, and coffee. Other agricultural exports include coconuts, tobacco, castor beans, and kapok. During 1965/66–1967/68 there was an expansion in production of these commodities, particularly in palm products, cotton, and groundnuts, as a result of recent investment and extension work undertaken with the assistance of certain public bodies and specialized foreign institutions.

Oil palm products.—In 1968, oil palm products accounted for over one half of the country's recorded exports. Wild palm groves covered an area of about 400,000 hectares in 1968, and plantations of selected oil palm varieties initiated since 1955 covered an area of about 15,000 hectares. The new varieties have both a thicker cluster for higher palm oil yields and a bigger kernel for higher palm kernel yields. The palm oil extraction rate from selected trees is estimated at 13 per cent, compared with 9 per cent for wild trees, and the palm kernel extraction rate is estimated at 50 per cent uniformly for all varieties of palm.

Since 1962 the National Rural Development Agency has implemented a successful palm plantation program with FAC and EDF financial assistance. It stepped up the rate of planting in 1964 and 1965 with the implementation of the Mono project, which covered 4,000 hectares, and so far some 13,000 hectares have been planted with selected varieties. It was expected that by 1969 an additional 3,950 hectares would be planted, of which 1,800 hectares would be included in the Grand Hinvi project (northwest of Porto-Novo) in southern Dahomey. This project, which will cover 6,000 hectares when completed, represents an investment of CFAF 1.85 billion and is to be financed jointly by FAC and IBRD. In addition, another project to be undertaken in 1970 at Agonvy (north of Porto-Novo) will extend over an area of 7,000 hectares at an estimated cost of CFAF 2.0 billion and will be financed by EDF.

Oil palms planted in the early 1960's are now beginning to be productive, and it was estimated that in 1969 the output of selected groves reached 31,000 tons.[1] The marketing of palm products is entrusted to the National Oil Mills Company (Société Nationale des Huileries du Dahomey, or SNAHDA), which operates four palm oil mills and a palm kernel oil mill. Market sales of palm products declined in 1966/67 owing to drought but rose significantly in 1967/68 and in 1968/69 (Table 5).

In 1967/68, world market prices continued to decline for palm oil because of increased production of close substitutes, but rose substantially for palm kernel oil. Consequently, the producer price for palm bunches remained unchanged at CFAF 2.75 per kilogram from the 1964/65 season, whereas for palm kernels it was increased from CFAF 19 per kilogram to CFAF 21 per kilogram in 1967/68. The rise in world market prices for palm kernel oil in 1967/68 left the National Oil Mills Company with a profit, which largely offset losses incurred on palm oil exports, and its cash position improved significantly. Palm

---

[1] Throughout this chapter the word "ton" refers to a metric ton of 2,240.6 pounds.

TABLE 5. DAHOMEY: MARKET SALES OF OIL PALM PRODUCTS, 1965/66–1968/69

(Quantity in thousands of metric tons; value in millions of CFA francs)

| | 1965/66 | | 1966/67 | | 1967/68 | | 1968/69 |
	Quantity	Value	Quantity	Value	Quantity	Value	Quantity[1]
Palm oil	11.4	697.1	6.7	384.1	9.7	466.6	11.9
Palm kernels	7.8	330.8	5.7	196.3	7.3	353.3	9.4
Palm kernel oil	17.6	1,203.7	18.6	1,139.3	23.5	1,964.9	23.1
Palm cake	18.5	427.6	19.2	367.4	22.7	446.8.	22.8

Source: Data provided by the Dahomean authorities.

[1] Value not available.

kernel oil is exported mainly to the United States; palm oil has been exported to France without any price support since 1965.

Cotton.—Cultivation of cotton is being developed by the Compagnie Française des Fibres Textiles (CFDT), which is responsible for providing advice to farmers and increasing both area and yields. The area under cotton expanded from 26,800 hectares in 1963/64 to 38,400 hectares in 1967/68. Production of seed (unginned) cotton more than trebled between 1963/64 and 1967/68, when it reached about 12,500 tons, and it was anticipated that the revised development plan target of 18,000 tons for 1970 would be exceeded in 1969 (Table 6).

The yields for the Allen variety (in the northern part of the country) are estimated at 800–900 kilograms of seed cotton per hectare and those of the Mono variety at 300–400 kilograms. The latter variety is considered of little interest, and its production is not being encouraged.

TABLE 6. DAHOMEY: PRODUCTION AND EXPORTS OF COTTON, BY VARIETY, 1965/66–1968/69

(In metric tons)

| | Allen Variety | | Mono Variety | |
	Production [1]	Exports [2]	Production [1]	Exports [2]
1965/66	4,057	1,551	2,360	506
1966/67	7,413	2,948	1,875	345
1967/68	11,078	3,450	1,494	202
1968/69 [3]	21,500	8,200	1,700	—

Source: Data provided by the Dahomean authorities.

[1] Seed (unginned) cotton.
[2] Ginned cotton.
[3] Forecasts.

Producer prices in 1968 for the Allen variety were CFAF 32.30 per kilogram in the north and CFAF 36.30 in the south, and for the Mono variety CFAF 29.80 in the center and CFAF 25 in the northwest. Compagnie Française des Fibres Textiles operates five ginning mills, the capacity of which will soon become insufficient in relation to the considerable expansion in cottonseed production. Exports of ginned cotton have been supported since 1963 (see "Agricultural price subsidies and support," below).

Groundnuts.—Production of groundnuts has fluctuated widely, as a result of both climatic variations and changes in area cultivated. Since 1965, however, production has increased steadily, owing partly to the implementation of a program to develop this cash crop, particularly in the northern part of the country; Société d'Aide Technique et de Coopération (SATEC) is responsible for carrying out this program, which is financed by FAC. Market sales of shelled groundnuts rose from 3,820 tons in 1965/66 to 6,236 tons in 1966/67 and further to 7,800 tons in 1967/68; continued expansion in groundnut production was expected in 1968/69. The quantity of shelled groundnuts exported followed a similar trend, reaching 7,600 tons in 1968 (Table 7). However, in view of the sharp drop in world market prices and the termination of the guaranteed price arrangements for groundnuts in the French market on January 1, 1968, the value of groundnut exports declined in 1967/68. The producer price, which averaged CFAF 14 per kilogram of unshelled groundnuts in 1965/66, remained unchanged in 1966/67 but was reduced to an average of CFAF 13 in 1967/68. In anticipation of a rise in world market prices in 1969, the producer price was increased to

TABLE 7.   DAHOMEY: QUANTITY OF MINOR AGRICULTURAL
PRODUCTS EXPORTED, 1965–68

(*In thousands of metric tons*)

	1965	1966	1967	1968 [1]
Shelled groundnuts	2.3	4.0	5.3	7.6
Sheanuts	4.9	3.8	5.6	6.7
Copra	1.8	1.3	0.7	0.6
Coffee	0.9	0.8	1.2	0.5
Coconuts	0.6	0.5	0.3	0.3

Source: Data provided by the Dahomean authorities.
[1] Until November 30, 1968.

CFAF 13.70 per kilogram for 1968/69 and to CFAF 14 per kilogram for 1969/70, a level considered to be satisfactory to farmers. However, if groundnut shelling costs could be reduced, the producer price might be increased.

A groundnut oil factory was scheduled for construction in 1969–70; plans called for an investment of CFAF 500 million and a capacity of 45,000 tons of unshelled groundnuts. It was expected that the establishment of this factory would result in an increase in the producer price because of the economies to be gained from industrial processing over the processing methods used in the subsistence sector.

Sheanuts.—Most of the sheanuts are produced in the northern and central parts of the country. Exports increased from 4,900 tons in 1965 to 6,700 tons in 1968 and were expected to reach 11,000 tons in the next few years (see Table 7). Owing to higher export prices, the producer price was raised from CFAF 6 per kilogram in 1966/67 to CFAF 14 in 1968/69. Recently a three-year sales contract was signed with Japan for the export of the bulk of this crop, and it was anticipated that the producer price will remain unchanged in the next two years.

Coffee.—Production of robusta coffee remained at a low level in view of the poor maintenance of plantations. Exports, after having risen from 900 tons in 1965 to 1,200 tons in 1967, declined to 500 tons in 1968. To encourage production, the Government raised the producer price from CFAF 60–70 per kilogram in 1965/66 to CFAF 90 in 1966/67 and 1967/68. With FAC assistance, the Government is studying the possibility of expanding coffee production so that Dahomey may utilize more fully its International Coffee Agreement (ICA) export quota of 2,000 tons.

Coconut products.—Coconut palms cover an area of about 12,000 hectares. Owing to low yields and increasing domestic consumption, the export of coconuts, grated coconut, and copra has declined in recent years.

Tobacco.—The exportable production of tobacco increased from 153 tons in 1965 to 730 tons in 1967. Tobacco production, which is encouraged by the Compagnie Agricole et Industrielle des Tabacs Africains (CAITA), could further be expanded. However, as Senegal and Ivory Coast, which were the main importers of Dahomean tobacco, have raised their import taxes on tobacco, the Government is studying other outlets for marketing the crop.

Cashew nuts.—The area covered by cashew trees is estimated at 8,000 hectares. Production increased from 75 tons in 1966 to 350 tons in 1968, the bulk of which was exported. In view of the increase in world demand, production was expected to reach 500 tons in 1969.

Agricultural Price Subsidies and Support

Subsidies for agricultural products are provided by the Stabilization Fund (Fonds de Stabilisation et de Soutien des Prix des Produits à l'Exportation, or FSSPPE), which in turn derives its receipts from levies on exports and EEC subsidies provided under the Yaoundé Convention of Association. Beginning in January 1968, the Stabilization Fund, previously managed by the Treasury, became an autonomous agency with an annexed budget.

EEC assistance aims at compensating Dahomey for the loss of bilateral support for its exports and at enabling it gradually to adjust production costs to world market conditions. This assistance is of two types: (1) price subsidies for groundnuts, cotton, and grated coconut and (2) support for structural improvement and diversification for oil palm products, groundnuts, cotton, coconuts, and coffee. EEC price subsidies for each commodity are computed on the basis of the actual export price per unit and the target cost established for the corresponding crop year (Tables 8 and 9). Target costs are calculated on the basis of producer prices, taxation, and other costs, including internal marketing costs. Under the EEC program, total price subsidies for agricultural exports during 1965–69 were estimated at CFAF 969 million.

In addition to EEC support, the Stabilization Fund provides subsidies out of its own resources (Table 10). In 1965/66 and 1966/67, all agricultural exports except palm products and tobacco were subsidized. Cotton, sheanuts, and kapok became competitive in 1968. Among the remaining subsidized cash crops (groundnuts, coffee, copra, and castor beans), only groundnuts continue to be subsidized to any significant extent.

The total price subsidy for shelled groundnut exports rose from CFAF 2.17 per kilogram, or 5 per cent of the c.i.f. export price in 1965/66, to CFAF 8.20, or 22.3 per cent of that price, in 1967/68.

TABLE 8. DAHOMEY: COST, EXPORT PRICE, AND SUBSIDIES OF
COTTON, 1965/66–1967/68

(*In CFA francs per kilogram*)

	1965/66	1966/67	1967/68
Allen			
Cost f.o.b. Cotonou	144.00	141.00	138.00
Export price f.o.b. Cotonou	127.53	133.01	143.58
Profit, or loss (−)	−16.47	−7.99	5.58
Mono			
Cost f.o.b. Cotonou	114.99	127.00	124.00
Export price f.o.b. Cotonou	107.00	114.09	124.37
Profit, or loss (−)	−7.99	−12.91	0.37
Total gross profit, or loss (−)	−24.46	−20.00	5.95
Reimbursements [1]	1.07	6.11	5.48
Total net profit, or loss (−)	**−22.39**	**−14.79**	**11.43**
Subsidies			
EEC	17.80	5.63	—
Domestic	4.58	9.16	—

Source: Data provided by the Dahomean authorities.

[1] From Compagnie Française pour le Développement des Fibres Textiles (CFDT) to the Stabilization Fund, on account of profits made on seed cotton exports and readjustments in the schedule of cotton yields based on actual yields at the end of the crop season.

There was an increase in both the EEC and the domestic component of the subsidy. The domestic subsidy has been higher than the EEC subsidy because of ceilings on EEC subsidies provided for in the Convention of Association. EEC price subsidies for groundnut exports

TABLE 9. DAHOMEY: COST, EXPORT PRICE, AND SUBSIDIES OF
SHELLED GROUNDNUTS, 1965/66–1967/68

(*In CFA francs per kilogram*)

	1965/66	1966/67	1967/68
Cost c.i.f. Cotonou			
Producer price	14.00	14.00	13.00
Taxes	6.76	6.76	6.76
Other costs	25.14	25.14	25.14
Total cost	45.90	45.90	44.90
Export price c.i.f. Cotonou	43.73	38.44	36.70
Loss	**−2.17**	**−7.46**	**−8.20**
Subsidies			
EEC	1.02	2.16	2.73
Domestic	1.15	5.30	5.47

Source: Data provided by the Dahomean authorities.

TABLE 10. DAHOMEY: STABILIZATION FUND BUDGET, 1965/66–1969 [1]

(In millions of CFA francs)

	1965/66	1966/67	1968	1969
Receipts				
Reserve funds	20.00	113.70	122.90	117.14
Palm kernel reserves	20.00	54.00	—	—
Support tax	43.50	66.20	112.00	136.00
Other levies	—	—	5.00	37.30
Sundry receipts	—	—	—	94.00
Refund on cotton prefinancing	40.00	50.00	59.64	52.00
Total receipts = total expenditures	**123.50**	**283.90**	**299.54**	**437.04**
Expenditures				
Operating costs				
Personnel	0.30 ⎫			
Material	0.20 ⎬	1.18	1.15	1.07
Insurance	0.18 ⎭			
Subscriptions	1.50	3.00	1.50	2.00
Price support				
Copra	3.00	6.00	2.00	1.00
Cotton	9.00	75.20	72.84	8.50
Sheanuts	27.00	4.70	—	—
Castor beans	2.50	3.20	1.60	1.00
Kapok	1.00	2.50	—	—
Coffee	5.00	2.70	1.00	1.00
Groundnuts	7.00	14.20	38.00	150.00
Palm kernels	20.00	10.00	—	—
Prefinancing of cotton	45.00	53.00	—	—
Sundry expenditures	1.82	2.82	67.91 [2]	115.18
Capital expenditures	—	—	—	50.00 [3]
Net surplus	—	105.40	113.54	107.29

Source: Data provided by the Dahomean authorities.

[1] The accounting year 1965/66 ended September 30, the accounting year 1966/67 ended December 31, and beginning in 1968, the accounting year coincides with the calendar year.

[2] Including interest payments of CFAF 4.41 million on loans.

[3] Investment in storage facilities for cotton.

amounted to CFAF 38.7 million during the three-year period. It was envisaged that in 1969 the amount of total subsidy to groundnut exports would further increase in view of the expected rise in production and the higher producer price.

Exports of ginned cotton have been supported since 1963/64 by both the EEC and the Stabilization Fund. However, the Stabilization Fund has been reimbursed by the Compagnie Française pour le Développement des Fibres Textiles (CFDT) for a part of its assistance. Net price support for Allen cotton declined from CFAF 16.47 per kilogram, or 13 per cent of the f.o.b. export price in 1965/66, to CFAF 7.99, or 6 per cent, in 1966/67; for Mono cotton, it increased from CFAF 7.99 per kilogram, or 7.5 per cent of the f.o.b. export price, in 1965/66 to CFAF 12.91, or 11.3 per cent, in 1966/67. EEC price subsidies for ginned cotton amounted to CFAF 53.4 million during the three years 1965–67. No price support was provided in 1967/68 as ginned cotton was exported at a profit estimated at CFAF 5.58 per kilogram for the Allen variety and CFAF 0.37 per kilogram for the Mono variety.

Livestock and Livestock Products

Although cattle are raised in Dahomey, mainly for the production of meat, substantial imports of cattle on the hoof are made from neighboring Niger and Upper Volta. The livestock population is estimated to have increased in recent years (Table 11). Various parasitic diseases are widespread, and campaigns against these diseases, particularly rinderpest, have been hampered by lack of budget resources. Per capita consumption of meat is relatively low (5–6 kilograms a year).

TABLE 11.   DAHOMEY: LIVESTOCK POPULATION, 1963–67

(*In thousands*)

	1963	1964	1965	1966	1967
Cattle	371	393	449	506	519
Sheep and goats	908	974	1,034	1,045	1,118
Pigs	303	332	353	300	347
Horses and donkeys	3	4	4	4	3

Source: Data provided by the Dahomean authorities.

Ranching could be developed in combination with expanded production of animal fodder (e.g., corn and groundnut cake). In 1968 the Government was considering the establishment of two ranches, at an estimated cost of about CFAF 600 million, with a capacity on each ranch for raising 5,000–10,000 head of cattle. Another project, which was under way with Swiss assistance, involved the raising of cows for milk production. Possibilities for livestock breeding in the north, where conditions appear favorable, were also being investigated.

Fishing and Forestry

Fishing, a major activity in Dahomey, supplies a basic item of the diet in the south and employs about 15,000 persons. The level of fishing activity, however, has not changed significantly in recent years. The deep-sea catch increased slightly in 1968, but the inland catch, which furnishes most of the fish, declined between 1965 and 1968 (Table 12) because the construction of the port of Cotonou changed the salinity of the water in the nearby lagoon. Imports of fish, mainly from neighboring countries, were estimated at 3,000 tons in 1966, 2,600 tons in 1967, and 2,800 tons in 1968. Construction of a fishing port at Cotonou is under way and is expected to be completed in 1971; financing is provided by EDF and Caisse Centrale de Coopération Economique (CCCE). In the next few years the Government plans to enlarge the deep-sea fishing fleet from 5 trawlers to 12; 3 are to be equipped with refrigeration facilities and another 3 are to specialize in tuna fishing. In addition, refrigerated storage will be established in up-country areas, particularly at Parakou and Kandi.

TABLE 12.   DAHOMEY: PRODUCTION OF FISH, 1965–68

(*In metric tons*)

	1965	1966	1967	1968
Coastal fishing	5,000	4,500	3,500	3,600
Inland fishing	20,000	17,000	17,000	17,000
Deep-sea fishing	1,500	1,000	1,500	1,800
Total	26,500	22,500	22,000	22,400

Source: Data provided by the Dahomean authorities.

Dahomey is deficient in forest resources, especially in the south. Reforestation projects under way include mainly teak and cashew nut plantings. In 1967, however, the planting program fell short of the development plan targets, mainly because of a lack of financing.

MINING

No mines were operating in 1968. Small deposits of alluvial gold, however, were being panned on an experimental basis. Prospecting for gold and other minerals (phosphates, limestone, and uranium) was expected to continue. In February 1968, the Union Oil Company of California found petroleum deposits offshore at about 29 kilometers southeast of Cotonou; work was proceeding toward their commercial exploitation. Investment in petroleum exploration was estimated at about CFAF 360 million in 1967 and CFAF 956 million in 1968.

MANUFACTURING

Before 1967, industrial activity in Dahomey was essentially confined to the processing of agricultural exports. The National Oil Mills Company (SNAHDA) operated four palm oil mills at Bohicon (east of Abomey), Avrankou (northeast of Porto-Novo), Ahozon (east of Ouidah), and Bada (north of Porto-Novo), with a total annual capacity of 20,000 tons, and a palm kernel oil mill, built at Cotonou in 1965, with an annual capacity of 40,000 tons and financed by a loan from the Kreditanstalt für Wiederaufbau. The Compagnie Française pour le Développement des Fibres Textiles (CFDT) operated five cotton ginning mills with a total annual capacity of 10,000 tons. In addition, there were small industrial units including a beer and soft drink factory, a soap factory, a plant making prefabricated building materials, and two assembly plants, one for transistor radios and the other for Citroën cars.

During 1967–68, several new manufacturing plants were established. The most notable of them was the factory of the Kenaf Company (Société Dahoméene du Kenaf, or SODAK). This project was financed by an Italian suppliers' credit of CFAF 3.0 billion, of which CFAF 500 million was for the development of kenaf cultivation. The Government holds 20 per cent of this mixed enterprise, and private Italian interests the remainder. At full capacity, this factory would employ about 1,200 workers and would produce 16,000 tons of kenaf fiber and 5,000 tons of bags. Not much progress, however, has been made in kenaf cultivation, and the factory operated in 1968 much below capacity. In order to increase the rate of capacity utilization, the Government is considering importing kenaf fiber, pending the production of locally cultivated kenaf.

Smaller industries include a plant for freezing shrimps, a noodle factory, a paint manufacturing plant, and a shoe factory. The shrimp plant involves an investment of CFAF 112 million, and has an annual capacity of 500 tons. The noodle factory, established at a cost of CFAF 40 million, can produce 30 tons of noodles annually at full capacity. The paint manufacturing unit represents an investment of CFAF 60 million and at full capacity produces 600 tons of painting oils a year for domestic use. The shoe factory was established at a cost of CFAF 50 million and can produce 600,000 pairs of sandals and shoes a year at full capacity.

Several new manufacturing projects were under way in 1969. A textile printing factory of the Cotton Industries of Dahomey (Industries Cotonnières du Dahomey, or ICODA) was being built at a cost of CFAF 500 million; its capital is CFAF 120 million, 20 per cent held by the Government and the remainder by French and German private interests. Its annual capacity was estimated at 600 tons and its employment at 120 workers. A cycle assembly plant is also under construction at a cost of CFAF 95 million. Additional projects under active consideration included a cement factory (Société du Ciment du Dahomey), estimated to cost CFAF 250 million, a cotton ginning mill estimated to cost CFAF 200 million, a groundnut oil mill requiring an estimated investment of CFAF 800 million, and an increase in the capacity of the Bada palm oil factory at an estimated cost of CFAF 100 million.

Dahomey has obtained the guarantee of the Fonds d'Entraide et de Garantie des Emprunts du Conseil de l'Entente for loans to finance three projects: the textile plant, the kenaf factory, and the groundnut oil mill.

The major bottlenecks to industrial development in Dahomey are the small size of its market and the shortage of entrepreneurship. In order to induce private investors into industrial ventures, the Government enacted an Investment Code in 1961; further liberalization of its provisions is being studied (see "Investment code," below).

TRANSPORTATION

The volume of operations of the port has been increasing since its construction in 1965. In 1968 the port handled on the average 50 ships per month and cargo totaling 480,000 tons for the year, about half of total capacity. The number of passengers declined from 9,200 in 1965 to 7,900 in 1967 but rose to 8,900 in 1968. Table 13 shows receipts and expenditures during 1965–67. Construction of the port of Lomé apparently has not affected the operations of the port of Cotonou since it handles traffic for Dahomey and Niger while the port of Lomé handles traffic for Togo and Upper Volta.

The railway network, which is operated by the Dahomey-Niger Railway and Transport System (Organisation Commune Dahomey-Niger

TABLE 13.   DAHOMEY: BUDGET OF THE PORT OF COTONOU, 1965–67

(*In millions of CFA francs*)

	1965	1966	1967
Receipts			
Current receipts	132.0	171.0	191.0
Subsidies [1]	15.0	—	2.5
Loans from Development Bank	140.0	—	—
Other	5.5	2.0	—
Total receipts = total expenditures	**292.5**	**173.0**	**193.5**
Expenditures			
Current expenditures	85.0	119.0	138.0
Reserves	54.0	16.0	23.0
Capital expenditures	153.5	38.0	32.5

Source: Data provided by the Dahomean authorities.

[1] From the central government budget in 1965; from FAC in 1967.

des Chemins de Fer et des Transports, or OCDN), covers 579 kilometers. The main line (418 kilometers), connecting Cotonou and Parakou, handles the traffic with Niger. The System also operates the road connections between Parakou and Niger (Opération Hirondelle). In 1966, its deficit on account of railway activities amounted to CFAF 126 million; this deficit was to be financed by a subsidy from the Dahomean Government, but it has not yet been paid. In 1967, the System had a surplus of CFAF 4.6 million because of an increase in freight following a bumper groundnut crop in Niger. In 1968, however, it again incurred a deficit estimated at CFAF 120 million. The System's financial operations on account of road transportation were balanced during the last three years.

Dahomey's road network (6,500 kilometers) consists of interstate roads, interregional roads, and track and feeder roads. The Ministry of Public Works is responsible for the maintenance of 3,500 kilometers of roads; 691 kilometers of them are paved and 1,624 kilometers are all-weather unpaved roads. The road network is generally in poor condition and has been deteriorating from inadequate maintenance in the recent past because of insufficient budgetary appropriations. In 1968, FAC provided some road maintenance equipment valued at CFAF 75 million, and granted CFAF 90 million for repairs of the Parakou-Malanville road (25 kilometers). Repair operations on this road were to continue into 1969. Reconstruction of the road from Porto-Novo northeast to Igolo (47 kilometers) was to be undertaken in 1969 under an EDF grant estimated at CFAF 300 million. The Government is currently preparing studies on road maintenance, and on the extension of the present network, for possible foreign financing.

POWER

A joint Togo-Dahomey electric company, the Communauté Electrique du Bénin (CEB), was established on July 27, 1968. The establishment of this company followed the agreement signed by Togo, Dahomey, and Ghana for the provision of electric power from Ghana. Under this agreement, Dahomey was to import 15 megawatts annually during the first two years and 50 megawatts annually after 1971. The company has a share capital of CFAF 500 million divided equally between Togo and Dahomey. A feasibility study on power transmission from Ghana was being undertaken; it was provisionally estimated that the investment involved might amount to CFAF 1.35 billion. Importation of power from Ghana may not result in a reduction of electricity rates in Togo and Dahomey because the joint company plans to utilize its profits to finance an expanded power distribution program. One of the consequences of the agreement with Ghana was the canceling of the proposed hydroelectric project on the Mono in Dahomey.

ECONOMIC DEVELOPMENT PLANNING

Economic planning was initiated in Dahomey soon after independence with the elaboration of the 1962–65 Plan. In recent years, changes have been made from time to time in the administrative machinery responsible for planning. In 1967 the previous Haut Commissariat du Plan became a Department of the Ministry of Finance, Economic Affairs, and Planning. After the present Government took office in August 1968, a Ministry of Planning was established directly under the President. In addition to responsibility for drawing up the plan, this Ministry controls its execution, coordinates development activities of other government departments, and for important projects or projects requiring foreign financing, assists in their preparation. The Ministry of

Planning also chairs the permanent interdepartmental committee in charge of granting concessions under the Investment Code.

1962–65 PLAN

The 1962–65 Plan provided for an average annual increase in GDP of 6.5 per cent. In 1964, however, this plan was abandoned as it became evident that the size of the proposed investment program exceeded available resources and was not in line with the ability of the existing administrative structure to prepare and implement development projects. The major achievements during the first plan period were (1) establishment of the National Rural Development Agency (SONADER), in charge of the palm planting program, and (2) construction of the port of Cotonou, completed in 1965.

1966–70 DEVELOPMENT PLAN

Dahomey is in the process of executing a second development plan covering 1966–70. Its general goals are threefold: (1) increase and diversify the productive capacity, especially in the rural sector; (2) balance the current budget by the end of the plan period and consolidate the floating debt of the Government; and (3) lay the foundations for long-term growth within a framework of regional cooperation. The 1966–70 Plan envisages an over-all annual economic growth rate of 4 per cent, based on an average annual increase of nearly 4 per cent in agriculture, 8 per cent in the secondary sector, and 3 per cent in services. To achieve these targets, the plan called for an over-all investment program of CFAF 35.3 billion, CFAF 25.6 billion in the public sector (Table 14). Although the 1966–70 Plan was prepared as a comprehensive investment program, including both the public and the private sectors, its targets for the private sector were only indicative. Total planned investment a year was to average about 16 per cent of the expected GDP, compared with 17 per cent in 1963.

The plan aimed at achieving early increases in production. Overriding priority was given to rural development, and 46 per cent of the total investment was to be channeled into this sector. More generally, emphasis was placed on directly productive investments in agriculture, manufacturing, and tourism; these sectors were to absorb about 47 per

TABLE 14. DAHOMEY: DEVELOPMENT PLAN 1966-70—PLANNED AND ACTUAL PUBLIC SECTOR INVESTMENT, 1966-67

(Amount in billions of CFA francs)

	Total Planned Investment, 1966-70		1966		1967		1966-67		
							Planned investment	Actual investment [1]	
	Amount	Per cent	Planned investment	Actual [1] investment	Planned investment	Actual [1] investment		Amount	Per cent of planned
Rural development	11.8	46.1	1.8	1.2	2.0	1.1	3.8	2.3	60.5
Industry and commerce	2.8	10.9	0.7	0.1	1.2	0.4 [2]	1.9	0.5	26.3
Infrastructure	8.4	32.8	1.1	0.3	2.0	0.6	3.1	0.9	29.0
Social overhead and administration	2.6	10.2	0.3	0.5	0.5	0.5	0.8	1.0	125.0
Total investment	25.6	100.0	3.9	2.1	5.7	2.6	9.6	4.7	49.0

SOURCE: Data provided by the Dahomean authorities.

[1] Data cover only actual investment financed by external sources; this represents approximately 80 per cent of total investment. Total actual investments, therefore, were higher than the amounts shown.

[2] In addition, a kenaf factory, which was not included in the plan and which represents an investment of CFAF 2.5 billion, was established in 1967-68.

cent of the total investments. For social and administrative purposes, investments were restrained so as to minimize the growth in the Government's current expenditures.

The plan relied mainly on foreign resources for financing, but it assumed that public enterprises, special Treasury funds, and local authorities would generate savings of CFAF 4.7 billion, or about 19 per cent of planned public investments. It also assumed that the ordinary budget deficit, which was to decline sharply until its eradication in 1970, would be covered by foreign grants. To reach a balanced budget, the plan envisioned a reduction over the five years of CFAF 900 million in personnel outlays and an increase of CFAF 1.3 billion in budget receipts from more efficient tax collection and higher taxes. It estimated foreign financing from official sources at CFAF 4.1 billion a year; this estimate is in line with the amount of foreign funds committed in the recent past. Private sector investment was estimated at an annual average of CFAF 2.0 billion, and over 63 per cent of the resources for such investment was expected to originate from domestic sources. The execution of the over-all investment program was divided into annual tranches. Public and private investment was planned to increase from CFAF 5.3 billion in 1966 to a peak of CFAF 8.8 billion in 1968 and to decline to CFAF 5.9 billion in the final year of the plan.

Data on the implementation of the Five-Year Development Plan during 1966 and 1967 have not yet been completed, and for 1968 even provisional figures are not yet available. Nevertheless, the indications from partial data are that, although there was a considerable gap between plan targets and actual performance, tangible progress was made, particularly in agriculture.

In 1966, agricultural production fell slightly short of plan targets; the over-all rate of achievement in agriculture was estimated at about 92 per cent, with highest results in some cash crops (cotton and groundnuts). In 1967, agricultural production targets were exceeded in cotton, groundnuts, sheanuts, kapok, and foodstuffs. Production of seed (unginned) cotton exceeded plan targets by 4,500 tons; the plan target for cotton production by 1970 was raised from 14,000 tons to 18,000 tons, but even this new figure probably was exceeded in 1969. In other sectors, notably fishing and manufacturing, production lagged substantially behind plan objectives in the first two years of the plan.

During 1966–67, actual public sector investment financed by external sources was estimated at CFAF 4.7 billion, or 49 per cent of planned public investment (see Table 14); however, some additional investment, probably not over CFAF 1.0 billion, was financed from domestic sources. The shortfall in investment was particularly pronounced in manufacturing, where the rate of realization was 26.3 per cent, and in infrastructure, where it was 29 per cent. None of the major industrial projects included in the plan (a cement factory, textile mills, a brick-yard, and a groundnut oil factory) were established during this period; on the other hand, a cotton ginning mill at Parakou that was to be started in 1969 was, in fact, built in 1966, owing to the rapid progress in cotton production. A kenaf factory, representing an investment of CFAF 2.5 billion, which was not included in the plan, was started in 1967 and completed in 1968. Actual infrastructure investments in transportation, mainly repairs and extension of the road network, were estimated at about 29 per cent of plan estimates. Actual public investment in rural development, including agriculture, amounted to 60.5 per cent of planned estimates; the rate of implementation was highest in agriculture, particularly for export commodities such as cotton and palm products. For social overhead and administration, the rate of realization was 125 per cent, mainly because of higher investments in education than planned.

It was in the financial objectives that performance lagged farthest behind plan targets, owing partly to a shortfall in foreign financing. The plan also assumed that the domestic savings ratio would double between 1965 and 1970 as a result of a lower annual growth rate in consumption, particularly public consumption, than in GDP. Available data indicate that domestic savings declined between 1965 and 1967 but rose again in 1968, when they amounted to over 4 per cent of GDP, compared with an average of 8.6 per cent envisaged in the plan. Moreover, the current budget deficit, though narrowed, remained substantial; in this respect, financial performance apparently fell short of the plan objective, which assumed a balanced budget by 1970. The plan also estimated that, owing to a substantial reduction in the trade deficit to be brought about, in part, by a decline in imports consequent to the Government's austerity program, the resource gap would narrow from 10.6 per cent of GDP in 1965 to 3.6 per cent of GDP in 1970. Available data indicate that although the resource gap declined from 14.5 per cent of GDP in 1965 to 12.9 per cent in 1966, it rose to 17.5 per cent in 1967.

The Government is seeking additional technical assistance from abroad in project preparation and appraisal, and has indicated its intention of strengthening the authority of the planning agency to help ensure that projects are soundly investigated before being taken up in the public sector.

INVESTMENT CODE

No data are available on the execution of the 1966–70 Development Plan in the private sector. To encourage new private investment, domestic and foreign, an Investment Code was enacted on December 31, 1961. The Code guarantees equitable compensation to all private enterprises in case of expropriation, nondiscriminatory treatment between foreign and Dahomean investors, repatriation of business profits and capital, and tax exemption on reinvested profits until 1975. In addition, the Code provides for three different types of preferential treatment classified in categories A, B, and C. Preferential treatments under categories A and B are granted to small ventures; category C is awarded to enterprises of particular importance to the Dahomean economy. Table 15 gives pertinent data on enterprises granted priority status during 1967–68.

Concessions under category A, granted for a period of 5 years, include (1) exemption of import taxes on imported equipment, machinery, and raw materials; (2) reduction in export taxes; and (3) exemption from the internal consumption tax. In addition to benefits under category A, preferential treatment under category B includes (1) exemption from the tax on industrial and commercial profits for a period of 5 years and (2) exemption from the license fees and the mining and real property royalty. Advantages under category C are specified in a separate agreement between the Government and the benefiting enterprise (*convention d'établissement*); they include, in addition to concessions under categories A and B, assurance of an unchanged tax burden for periods ranging from 5 to 15 years.

In order to obtain the concessions under the Investment Code, enterprises must be approved by a special interdepartmental committee chaired

TABLE 15. DAHOMEY: PRIORITY ENTERPRISES UNDER THE INVESTMENT CODE, 1967/68

	Planned Investment	Capacity	Number of Employees	Duration of Concessions
	Million CFA francs	*Metric tons, except as noted*		*Years*
Fabric printing factory	500	600	124	15
Cement factory	270	100,000	35	15
Kenaf factory [1]	2,500	16,000 / 5,000 [2]	1,177	15
Fishing	370	4,000	58	5
Shrimp freezing	113	600	101	5
Paint manufacturing	40	600	30	5
Shoe factory	51	600,000 [3]	25	5
Plastics factory	98	250,000	22	5
Stationery	48	. . .	49	3
Cycle assembly plant	95	8,800 [4]	44	5
Tire recapping factory	36	3,000 [5]	17	4
Noodles factory	12	200	20	2½
Laundry	13	. . .	20	3

Source: Data provided by the Dahomean authorities.
[1] The kenaf factory operates much below capacity with about 40 employees.
[2] Bags, in addition to fiber.
[3] Pairs.
[4] Bicycles and motorcycles.
[5] Tires.

by the Ministry of Planning. A new Investment Code, more liberal than the present Code, is currently under preparation. It is expected that in the new Code, advantages granted under category C will be extended for a period of 25 years.

PRICES, WAGES, AND EMPLOYMENT

PRICES

Data on price developments in Dahomey are scanty. No official consumer or wholesale price indices are available. A retail price index in urban and rural areas was constructed by a foreign technical aid expert for 1957–65 but has not been continued. A consumer price index is currently under preparation with the assistance of the French Institut National de la Statistique et des Etudes Economiques. In this connection, the consumption pattern of an average African family was surveyed in 1968, and it was expected that a consumer price index would be available about mid-1969.

At present the only available indication of general price movements is contained in surveys compiled by the Labor Bureau at irregular intervals. These surveys determine the level of yearly consumption expenditures of an unmarried African worker living in Cotonou and are used as a basis for the calculation of the legal minimum wage (*salaire minimum interprofessionnel garanti*, or SMIG). The last of such surveys by the Labor Bureau were made in December 1968 and the one previous to that in April 1966.

Price Developments During 1964–68

Between January 1964 and January 1966 the Labor Bureau surveys indicated a rise in the cost of living of about 18 per cent, reflecting increases in expenditures on food, clothing, furniture, amusement, and taxes (Table 16). In 1967, no survey was made, but as prices of most foodstuffs are reported to have remained generally stable, no substantial change in the cost of living is likely to have occurred. A survey made

TABLE 16.   DAHOMEY: CALCULATION OF THE COST OF LIVING FOR ESTABLISHING
THE MINIMUM WAGE RATE (SMIG),[1] 1964–68 [2]

(In thousands of CFA francs)

	1964 (January)	1965 (August)	1966 (January)	1968 (December)	Per Cent of Change, January 1964– December 1968
Food	45.39	35.76	36.27	43.94	−3.2
Fuel	3.95	5.92	4.13	4.10	3.9
Lighting	0.69	0.71	0.69	0.74	7.2
Clothing	6.00	11.69	12.08	6.00	—
Bedding	1.81	2.22	1.99	1.75	−3.4
Furniture	2.63	3.63	4.62	3.74	42.2
Upkeep	0.78	1.40	1.41	0.77	−1.3
Rent	18.00	30.00	30.00	18.00	—
Laundry	1.50	1.31	1.56	1.32	−12.0
Hygiene	3.51	4.20	4.49	4.37	24.5
Amusement	6.24	6.24	8.84	5.85	−0.6
Taxes	2.09	1.69	3.75	2.19	4.7
Total	92.59	104.77	109.83	92.77	0.2

Source: Data provided by the Dahomean authorities.

[1] *Salaire minimum interprofessionnel garanti.*

[2] Estimated expenditures of an unmarried African worker in Cotonou on items shown.

in December 1968 showed a decline in the cost of living of about 16 per cent from January 1966; the decline occurred mainly in expenditures on clothing, rent, and amusement, largely because of substantial decreases in prices of imported goods following the reduction in import taxes in early 1968. Food expenditures, however, increased in 1968, reflecting shortages in some locally produced staples, as a result of flood damage to food crops.

Price Controls

Since June 23, 1965 the Government has introduced price controls for certain products, mainly with a view to deterring dealers from undertaking speculative activities or overcharging. Price controls are exercised mainly through administrative directives. An ordinance issued on July 5, 1967, which constitutes the basic text of these regulations, provided for the establishment of a national price committee and regional price committees to advise the Government on price control measures. It also gave the Ministry of Finance, Economic Affairs, and Planning the authority to fix the prices of certain essential agricultural goods which are produced locally, to establish price ceilings, and to fix profit margins and *homologation de prix* (which involves the establishment of prices on the proposal of private dealers and with the concurrence of the Government) for certain other commodities. The Ministry is also empowered to control stocks at the wholesale level.

In 1969, sugar, soft drinks, and beer were subject to price ceilings; rice, wheat flour, potatoes, and shoes were subject to profit margins at the wholesale and retail levels; and prices of textiles, pharmaceutical products, and other essential imported consumer and intermediate foods were subject to *homologation de prix*.

In general, price controls are limited to the major urban centers, and the government bureau in charge of administering price controls is understaffed. Price controls in Dahomey do not appear to have been very effective in periods of commodity shortages.

WAGES

Minimum wages are established in Dahomey by joint commissions composed of representatives of labor, management, and the Government. They are determined on the basis of the aforementioned surveys compiled by the Labor Bureau. Two guaranteed minimum wages are enforced: SMIG (*salaire minimum interprofessionnel garanti*) for nonagricultural employment and SMAG (*salaire minimum agricole garanti*) for agricultural occupations; these vary according to three labor zones (the coastal urban centers, the central region, and the rest of the country). However, since the labor force in agriculture is predominantly composed of self-employed farmers, the SMIG rate is the most widely applied minimum wage. In the private sector, according to a survey made in 1965, the SMIG rate was paid to 2,243 workers out of a total of 7,020. Legal salary scales are established on the basis of SMIG, taking into account job qualifications. Social security benefits are granted to permanent employees in accordance with a new Labor Code promulgated in December 1967.

Although the cost of living seems to have risen in recent years, SMIG rates have remained unchanged since October 1966 at the level of CFAF 38.08 per hour in the coastal urban centers, CFAF 31.02 in the central region, and CFAF 26.65 in the rest of the country; corresponding SMAG rates are CFAF 32.92, CFAF 26.88, and CFAF 23.85. After discussion between the Government and representatives of the private sector, it was recently decided to grant an across-the-board increase of 4 per cent in minimum wages paid in the private sector. This increase, effective February 1, 1969, is not subject to the national solidarity tax levied on wages and salaries. The increase in minimum wages in the private sector did not alter the legal minimum wages; so far no change in the minimum wages in the public sector has been made.

The SMIG rate in Dahomey is among the highest in the BCEAO area, ranking third after SMIG rates in Senegal and Ivory Coast. According to a study made by the Ministry of Labor in 1967, total wages and salaries were estimated at about CFAF 8.0 billion, of which about CFAF 2.0 billion was paid in the private sector. In addition, family allowances in the private sector amounted to CFAF 319 million, and retirement allowances in the public and private sectors to CFAF 1.7 billion. According to the same study the average annual salary (including social benefits) in 1967 was estimated at CFAF 300,000 in the public sector, and at CFAF 220,000 in the private sector.

EMPLOYMENT

Urban unemployment remains a major problem of the Dahomean economy. Underemployment in agriculture also continues to be widespread. With the achievement of independence in 1960, large numbers of expatriate Dahomeans lost their jobs in neighboring countries and were repatriated. The Government absorbed a large proportion of the civil servants into the public sector; however, many repatriates remained unemployed, and efforts to induce them to enter agricultural occupations were not successful. Moreover, migration from rural to urban areas, particularly to Cotonou, adds further pressure on the labor market. Completion of the port of Cotonou in 1965 and the virtual freeze on new recruitment in the public sector which began in 1966 substantially reduced employment opportunities. One of the major labor-intensive sectors, building and public works, experienced a slowdown in 1966-67. During this period, the number of urban unemployed rose by 2,500 a year, and in 1967 it was estimated at 10,000. Although statistics of unemployment are not available beyond 1967, the creation of a few industries and the recovery in economic activity are reported to have alleviated somewhat the unemployment pressure in 1968. The outlook for 1969 was for further improvement, mainly because of expected increases in public sector investments (e.g., construction of the fishing port, road maintenance, construction of a cement factory and a textile mill, and acceleration of investments in the cultivation of palms and cotton).

In 1967 the number of wage earners was estimated at 28,455 (Table 17), compared with 30,138 in 1965. About 67 per cent of total wage earners in 1967 were employed in the public sector, mostly in the Central Government. Tertiary activities, manufacturing and construction, accounted for most of the salaried employment in the private sector.

Employed wage earners are organized into four labor unions, which, since 1965, have been relatively active and have opposed government economy measures, in particular, the national solidarity tax on wages and salaries. Although this tax was recently reduced, the labor unions have continued to demand its elimination.

TABLE 17. DAHOMEY: NUMBER OF WAGE EARNERS BY CATEGORY
OF ACTIVITY, END OF 1967 [1]

Private sector	
Agriculture and fishing	150
Mining	50
Manufacturing	1,950
Building and public works	1,100
Power	150
Commerce, insurance, and banking	2,500
Transport and communications	3,250
Miscellaneous	225
Total private sector	9,375
Public sector	19,080
Central Government	*13,930*
Total wage earners	28,455

Source: Data provided by the Dahomean authorities.

[1] Comparable data by category of wage earners are not available for previous years.

GOVERNMENT FINANCE

STRUCTURE OF THE PUBLIC SECTOR

The public sector in Dahomey comprises the Central Government, the post and telecommunications office, six provinces (*départements*)— Ouémé (Southeast), Alantique (South), Mono (Southwest), Zou (Central), Dorgou (Northeast), and Atakora (Northwest); six municipalities (Porto-Novo, Cotonou, Ouidah, Abomey, Parakou, and Djougou); and several autonomous and semipublic agencies. The leading autonomous and semipublic agencies are the Port Authority of Cotonou, the Dahomey-Niger Railway and Transport System, the National Oil Mills Company (SNAHDA), Agricultural Marketing Office (OCAD), and National Rural Development Agency (SONADER). Most of these agencies have financial autonomy and derive their revenues from fiscal or parafiscal levies, government subsidies, and commercial activities. They are expected to meet their expenditures out of their own revenues or borrowings. In addition, a number of special funds outside the central budget are financed mainly by earmarked revenues and special levies, e.g., Stabilization Fund for Agricultural Exports (Fonds de Soutien des Prix des Produits à l'Exportation), the Social Security Fund (Fonds National des Retraites du Dahomey), and the Amortization Fund (Caisse Autonome d'Amortissement). Most of the autonomous and semipublic agencies, as well as the special funds, deposit their cash balances with the Treasury.

The principles governing the budget operations of the Central Government are set out each year in a Finance Law, which is usually enacted on the last day of the calendar year on the proposal of the Council of Ministers and which is normally published within one month after enactment.

The Central Government has an ordinary budget which covers mainly the current transactions of the Central Government. Although most current transactions of the Central Government are recorded in the ordinary budget, a smaller but not unimportant part of current revenue and expenditure is kept outside the ordinary budget and handled through annexed budgets and special accounts in the Treasury.

Before 1966, investment ᴐf the Central Government was channeled through special funds kept with the Treasury, e.g., Road Fund (Fonds Routier), National Investment Fund (Fonds National d'Investissement), and the Regional Investment Fund (Fonds d'Aménagement Régional). In 1966, however, the Government established an investment budget, and most of the special funds for investment purposes were integrated in the investment budget. The remaining investment funds which were not integrated in the investment budget and which in general were of limited importance were to be gradually phased out.

Formulation of an investment budget was discontinued after 1966, and investment expenditures of the Central Government have since been channeled through a Special Reserve Fund (Fonds Spécial de Réserve) and a Special Investment Fund (Fonds Spécial d'Equipement et d'Investissement), both kept with BCEAO. However, the major part of public sector investment and technical programs, which for the most part are financed directly by external sources and are the responsibility of various autonomous enterprises, are not reflected in the budget and Treasury accounts.

The regional and municipal authorities have separate budgets of their own. These authorities derive their revenues entirely from certain local resources (e.g., local taxes, receipts from public property, and payments for services rendered). Assessment and collection of some of the local taxes are handled by the Central Government. At the beginning of the fiscal year, the regional and municipal authorities prepare an ordinary

budget which sets out their annual receipts and expenditures. In addition, each authority prepares a supplementary budget that indicates
both the outstanding amount of revenue arrears relating to the previous
fiscal year and the outstanding amount of authorized spending for
which no actual payments were made during the previous fiscal year. In
1966 the actual receipts of the regional and municipal authorities
amounted to 16.2 per cent of the actual revenues of the Central Government and their actual expenditures to 13.7 per cent of the actual
expenditures of the Central Government.

BUDGET CONTROL

The system of public accounting used since 1963 is the extended
cash period system (*règle de la gestion prolongée*). Under this system,
revenues are recorded in the fiscal year (calendar year) in which they
are actually received. To bring expenditures closer to a cash basis, the
Government must issue purchase orders for materials and supplies
before December 15; also, outstanding commitments for which payment
vouchers have been issued before the end of the fiscal year are paid out
up to the end of January of the following year and are written back
into the accounts of the year of authorization.

Specific regulations are laid down for committing different categories
of expenditures, and the expenditure control procedure is performed at
different levels of the Government. The authority of the disbursement
officer in the various government departments is limited to initiating
commitments for expenditures on materials and supplies, which amount
to about 13 per cent of total government expenditures. A central personnel office deals with personnel expenditures such as those for salaries and allowances; and the Budget Bureau deals with all other payments (e.g., for public debt, transfers, and subscriptions to international
bodies). However, for all categories of expenditures, other than those
mentioned, cash disbursements made by the Treasury are preceded by
three consecutive expenditure control operations: (1) The requisition
for funds or commitments (*engagement de dépense*) is initiated by
each government department within the limits of its budgetary appropriations. (2) Verification or pre-audit (*liquidation*), the inquiry into
the existence and accuracy of the expenditure commitment, is done successively by the Bureau of the Budget and the Director of Accounts

(Directeur de la Comptabilité) and is certified by the Controller of Finance (Contrôleur des Finances). The Controller of Finance charges the amount of the expenditure commitment to the proper budgetary account and certifies that the nature of the expenditure and the amount requested is within the limits of the budgetary appropriation and the balance of the funds available. The original requisition is returned to the government department that drew up the requisition for funds; the department then prepares a purchase order (*bon de commande*).[2] (3) Provisional disbursement is performed in the government department where the expenditure commitment was initiated and involves the issuance of a "draft pay order" or "disbursement order" (*projet de mandat*), which repeats most of the information previously submitted with the original requisition for funds. To this pay order are attached the bills for the merchandise received, as well as either the advice of payment or the cash warrant according to the way the final disbursement will be made. The pay order is checked by the Controller of Finance; it is then rechecked by the Director of Accounts in his capacity of Paymaster, after he issues a payment voucher (*mandat*) and submits it to the Treasury for final disbursement (*paiement*). The Treasury has the responsibility of ensuring that the successive steps in the expenditure control procedure have been properly performed.

The Dahomean Treasury records only those expenditures for which payment vouchers (*mandats*) have been issued. These are shown in Table 18. Until 1967, additional expenditure obligations and commitments undertaken by government departments (for which payment vouchers had not been issued by the Treasury) constituted the Government's payment arrears and were not recorded by the Treasury as part of budgetary expenditures. Such expenditure obligations (*dépenses non-mandatées*) arose either because the amounts were not appropriated in the budget or because the expenditure control process was not completed for them. The amount of expenditure obligations for which payment vouchers had not been issued and for which therefore no payments had been made was relatively large during 1966–67 but declined significantly in 1968.

---

[2] It should be noted that there is no centralized purchasing in Dahomey and that even for overseas purchases each government department directly makes the purchases.

TABLE 18. DAHOMEY: ORDINARY BUDGET, 1966–69

(In millions of CFA francs)

	1966 Budget estimates	1966 Actual	1967 Budget estimates	1967 Actual [1]	1968 Budget estimates	1968 Actual	1969 Budget Estimates
Revenue [2]							
Tax revenue							
Direct taxes							
Income taxes	901	501	1,333	669	1,682	…	…
Other direct taxes	57	48	316	221	229	…	…
Total direct taxes	958	549	1,649	890	1,911	2,423	1,900
Indirect taxes							
Import taxes	3,180	2,822	2,986	3,077	3,175	…	…
Export taxes	148	63	189	131	210	…	…
Internal excise taxes	958	738	765	703	741	…	…
Other indirect duties and fees	147	124	10	10	9	…	…
Total indirect taxes	4,433	3,747	3,950	3,921	4,135	2,820	4,193
Registration and stamp duties	94	105	95	90	97	157	328
Other ordinary revenue							
Public property	70	67	66	66	57	…	…
Administrative receipts	455	330	284	318	282	…	…
Transfers from local budgets and public institutions	280	167	247	120	141	…	…
Total other ordinary revenue	805	564	597	504	480	165	148
Unclassified revenue [3]	624	566	567	676	538	786	745
Total revenue	6,915	5,531	6,858	6,083	7,161	6,351	7,314

Expenditure [4]							
Personnel	4,631	4,047	4,638	4,188	5,513	5,038	5,649
Material	1,374	1,448	1,405	2,467	1,359	1,562	1,328
Public debt	154	151	136	92	138	112	170
Other [5]	2,024	1,638	1,383	137	1,226	964	1,576
Total expenditure	8,183	7,284	7,562	6,884	8,236	7,676	8,723
Budget deficit	1,268	1,753	704	801	1,075	1,325	1,409

Source: Information supplied by the Dahomean authorities.

[1] Owing to problems with the automatic data processing program which was installed at the beginning of 1967, detailed actual figures of 1967 have not been compiled. However, in July 1968, the authorities reviewed the available data and prepared revised estimates of total receipts and expenditures which have since been considered as the final accounts for that fiscal year. The detailed breakdown of revenues and expenditures are estimates.

[2] Excluding foreign budgetary aid.

[3] Covers revenues relating to previous fiscal year.

[4] Represents only Treasury expenditures. Does not include expenditure obligations incurred but not authorized by the Treasury.

[5] Including maintenance, transfers, and unclassified expenditure.

Since Dahomey has no separate Court of Account, an audit section of the Supreme Court was created to handle the task of post audit. However, it has not been active in recent years.

TREASURY OPERATIONS

Management of the cash resources of the public sector is centralized in the Treasury, enabling the Treasury to act as both cashier and banker for the public sector. It also functions as an important instrument of financial control. The Treasury carries out not only regular budget operations but also extrabudgetary operations involving mainly the operation of special accounts outside the ordinary budget and financing operations. These special accounts cover a wide range of transactions and are distinguished by the fact that their revenues are earmarked for particular expenditures. Generally speaking, the extrabudgetary operations carried out by the Treasury are subject to the same rules that govern the operations of the ordinary budget.

To finance government operations, the Treasury may have to use its deposit resources (mainly administrative deposits and deposits with the Postal Checking System) or advances from the Central Bank.

Until December 10, 1968, BCEAO provided direct financing to the Treasury through two means: (1) Advances for ways-and-means purposes may be made up to an amount of 10 per cent of the previous year's actual budgetary revenue (including the earmarked revenues of the Amortization Fund and the Stabilization Fund for Agricultural Exports). BCEAO advances mature in 240 days, but the period can be extended up to the first working day of the following fiscal year upon justification being provided. This limit on BCEAO advances to the Treasury was raised from 10 per cent to 15 per cent of actual fiscal receipts of the previous year with effect from December 10, 1968, but the utilization of the additional 5 per cent requires specific justification. In June 1969, BCEAO agreed to the utilization of the additional 5 per cent by Dahomey. (2) The discount may be made of 90-day customs bills representing claims of the Treasury on importers.

REVENUE STRUCTURE

The Dahomean revenue structure is characterized by heavy reliance on customs duties and other indirect taxes. In 1967, total government revenue amounted to 12 per cent and tax revenues to about 11 per cent of GDP. Customs duties and other indirect taxes accounted for nearly 65 per cent of total ordinary budget revenue in 1967; direct taxes for less than 15 per cent; registration and stamp duties for 1 per cent; revenue from public property, administrative receipts, and transfers from local budgets and public institutions, for 8 per cent; and unclassified revenue for the remaining 11 per cent (see Table 18).

Indirect Taxes

Customs duties and other import taxes.—Taxation of imports is the mainstay of the revenue structure in Dahomey and amounted in 1967 to about 51 per cent of total ordinary budget revenue. The importance of the foreign trade sector, which accounted for about 30 per cent of the GDP in 1967, explains, in part, the large share of import taxation in Dahomey's total revenue.

Control and prevention of smuggling is an important consideration in the administration of customs duties in Dahomey. In the past, smuggling has occurred mainly because of the differential between the structure of customs duties in Dahomey and that in Togo, which does not belong to the West African Customs Union (Union Douanière des Etats de l'Afrique de l'Ouest, or UDEAO). Formerly, the import tariff of Dahomey significantly exceeded that of Togo, providing an incentive to smuggle certain items from Togo into Dahomey. In early 1968, the Dahomean Government substantially reduced its import tariffs in line with Togolese tariffs and, for some commodities, even below the level in Togo. Some increase in smuggling from Nigeria in recent years has also been reported.

The prevailing classification of the customs tariff is in accordance with the Brussels tariff nomenclature. For the purpose of levying the duties, the c.i.f. concept is considered as the basis of value. The tariff rate structure differentiates among (1) essential foods, raw materials, and capital goods—all generally exempt from duty; (2) commodities regarded as nonessential and subject to varying rates according to the degree of nonessentiality; and (3) certain commodities subject to higher duties for protective purposes. The combined revenues from duties on all imports (including duty-free goods) averaged 28.6 per cent of their c.i.f. value for the fiscal year 1967.

On January 1, 1967 the authorities consolidated a wide variety of taxes and duties on imports and exports with a view to simplifying the tax system for imports and exports. As a result of this reform, the fiscal fee, the turnover tax, the statistical tax, the fiscal tax, and the "condition" tax were eliminated and consolidated into fiscal duties.[3] Currently imports are subject to (1) customs duties, (2) fiscal taxes, and (3) certain other minor taxes.

(1) Customs duties are applied ad valorem on all imports originating from countries outside UDEAO, as well as EEC and associated countries. Imports from countries to which Dahomey accords the most-favored-nation treatment are subject to the minimum ad valorem rates of customs duties. Imports from all other countries are subject to the general rates of customs duties, which are three times the minimum rate. However, Dahomey has drawn up on a unilateral basis a list of products which receive the benefit of the minimum customs tariff even though most-favored-nation treatment is not granted to the country of origin of such imports.

(2) Fiscal taxes are applicable irrespective of the country of origin of imports except that imports from UDEAO member countries are subject to a preferential tariff which is 50 per cent of the fiscal tax normally applied. It should also be noted that Dahomey has entered into a bilateral convention with certain other UDEAO member countries to exempt specific products from the application of the fiscal tax (e.g., the convention between Dahomey and Niger).

(3) Other import taxes include a customs stamp duty of 4 per cent levied on the total amount of fiscal taxes and customs duties assessed; a specific tax (*taxe spécifique au profit du fonds de soutien des produits à l'exportation*) levied for the purpose of the Stabilization Fund for Agricultural Products; and a special tax (*taxe spéciale d'amortissement*), which is levied on the import value and is earmarked for the Amortization Fund. The special tax is a tax on both imports and internal consumption; at the import stage, it is 5 per cent of the c.i.f. value. It

---

[3] The various duties on imports and exports that have been consolidated were the *droit fiscal d'entrée,* the *taxe de statistique,* the *taxe forfaitaire à l'importation,* the *taxe fiscale,* the *taxe forfaitaire représentative de la taxe sur les transactions à l'exportation,* and the *taxe de conditionnement.*

should be noted further that the turnover tax (discussed below) as well as tax on petroleum products, is also applicable to foreign purchases at the import stage.

Export duties.—Taxes are levied on certain exports for fiscal reasons. Since January 1, 1967 the various export duties have been consolidated into a single levy covering the previous fiscal duty, export turnover tax, statistical tax, fiscal tax, and "condition" tax. In addition, exports are also subject to a customs duty stamp of 4 per cent assessed on the amount of payable customs duties and taxes as well as to a specific tax for the purpose of the Stabilization Fund for Agricultural Products.

Taxes and levies on internal transactions.—Dahomey has different taxes and levies on internal transactions, which in 1967 amounted to 13.2 per cent of total ordinary budget revenues. They include stamp and registration taxes, the tax on petroleum products, the excise tax, and turnover tax, which is collected at the manufacturers' level for domestic production and at the import level for imports.

The tax on petroleum products (*taxe sur les hydrocarbures*) is levied as a specific tax at the manufacturers' level. The tax is calculated on gross sales, but particular categories of taxpayers are assessed on a fixed turnover basis (*régime du forfait*). The rates amount to CFAF 7.58 per liter for gasoline, CFAF 7.77 per liter for petroleum, CFAF 3.43 per liter for gas oil, and CFAF 15 per kilogram for automobile oil.

The internal excise tax (*taxe intérieure sur les boissons alcooliques, boissons gazeuses ou fermentées*) is a specific tax, ranging from CFAF 7 to CFAF 19 per liter, assessed on soft drinks and alcoholic beverages at the manufacturers' level.

The internal turnover tax (*impôt sur le chiffre d'affaires intérieur*) is imposed on gross sales of goods by agricultural processors and manufacturers and on a restricted list of services. The tax is levied at a basic rate of 8.4 per cent (tax excluded) or 9.17 per cent (tax included).

Direct Taxes

Direct taxes in the central government budget consist mainly of various taxes on income. The most important of these is a schedular income tax system applying different rates to different sources of income. Revenue from direct taxes amounted to 15 per cent of total ordinary budget revenue in 1967.

For wage and salary earners, a tax on wages and salaries (*impôt sur les traitements et salaires*) is assessed at a progressive scale, ranging from 1 to 6 per cent, depending on the taxpayer's salary. Annual wages and salaries up to CFAF 120,000 are exempt from the tax. In addition, a national solidarity tax (*impôt de solidarité nationale*) is assessed on the same source of income at a flat rate of 20 per cent for incomes of more than CFAF 22,350 a month; for incomes below that, progressive rates, ranging from 4 to 17 per cent, are applicable.

Net profits of individual taxpayers and corporations engaged in trade, industry, handicrafts, agriculture, and mining are subject to a tax (*impôt sur les bénéfices industriels, commerciaux, artisanaux et agricoles*). The tax is a flat rate of 35 per cent for corporations and all businesses with an annual turnover of more than CFAF 20 million. For profits of non-incorporated enterprises and individuals with an estimated annual turnover of less than CFAF 20 million, the tax is 6 per cent on estimated taxable profits below CFAF 100,000, 12 per cent for profits of CFAF 100,000–300,000, and 25 per cent for profits exceeding CFAF 300,000 a year. For all taxpayers there is a minimum tax liability of either 0.5 per cent, or 1 per cent of the business turnover on gross receipts, according to the nature of their activities; for corporations the minimum tax liability is CFAF 200,000. On all profits, tax exemptions are granted on the grounds of specified reinvestment.

The net profits of liberal professions are subject to the same tax rate as business profits except that their minimum tax liability amounts to 4 per cent of gross annual receipts.

Corporate dividends and interest are subject to a tax on unearned income (*impôt sur le revenu des valeurs mobilières*) assessed at rates ranging from 8 to 25 per cent.

In addition to the above-mentioned schedular taxes, a general income tax (*impôt général sur le revenu*) is assessed on all sources of income in excess of CFAF 80,000 received by individuals. The tax has two tiers, first a proportional tax of 1 to 2.5 per cent on taxable income and, second, a progressive tax rate schedule of 6 to 60 per cent for family incomes, with a maximum deduction for dependents of 40 per cent of the taxable income and, for single persons with no dependents, tax rates ranging from 7.8 to 78 per cent.

There is also a number of small direct taxes such as a property tax payable by religious missions (*taxe des licences de main morte*), a tax on firearms (*taxe sur les armes à feu*), and a tax on apprenticeship (*taxe d'apprentissage*).

BUDGETS AND DEFICIT FINANCING, 1966–69

Recent budgets have been characterized by a large excess of ordinary expenditures over revenues and overestimation of both revenues and recorded expenditures in the ordinary budget (Table 19). In each fiscal year during 1966–68, actual revenues were below budget estimates. Although actual expenditures recorded by the Treasury were also below budget estimates in each fiscal year, they do not take account of payment arrears incurred by government departments for which Treasury authorization was not provided. Such payment arrears (see "Budget control," above, and "Payment arrears," below) were relatively high in 1966 and 1967, but declined in 1968.

Deficits during 1966–68 were financed mainly by foreign budgetary aid, BCEAO advances, deferment of payments to the private sector, and other Treasury operations (see Table 19).

Fiscal Year 1967

In the 1967 budget, ordinary revenue was estimated at CFAF 6.9 billion and expenditure at CFAF 7.6 billion, leaving an estimated deficit of CFAF 0.7 billion (see Table 18). In preparing the budget, expenditure requests of the various government departments were carefully scrutinized. Total ordinary expenditure was budgeted somewhat above its actual level in 1966 because of an increase in the outlays for personnel. However, outlays for maintenance, transfers, and unclassified expenditure were budgeted somewhat below their actual 1966 level. Ordinary revenue was expected to exceed considerably its actual level in 1966, mainly because of an anticipated substantial increase in the revenue from the national solidarity tax. No significant new tax measures were proposed in the 1967 budget.

TABLE 19. DAHOMEY: BUDGET DEFICIT AND FINANCING, 1966–68

(*In millions of CFA francs*)

	1966	1967	1968
Ordinary budget expenditure	−7,284	−6,884	−7,676
Investment budget expenditure [1]	−357	—	—
Total budget expenditure [2]	−7,641	−6,884	−7,676
Ordinary budget revenue	5,531	6,083	6,351
Investment budget revenue [1]	79	...	...
Deficit	−2,031	−801	−1,325
Net unclassified revenues [3]	266	—	—
Extrabudgetary operations	422	−296	−136
Over-all Treasury deficit [2]	−1,343	−1,097	−1,461
Financing			
Foreign: French budgetary aid	850	500	555
Domestic			
Central Bank (BCEAO) advances	505	−5	
Portfolio of customs duty bills	−82	125	
Deferment of payments to private sector	202	102	
Foreign aid projects account	−27	48	
Other	97	19	906
Current account with French Treasury	−24	184	
Miscellaneous, including changes in cash balances and errors and omissions [4]	−178	124	

Source: Data provided by the Dahomean authorities.

[1] An investment budget was introduced in 1966. It was not continued in subsequent years.

[2] Does not take account of expenditure obligations incurred but not authorized by the Treasury.

[3] With the establishment of automatic data processing in 1967, this item was eliminated because of a reorganization of accounts.

[4] Miscellaneous is a balancing item and includes mainly variations in postal checking deposits and Treasury cash balances (including the current account with domestic branch offices).

At the beginning of the fiscal year an automatic data processing program was installed to process public accounts. Since then the Dahomean authorities have experienced considerable difficulties and delays in the processing of the budgetary data. Thus, for example, detailed figures of the actual budgetary outcome for 1967 could not be compiled. In July 1968, the Dahomean authorities reviewed the available data and issued estimates of the main aggregates of receipts and expenditures; these figures have since been considered as the final accounts for that fiscal year.

Actual revenue in 1967 (CFAF 6.1 billion) remained considerably below budget estimates though 10 per cent higher than in 1966.

Despite the fact that actual receipts from the national solidarity tax, the tax on business profits, and the general income tax were considerably below the budget estimates (because of difficulties in tax enforcement and collection), the share of direct taxes in total ordinary budget revenue in 1967 rose to CFAF 0.9 billion, or 15 per cent (compared with CFAF 0.5 billion, or 10 per cent, in 1966). Indirect taxes accounted for about 65 per cent of total ordinary budget revenue, or CFAF 3.9 billion in 1967 (compared with 68 per cent, or CFAF 3.7 billion in the previous year). "Other ordinary revenue" (see Table 18) was 12 per cent below the previous year, while "unclassified revenue" was slightly above the 1966 level.

Actual expenditure in the ordinary budget in 1967 was also substantially below budget estimates, decreasing by 6 per cent from actual expenditures of the previous year. Outlays for personnel rose to CFAF 4.2 billion, or 61 per cent of total ordinary expenditure (compared with CFAF 4.0 billion, or 56 per cent, in 1966). There was almost no new recruitment initially in the lower grades; however, the growing population and school attendance required larger outlays for public health and education, as well as the recruitment of some new personnel. Outlays for materials were considerably above budget estimates and rose to CFAF 2.5 billion, or 70 per cent above the actual 1966 level. Outlays for maintenance, transfers, and unclassified expenditure were substantially below budget estimates and amounted to only CFAF 0.1 billion, or 2 per cent of total expenditures (compared with CFAF 1.6 billion, or 22 per cent of total expenditures in 1966). Public debt expenditure was also below budget estimates.

The over-all deficit for the fiscal year amounted to CFAF 1.1 billion (see Table 19) without taking into account the increase in expenditure obligations, estimated at approximately CFAF 1,490 million, which were not authorized for payment by the Treasury (*dépenses non-mandatées*). The deficit was financed mainly by foreign budgetary aid to the extent of CFAF 0.5 billion, deferment of payments on payment vouchers authorized by the Treasury of CFAF 0.1 billion, reduction in the portfolio of customs duty bills by CFAF 0.1 billion, foreign aid funds of less than CFAF 0.1 billion temporarily deposited with the Treasury in anticipation of the execution of the projects concerned, and the current account with the French Treasury of nearly CFAF 0.2 billion. Since BCEAO advances in 1966 had not been repaid upon maturity before the close of that calendar year, the Treasury could not use this method of financing during the fiscal year 1967.

Fiscal Year 1968

The 1968 ordinary budget estimated revenue at CFAF 7.2 billion— nearly 18 per cent higher than actual collections in 1967—and ordinary expenditure at CFAF 8.2 billion—20 per cent higher than actual expenditure in 1967—leaving an ordinary budget deficit of nearly CFAF 1.1 billion (see Table 18). Tax measures enacted in 1968 included a substantial reduction in customs duties with a view to bringing Dahomey's tariff rate structure in line with neighboring Togo's. The Government also considered certain measures to improve the process of tax enforcement and collection, mainly for direct taxes. In July 1968 it created the National Center for Tax Collection (Centre National de Recouvrement) and centralized responsibility for tax collections in this agency.

The 1968 budget estimate for direct taxes was CFAF 1.9 billion, compared with actual collection of only CFAF 0.9 billion in 1967. In part the higher tax figure was the result merely of an accounting adjustment; it included the estimated revenue from the national solidarity tax assessed on wage and salary earners in the public sector, which, beginning in 1968, was shown as a revenue item in the budget; previously the receipts of the tax had been treated as a deduction from expenditures. In part, however, it reflected the expectation of greater revenue from improved tax enforcement and collection. Indirect taxes accounted for CFAF 4.1 billion, or 58 per cent of all estimated revenue in the ordinary budget, some 5 per cent higher than the 1967 actual collections. Import taxes alone accounted for CFAF 3.2 billion, or 44 per cent of total revenues.

Outlays for personnel were estimated at CFAF 5.5 billion, or 67 per cent of total ordinary expenditure, compared with 1967 actual expenditures of CFAF 4.2 billion. Outlays for maintenance, transfers, and unclassified expenditure were increased from the extremely low level of the previous year and accounted for CFAF 1.2 billion, or 15 per cent of total estimated ordinary expenditure. Estimated outlays for materials accounted for CFAF 1.4 billion, considerably below the 1967 actual expenditures.

Recently available figures on actual revenues and expenditures show an over-all deficit of CFAF 1.3 billion in 1968. Receipts amounted to CFAF 6.4 billion (excluding foreign budgetary aid of CFAF 555 million) and were about 6 per cent higher than 1967 actual receipts. Expenditures amounted to CFAF 7.7 billion and were about 12 per cent above actual expenditures in the previous year. The resulting deficit was financed mainly by French budgetary assistance.

The deficit is as recorded by the Treasury. In addition, the amount of expenditure obligations for which payments were not authorized by the Treasury increased by CFAF 0.3 billion, compared with CFAF 1.4 billion in 1966 and CFAF 1.5 billion in 1967. If this increase in expenditure obligations were to be included, the over-all deficit in 1968 would be about CFAF 1.6 billion.

In 1969 the Dahomean Government was considering a broad administrative reform aimed at reducing government overstaffing and strengthening the general government structure. Proposals included transfer of particular government activities to self-supporting autonomous public agencies; shift of surplus government employees from the central government administration to areas where they can be more productively employed; early retirement of government employees in the lower grades; and modification of the existing pension rights for all government employees.

The 1969 Budget

The authorities have stated that the main objective of the 1969 budget is to initiate a process of corrective action in public finance, in line with the Government's policy of achieving a balanced budget by 1971. For the 1969 budget, the authorities have estimated revenues at CFAF 7.5 billion (not taking into account any possible foreign budgetary aid), an increase of about 1 per cent over the revenue estimates of the previous budget but 14 per cent over the projected actual revenues for 1968 (see Table 18). Expenditures have been estimated at CFAF 8.7 billion, or 6 per cent higher than the 1968 budget estimates but 13 per cent higher than the actual expenditures, including payment arrears, for 1968.

The Dahomean authorities have proposed a number of tax measures under the 1969 budget to improve the budget situation. These measures include the introduction of a tax on property income, a port and harbor tax, a surtax on motor vehicles, and a tax on interest from bank accounts. Furthermore, there has also been a selective adjustment of the customs duties to increase certain rates which in 1968 had been brought below the level prevailing in neighboring countries. Offsetting these tax increases, the tax on reserve funds of corporations was abolished,[4] and the rate of the national solidarity tax on wages and salaries was reduced from 25 per cent to 20 per cent. It was estimated that the over-all effect of these tax changes would increase revenue by a net CFAF 0.3 billion and that a further increase of CFAF 0.7 billion would accrue from improved tax collection and enforcement. Special measures to this end were planned including, among other things, the establishment of a bonus system for the tax officials as an incentive in tax collection, and an organized administrative effort under the direction of the National Center for Tax Collection. The Government intends also to launch a campaign to get the support of the business community and the general public for these efforts.

In the 1969 budget, the great bulk of expenditures continued to be allocated to education, public health, and defense—together accounting for about 47 per cent of total ordinary expenditures. Expenditures on material and supplies for administrative purposes were reduced virtually across the board by 30 per cent and represented only about 13 per cent of total expenditures, against 24 per cent in 1968. It has been indicated in the budget, however, that if revenues should exceed the budget estimates and further need should arise for expenditures on account of material and supplies, additional expenditures would be authorized. Estimates for personnel expenditures were only 2 per cent higher than the 1968 budget estimates, mainly reflecting new recruitment in public health and education, offset partly by the reduction of personnel in the Department of Defense. The total number of government employees in the 1969 budget was estimated at 14,411, compared with 13,927 in 1968.

For the fiscal year 1969 the ordinary budget deficit was estimated at

---

[4] The tax on reserve funds was assessed on the retained profits of corporations. However, the revenue collected from this levy was insignificant.

CFAF 1.4 billion, or about 16 per cent of estimated expenditures. The budget does not indicate how the deficit would be financed.

PAYMENT ARREARS

Past budgetary difficulties and weak expenditure controls led to a gradual accumulation of payment arrears. These arrears are of two types: (1) deferred payments which represent expenditures authorized by the Treasury (*dépenses mandatées*) but not paid; and (2) other expenditure obligations which were not authorized for payment by the Treasury (*dépenses non-mandatées*).

To clear up the amounts outstanding on payment arrears, the Government established the autonomous Amortization Fund (Caisse Autonome d'Amortissement) in August 1966 for the purpose of liquidating government debts to the private sector outstanding on January 1, 1966. The revenue of the Fund results mainly from a special levy called *taxe spéciale d'amortissement*. The Fund does not have an account with the Treasury and is not allowed to give advances to the Treasury. It has an account with BCEAO, which pays it interest at the rate of 3.5 per cent for the Fund's cash balances. The *taxe spéciale d'amortissement* is levied on the gross value of commercial transactions in Dahomey of importers, producers, and all other persons supplying services. Since its introduction, revenues from the tax have averaged about CFAF 225 million a year. During November 1966–December 1968 the Fund disbursed CFAF 542 million.

When the Amortization Fund began operations, the outstanding public debt to the private sector, mostly short term, was about CFAF 2.0 billion. During 1966–68 the Government increased these arrears, bringing the total to CFAF 5.6 billion by the end of 1968. Deferred payments represented CFAF 0.4 billion of the increase and expenditure obligations not authorized for payment by the Treasury represented CFAF 3.2 billion.

It should be noted that in 1968 the Dahomean authorities had more success in curtailing the growth in payment arrears, which amounted to only CFAF 0.3 billion in 1968, compared with a growth of CFAF 3.2 billion during the preceding two years.

In July 1969 the Amortization Fund was authorized to float a loan of CFAF 750 million to meet its debt amortization obligations.

MONEY AND BANKING

MONETARY SYSTEM

Dahomey belongs to the franc area. It is also a member of the West African Monetary Union (Union Monétaire Ouest Africaine, or UMOA), together with six other West African countries (Ivory Coast, Mauritania, Niger, Senegal, Togo, and Upper Volta). These countries have a common currency, the CFA franc, and a common central bank, the Banque Centrale des Etats de l'Afrique de l'Ouest (BCEAO), which is the issuing authority of UMOA and keeps its external reserves. The CFA franc is freely convertible into French francs at the rate of CFAF 1.00 = F 0.02. On August 10, 1969, the rate against the U.S. dollar became CFAF 277.710 per dollar; previously, since January 1, 1960, the rate had been CFAF 246.853. (For details on the operation of BCEAO, see Chapter 4, and for information on the change in the par value, see Chapter 6.)

STRUCTURE OF THE BANKING SYSTEM

The monetary system of Dahomey includes a central bank (BCEAO), which it shares with the other UMOA members; three commercial banks; and the Development Bank (Banque Dahoméenne de Développement, or BDD). BCEAO operates in Dahomey, as in the other UMOA countries, through a local agency. Decisions concerning the implementation of BCEAO policies in Dahomey are taken by the National Monetary Committee. The Director of the local BCEAO agency, who sits on the National Monetary Committee in an advisory capacity, is responsible for the application of these policies.

The Treasury of Dahomey also performs certain banking operations. It accepts customs duty bills (*obligations cautionnées*) with a maturity of four months in payment of certain indirect taxes, principally customs duties. These bills are discountable at BCEAO. The Treasury may receive deposits from public and semipublic institutions.

In addition to credit extended by banks, the Caisse Centrale de Coopération Economique (CCCE), a French public institution, extends medium-term and long-term credit and contributes to the financing of the Development Bank's credit operations. In addition, it acts as the authorized agent of the Fonds d'Aide et de Coopération (FAC) and the European Development Fund (EDF, or Fonds Européen de Développement, or FED) for local aid disbursements.

BANKING LEGISLATION AND REGULATIONS

On July 8, 1965 the Dahomean Government enacted a Law No. 65–22, which was designed to establish banking law in accordance with the guidelines set by the Executive Board of BCEAO for the whole UMOA area. The main features of the banking law include determination of liquidity ratios for banks; fixation of interest rates, commissions, and service fees charged by banks; and establishment of special requirements concerning the capital and reserves of banks and other financial institutions. The law also provides for the establishment of three institutions to supervise the banking and financial sector: (1) National Credit Council, which studies credit policies, advises the Government on regulations to be adopted, and takes decisions on matters of credit and banking regulations which become applicable on approval of the Minister of Finance; (2) Banks and Financial Institutions Committee, which controls the implementation of regulations governing banking and credit matters; and (3) the Association of Banks and Financial Institutions, a professional association which acts as an intermediary between the Government, the two above-mentioned committees, and the managements of banking and financial enterprises.

The few recent changes in the banking system of Dahomey include an amendment to BCEAO's statutes, a change in the policy of determining the limits on rediscount ceilings for commercial banks, and a change in the interest rate structure, as described below.

CENTRAL BANK OPERATIONS

Operations of the Central Bank in Dahomey during 1962–69 are summarized in Table 20.

Foreign Assets

Foreign assets of BCEAO for Dahomey consist essentially of Dahomey's share in BCEAO's balance of operations account with the French Treasury and of the gold tranche of Dahomey's IMF subscription. The latter rose from CFAF 185 million in 1963 to CFAF 347

TABLE 20. DAHOMEY: ASSETS AND LIABILITIES OF THE CENTRAL BANK, 1962–69

(In millions of CFA francs; end of period)

	1962	1963	1964	1965	1966	1967		1968				1969		
						Sept.	Dec.	Mar.	June	Sept.	Dec.	Mar.	June	Sept.
Foreign assets (net)														
Foreign exchange	2,464	2,445	2,254	2,319	2,055	1,690	1,722	1,295	1,324	1,651	2,077	2,229	1,863	1,841
IMF	—	185	185	185	216	247	247	247	278	278	278	278	309	347
Total foreign assets (net)	2,464	2,630	2,439	2,504	2,271	1,937	1,969	1,542	1,602	1,928	2,355	2,507	2,172	2,188
Claims on Government	214	87	192	214	679	725	732	811	909	928	875	828	842	1,110
Less government deposits	-333	-247	-358	-173	-198	-321	-427	-404	-465	-261	-515	-629	-466	-734
Total claims on Government (net)	-119	-160	-166	41	481	404	305	407	444	667	360	199	376	376
Claims on banks														
Rediscounts, short-term	...	780	1,051	805	694	635	1,060	1,342	1,060	628	695	1,219	1,278	898
Rediscounts, medium-term	...	150	200	96	50	45	—	—	4	4	70	82	89	263
Total claims on banks	852	930	1,250	901	744	680	1,060	1,342	1,064	632	765	1,301	1,367	1,161
Assets = liabilities	3,197	3,400	3,522	3,446	3,496	3,021	3,334	3,291	3,110	3,227	3,480	4,007	3,915	3,725
Currency and bank deposits	3,197	3,400	3,522	3,446	3,496	3,020	3,334	3,291	3,110	3,227	3,479	4,006	3,914	3,725
Currency outside banks	3,027	3,259	3,369	3,307	3,285	2,919	3,149	3,189	3,007	3,083	3,325	3,912	3,789	3,544
Other items (net)	—	—	—	—	—	1	—	—	—	—	1	1	1	-1

Source: Data supplied by BCEAO.

million in September 1969, when Dahomey completed gold payments for an increase in its quota to which it consented in May 1966, and following the devaluation of the CFA franc in August 1969.

In September 1969, BCEAO's net foreign assets amounted to CFAF 2.19 billion. After decreasing in 1966 and 1967, they increased by almost 20 per cent in 1968, as a result mainly of higher export earnings in the last quarter of 1968.

Credit to the Government

BCEAO's credit to the Government consists mainly of direct advances and of discounts of customs duty bills. In December 1968, Article 15 of the statutes of BCEAO was modified, by special decision of its Executive Board, so as to allow BCEAO to increase its direct advances to member governments from the previous 10 per cent to 15 per cent of the actual fiscal receipts of the previous budget year. The statutes provide that the limit on such advances shall be reduced automatically by the amount of Treasury bills held by BCEAO and by the amount of government borrowing from commercial banks and other credit institutions which have rediscount facilities with BCEAO. In order to use the additional 5 per cent credit facility, the member government must provide specific justification to the Board. After a study of the fiscal and monetary situation, the Board will decide the length of the period for which such additional credit would be granted. In any event, this period cannot exceed the limit previously applied to BCEAO's direct advances to member governments and not modified by the new amendment. This limit remains fixed at 240 days, but it can be extended by a special waiver of the Board until the first working day of the next calendar year, on presentation of justification from the government concerned. It is estimated that the larger credit facility would increase the Dahomean Government's borrowing facility with BCEAO by about CFAF 300 million in 1969.

BCEAO's net claims on the Government rose after 1964, although they declined slightly in 1967 and were less in September 1969 than in September 1968. Growth in credit to the Government has been mainly in the form of direct advances and reflects the growing needs of the Treasury to finance budgetary deficits incurred during this period.

Credit to the Private Sector

BCEAO's credit operations consist of rediscounts of short-term and medium-term claims of the other banks on the private sector. The Monetary Committee establishes a rediscount ceiling for each bank consistent with the global rediscount ceiling fixed by BCEAO's Executive Board. The global rediscount ceiling, which is fixed on submission of proposals by the Monetary Committee for a period of six months, can be revised only by the Executive Board. Global rediscount ceilings are established separately for short-term and for medium-term credits.

For short-term credit, BCEAO's Executive Board fixes an over-all rediscount ceiling for each member country, on proposals by the Monetary Committee and based on the estimated needs of the economy in the forthcoming half year. In arriving at this ceiling the Board takes into account the banks' own resources in order to ensure that the banks will use their own resources fully before resorting to the rediscount facilities of BCEAO. The Monetary Committee earmarks part of the over-all rediscount ceiling for the Treasury to enable it to discount customs duty bills with BCEAO. In the past, Dahomey has utilized only part of the amount reserved for the Treasury. Another part of the over-all rediscount ceiling is earmarked for the banks; the remainder is left as a margin against unforeseen needs which may arise during the forthcoming half year.

The major part of the over-all rediscount ceiling is reserved for the banks. Consistent with the over-all ceiling, the Monetary Committee establishes individual rediscount ceilings for each bank, taking into account the bank's expected credit operations and its own resources. In the past, the individual ceilings for the banks' rediscounts with BCEAO have been subject to a maximum limit of 50 per cent of the banks' expected credit operations, which could be raised to 65 per cent during the crop season to finance seasonal needs. To tighten credit, the Executive Board of BCEAO decided in September 1968 that the banks could exceed the limit of 50 per cent only to finance crops of individually designated products which are of particular importance to a member country. These products were designated separately for each member country, and BCEAO could rediscount up to 80 per cent of the financing of the crops of such products. For Dahomey, only cotton was designated to take advantage of this facility.

In addition to rediscount ceilings for each bank, the Monetary Committee also establishes individual credit limits for each enterprise on the basis of its financial situation. Bank loans to the private sector are rediscountable only up to the limits established for each enterprise.

For medium-term credit BCEAO's Executive Board establishes rediscount ceilings for each member country on the basis of the estimated number of investment projects likely to be financed by medium-term credit. This ceiling is not distributed among the banks. However, for each financial institution, a limit is fixed on the medium-term credit, whether rediscountable or not, which it can extend during a certain period of time. Medium-term credit can be rediscounted with BCEAO only if the credit has received the prior approval of the Monetary Committee. The approval is given on the basis of examination of the financial situation of the enterprise applying for credit. Moreover, the project to be financed by medium-term credit must be in line with the general development policy of the country and must yield sufficient returns to reimburse the credit.

The bulk of central bank credit to the private sector consists of rediscounts of short-term paper. The amount of short-term paper rediscounted varies seasonally with the need for financing export crops. During 1962–68 the amount of short-term paper rediscounted by the deposit banks represented on the average approximately 21 per cent of the total amount of short-term credit extended by them to the private sector. In September 1969, however, this percentage increased to about 44 per cent.

Rediscounts of medium-term paper have declined steadily since 1964, reflecting the trend of decreasing medium-term and long-term credit extended by the banks as explained below.

BCEAO's liabilities consist mainly of its currency in circulation, which has remained stable over the last five years. Most of the increase in money supply since 1963 occurred in the form of a growth in demand deposits.

OPERATIONS OF COMMERCIAL BANKS AND THE DEVELOPMENT BANK

Two of Dahomey's three commercial banks are foreign; besides these there is the Development Bank.

The Development Bank extends long-term, medium-term, and short-term credit to public and private enterprises and subscribes to their capital. It has a subscribed capital of CFAF 300 million, of which CFAF 250 million was paid up at the end of 1968. The capital subscription is distributed as follows: Government of Dahomey 55.2 per cent, CCCE 33.5 per cent, BCEAO 10 per cent, and local private shareholders 1.3 per cent. Aside from its capital, the main resources of the Development Bank are loans from CCCE, rediscounts with BCEAO, and deposits received from public and semipublic organizations. CCCE extends two types of loans to the Development Bank: global advances and special advances to finance a given project; these advances are fully guaranteed by the Dahomean Government in French francs. The rate of interest paid by the Development Bank on CCCE loans depends on the nature of the operation: it is 3.5 per cent for credit to the Government, 4.25 per cent for credit to enterprises engaged in rural development, and 5 per cent for credit to the private sector.

The Development Bank has had some financial difficulties in recent years. In 1967–69, however, efforts were made to restore the Bank's financial position: the accounting system was reorganized, less profitable operations were curtailed, and the Bank's personnel was reduced in view of the reduced volume of lending operations. The Development Bank also increased its capital from CFAF 300 million to CFAF 400 million, to be subscribed mainly by the Government and the remainder by BCEAO and a local commercial bank. It is hoped that these measures of reorganization will enable the Bank to resume full activity and that CCCE will soon continue its global advances, which were suspended in 1965.

The bulk of the banks' operations consists of the extension of credit, largely short-term credit, to the private sector (Table 21). Credit to the Government represents only a very small part of their total credit operations and has not varied much over the past few years. Short-term credit to the private sector is used mainly to finance export crops and

TABLE 21. DAHOMEY: ASSETS AND LIABILITIES OF THE COMMERCIAL BANKS AND THE DEVELOPMENT BANK, 1962–69

(In millions of CFA francs; end of period)

	1962	1963	1964	1965	1966	1967		1968				1969		
						Sept.	Dec.	Mar.	June	Sept.	Dec.	Mar.	June	Sept.
Reserves	80	126	78	95	154	75	144	62	72	102	140	90	110	139
Foreign assets (net)	−688	−1,163	−1,300	−1,191	−603	−642	−878	−826	−12	316	−565	−840	−570	−339
Claims on Government	—	5	14	6	16	27	9	21	29	17	20	40	40	285
Less government deposits	−91	−120	−115	−154	−139	−125	−120	−120	−125	−144	−128	−145	−140	−157
Total claims on Government (net)	−91	−115	−101	−148	−123	−98	−111	−99	−96	−127	−108	−95	−100	−128
Claims on private sector [1]														
Short-term	…	3,394	3,682	3,344	3,256	3,248	4,011	4,272	3,930	3,562	4,356	…	…	…
Medium-term	…	484	526	425	318	209	152	160	157	139	130	…	…	…
Long-term	…	550	619	732	684	431	410	443	413	417	402	…	…	…
Total claims on private sector	3,866	4,428	4,827	4,501	4,257	3,888	4,573	4,876	4,500	4,117	4,888	5,711	6,010	5,151
Assets = liabilities	3,167	3,276	3,504	3,257	3,685	3,223	3,728	4,013	4,464	4,408	4,355	4,866	5,450	5,079
Demand deposits	2,140	2,146	2,025	2,241	2,664	2,432	2,435	2,247	2,859	3,220	3,133	3,028	3,460	3,336
Time deposits	168	140	214	107	75	133	268	287	297	390	364	312	350	288
Credit from Central Bank	850	930	1,250	901	744	680	1,060	1,337	1,064	629	765	1,301	1,370	1,161
Other items (net)	9	61	15	7	202	−22	−35	141	245	170	94	225	270	294

Source: Data supplied by BCEAO.

[1] Including miscellaneous debtors.

202 SURVEYS OF AFRICAN ECONOMIES, VOL. 3
imports. Although short-term credit declined in 1965 and 1966, it rose
in subsequent years. The decline was due mainly to generally slower
business activity and to some extent also to the reluctance of enterprises
to undertake government contracts following the large accumulation of
unpaid government bills. The pronounced growth in short-term credit in
1968 and in early 1969 reflects essentially the general revival of economic activity, particularly in the export sector.

Medium-term and long-term credit has been provided mainly by the
Development Bank. The total amount of medium-term and long-term
credit declined steadily, from CFAF 1.0 billion at the end of 1963 to
less than CFAF 0.6 billion in December 1968. The decline was particularly marked in the public works sector as a result of the termination of
some large investment projects (Table 22). However, it was also
important in the three sectors of housing, industry, and agriculture
(including fishing and forestry). The decrease in the medium-term and
long-term credit to the private sector reflects partly the lack of expansion in the economy in recent years and partly the financial difficulties
of the Development Bank.

The foreign exchange position of the banks improved markedly over
the past five years, largely in 1966 and 1968. In 1966, however, it was
accompanied by a decrease in credit to the private sector; in 1968,
credit to the private sector rose. Both demand and time deposits of the
banks increased during 1963–68. However, time deposits rose faster
than demand deposits, reflecting a change in the public's preference for
deposits earning interest. During the first nine months of 1969, the
foreign exchange position of the banks deteriorated somewhat and in
September 1969 their foreign liabilities exceeded their foreign assets
by CFAF 339 million.

RATES OF INTEREST

On June 30, 1966 the Government issued Decree No. 266 regulating
interest charges on credit operations of the banks. This Decree covers
the operations of the commercial banks, the Development Bank, and
other financial institutions of a commercial type. The new regulation is
primarily expected to allow easier access to bank credit by small and
medium-sized enterprises by putting more emphasis on criteria of general economic utility and eligibility for rediscount, and less on those of

TABLE 22.   DAHOMEY: DISTRIBUTION OF MEDIUM-TERM AND LONG-TERM CREDIT,
BY MAIN ECONOMIC SECTORS, ON JUNE 30, 1963–68 [1]

(*In millions of CFA francs*)

	1963	1964	1965	1966	1967	1968
Agriculture, fishing, and forestry	48	87	52	38	27	26
Industry	100	80	91	67	55	45
Public works	68	18	20	11	13	10
Housing	65	72	68	47	38	11
Transportation and auxiliary services	29	26	93	152	138	134
Commerce and other services	300	267	272	203	190	154
Imports and distribution of fuels	*138*	*140*	*97*	*51*	*45*	—
Hotels and restaurants	*155*	*127*	*150*	*132*	*131*	*133*
Cooperatives and mutual credit organizations	1	—	31	33	—	—
Total	611	550	627	551	461	380

Source: Data supplied by BCEAO.

[1] Excludes enterprises with total indebtedness of less than CFAF 10 million.

creditworthiness and financial guarantees which these enterprises could not always meet.

Interest rates set by the new regulation are of the following types: (1) a uniform basic rate (*taux de référence*), (2) an additional rate varying with the different categories of credit specified in the regulation, and (3) a 0.25 per cent commission (*commission d'engagement*) to BCEAO on rediscountable medium-term credit. At present, the basic rate is equal to the rediscount rate of BCEAO, 3.5 per cent; however, if BCEAO's foreign assets should decline below the level which calls for readjustment measures under the bank statutes, the Government may authorize BCEAO to establish a basic rate different from its rediscount rate.

Initially the new regulation provided interest rates on deposits with commercial banks as follows: nil to 2.5 per cent annually on demand deposits of less than six months, depending on the size of the deposit; up to 3 per cent on time deposits of more than six months; and a uniform rate of 3.25 per cent on savings deposits. In November 1968, as proposed by BCEAO's Executive Board, the Government authorized increases in the interest rates paid on time deposits for periods over six months in order to discourage an outflow of capital. The rate of interest was increased from 2.5 per cent to 3.5 per cent for deposits ranging from CFAF 200,000 to CFAF 5.0 million, and from 3 per cent to 4.5 per cent for deposits above CFAF 5.0 million. No interest rates are paid for deposits below CFAF 200,000.

For short-term credit under the previous system, the banks fixed a minimum rate of 6 per cent annually by a multilateral agreement. In practice, however, this rate was subject to variation, depending on the nature of the risk involved, the creditworthiness of the debtor, and the guarantees offered. Generally the rate on outright advances ranged from 6 to 8 per cent, but, in a few circumstances, it was as low as 4.75 per cent. Discount rates on commercial bills had a similar range, except that the rate for each category was 0.25 per cent less than the corresponding rates on outright advances. There was only a minor surcharge ($\frac{1}{12}$ of 1 per cent) on credits noneligible for rediscount.

The new regulation contains certain innovations in the matter of interest rates charged on short-term credit. It fixes the interest rates to be charged on certain categories of credits, without specific reference to creditworthiness or guarantee criteria. The rates specified are as follows: (1) 4.5 to 5.25 per cent annually on credits to public enterprises for crop marketing and to priority enterprises; (2) 5.0 to 6.0 per cent on advances for goods under warranty which are generally related to export trade; (3) 5.0 to 6.0 per cent on discounts of certain categories of commercial bills (e.g., documentary bills issued on export operations); and (4) 5.5 to 6.5 per cent on all other credits eligible for rediscount. Moreover, the new regulation strongly penalizes credits granted beyond the rediscount limits set by BCEAO for each enterprise; such credits are to be extended only at a uniform 8 per cent annually.

The new regulation introduces similar considerations for medium-term rates. The rates are primarily determined on the basis of the economic utility of the project, without placing emphasis on the usual bankers' criteria. However, it is required that such credit should be rediscountable; noneligibility for rediscount is strongly penalized. The rates specified for different types of medium-term credit are as follows: (1) 5.5 to 6.0 per cent annually on investment credits to priority enterprises or for real estate projects of social utility, (2) 5.5 to 6.25 per cent on industrial or commercial credits for productive purposes, and (3) 7.25 to 7.75 per cent on real estate credits. Credits underwritten by the Government are free from the 0.25 per cent BCEAO commission. All medium-term credits not eligible for rediscount are charged 8.0 to 8.5 per cent. Interest rates charged on operations not covered by the decrees in question have to be specifically approved by the National Credit Council. The Development Bank charges interest rates from 6 to 8 per cent a year on real estate credit and an additional 2 per cent on credit for houses built for rent. Credits to agriculture extended by the Development Bank carry interest at a rate of 4 to 6 per cent annually and those to commerce, industry, and handicrafts interest at a rate of 5 to 8 per cent. Loans on small equipment and building materials carry an interest rate of 5 per cent.

RECENT MONETARY AND CREDIT DEVELOPMENTS

Over the six years ended December 31, 1968, money supply rose at an average rate of 4 per cent and net domestic credit at 6 per cent, while net foreign assets of the banking system were at the same level in December 1968 as in December 1962 (Table 23). The average annual increase in total domestic credit includes a marked rise in credit to the Government. Movements in credit to the private sector have been more uneven. Credit to the private sector rose substantially in 1963 and 1964, declined over the next two years, and remained relatively stable in 1967. However, in 1968, credit to the private sector was higher at the end of each calendar quarter, compared with the previous year, and rose by 6 per cent over the year as a whole. Even so, at the end of 1968, credit to the private sector was only about 1 per cent higher than at the end of 1964; in the next nine months it rose by 12 per cent. Quasi-money increased by an average of 20 per cent a year during 1963–68.

Net foreign assets of the banking system rose in 1966 and 1968, but declined in 1967. In that year the decline in net foreign assets more than offset the rise in net domestic credit; as a result, money supply declined by nearly 6 per cent in 1967.

Monetary and credit developments were relatively much more buoyant in 1968, particularly in the last quarter of the year. Net domestic credit rose by more than 7 per cent in 1968 and net foreign assets of the banking system by 64 per cent. The sharp increase in foreign assets

TABLE 23. DAHOMEY: MONETARY SURVEY, 1962–69

(In millions of CFA francs; end of period)

	1962	1963	1964	1965	1966	1967 Sept.	1967 Dec.	1968 Mar.	1968 June	1968 Sept.	1968 Dec.	1969 Mar.	1969 June	1969 Sept.
Foreign assets (net)	1,777	1,467	1,139	1,314	1,668	1,295	1,091	716	1,590	2,244	1,790	1,668	1,601	1,487
Domestic credit														
Claims on Government (net)	-58	-53	-2	127	519	541	393	484	529	743	480	316	518	715
Claims on private sector	4,176	4,709	5,085	4,761	4,540	4,122	4,836	5,157	4,756	4,375	5,137	5,748	6,228	5,764
Total domestic credit (net)	4,118	4,656	5,083	4,888	5,059	4,663	5,229	5,641	5,285	5,118	5,617	6,064	6,746	6,479
Assets = liabilities	5,895	6,123	6,222	6,202	6,727	5,958	6,320	6,357	6,875	7,362	7,407	7,732	8,347	7,966
Money														
Currency	3,027	3,259	3,369	3,307	3,285	2,919	3,149	3,189	3,007	3,083	3,325	4,006	3,914	3,544
Demand deposits	2,655	2,660	2,597	2,772	3,140	2,918	2,908	2,708	3,299	3,686	3,614	3,415	3,828	3,798
Total money	5,682	5,919	5,966	6,079	6,425	5,837	6,057	5,897	6,306	6,769	6,939	7,421	7,742	7,342
Quasi-money	168	140	214	107	75	133	268	287	297	390	364	312	351	288
Other items (net)	45	64	43	16	227	-12	-5	174	273	202	103	-1	254	336
SAVINGS BANKS														
Deposits	250	274	294	317	327	344	336	358	368	367	368	372	379	383

Source: Data supplied by BCEAO.

largely reflected higher export receipts. Most of these receipts were deposited with the commercial banks. Over the whole year, the increase in the banking system's net foreign assets (about CFAF 0.7 billion) was reflected mainly in a growth of money supply, particularly in demand deposits, which rose by 24 per cent. Quasi-money rose by 36 per cent.

In the first nine months of 1969 credit to the private sector continued to expand, reflecting increased crop financing, mainly of palm products. In September 1969, credit to the private sector was 32 per cent higher than a year before. Credit to the Government, on the other hand, remained at approximately the same level as in the third quarter of 1968. Net foreign assets of the banking system declined by 34 per cent over the year ended September 1969, when they amounted to CFAF 1.5 billion. This decline mainly reflects a decrease in the banks' foreign assets. During the same period, money supply rose by 8 per cent, while quasi-money declined by about 25 per cent.

FOREIGN TRADE, AID, PAYMENTS, AND DEBT

FOREIGN TRADE

Value and Composition of Trade

Exports adjusted for estimated unrecorded trade rose by over 50 per cent in value during 1965–68 (Table 24). The rise was particularly marked in 1968, when total exports grew by almost 35 per cent as a result of increased exports of palm products, cotton, and groundnuts. Unrecorded exports are estimated to have increased as well during 1968. Imports adjusted for estimated unrecorded trade rose by approximately 40 per cent during 1965–68. Part of the growth in imports is directly attributable to an increase in imports financed by foreign aid and private capital inflow.

Unrecorded trade during 1965–67 is estimated to have represented about 20 per cent of recorded exports and 15 per cent of recorded imports. Unrecorded imports, besides the traditional imports of cattle from Niger and Upper Volta, have consisted mainly of manufactured goods, such as textiles, cigarettes, and alcoholic beverages. Illegal

TABLE 24. DAHOMEY: VALUE OF RECORDED AND ADJUSTED FOREIGN TRADE, 1965–68

	Exports		Imports		Trade Balance		Ratio of Exports to Imports	
	Recorded	Adjusted	Recorded	Adjusted	Recorded	Adjusted	Recorded	Adjusted
	Billion CFA francs						*Per cent*	
1965	3.37	4.51	8.49	9.99	−5.12	−5.48	40	45
1966	2.59	4.80	8.27	10.90	−5.69	−6.10	31	44
1967	3.75	5.20	11.98	13.80	−8.23	−8.60	31	38
1968	5.51	6.90	12.21	14.00	−6.70	−7.10	45	49

Sources: Ministère de l'Economie et des Finances, *Aspects Economiques 1967* and *Bulletin de Statistique.*

importing of these items occurred because of differences in the customs duties and taxes, which were considerably lower in the neighboring countries than in Dahomey. Unrecorded exports have included beer produced in Dahomey, food crops, and re-exports to Nigeria of manufactured goods. Until 1967, unrecorded imports were estimated to have been approximately twice as high as unrecorded exports. In 1968, however, unrecorded imports are estimated to have declined sharply as a result of changes in Dahomey's taxation and customs duty structure (see "Indirect taxes," above) which considerably reduced the incentive to smuggle. On the other hand, unrecorded exports are estimated to have increased as Dahomey has benefited from the introduction of import restrictions in Nigeria. Consequently, it is estimated that unrecorded exports might have been as high as unrecorded imports during 1968, or even higher. Composition of exports and imports is available only on the basis of customs data (i.e., excluding unrecorded trade).

Exports.—Palm products continue to lead Dahomey's exports, although their share in total recorded exports fell from a peak of 74 per cent in 1964 to 50 per cent in 1968 (Table 25). This decline was due mainly to a reduction in palm production in 1966–67, but also to the increase in exports of cotton and groundnuts. In 1968, however, the value of palm product exports rose by about 74 per cent as a result of a 25 per cent greater production and substantially higher world prices of palm kernels.

Cotton accounted for 9 per cent of total recorded exports in 1967. Exports of this crop, which have been growing steadily since 1964, were expected to continue to expand for some years. Other export crops in the order of their importance are groundnuts (6 per cent), sheanuts (5 per cent), coffee (4 per cent), and tobacco (3 per cent). Exports of both groundnuts and sheanuts increased in 1968 and were expected to increase further in 1969.

Imports.—The composition of Dahomey's imports has not changed greatly since 1962 despite a substantial growth in imports (Table 26). Two import categories—food and beverages and other consumer goods (e.g., textiles and leather articles)—represented about 65 per cent of the total value of imports in 1968, compared with 59 per cent in 1961. During 1962–66, however, the share of food and beverages ranged from 20 to over 23 per cent, declining to 17 per cent in 1967, despite a

TABLE 25. DAHOMEY: RECORDED EXPORTS, BY COMMODITIES, 1961–68

	1961	1962	1963	1964	1965	1966	1967	1968
VOLUME *(thousand metric tons)*								
Palm products								
Palm kernels	48.5	43.9	50.6	56.2	16.7	5.8	4.0	7.2
Palm oil	11.0	9.3	9.3	12.7	13.3	9.9	8.5	10.5
Palm kernel oil	—	—	—	—	16.7	11.7	16.9	22.7
Palm cakes	—	—	—	—	16.1	11.7	21.7	...
Groundnuts (shelled)	12.5	4.3	6.6	4.0	2.3	3.2	5.5	8.0
Coffee	1.7	1.2	1.0	1.1	0.9	1.0	1.1	0.5
Cotton (ginned)	1.3	0.7	1.4	1.1	1.3	2.3	2.6	4.8
Sheanuts	...	...	1.0	7.4	5.0	2.8	6.4	8.1
Copra	...	...	0.6	1.5	1.7	1.1	0.6	0.7
VALUE *(million CFA francs)*								
Palm products								
Palm kernels	1,356	1,155	1,631	1,747	599	279	142	...
Palm oil	519	467	470	654	751	450	270	...
Palm kernel oil	—	—	—	—	990	602	897	...
Palm cakes	—	—	—	—	127	98	258	...
Total palm products	1,875	1,622	2,101	2,401	2,468	1,430	1,567	2,730
Groundnuts (shelled)	548	194	287	153	88	114	235	...
Coffee	272	243	126	153	108	90	142	...
Cotton (ginned)	179	86	164	124	158	274	339	...
Sheanuts	57	54	25	104	98	44	177	...
Copra	54	57	57	78	94	78	31	...
Other	596	444	395	241	354	556	1,359	...
Total exports	3,581	2,700	3,155	3,254	3,367	2,585	3,850	5,505

PER CENT OF TOTAL VALUE

Palm products	37.9	42.8	51.7	53.7	17.8	10.8	3.7	⋮
Palm kernels	14.5	17.3	14.9	20.1	22.3	17.4	7.0	⋮
Palm oil	—	—	—	—	29.4	23.3	23.3	⋮
Palm kernel oil	—	—	—	—	3.8	3.8	6.7	⋮
Palm cakes								49.6
Total palm products	52.4	60.1	66.6	73.8	73.3	55.3	40.7	⋮
Groundnuts (shelled)	15.3	7.2	9.1	4.7	2.6	4.4	6.1	⋮
Coffee	7.6	9.0	4.0	4.7	3.2	3.5	3.7	⋮
Cotton (ginned)	5.0	3.2	5.2	3.8	4.7	10.6	8.8	⋮
Sheanuts	1.6	2.0	0.8	3.2	2.9	1.7	4.6	⋮
Copra	1.5	2.1	1.8	2.4	2.8	3.0	0.8	⋮
Other	16.6	16.4	12.5	7.4	10.5	21.5	35.3	⋮
Total exports	100.0	100.0	100.0	100.0	100.0	100.0	100.0	100.0

Sources: Ministère des Finances et de l'Economie, *Aspects Economiques*, and BCEAO, *Notes d'Information et Statistiques.*

TABLE 26. DAHOMEY: RECORDED IMPORTS BY COMMODITY GROUPS, 1961–68

	1961	1962	1963	1964	1965	1966	1967	1968
	VALUE (million CFA francs)							
Food and beverages	1,181	1,547	1,702	1,692	1,680	1,785	2,019	2,443
Other consumer goods	2,541	2,586	3,796	3,656	4,090	3,893	5,226	5,470
Raw materials and semiprocessed goods	514	627	741	722	798	699	983	765
Fuels and lubricants	528	529	503	466	470	368	465	572
Machinery and transport equipment	1,510	1,338	1,507	1,226	1,452	1,525	3,290	2,960
Total	6,276	6,627	8,249	7,762	8,491	8,270	11,983	12,210
	PER CENT OF TOTAL VALUE							
Food and beverages	18.9	23.3	20.7	21.8	19.8	21.6	16.8	20.0
Other consumer goods	40.5	39.0	46.0	47.1	48.2	47.1	43.6	44.8
Raw materials and semiprocessed goods	8.2	9.5	9.0	9.3	9.4	8.5	8.2	6.3
Fuels and lubricants	8.4	8.0	6.1	6.0	5.5	4.4	3.9	4.7
Machinery and transport equipment	24.0	20.2	18.2	15.8	17.1	18.4	27.5	24.2
Total	100.0	100.0	100.0	100.0	100.0	100.0	100.0	100.0

Source: BCEAO, Notes d'Information et Statistiques.

rise in absolute value in that year. Other consumer goods followed a similar trend, rising to a peak of 48 per cent of total import value in 1965 and declining to 45 per cent in 1968. Among the remaining categories of imports, the share of raw materials and semiprocessed goods declined from 8 per cent to 6 per cent and that of fuels and lubricants from 8 per cent to 5 per cent during the period 1961–68. Machinery and transport equipment, which had represented 24 per cent of total imports in 1961, declined to 16 per cent in 1964 but rose steeply in 1967 to 28 per cent and again reached 24 per cent in 1968.

Direction of Trade

France continues to hold a dominant position in Dahomey's foreign trade, although its relative importance has declined since 1961 (Table 27). Exports to France accounted for 72 per cent of Dahomey's total recorded exports in 1961, but for only 37 per cent in 1968. The French share in Dahomey's recorded imports also declined—from 59 per cent to 42 per cent. EEC countries other than France benefited most from Dahomey's reoriented trade; their share in Dahomey's exports went up from 3 per cent to 17 per cent and their share in Dahomey's imports from 7 per cent to 24 per cent. For the most part, this growth reflects larger exports of palm products to Germany, Italy, and the Netherlands and liberalization of Dahomean imports from EEC countries other than France. The dollar area has also enlarged its share in Dahomey's foreign trade, particularly for exports, as a result of taking increased exports of Dahomean palm products.

Dahomey's negative balance of recorded trade with the franc area grew from CFAF 1.6 billion in 1961 to CFAF 4.6 billion in 1967 and with EEC countries other than France, from CFAF 0.4 billion to CFAF 2.5 billion (Table 28). In the same period, Dahomey's trade gap with the sterling area widened slightly and with the dollar area narrowed slightly.

FOREIGN FINANCIAL ASSISTANCE

Foreign aid consists principally of (1) grants for budgetary support; (2) grants, mainly from FAC and EDF, for financing development projects; and (3) technical assistance provided to Dahomey. In 1968

TABLE 27.　DAHOMEY: DIRECTION OF RECORDED FOREIGN TRADE, 1961–68

(*Value in millions of CFA francs*)

	1961	1962	1963	1964	1965	1966	1967	1968	Per Cent of Total 1961	Per Cent of Total 1968
EXPORTS BY DESTINATION										
France	2,583	1,901	2,255	2,442	1,845	1,365	1,300	2,015	72.1	36.6
EEC excluding France	107	182	440	413	882	377	1,025	960	3.0	17.4
United Kingdom	15	3	30	61	46	35	6	157	0.4	2.9
United States	—	—	3	1	92	242	529	1,192	—	21.7
West African Customs Union (UDEAO)	556	309	239	104	187	300	336	519	15.5	9.4
Nigeria	142	129	64	46	77	127	169	304	4.0	5.5
Other	178	176	124	187	238	139	385	358	5.0	6.5
Total exports	3,581	2,700	3,155	3,254	3,367	2,585	3,750	5,505	100.0	100.0
IMPORTS BY ORIGIN										
France	3,726	3,936	5,110	4,534	4,653	4,299	5,328	5,115	59.3	41.9
EEC excluding France	444	518	685	670	1,158	1,270	3,479	2,923	7.1	23.9
United Kingdom	137	120	266	258	293	283	251	472	2.2	3.9
United States	151	138	124	167	207	395	453	470	2.4	3.8
West African Customs Union (UDEAO)	657	858	724	614	654	659	866	884	10.5	7.2
Nigeria	138	149	372	345	212	172	178	249	2.2	2.0
Other	1,025	908	968	1,174	1,314	1,192	1,428	2,098	16.3	17.3
Total imports	6,276	6,627	8,249	7,762	8,491	8,270	11,983	12,211	100.0	100.0

Sources: Ministère des Finances et de l'Economie, *Aspects Economiques*, and BCEAO, *Notes d'Information et Statistiques.*

TABLE 28. DAHOMEY: BALANCE OF RECORDED FOREIGN TRADE, BY REGIONS, 1961–68

(In millions of CFA francs)

	1961	1962	1963	1964	1965	1966	1967	1968
Franc area	−1,590	−2,705	−3,479	−2,781	−3,396	−3,293	−4,560	...
France	−1,098	−1,974	−2,785	−2,038	−2,808	−2,882	−3,863	...
Dollar area	−493	−435	−354	−318	−191	−423	−267	...
Sterling area	−302	−336	−758	−739	−464	−206	−511	...
Other areas	−311	−452	−504	−669	−1,073	−1,763	−2,895	...
EEC excluding France	−338	−337	−347	−257	−276	−893	−2,454	−1,963
Total	−2,696	−3,928	−5,094	−4,508	−5,124	−5,685	−8,233	−6,706

Sources: Ministère de l'Economie et des Finances, *Aspects Economiques*, and *Bulletin de Statistique*.

the grant for budgetary support amounted to CFAF 0.4 billion, FAC
and EDF grants to CFAF 2.3 billion, and the cost of technical assistance to an estimated CFAF 1.0 billion.

BALANCE OF PAYMENTS

Table 29 summarizes balance of payments developments during
1965–68. Official balance of payments data were published only for

TABLE 29. DAHOMEY: BALANCE OF PAYMENTS, 1965–68

(In billions of CFA francs)

	1965	1966 [1]	1967 [1]	1968 [2]
A. Goods and services (net)				
Imports c.i.f. [3]	−9.99	−10.90	−13.80	−14.00
Exports f.o.b. [3]	4.51	4.80	5.20	6.90
Trade balance	−5.48	−6.10	−8.60	−7.10
Investment income (net)	—	−0.03	−0.10	−0.10
Government, n.i.e. (net)	0.71	−0.30	0.90	0.80
Other services (net)	0.05	—	0.20	0.10
Total goods and services (net)	−4.72	−6.43	−7.60	−6.30
B. Transfer payments (net)				
Private	0.53	0.76	0.70	0.50
Central Government	3.92	4.05	4.30	4.50
Total transfer payments (net)	4.45	4.81	5.00	5.00
C. Capital movements (net)				
Private	0.13	0.32	2.20	2.30
Official				
Receipts	1.25	0.05	—	—
Payments	−0.17	−0.23	−0.20	—
Total official	1.08	−0.18	−0.20	—
Total capital movements (net)	1.21	0.14	2.00	2.30
D. Net errors and omissions	−0.86	1.73	−0.20	−0.20
E. Over-all balance (A+B+C+D)	**0.08**	**0.25**	**−0.80**	**0.80**
F. Monetary movements (net)				
Commercial banks	−0.11	−0.59	0.28	−0.42
Central Bank	−0.07	0.24	0.30	−0.39
Other institutions	0.10	0.10	0.22	0.01
Total monetary movements (net)	−0.08	−0.25	0.80	−0.80

Sources: Data supplied by BCEAO and the Dahomean authorities.
[1] Provisional.
[2] Estimates.
[3] Figures for imports and exports differ from those in Tables 25–28 mainly
because of the inclusion of an estimate of unrecorded transactions with neighboring countries.

1965, but provisional estimates have been compiled by BCEAO for 1966 and 1967. Estimates for 1968 are of a very tentative nature and have been prepared on the basis of information provided by the authorities.

During 1965–68 Dahomey's balance of payments was characterized by large deficits in goods and services; except in 1967, these deficits were more than offset by net transfer payments and capital inflow. For services, there was a small surplus with the exception of the slight deficit in 1966. The deficit in trade increased from CFAF 5.5 billion in 1965 to an estimated CFAF 7.1 billion in 1968. Over this period, the ratio of exports to imports averaged about 44 per cent, including estimates for unrecorded trade with neighboring countries.

To a considerable extent, the trade deficit was merely the counterpart of the fairly substantial inflow of net transfer payments and capital into Dahomey. Transfer payments consisted of foreign grants for budgetary support and the financing of development projects. The estimated cost of technical assistance was also included in these transfers. Since most foreign assistance was in the form of grants rather than loans, the official inflow of capital was small, except in 1965, when it included CFAF 0.9 billion advances from the French Treasury. The increase in the inflow of private capital (net) in 1967 and 1968 relates to the construction of the kenaf factory, financed by a suppliers' credit from Italy, and to investments made in petroleum prospecting.

The over-all balance of payments of Dahomey was in approximate balance in 1965 and a slight surplus occurred in 1966. In 1967 there was a deficit of CFAF 0.8 billion, as sharply increased imports were only partly offset by increased exports and capital receipts. Estimates for 1968 indicate a balance of payments surplus of about CFAF 0.8 billion, mainly as a result of increased export receipts. Estimates for 1969 indicate further improvement in Dahomey's balance of payments based on expected increases in exports of cotton and groundnuts, more than offsetting a probable decrease in palm production. Larger net transfer payments and capital receipts in 1969 were anticipated with the start of some new investment projects, financed mostly by external resources; but it was expected that this increase would be offset by corresponding imports.

TABLE 30. DAHOMEY: EXTERNAL PUBLIC DEBT AND ESTIMATED DEBT SERVICE, 1969–82 [1]

(In millions of CFA francs)

	Indebtedness on December 31, 1967		Debt-Service Payments															
	Total commitments	Amount disbursed	1969			1970			1971			1972			1973–82		
			Principal	Interest	Total	Principal	Interest	Total	Principal	Interest	Total	Principal	Interest	Total	Principal	Interest	Total
Private	2,445	1,913	493	129	622	493	94	587	493	58	551	454	22	476	6	2	8
Suppliers' credits	*2,109*	*1,877*	*432*	*117*	*549*	*432*	*85*	*517*	*432*	*53*	*485*	*393*	*20*	*413*	*—*	*—*	*—*
Official	7,643	7,352	271	47	318	258	39	297	245	33	278	253	38	291	1,381	291	1,672
Total	10,088	9,265	764	176	940	751	133	884	738	91	829	707	60	767	1,387	293	1,680

Source: Data provided by the Dahomean authorities to the IBRD.

[1] Includes estimated debt service on the undisbursed portion of debt committed on December 31, 1967, except for CFAF 3,450 million, representing amounts owed to France on account of certain official debts and to Italy in connection with suppliers' credit, for which repayment terms have not yet been agreed upon.

EXTERNAL DEBT

At the end of 1967, on the basis of commitments, Dahomey's external debt amounted to CFAF 10.1 billion, of which CFAF 9.3 billion had been disbursed (Table 30). Suppliers' credits represented approximately 20 per cent of the total debt; the remainder consisted essentially of official debts owed mainly to France. Interest and amortization of external debt represented about 14 per cent of Dahomey's export earnings in 1967, including estimated debt service on the undisbursed portion of debt committed as of the end of 1967. This amount, however, does not include service of debts (totaling CFAF 3.5 billion) owed mainly to France on account of certain official debts, including arrears of the Postal Checking System, and to Italy in connection with a suppliers' credit, for which repayment terms have not yet been agreed on.

CHAPTER 8

Ivory Coast

GENERAL SETTING

Ivory Coast gained its independence on August 7, 1960. On March 11, 1963 it became a member of the International Monetary Fund (IMF); its present quota is $19,000,000 (April 1970). On the same day it joined the International Bank for Reconstruction and Development (IBRD, or World Bank), present subscription $20,000,000; the International Development Association (IDA), subscription $1,010,000; and the International Finance Corporation (IFC), subscription $111,000. Among other international organizations, it is a member of the United Nations (UN); the Food and Agriculture Organization (FAO); the UN Educational, Scientific, and Cultural Organization (UNESCO); the UN Economic Commission for Africa (ECA); the General Agreement on Tariffs and Trade (GATT); the African Development Bank (ADB); and the Common Organization of African and Malagasy States (Organisation Commune Africaine et Malgache, or OCAM). With Dahomey, Mali, Mauritania, Senegal, and Upper Volta, it is joined in the West African Customs Union (Union Douanière des Etats de l'Afrique de l'Ouest, or UDEAO). With Dahomey, Mauritania, Niger, Senegal, Togo, and Upper Volta, it is joined in the West African Monetary Union (Union Monétaire Ouest Africaine, or UMOA), sharing a common central bank, the Banque Centrale des Etats de l'Afrique de l'Ouest (BCEAO), and a common currency, the CFA franc.

Ivory Coast has an area of 322,460 square kilometers (127,520 square miles), about three fifths of the size of France. It has common boundaries with Liberia and Guinea on the west, Mali and Upper Volta on the north, and Ghana on the east. On the south it borders the Gulf of Guinea and the Atlantic Ocean.

Most of the country is a plateau, tilting gently toward the Atlantic. Along the northwestern border, however, where the Guinea Highlands extend southward into the country, some peaks rise as high as 1,560 meters (5,000 feet).

The four major rivers flow roughly parallel from north to south but have little value for transportation because of falls and cataracts: (1) the Cavally, forming part of the Liberian border; (2) the Sassandra, with its chief tributaries, the Bafing and the Lobo; (3) the Bandama, with its chief tributaries, the Bandama Rouge and the Nzi; and (4) the Komoé. Two smaller rivers—the Baoulé and the Bagoé—drain northward into Mali. Two other rivers, flowing mainly in Ghana, form part of the eastern boundary—the Volta Noire in the northeast and the Tanoé (Tano) in the southeast; the Nuon, flowing mainly in Liberia, forms part of the southwestern boundary.

There are three main climatic regions: (1) Bordering the coast is the hot, humid region of heaviest rainfall—2,000–3,000 millimeters (80–120 inches) annually—and least range in average temperature (73°–80° F.). It has a long dry season (December to mid-May), folowed by heavy rains (mid-May to mid-July), a short agreeable dry season (mid-July to October), and a short season of light rains (October–November). With exploitation of the original tropical forest, more land is becoming available for growing coffee, cocoa, bananas, pineapples, oil palms, and rubber trees. (2) The central forest region has less but still plentiful rainfall—1,325–2,500 millimeters (53–100 inches)—almost continuously high humidity, and less distinct seasons. The principal dry season is earlier and shorter than on the coast (November to mid-March) and is followed by a short wet season (mid-March to mid-May), a short dry season (mid-May to mid-July), and the heavy rains (mid-July to mid-November). Here, forests alternate with grass-lands. Cotton, as well as rice, yams, and other food crops, are pro-duced. (3) In the northern or savanna region, temperatures are high, the maximum averaging 90° to 94° and the minimum 57°. The long dry season (November to May) is followed by a long wet season (June to October). Cattle raising and production of cereals (corn, rice, and sorghum) are the main activities.

The population in 1969 may be estimated at 4.9 million (based on an average growth of 2.9 per cent since 1965, when the population was stated as 4.3 million). This figure includes some 15,000 Europeans. The capital, Abidjan, which is also the largest city and main port, has an estimated population of 500,000. Other important towns are Bouaké (population, 80,000 in 1964), Gagnoa, Agboville, Korhogo, Daloa, and Dimbokro, together with the ports of Grand-Bassam, Sassandra, and Tabou.

The ethnic composition of the African population is complex; most of the people belong to six main groups—Agnis-Ashantis, Kroumen, Mandé, Baoulé, Dan-Gouro, and Koua. Many languages are spoken, but French is the official language. About one fourth of the population are Muslims and one eighth Christians.

STRUCTURE OF THE ECONOMY

GROSS DOMESTIC PRODUCT

The economy of Ivory Coast has made rapid progress since inde-pendence although the growth rate has fluctuated considerably. From 1960 to 1965, the gross domestic product (GDP) at market prices rose from CFAF 142.6 billion to CFAF 239.6 billion, or by an average annual rate of over 11 per cent (Table 1). According to estimates, which show an average rise in domestic prices of about 3 per cent a year, the increase in GDP at constant prices averaged 8 per cent a year.

During 1966–68 the average annual growth rate at current prices

TABLE 1. IVORY COAST: PRODUCTION AND INCOME, 1960–68

	1960	1961	1962	1963	1964	1965	1966	1967	1968
TOTAL VALUE (billion CFA francs)									
Gross domestic product	142.6	161.4	168.3	197.8	239.7	239.6	258.0	275.7	326.5
Less net payments to external factors[1]	-3.7	-4.9	-6.5	-9.3	-9.3	-11.5	-8.5	-9.4	-10.3
Gross national product	138.9	156.5	161.8	188.5	230.4	228.1	249.5	266.3	316.2
Less depreciation	-5.4	-6.1	-6.5	-7.0	-7.5	-8.5	...	...	...
National income at market prices	133.5	150.4	155.3	181.5	222.9	219.6	240.4	256.8	305.2
Less indirect taxes net of subsidies	-18.8	-23.5	-27.1	-34.4	-43.3	-38.2	-42.2	-46.6	-56.7
National income at factor costs	114.7	126.9	128.2	147.1	179.6	181.4	198.2	210.2	248.4
PER CAPITA VALUE (CFA francs)									
National income[2]	30,703	33,043	32,508	36,333	43,115	42,176	44,750	46,094	52,136

Sources: Ministère du Plan, *Les Comptes de la Nation—Principaux Résultats, 1960–65*, *Les Comptes de la Nation, 1966–67*, and *Les Comptes de la Nation, 1968*.

[1] Includes net value added of foreign administration and households, on the basis of salary payments.
[2] Based on total population (including permanently employed foreigners working in Ivory Coast) as follows (in thousands): 3,735 (1960), 3,840 (1961), 3,954 (1962), 4,050 (1963), 4,165 (1964), 4,300 (1965), 4,430 (1966), 4,560 (1967), and 4,765 (1968).

was still 11 per cent. In 1968, however, the increase was much larger (18 per cent) than in 1965 and 1967 (7–8 per cent), largely because of an excellent coffee crop in 1967/68, compared with a very poor one in the preceding year. Domestic prices are believed to have increased by about the same amount so that the growth rate of GDP at constant prices continued to average 8 per cent.

Per capita national income, which had risen at an average annual rate of just under 7 per cent through 1965, continued upward at a slightly higher rate (over 7 per cent), taking into account an annual average of population growth of about 3 per cent. In real terms, per capita income rose by an average of at least 4 per cent a year during the entire period 1960–68, with an exceptional increase of about 10 per cent in 1968.

Preliminary estimates for 1969 indicate some slowdown, compared with the extremely high growth rate of the economy in 1968. However, the trade surplus according to customs data increased from CFAF 27 billion in 1968 to CFAF 32 billion in 1969.

Consumption and Investment

Since 1960 there has been a high rate of investment in Ivory Coast, especially in 1960–65. A total of CFAF 324 billion was invested during 1960–68, public investment accounting for about 30 per cent of the total. The share of gross investment in GDP rose from 13 per cent in 1960 to over 16 per cent in 1968 (Table 2). In 1960–65, the average annual rate of increase in gross investment was 19 per cent, while that of consumption was only 11 per cent. Over the following three years, the average annual rate of increase in gross investment declined to 8 per cent and that of consumption to 9 per cent. In 1966 and 1967, these rates were much lower than the three-year average and in 1968 much higher (18 per cent for gross investment and 12 per cent for consumption).

For private investment alone the average annual rate of increase was as high as 22 per cent during 1960–65 and that of public investment much smaller, or about 13 per cent. In the subsequent three-year period both rates of investment declined, averaging 7 per cent and 9 per cent, respectively. In 1965–68, opposite trends appeared: private investment rising sharply in 1968 and public investment declining

TABLE 2. IVORY COAST: SUPPLY AND USE OF RESOURCES, 1960-68

	1960	1961	1962	1963	1964	1965	1966	1967	1968
	VALUE (billion CFA francs)								
Consumption									
Private [1]	107.8	124.3	134.9	146.8	171.2	180.0	188.7	207.2	231.0
Public	5.7	7.4	6.3	7.3	8.0	8.9	10.6	11.5	14.1
Total consumption	113.5	131.7	141.2	154.0	179.2	188.9	199.3	218.7	245.1
Gross investment									
Private	12.0	13.9	16.9	20.8	29.1	31.9	31.3	30.6	38.9
Public	7.1	10.4	8.3	7.6	10.1	11.7	13.3	15.3	15.1
Total gross investment	19.1	24.3	25.2	28.4	39.2	43.6	44.6	45.9	54.0
Change in stocks	1.3	3.1	-3.7	3.8	5.7	1.3	5.5	1.6	3.0
Exports of goods and services	45.5	53.1	53.8	63.4	81.4	73.5	81.7	87.2	115.3
Less imports of goods and services	-36.8	-50.8	-48.2	-51.8	-65.8	-67.7	-73.1	-77.7	-89.4
Net GDP	142.6	161.4	168.4	197.8	239.7	239.6	258.0	275.7	326.5
	PER CENT OF GDP								
Consumption									
Private [1]	75.6	77.0	80.1	74.2	71.4	75.1	73.1	75.1	70.1
Public	4.0	4.6	3.7	3.7	3.3	3.7	4.1	4.2	4.3
Total consumption	79.6	81.6	83.8	77.9	74.7	78.8	77.2	79.3	74.4
Investment									
Private	8.4	8.6	10.0	10.5	12.1	13.3	12.1	11.0	11.9
Public	5.0	6.4	4.9	3.8	4.2	4.9	5.2	5.6	4.6
Total investment	13.4	15.1	15.0	14.3	16.3	18.2	17.3	16.6	16.5
Change in stocks	0.9	1.9	-2.2	1.9	2.4	0.2	0.2	0.6	0.8
Exports of goods and services	31.9	32.9	31.9	32.1	34.0	30.7	31.7	31.6	35.3
Less imports of goods and services	-25.8	-31.5	-28.6	-26.2	-27.5	-28.2	-28.3	-28.1	-27.4
Net GDP	100.0	100.0	100.0	100.0	100.0	100.0	100.0	100.0	100.0

Sources: Ministère du Plan, *Les Comptes de la Nation—Principaux Résultats, 1960–65, Les Comptes de la Nation, 1966–67*, and *Les Comptes de la Nation, 1968*.

[1] Includes consumption by domestic and foreign government agencies, private nonprofit institutions, and households (on the basis of the value added) of this sector.

sharply. After a rise in both private and public consumption at about the same pace until 1965, public consumption speeded up during 1965–68 to an average annual growth rate of 17 per cent, in contrast to 9 per cent for private consumption. For both public and private consumption, the highest increases occurred in 1968.

Production by Sectors

All sectors of Ivory Coast economy have contributed to its economic expansion since 1960, but the growth rate has been considerably greater in the secondary sector of the economy than in the other sectors, reflecting the rapid expansion of manufacturing, energy, and construction (Table 3). During 1960–65 the annual average increase of production was about 7 per cent in the primary sector, about 15 per cent in the secondary sector, and about 12 per cent in the services sector. As a result, the share of the primary sector in total GDP fell from some 43 per cent in 1960 to some 35 per cent in 1965, while that of the secondary sector rose from 14 per cent to 17 per cent and that of services from 43 per cent to 48 per cent.

Since 1965, annual increases in production have averaged about 6 per cent for the primary sector, 16 per cent for the secondary sector, and 15 per cent for the tertiary sector. The primary sector's share of total GDP for 1968 declined slightly (from some 35 per cent to 31 per cent), against a rise in the secondary sector (from 17 per cent to about 19 per cent) and in services (from 48 per cent to 50 per cent). These shares of total GDP indicate some stabilization in relative importance since they are about the same as in the previous year.

AGRICULTURE, FISHING, AND FORESTRY

In spite of the rapid development of industry and construction, more than 80 per cent of the population of working age of 2.1 million is engaged in the primary sector of the economy, which is also responsible for some 85 per cent of the value of total exports. Subsistence agriculture, livestock, and fishing make up about half of the output of the sector, with cash crops and forestry providing the other half.

Although the increase in production of food crops, meat, and fish has continuously been insufficient to meet a growing demand, imports of foodstuffs, beverages, and tobacco, which had increased from about

TABLE 3. IVORY COAST: GROSS DOMESTIC PRODUCT BY ORIGIN, 1960–68

(In billions of CFA francs)

	1960	1961	1962	1963	1964	1965	1966	1967	1968
Domestic production									
Primary sector									
Subsistence agriculture and livestock	31.6	30.9	34.9	37.0	38.9	42.3	41.5	43.7	44.8
Cash crops	24.8	25.5	18.5	28.4	36.3	31.3	35.6	29.6	40.1
Forestry	3.6	4.6	5.5	7.4	10.4	8.9	9.0	11.5	13.9
Fishing	1.2	1.3	1.3	1.6	1.7	1.9	1.9	1.9	1.9
Total primary sector	61.0	62.3	60.2	74.4	87.2	84.4	88.1	86.8	100.7
Secondary sector									
Manufacturing	11.0	14.0	15.5	17.8	21.5	22.9	24.7	27.5	31.6
Energy and water	2.1	2.7	2.9	3.3	3.5	4.9	10.6	11.3	14.0
Construction	6.8	8.0	9.0	9.1	11.0	12.8	13.9	14.4	16.8
Total secondary sector	19.9	24.7	27.4	30.2	36.0	40.6	49.1	53.2	62.4
Tertiary sector									
Transport	9.9	12.2	12.9	14.3	17.9	19.4	20.3	22.0	24.5
Commerce	33.4	40.0	42.0	50.2	63.5	55.6	58.6	67.7	87.5
Housing and other services	6.3	7.9	8.5	9.9	12.3	14.0	16.6	17.6	21.0
Total tertiary sector	49.6	60.1	63.4	74.4	93.6	89.0	95.5	107.3	133.0
Total domestic production	130.5	147.2	151.1	179.0	216.8	214.0	232.7	247.3	296.1
Financial intermediaries, government agencies, and households [1]	12.1	14.2	17.3	18.8	22.9	25.6	25.3	28.4	30.4
Gross domestic product	142.6	161.4	168.4	197.8	239.7	239.6	258.0	275.7	326.5

Sources: Ministère du Plan, *Les Comptes de la Nation—Principaux Résultats, 1960–65, Les Comptes de la Nation, 1966–67,* and *Les Comptes de la Nation, 1968.*

[1] Value added by this sector, based on salary payments, is not considered part of production by the national accounting system used in Ivory Coast.

CFAF 5 billion in 1960 to CFAF 13 billion in 1966, declined to CFAF 11.8 billion in 1968.

Crops Mainly for Food

Basic food crops include cereals (mainly rice, maize, and millet), plantains, and root crops (such as yams, cassava, and taro).

There has been an annual increase in production of food crops averaging almost 3 per cent between 1960 and 1968 (Table 4). To the extent that estimates of food crops may approach reality, there has not been much progress in this sector. Farmers generally plant only enough for their own requirements, allowing a small margin for emergencies in the form of cassava; this root crop can remain in the ground for several years and be harvested in case other crops fail. In the south, many farmers rely on coffee or cocoa for money income, since these require less work than food crops. Most of the land available for expanding the output of food is in the northern and central regions, where, however, the population is sparse and many young persons migrate to the more prosperous south. Lack of outlets for agricultural surpluses in the north also discourages expansion of the cultivated area. It is estimated that only about 10 per cent of food produced (excluding rice) is marketed;

TABLE 4. IVORY COAST: ESTIMATED FOOD CROP PRODUCTION, 1960–68

(*In thousands of metric tons*)

	1960	1961	1962	1963	1964	1965	1966	1967	1968
Cereals									
Rice									
(paddy) [1]	160	156	230	220	248	250	275	347	365
Maize	147	99	170	168	176	200	215	223	206
Millet	42	27	36	34	34	35	36	37	35
Sorghum	10	8	11	10	10	11	11	11	12
Fonio	5	4	5	9	8	7	7	7	7
Other food crops									
Yams	1,150	1,050	1,200	1,230	1,260	1,300	1,320	1,350	1,388
Plantains	490	500	570	550	580	600	615	620	625
Cassava	450	460	500	470	490	500	515	520	530
Taros	135	120	150	152	156	160	160	162	160
Sweet									
potatoes	18	17	18	19	20	20	20	21	21
Groundnuts	24	20	29	31	29	28	30	30	32

Source: Data supplied by the Ivory Coast Ministry of Agriculture.
[1] Hulled rice is equivalent to about 65 per cent of paddy.

the result has been seasonal shortages in urban areas, which have caused wide fluctuations in prices.

According to initial estimates for the new plan 1971–75, requirements for locally produced foodstuffs will grow rapidly, taking into account both the growth of the population and its changing distribution between cities and country. Among the implications of growing requirements, two are of particular importance: first, the extra amount of food needed will have to be produced by a smaller and more productive rural population, and second, the food once produced will have to be distributed properly which so far has not been the case (most of the crops are highly perishable and there is no adequate system of collection and storage). It may be difficult to raise labor productivity through an improved technology in so traditional an activity as agriculture by a sufficient margin and at a rapid enough pace. The Government might also consider measures which would increase earnings of the farmers and direct population movements toward the most productive areas.

Among food crops, rice requires special attention since its production has been greatly increased in recent years. The production of paddy more than doubled between 1960 and 1968 (from 160,000 tons [1] to 365,000 tons), particularly in 1966–68, when the increase was 25 per cent. However, production during 1960–68 did not keep pace with increasing domestic requirements, and rice imports with some fluctuations averaged 50,000 tons between 1960 and 1968. In 1969, production dropped from 365,000 tons to 320,000 tons as a result of a particularly dry season. For that reason and also because of an increase in domestic demand, rice imports which had declined since 1966, rose again to 56,000 tons. The Government's present production target is 550,000 tons by 1975, at which time production should cover demand. Over-all implementation of the rice program in the last five years has been in the hands of a government agency, the Agricultural Modernization Agency (Société pour la Modernisation Agricole de la Côte d'Ivoire, or SATMACI), created to set up infrastructure, train farmers, provide seed and fertilizer, and to arrange for collection, processing, and marketing. The Agency operates four rice mills with a capacity of 70,000 tons, at present, however, underutilized.

---

[1] The word "ton" refers to a metric ton of 2,204.6 pounds.

Ivory Coast produces rice under three cultural methods: upland rice, which represents 90 per cent of the cultivated area; irrigated rice; and flood rice. Present efforts emphasize extension of the irrigated rice area. One problem will be financing the rice extension services, which are extremely costly.

Although yields per hectare have increased considerably in recent years, the cost of locally produced rice remains higher than that of imported rice. However, the retail price of both domestic and imported rice has been fixed at CFAF 55 per kilogram, with the profits resulting from the sale of imported rice being used by the Caisse de Péréquation du Riz (which acts as a price stabilization fund) to subsidize local production.

Crops Mainly for Export

Coffee and cocoa have traditionally been Ivory Coast's principal export crops. In 1967, they accounted for over half the value of merchandise exports and, combined with timber and bananas, for 80 per cent. These products provide money income for a large part of the active population, and rapid expansion in production of these products in 1960–64 was one important factor in the country's development of those years. More recently, this expansion has generally slowed down, owing mainly to conditions in world markets. Despite developments in production of palm oil, pineapple, and other products (see below), traditional exports will continue to play an important role in Ivory Coast economy for the next few years.

Coffee and cocoa.—Production of coffee and cocoa involves at least one half of Ivory Coast's active population, and provides seasonal employment for an additional 275,000 farmhands, mainly foreign laborers. According to an official study of the coffee industry, the area under coffee trees would be over 600,000 hectares. Cocoa trees take up an estimated 560,000 hectares.

Both coffee and cocoa are grown mainly on small family-type holdings, most growers producing both crops. Output has fluctuated widely according to the weather; prolonged drought in 1966 affected the cocoa crop of 1965/66 and the coffee crop of 1966/67. In 1967/68 the coffee crop reached a peak as a result of extremely favorable weather, but dropped in 1968/69 while the 1969/70 crop was forecast at a high level

(Table 5). Cocoa production increased in 1966/67 and remained at the same level through 1968/69; in 1969/70, however, there was a much larger crop as new plantings came into bearing. All cocoa harvested in recent years has been exported. Coffee production, on the other hand, has exceeded exports, and stocks have accumulated.

TABLE 5. IVORY COAST: PRINCIPAL EXPORT CROPS—COMMERCIAL PRODUCTION AND EXPORTS, 1964–70

(In thousands of metric tons)

	1964	1965	1966	1967	1968	1969	1970 (Fore-cast)
Coffee [1]							
Production	261	202	272	131	288	210	265
Exports	258	172	177	165	198	177	...
To countries outside Agreement	55	40	40	15	25	8	...
Cocoa beans [1]							
Production	116	148	113	150	147	144	170
Exports	120	126	124	148	145	140	145 [2]
Bananas							
Production	164	153	163	173	195	180–190	...
Exports [3]	102	117	119	152	36	135	...
Kolanuts (exports)	17	23	28	26	25	...	...
Pineapple products (exports)							
Fresh fruit	4	5	7	10	14	14	...
Canned fruit	11	13	19	24	23	...	...
Canned juice	7	8	8	8	9	...	...

Sources: BCEAO, *Conjoncture Ouest Africaine, Côte d'Ivoire,* and data provided by the Ivory Coast authorities.

[1] Crop year ended September 30.
[2] A processing factory in Abidjan will absorb the remainder of production.
[3] Net weight of hands packed in cartons; crop year ending August 31.

Under the first International Coffee Agreement (ICA) covering the period 1962–68, Ivory Coast's share of world coffee exports was 5.0 per cent, and this share was raised to 5.6 per cent under the new agreement for the period 1968–73.

On October 1, 1967, Ivory Coast had accumulated coffee stocks of 113,000 tons. In 1967/68 and 1968/69, when stocks continued to pile up, the authorities ordered the destruction of as much as 140,000 tons, most of which had lost part of its value because of inadequate storage facilities. At the end of December 1969, stocks were estimated at 85,000 tons, one half stored by the producers and the rest by the exporters.

As a result of recent ICA decisions, coffee-producing countries are now required to follow certain levels of production and stocks. Accordingly, Ivory Coast production should be limited to about 212,000 tons in 1972/73 and stocks should not exceed 140,000 tons. Since world coffee consumption increases by about 2.2 per cent annually, Ivory Coast's quota will be raised proportionately.

In keeping with the production targets established under the ICA diversification program, the Ivory Coast authorities intend to maintain production at about its present average annual level of some 250,000 tons through 1972/73. In implementation of this objective, the Government intends to reduce the area under cultivation and to concentrate initially on rehabilitation of some existing plantations. After 1971 it envisages bringing 20,000 hectares a year of new land into cultivation, using high-yield varieties. The Government is also considering a major reform of processing and marketing of coffee production, including the improvement of storage facilities, particularly in the interior. In an initial report issued by the Ministry of Agriculture, it is also recommended that decortication and sorting of the berries should be improved in order not only to meet required quality standards but also to meet keen competition from Brazil on the world market.

The Agricultural Modernization Agency has conducted a cocoa program since 1962, with a production target of 300,000 tons by 1980, largely by replacing and reviving old plantations. The cocoa program, well under way, includes technical assistance by the Agency, regeneration of 38,000 hectares by 1972, and the planting of 60,000 hectares by 1975 with selected planting material under intensive cultivation. IBRD approved in May 1970 a project which would include the financing of the Agency's technical assistance, as well as the planting of 19,000 hectares and the rehabilitation of about 38,000 hectares of young cocoa plantations.

To stabilize producers' incomes, the Government has established the Stabilization Fund (Caisse de Stabilisation et de Soutien des Prix des Productions Agricoles). At present, the Stabilization Fund has authority over marketing arrangements for coffee, cocoa, and cotton; it also plays a role in the regeneration of coffee and cocoa plantations and in other methods of modernizing agriculture.

Producer prices for coffee and cocoa are fixed at the beginning of each crop year in the light of the expected harvest and of world market conditions. Since 1963, producer prices have been uniform throughout the country, the Stabilization Fund financing extra transport costs from the interior. For coffee, producer prices are based on beans at an intermediate stage of processing (hulled and partly cleaned), and for cocoa on fermented beans. In view of the large harvest expected in 1965/66, producer prices were reduced at the beginning of that crop year from CFAF 90 to CFAF 75 per kilogram for coffee and from CFAF 70 to CFAF 55 per kilogram for cocoa. For the crop year 1966/67, producer prices were raised again to their former levels, since that year's harvest was expected to be a poor one, and remained unchanged until 1969/70, when they were raised to CFAF 95 for coffee and CFAF 80 for cocoa. Exporters may purchase coffee and cocoa only at the producer price. However, the Government does not guarantee purchase of the entire harvested crop.

Coffee and cocoa are subject to an export tax, which was first raised in the crop year 1966/67 from CFAF 22.38 per kilogram to CFAF 25.74 per kilogram, then raised again in 1969/70, the increase for cocoa being much larger. The Stabilization Fund benefits from the difference between the price paid to producers (plus the export tax and most of the cost of domestic transport) and the actual export price received. It also receives a rebate on coffee and cocoa export taxes; this rebate was raised from CFAF 3.75 to CFAF 4.325 per kilogram beginning with the 1966/67 crop year but was discontinued with effect from January 1, 1969.

In the crop year 1965/66, the Stabilization Fund sustained a loss of about CFAF 2.3 billion, largely as a result of the sharp decline in world cocoa prices in 1965 (Table 6). In 1966/67, the world cocoa price nearly doubled and the coffee price rose by about 20 per cent. As a result, the Stabilization Fund profited from both crops, making a total net operating gain of more than CFAF 3.1 billion. In 1968/69, there was a negative balance on price stabilization for coffee from the cost of coffee destruction, amounting to CFAF 1.9 billion and entirely chargeable to accounts for that crop year. However, over-all operations of the Fund were again in surplus as a result of a 20 per cent increase in cocoa export prices. Preliminary results for 1969/70 indicated that the operations of the Fund would again be largely beneficiary.

TABLE 6. IVORY COAST: STABILIZATION FUND OPERATIONS,
CROP YEARS 1965/66–1968/69

	1965/66	1966/67	1967/68	1968/69 [1]
UNIT VALUE (*CFA francs per kilogram*)				
Coffee				
Export price f.o.b.	135.69	163.01	155.37	151.23
Export cost f.o.b.	116.23	134.70	134.39	134.11
Net profit	19.46	28.31	20.98	17.12
Cocoa				
Export price f.o.b.	62.07	113.78	144.76	180.89
Export cost f.o.b.	92.96	110.84	111.53	111.64
Net profit, or loss (−)	−30.89	2.94	33.21	69.25
TOTAL VALUE (*million CFA francs*)				
Total exports				
Coffee	24,068	26,916	. . .	. . .
Cocoa	7,002	16,853	. . .	. . .
Financial results				
Balance on price stabilization				
Coffee [2]	2,602	4,335	1,593	−649
Cocoa [2]	−3,462	493	4,878	9,773
Cotton	−72	−5	27	32
Net balance on price stabilization	−932	4,823	6,498	9,155
Administrative costs net of income from invested funds	−209	−442	−409	−596
Transport and other subsidy payments	−1,167	−1,255	−1,076	−1,099
Net operating profit, or loss (−)	−2,309	3,126	5,013	7,460
Contribution to the investment budget	−1,300	−3,000	−2,000	−1,570
Net income, or outgo (−)	−3,609	126	3,013	5,890

Source: Data supplied by the Ivory Coast authorities.

[1] Provisional.

[2] Net of the export tax of CFAF 22.830 per kilogram in 1965/66 and CFAF 25.740 in 1966/67, less CFAF 3.75 per kilogram in 1965/66 and CFAF 4.3225 per kilogram in 1966/67 returned to the Stabilization Fund. This rebate to the Stabilization Fund, however, was discontinued as of January 1, 1969.

A provisional budget for the Stabilization Fund is established at the beginning of each crop year on the basis of expected receipts, expenditures for subsidies and other costs, contributions to international organizations, and stabilization requirements. Beginning in 1967 the Stabilization Fund has been required to place in reserve 60 per cent of its current profits and to transfer the remaining 40 per cent to the Government. With current profits growing at a rapid pace, it was agreed that for the fiscal year 1970 the Stabilization Fund would allocate to the investment budget CFAF 8–10 billion. The Stabilization Fund has also continuously provided direct financial assistance to extension services for coffee and cocoa, as well as sprayers and fertilizers; these operations totaled about CFAF 5 billion during 1962–70.

Bananas.—Ranking fourth among Ivory Coast's exports by value (after coffee, timber, and cocoa), bananas are grown mainly on a few hundred, medium-sized plantations, some owned by Europeans. The industry provides employment for about 10,000 persons. After rapid expansion between 1960 and 1964, when output doubled to 164,000 tons, it leveled off in 1965–67. In 1968, output reached 195,000 tons and declined slightly in the following year (see Table 5). More land suitable for bananas is available for planting, but further expansion of production depends largely on export possibilities. Although the quality of the exported fruit has been improved in recent years, Ivory Coast's bananas are still not competitive on the world market. Most of the exports go to France under preferential treatment. A government program now under way aims at rendering Ivory Coast's bananas fully competitive both in terms of price and quality. In spite of the difficulty of breaking into new markets in a commerce governed by long-established connections, restrictions, and keen competition, some 44,000 tons of bananas were sold to Italy in 1967/68, or about 37 per cent of total exports for that crop year and 11,000 tons to Algeria.

Production for export is strictly regulated by the Ministry of Agriculture, working with the producers' trade cooperative COFRUCI. Permits for new planting are subject to conformity with specified cultivation standards; plantations must be within a maximum distance of 200 kilometers from the port, and must give a minimum yield of high-quality fruit. The National Packing Agency (Société Nationale de Conditionnement, or SONACO) was created in 1965 to improve methods of preparing the fruit for export. By the end of 1969, the Agency had established 19 packing centers in the fruit area and a factory to produce cartons for packing. The fruit, which was previously shipped on stems in plastic bags, is now cut into hands, chilled, and packed in cartons which are transported by refrigerated trucks to the new banana port at Abidjan. This port has a modern chilling and conveyer system for rapid loading, and freight charges are expected to decline. A new organization, SODEFEL, has recently been set up to assist in training producers in modern techniques. Improved methods of cultivation, involving irrigation of plantations, are expected to result in better timing of production and less waste. In the past, output has been too heavy in certain seasons, and quotas had to be placed on deliveries. More regular supplies of fruit, will allow more efficient utilization of packing and shipping facilities and economies in cost. The Stabilization Fund is not involved in price support for bananas, but it promotes banana sales in Europe through its organization. Experiments are also under way to find profitable methods of processing bananas into products such as flour, chips, and oil and to use the skins for manufacturing fertilizer.

Kolanuts and other export products.—Kolanuts are a source of money income for farmers in the forest regions, where they are picked from wild trees. Part of the harvest is consumed domestically; the rest is exported. In recent years, recorded exports have amounted to about CFAF 1 billion annually. These exports, however, are believed to represent less than half of total exports, since substantial amounts are known to be exported without control. Other agricultural exports include palm oil, pineapple products, and rubber, which are being developed under the agricultural diversification program.

Agricultural Diversification

The Development Plan, 1960–70 considered agricultural diversification as an essential requirement for raising standards of living and lessening the country's dependence on traditional exports. It called for public investment in agriculture totaling CFAF 38 billion for the 10-year period. Diversification effort was to be concentrated on a few major products: oil palms, to provide new export products in future years; rice, to improve nutrition and eliminate costly imports; cotton and rubber, to supply domestic industries and for export; pineapples, for both local consumption and export; and sugar, to satisfy domestic requirements. During 1960–66, public investment in agriculture remained considerably below the original plan estimates, totaling CFAF 11.1 billion over the period. However, certain sections of the diversification program were implemented with considerable success. The oil palm program, in particular, has proceeded well according to schedule, and production targets for future years have actually been raised. Production of rice, cotton, and pineapples has also reached expected levels, but the sugar program has barely started. Investment has thus far been concentrated in certain areas, especially of the south. In the coming years, efforts will be made to modernize agriculture in the northern and central regions. It is hoped to stem the migration of labor from these less favored regions by increasing local cash revenues and thus hastening development.

To carry out the diversification program, a number of government organizations have been set up, each charged with responsibility for one or more products. As explained earlier, the Agricultural Modernization Agency (SATMACI) is in charge of the rice program; the Société pour le Développement et l'Exploitation du Palmier à Huile (SODEPALM) of the oil palm and coconut programs; and SODEFRUIT of the pineapple and other fruit programs. These concerns are responsible for tasks which range from deforestation, initial preparation of land, building dams, and irrigation facilities to training farmers and supervisors and providing cultivation needs such as improved seeds and plants, fertilizers, and insecticides.

In 1966 a new organization, MOTORAGRI, was created for the purpose of expanding mechanization in agriculture. Provided with an initial capital of CFAF 1 billion from the Stabilization Fund, MOTORAGRI has acquired equipment and has hired technical advisors. It now operates stations in various part of the country for leasing farm machinery to small landholders. MOTORAGRI is expected to pay its way, charging state organizations, such as the Agricultural Modernization Agency and SODEPALM, for its services.

Oil palms.—The oil palm project, launched in 1962, is by far the largest under the agricultural diversification program, having received by the end of 1967 about 40 per cent of total public investment in agriculture. By the end of 1966 the area planted with new high-yielding trees had reached 28,500 hectares and as much as 59,700 hectares by the end of 1968 (Table 7). Newly planted oil palms begin to produce in 4 years, reach a maximum production in about 8 years, and continue to bear fruit up to 25 years. Production from the new plantations reached some 22,000 tons of oil and 6,000 tons of palm kernels by 1969. Exports of palm oil and kernels started in 1968 with 500 tons of oil and 10,000 tons of kernels. Eight oil-processing plants are to be installed by 1973; three were already in operation at the beginning of 1970.

TABLE 7. IVORY COAST: AREA, PRODUCTION, AND EXPORTS OF PRODUCTS
UNDER THE AGRICULTURAL DIVERSIFICATION PROGRAM, 1965–69

	1965	1966	1967	1968	1969
CUMULATIVE AREA, NEW PLANTED (*thousand hectares*) [1]					
Oil palms					
Planted	21.0	28.0	37.0	51.2	...
Realized	19.1	28.5	39.5	51.0	59.7
Cotton (Allen) [2]	6.4	11.8	13.8	39.0	48.0
Rubber	11.0	11.6	12.2	13.0	12.6
Coconut palms	10.0	10.0	10.5	12.4	...
QUANTITY (*thousand metric tons*)					
Oil palms					
Oil production	9.8	10.6	13.4	14.8	21.6
Kernel production	4.3	3.2	4.0	4.8	6.3
Cotton					
Production, seed (unginned)	5.5	9.1	22.0	32.2	41.7
Exports (ginned)	—	1.7	8.5	11.3	...
Rubber					
Production (latex)	3.5	5.6	5.9	7.0	8.6
Exports	2.8	5.5	5.8	7.0	8.6

Source: Data supplied by the Ivory Coast authorities.

[1] Cumulative.

[2] Crop year ending September 30.

New plantations fall into two categories, the industrial plantations and the village plantations for which SODEPALM carries the entire responsibility to establish groves and to provide plants, fertilizers, and technical supervision. An oil mill is to be established at the site of each industrial plantation, which acts as training and guidance for small village cooperatives and individual farms in the 20 kilometers surrounding the mill. For the two years 1968–69, over 20,000 hectares of selected oil palms were planted, more than 60 per cent on industrial plantations. The size of the planned industrial plantations has been somewhat reduced in order to meet the demand for an additional 3,000 hectares annually of small private groves. SODEPALM has been spending an average of over CFAF 100,000 per hectare to establish groves and provide various services. Farmers are to reimburse one half this cost after the trees start to bear; repayments will go into a Special Fund for Extension and Renewal of Plantations.

To help finance the oil palm program, which is estimated to cost some CFAF 25 billion (including CFAF 8 billion for oil mills), Ivory Coast is receiving various financial assistance. The investment budget and the Amortization Fund (Caisse Autonome d'Amortissement, or

CAA) have participated for an amount of CFAF 3.6 billion; the balance is to come from external aid. As of the end of 1969, CFAF 12 billion had been financed by the European Economic Community (EEC), mostly European Development Fund (EDF) grants. In 1969, IBRD agreed to participate in the financing for $13 million under a project to be carried out by SODEPALM and two other newly created and state-controlled institutions, PALMIVOIRE and PALMINDUSTRIE. The French CCCE and FAC have also contributed a little over $10 million.

Cotton.—Cotton production has progressed rapidly in recent years. Starting in 1963, research was placed under the French Institut de Recherches du Coton et des Textiles Exotiques (IRCT), marketing under the Stabilization Fund, and all other aspects of the program under the Compagnie Française pour le Développement des Fibres Textiles (CFDT). Some Mono cotton has always been grown in the north, and this production is expected to be reduced and to disappear by 1975. The new program involves the high-grade Allen variety of cotton, which has a longer fiber and yields up to a metric ton per hectare, or about ten times as much as the traditional culture. Ginning yields, now about 39.5 per cent, are planned to increase to as much as 42.5 per cent in the future. The area under cultivation has expanded at a spectacular rate; between 1966 and 1969, 36,200 hectares of Allen type cotton were newly planted and production of cotton doubled. Most of the cotton is grown in the northern and central savanna regions, in small family plantations, averaging about half a hectare, capable of being cared for without outside help. Only one crop a year is possible in the north, but in the central regions, where there are two rainy seasons, cotton can be grown in rotation with corn and peanuts each year.

It is believed that in the future the domestic textile industry will absorb all of the expected annual output of seed cotton. Thus far, the textile industry has expanded less rapidly than cotton production; some 8,500 tons of cotton were exported in 1967 and 11,000 tons in 1968.

Regardless of quality, the produced price had been fixed in 1964/65 at CFAF 33.50 per kilogram for seed (unginned) cotton delivered by farmers to established collection centers. For the crop year 1969/70, two prices were set, CFAF 35 per kilogram for first-quality grade and CFAF 30 for second-quality grade.

After the Stabilization Fund had suffered a CFAF 5 million loss on cotton operations in 1966/67, it was able to balance its account with even a small surplus in the two following crop years. The cotton program calls for an investment of nearly CFAF 2.0 billion, excluding expenditures required for the expansion of ginning facilities. The Ivory Coast investment budget and the French FAC have both contributed to the financing.

Other products.—(1) Pineapples do well on the relatively poor soil of the southern regions, and the area under production has expanded rapidly. Under the general supervision of the French Institut Français de Recherches Fruitières Outre-Mer (IFAC), which conducts research and advises growers, fruit of excellent quality is produced. This assistance has enabled Ivory Coast to meet the stiff competition in Europe from fruit of lower quality and lower prices originating in Guinea and the Caribbean Islands. Two commercial canning firms operate large plantations of their own and assist private growers established in the areas around their factories. In 1963 commercial plantations produced about 11,000 tons of fruit, and farm plantations another 8,000 tons. By 1967, commercial plantations were providing only about 30 per cent of the total output of 75,000 tons; about 10,000 tons were exported as fresh fruit and 32,000 tons as canned fruit and juice, mostly to France, Germany, and Italy. In 1968 and 1969, fresh fruit exports increased substantially (see Table 5). Producer prices are fixed by the canning companies at time of planting, i.e., two years before the harvest. No subsidies are involved in marketing operations. The two commercial firms, considering good prospects for exports of canned fruit, have decided on new investments to raise their almost fully used canning capacity to about 120,000 tons in 1971. Furthermore, a new factory with German capital is now under construction.

(2) Rubber tree planting began in earnest in 1963 and by the end of 1967 covered an area of about 12,000 hectares. Most of the new plantations belong to two large companies; in one, the Government has a 50 per cent participation. These companies operate their own processing facilities. Output of latex reached 5,900 tons in 1967 and 8,600 tons in 1969. Future development will depend on two projects now under consideration by commercial firms, Goodyear and Michelin. Such projects would call for plantations of about 20,000 hectares and pro-

cessing factories. At present, latex production, which increased by 35 per cent between 1966 and 1969, is almost totally exported. Competition from synthetic rubber is not too serious a danger since the latex produced in Ivory Coast is of excellent quality. World prices, which fell in 1969, are, however, a matter of concern.

(3) Until recently coconut palm exploitation has been mainly a family industry; the farmers gather fruit from small plantations and wild groves, prepare copra in home furnaces, use part of the product at home for oil, and sell the rest to local mills for making soap and margarine. In 1965, such plantations covered about 10,000 hectares. Research carried on by the Institut Recherches pour les Huiles et Oléagineux has shown that by improving cultivation and applying fertilizers, the output from these plantations can be raised from 800 kilograms to 2,000 kilograms of copra per hectare annually. Since 1967, SODEPALM has been engaged in establishing commercial coconut plantations, using high-yielding varieties, along the lines of those described for the oil palm scheme.

At the end of 1968, total cumulative plantings had reached 12,400 hectares, and by 1971 it is expected to add 15,000 hectares of new industrial and village plantations. Copra production, estimated at 6,800 tons in 1967, was expected to rise to 9,000 tons by 1970. Financing of the program, estimated at CFAF 4 billion by 1972, is secured by the investment budget, the IBRD, and the French CCCE. SODEPALM is preparing for 1971 a further project for planting 10,000 hectares in coconut palms with hybrid seeds; the financing for this project, however, has not yet been secured.

(4) Experimental sugarcane groves have been set out as the beginning of a project to make the country self-sufficient in sugar, but progress thus far has been slow. (5) High-quality, grafted mangoes are entering into production in the north, but the fruit is fragile and difficult to transport. Research has been undertaken to devise techniques of using the fruit for jams, preserves, and soft drinks and in dried form. Other studies are being conducted on oranges, mandarins, and pomelos. (6) For some years avocados have been the subject of research, and in 1967 a joint private-state organization, the Société d'Etudes pour la Production de l'Avocat en Côte d'Ivoire (SOPRODAV) was set up to supply technical advice to growers. A plantation and a pilot plant to

extract oil are also being established. (7) Tobacco is produced in the central regions for the local cigarette industry, but it is of relatively poor quality; production is still insufficient to satisfy domestic require-ments. (8) Planting of cashew trees is also being considered to supple-ment local diets, to provide nuts for export, and to supply valuable wood.

Livestock and Livestock Products

Livestock raising continues to be relatively unimportant in Ivory Coast, although rising standards of living have been expanding demand for meat by about 5 or 6 per cent annually. Except for pork and chicken, which are produced domestically in sufficient quantity, Ivory Coast depends substantially on imports to satisfy domestic meat requirements. In 1966, meat consumption was estimated at some 65,000 tons, of which more than 50,000 tons, valued at some CFAF 6 billion, were supplied by imports. Only about one sixth of the beef and one half of the mutton and goat meat consumed in Ivory Coast now comes from the national herd; the rest is imported.

Some fresh and frozen meat is imported from other African countries and from Europe, but most imports are in the form of live animals from neighboring countries, not recorded in the customs statistics. Slaughterhouse facilities in Ivory Coast are inadequate, and new ones are planned to meet enlarged demand. There are a number of projects intended to improve the size and quality of domestic herds, train farm-ers in modern cattle-raising methods, and provide better control of dis-ease, which seems to be one of the chief obstacles to livestock develop-ment.

Fishing

Although fishing still accounts for less than 1 per cent of GDP, the prospects are that it will grow in importance in the coming years. At present about 60,000 people earn at least part of their livelihood from the industry, and fish is a valuable source of food, easily merchandized in smoked or dried form and costing only about one fifth as much as meat. Compared with about 50,000 tons in 1960, output in the past few years has averaged about 65,000 tons. The present target is an annual output of 130,000 tons by 1975. This level of production would permit an increase of one third in annual per capita consumption, now about 18–19 kilograms, and would eliminate the need of importing smoked fish from neighboring countries.

Despite the Government's training school for fishermen, mechanics, and boat operators, fishing has never been a popular occupation in Ivory Coast; about 80 per cent of workers in the industry are foreign nationals. A considerable expansion of the fleet is planned, both small craft for coastal and lagoon waters and larger boats for deep-water ocean fishing. In addition, the fishing port at Abidjan is to be improved; berthing capacity and storage and freezing facilities are to be enlarged. Systems of distributing and storing fish in the interior of the country also are to be provided, and existing commercial establishments are to be improved.

Deep-sea tuna fishing offers prospects for rapid development. Now that limitations are imposed on tuna fishing in the Pacific Ocean, more foreign ships come to the Gulf of Guinea in the tuna season and make Abidjan their home port. Part of their catch is placed in cold storage in port to await the arrival of refrigerated ships, and part is transferred from trawlers to cargo ships, using Abidjan docking equipment. Prospects for increased output of fresh-water fish are also good. In 1969, an Ivory Coast company started exploring the shrimp resources with some success. An experimental plant was opened for using sardines and other small readily available species to produce nuoc-mam sauce, a dietary supplement of high nutritional value, which is much appreciated for flavoring rice and beans.

Forestry

Forestry has developed rapidly in recent years. In 1967 and 1968, timber accounted for about 25 per cent of total exports, second in importance only to coffee. In 1969, however, exports of timber rose to CFAF 35.1 billion and exceeded for the first time the value of coffee exports. However, the current rate of exploitation would exhaust the most valuable species in about 15 years. Some 3.5 million cubic meters of trees were felled in 1968, compared with about 1 million cubic meters in 1960 (Table 8). A major recent development has been the expansion of sawmills and wood processing; as a result, exports in the form of logs declined from some 82 per cent of total exports in 1960 to 67 per cent in 1968.

TABLE 8. IVORY COAST: FORESTRY PRODUCTION
AND EXPORTS, 1960 AND 1965–68

	Felling	Exports		Total value
		Logs	Timber	
	Thousand cubic meters →			*Billion CFA francs*
1960	1,003	823	—	...
1965	2,538	1,905	153	...
1966	2,608	1,822	182	...
1967	3,022	2,173	183	21.8
1968	3,470	2,620	188	25.8

Source: Data provided by the Ivory Coast authorities.

In the past, less than 10 per cent of the forest species were commercialized, exports being practically limited to the more valuable red woods—sipo, mahogany, aboudikrou, and avodiré. As these species have become more scarce and expensive, certain other types have been exported. Changes in taste have also created demand for more light-colored woods, such as the samba, and two new types, lengué and aningueri, which are now being exported. Nevertheless, demand remains concentrated on a narrow range of species and on first-grade logs, limiting the profitability of forest exploitation.

Large, integrated, foreign-owned companies still account for about 70 per cent of total production. In addition, some 80 small companies, about 60 owned by Ivorians, are operating, but most of them lack the organization and financing necessary to compete successfully on export markets. Since foreign-owned companies usually have mills in Europe that are more efficient and operate at lower cost than African mills, the companies prefer to ship wood in the form of logs. However, the Government is encouraging the further expansion of domestic processing. Not only does the export of processed wood earn about two and a half times as much foreign exchange per cubic meter of trees felled, but processing provides employment and training of workers in technical skills. Recently the Government made the granting of forest licenses contingent upon the local processing of a certain proportion of trees felled. In addition, to limit exports of the most valuable woods, the

Government increased the tax on exports of such species from 13 per cent to 17 per cent and on the exports of other species to only 15 per cent. Investment in sawmills has boomed in recent years, but many mills still operate far below capacity. In 1967, local mills processed about 850,000 cubic meters of wood, producing about 300,000 cubic meters of processed wood such as veneer, plywood, panels, and wood-work. In 1968 and 1969 only 25 per cent of the production was processed in Ivory Coast. The domestic market absorbs about 100,000 cubic meters of timber annually, and nearly all of the finished plywood.

Freight rates for wood exported from Africa to Europe have traditionally been higher than rates charged for shipments from the Far East. It is estimated that costs of delivering Ivory Coast wood to the harbor average CFAF 7,200 per cubic meter; taxes and loading charges add CFAF 1,800 and freight to Europe CFAF 5,500 per cubic meter. At present costs, a number of species are barely competitive with North European woods, and any further increase in prices is likely to affect demand for these species. Prices for most African woods have changed very little in recent years, the comparative cost of European oak being the limiting factor. Competition from metals and plastics in construction and furniture is also a factor influencing demand.

The United Kingdom is the largest market for Ivory Coast's processed wood, since import duties there are the same for logs as for sawn timber. By contrast, import duties in Common Market countries are negligible on logs and other rough timber, whereas they total 6 to 8 per cent for sawn lumber and veneer from Africa and 10 per cent for plywood.

In view of the rapid depletion of forest resources, the Government has undertaken a reforestation program, implemented by a new forest development organization, SODEFOR, established for this purpose and financed partly by the 2 per cent felling tax, which was raised to 3 per cent in early 1970 so that SODEFOR would have the means to embark on a new program of *"délimitation du domaine de l'Etat."* The rate of reforestation has been stepped up since 1967 by about 7 per cent, with a coverage of 2,400 hectares in 1968, mainly teak and mahogany. However, the proposed target of annual average reforestation remains much higher, or 5,000 to 6,000 hectares.

MINING

The small mineral production in Ivory Coast is limited to manganese ore and industrial diamonds (Table 9). In 1967, manganese production declined with a drop in U.S. demand and consequent lower prices. In 1968 and 1969 the world market for manganese deteriorated further, and Ivory Coast discontinued production in early 1970, after operations showed a deficit. Diamond production has increased slightly since 1967, but because known resources are quite small, exploitation is expected to continue for only seven or eight more years. Production of colombite, valued at CFAF 3.7 million in 1966, ceased altogether in 1967.

Although considerable geological research has been done in recent years, no important new mineral reserves have been discovered. Small deposits of gold and tantalite are known to exist, but none are suitable for exploitation. A deposit of iron ore has also been found in Bangolo (northwest of Daloa); it may warrant production of iron pellets by modern techniques.

TABLE 9.   IVORY COAST: ESTIMATED MINERAL PRODUCTION, 1965–69

(Value in millions of CFA francs)

	Manganese			Diamonds		
	Production		Known reserves	Production		Known reserves
	Value	Quantity		Value	Quantity	
	Thousand metric tons			*Thousand carats*		
1965	750	165	. . .	914	204	. . .
1966	820	156	. . .	846	178	. . .
1967	542	123	1,000	893	884	1,300
1968	414	119	1,000	937	190	1,300
1969	. . .	71	1,000	. . .	197	1,300

Source: Data provided by the Ivory Coast authorities.

MANUFACTURING

Industrial activity has progressed rapidly in recent years. In 1966, value added by the secondary sector (manufacturing, energy, water, and construction) provided about 19 per cent of GDP, compared with some 14 per cent in 1960. The leading industry is that producing food, beverages, and tobacco, followed by the wood processing industry (Table 10). Between 1960 and 1966, total manufacturing production

TABLE 10. IVORY COAST: VALUE OF INDUSTRIAL PRODUCTION, 1960–66

(*In millions of CFA francs*)

	1960	1961	1962	1963	1964	1965	1966
Manufacturing [1]							
Food, beverages, and tobacco	3,313	4,961	5,857	7,418	8,590	11,926	14,542
Wood processing	1,605	1,977	2,560	3,420	4,586	6,375	7,825
Chemicals, oils, and fats	2,221	2,518	2,995	3,923	4,871	5,659	6,162
Textiles	1,648	2,008	2,166	3,167	4,127	4,320	5,421
Metal products	1,103	1,299	1,905	2,677	3,316	3,665	4,211
Mining (processing)	1,038	1,460	1,367	1,343	1,559	1,812	1,734
Other	628	817	1,005	1,333	1,915	2,379	4,112
Total	11,556	15,040	17,855	23,281	28,964	36,136	44,007
Energy and water	1,163	1,614	1,871	2,365	2,632	4,350	7,354
Grand Total	12,719	16,654	19,726	25,646	31,596	40,486	51,361

Source: Chamber of Industry, *Bulletin Mensuel.*

[1] Excluding rubber industries.

increased by about 25 per cent annually with higher rates for wood-working (more than 30 per cent); and other industries (38 per cent). The annual rate of expansion was less than the over-all average in the chemicals, oils, and fats industries (19 per cent) and in textiles (23 per cent). Over this period, manufacturing created an average of 3,000 new jobs a year, its share of total private employment rising from 9 per cent to nearly 15 per cent.

Although no comparable figures are available for production after 1966, expansion in the industrial sector continued according to data expressed in value added. By 1968 the industrial sector had received CFAF 42 billion in cumulative investment, including as much as CFAF 5 billion in 1968 alone. The three groups with the largest value added in 1968 were wood processing, textiles, and food, beverages, and tobacco—together accounting for about 43 per cent of the total value added.

In 1967, total value added in the industrial sector rose by 9 or 10 per cent and in 1968 by more than 20 per cent. Only in the mining sector has there been a decline in value added since 1966.

A relatively large inflow of foreign capital has been the main factor in the expansion of manufacturing in Ivory Coast. This inflow has been attracted by liberal tax and other benefits granted to approved industries under the Investment Code and by government participation in the capital of certain industries, especially those processing raw materials for export. A number of new industries were granted approved status under the Investment Code in 1966, the largest being connected with cotton textiles, woodworking, metal containers, jute bags, and tuna processing. In 1967, two new textile plants were granted approved status for a proposed total investment of CFAF 4.4 billion.

In order to attract more Ivorian nationals into industrialization of the country, the Government recently created more institutions for the promotion of small Ivorian firms. It is also intended to revise the Investment Code so that it would provide a more flexible tool and the Government could then grant benefits to a specific project according to its real needs.

With few exceptions, notably the flour mill and the cement plants during the construction season, manufacturing installations are running at less than full capacity, particularly lumbering. Infant industries have been granted tariff protection and export taxes are kept substantially higher on raw materials than on processed goods. For example, the export tax is 15 to 17 per cent on timber in the form of logs but only 0.5 per cent on sawn timber.

Except for the output of the wood industry and some food processing and packing industries, the bulk of industrial production is sold on the domestic market. It is the intention of the authorities to encourage investment in export industries, not only in facilities for further processing of domestic raw materials but also in industries producing commodities now imported in large quantities. It is also stated that a more export-oriented industry could be best achieved by signing bilateral agreements with neighboring countries and by developing exporting industries with a large local manpower input. In 1969, a Bureau for Industrial Development began operations, and a regional commission to promote industrialization was set up between Ivory Coast, its Conseil de l'Entente partners, and Ghana.

TRANSPORTATION AND POWER

Ivory Coast has a relatively well developed transportation system. Expansion in production of wood and cash crops was accompanied by a rapid extension of the road network, which at present comprises about 32,000 kilometers (20,000 miles)—11,000 kilometers of all-weather roads and nearly 1,000 kilometers of hard-surfaced roads. The number of motor vehicles in Ivory Coast more than doubled from 24,000 in 1960 to 51,000 in 1964. For both 1967 and 1968, nearly 10,000 vehicles were newly registered. During 1960–64, investment in new roads totaled CFAF 10.2 billion—CFAF 7.9 billion financed by the Government, CFAF 1.8 billion by EDF, and CFAF 0.5 billion by France. Maintenance of the road network requires an outlay of CFAF 1.5 billion a year. Inland water transportation is of importance in the coastal lagoons, mainly for shipping logs and manganese to Abidjan.

A 1,300-kilometer railroad linking Abidjan to Ouagadougou is operated by the Régie du Chemin de Fer Abidjan-Niger (RAN), jointly owned by the Governments of Ivory Coast and Upper Volta. The railroad has made an annual profit, which has been used for improvements.

The country has an international airport at Abidjan, another major airport at Bouaké, and 19 secondary airports. The Government is part owner of Air Afrique, the international airline organized by most of the African franc area countries. It also holds a 66 per cent share of the capital of Air Ivoire, which began operations in 1964 to provide domestic air transportation.

Abidjan has a modern deep-water seaport built in 1950 and expanded in recent years at a total cost of CFAF 3.4 billion, mainly by government financing. The port handled 3.6 million tons of merchandise in 1965, against 0.9 million tons in 1960. In 1967 this volume rose to 4.1 million tons and in 1968 to 4.7 million. The port of Sassandra handled about 0.2 million tons in 1964 and 0.4 million in 1968.

Planned investments during 1966–70 to extend the country's transportation network and its water supply system, estimated at CFAF 50 billion, included the following projects: paving of 800 kilometers of roads, construction of additional secondary roads and bridges to replace existing ferries, improvement of existing roads, construction of irrigation works and drinking water systems, expansion of the port of Abidjan, and construction of a new seaport at San-Pédro to open up the southwestern part of the country, which contains substantial unexploited wood reserves and land suited for agricultural production.

The electric power system has grown very rapidly in recent years. Total production increased from 276,000 kilowatt-hours in 1966 to 372,000 kilowatt-hours in 1968, with a corresponding rise in consumption from 241,000 kilowatt-hours to 317,000 kilowatt-hours. In order to meet the growing demand, an extensive hydroelectric project—consisting of a large dam, power station, and distribution system on the Bandama River near Kossou (northeast of Bouaflé)—was initiated in 1969, after financing (about CFAF 26 billion) had been secured.

ECONOMIC DEVELOPMENT PLANNING

EARLY DEVELOPMENT PLANNING

The broad lines of development policy in Ivory Coast were first laid down in the early 1960's in a long-range development plan, the *Perspectives Décennales de Développement Economique et Social, 1960–70.* This plan consisted essentially of a series of interrelated national accounts projections. It included broad sectoral investment targets for the private sector and a more specific program for public sector investment, the latter being intended to provide guidelines for the preparation of the annual investment budgets. Priority was given to (1) diversification of agricultural production, (2) encouragement of local processing of agricultural produce, and (3) establishment of manufacturing industries producing substitutes for imports. A program for creation of physical and social infrastructure was designed to complement these objectives. An average annual growth rate of GDP at constant prices of 7.9 per cent was projected for the ten-year period.

During 1960–65 the target over-all growth rate was actually slightly exceeded, but certain significant departures from the plan occurred in the distribution of investment. Although total private investment substantially exceeded the plan's expectations, public investment lagged behind. Public investment in agriculture, economic infrastructure, education, and health remained well below the plan projections, while investment in administrative construction went considerably above. Furthermore, investment during the period was largely concentrated in and around Abidjan, while the countryside—particularly in the western and northern regions—benefited relatively little.

DEVELOPMENT PLAN, 1967–70

To redirect investment and to some extent correct the over-all distribution of resources during the last four years of the original plan, the Ivory Coast authorities issued a new plan in 1967, Development Plan, 1967–70 (*Loi Plan de Développement Economique, Social et Culturel, 1967–70*). This is considered a transitional plan, leading to a further plan covering the period 1971–75, to be ready by mid-1970. The over-all growth targets for 1967–70 were an annual increase in GDP at constant prices of 7.7 per cent, and in real income per capita of 4.8 per cent. These targets are generally consistent with those of the earlier *Perspectives Décennales,* after taking account of the growth achieved in the years since 1960.

The Development Plan, 1967–70, sets out only broad sectoral targets for private and public investment during the period. The investment projected for 1967–70 at constant 1965 prices is compared with that realized during the period 1960–66 in Table 11. For the four years 1967–70, total investment is estimated at CFAF 224 billion, or an

TABLE 11. IVORY COAST: PRIVATE AND PUBLIC INVESTMENT,
1960–66 AND 1967–70

(*In billions of CFA francs at constant 1965 prices*)

	Realized 1960–66 [1]		Plan Target 1967–70	
	Total	Annual average	Total	Annual average
Private investment	108.0	15.4	108.0	27.0
Industry	*31.0*	*4.4*	*39.0*	*10.0*
Public investment				
Agriculture	11.1	1.6	34.5	8.6
Economic infrastructure	42.9	6.1	45.4	11.3
Education	8.1	1.1	8.5	2.1
Health	1.9	0.3	5.8	1.5
Special development	0.3	0.1	0.7	0.2
Administration	16.7	2.4	8.8	2.2
Participation	6.6	0.9	7.3	1.8
Studies and research	5.3	0.8	4.8	1.2
Total public investment	93.2	13.3	116.0	29.0
Total investment	201.2	28.7	224.0	56.0

Source: Ministère du Plan, *Loi Plan 1967–70.*

[1] These figures differ from the estimates presented in the national accounts (Table 2) because they are at constant 1965 prices, and also because of differences in classification criteria.

average of CFAF 56 billion a year. This represents nearly a doubling of the average annual rate of investment achieved in the seven years 1960–66. However, compared with the investment realized in the latter part of the 1960–66 period, the projected increase averages less than 50 per cent. During 1967–70, private investment was expected to average about CFAF 27 billion a year. A larger proportion of private investment than in the past was projected for industries processing local raw materials for export, as opposed to those manufacturing import substitutes for the domestic market.

Private industrial projects foreseen in the plan included fiber board and paper plant (CFAF 6 billion), other forest-based industries (CFAF 2 billion), textile industries (CFAF 4 billion), and food-processing industries (some CFAF 3 billion). The remainder of projected investment consisted mainly, in approximately equal proportions, of construction and normal replacement of existing plant and equipment.

Public investment was expected to average about CFAF 29 billion annually during 1967–70. The largest part of the planned increase was for agriculture, but substantial increases were also planned in all other broad categories of public investment, except administration and studies and research, for which there were declines. Total public investment for 1967–70 (CFAF 116 billion) was divided into a "guaranteed core" of CFAF 101 billion, consisting of projects considered essential to realization of the plan's objectives, and an "optional tranche" of CFAF 15 billion, consisting of additional investments to be executed if and when resources become available. Major infrastructural projects to be initiated in the public sector during 1967–70 included (1) the Port of San-Pédro, which, together with related road and urban developments, would require an investment of some CFAF 7.4 billion (US$30 million) over the three years 1968–70, and (2) the Kossou Dam (on the Bandama), a hydroelectric and irrigation project, which was expected to cost some CFAF 26 billion ($105 million), to be constructed over the years 1969–72.

In keeping with the principles originally laid down in the *Perspectives Décennales*, the 1967–70 Plan relied mainly on private initiative and on the maintenance of a favorable investment climate to realize the planned private investment. A policy of government participation in selected private industrial ventures was foreseen for 1967–70, and a total of CFAF 7.3 billion in public investment was provided for this purpose.

Concerning public investment, an innovation introduced under the new plan is the provision for an annual *Loi Programme,* covering the public investment program for successive periods of three years. This is intended to provide an opportunity for annual reviews of the projected program in the light of actual implementation up to that point and expectations for the immediate future. Thus far, two of these reviews, covering the periods 1967–69 and 1968–70, have been issued; these have introduced only minor changes in the magnitude and timing of public investment originally envisaged over the remaining years of the plan period. Table 12 shows the public investment program for each of the four years 1967–70 as detailed in the *Loi Programme 1968–70,* with breakdowns by major economic sector and "guaranteed core" and optional tranche. Total public investment was expected to reach a peak

TABLE 12. IVORY COAST: PROJECTED PUBLIC INVESTMENT PROGRAM, 1967–70

(In billions of CFA francs at constant 1965 prices)

	Estimated 1967	Programed 1968	Programed 1969	Programed 1970	Total, 1967–70
Agriculture					
"Guaranteed core"					
Existing programs	8.6	7.7	5.6	2.6	24.5
New programs	—	1.6	1.2	1.4	4.2
Optional tranche	—	0.6	2.2	3.0	5.8
Total	8.6	9.9	8.9	7.0	34.5
Economic infrastructure					
"Guaranteed core"					
Existing programs	9.3	9.1	6.5	5.3	30.2
New programs	—	2.9	4.3	3.5	10.8
Optional tranche	—	0.9	1.7	1.8	4.5
Total	9.3	13.0	12.6	10.6	45.4
Other					
"Guaranteed core"					
Existing programs	7.6	5.5	3.7	2.9	19.7
New programs	—	3.6	4.5	3.5	11.6
Optional tranche	—	0.8	1.9	2.0	4.7
Total	7.6	9.9	10.1	8.4	36.0
Total public investment					
"Guaranteed core"					
Existing programs	25.5	22.3	15.8	10.8	74.1
New programs	—	8.1	10.1	8.4	26.8
Optional tranche	—	2.4	5.8	6.8	15.0
Grand Total	25.5	32.9	31.6	26.0	116.0

Source: Ministère du Plan, *Loi Programme 1968–70.*

in 1968 of CFAF 33 billion, and to decline to CFAF 26 billion in
1970. Of the projected "guaranteed core" investment, about three
fourths was to be made under programs which were already in existence at the beginning of 1968.

PUBLIC INVESTMENT EXPENDITURES 1967–70

The *Loi Plan 1967–70* projected total public investment of CFAF 116
billion at constant prices over the four years, an annual average of
CFAF 29 billion (Table 13). On the basis of actual results for 1967

TABLE 13. IVORY COAST: PLANNED AND ESTIMATED ACTUAL PUBLIC
INVESTMENT, BY SECTORS, AND FINANCING, 1967–70

(Amount in billions of CFA francs)

	Plan Targets [1]		Estimated Actuals [2]	
	Amount	Per cent	Amount	Per cent
Public investment				
Economic infrastructure	45.4	39.1	59.1	45.3
Ports and waterways	*6.5*	*5.6*	*9.5*	*7.3*
Electricity	*7.2*	*6.2*	*16.4*	*12.6*
Agriculture	34.5	29.7	33.7	25.8
Administration	8.8	7.6	10.5	8.0
Education and cultural	8.8	7.6	8.5	6.5
Participation	7.3	6.3	7.8	6.0
Health	5.8	5.0	3.8	2.9
Studies and research	4.8	4.1	6.5	5.0
Other	0.7	0.6	0.6	0.5
Total public investment	**116.0**	**100.0**	**130.5**	**100.0**
Financed by				
Domestic resources				
Investment budget revenue	47.7	41.1	57.6	44.1
Retained earnings of pub-				
lic enterprises	7.5	6.5	10.3	7.9
Contributions of local				
authorities	7.5	6.5	—	—
Domestic loans	4.8	4.1	4.3	3.3
Total domestic resources	67.5	58.2	72.2	55.3
External resources				
Grants	16.5	14.2	14.1	10.8
Loans	32.0	27.6	44.2 [3]	33.8
Total external resources	48.5	41.8	58.3	44.6

Sources: Ministère du Plan, *Loi Plan 1967–70*, and data provided by the Ivory
Coast authorities and by IBRD.

[1] At constant 1965 prices.
[2] At current prices.
[3] Includes CFAF 3.0 billion in 1970, for which loan financing has not been
found.

and 1968, provisional results for 1969, and estimates for 1970,[2] prepared by the Planning Ministry, it appears that total public investment
expenditure during this period will amount to about CFAF 130 billion
at current prices (i.e., about 112 per cent of the original expenditure
target), which, when deflated roughly by 3 per cent per annum to allow
for price increases over the period, corresponds roughly to 100 per cent
on a constant-price basis. Distribution of public investment by sector
during this period, however, has deviated considerably from that envisaged in the original *Loi Plan*. In broad terms, investment in agricultural
and social development projects lagged behind the planned targets,
while that for infrastructural development (actually accounting for
nearly one half of the total spent) was 30 per cent ahead. In the latter
category, the overexpenditure of plan targets was due almost entirely to
larger-than-anticipated expenditures on two large projects—the Port of
San-Pédro and the Bandama River hydroelectric complex. The first of
these projects accounts for most of the CFAF 3 billion increase over
plan targets in the item "ports and waterways" and the second for most
of the CFAF 9.2 billion increase in "electricity" in Table 13. It is estimated by the authorities that roughly 80 per cent of those public-
investment expenditures specifically envisaged in the original *Loi Plan*
will be realized during the period; the rest represents nonplanned
expenditures, relating mainly to these two projects.

Estimates of actual private investment comparable to those projected
in the *Loi Plan 1967–70* have not yet been published.

FINANCING OF PUBLIC INVESTMENT

The financing of public investment during 1967–70, as projected in
the *Loi Plan,* is summarized in the second part of Table 13, together
with the estimated actual financing in this period, based upon results
for 1967 and 1968 and estimates for 1969 and 1970. Apparently
domestic resources have financed a slightly smaller, and external
resources a slightly larger part of public investment than was originally

---

[2] The estimate for 1970 (CFAF 46.6 billion) is the figure provided for in the
Loi Programme 1970–72, the basis for the draft investment budget for 1970. This
figure represents an increase of about CFAF 16 billion over the estimated 1969
actual. However, the final investment budget for 1970 was not yet determined
when this chapter was completed.

anticipated. The shortfall in domestic resources has been due to reduced contributions from local authorities and from domestic loans. The latter, however, increased from CFAF 1.4 billion in 1967 to CFAF 3.7 billion in 1969, indicating a favorable trend. Among external resources, grants fell considerably below expectations, while loans financed 33.8 per cent of total expenditures, compared with 27.6 per cent anticipated in the *Loi Plan*. A large part of the increased external borrowing has been on account of the two large projects mentioned earlier.

Comparison of the estimated actual financing for 1967–70 with the realized financing during 1960–65, shows sharply increased contributions in all categories of financing during 1967–70. Budgetary savings rose from an average annual rate of CFAF 7 billion in 1960–65 to CFAF 14.4 billion in 1967–70. Recourse to domestic and to external borrowing also more than doubled between the two periods.

PRICES, WAGES, AND EMPLOYMENT

PRICES

On the whole, price increases have been relatively small in recent years. Two indices of cost of living in Abidjan are computed; one covers 100 items consumed by a typical African family of four, and the other 140 articles typically consumed by a family of European living standards. Neither index is considered very satisfactory, since their composition has not been revised since 1960 to take account of the changes that have intervened in consumption patterns; nevertheless they do indicate the general trend of prices. During 1960–67 the annual increase in the cost of living averaged 2.8 per cent for African families and about 3 per cent for non-African families (Table 14). In 1968, however, living costs rose by 5 per cent for the former and 4 per cent for the latter. For African families, apparently the large increase in 1968 came mainly from food prices. During the first six months of 1969, again mainly because of a considerable increase in food prices, the African index of consumer prices rose by 5.3 per cent, compared with 3.2 per cent in the first six months of 1968.

TABLE 14. IVORY COAST: INDICES OF CONSUMER PRICES IN ABIDJAN, 1963–68

(Annual Averages)

	Number of Items	Weight	1963	1964	1965	1966	1967	1968
AFRICAN CONSUMPTION (February 1960 = 100)								
Food	47	51.1	118.3	118.9	122.4	127.6	126.6	134.8
Housing	2	11.6	108.8	109.3	113.6	114.6	122.6	126.7
Utilities	6	8.1	102.9	105.6	110.1	102.8	108.0	109.8
Household utensils	13	7.3	103.8	107.8	106.2	110.9	115.4	124.1
Clothing	12	8.4	112.3	120.2	128.1	132.0	128.9	132.1
Services	9	8.5	102.7	98.4	94.1	94.9	94.9	107.5
Other	11	5.0	104.9	112.5	118.1	156.2	191.5	193.6
Total or average	100	100.0	112.4	113.9	117.0	122.0	124.6	131.4
EUROPEAN CONSUMPTION (1960 = 100)								
Food	57	50.0	105.7	109.6	115.4	118.6	119.5	120.5
Utilities	5	4.0	99.6	97.9	97.6	95.1	94.2	94.1
Textiles and household utensils	28	8.0	121.3	123.9	130.1	133.3	128.3	144.1
Maintenance and health	22	10.0	113.5	114.8	118.5	122.2	123.2	145.2
Servants	2	8.0	110.0	117.0	117.0	117.0	120.0	125.8
Other	26	20.0	114.9	119.9	123.8	125.4	128.3	131.4
Total or average	140	100.0	109.5	113.5	118.0	120.8	122.3	126.7

Sources: Ministère de l'Economie et des Finances, *Bulletin Mensuel de Statistique*, and data supplied by the Ivory Coast authorities.

Prices of a number of goods and services have been under government control since 1961. Three types of control are used: (1) Prices of some basic consumer goods (bread, rice, meat, edible oils, soap, beer, gas and oil products, cigarettes, matches, and cotton fabrics) and certain services (taxis, cinemas, hotel rooms, and restaurant meals) are fixed directly by the Government. (2) For a list of imports and goods manufactured domestically specified by priority enterprises enjoying fiscal privileges, the control is applied by setting profit margins at the wholesale and retail levels (e.g., wheat flour, sugar, canned milk, salt, potatoes, some fabrics, and jute bags). (3) For other imported goods, retail prices must be registered and approved by the price control office, but not necessarily prior to their application.

For the most part, price controls are not very effectively enforced. In Abidjan, competition at the retail level is sufficient to prevent excessive profiteering. In the interior, where distribution is less satisfactory and prices tend to be higher, enforcement of controls is almost impossible. The Government is seeking to encourage better distribution of goods in the interior.

In 1969 the price situation was upset by the devaluation of the French franc in August. After prices started to increase, the Government decreed an over-all price freeze, providing, however, for ad hoc adjustments. In fact since the end of 1969 a particular effort has been made to keep the level of prices for consumption goods steady, while the control was less strictly applied for other products.

It appears that import prices for goods originating in France increased more than one might have expected as a result of the devaluation. In addition, the cost of freight and various services also increased in 1969. As for goods manufactured in Ivory Coast, but including imported raw materials, prices rose by 4 to 5 per cent, as a result of increased production costs.

WAGES

There is a legal minimum wage rate, the *salaire minimum interprofessionnel garanti* (SMIG). For nonagricultural workers, SMIG remained unchanged from November 1963 through March 1968 at CFAF 42.40 per hour in the Abidjan area and CFAF 38.20 in the rest of the country. On April 1, 1968 the wage zones were abolished, and the Abidjan area rate became applicable throughout the country; on July 1, 1968 the over-all SMIG was raised from CFAF 42.40 per hour to CFAF 46.64, or by 10 per cent.

For agricultural workers also, wage zones were abolished on July 1, 1968. Their legal minimum wages had since 1958 been fixed at a scale ranging from CFAF 26.00 to CFAF 19.50 per hour, according to region. Furthermore, on July 1, 1968, Ivory Coast introduced new legal minimum wages of CFAF 21.50 and CFAF 24.50 per hour for agricultural workers, according to their occupation.

For salaried workers, minimum wage scales for various classes in different sectors of the economy are fixed by joint commissions representing labor, employers, and the Government; on July 1, 1968 these scales, which had not previously been changed since 1961, were also adjusted upward by 10 per cent. Wage scales for government employees, however, have remained the same since 1963.

The significance of the minimum wage rates, however, has tended to decline in recent years, as fringe benefits have increased, and wage adjustments by reclassification have been common. Over-all, average actual remunerations (i.e., total amount of wages paid divided by the estimated number of wage earners) are believed to have increased by some 8 per cent a year during 1961–66, with annual increases exceeding 10 per cent in the three years 1964–66.

In early 1970, however, major changes took place. For all labor categories mentioned, the Government raised SMIG, as of January 1, 1970, by 25 per cent above its 1968 level, or an estimated additional cost of CFAF 11.0 billion for firms. It also increased the wage scales of its own employees by an estimated additional cost of CFAF 1.6 billion.

EMPLOYMENT

The available estimates indicate that employment has been increasing less rapidly than GDP in recent years. Although GDP rose by an average of more than 10 per cent a year during 1960–66, the total number of wage earners rose by only about 5 per cent a year. The largest increase in employment was in industry and energy, which created jobs at an average annual rate of 11 per cent. The smallest expansion was in agriculture, forestry, and fishing, where the number of salaried employees rose by about 2 per cent a year (Table 15). For the public sector, growth in employment averaged about 4 per cent through 1965, but in 1966 it approached 18 per cent, because a body of workers previously classed as temporary were transferred to the role of permanent civil servants.

The difference in growth rates of production and of employment is believed to result mainly from increased productivity, especially in agriculture, modernization of procedures in industry, and employment of more specialized and less unskilled labor.

Ivory Coast has always provided work for large numbers of laborers from neighboring countries, most of them in agriculture. Some workers have migrated from the farm to Abidjan, where a certain level of unemployment exists among unskilled workers, while shortages of skilled workers continue. Official programs to increase technical training have been established, and industry has provided some on-the-job training aimed at upgrading its employees. Most of the managerial staff and technicians' jobs and a large part of the foremen's jobs are held by foreigners of non-African origin (Table 16).

Work permits, though required for all foreigners, are given liberally. The authorities have no intention of limiting the inflow of foreigners, or of introducing any official systematic preference favoring employment of Ivorian nationals.

TABLE 15. IVORY COAST: ESTIMATED NUMBER OF PERMANENT
WAGE EARNERS, BY SECTOR, 1960 AND 1964–67

(*In thousands*)

	1960	1964	1965	1966	1967
Private sector					
Agriculture, forestry, and fishing	78.4	90.3	91.0	91.6	92.1
Industry and energy	11.1	25.1	27.1	29.4	32.6
Construction and public works	16.3	16.5	15.4	13.1	18.5
Transportation	13.4	16.9	19.0	19.9	21.3
Commerce and services	25.6	30.1	33.9	31.3	33.8
Total private sector	144.9	178.9	186.4	185.3	198.2
Public sector	24.9	30.0	30.4	35.9	37.5
Grand Total	169.8	208.9	216.8	221.2	235.8

Source: Data supplied by the Ivory Coast authorities.

TABLE 16. IVORY COAST: DISTRIBUTION OF WAGE EARNERS BY QUALIFICATION AND ORIGIN, 1964, 1966, AND 1967 [1]

	Total Number of Wage Earners			Per Cent of Total by National Origin								
				Ivorian nationals			Foreigners of African origin			Foreigners of non-African origin		
	1964	1966	1967	1964	1966	1967	1964	1966	1967	1964	1966	1967
Managerial staff	1,649	1,622	1,616	10.1	9.8	7.1	4.5	3.5	1.5	85.4	86.6	91.3
Technicians	2,947	2,858	2,915	15.7	12.1	14.3	2.5	2.8	3.9	81.7	85.0	81.7
Foremen	3,265	3,943	4,298	28.3	32.1	34.7	11.1	10.9	10.4	60.5	57.0	54.9
Employees	18,943	18,211	18,605	69.6	68.8	68.6	21.9	21.5	21.6	8.4	9.6	9.9
Skilled workers	27,565	34,709	38,275	69.2	64.1	68.5	30.0	35.0	30.8	0.8	0.8	0.7
Apprentices and unskilled workers	57,880	59,908	63,975	33.7	31.6	34.3	66.3	68.3	65.7	—	0.1	—
Total or average	112,249	121,251	129,684	47.5	45.8	48.5	45.7	47.5	45.1	6.8	6.7	6.4

Source: Data supplied by the Ivory Coast authorities.

[1] Based on declarations by enterprises to the Office de la Main d'Oeuvre. The number of wage earners shown in this table is lower than the estimates shown in Table 15 since detailed declarations concerning the agricultural sector, public services, and house servants are incomplete.

GOVERNMENT FINANCE

BUDGETARY SYSTEM

Most budgetary operations of the Central Government are recorded in the ordinary budget (*budget général*) and the investment budget (*budget spécial d'investissement et d'équipement*). The service of the public debt is entrusted to a special public agency, the Amortization Fund (Caisse Autonome d'Amortissement, or CAA), and is not included in the government budgets except as an ordinary budget appropriation for the debt contracted by public entities under the government guarantee. In addition, there are the annexed budgets for seven special public agencies and the budgets of the municipalities.

The investment budget includes only that part of government capital expenditure which is financed by fiscal revenue and by borrowing by the Amortization Fund as authorized in this budget. Capital expenditure not entered in the government budgets consists essentially of that financed by (1) foreign development grants, such as those of the French FAC and EEC/EDF; (2) proceeds from voluntary and compulsory domestic savings collected by two public institutions, the National Investment Fund (Fonds National d'Investissement, or FNI) and the National Finance Company (Société Nationale de Financement, or SONAFI); and (3) other foreign loans contracted by the Amortization Fund.

The seven special public agencies which are governed by annexed budgets are Ivory Coast's Radio-Television, the News Agency, the Port of Abidjan, the Post Office, the University Hospital, the Sassandra Wharf, and the Machinery Unit (Arrondissement d'Outillage Mécanique). In 1967, their total expenditure was estimated at some 12.5 per cent of ordinary budget expenditure of the Central Government; about 40 per cent of their expenditure was for investment purposes, mainly by the Port of Abidjan and the Post Office. For 1970, their total expenditures are estimated at CFAF 7,020 million (or about 12 per cent of the ordinary budget expenditure), and about 30 per cent of these expenditures are for investment purposes. As a rule, these seven agencies finance their operations from their own operating revenues, but they may also receive subsidies appropriated in the ordinary budget; in 1967 these subsidies represented about 10 per cent of the combined revenue of the seven agencies (14 per cent for 1970 estimates) and were directed mainly to the annexed budget of the Radio-Television, the News Agency, and the University Hospital. Moreover, their deficit, if any, has been financed by the Treasury itself, from its own reserves.

The municipal budgets are of minor significance; the largest one, for the City of Abidjan, equals some 4 per cent of the ordinary budget expenditure of the Central Government.

A specified proportion of all revenue from certain direct and indirect taxes is earmarked directly for the investment budget. Other tax revenue is earmarked for the Amortization Fund for servicing the public debt and is not entered in the ordinary budget. Similarly, part of the receipts from the export tax on coffee and cocoa was rebated to the Stabilization Fund until January 1969, other revenue is earmarked for the Road Fund, and other tax rebates are made to the municipalities and other public entities. Total earmarked tax revenue has accounted for about 30 per cent of total government revenue in recent years (Table 17).

The principles governing the budgetary operations of the Central Government are set out each year in a Finance Law (*Loi de Finance*), which specifies (1) the amount of authorized expenditure under the ordinary budget and the annexed budgets and (2) the taxes

TABLE 17. IVORY COAST: EARMARKED TAX REVENUE, 1966–69

	1966	1967	1968	1969 (Estimate)
VALUE (*billion CFA francs*)				
Earmarked tax revenue for				
Investment budget	7.1	7.2	10.8	10.9
Amortization Fund and FNI				
(Public Debt Department)	4.3	5.3	7.5	7.1
Stabilization Fund	1.1 [1]	1.3 [1]	1.2	...
Road Fund	1.2	1.1	1.1	1.5
Municipalities and others	0.9 [1]	1.0 [1]	0.8	1.0
Total	14.6	15.9	21.4	20.5
PER CENT OF TOTAL GOVERNMENT REVENUE				
Total earmarked revenue	29.0	30.6	32.4	...

Sources: *Loi de Finance 1968,* and data provided by the Ivory Coast authorities.
[1] Partly estimated.

and other revenue to be collected to attain general fiscal equilibrium. The government budgets are established on a calendar-year basis. Before 1968, however, the ordinary budget, was executed over a period of 15 months as the budget accounts were not closed until March 31 of the following calendar year (complementary period). The investment budget is approved by Parliament under a separate law and is executed on a calendar-year basis, as the ordinary budget is now.

In Ivory Coast, budgetary and other financial operations of the Government are managed by two main executive agencies, the Treasury itself and the Amortization Fund.

TREASURY

The Treasury is responsible for the execution and control of the ordinary budget, that part of the investment budget which is financed by the Government's earmarked tax revenue, and generally the annexed budgets. The Treasury collects all tax revenue, including that earmarked for the investment budget and other agencies, with the exception of the Post Office. It also executes that part of investment budget expenditure which is financed by fiscal revenue, and centralizes in its accounting system the operations which are executed by the Amortization Fund. This centralization, however, is of a purely accounting nature, and there is no corresponding cash flow in the Treasury.

All budgetary operations carried out by the Treasury are recorded in either definitive accounts (*comptes d'imputation définitive*), budgetary suspense accounts (*comptes d'exécution recettes et d'exécution dépenses*), or the Treasury's suspense accounts (*opérations à classer*). At the end of the calendar year, the balances in the suspense accounts are transferred to the following year's accounts, unless these operations have been legally identified, and thus transferred to the definitive accounts.

The budgetary suspense accounts record not only ordinary budget operations, but also receipts and expenditure to be allocated to the investment budget and the annexed budgets.

In addition to budgetary revenue, the resources at the disposal of the Treasury include mainly deposits of certain public agencies and the municipalities. The Treasury maintains transfer accounts for earmarked tax revenue to be transferred to the Amortization Fund and other agencies (e.g., National Investment Fund, or FNI). To the extent that this revenue is not immediately transferred, it becomes a source of short-term financing for the Treasury.

The Treasury maintains a free cash flow with the Post Office, as the latter acts also as agent for the Treasury in certain financial operations. The Post Office keeps its liquid funds (other than cash on hand) with the Treasury, while private deposits in the Postal Checking System and savings accounts are transferred to the Amortization Fund. However, the Treasury has so far had a net claim on the Post Office and therefore the latter has not provided liquid funds for the Treasury's use. The Treasury maintains the same free cash flow relationship with the various government accounts (e.g., *comptables publics, trésoriers particuliers,* and *percepteurs et receveurs des régies financières*). It may extend temporary advances to certain government agencies, to agencies in charge of the execution of projects to be financed by foreign aid, and to civil servants.

OVER-ALL BUDGET DEVELOPMENTS AND FINANCING SINCE 1965

Table 18 shows the over-all fiscal performance of the Central Government during 1965–69 and the financing of the over-all deficit through budget savings, the Treasury, the Amortization Fund, and the Stabilization Fund. Under the present public accounting system of Ivory Coast, a consolidation of cash transactions can be obtained after including transactions registered in suspense accounts in each calendar year, for which certain assumptions must be made. For the investment budget, the expenditures presented in Table 18 are obtained by combining the actual borrowing by the Amortization Fund during each year, the tax revenue earmarked for the investment budget, and the net balance of receipts and expenditures under the investment budget as registered by the Treasury's accounts.

In 1967, total revenue for ordinary and investment budgets amounted to CFAF 46.4 billion, a gain of about 5 per cent over 1965; and total current government expenditure amounted to CFAF 41.5 billion, a gain of 21 per cent. As a result, the surplus of total government revenue over current expenditure fell from CFAF 10.0 billion in 1965 to CFAF 4.9 billion in 1967. In the same period, investment budget expenditure rose by more than 20 per cent to CFAF 16.6 billion in 1967. The over-all deficit to be financed by the Treasury, the Amorti-

TABLE 18. IVORY COAST: OVER-ALL BUDGETARY AND EXTRABUDGETARY CASH TRANSACTIONS OF THE CENTRAL GOVERNMENT, AND FINANCING, 1965–69

(In billions of CFA francs)

	1965	1966	1967	1968	1969
Revenue					
Ordinary budget	36.9	39.0	38.4	49.1	50.6
Investment budget	7.3	7.4	8.0	9.8	11.5
Total revenue	44.2	46.4	46.4	58.9	62.1
Expenditure					
Ordinary expenditure (including annexed budgets net)	34.3	39.2	40.6	49.5	50.2
Outside the budget	−0.1	1.3	0.9	1.0	1.7
Total expenditure	34.2	40.5	41.5	50.5	51.9
Budget savings	10.0	5.9	4.9	8.4	10.2
Investment budget expenditure	13.2	13.7	16.6	19.9	23.1
Over-all deficit	**−3.2**	**−7.8**	**−11.7**	**−11.5**	**−12.9**
Financing					
By Treasury					
Changes in Treasury's accounts [1]	−3.2	0.3	1.9	6.8	...
Central Bank's advances [2]	—	1.2	1.5	−2.5	—
Changes in Treasury's cash balances	2.0	1.0	0.1	−1.2	...
Total Treasury	−1.2	2.5	3.5	3.1	0.1
By Amortization Fund					
Long-term borrowing	0.9	0.8	1.7	3.8	8.2
Règlements sur Convention à paiements différés [3]	3.5	3.2	3.5	2.4	3.0
Total CAA	4.4	4.0	5.2	6.2	11.2
By Stabilization Fund [4]	—	1.3	3.0	2.2	1.6

Source: Data provided by the Ivory Coast authorities.

[1] Mainly changes in holdings of public agencies with the Treasury and in the balances of the Public Debt Department of the Amortization Fund (Caisse Autonome d'Amortissement, or CAA).

[2] The discrepancy between total advances by the Central Bank to the Treasury as of the end of 1967, as registered in the Treasury's accounts (CFAF 2.7 billion), and the Central Bank's claims on Government in the monetary statistics (CFAF 1.8 billion) is due largely to the Treasury's drawing in the last days of 1967 which could not be registered in the Central Bank's accounts before the end of the year.

[3] Consists largely of suppliers' credits.

[4] Caisse de Stabilisation et de Soutien des Productions Agricoles.

zation Fund, and the Stabilization Fund grew from CFAF 3.2 billion in 1965 to CFAF 11.7 billion in 1967.

The tax revenue earmarked for the investment budget remained virtually unchanged at some CFAF 8 billion annually between 1965 to 1967, and the increase in investment budget expenditure was financed by contributions of the Stabilization Fund (CFAF 1.3 billion in 1966 and CFAF 3.0 billion in 1967), by net borrowing by the Amortization Fund (CFAF 4.4 billion in 1965, CFAF 4.0 billion in 1966, and CFAF 5.2 billion in 1967), and by Treasury resources. Ordinary budget operations (including expenditure outside the budget) moved from a surplus of CFAF 2.7 billion in 1965 to a deficit of CFAF 3.1 billion in 1967. As a result, the Treasury's cash balances declined sharply, and the Treasury had recourse to temporary advances from BCEAO in both 1966 and 1967. However, resources at the disposal of the Treasury slightly improved in 1966 and 1967.

In 1968, as a result of some changes in the accounting methods, the figures for 1968 and 1969 are not quite comparable with those of the previous years. However, revenue apparently increased sharply in 1968, while ordinary expenditure rose at a lower pace. Consequently, the budgetary savings increased to CFAF 8.4 billion.

Developments during 1969 were less favorable. The rise in revenue was much smaller than in the preceding years, and though budgetary savings showed a further increase from CFAF 8.4 billion to CFAF 10.2 billion, the over-all deficit was larger than in the preceding year. The 1970 budget deficit is expected to be about three times as large as that recorded in 1969. The large deficit for that year was due entirely to a substantial expansion of investment expenditures. In financing the 1970 budget, the Government will increase reliance on foreign borrowing, and will obtain a substantial loan from the Stabilization Fund, whose resources have greatly expanded in recent years through profits earned on coffee and cocoa marketing.

Ordinary Budget Developments

Ordinary budget revenue and expenditure on an accrual basis for 1965–68 are shown in Table 19. In the three years 1965–67, ordinary revenue rose by 5 per cent to CFAF 39.1 billion, while ordinary expenditure rose by 18 per cent to CFAF 40.7 billion, moving the budget from a surplus of CFAF 2.7 billion in 1965 to a deficit of CFAF 1.6 billion in 1967. The ordinary budget position improved in 1968 and, excluding extrabudgetary expenditures, the deficit was only CFAF 0.1 billion. However, in 1969 the deficit was again at about its 1967 level of CFAF 1.5 billion. For 1970 ordinary budget estimates have been balanced at CFAF 57.0 billion.

TABLE 19. IVORY COAST: ORDINARY BUDGET, 1965–68 [1]

	Actual		Estimates	
	1965	1966	Revised 1967	Original 1968
VALUE (*billion CFA francs*)				
Revenue				
Taxes on income and profits	3.8	5.1	4.9	5.9
Taxes on property	2.0	2.2	2.4	2.0
Value-added tax	7.3	6.9	7.0	9.9
Taxes on international trade	21.7	22.3	22.3	22.2
Other taxes	0.7	0.7	0.8	0.7
Nontax revenue	1.6	2.0	2.4	2.5
Total revenue	37.1	39.2	39.8 [2]	43.2
Expenditure				
General services	12.8	13.5	13.4	14.3
Defense	*2.8*	*3.3*	*3.6*	*3.8*
Social services	9.8	11.6	12.0	13.6
Education	*6.2*	*7.2*	*7.5*	*8.8*
Health	*3.3*	*4.0*	*4.2*	*4.5*
Economic services	7.3	8.0	8.5	9.3
Agriculture	*1.6*	*2.0*	*1.9*	*2.3*
Public works	*4.5*	*4.6*	*5.0*	*5.2*
Other [3]	4.5	5.1	5.9	6.0
Total expenditure	34.4	38.2	39.8 [2]	43.2
Surplus, or deficit (−)	2.7	1.0	−1.6	—
PER CENT OF TOTAL EXPENDITURE [4]				
Wages and salaries [5]		43.4	44.5	45.3
Maintenance and materials		35.6	34.7	34.8
Subsidies and transfers		21.0	20.8	19.9
Total expenditure		100.0	100.0	100.0

Sources: *Loi de Finance 1968*, and data provided by the Ivory Coast authorities.

[1] By budget year, i.e., calendar year plus complementary period.
[2] Actual, 1967: total revenue CFAF 39.1 billion, total expenditure CFAF 40.7 billion.
[3] Mainly joint expenditure.
[4] Based on original budget estimates.
[5] Including travel, pensions, and guarantees.

Revenue.—The relatively small increase (5 per cent) in ordinary budget revenue between 1965 and 1967 may be attributed to a general slowing down in the growth of foreign trade. No significant increase in taxation was enacted during this period. The increase in revenue occurred in the 1966 budget (revenue declined slightly in 1967) and resulted almost entirely from a sharp rise in revenue from taxes on income and profits.

Under the 1968 budget, a number of tax measures were introduced which were expected to produce most of the increase in budgeted revenue for the year. These measures included a 14.8 per cent increase in the tax on coffee and cocoa exports; an increase in the rates of the value-added tax, averaging 28 per cent on imported goods and at least 25 per cent on most locally produced goods; and a 25 per cent increase in the excise taxes on gasoline. Furthermore, the withholding procedure for the general income tax was extended to wages and salaries, and the rate of the schedular income tax on profits was raised from 25 per cent to 32 per cent. The increase in the latter tax, however, was not expected to result in an increase in revenue as it was accompanied by the repeal of the tax on income from interest and dividends. As a result of these various measures and a good coffee and cocoa crop, the ordinary budget revenue rose sharply to CFAF 49.1 billion (from CFAF 38.4 billion in 1967) and continued upward in 1969 to CFAF 50.6 billion.

Indirect taxes continue to account for about 75 per cent of all revenue in the ordinary budget and for a somewhat larger share of total government revenue (Table 20). Export and import taxes alone account for some 56 per cent of ordinary budget revenue and the value-added tax for an additional 18 per cent. The revenue from excise taxes and a portion of the revenue from the value-added tax is earmarked for the investment budget and the Amortization Fund; this revenue accounts for about 20 per cent of total government revenue.

The share of direct taxes in total ordinary budget revenue rose by more than 2 percentage points to 18 per cent in 1966 and has since remained approximately unchanged. Nontax revenue (e.g., administrative fees and government property) represents some 5 per cent of ordinary budget revenue; its relative importance has increased somewhat in recent years.

From 1960 to 1965 the growth of government revenue exceeded the growth of the economy. The burden of taxation, as measured by the ratio of total government revenue to GDP rose from 18 per cent in 1960 to 20 per cent in 1965. This increase represented in part the application of new taxes (e.g., the value-added tax) and better enforcement and, to a smaller extent, the built-in progression of the tax system. Since 1965, however, total revenue apparently has increased less rapidly than the economy as a whole; its ratio to GDP declined to

19 per cent in 1966 and declined somewhat further in 1967, but rose again to 21 per cent in 1968.

Expenditure.—All major categories of expenditure contributed to the 18 per cent increase in ordinary budget expenditure between 1965 and

TABLE 20. IVORY COAST: GOVERNMENT REVENUE AND AMOUNT EARMARKED FOR THE INVESTMENT BUDGET AND THE AMORTIZATION FUND, 1965–68 [1]

(In billions of CFA francs)

	Actual		Estimates	
	1965	1966	Revised 1967 [2]	Original 1968
Ordinary budget				
Taxes on income and profits	3.8	5.1	4.9	5.9
Property taxes				
Real estate	0.6	0.6	0.9	0.9
Other [3]	1.4	1.6	1.5	1.0
Total property taxes	2.0	2.2	2.4	2.0
Value-added tax	7.3	6.9	7.0	9.9
Taxes on foreign trade				
Import duties	11.7	12.0	12.4	12.8
Export duties	10.0	10.3	9.9	9.4
Total taxes on foreign trade	21.7	22.3	22.3	22.2
Business tax and licenses	0.6	0.6	0.8	0.7
Other taxes	0.1	0.1	—	—
Administrative fees, service charges, etc.	1.2	1.6	1.9	2.1
Government property income	0.4	0.4	0.4	0.4
Total ordinary budget	37.1	39.2	39.7 [4]	43.2
Investment budget				
Taxes on income and profits	1.2	1.4	1.4	...
Real estate taxes	0.1	0.1	0.1	...
Taxes on production, consumption, and domestic transactions				
Value-added tax	2.6	2.6	2.5	...
Excise taxes				
Tobacco	0.2	0.3	0.3	...
Alcoholic beverages	0.2	0.2	0.4	...
Gasoline	1.5	1.6	1.5	...
Timber tax	0.7	0.5	0.6	...
Total	5.2	5.2	5.3	...
Business tax and licenses	0.1	0.1	0.4	...
Other taxes	1.0	0.3	—	...
Total investment budget	7.6	7.1	7.2	...
Amortization Fund [5]				
Taxes on production, consumption, and domestic transactions				
Value-added tax	1.8	1.9	2.1	...
Excise taxes				
Tobacco	1.4	1.4	1.5	...
Alcoholic beverages	1.0	1.0	1.0	...
Total Amortization Fund	4.2	4.3	4.6	...

TABLE 20 (*concluded*). IVORY COAST: GOVERNMENT REVENUE AND AMOUNT
EARMARKED FOR THE INVESTMENT BUDGET AND THE AMORTIZATION FUND,
1965–68 [1]

(*In billions of CFA francs*)

	Actual		Estimates	
	1965	1966	Revised 1967 [2]	Original 1968
Total revenue, recapitulation				
Taxes on income and profits	5.0	6.5	6.3	...
Taxes on property	2.1	2.3	2.5	...
Taxes on production, consumption, and domestic transactions	16.7	16.4	16.9	...
Taxes on foreign trade	21.7	22.3	23.2	...
Business taxes and licenses	0.7	0.7	1.2	...
Other taxes	1.1	0.4	—	...
Administrative fees, service charges, etc.	1.2	1.6	1.9	...
Government property income	0.4	0.4	0.4	...
Grand Total	48.9	50.6	51.5 [4]	...

Sources: *Loi de Finance 1968*, and data supplied by the Ivory Coast Treasury
and the Amortization Fund.

[1] Figures for ordinary budget revenue are by budget year (i.e., calendar year
plus complementary period).
[2] Actual figures for investment budget and Amortization Fund (Caisse Autonome d'Amortissement, or CAA).
[3] Death, gift, and property transfer taxes.
[4] Actual 1967, total ordinary budget revenue CFAF 39.1 million and grand
total CFAF 50.9 million.
[5] Refers to Amortization Fund's Public Debt Department, for which specified
tax revenue is earmarked for service of the public debt.

1967. However, the increase in expenditure for education and health
was somewhat larger than average and for economic and general services was smaller (see Table 19). No significant changes have occurred
in recent years in the distribution of ordinary budget expenditure
appropriations between wages and salaries (some 44 per cent), maintenance and materials (35 per cent), and subsidies and transfers (21 per
cent). In 1967 the Government imposed a flat 20 per cent cut on nonpersonnel expenditure. At the same time, however, temporary government personnel, hitherto paid out of the nonpersonnel budget
appropriations, were transferred to the payroll of regular civil servants;
this transfer largely explains the changes that occurred in the percentage distribution of ordinary budget expenditure in that year.

Between 1965 and 1967 the proportion of general service expenditure in total ordinary budget expenditure declined from some 37 per
cent to 34 per cent, or from 50 per cent to 48 per cent when joint

expenditure, representing a kind of overhead, is taken into account. In the same period, the proportion of expenditure for social services (mainly education and health) rose from 28 per cent to 30 per cent. Economic services (mainly in agriculture and public works) absorbed the remaining 22 per cent of total ordinary budget expenditure.

The 1970 ordinary budget estimates indicate an increase of CFAF 7.0 billion in expenditures over 1969, or about 15 per cent. This increase is due mainly to (1) a general increase in the civil service salaries (about CFAF 1.6 billion), (2) a transfer of technical assistance expenditure from the investment budget to the ordinary budget (about CFAF 1.0 billion), (3) an increase in the guaranteed debt of public entities (about CFAF 0.5 billion), (4) appropriations for the four new ministries created at the end of 1969 (about CFAF 0.8 billion), (5) a grant to the newly created public entities—the Bandama Valley Authority, the South West Area Authority, etc. (about CFAF 0.6 billion), and (6) an increase in subsidies, transfers, and in the current costs of administration.

Investment Budget

In the three years 1965–67, expenditure authorized in the investment budget rose from CFAF 12.7 billion to CFAF 17.6 billion (Table 21).

TABLE 21. IVORY COAST: INVESTMENT BUDGET ESTIMATES, 1965–70

(In billions of CFA francs)

	1965	1966	1967	1968	1969	1970
Receipts						
Tax revenue	7.2	9.6	7.8	8.6	10.1	13.1
Contribution of Stabilization Fund	—	1.3	3.0	2.1	2.1	13.5
Authorized borrowing	5.5	4.3	6.8	9.3	15.0	17.5
Total receipts = total expenditures	**12.7**	**15.2**	**17.6**	**20.0**	**27.2**	**44.1**
Expenditure						
Agriculture and industry	4.4	5.2	6.5	9.1	12.1	13.1
Transport and infrastructure	4.3	3.5	5.3	5.4	3.1	20.4
Administrative infrastructure	2.4	2.5	2.8	2.8	2.3	3.8
Education and health	0.3	2.7	1.7	1.5	1.5	5.3
Studies and research	1.3	1.3	1.3	1.2	2.2	1.5[1]

Source: Ivory Coast, "Budget Spécial d'Investissement et d'Equipement," *Journal Officiel.*

[1] CFAF 1.0 billion transferred to the ordinary budget in 1970.

The financing of this expenditure came from tax revenue earmarked for the investment budget, from contributions of the Stabilization Fund, and from borrowing by the Amortization Fund.

The 1968 investment budget provided for total expenditure (*prévisions d'emploi*) of CFAF 20.0 billion. This figure does not include carry-overs of nonutilized appropriations from previous years, amounting on December 31, 1967 to CFAF 6.9 billion. To finance the expenditure authorized in 1968, an increase was made in the tax revenue earmarked for the investment budget, in the Stabilization Fund contribution, and in borrowing by the Amortization Fund.

For 1969, total investment budget expenditure was raised to CFAF 27.2 billion, mainly because of two major projects—the hydroelectric complex on the Bandama and the new deep-water Port of San-Pédro—accounting for about one third of the estimated expenditure. These figures show that the investment budget expenditure is growing at a faster rate than ordinary budget expenditure; in 1969 it was equivalent to 58 per cent of the ordinary budget expenditure, compared with 46 per cent in 1968 and 44 per cent in 1967.

In 1970 estimated investment expenditures represent an increase of about 80 per cent over actual expenditures of 1969. Implementation of the San-Pédro and Kossou projects account for most of the increase with allocations for transport and infrastructure being projected to rise from CFAF 9.1 billion in 1969 to CFAF 20.4 billion, an increase of about 125 per cent.

PUBLIC DEBT AND THE AMORTIZATION FUND

The public debt comprises essentially the Central Government's debt and the debt contracted direct by public and semipublic enterprises. Management of the Central Government's debt is entrusted to the Public Debt Department of the Amortization Fund (Caisse Autonome d'Amortissement, or CAA). The Amortization Fund ensures the service of the public debt, for which it receives earmarked tax revenue. It is also authorized to contract domestic or foreign public debt required for the execution of the investment budget.

Furthermore, through its separate Banking Department, the Amortization Fund acts as a banker for public institutions, such as the Stabilization Fund, the Postal Checking System, the National Investment

Fund (FNI), and the National Finance Company (SONAFI); it holds their deposits and extends long-term credit (see "Money and banking," below). The Amortization Fund is not allowed to extend credit to the Treasury, with which it holds no current account; and its Banking Department may not make advances to its Public Debt Department. Thus far, the earmarked tax revenue transferred to the Public Debt Department has generally exceeded the public debt charges for interest and amortization, and the surplus has been deposited with the Banking Department.

Most of the public debt consists of medium-term and long-term debt contracted abroad. Disbursed foreign debt outstanding at the end of 1968 amounted to $172.7 million; an additional $151.9 million had been contracted but was still undisbursed (Table 22). A breakdown of

TABLE 22. IVORY COAST: EXTERNAL MEDIUM-TERM AND LONG-TERM
PUBLIC DEBT OUTSTANDING ON DECEMBER 31, 1968 [1]

(*In thousands of U.S. dollars*)

	Disbursed	Including Undisbursed
Publicly issued bonds	20,771	20,771
Privately placed debts		
Suppliers' credits	42,197	96,301
Private bank credits	13,100	19,300
Total privately placed debts	55,297	115,601
Loans from European Investment Bank	607	607
Loans from IBRD	—	5,800
U.S. Government loans		
(Export-Import Bank and AID)	12,235	54,134
Loans from other governments		
Denmark	—	2,000
France	75,287	88,968
Germany	3,791	13,750
Israel	—	2,000
Italy	1,955	14,656
Lebanon	2,800	3,800
Norway	—	2,520
Total loans from other governments	83,833	127,694
Grand Total [2]	172,743	324,607

Source: IBRD, Statistical Services Division.

[1] Debt with an original or extended maturity of one year or more, repayable in convertible currency as defined to include the CFA franc.

[2] Includes, whenever it applies, debt payable in French francs and CFA francs, which are converted at the exchange rate as devalued in August 1969.

interest and amortization charges on the foreign debt contracted as of the end of 1968 is given in Table 23. For 1969, these charges totaled $28.4 million, roughly 10 per cent of the value of exports for the same year. These charges were scheduled to rise sharply until 1972 and then to decline in the following years.

Debt of the Central Government

On December 31, 1967 the outstanding medium-term and long-term debt of the Central Government managed by the Amortization Fund totaled CFAF 25.5 billion, an increase of 6 per cent over 1966 (Table 24). Debt contracted but still undisbursed on that date totaled CFAF 4 billion. The outstanding debt consisted almost entirely of foreign long-term loans and bonds, and suppliers' credits.

About 70 per cent of all contractual borrowing outstanding (CFAF 10.8 billion) on December 31, 1967 was due to France. The main creditor

TABLE 23. IVORY COAST: ESTIMATED CONTRACTUAL SERVICE PAYMENTS ON EXTERNAL MEDIUM-TERM AND LONG-TERM PUBLIC DEBT OUTSTANDING ON DECEMBER 31, 1968 [1]

(In thousands of U.S. dollars)

	Debt Outstanding at Beginning of Period Including Undisbursed	Payments During Period		
		Amortization	Interest	Total
1969	313,006	21,014	7,378	28,392
1970	291,992	25,635	8,977	34,612
1971	266,357	25,003	9,596	34,599
1972	241,354	27,883	9,676	37,560
1973	213,470	23,211	9,005	32,216
1974	190,259	21,935	8,304	30,238
1975	168,325	17,431	7,353	24,784
1976	150,893	15,938	6,567	22,504
1977	134,956	14,066	5,852	19,918
1978	120,890	13,935	5,181	19,116
1979	106,955	12,582	4,521	17,103
1980	94,372	12,296	3,930	16,226
1981	82,076	9,634	3,365	12,999
1982	72,442	9,331	2,900	12,231
1983	63,111	9,089	2,439	11,528

Source: IBRD, Statistical Services Division.

[1] Includes service on all debts listed in Table 22 except the following loans totaling $11,601,000, for which repayment terms are unknown: (1) suppliers' credits $1,195,000, (2) private bank credits $3,000,000, and (3) loans from governments totaling $7,406,000.

TABLE 24. IVORY COAST: CENTRAL GOVERNMENT MEDIUM-TERM AND LONG-TERM
DEBT (MANAGED BY THE CAISSE AUTONOME D'AMORTISSEMENT)
OUTSTANDING ON DECEMBER 31, 1967

(In billions of CFA francs)

Serviced with earmarked tax revenue	
Contractual loans	9.7
Publicly issued bonds	4.5
Suppliers' credits	9.4
Total	23.6
Serviced with resources supplied by beneficiaries	
Publicly issued bonds	0.8
Contractual loans	1.1
Total	1.9
Grand Total	25.5

Source: Data provided by the Public Debt Department of the Amortization
Fund (Caisse Autonome d'Amortissement).

was the French CCCE, whose outstanding claims consisted of a number of long-term, low-interest loans totaling CFAF 6.7 billion. This borrowing also included consolidated advances of the French Treasury, the French Caisse des Dépôts et Consignations, and the French Fonds d'Aide et de Coopération (FAC).

The publicly issued debt consisted mainly of long-term bonds floated by Ivory Coast on the Paris market since 1959 and generally carrying an interest rate of 5 per cent. At the end of 1967, such issues totaled CFAF 6.0 billion, of which CFAF 4.5 billion was outstanding. Other publicly issued debt included bonds with a 40-year maturity issued by the Amortization Fund in Ivory Coast (CFAF 0.8 billion) in replacement of National Investment Fund (FNI) certificates, carrying an interest rate of 2.5 per cent.

Suppliers' credits outstanding (CFAF 9.4 billion) consisted largely of credit extended to the Government by private firms engaged in research or public works in Ivory Coast. The duration of these credits is at least double that of the execution of the works. Generally, the suppliers obtain the necessary capital from foreign banks or financial groups and have access to credit insurance facilities in the exporting country.

In Table 24, the debt of the Central Government outstanding at the end of 1967 is broken down in two major categories: (1) debt contracted by the Public Debt Department of the Amortization Fund or the Ivory Coast Government and serviced by the Amortization Fund out of its own resources (i.e., earmarked tax revenue) and (2) debt contracted by the Amortization Fund for the financing of specific projects and serviced by the Fund through resources provided by those agencies or enterprises which are the beneficiaries of the borrowed funds. In 1967 the interest and amortization charges on the first category of debt totaled CFAF 4.9 billion, or nearly 10 per cent of total government revenue.

Debt of Public and Semipublic Enterprises

At the end of 1966 the medium-term and long-term debt outstanding owed by Ivory Coast's public and semipublic enterprises totaled some CFAF 13.4 billion. It consisted almost entirely of foreign long-term contractual loans and suppliers' credits provided mainly by the French CCCE. This debt is serviced directly by the contracting enterprises which are legal entities distinct from the Central Government. The Government authorizes these enterprises to contract loans only when it is satisfied that they will be able to provide for the amortization of the debts from their own resources. Some loans contracted by public and semipublic enterprises, however, are covered by government guarantees (*avals*); in 1966 these loans represented about half of the total debt.

The total amount of the debt increased to CFAF 32.9 billion at the end of 1968, of which central government debt accounted for 85 per cent.

In November 1969, CAA issued bonds for the first time on the local market, the proceeds of which will be used for investment financing needs. These bonds bearing an interest rate of 7 per cent have an attractive lottery feature and are tax exempt.

The service payments on the debt managed by the CAA will reach a peak in 1971 and 1972 and will begin declining again only after 1972, as a result of the first payments coming due on a Euro-dollar loan of CFAF 1.1 billion and two German loans used in connection with the San-Pédro port construction. Earmarked revenue will be insufficient to cover the scheduled payments in these years; the deficits are expected to be met from a reserve set aside from the surpluses of earlier years.

MONEY AND BANKING

MONETARY SYSTEM

Ivory Coast is a member of the franc area. It is also a member of the West African Monetary Union (Union Monétaire Ouest Africaine, or UMOA), together with six other countries (Dahomey, Mauritania, Niger, Senegal, Togo, and Upper Volta). These countries have a common currency, the CFA franc, and a common central bank, the Banque Centrale des Etats de l'Afrique de l'Ouest (BCEAO), which is the issuing authority for UMOA and keeps its external reserves. The CFA franc is fully convertible into French francs at the rate of CFAF 1 = F 0.02. On August 10, 1969 the rate against the U.S. dollar became CFAF 277.710 per dollar; previously, since January 1, 1960, the rate had been CFAF 246.853. (For further details on the operation of BCEAO, see Chapter 4, and for information on the change in par value, see Chapter 6.)

STRUCTURE OF THE BANKING SYSTEM

Central Bank Operations

BCEAO operates in Ivory Coast, as in the other UMOA countries, through a local agency. Decisions concerning the implementation of BCEAO policies in Ivory Coast are taken by the National Monetary Committee. The Director of the local BCEAO agency, who serves on the National Monetary Committee in an advisory capacity, is responsible for the application of these policies.

Assets and liabilities of the Central Bank are shown in Table 25, and its credit operations are discussed with those of other institutions below.

Operations of Commercial Banks and Other Financial Institutions

Besides BCEAO, the Ivory Coast's banking system includes four commercial banks and four specialized public credit institutions. The four commercial banks are the Banque Internationale pour l'Afrique Occidentale (BIAO), which also operates in neighboring countries; the Banque Internationale pour le Commerce et l'Industrie en Côte d'Ivoire (BICICI); the Société Générale de Banques en Côte d'Ivoire

TABLE 25. IVORY COAST: ASSETS AND LIABILITIES OF THE CENTRAL BANK, 1962–69

(In billions of CFA francs; end of period)

	1962	1963	1964	1965	1966	1967			1968				1969		
						Sept.	Dec.	Mar.	June	Sept.	Dec.	Mar.	June	Sept.
Assets															
Foreign assets	8.93	10.07	9.52	14.89	14.99	16.44	17.08	19.92	18.23	18.68	19.29	19.53	20.17	18.14
Claims on Government	—	0.76	—	—	1.16	—	1.82	—	—	—	0.37	—	—	—
Claims on deposit money banks	10.23	12.34	17.84	11.99	13.32	7.29	12.66	18.84	15.38	11.29	15.65	22.89	15.38	12.49
Assets = liabilities	**19.16**	**23.17**	**27.36**	**26.88**	**29.47**	**23.73**	**31.56**	**38.76**	**33.61**	**29.97**	**35.31**	**42.42**	**35.55**	**30.63**
Liabilities															
Reserve money	18.61	21.98	24.99	25.40	28.84	22.39	30.85	36.53	31.11	27.69	33.32	38.97	32.46	27.90
Currency outside banks	*17.94*	*20.88*	*23.43*	*22.85*	*26.36*	*20.28*	*27.60*	*34.58*	*28.81*	*25.12*	*30.60*	*34.89*	*2.19*	*25.36*
Government deposits	0.26	0.28	2.18	1.20	0.56	1.14	0.57	1.93	2.34	1.80	0.89	3.15	2.36	2.57
Foreign liabilities	0.66	1.28	0.18	0.27	0.07	0.19	0.11	0.30	0.17	0.46	1.08	0.30	0.59	0.15
Other items (net)	−0.37	−0.37	—	0.01	0.02	0.01	0.03	—	—	0.01	0.01	—	0.14	—

Source: IMF, *International Financial Statistics.*

(SGBCI); and the Société Ivoirienne de Banque (SIB)—all predominantly foreign owned, with French banks holding a majority
interest. Ivory Coast holds a 10 per cent equity interest in the first
three banks through the National Finance Company (SONAFI). All
commercial banks have their main offices in Abidjan and maintain
branch offices in other centers. Between December 1965 and September
1969, the number of permanent commercial banking offices increased
from 20 to 29.

At the end of September 1969 the commercial banks accounted for
61 per cent of the total deposits and 73 per cent of the total credit of
the banking system.

Among the four credit institutions with specialized functions—all
under public or semipublic ownership (Table 26)—the most important
in size of operations is the Banking Department of the Amortization
Fund, which acts as banker to most public sector enterprises. Through
a separate department, the Fund also manages the public debt (see
"Government finance," above). Most public agencies and institutions are
required to deposit their surplus funds with the Fund's Banking Department; these include the Stabilization Fund, the Social Security Fund,
the National Finance Company, the National Investment Company
(FNI), the Postal Checking System, and the Amortization Fund's own
Public Debt Department. Most loans of the Amortization Fund are
made to public or semipublic enterprises; some are made to banks or
private enterprises for financing development projects. The Fund is for-
bidden to make direct loans to the Treasury but does rediscount customs duty bills held by the Treasury. At the end of September 1969 the
Fund's Banking Department accounted for 91 per cent of the total
deposits and 39 per cent of the total credit of the public and semipublic
credit institutions combined.

Two institutions provide medium-term and long-term credit for
industry. (1) The Industrial Development Bank (Banque Ivoirienne de
Développement Industriel, or BIDI) was established in February 1965.
On September 30, 1967 the medium-term and long-term credit extended
by this institution totaled about CFAF 950 million, or CFAF 345
million above the level of one year earlier. It is intended to concentrate mainly on larger industrial loans. (2) The longer established
Credit Bank (Crédit de la Côte d'Ivoire, or CCI) now concentrates its

TABLE 26. IVORY COAST: PUBLIC AND SEMIPUBLIC CREDIT INSTITUTIONS, 1969 [1]

	Year of Establishment	Capital	Capital Participation		Type of Operation
		Million CFA francs	Government	Other	
			← Per cent →		
Caisse Autonome d'Amortissement—Banking Department (CAA)	1959	630 [2]	100	—	Banker for public institutions
Banque Ivoirienne de Développement Industriel (BIDI)	1964	700	21	79 [3]	Medium-term and long-term credits to industrial enterprises
Crédit de la Côte d'Ivoire (CCI)	1955	800	75	25 [4]	Medium-term loans for private construction and small industrial enterprises
Banque Nationale de Développement Agricole (BNDA)	1968	700	67	33 [5]	Agricultural credit

Source: BCEAO, Annuaire des Banques de l'Union Monétaire Ouest Africaine, 1969.

[1] These institutions are those classified as "business and development banks," under the Ivory Coast's banking legislation and are included in "deposit money banks" in IMF banking statistics. Certain other public financial institutions not so classified are indicated in the text.
[2] Reserves.
[3] CCCE 11 per cent, BCEAO 6 per cent, IFC 6 per cent, Banque Française du Commerce Extérieur 5 per cent, Chase International Investment Company 9 per cent, Lazard Frères & Company of New York 9 per cent, Ivory Coast private shareholders 14 per cent, French private shareholders 14 per cent, and U.S. private shareholders 3 per cent.
[4] CCCE 17 per cent and BCEAO 8 per cent.
[5] Stabilization Fund 17 per cent, BCEAO 8 per cent, and CCCE 8 per cent.

new loans in small industrial, handicraft, and private construction ventures. Besides its capital, it has received long-term resources from CCCE for relending. At the end of February 1968 its outstanding loans (mostly long-term) amounted to CFAF 4.6 billion.

Functions of the Caisse Nationale de Crédit Agricole (CNA), formed in 1959, with 100 per cent government equity, to make medium-term loans to farmers, were taken over by the new National Agricultural Development Bank (Banque Nationale de Développement Agricole, or BNDA), established early in 1968. The new Bank makes loans for agricultural projects mainly through the official agencies dealing with various aspects of agricultural production.

Assets and liabilities of the commercial banks are shown separately in Table 27 from those of the specialized public credit institutions—the Amortization Fund (CAA), the Industrial and the Agricultural Development Banks (BIDI and CNA), and the Credit Bank (CCI). These data are given for the end of September in the years 1965–69.

Table 28 shows the combined assets and liabilities of these institutions at the end of the years 1962–67, and since then by quarters (through September 1969), together with the Treasury's claims on the private sector and the deposits of the Postal Checking System and savings banks.

In addition to the banks and credit institutions described above, certain specialized financial institutions are normally not included in monetary statistics. These institutions include the National Finance Company (Société Nationale de Financement, or SONAFI), which holds government equity participations in industrial enterprises and also extends some long-term loans to industry, and the National Investment Fund (Fonds National d'Investissement, or FNI), which collects private funds through a compulsory scheme largely for the financing of development projects.

The National Finance Company was created in November 1963 with the primary objective of mobilizing voluntary domestic savings through long-term bond sales to private individuals and enterprises. Another objective was the creation of a basis for a domestic capital market. Its bonds mature in 20 years and bear 6 per cent interest, tax free. Although in principle its resources may be used for various investments, in practice they have been utilized mainly for government participations

TABLE 27. IVORY COAST: ASSETS AND LIABILITIES OF COMMERCIAL BANKS AND SPECIALIZED PUBLIC CREDIT INSTITUTIONS, END OF SEPTEMBER, 1965–69

(In billions of CFA francs)

	Commercial Banks					Specialized Public Credit Institutions					Total				
	1965	1966	1967	1968	1969	1965	1966	1967	1968	1969	1965	1966	1967	1968	1969
Reserves	0.6	0.5	0.6	0.7	0.7	1.1	1.2	1.2	1.8	1.4	1.7	1.7	1.8	2.5	2.1
Foreign assets	1.3	1.9	1.6	2.1	2.6	12.3	9.6	2.4	5.5	17.1	13.6	11.5	4.0	7.6	19.7
Claims on private sector	32.9	32.5	33.6	43.8	47.1	8.0	9.2	11.3	12.2	14.4	40.9	41.7	44.9	56.0	61.5
Assets = liabilities	**34.8**	**34.9**	**35.8**	**46.6**	**50.4**	**21.4**	**20.0**	**14.9**	**19.5**	**32.9**	**56.2**	**54.9**	**50.7**	**66.1**	**83.3**
Deposits															
Demand deposits	15.2	17.2	17.9	22.9	26.0	1.5	1.0	1.3	1.7	2.3	16.7	18.2	19.3	24.5	28.3
Time deposits	0.5	1.8	2.8	2.4	2.3	9.3	6.1	5.0	8.6	15.4	9.8	7.9	7.8	11.0	17.7
Government deposits	0.3	0.3	0.3	0.4	0.3	9.2	11.1	7.3	7.7	8.3	9.4	11.4	7.7	8.1	8.6
Total deposits	15.9	19.3	21.0	25.6	28.6	20.0	18.2	13.6	18.0	26.0	35.9	37.5	34.8	43.6	54.6
Foreign liabilities	4.1	4.0	3.7	4.7	4.9	2.6	3.2	3.4	3.6	4.6	6.7	7.2	7.1	8.3	9.5
Credit from Central Bank	12.4	8.4	6.6	10.7	11.7	0.2	0.5	0.7	0.6	0.8	12.6	8.9	7.3	11.3	12.5
Interbank obligations (net)	1.4	1.5	3.1	3.9	3.3	−1.4	−1.5	−3.1	−3.9	−3.3	—	—	—	—	—
Capital	1.1	1.2	1.3	1.3	1.3	1.3	1.3	1.5	{ 1.2	4.8	2.4	2.5	2.8	{ 2.9	
Other items (net)	−0.2	0.5	—	0.4	0.6	−1.2	−1.6	−1.3			−1.4	−1.2	−1.3		6.7

Source: Information provided by BCEAO.

TABLE 28. IVORY COAST: ASSETS AND LIABILITIES OF COMMERCIAL BANKS, SPECIALIZED PUBLIC CREDIT INSTITUTIONS, AND OTHER FINANCIAL INSTITUTIONS, 1962–69

(In billions of CFA francs; end of period)

	1962	1963	1964	1965	1966	1967	1968				1969		
							Mar.	June	Sept.	Dec.	Mar.	June	Sept.
COMMERCIAL BANKS AND SPECIALIZED PUBLIC CREDIT INSTITUTIONS													
Reserves	0.65	0.93	1.29	2.37	2.20	2.81	1.48	2.15	2.48	2.61	3.78	2.89	2.06
Foreign assets	−2.85	7.15	12.58	8.54	11.37	5.87	9.10	8.66	7.56	14.59	17.02	17.02	19.67
Claims on private sector	26.27	33.49	44.79	41.64	45.75	52.24	62.43	61.33	55.96	62.36	71.28	66.42	61.54
Assets = liabilities	**24.07**	**41.57**	**58.66**	**52.55**	**59.34**	**60.92**	**73.01**	**72.14**	**66.00**	**79.56**	**92.08**	**86.33**	**83.27**
Demand deposits	10.05	11.86	15.94	18.09	18.97	19.64	23.34	22.66	24.47	27.18	29.16	30.09	28.31
Time deposits	2.19	2.23	8.92	6.62	7.54	9.71	12.45	13.45	11.04	13.44	17.30	17.05	17.75
Government deposits	2.78	6.92	5.68	8.40	11.28	9.02	9.23	7.86	8.11	9.55	8.80	8.17	9.50
Foreign liabilities	...	8.31	9.38	7.51	7.23	8.39	8.23	10.91	8.28	10.44	9.31	11.09	8.58
Credit from Central Bank	10.14	12.36	17.84	11.99	13.34	12.66	18.84	15.36	11.29	15.64	22.89	15.38	12.48
Other items (net)	−1.09	−0.11	0.91	−0.05	0.96	1.51	0.91	1.89	2.81	3.30	4.62	4.55	6.65
OTHER FINANCIAL INSTITUTIONS													
Treasury: Claims on private sector	2.88	2.78	2.54	3.09	2.42	2.53	3.10	3.12	2.35	3.15	3.04	2.78	2.69
Postal Checking System: Deposits	1.17	1.20	1.20	1.30	1.08	1.28	1.36	1.35	1.34	1.32	1.72	1.83	1.59
Savings banks: Deposits	0.37	0.39	0.44	0.48	0.52	0.61	0.70	0.72	0.70	0.74	0.78	0.81	0.78

Source: IMF, *International Financial Statistics.*

in enterprises and to promote new enterprises by capital participations or lending.

In 1962 the National Investment Fund was created to collect private funds through a compulsory plan, with the objective of utilizing domestically part of the profits of foreign enterprises which would otherwise be transferred abroad. Its resources are derived from a 10 per cent levy on business income and a 16 per cent levy on real property, both in the form of compulsory subscriptions to noninterest-bearing certificates with no specific maturity. The certificates may be redeemed at three times their face value for approved productive investments or may be converted into National Finance Company bonds if an equal amount is invested in cash. If not used for these two purposes, the certificates are to be converted into 40-year 2.5 per cent bonds of the Amortization Fund. The Investment Fund redeems certificates collected by the Amortization Fund, which transfers the cash received to the National Finance Company. Its establishing legislation allows the National Investment Fund to spend 10 per cent of its resources on development research and to use the remainder for financing development projects, keeping its liquid resources as time deposits with the Amortization Fund.

Finally, the Société Africaine de Crédit Automobile (SAFCA) and the Société Ivoirienne de Financement (SIF) provide short-term credit mainly to finance purchases of vehicles, equipment, and consumer items. The French CCCE makes certain direct medium-term and long-term loans to public and private enterprises in Ivory Coast. Deposits from the private sector are also collected in the Post Office, Savings Bank, and Checking System; these are mostly redeposited with the Amortization Fund.

In 1968 the Government established the Fonds de Garantie des Crédits aux Entreprises Ivoiriennes to provide guarantees for commercial bank credit to local enterpreneurs; its operations, started in 1969, have so far reached only a modest volume.

The Treasury of Ivory Coast also performs certain banking operations. It accepts customs duty bills (*obligations cautionnées*) with a maturity of four months in payment of certain indirect taxes, principally customs duties. These bills are discountable at BCEAO. The Treasury may receive deposits from public and semipublic institutions.

Besides credit extended by banks, the Caisse Centrale de Coopération

Economique (CCCE), a French public institution, extends medium-term and long-term credit and contributes to the financing of the Development Bank's credit operations. In addition, it acts as the authorized agent of the Fonds d'Aide et de Coopération (FAC) and the European Development Fund (EDF, or Fonds Européen de Développement, or FED) for local aid disbursements.

BANKING LEGISLATION AND REGULATIONS

After establishing UMOA, member governments undertook to adopt basically uniform banking legislation and terms. In Ivory Coast, banking legislation introduced on August 4, 1965 and subsequently elaborated in decrees specified the basic conditions and regulations governing banks and other credit establishments. Among other things, it prescribed banks' solvency requirements, by establishing minimum capital requirements and by limiting equity participations.

While BCEAO has certain regulatory powers over banks and financial institutions, the legislation of August 4, 1965 contemplated and government decree (September 5, 1966) established (1) a Banking Control Commission responsible for general supervision over the application of banking regulations and for advising the Minister of Economic and Financial Affairs on the admission of new banks and the expansion of banking facilities; and (2) a National Credit Council, a consultative body that may be charged by the government with the preparation of studies concerning the orientation of credit policy, credit distribution, and the organization of the banking profession. The Minister of Economic and Financial Affairs presides over the Council, which is composed essentially of representatives of the country's economic and financial ministries, its banking sector, and BCEAO.

INTEREST RATES

Since the establishment of UMOA, BCEAO's discount rate has remained unchanged at 3.5 per cent annually, and the rate for documentary credit relating to financing of exports at 3 per cent. Until May 1966, banks charged uniform interest rates determined in relation to customers' creditworthiness; consequently interest rates for small customers tended to be relatively high. At that time, however, the structure of interest rates charged by banks was first revised by relating interest rates to the nature of the operation financed. All rates on credit operations are computed on the basis of the present official discount rate of BCEAO, to which specified percentage points are added. Effective interest rates of 4.5 to 5.25 per cent are charged on short-term credit to finance crops, and on short-term and medium-term credit for productive purposes and for enterprises which have received priority status under the Investment Code. Interest rates of 7.0 to 7.5 per cent are charged on real estate operations not declared of social interest. Penalty rates of 8.0 to 8.5 per cent are charged on all credit operations in excess of individual rediscount limits with BCEAO.

In May 1969, BCEAO's Board raised from 8 per cent to 9 per cent the discount rate on rediscountable credit granted to enterprises in excess of their short-term individual ceilings. The same new regulation applies to short-term nonrediscountable credits for amounts in excess of CFAF 5 million, compared with CFAF 1 million under the previous regulation.

MONETARY AND CREDIT DEVELOPMENTS

Monetary and credit developments in Ivory Coast are subject to marked seasonality because of crop financing requirements; usually credit rises to a peak during the early part of the year and falls to its lowest level around September (Table 29).

Money Supply

Money supply increased but at a declining rate during 1964–67. After reaching nearly 20 per cent in the year ended September 1964, the rate of increase dropped to 9 per cent in the next year and to 4 per cent in the year ended September 1967. Since currency in circulation changed relatively little between 1965 and 1967, the expansion of money supply involved mainly changes in demand deposits. In the same period, quasi-money declined by nearly 25 per cent as a result of a fall in deposits of public sector enterprises. In the year ended September 1968, however, money supply expanded by 25 per cent and quasi-money by 42 per cent, largely reflecting the economic activity generated by the excellent coffee crop. In the next year, money supply rose by 9 per cent and quasi-money by 61 per cent. The rapid expansion in quasi-

TABLE 29. IVORY COAST: MONETARY SURVEY, 1962–69

(In billions of CFA francs; end of period)

	1962 Sept.	1963 Sept.	1964 Sept.	1965 Sept.	1966 Sept.	1967 Sept.	1967 Dec.	1968 Mar.	1968 June	1968 Sept.	1968 Dec.	1969 Mar.	1969 June	1969 Sept.
Assets														
Foreign assets (net)														
Central Bank	...	...	7.7	7.5	13.3	16.3	17.0	19.6	18.1	18.2	18.2	19.3	19.6	18.0
Other banks	...	...	5.0	6.9	4.2	−3.1	−2.5	0.9	−2.2	−0.7	4.2	7.7	5.9	10.2
Total foreign assets	9.2	6.9	12.7	14.4	17.5	13.2	14.5	20.5	15.8	17.5	22.4	27.0	25.5	28.2
Domestic credit														
Claims on Government (net)	−3.2	−5.8	−9.8	−8.4	−10.7	−7.8	−6.8	−10.6	−10.1	−9.1	−10.3	−13.1	−11.3	−12.0
Claims on private sector	22.2	29.6	40.0	43.7	44.3	47.2	54.8	65.5	64.5	58.3	65.5	74.3	69.2	64.2
Total domestic credit	19.0	23.8	30.2	35.2	33.6	39.4	48.0	54.9	54.4	49.2	55.2	61.2	57.9	52.3
Assets = liabilities	**28.2**	**30.7**	**42.8**	**49.6**	**51.1**	**52.6**	**62.5**	**75.4**	**70.2**	**66.7**	**77.6**	**88.2**	**83.4**	**80.5**
Liabilities														
Money														
Currency outside banks	14.0	15.8	18.9	19.2	20.0	20.3	27.6	34.6	28.9	25.1	30.6	34.9	29.2	25.4
Demand deposits [1]	11.2	12.4	14.9	18.0	19.3	20.4	20.9	24.8	24.0	25.8	28.5	30.9	31.9	28.3
With Post Office	—	—	*1.2*	*1.3*	*1.1*	*1.2*	*1.3*	*1.4*	*1.3*	*1.3*	*1.3*	*1.7*	*1.8*	*1.6*
Total money	25.2	28.2	33.8	37.3	39.3	40.7	48.5	59.4	52.9	50.9	59.1	65.8	61.2	55.3
Quasi-money [1]	2.1	2.3	8.2	9.8	7.9	7.8	9.7	12.5	13.5	11.1	13.5	17.3	17.1	17.8
Other items	0.9	0.2	0.8	2.6	3.9	4.1	4.2	3.5	3.8	4.7	5.0	5.1	5.1	7.4

Sources: IMF, *International Financial Statistics*, and data provided by BCEAO.

[1] Includes certain deposits not separately shown.

money since September 1967 is attributable mainly to the increase in term deposits of the Stabilization Fund with the Amortization Fund.

Before September 1965 the gain in money supply resulted from the continued expansion of both net foreign assets and domestic credit. In the year ended September 1966, however, domestic credit actually declined slightly as a result of an increase in the Government's net creditor position with the banking system, which outweighed the small upturn in credit to the private sector, while net foreign assets continued to increase. By September 1967, domestic credit had resumed its expansion, and this trend strengthened in 1968. The Government's net creditor position was slightly reduced between September 1966 and September 1968, and credit to the private sector rose by 32 per cent. In the year ended September 1969, credit to the private sector rose by only 6 per cent.

Net foreign assets of the banking system, which fell by 25 per cent in 1967, regained their 1966 level in September 1968 and rose further to CFAF 28.2 billion in September 1969. Net foreign assets held by BCEAO increased considerably during 1965–67, and those held by other banks declined sharply in 1967 (see Tables 26 and 28). The net foreign asset position of the commercial banks has generally been negative (see Table 27). Since September 1967, BCEAO's net foreign assets have changed relatively little, and the bulk of the increase has occurred almost entirely in the holdings of the specialized credit institutions, reflecting mainly the placement abroad of surplus liquidity of the Amortization Fund from the sharply increased deposits of the Stabilization Fund and other public agencies with the Amortization Fund.

Credit to the Economy

Apart from seasonal fluctuations, total short-term credit remained relatively unchanged between 1965 and 1967. The four commercial banks continued to supply most of this credit (Table 30), including virtually all the credit required for seasonal crop financing. Relatively small amounts of short-term credit were extended to the private sector by specialized credit institutions, and by the Treasury in the form of short-term customs duty bills; this credit has remained virtually unchanged since 1965. Rediscounts by BCEAO of short-term credit tended to fluctuate with seasonal financing requirements but, on the

TABLE 30. IVORY COAST: CREDIT TO THE ECONOMY, 1965–69

(In billions of CFA francs; end of period)

	1965	1966		1967		1968		1969	
	(Sept.)	Mar.	Sept.	Mar.	Sept.	Mar.	Sept.	Mar.	Sept.
CREDIT EXTENDED									
Commercial banks									
Short-term	31.3	35.0	30.5	35.6	31.2	48.0	40.8	54.4	43.5
Medium-term and long-term	1.6	1.6	1.9	2.0	2.3	2.1	3.0	3.3	3.6
Total commercial banks	31.9	36.6	32.5	37.6	33.5	50.1	43.8	57.7	47.1
Specialized public credit institutions									
Short-term	2.3	2.4	2.2	2.5	2.5	2.7	2.2	2.8	...
Medium-term and long-term	5.7	6.4	7.0	7.6	8.8	9.5	10.9	10.7	...
Total specialized public credit institutions	8.0	8.8	9.2	10.1	11.3	12.2	13.1	13.5	14.4
Treasury (short-term) [1]	2.8	3.3	2.6	2.2	2.5	3.1	2.4	3.0	2.7
Total credit extended	43.7	48.7	44.3	49.9	47.3	65.5	58.3	74.2	64.2
Short-term	*36.4*	*40.7*	*35.4*	*40.3*	*36.2*	*53.9*	*45.4*	*60.2*	...
Medium-term and long-term	*7.3*	*8.0*	*8.9*	*9.6*	*11.1*	*11.6*	*12.9*	*14.0*	...
CREDIT REDISCOUNTED AT BCEAO									
Commercial banks									
Short-term	11.3	11.4	6.8	9.3	5.0	16.9	8.7	20.0	9.1
Medium-term and long-term	1.1	1.5	1.6	1.4	1.6	1.2	2.0	2.3	2.6
Total commercial banks	12.4	12.9	8.4	10.7	6.6	18.1	10.7	22.3	11.7
Specialized public credit institutions									
Short-term	—	0.1	—	—	—	—	—	—	...
Medium-term and long-term	0.2	0.5	0.5	0.7	0.7	0.8	0.6	0.6	...
Total specialized public credit institutions	0.2	0.5	0.5	0.7	0.7	0.8	0.6	0.6	...
Total credit discounted	12.6	13.4	8.9	11.4	7.3	18.9	11.3	22.9	...

Source: Data supplied by BCEAO.

[1] Customs duty bills, which are short-term claims on the private sector.

whole, declined rather sharply during 1966–67. In 1968, however, short-term credit rose by 25 per cent, mainly because of large increases in credit supplied by commercial banks, and continued upward but more slowly in 1969. This trend was reflected in rediscounts.

Medium-term and long-term credit to the economy rose steadily, without appreciable seasonal variation during 1965–69, increasing by 22 per cent in the year ended September 1966, by a further 25 per cent in the next year, and at a slower rate thereafter. This credit is supplied principally by the specialized credit institutions. Most of the medium-term credit provided by commercial banks was rediscounted with BCEAO, while specialized credit institutions had little recourse to rediscounting.

Table 31 shows distribution by economic sectors of total credit, including medium-term and long-term credit extended directly by CCCE to enterprises in Ivory Coast but excluding small bank loans. (The figures therefore differ somewhat from those presented in Table 30.) Roughly two thirds of the total short-term credit went to the commercial sector, including crop marketing; this credit varied widely by seasons, depending on the value and timing of the crops. Industry and agriculture absorbed an increasing amount of short-term credit during 1965–67, while credit to construction remained virtually stable. The trend in medium-term and long-term credit was also upward, with industry and construction receiving a large share of the total. Short-term credit was directed largely to the private sector companies, but much of the medium-term and long-term credit (about 56 per cent at the end of September 1967) was extended to public and semipublic enterprises. In September 1969, roughly 40 per cent of the total credit surveyed consisted of short-term credit to commercial enterprises. This proportion had declined from 66 per cent in September 1967, indicating the increased relative importance of other sectors in the credit distribution. The most volatile element in credit to commercial enterprises is that provided to exporters of coffee and cocoa: this credit generally rises sharply in March, during the height of the exporting season, and falls to a seasonal low in September. Short-term credit to agriculture and forestry rose about 40 per cent over 1967–69, but remained a rather small part (about 5 per cent) of the total credit surveyed. In the remaining categories of industry and construction/public works, there

TABLE 31.   IVORY COAST: CREDIT BY ECONOMIC SECTOR, 1965–69 [1]

(In billions of CFA francs; end of period)

	1965	1966	1967		1968		1969	
			Mar.	Sept.	Mar.	Sept.	Mar.	Sept.
Short-term								
Commerce	20.6	22.2	22.9	18.0	32.3	24.1	34.1	23.7
Industry	4.3	4.8	5.3	4.8	6.3	5.6	6.8	6.6
Construction and public works	2.6	2.4	2.7	2.7	2.8	3.0	3.4	3.8
Agriculture	0.9	1.1	1.4	2.1	2.2	2.2	3.1	2.8
Other	2.2	2.0	2.5	2.4	....	....	....	....
Total short-term	30.6	32.5	34.8	30.0	46.8	37.8	51.3	40.2
Medium-term and long-term								
Industry	5.1	5.5	5.0	5.2	5.2	5.6	5.6	6.3
Construction and public works	5.1	4.9	5.3	5.5	6.3	6.3	6.5	6.5
Other	3.3	3.6	3.7	4.8	4.3	4.9	5.3	5.5
Total medium-term and long-term	13.5	14.0	14.0	15.5	15.8	16.8	17.4	18.3
Total credit	44.1	46.5	48.8	45.5	62.6	54.6	68.7	58.5

Source: Information provided by BCEAO.

[1] Includes medium-term and long-term credits extended directly by CCCE to enterprises, but excludes credits of less than CFAF 10 million.

has been a steady growth in both short-term and medium-term to long-term credit.

Credit extended by BCEAO.—The amount of credit rediscounted at BCEAO declined considerably during 1965–67 (see Table 30) with the increase in lending capacity of the commercial banks. The rediscount ceilings applied by BCEAO to short-term credit to the economy vary with seasonal requirements. At the end of September 1967, these ceilings totaled CFAF 5.3 billion and actual rediscounts CFAF 5.0 billion. BCEAO reduced the short-term rediscount ceilings for commercial banks early in 1967, when the Banking Department of the Amortization Fund placed CFAF 3 billion on deposit with the commercial banks to augment their liquidity. At the end of September 1967 the rediscount ceiling for medium-term credit (operations initiated in Ivory Coast) totaled CFAF 8 billion. Authorizations for rediscounts granted by BCEAO reached CFAF 2.6 billion, while actual rediscounts totaled CFAF 2.3 billion. The major part of the unutilized medium-term rediscount facilities at that date were for approved operations financed by specialized credit institutions, particularly the Banking Department of the Amortization Fund and the Industrial Development Bank (BIDI). Rediscount ceilings for medium-term credit have been raised each year in response to the increasing demand for this type of credit.

The main feature of BCEAO's operations in Ivory Coast during the two years ended September 1969 has been a gradual increase in rediscounts of nonseasonal commercial bank credit (see Table 26). These rediscounts stood at an unusually low level (CFAF 7.3 billion) at the end of September 1967, following the placement by the Amortization Fund during 1967 of the CFAF 3 billion on term deposit with the commercial banks, mentioned above. Subsequently, the total amount rediscounted rose quite substantially from this low base. However, the relationship of rediscounts of commercial bank credit to total commercial bank credit has remained relatively stable, i.e., 20 per cent in September 1967, 24 per cent in September 1968, and 25 per cent in September 1969. Rediscounts of credits provided by the specialized credit institutions, relatively insignificant in amount, have changed little over the period.

BCEAO rediscounts have continued to play an important role in financing the seasonal peaks of credit requirements. The bulk of the seasonal increase in short-term credit provided by the commercial banks is generally rediscounted with BCEAO. At the seasonal peak in March 1968, and again in March 1969, such rediscounts stood at CFAF 11 billion to CFAF 12 billion above the levels of the seasonal lows six months previously.

In recent years, BCEAO's claims on the Government have varied from month to month but have been relatively small, consisting mainly of short-term ways-and-means advances to the Treasury, which have always been used for less than 240 days in each calendar year.

Credit extended by commercial banks.—At the end of September 1966, total credit by commercial banks was at approximately the level reached in September 1965 (see Table 29), but increased slightly during the next year. At the same time, rediscounts from BCEAO declined sharply. Since commercial banks' foreign liabilities (largely borrowings from foreign banks) declined somewhat, the resources required to maintain credit to the private sector in face of reduced rediscounts came from the increase in deposits of the private sector. In fact, demand and time deposits with commercial banks rose during the period by amounts comparable to the decline in BCEAO rediscounts. As mentioned above, other resources for the commercial banks came from the CFAF 3 billion made available by the Banking Department of the Amortization Fund early in 1967; this amount was to a considerable extent utilized in place of rediscounting with BCEAO. An increase in the share capital of commercial banks from CFAF 1.1 billion in 1965 to CFAF 1.3 billion in 1967, made in response to the increase in minimum capital requirements in the new banking legislation, also contributed to the increase in resources available to commercial banks.

Credit provided by the commercial banks expanded 30 per cent in the year ended September 1968 and 11 per cent in the following year. Financing for this expansion was provided mainly from annual increases in private deposits of about 12 per cent and from greater resort to BCEAO rediscounts, which rose more rapidly in the first than in the second year. Amortization Fund deposits with commercial banks and their net foreign asset position did not change significantly during the period. The figures mentioned above represent roughly the non-seasonal credits to the economy: at the seasonal peaks in credit requirements in March each year, short-term credit provided by the commercial banks rose substantially above the September levels, with the bulk of the increases being rediscounted with BCEAO.

Credit extended by specialized credit institutions.—The share of bank credit to the economy supplied by the specialized credit institutions rose from CFAF 8.0 billion, or about 20 per cent of the total, in September 1965 to CFAF 11.3 billion, or 25 per cent, in September 1967 (see Table 30). This credit continued upward in absolute terms over the two following years, reaching CFAF 14.4 billion, but because of the more rapid increase in commercial bank credit, its relative share declined to 22 per cent. Much of this credit is supplied by the Banking Department of the Amortization Fund, mainly in loans to public sector enterprises and in discounts of customs duty bills. Not included in these totals is the CFAF 3 billion made available by the Amortization Fund to the commercial banks early in 1967, and maintained at approximately that level thereafter.

Deposits in these institutions (principally deposits of government and public sector enterprises with the Amortization Fund) declined from CFAF 19.8 billion in September 1965 to CFAF 13.6 billion in September 1967. At the same time, their foreign assets fell from CFAF 12.3 billion to CFAF 2.4 billion, as surplus funds previously held abroad were repatriated for domestic use, and the net foreign asset position of the institutions turned negative. In the two years ended September 1969, total deposits with the specialized credit institutions approximately doubled, reaching CFAF 26 billion. Most of this expansion was caused by larger Amortization Fund deposits, representing increases in the deposits of public and semipublic entities; the Stabilization Fund accounted for about CFAF 8.5 billion of the increase and the Social Security Fund for about CFAF 1.0 billion. The former's deposits with the Amortization Fund totaled about CFAF 12.5 billion in September 1969 and rose to about CFAF 20 billion by early 1970 as a result of operations in the first part of the 1969/70 crop year.

FOREIGN TRADE, AID, AND PAYMENTS

FOREIGN TRADE

Ivory Coast's official foreign trade statistics, based on customs data, are incomplete because of valuation problems and certain omissions.

The sale price of certain export commodities (timber, bananas, and minerals) is usually not known at the time of shipment; for customs purposes these exports are valued at standard values fixed by the Government (*valeurs mercuriales*). Since the standard values are usually lower than market prices, these exports tend to be undervalued in customs statistics. Furthermore, border trade is not recorded by the official trade statistics. Traditionally, Ivory Coast has a deficit in this trade, owing to relatively large imports (livestock, dried fish, and other staple food items) from neighboring countries to the north, imports which are only partly offset by unrecorded exports (mainly of kolanuts and manufactured goods) to these countries. In 1968, official adjustments to take these various factors into account raised the value of exports as recorded by customs (CFAF 104.9 billion) by approximately 5 per cent and the value of imports (CFAF 77.6 billion) by approximately 9 per cent, both mainly for coverage and to a less extent for valuation. Adjusted figures are used in the balance of payments, below. The trade statistics presented in this section are based on unadjusted customs data, since these alone provide a detailed breakdown required for purposes of analyzing recent trade developments.

Value and Composition of Trade

Exports.—Between 1963 and 1968, exports (as reported in customs data) rose from CFAF 56.8 billion to CFAF 104.9 billion (Table 32). The country's recent export earnings have been determined largely by developments in the exports of three commodities—coffee, tropical woods, and cocoa. In 1968, coffee accounted for 34 per cent of the recorded value of exports, tropical woods for 25 per cent, and cocoa for 18 per cent, or for a total of 77 per cent.

In 1955 the export value of coffee went down from CFAF 31.7 billion to CFAF 25.9 billion as a result of declines in both volume and average price. Higher export prices in 1966 raised this value considerably despite some decline in volume. Although prices continued to improve in 1967, the export value declined because of the smaller volume. As surplus coffee stocks existed during most of that year, the major factor slowing coffee exports apparently was limited market possibilities. In 1968, however, the total value of coffee exports reached its

TABLE 32. IVORY COAST: EXPORTS BY MAJOR COMMODITIES, 1963–68

	1963	1964	1965	1966	1967	1968 Total	1968 Per cent of total
			VALUE *(billion CFA francs)*				
Agricultural products							
Coffee	24.5	31.7	25.9	30.2	25.4	35.4	33.7
Cocoa	11.3	14.5	10.9	13.1	13.9	19.4	18.5
Bananas	3.5	3.1	2.8	2.8	3.0	3.1	3.0
Pineapple products [1]	1.0	1.4	1.3	1.9	2.1	2.2	2.1
Kolanuts	0.4	0.7	0.9	1.1	1.1	1.0	1.0
Oil palm products	0.3	0.3	0.5	0.3	0.3	0.4	0.4
Rubber	—	0.2	0.3	0.6	0.6	0.6	0.6
Cotton	—	—	0.1	0.3	0.9	1.4	1.3
Total agricultural products	41.0	51.9	42.7	49.1	47.3	63.5	60.5
Tropical woods	12.4	17.8	18.5	18.6	21.8	25.8	24.6
Manganese	0.4	0.5	0.7	0.8	0.5	0.4	0.4
Diamonds	0.4	0.5	0.4	0.4	0.4	0.4	0.4
Other	2.6	3.8	6.1	7.8	10.3	14.8	14.1
Total value	56.8	74.5	68.4	76.7	80.3	104.9	100.0
			VOLUME *(thousand metric tons)*				
Coffee	182	200	186	181	149	212	
Cocoa	100	119	124	124	105	121	
Bananas [2]	120	102	117	125	143	147	
Tropical woods	1,155	1,526	1,566	1,568	1,840	2,175	
		AVERAGE UNIT PRICE *(thousand CFA francs per metric ton)*					
Coffee	135	158	139	167	170	167	
Cocoa	113	122	88	106	132	185	
Bananas	29	30	24	22	21	21	
Tropical woods	10.7	11.7	11.8	11.8	11.8	11.9	

Sources: Ministère de l'Economie et des Finances, *Bulletin Mensuel de Statistique,* and data provided by the Ivory Coast authorities.
[1] Fresh and processed.
[2] Net weight of hands packed in cartons.

highest level (CFAF 35.4 billion) following the outstanding 1967/68 crop and a record volume of exports.

Since cocoa exports remained approximately stable in volume during 1964–66, the drop in export value in 1965 to its lowest level in recent years almost entirely reflected price changes. Thereafter, prices recovered; the export value rose in 1967, despite a decline in volume, reaching a peak of CFAF 19.4 billion in 1968, when export prices rose very sharply.

The export value of tropical woods more than doubled during 1963–68, largely reflecting an increase in volume, but the average unit price also increased by some 10 per cent. Some of this expansion was due to the interruption of competing timber exports from Nigeria, which increased the demand for Ivory Coast products.

In 1969, exports from Ivory Coast rose by about 13 per cent, to CFAF 118 billion, and for the first time tropical wood became the most important export commodity, superseding coffee. Wood exports amounted to CFAF 35 billion, which represented an increase of 36 per cent in export value over 1968, while coffee exports amounted to CFAF 30 billion, a decline from the preceding year on account of a much smaller volume shipped. Exports of cocoa, which ranked third, amounted to CFAF 26 billion, or an increase of 34 per cent over 1968, on account of very favorable export prices.

Among exports of other products which also increased during 1963–68 were pineapple and oil palm products and rubber; these exports are expected to rise substantially over the next few years under the agricultural diversification program now under way. The increase in the value of kolanut exports may be partly due to improved reporting. Banana exports have risen in volume but not correspondingly in value; export prices have declined, partly because of reduced protection in the French market.

Imports.—During 1963–68 the total recorded import value increased by 85 per cent (Table 33). Most of the increase occurred in 1964; imports remained virtually unchanged in 1965 but rose moderately in 1966 and 1967 and sharply in 1968 and 1969. All major categories of commodities contributed to this expansion; imports of foodstuffs rose to a peak in 1966, reflecting mainly the growing demand for imported foodstuffs created by the rapidly increasing urban population, declined

TABLE 33. IVORY COAST: IMPORTS BY MAJOR CATEGORIES
AND SELECTED COMMODITIES, 1963–68

(*In billions of CFA francs*)

	1963	1964	1965	1966	1967	1968
Foodstuffs, beverages, and to-						
bacco	6.9	10.0	10.3	12.6	9.4	11.8
Rice	*0.8*	*2.0*	*2.2*	*3.1*	*1.1*	*1.9*
Wheat	*0.5*	*1.5*	*1.3*	*2.3*	*1.2*	*1.4*
Beverages	*1.4*	*1.6*	*1.6*	*1.6*	*1.6*	*1.8*
Dairy products	*0.9*	*1.0*	*1.1*	*1.2*	*1.6*	*1.6*
Other consumer goods	14.3	20.0	19.7	20.0	22.4	25.1
Cotton products	*3.8*	*5.4*	*5.5*	*4.6*	*5.0*	*5.8*
Clothing	*1.2*	*2.0*	*1.8*	*2.0*	*1.8*	*2.1*
Automobiles and spare parts	*2.3*	*4.1*	*3.6*	*3.7*	*4.5*	*4.6*
Raw materials and semifinished						
products	9.3	13.4	13.3	15.4	17.4	21.1
Cement and lime	*0.7*	*0.7*	*1.1*	*1.1*	*1.0*	*1.1*
Chemicals	*1.0*	*1.2*	*1.4*	*1.7*	*3.1*	*2.7*
Paper	*0.9*	*1.7*	*1.6*	*2.2*	*2.5*	*2.5*
Metals	*1.8*	*2.8*	*2.3*	*2.5*	*3.0*	*3.3*
Fuels and lubricants	*2.2*	*2.7*	*3.2*	*3.4*	*3.5*	*5.9*
Equipment goods	11.4	15.5	15.0	15.6	15.8	19.6
Machinery	*3.2*	*4.6*	*4.7*	*5.4*	*5.0*	*6.6*
Trucks	*0.9*	*1.7*	*1.9*	*1.8*	*1.8*	*1.9*
Other transport	*2.8*	*3.3*	*2.7*	*3.3*	*3.6*	*4.3*
Grand Total	41.9	58.9	58.3	63.6	65.0	77.6

Sources: Ministère de l'Economie et des Finances, *Bulletin Mensuel de Statistique*, and data provided by the Ivory Coast authorities.

in 1967, and increased in 1968. Imports of other consumer goods went up less sharply than total imports and most imports of raw materials and semifinished products more sharply over the period as a whole. In 1969, the value of imports increased by about 11 per cent, mainly equipment goods. Most of this increase took place toward the end of the year, largely as a result of the French franc devaluation.

Direction of Trade

France remains Ivory Coast's principal trading partner, although its relative importance in total Ivory Coast trade has declined in recent years. Between 1963 and 1968 the proportion of exports to France fell from 47 per cent to 35 per cent of the total, and imports from 65 per cent to 50 per cent (Table 34). Trade with the French franc area as a

TABLE 34. IVORY COAST: DIRECTION OF TRADE, 1963 AND 1966–68

(Value in billions of CFA francs)

	Value				Per Cent of Total	
	1963	1966	1967	1968	1963	1968
EXPORTS						
Coffee exports						
France	14.6	13.6	12.5	15.7	59.6	43.7
Other EEC	0.9	2.8	1.4	1.7	3.7	4.8
United States	4.9	8.6	7.1	12.4	20.0	34.5
Japan	—	1.8	0.7	1.6	—	4.5
Other	4.1	3.4	2.7	4.5	16.7	12.5
Total coffee exports	24.5	30.2	25.4	35.9	100.0	100.0
Cocoa exports						
France	3.5	3.9	3.4	3.8	31.0	19.6
Other EEC	4.5	5.5	7.1	11.6	39.8	53.8
United States	2.6	3.2	2.3	2.3	23.0	11.9
Other	0.7	0.5	1.1	1.7	6.2	8.7
Total cocoa exports	11.3	13.1	13.9	19.4	100.0	100.0
Wood exports						
France	4.2	5.5	6.2	7.4	33.9	28.7
Other EEC	6.1	8.1	10.0	11.8	49.2	45.7
United Kingdom	0.6	1.9	1.8	2.3	4.8	8.9
Other	1.5	3.1	3.8	4.3	12.1	16.7
Total wood exports	12.4	18.6	21.8	25.8	100.0	100.0
Total exports						
France	26.6	29.7	30.0	36.2	46.8	34.5
Other franc area	5.1	6.4	7.4	8.5	8.9	8.1
EEC (except France)	13.3	17.2	21.9	29.9	23.4	28.5
United States	7.8	13.0	11.0	15.8	13.7	15.0
Sterling area	1.7	3.8	3.3	4.4	3.0	4.2
Japan	0.4	2.9	1.4	2.6	0.7	2.5
Other	1.9	3.7	5.3	7.5	3.4	7.2
Total exports	56.8	76.7	80.3	104.9	100.0	100.0
IMPORTS						
Total imports						
France	27.1	36.3	35.4	38.9	64.7	50.1
Other franc area	4.5	6.7	6.7	10.0	10.7	12.9
EEC (except France)	4.2	8.7	11.0	14.8	10.0	19.1
United States	2.0	4.9	4.9	4.7	4.8	6.1
Sterling area	2.1	1.4	1.7	1.9	5.0	2.4
Japan	0.1	0.3	0.8	1.3	0.2	1.7
Other	1.9	5.3	4.5	6.0	4.5	7.7
Total imports	27.1	63.6	65.0	77.6	100.0	100.0

Source: Ministère de l'Economie et des Finances, *Bulletin Mensuel de Statistique.*

whole was approximately in balance in 1963, but had a deficit averaging CFAF 4.5 billion in 1967–68. The surplus in the trade with non-franc area countries grew from about CFAF 15 billion in 1963 to CFAF 26 billion in 1967–68. The increase in exports to non-franc area countries was directed mainly to the United States, Japan, and more recently the EEC countries other than France. For imports, the EEC countries other than France, together with the United States, were the major countries that increased their shares as suppliers to Ivory Coast between 1963 and 1968. Imports from the sterling area declined both absolutely and relatively, while the small imports from Japan increased slightly.

France is the principal buyer of Ivory Coast's coffee, although its share of total coffee exports declined from 60 per cent in 1963 to 44 per cent in 1968. Instead, Ivory Coast shipped an increasing proportion of coffee to the United States, Japan, and other non-EEC countries, which together accounted for 52 per cent of total coffee exports in 1968, compared with 37 per cent in 1963. Cocoa exports to France declined while those to other EEC countries accounted for about 54 per cent of total cocoa exports in 1968. Tropical woods are exported largely to France and the other EEC countries, but their combined share in total exports declined from 83 per cent in 1963 to 74 per cent in 1968. In recent years the United Kingdom has been Ivory Coast's principal new market for tropical woods; its share in the total wood export rose from about 5 per cent in 1963 to 9 per cent in 1968.

FOREIGN FINANCIAL ASSISTANCE

Aid payments to the Central Government, which totaled CFAF 5.4 billion in 1965, declined to CFAF 3.8 billion in 1968 (Table 35). They consisted largely of financial and technical assistance grants from France, and financial grants from EDF. They included also some grants from the United States, technical assistance from Israel, and small grants from private institutions.

Aid from France

Aid from France consists essentially of financial grants from FAC and technical assistance. Furthermore, the French CCCE extends medium-

TABLE 35.   IVORY COAST: AID PAYMENTS TO CENTRAL GOVERNMENT, 1964–68 [1]

(*In billions of CFA francs*)

	1964	1965	1966	1967	1968
France					
Technical assistance					
Value of services	2.3	2.6	3.0	3.5	4.1
Ivory Coast contribution	−0.9	−1.1	−1.1	−2.2	−1.5
Total technical assistance	1.4	1.5	1.9	1.3	2.6
FAC grants	1.4	1.0	} 1.5	1.2	1.3
Other	0.1	0.4			
Total France	2.9	2.9	3.4	2.6	3.9
EDF grants	1.5	2.3	2.6	1.7	2.1
United States (grants)	0.3	0.2	0.1	0.2	—
Israel (technical assistance)	—	0.1	0.2	0.2	0.2
Subtotal	4.7	5.5	6.3	4.6	6.2
Grants from private institutions	—	0.1	0.2	0.1	0.2
Contributions to international					
organizations	−0.5	−0.2	−0.3	−0.1	−0.8
Current transfers abroad	—	—	−1.4	−1.0	−1.8
Total	4.2	5.4	4.8	3.6	3.8

Source: IMF, *Balance of Payments Yearbook*, and data provided by the Ivory Coast authorities.

[1] Positive figures are credits; negative figures are debits.

term and long-term loans at low rates of interest to the Government, public and semipublic institutions, and private enterprises. In recent years, net disbursements of CCCE loans have been small and, in the balance of payments, are included in government nonmonetary capital.

During 1960–68, disbursement of FAC financial grants is estimated to have totaled some CFAF 12.4 billion, averaging about CFAF 1.2 billion annually. The French technical assistance program increased from CFAF 3.0 billion in 1966 to CFAF 3.5 billion in 1967 and to CFAF 4.1 billion in 1968 (including Ivory Coast's contribution to the cost of these programs of CFAF 1.1 billion, CFAF 2.2 billion, and CFAF 1.5 billion in these years). The Ivory Coast Government contributes CFAF 60,000 per expert monthly and provides housing. The remainder of the experts' salaries, transport, and other costs are paid by the French Government.

Aid from EEC

Since 1961, EEC has extended financial grants under the first and second EDF programs, totaling some CFAF 19 billion at the end of 1968. This aid has been directed largely to the preparation and execution of transport, education, and social infrastructure projects, but also under the Yaoundé Convention of Association of African States to EEC, to a program of aid to agricultural production and diversification. Although disbursements have lagged behind commitments, particularly in 1966–67, there has been some acceleration; and as of mid-1968, 70 per cent of total cumulative EEC commitments had been disbursed.

Other Aid

U.S. aid, which averaged CFAF 1.0 billion annually between 1960 and 1965 for projects in agriculture and transportation, has increased since 1967 but has taken the form of loans only, grants being discontinued. The United States lent the Industrial Development Bank (BIDI) over CFAF 1.0 billion, from which disbursements started in 1968. In addition, in 1968 the Export-Import Bank extended a CFAF 9.0 billion loan to help in financing the Bandama dam.

Ivory Coast has also received technical assistance from Israel. The UN Development Program, which committed a total of about CFAF 1.6 billion between 1960 and 1966, has continued to allocate funds for a number of small projects usually requiring implementation over a few years. At the end of 1969, disbursements were rather small. Since 1967 the Federal Republic of Germany has extended fairly large development loans, including CFAF 6.0 billion to the Industrial Development Bank, CFAF 1.5 billion to help finance the Port of San-Pédro, and CFAF 0.8 billion to expand the Port of Abidjan. In 1967–68, Italy extended two loans, suppliers' credits in an amount of CFAF 1.0 billion for the Port of San-Pédro and CFAF 9.0 billion for partial financing of the Bandama dam. Finally, some small grants and technical assistance aid, still largely undisbursed, has been extended in recent years by several countries, including Switzerland, the Netherlands, the United Kingdom, and Canada. Except for assistance from Israel, the cost of these small grants is not included in the balance of payments figures below.

BALANCE OF PAYMENTS

Balance of payments data are presented in Table 36 covering total transactions with all countries for 1963–68 and in Table 37 covering transactions by regions for 1968. Because of improvements in the methods of recording, the figures for some items are not fully comparable throughout the period covered, nor can the over-all figures be fully reconciled with the national accounts statistics presented in "Structure of the economy," above. Data for 1965–68 are considered generally more accurate and more comparable than those for the preceding years.

The principal features of Ivory Coast's balance of payments are the relatively large surpluses on trade and nonmonetary capital transactions and the large deficits on services and unrequited transfers. There was an over-all surplus in the balance of payments in every year during 1963–68 except in 1967. This surplus, which averaged CFAF 4.8 billion in 1963–64, declined to an annual average of CFAF 3.0 billion in 1965–66. After an over-all deficit of CFAF 6.3 billion in 1967, a surplus emerged again in 1968 totaling CFAF 8.7 billion.

Ivory Coast's trade surplus (according to the customs data as adjusted for balance of payments purposes) approximated the deficit in services and unrequited transfers during 1963–64, and the over-all surplus was proportionate to the net inflow of nonmonetary capital. In 1965 the trade surplus declined to CFAF 7.6 billion and the deficit in services rose, leaving a deficit in combined goods and services and a sharply reduced over-all balance of payments surplus. Considerable recovery in the trade balance in 1966 was not sufficient to offset growing deficits in services and unrequited transfers and a decline in nonmonetary capital inflow; therefore the balance of payments surplus remained small. The over-all deficit in the balance of payments for 1967 resulted from the decline in the trade surplus, together with continued trends in the movements of other elements. In 1968 a record trade surplus (CFAF 25.7 billion), together with a larger inflow of nonmonetary capital (CFAF 6.6 billion), produced the over-all balance of payments surplus of CFAF 8.7 billion, even with slightly greater deficits in the other elements (CFAF 16.7 billion in services and CFAF 5.4 billion in unrequited transfers).

Among the items in the services account, transport and insurance (excluding charges related to imports) have been in substantial surplus

TABLE 36. IVORY COAST: BALANCE OF PAYMENTS, 1963–68 [1]

(In billions of CFA francs)

	1963	1964	1965	1966	1967	1968
A. Goods and services (net)						
Exports f.o.b.	58.6	74.9	70.5	80.2	83.3	110.0
Imports c.i.f. [2]	−49.6	−64.6	−62.9	−68.6	−73.3	−84.2
Trade balance	9.0	10.3	7.6	11.6	9.8	25.7
Transport and insurance	0.2	3.4	4.8	5.3	5.9	7.6
Travel	−1.9	−4.7	−4.7	−5.9	−5.9	−6.5
Investment income	−5.1	−6.8	−6.6	−8.4	−8.9	−9.5
Government, n.i.e. [3]	0.2	4.8	0.9	−0.1	−0.2	0.3
Other services	−2.0	−3.8	−3.8	−5.3	−6.2	−8.6
Total services	−8.5	−7.2	−9.4	−14.3	−15.3	−16.7
Total goods and services	0.5	3.1	−1.8	−2.7	−5.5	9.0
B. Unrequited transfers (net)						
Private	−5.4	−7.3	−7.5	−8.7	−8.9	−9.2
Central Government [4]	4.4	4.2	5.4	4.8	3.6	3.8
Total unrequited transfers	−1.0	−3.1	−2.1	−3.9	−5.3	−5.4
C. Nonmonetary capital (net)						
Direct investment	2.6	2.9	4.7	−0.4	1.6	3.0
Other private long-term	2.1	1.8	−0.3	0.8	1.4	1.0
Other private short-term	—	0.3	−1.3	2.7	0.1	−2.1
Government	1.2	1.0	3.3	0.6	—	4.7
Total nonmonetary capital	5.9	6.0	6.4	3.7	3.1	6.6
D. Total A + B + C	5.4	6.0	2.5	−2.9	−7.7	10.2
E. Errors and omissions [5]	−1.0	−0.8	0.4	6.0	1.4	−1.5
F. Over-all balance (D + E)	4.4	5.2	2.9	3.1	−6.3	8.7
G. Monetary movements (net)						
Commercial banks [6]	−3.3	−6.0	2.4	−2.8	8.3	−7.5
Central Bank	−1.1	0.8	−5.3	−0.3	−2.0	−1.2
Total monetary movements	−4.4	−5.2	−2.9	−3.1	6.3	−8.7

Source: IMF, *Balance of Payments Yearbook*.

[1] Positive figures are credits; negative figures are debits.

[2] Including imports of nonmonetary gold, totaling CFAF 0.1 billion in each of the years shown, except in 1967, for which it was CFAF 0.2 billion.

[3] Not included elsewhere.

[4] Credit entries include grants of technical assistance, which are counterentries to the services entered as debits in the item "Government, n.i.e."

[5] Including multilateral settlements and regional adjustments.

[6] Including the specialized public credit institutions, the Post Office, and the Savings Bank.

TABLE 37. IVORY COAST: REGIONAL BALANCE OF PAYMENTS, 1968 [1]

(In billions of CFA francs)

	United States and Canada	France	Other Franc Area Countries	Other OECD Countries	Other Countries and Unallocated	Total
A. Goods and services (net)						
Exports f.o.b.	15.5	38.8	8.9	34.9	11.9	110.0
Imports c.i.f.	−5.0	−41.0	−15.9	−16.1	−6.2	−84.2
Trade balance	10.5	−2.3 [2]	−7.0	18.8	5.7	25.8 [2]
Transport and insurance	−0.3	−1.1	7.6	1.0	0.4	7.6
Travel	−0.3	−5.8	0.1		−0.5	−6.5
Investment income	−0.2	−7.6	−0.3	−0.4	−1.0	−9.5
Government n.i.e. [3]	0.3	−0.4	0.1		0.3	0.3
Other services	−0.5	−6.9	−1.9	0.7		−8.6
Total services	−1.0	−21.8	5.6	1.3	−0.8	−16.7
Total goods and services	9.5	−24.1	−1.4	20.1	4.9	9.0
B. Unrequited transfers (net)						
Private		−2.0	−5.4		−1.8	−9.2
Central Government		3.6	−0.2	2.1	−1.7	3.8
Total unrequited transfers		1.6	−5.6	2.1	−3.5	−5.4
C. Nonmonetary capital (net)						
Direct investment	0.1	1.9	0.3	0.8	−0.1	3.0
Other private long-term capital	−0.4	−0.2	0.4	0.7	0.5	1.0
Other private short-term capital		−1.3	−0.8	−0.1	0.1	−2.1
Government		2.1	0.1	−2.3	0.2	4.7
Total nonmonetary capital	−0.3	2.5		3.7	0.7	6.6
D. Total A + B + C	9.2	−20.0	−7.0	25.9	2.1	10.2
E. Errors and omissions (net) [4]	−7.1	27.1	6.5	−26.0	−2.0	−1.5
F. Over-all balance (D + E)	2.1	7.1	−0.5	−0.1	0.1	8.7
G. Monetary movements (net)						
Commercial banks	−2.1	−5.4	0.7	0.1	−0.8	−7.5
Central Bank		−1.7	−0.2		0.7	−1.2
Total monetary movements	−2.1	−7.1	0.5	0.1	−0.1	−8.7

Source: IMF, *Balance of Payments Yearbook.*

[1] Positive figures are credits; negative figures are debits.
[2] Including imports of nonmonetary gold, totaling CFAF 0.1 billion.
[3] Not included elsewhere.
[4] Including multilateral settlements and regional adjustments.

since 1964 mainly because of the inclusion from that year of the net foreign earnings of Air Afrique, a multinational airline partly owned by Ivory Coast and legally domiciled in Abidjan. In 1968 this surplus reached CFAF 7.6 billion. All passenger fares of Air Afrique except those sold in Ivory Coast are entered in the balance of payments as foreign receipts of a local company. Foreign travel, however, has involved an increasing net deficit, which totaled CFAF 6.5 billion in 1968. Transfers of investment income have gradually increased in line with increasing returns to investment generated by foreign-owned companies in Ivory Coast. Other private service items have resulted in rising deficit, and so have government service transactions; the latter include as debit items the countervalue of the total cost of technical assistance programs, which are entered as credit items in unrequited transfers of the Central Government.

Private unrequited transfers increased by more than 20 per cent during 1965–68. The bulk of these payments consists of remittances by foreigners working in Ivory Coast. These remittances totaled CFAF 10.3 billion in 1966 and CFAF 10.9 billion in 1968. African workers accounted for CFAF 6.8 billion, or over 60 per cent. Estimates of remittances by African workers are based largely on repurchases from neighboring countries of banknotes issued in Ivory Coast. Remittances abroad by non-Africans (mostly Europeans employed in the private sector) are estimated to be equal to two months of their annual salary. Net private unrequited transfers rose to CFAF 9.2 billion in 1968. Net receipts from official unrequited transfers reached a peak of CFAF 5.4 billion in 1965; thereafter they declined, totaling CFAF 3.8 billion in 1968.

During 1963–65 the net inflow of nonmonetary capital was relatively large and gradually increased. In 1966 and 1967 this inflow dropped rather sharply but exceeded the 1965 level in 1968 (CFAF 6.6 billion). One element in the decline appears to have been a shift in net direct private investment, from CFAF 4.7 billion in 1965 to a negative CFAF 0.4 billion in 1966. Other private capital increased in 1966 with the net inflow of long-term capital and, more importantly, a reversal of short-term movement (from a net outflow of CFAF 1.3 billion in 1965 to a net inflow of CFAF 2.7 billion in 1966). The latter movement reflects in part the repatriation during 1966 of funds belonging to the

Stabilization Fund (CFAF 1.7 billion). Direct private investment became a net inflow in 1967 and increased to CFAF 3.0 billion in 1968. Other private short-term capital reversed its trend and became a negative CFAF 2.1 billion in 1968. The net inflow of official long-term capital, which reached CFAF 3.3 billion in 1965, was sharply reduced in 1966 and 1967 as new loans were offset by loan repayments and other debit entries. The bulk of the new loans came from France (CFAF 3.0 billion in 1965 and CFAF 2.6 billion in 1966), other European countries (CFAF 2.4 billion in 1965 and CFAF 2.2 billion in 1966), and the United States (CFAF 0.7 billion in 1965 and CFAF 1.4 billion in 1966). In 1968 the net inflow of official capital rose to CFAF 4.7 billion and, together with direct investment, accounted for most of the improvement in the net inflow of nonmonetary capital.

Complete data on the 1969 balance of payments are not yet available. Unadjusted foreign trade statistics point, however, to an increased trade surplus of CFAF 32.0 billion, compared with CFAF 27.0 billion in 1968. In addition, the increase in the net foreign assets of the banking system in the first nine months of 1969 almost equaled that in the corresponding period of 1968. This could point to an improvement, particularly in the nonmonetary capital items, of the balance of payments.

CHAPTER 9

Mauritania

GENERAL SETTING

Mauritania, formerly a member of the French West African Federation, became an independent republic on November 28, 1960. On September 10, 1963 Mauritania became a member of the International Monetary Fund (IMF), current quota $10,000,000 (April 1970). On the same day, it joined the International Bank for Reconstruction and Development (IBRD, or World Bank), current subscription $10,000,000, and the International Development Association (IDA), current subscription $500,000, and on December 29, 1967 the International Finance Corporation (IFC), current subscription $55,000. Among other organizations, Mauritania belongs to the United Nations (UN), the Food and Agriculture Organization (FAO), the UN Educational, Scientific, and Cultural Organization (UNESCO), the General Agreement on Tariffs and Trade (GATT), the UN Economic Commission for Africa (ECA), and the African Development Bank (ADB). With Guinea, Mali, and Senegal it is a member of the Organization of Senegal River States (Organisation des Etats Riverains du Sénégal, or OERS). With Dahomey, Ivory Coast, Mali, Senegal, and Upper Volta, it is joined in the West African Customs Union (Union Douanière des Etats de l'Afrique de l'Ouest, or UDEAO). With Dahomey, Ivory Coast, Niger, Senegal, Togo, and Upper Volta it is joined in the West African Monetary Union (Union Monétaire Ouest Africaine, or UMOA), having a common central bank (Banque Centrale des Etats de l'Afrique de l'Ouest, or BCEAO) and a common currency, the CFA franc.

Mauritania has an area of nearly 1.1 million square kilometers (419,000 square miles), or almost twice the area of France. In the west it borders the Atlantic Ocean; in the northwest and the northeast, the Spanish Sahara and Algeria; in the east, Mali; and in the south, Senegal (from which it is separated by its principal river, the Sénégal) and Mali (see map). The area north of a line extending from Nouakchott to Néma lies within the Sahara Desert and has an arid climate. South of this line down to the Senegal Valley, the area is known as the Sahelian or sub-Saharan region and has an average annual rainfall of 150 millimeters (6 inches). Vegetation in this region consists mostly of gum trees and grass except in the oases (in the central and northern parts of the country), where palm trees grow. The Senegal Valley, with an annual rainfall of up to 500 millimeters (20 inches), is the most fertile region.

The country's population is estimated at 1.2 million. According to a survey based on a sample of approximately one seventh of the population and completed in 1965 by the French Société d'Etudes pour le Développement Economique et Social, the estimated population in 1965 was 1.1 million, of which 80 per cent were nomadic Moors. The annual rate of population growth was estimated at 1.7 per cent. The active age group of 15–59 years in 1967 represented about 47 per cent of the population and was engaged chiefly in livestock raising (Table 1). Most of the rest carried on other agricultural activities. The population density is roughly 0.1 per square kilometer in the northern part of the country, 2.2 per square kilometer in the southwest, and 35 per square kilometer in the Senegal Valley.

Five cities have between 10,000 and 32,000 inhabitants: Nouakchott, the capital, with a population of about 32,000; Nouadhibou (Port-Etienne), 13,000; Kaédi and Rosso, 12,000; and Zouîrât, 10,000.

Approximately 10 per cent of school-age children are in school. In

TABLE 1. MAURITANIA: ESTIMATED POPULATION AND DISTRIBUTION, 1965–69

(In thousands)

	1965	1966	1967	1968	1969
Total population	1,065	1,083	1,102	1,120	1,140
Urban population	*110*	*120*	*130*	*140*	*150*
Active population					
Agriculture	143	147	151	154	156
Livestock raising	372	378	384	391	398
Salaried [1]	19	20	19	19	19
Total active population	534	545	554	564	573

Source: Data provided by the Mauritanian authorities.

[1] Including about 9,000 in the private sector, of which 4,000 were employed in mining.

1969 there were 28,500 students enrolled in the primary school system but only 2,663 in the secondary school system. The Second Development Plan, 1970–73 includes the following objectives in education: (1) reduction in the cost of education (now about 20 per cent of the current budget); (2) better reconciliation of the objectives of primary and secondary education; (3) regrouping of primary and secondary schools, especially in rural areas to utilize teachers more efficiently; and (4) centralization of secondary schools providing education of the "primary cycle" type. The secondary schools ("second cycle") at Nouakchott and Rosso are to become national educational centers. A teacher training college (*école normale supérieure*) is also planned for Nouakchott to train teachers for the secondary school system. In addition, there is also a nurses' training school at the hospital in Nouakchott.

At present those who leave secondary school are not always able to find suitable employment. Because of this situation and because of the need for certain skills, the Government compiles each year a list of priorities for education and manpower training and channels students into courses by means of scholarships. The National School of Administration, for example, in 1969 opened courses to train civil servants for the customs office and for the Postal and Telecommunications Office. In 1969, when a shortage of secretaries, typists, and accountants was noted, the National School of Administration decided to open courses to train people for these occupations. In addition, facilities will be provided to train people for work in the Public Works Office and in mining.

STRUCTURE OF THE ECONOMY

Most of the increases in gross domestic product (GDP) were concentrated in the modern sector of the economy, which increased by 457 per cent from CFAF 5.1 billion to CFAF 28.4 billion between 1959 and 1968 (Table 2). This increase resulted mainly from a rapid rise in the mining and construction sector from CFAF 0.7 billion in 1959 to CFAF 8.7 billion in 1964 and finally to CFAF 16.5 billion in 1968; this rapid increase reflects principally the exploitation of the iron ore deposits by the Mining Company (Société des Mines de Fer de Mauritanie, or MIFERMA). Apart from mining and construction, other sectors (government, transport and commerce, and services) within the modern sector of the economy increased by 170 per cent from CFAF 4.4 billion to CFAF 11.9 billion between 1959 and 1968.

Growth in the traditional sector of Mauritania's economy has been steady, although, of course, less spectacular than that resulting from the opening of the iron ore mines. Between 1959 and 1968 the nonmonetary sector of the economy (mainly subsistence farming and livestock trading)

TABLE 2. MAURITANIA: GROSS DOMESTIC PRODUCT, 1959, 1964, AND 1968

(In millions of CFA francs; except where noted)

	1959	1964	1968
Traditional sector			
Nonmonetary sector	6,865	8,425	10,560
Monetary sector	4,396	5,795	8,213
Agriculture	*520*	*925*	*1,380*
Livestock	*2,798*	*3,247*	*4,220*
Dairying	*400*	*600*	*700*
Fishing	*320*	*583*	*1,248*
Handicrafts	*328*	*400*	*613*
Others	*30*	*40*	*52*
Total traditional sector	11,261	14,220	18,773
Modern sector			
Mining and construction	737	8,695	16,502
Transport and commerce	1,493	5,595	5,445
Services	202	499	1,150
Public enterprises	—	213	1,236
Government salaries	2,690	5,358	4,038
Total modern sector	5,122	20,360	28,371
Gross domestic product (GDP)	16,383	34,580	47,144
GDP per capita (in CFA francs)	17,500	33,800	41,350

Source: Ministère de la Planification et du Développement Rural, *Comptes Economiques de la République Islamique de Mauritanie.*

increased by 54 per cent from CFAF 6.9 billion to CFAF 10.6 billion, or about 6 per cent a year. The monetary sector of the traditional economy (mainly recorded sales of agricultural and animal products, but also including handicrafts) increased by 86 per cent, from CFAF 4.4 billion to CFAF 8.2 billion between 1959 and 1968. Over all, therefore, the traditional sector increased by 66 per cent, from CFAF 11.3 billion to CFAF 18.8 billion, between 1959 and 1968, while the modern sector (largely as a result of mining) increased by 457 per cent.

AGRICULTURE, LIVESTOCK, AND FISHING

Crops

Owing to the almost complete absence of rain in most regions, less than 1 per cent of the country's surface is arable; and less than one third of this limited area is being cultivated. Most of the agriculture in Mauritania, other than nomadic livestock raising, represents subsistence farming. Only a small part of the crops is marketed. Except for gum arabic, no crops are exported on a significant scale. Most of the settled agriculture is in a relatively narrow, fertile strip along the northern bank of the Sénégal. This area includes about 350,000 hectares of arable land, of which 260,000 hectares are under millet. Although the region along the border with Mali has ample rainfall of up to 500 millimeters (20 inches) a year, production is limited because the region is isolated from potential markets by lack of roads. The central and northern parts of the country are dotted with a few oases, where dates and some vegetables are grown.

The physical limitations, as well as pestilence, poor marketing and distribution facilities, and rudimentary modes of cultivation, have restricted yields and agricultural expansion. Except for fluctuations owing to weather, production of major crops (e.g., millet, beans, maize, potatoes, and dates) have changed little during recent years (Table 3). In an average year, Mauritania consumes 130,000 tons [1] of millet, of which 100,000 tons are produced locally and the rest is imported, mainly from Mali. Although the Mauritanian authorities encourage local production of millet, they do not expect self-sufficiency in the fore-

---

[1] Throughout this chapter, the word "ton" refers to a metric ton of 2204.6 pounds.

TABLE 3.   MAURITANIA: ESTIMATED AREA AND PRODUCTION
OF PRINCIPAL CROPS, 1963–69

	1963	1964	1965	1966	1967	1968	1969
AREA CULTIVATED (*thousand hectares*)							
Millet	245.0	245.0	250.0	250.0	260.0	260.0	260.0
Beans	3.0	3.0	3.0	3.3	3.3	2.2	3.3
Wheat	0.8	0.8	0.8	0.8	0.8	—	0.8
Groundnuts	1.6	1.6	1.6	1.6	1.6	—	1.6
Maize	6.5	6.5	6.5	6.7	4.0	—	4.0
Potatoes	2.0	2.0	2.0	2.0	2.0	—	2.0
Rice	0.4	0.4	0.3	0.4	0.4	0.5	0.6
Dates	5.0	5.0	3.4	3.4	3.4	3.4	3.4
Vegetables	—	0.1	0.1	0.1	0.2	0.2	0.3
PRODUCTION (*thousand metric tons*)							
Millet	90.0	100.0	110.0	90.0	104.0	50.0	100.0
Beans	0.9	1.0	1.0	1.1	1.1	0.5	1.1
Wheat	0.3	0.3	0.3	0.3	0.3	—	0.3
Groundnuts	0.8	0.8	0.8	0.8	0.8	—	0.8
Maize	3.7	4.0	3.8	4.0	4.0	—	4.0
Potatoes	1.9	2.0	2.0	2.0	2.0	—	2.0
Rice	0.6	0.7	0.7	0.7	0.6	0.8	1.0
Dates	20.0	20.0	15.0	15.0	15.0	15.0	17.0
Vegetables	—	0.8	0.9	0.9	0.3	0.3	0.4

Source: Data provided by the Mauritanian authorities.

seeable future. Millet imports come from Mali at relatively low prices (CFAF 5–10 per kilogram). Millet movements across the border with Senegal take the form of seasonal price arbitrage. Owing to an adequate supply of millet at relatively stable prices from Mali, it is estimated that only during the drought of 1968, when Mauritanian production of millet fell to 50,000 tons, was there a net inflow from Senegal.

Gum arabic is collected from a species of the acacia tree in the southern region adjoining the Sénégal. Production, virtually all of which is exported, increased from 4,398 tons in 1967 to 5,220 tons in 1968 and 10,874 tons in 1969. Export prices increased from CFAF 70 per kilogram in 1967 to CFAF 85 in 1969.

Dates are the largest single crop produced outside the Senegal Valley. The principal centers of production are the oases of Adrar, Tagant, and Assaba in central Mauritania. In 1966–68, annual production reached 15,000 tons, of which 60 per cent was consumed by the growers, 20 per cent was marketed for domestic consumption, and 20 per cent was exported. It is estimated that in 1969, date production increased to 17,000 tons. The date palm is less productive in Mauritania than in other producing countries, yielding about 10 kilograms per palm, compared with a normal average yield of 22 kilograms. The Government is engaged in developing and improving the date crop through irrigation and replacement of old palms with new species. A project to fight parasites has been undertaken, and financial assistance has been received from the Fonds d'Aide et de Coopération (FAC). A conditioning plant was constructed in Atar to process dates for both export and local consumption. The plant has an annual capacity of 50 tons of dates, which could easily be doubled. In 1967, its first year of operation, it received 25 tons of dates; 20 tons were utilized in making date powder, which is used for fodder and marketed at a price of CFAF 50 per kilogram. The 5 tons of dates processed for export brought a price of CFAF 160 per kilogram.

Experiments have been carried out to determine whether cotton is suitable for cultivation in Mauritania. So far no cotton has been grown commercially because of the relatively high cost of production and the absence of a ready market.

Mauritania imports annually about 12,000 tons of rice. Cultivation of rice started in 1969 on a pilot farm with an area of 600–800 hectares in the Rosso region. The average yield for this project, supported by mainland China, is expected to be about 1.5 to 2 tons per hectare, in comparison with the present average of 0.8 tons. In addition to the pilot farm, Chinese experts are providing supervision and management for an additional 4,000 hectares. Although the first crop has not yet been harvested, it is estimated that production will rise to about 6,000 tons annually by the end of the 1970–73 plan period.

The Government is making efforts to increase agricultural production and to enhance the role of agriculture in the country's development effort. An Agricultural Education and Training Center for about 25 trainees with financing from FAC and the UN Development Program has been established at Kaédi, and the Government is planning to develop it into an institution with a four-year course in agriculture and animal husbandry.

Cooperatives have been established to facilitate the purchase of equipment and the marketing of agricultural products and to encourage production of certain agricultural products. In Hodh-Oriental, 38 groups of farmers combined to coordinate purchases of equipment and to market the agricultural products. In the region adjoining the Sénégal, the Government's Cooperation Service (Service de Coopération) established 22 producer cooperatives for the storage and marketing of millet and sorghum. Other cooperatives include those in the Atar region, established to encourage date and vegetable production. Despite the recognized need for cooperatives, these have not proved viable; owing to defaults, agricultural credit, which until 1966 was available to the cooperatives through the Mauritanian Development Bank, has decreased sharply in recent years.

The Government is undertaking two major irrigation projects. The Bogué (Boghé) project includes the irrigation of about 600 hectares for production of foodstuffs; work on this project, which is financed by the EEC's European Development Fund (EDF), is under way. Another project, still in the planning stage, is in the Gorgol Valley; it entails the construction of dams for the irrigation of 10,000 hectares to be planted with rice and 3,000 hectares to be planted with sugarcane.

Livestock Raising

Livestock raising, mostly by nomads, occupies nearly 70 per cent of the active labor force. The total livestock population is not known but is estimated at about 2 million head of cattle, 7 million sheep and goats, 700,000 camels, 150,000 donkeys, and 15,000 horses. The livestock population has increased only moderately in recent years as the natural increase, estimated at 6 per cent for cattle and 10 per cent for sheep and goats, has almost been matched by slaughtering and live exports. Only a small part of the slaughtering and exports is recorded (Table 4). A substantial increase in the livestock population would require improved breeding methods, more pastures, an increased number of wells and watering stations, and storage facilities for fodder.

Most of the meat is consumed domestically; annual per capita consumption is estimated at 15 kilograms. A combined slaughterhouse and cold storage plant has been constructed in Kaédi at a total cost of CFAF 200 million, financed by FAC (CFAF 178 million) and the capital budget (CFAF 22 million). It has an annual capacity of 3,000 tons and began operations in March 1969. In that year it processed 297 tons of meat and was expected to process 450 tons in 1970. The break-even point of the plant is estimated to be 1,000 tons a year. Diffi-

TABLE 4. MAURITANIA: LIVESTOCK SLAUGHTERING AND EXPORTS, 1964–69

(*In thousand head*)

| | Cattle | | Sheep and Goats | | Camels | |
	Recorded slaughter	Recorded exports	Recorded slaughter	Recorded exports	Recorded slaughter	Recorded exports
1964	13	—	34	—	4	—
1965	17	16	38	177	6	3
1966	14	20	40	163	5	1
1967	15	19	34	112	4	2
1968	18	18	35	69	5	0.8
1969	19	28	31	67	6	0.3

Source: Data provided by the Mauritanian authorities.

culties for the plant include reorienting cattle drives away from the traditional market at Dakar to the plant at Kaédi and foreign competition in foreign as well as domestic meat markets. In January 1970, increased tariffs were imposed to protect the Kaédi plant in the Mauritanian market.

At present, most livestock are exported on the hoof; exports of frozen meat are hampered by rinderpest and sanitary problems, as well as by competition in potential markets from other meat-exporting countries. Studies are under way with EDF financial assistance to find solutions to these problems.

Fishing

Despite the abundance of fish in coastal waters, fishing in the past has made only a modest contribution to Mauritania's economy. Mauritanian fishermen have confined themselves mostly to the waters of the Sénégal, while the resources of the sea were exploited by foreign fishing vessels. The catch from the Sénégal averages about 15,000 tons a year; about 10,000 tons are consumed by the population adjoining the river, and the rest is sold in inland Mauritania or in Senegal.

In 1968, 16,400 tons of fish were unloaded at Nouadhibou for drying. It is estimated that, after drying, there must have been about 6,400 tons of fish. Of this amount, 5,500 tons were recorded as exports, mainly to the Democratic Republic of Congo, the People's Republic of the Congo, Gabon, and Ghana. Much of the remaining 900 tons of dry fish was probably exported to nearby Mali and Senegal; however, this trade was not recorded. In addition, the recently established modern fishing industry exported 5,200 tons of fresh and frozen fish to Italy, France, and Greece in 1968 and 6,200 tons in 1969, and in 1969, 90 tons of live lobster were exported to France. Fish exports, which almost tripled between 1966 and 1969, still represent only a small part of the total catch along the Mauritanian coast. Foreign-owned boats equipped with processing and freezing facilities are estimated to take as much as 300,000 tons of fish annually, marketing the catch with only small benefits to Mauritania.

To improve the fishing industry, the Government has drawn up a program of action to increase the benefits that should accrue to Mauritania from the exploitation of this natural resource. Fishing by foreign vessels in territorial waters (within 12 miles of the shore) has been made subject to ministerial approval, requiring the catch to be treated locally, except for fishing covered by bilateral agreements. The Government has concluded bilateral cooperation agreements with Spain and Greece. The agreement with Spain, signed in February 1964, grants Spanish fishermen the right to fish in Mauritanian territorial waters in exchange for undertakings by the Spanish Government to (1) build a plant for salting and drying fish with an annual capacity of 6,000 tons, (2) set up a fish-canning factory with an annual capacity of 3,000 tons, (3) build a factory for fishmeal equipped to process 100 tons of fish daily, (4) register at least 20 fishing vessels in Mauritania (the number of registered vessels may be raised to 50), (5) extend scholarships to Mauritanians for training at Spanish vocational institutes related to fishing, and (6) accept on Spanish vessels Mauritanian citizens as crew members under the same conditions as Spaniards. The Spanish vessels may sell their catch in Nouadhibou at freely negotiated prices, and the Spanish enterprises will receive preferential tax and tariff treatment and will be authorized to transfer their profits freely. The plants provided for in the agreement have been constructed, and the other terms of the agreement are coming into force.

The agreement with Greece, signed in July 1966, permits Greek vessels, the number of which may be limited by the Mauritanian Government, to fish in Mauritanian waters provided that they (1) pay an annual registration fee of $15 per ton, (2) sell 25 per cent of the catch in the local market at current prices, (3) store or treat the

remainder of the catch with local enterprises before exporting it, and
(4) recruit one fourth of the crew from Mauritanian nationals. This
agreement has not yet been ratified by either country.

An agreement was reached with Japan in early 1970 whereby Japan
would be allowed to fish in Mauritanian waters upon payment of a tax
to Mauritania. In addition, Japan guaranteed to purchase processed fish
offered by the processing plants at Nouadhibou. The agreement was for
a single year only but is renewable by mutual consent.

The Société Mauritanienne d'Armement à la Pêche (SOMAP), a semipublic enterprise, was established to ensure Mauritanian participation in
fishing. This enterprise operated 14 vessels, 4 of which were equipped
with freezing facilities. Investment in these vessels amounted to about
CFAF 2,500 million, financed as follows: CFAF 280 million from the
company's capital, CFAF 88 million by FAC, and the remainder by
a Netherlands bank, L. Dryfus, and by suppliers' credits. Unprofitable
operations forced the closing of SOMAP in 1968, and by early 1970
all except 2 boats had been liquidated. The Government has guaranteed
the repayment of SOMAP's debt of CFAF 2,250 million remaining
at the end of 1969.

Another semipublic enterprise, the Société Mauritanienne des Industries de la Pêche (SOMIP), was set up to run a fishmeal factory, which
began operating in 1969 with a daily capacity of 600 tons of fish. A
freezing plant also started operations in 1969; the financing by EDF
amounted to CFAF 345 million. The total capital of the two fishing
enterprises (CFAF 400 million) was contributed by the Mauritanian
Government (50 per cent), the Development Bank (5 per cent), and
private investors (45 per cent). The Government's share was partly
financed by the Caisse Centrale de Coopération Economique (CCCE),
to the extent of CFAF 120 million. A project for the construction of
a fishing harbor and supporting facilities in Nouadhibou for about
25,000 tons of fish annually was completed in 1968. The harbor, which
services fishing vessels from all nations, was partly financed by an
EDF grant amounting to CFAF 1,270 million. Plans have been made
to increase the port's fish-handling capacity to 55,000 tons annually,
but work is not expected to begin before 1971. A private company,
the Société Guelfi Survif (GUELFI), has operated a freezing plant
since 1966 for exports of frozen fish. Its investment of CFAF 750

million was financed by a CCCE loan (CFAF 120 million) and by private sources (CFAF 630 million).

MINING

Iron Ore

The decision in the early 1950's to exploit the large iron ore deposits discovered in 1935 at Fdérik (Fort-Gouraud) has had considerable impact on the economy. Proven deposits with a metal content of at least 60 per cent now amount to 150 million tons. Additional deposits with a lower metal concentration have been found north of the present mining sites. A new enrichment process for the less concentrated ore is being developed; if this process proves feasible, the usable iron ore reserves could easily double.

To exploit the iron ore deposits an international company, the Mining Company (Société des Mines de Fer de Mauritanie, or MIFERMA) [2] was established in 1952 with an initial capital of CFAF 30 million; the capital was increased to CFAF 13.3 billion in 1960. In 1964 the Mauritanian Government bought a 5 per cent share in the company. Other shareholders include the Bureau de Recherches Géologiques et Minières, a French semipublic institution (24 per cent); French private steel and financial interests (32 per cent); and other steel firms of the United Kingdom (19 per cent), Italy (15 per cent), and Germany (5 per cent).

From 1960 to mid-1963 the Mining Company spent over CFAF 40 billion on infrastructure and supporting facilities, including 635 kilometers of railroad linking the mines with the Atlantic Ocean, the mineral port of Cansado near Nouadhibou, storage facilities for 1 million tons of ore, an airport at Fdérik and several airstrips along the railroad, a telecommunications system, and residential quarters for its employees at the mining site and in Nouadhibou. In addition to using its own capital, the Mining Company financed these investments by an IBRD loan of CFAF 16.3 billion ($66 million), two CCCE loans of CFAF 2.5 billion and CFAF 5.25 billion (the latter guaranteed in part by the French Government and disbursed in two tranches), advances of

---

[2] For a description of the concession payments, see "Indirect taxes—(2) Taxes on mining concessions," below.

CFAF 3.5 billion from the Mining Company's shareholders, and a medium-term credit of CFAF 3.5 billion from a consortium of French banks rediscountable with the French Crédit National. The IBRD loan carries interest at the rate of 6.25 per cent in addition to the customary commitment charge and is repayable in 20 semiannual installments over the period 1966–75. The CCCE loan of CFAF 2.5 billion carries interest at the rate of 3 per cent and is repayable in 24 equal installments between 1966 and 1989. The first tranche of the other CCCE loan, CFAF 3.5 billion, carries a 5.6 per cent interest charge, and is repayable in 13 installments between 1965 and 1977. The second tranche of CFAF 1.75 billion is repayable over 12 years from 1967–78, and is subject to interest charges that increase over time from 6 per cent to 6.5 per cent. The interest rate for the medium-term bank loan, repayable by August 30, 1968, is 0.8 per cent in addition to the rate charged by the Crédit National (4.75 per cent at mid-1966).

At present the Mining Company operates at four sites. The Tazadit deposits began to be exploited in 1961, the original Fdérik deposits in 1963, the Rouessa deposits in 1965, and the new Fdérik deposits in 1967. The Company started the mining in Rouessa merely by connecting it to the mine at Tazadit so that the Tazadit facilities could be utilized. The investment was, therefore, very small, involving only the construction of a road. The development of the new Fdérik mine involved an investment of CFAF 5 billion, which was financed with funds generated through the Mining Company's own operations. Production from the Fdérik mine began in January 1967 and was expected to reach 1.2 million tons in 1968 and 1.5 million tons annually thereafter. To handle additional tonnage, the Mining Company expanded the port at Nouadhibou and equipped it for the wider range of ore grades required because of world market demand. The cost of the improved port facilities (CFAF 1 billion) was financed from the Company's own resources.

Although production of iron ore began in early 1963, export shipments did not start until mid-1963, after a stockpile of 1 million tons had been built up. Since then the volume and value of production and exports have risen steadily (Table 5). Production and exports, which were slightly above 8 million tons in 1969, are expected to reach 9 million tons in 1970. The Mining Company is contemplating an additional CFAF 7.4 billion investment to increase production to 12 million tons annually by 1972. An additional CFAF 1.4 billion will be spent in 1970 to enlarge the Company's port at Consado so as to increase its handling capacity to 12 million tons annually. Improved management will enable the present railway to handle up to 12 million tons annually, but it is believed that any increases in production above that load will require the doubling of the present single-track line.

TABLE 5.   MAURITANIA: IRON ORE PRODUCTION AND EXPORTS, 1963–69

		Exports	
	Production	Quantity	Value
	←——Million metric tons——→		*Billion CFA francs*
1963	2.3	1.3	2.7
1964	4.7	5.0	10.6
1965	6.2	6.0	13.1
1966	7.2	7.1	15.6
1967	7.0	7.5	15.4
1968	8.1	7.7	15.3
1969 [1]	8.3	8.2	17.5

Source: Data provided by the Mauritanian authorities.
[1] Estimated.

The Mining Company's contracts with buyers are subject to discussion each year, but it does not appear to have marketing problems. About 95 per cent of its exports are to the United Kingdom and the EEC countries. A new market was opened in Japan, which took 5 per cent of the iron ore exports in 1967. Special rates are granted to customers who guarantee a minimum purchase of 500,000 tons annually.

Copper

In 1931, copper deposits were discovered near Akjoujt, about 240 kilometers northeast of Nouakchott. These deposits consist of a layer containing an estimated 7 million tons of oxidized copper ore with a copper content of 2.6 per cent, and of about 20 million tons of sulphuric ore with a copper content of 1.8 per cent. The deposits also contain small quantities of gold.

The physical properties of the ore necessitate a special process of refining before economic exploitation can commence. During 1953–64 the Société des Mines de Cuivre de Mauritanie tried to find such a method, but its work was inconclusive. In 1964 a new company, the

Société de Cuivre de Mauritanie (SOCUMA) was formed with participation by the Mauritanian Government, as well as Canadian, U.S., and
French interests. This company was given an option for 18 months to
complete its studies. Experiments carried out by the company in the
United States proved successful, and a pilot plant near Akjoujt started
to produce concentrate having a copper content of 85–90 per cent, which
is regarded as satisfactory for commercial purposes. Another obstacle
to the exploitation of the copper deposits was overcome when an underground source of water, estimated at 100 million cubic meters, which
would be adequate for the refining of the copper ore, was discovered
120 kilometers west of Akjoujt. The company's option lapsed at the end
of 1965.

Various interested parties regrouped themselves and submitted new
proposals to the Government. In November 1966 the Mauritanian
authorities granted Charter Consolidated, a subsidiary of the Anglo-
American Company, the right to exploit the copper deposits. The Copper
Company (Société Minière de Mauritanie, or SOMIMA) was formed in
March 1967 with a capital of CFAF 2 billion. The major shareholders
are Charter Consolidated (44.6 per cent), the Mauritanian Government
(22 per cent), and IFC (15 per cent). The remaining 18.4 per cent is
divided among the Bureau de Recherches Géologiques et Minières (6.13
per cent); the French mining company, Pennaroya (6.57 per cent); the
Banque de Paris et des Pays Bas (3.77 per cent); and the Compagnie
Financière pour l'Outre-Mer (1.93 per cent). Apart from the capital
participation, the Copper Company will require its shareholders to lend
it a total amount of CFAF 3.75 billion to be prorated among them.

Total planned investments by the Copper Company are estimated at
CFAF 14.25 billion, and will be financed by CFAF 2.00 billion from
capital and CFAF 3.75 billion from shareholders' loans, by a loan of
CFAF 2.75 billion from the European Investment Bank, CFAF 1.61
billion from the First National City Bank of New York, and CFAF 4.14
billion from IFC.

According to the agreement with the Mauritanian Government, the
Copper Company is to produce and export a minimum of 450,000 tons
of copper concentrate from the Akjoujt deposits during an exploitation
period of about 18 years. Once its exports of oxidized copper concentrate reach 140,000 tons, the Company is to exploit the sulphuric ore.

Cash deposits and bank guarantees amounting to CFAF 1.25 billion will be forfeited to the Government in case of nonperformance. The Company will participate with the Government in paving the Nouakchott-Akjoujt road at a total cost of about CFAF 1,825 million, with contributions over a period of 7 years of CFAF 750 million from the Government and CFAF 1,075 million from the Company. The Government will pay annual maintenance costs up to CFAF 10 million; any excess will be borne by the Company. The Government has undertaken the construction of the expansion of the wharf in Nouakchott. The total cost, estimated at about CFAF 700 million, is being financed mainly by a loan of $2,754,000 from the European Investment Bank. The Government will invest CFAF 738 million in the infrastructure installations at the wharf. To this end, the Government will receive loans from the Company (CFAF 180 million), FAC, CCCE, and the Development Bank. The Copper Company has undertaken the construction within 3 years of the required water installations for refining copper ore.

Production, to start in 1970, is expected to provide annual exports averaging 50,000 tons over the following 18 years. The total value of potential exports during the period is estimated at about CFAF 77 billion. The revenue accruing to the Government during the 3-year construction period and the 18-year exploitation period is estimated at CFAF 15.5 billion, including revenues from the export duty, import duties on consumption goods, and income taxes on wages and salaries during the period of installation, and revenues from a 35 per cent tax on profits and dividends, as well as additional indirect benefits of about CFAF 100 million a year from expenditures by the Copper Company and its employees during the 18 years of exploitation. The Company is expected to employ about 500 workers at the mine, of which about 200 will be employed during the first 2 to 3 years. Mauritanian employees will receive in-service training by the Company according to the agreement with the Government.

Other Minerals

Prospecting for petroleum has been carried out in the coastal region and in the Tindouf Basin along the Algerian border. Prospecting permits for the coastal region were granted to two companies: the Société Africaine des Pétroles, which invested about CFAF 350 million, and the Société des Participations Pétrolières (PETROPAR), which invested nearly CFAF 500 million in prospecting. Although some signs of petroleum were found near Nouadhibou, both companies in 1964 surrendered their permits prior to their expiration. The Tindouf Basin was prospected by the Société des Pétroles de Valence, which invested about CFAF 75 million before abandoning its exploitations in mid-1964. A new permit was granted to the Planet Oil and Mineral Corporation (United States) for prospecting in the area near Nouadhibou, where PETROPAR was active, and for offshore exploration. The Planet Oil and Mineral Corporation started prospecting in September 1966 with a pledge to spend CFAF 375 million over the next five years. Toward the end of 1967 the Corporation ceded 80 per cent of its exploration rights to the American Oil Company, which was granted a prospecting permit in November 1967. The Standard Oil Company of New Jersey has been given an oil exploration permit on the southern coast. Until now all exploration in Mauritania has taken the form of geological surveys and no drilling has taken place.

Salt is still produced by traditional methods, and the resulting quality has not enabled Mauritanian producers to compete successfully with the marine salt imported from Senegal and the Canary Islands. Production, which declined during the last decade from 10,000 tons to about 700 tons annually, was 900 tons in 1969. Large-scale salt production would be economical only if a sufficiently large market could be found. Prospects for exports are not promising because the West African market is saturated with Senegalese supplies. Although the processing of the copper ore will require 7,000–10,000 tons of salt annually, it appears that it will be cheaper to use imported salt than to refine local salt to a degree that would make it usable.

Proven gypsum deposits, estimated at 3.4 million tons, are located 60–100 kilometers from Nouakchott. Their exploitation is technically possible with a relatively small capital investment, but domestic demand is not adequate. The Government has an agreement with the Société d'Equipement de Mauritanie for a study of the feasibility of gypsum production and marketing.

An yttrium deposit at Bou Naga, 150 kilometers southeast of Akjoujt, was discovered by the French Bureau de Recherches Géologiques et

Minières and the Société Péchiney-Saint Gobain with the aid of FAC financing. Yttrium is mainly used in color television tubes. The Société d'Exploitation Minière et de Recherches de Mauritanie (SOMIREMA), formed in June 1967, was granted a prospecting permit. The Mauritanian Government agreed to a 20 per cent share in the company. The yttrium deposit so far discovered amounts to about 1,850 tons with an average mineral content of 3.66 per cent, and mine installations have been completed since March 1967. Production, which was 56 tons in 1967, reached 600 tons in 1968; the price of the ore was estimated at about CFAF 100,000 per ton in Nouakchott. The ore was exported to France, where the mineral was extracted chemically. Because of inadequate demand for yttrium, exploitation of the mine was discontinued in 1969.

The Compagnie de Phosphates de Thiès was granted a general permit in May 1966 for prospecting uranium, phosphate, and sulphur. Geological surveys, financed by FAC, are carried out mainly by the Bureau de Recherches Géologiques et Minières and the Compagnie Générale de Géophysique. Aid from the UN Development Program is also available for such projects, but it requires contributions from the Mauritanian Government to cover the local costs.

MANUFACTURING

Manufacturing industry is limited because of the small domestic market, lack of transport facilities, scarcity of raw materials suitable for processing, deficient supply of water and electric power, dearth of managerial skills, and competition from Senegalese products. The electric power problem in Nouakchott, while helped by the construction of the water desalination plant, still requires additional operating capacity. The workshops operated by the Mining Company, the fish processing enterprises in Nouadhibou, the freezing plant in Kaédi, and the slaughterhouse supplemented by a tannery, indicate that manufacturing industry is beginning to develop. The plants in Kaédi started operations in 1968. A plant for the treatment and packaging of dates started operating in Atar in 1967 with an initial annual capacity of 50 tons. The Société Air Liquide, a Senegalese company and a long-time supplier to Mauritania of industrial gas from Dakar, in 1968 constructed a plant in Nouadhibou close to the installations of the Mining Company, its principal consumer.

Three new manufacturing projects are under consideration. A plant for the processing of imported raw sugar into cubes may be constructed in the industrial area at the Nouakchott wharf, with an initial capacity of 80 tons daily to be increased later to 120 tons. The required investment is estimated at CFAF 600 million; the Government intends to take a 20 per cent participation in the prospective company, the remainder of the capital to be private. The possibility for a soft drink bottling plant, utilizing the sugar processed locally, is being studied. The second project, costing CFAF 75 million, concerns a match factory also to be installed in the wharf's industrial area. All the raw material would be imported. A third investment project for the Nouakchott wharf area is a sawmill to utilize imported timber. A textile bleaching, dyeing, and finishing plant is being considered for Rosso; realization will depend, in part on the quality of the water supply. The plant, estimated to cost CFAF 20 million, would employ 300 persons and treat 12 million meters of cloth annually.

CONSTRUCTION

Apart from the operations of the Mining Company and the Copper Company, the most important construction project since independence has been the construction of the capital city of Nouakchott during 1959–64. Most of the work was undertaken by the Government through the Société d'Urbanisme et de Construction Immobilière de Nouakchott (SUCIN), specifically established for this purpose. Investments, totaling CFAF 3 billion, were financed equally by CCCE and FAC.

In 1965, SUCIN was succeeded by the Société d'Equipement de Mauritanie (SEM), a company with a capital of CFAF 35 million, of which the Government holds CFAF 16 million and the Caisse des Dépôts et Consignations CFAF 7.95 million, while the remainder is distributed between the Mining Company and various other institutions. The company merely acts as a contractor and does not extend credit. The main financing sources for its projects are FAC, the government capital budget, funds of the Social Security Fund, and loans from the Development Bank. Project financing by FAC includes local currency costs. Credits by the Development Bank for private construction are extended up to 80 per cent of construction costs for a maximum period of ten years. The annual rate of interest ranges from 4.5 to 9 per cent, depending on the total amount of the investment. The new company operates in all parts of Mauritania and has a wider scope of activities than its predecessor; in addition to public construction work, it includes private residential and industrial construction, management and maintenance of public and private buildings, and research and feasibility studies for projects to be financed by the Development Bank. Outlays by the company in 1967 totaled CFAF 462 million including a housing development in Nouakchott (CFAF 132 million), slaughterhouse and freezing plant construction in Kaédi (CFAF 80 million), and some administrative buildings in Nouadhibou (CFAF 60 million). In 1968 and 1969, 21 new small-scale construction firms came into existence. Most of these were engaged in housing construction near the installations of the Société Minière de Mauritanie in Akjoujt.

ELECTRIC POWER

Consumption of electricity increased during 1965–68 from 28.8 million kilowatt-hours to 42.8 million kilowatt-hours (Table 6), of which the Mining Company consumed about 80 per cent. The total installed capacity of 21,390 kilowatts is barely adequate to meet the rapidly increasing demand under normal working conditions.

In 1967 the Nouakchott power plant had a capacity of 1,500 kilowatts, then adequate for current requirements, which were equivalent to 9 per cent of annual consumption in the country. Completion in late 1968 of the water desalination plant raised the capacity to nearly 2,000 kilowatts. By 1969, consumption had increased to the point where this capacity was barely adequate, and plans were initiated for increasing the generating capacity at Nouakchott.

Until 1968 the companies producing electricity were privately owned. However, the Société Africaine d'Electricité (SAFELEC) had the distribution concession for electric power from all power plants other than those owned by the Mining Company. In 1968 a semipublic company, the Société Mauritanienne d'Electricité (MAURELEC), was created to replace SAFELEC, and it is now responsible for the distribution of

TABLE 6. MAURITANIA: PRODUCTION AND CONSUMPTION OF ENERGY, 1965–69

	Capacity	Electric Power			Consumer price		Petroleum Products Consumption	
		Production	Consumption		High voltage	Low voltage	Total	Mining Company
			Total	Mining Company				
	Kilowatts	*Thousand kilowatt-hours*			*CFA francs per kilowatt-hour*		*Cubic meters*	
1965	21,390	29,562	28,760	23,726	35	35	52,842	37,963
1966	21,390	35,229	34,204	27,398	29	34	63,049	46,379
1967	21,390	37,888	37,075	28,497	29	34	81,139	48,638
1968	21,740	43,883	42,825	33,780	29	34	100,583	54,915
1969	21,740	—	—	—	29	34	112,655 [1]	59,206 [1]

Source: BCEAO, *Notes d'Information et Statistiques*, March 1968.

[1] Estimate.

electricity, as well as for electricity generation in Rosso, where it has purchased the electric plant.

In 1970 the generating capacity of other towns was 360 kilowatts at Rosso, 450 kilowatts at Kaédi, and 2,500 kilowatts at Nouadhibou.

The price of electricity per kilowatt-hour in Nouakchott was lowered from CFAF 38 to CFAF 35 in May 1965 and again in July 1966, when the old rate was differentiated into rates of CFAF 29 for high-voltage and CFAF 34 for low-voltage power. These prices remained unchanged through 1969.

WATER

Insufficient water is one of the serious problems facing the towns and villages in Mauritania. The Mining Company transports water to Nouadhibou, where the Société Anonyme de Production et de Distribution d'Eau en Mauritanie distributes it. A pipeline completed in 1969 was built from Boû Lanouar to Nouadhibou, at a cost of CFAF 1.3 billion. Boû Lanouar, almost 100 kilometers from Nouadhibou, supplies the current needs of the port and the mines. The Société des Eaux de Béni-Chab will provide water for the copper mines at Akjoujt from an underground reservoir at a distance of 120 kilometers. The Copper Company will build a water pipeline for this purpose at a cost of CFAF 500 million to be financed by FAC.

The serious water shortage in Nouakchott resulted in a temporary ban on all further public construction and the limitation of new private building permits to five a month. To remedy the situation, a seawater desalination plant, with a daily capacity of 3,400 cubic meters of drinking water, was constructed and put into operation in late 1968. This construction required an investment of about CFAF 1.2 billion, financed mostly by FAC and the remainder (about CFAF 100 million) by suppliers' credits repayable over five years at 6.5 per cent interest. The average price per cubic meter for water from this plant is estimated at about CFAF 190, compared with the consumer price of CFAF 120 in 1967 (Table 7). It is operated by the Electric Company (SAFELEC).

TRANSPORTATION

Mauritania's road network in 1967 had an over-all length of about 6,100 kilometers, of which only 185 kilometers were paved (Table 8).

TABLE 7. MAURITANIA: PRODUCTION AND CONSUMPTION OF WATER, 1965–69

	Production	Consumption	Consumer Price at Nouakchott
	←——Thousand cubic meters——→		CFA francs per cubic meter
1965	1,042	622 [1]	120
1966	1,141	1,070	120
1967	1,237	1,162	120
1968	1,342	1,254	120
1969	1,524	1,310	120

Source: BCEAO, *Notes d'Information et Statistiques,* March 1968.
[1] Excluding Nouakchott.

Existing main roads run north to south connecting Mauritania with its traditional markets in Mali and Senegal. The few lateral roads are impassable during most of the rainy season (July–December). Until the recent completion of the wharf at Nouakchott, most imports directed to central and southern parts of the country were channeled through the port of Dakar in Senegal, as road connections with Nouadhibou (Port-Etienne) in the north were inadequate. The Government's objective is to link the east and the west with all-weather roads, and to provide good road connections from the ports on the Atlantic coast to the interior.

Owing to a policy of budgetary austerity, funds available for maintenance of the existing road network (about CFAF 70 million in 1967) have been less than adequate. In order to provide for improved maintenance, a special Road Fund (Fonds Routier) was established in June 1968. To this fund IDA is contributing $3 million and Mauritania is committed to providing CFAF 200,000 in 1970, CFAF 273,000 in 1971, CFAF 275,000 in 1972, and CFAF 300,000 in 1973. As part of the highway maintenance effort, the Bureau Central d'Etudes pour les

TABLE 8. MAURITANIA: ROAD NETWORK, 1966–69

(*In kilometers*)

	1966	1967	1968	1969
Paved roads	96	96	96	185
Unpaved roads	980	1,105	1,105	1,016
Regional tracks	2,058	2,065	2,065	2,065
Local trails	2,815	2,860	2,860	2,860
Total	5,949	6,126	6,126	6,126

Source: Data provided by the Mauritanian authorities.

Equipements d'Outre-Mer (BCEOM), a French organization, will staff a training center for a four-year period to train and direct Mauritanian road maintenance personnel.

The main axis is the Rosso–Fdérik (Fort-Gouraud) road which links the Dakar–Saint-Louis road in Senegal with the Algerian border. Built in 1941, the road is approximately 1,000 kilometers long consisting of the following links: Rosso–Nouakchott (214 kilometers), Nouakchott–Akjoujt (278 kilometers), Akjoujt–Atar (198 kilometers), and Atar–Fdérik (307 kilometers). The heaviest traffic, about 50 cars daily, is on the road linking Nouakchott and Rosso. In 1964 and 1965, the Government signed conventions with EDF and IDA for rebuilding the Nouakchott–Rosso road at a total cost of CFAF 2.5 billion. The Government was to contribute CFAF 25 million, and the rest was to be financed by IDA (65 per cent) and EDF (35 per cent). IDA participation takes the form of a 50-year loan. Work began in June 1967, and about CFAF 214 million had been disbursed by December 1967. By early 1970, 60 of the 204 kilometers between Nouakchott and Rosso had been rebuilt and bituminized, and it was estimated that the entire project would be financed by the end of the year. Other projects for the north-south axis include the paving of the 256-kilometer Nouakchott–Akjoujt road at a total cost of over CFAF 2 billion, to be financed jointly by the Mining Company and the Government. The road extending 900 kilometers north of Fdérik toward the Algerian frontier is in poor condition.

The road from Rosso in the southwest to Néma in the southeast, about 1,165 kilometers in length, has the following links: Rosso–Bogué (215 kilometers), Bogué–Kaédi (105 kilometers), Kaédi–Mbout (115 kilometers), Mbout–Kiffa (195 kilometers), Kiffa–'Ayoûn el 'Atroûs (240 kilometers), 'Ayoûn el 'Atroûs–Timbédra (180 kilometers), and Timbédra–Néma (115 kilometers). The road between Rosso and Kaédi can only be used during the dry season (January–June). Between Kiffa and Néma, the road passes through terrain which is alternatively sandy, swampy, and rocky and which presents serious difficulties for traffic. A segment of 420 kilometers of this axis has been improved with the help of an EDF grant.

The country's only railroad, about 635 kilometers long, connects Fdérik (Fort-Gouraud) with Nouadhibou (Port-Etienne). Although it services the Mining Company primarily, some space for general cargo is available, and passenger coaches are added in case of demand. Maintenance of this railroad has proved more difficult than originally anticipated: wear and tear caused by wind and sand have made it necessary to replace part of the tracks much earlier than envisaged. Owing to rapid growth in the volume of the Mining Company's iron ore exports, the railroad is nearing its capacity and the Company is considering doubling the tracks.

Mauritania has three ports on the Sénégal: Rosso, Bogué, and Kaédi. Rosso and Kaédi each have a pier and a warehouse. Construction of port installations at Bogué is being studied. The three ports are served by Senegalese shipping lines from Saint-Louis. Rosso is served all the year round, while Kaédi is accessible only during the flood season between July and September. Bogué is served for five months by boats and during the rest of the year by lighters. Canoes are also used for transporting millet, wood, and cement.

Mauritania's ports on the Atlantic coast are Nouadhibou, Cansado, and Nouakchott. Nouadhibou, the only natural harbor, is gaining importance with the rapid development of the fishing industry. In 1969 its utilized capacity totaled 84,000 tons. A study was begun in 1970 to assess the feasibility of expanding the port's fish-handling capacity from 25,000 tons to 55,000 tons annually. The handling tariff ranges from CFAF 500 per ton for foodstuffs and cement to CFAF 7,500 per ton for fresh and frozen fish. Cansadò, constructed by the Mining Company for the export of iron ore, is equipped with the most modern loading equipment. The wharf at Nouakchott, completed in October 1966, can handle 100,000 tons annually. Imports handled at Nouakchott increased from 11,000 tons in 1966 to 58,000 tons in 1969. Exports leaving the wharf remained negligible through 1969; however, in 1970, the Copper Company expects to export 15,000 tons of copper concentrates. In order to meet the anticipated long-term growth in traffic, mainly from shipments of copper ore, the wharf's capacity is being increased to 200,000 tons annually by an extension of the pier and the addition of cranes, as well as barges and tugs. The increase in the port's capacity, costing about CFAF 700 million, is being financed by the European Investment Bank. The Copper Company is purchasing CFAF 107 million worth of equipment and is building a warehouse for its imports, which will add 2,000 square meters of storage surface to the existing 800 square meters.

Although receipts from wharf handling charges in 1967 amounted to CFAF 137.4 million, actual government revenue was less because of the Treasury's refunds of charges on goods destined for Rosso. This refund is designed to compensate for the high cost of inland transport to Rosso in line with the Government's policy of minimizing interregional price differences. Two thirds of the imports by the National Import and Export Company (Société Nationale d'Importation et d'Exportation, or SONIMEX) in 1967 actually benefited from this refund. The wharf's charges range from CFAF 3,600 to CFAF 6,000 per ton according to the merchandise handled. A charge of about CFAF 3,000 per ton covers the wharf's current expenses at the present rate of utilization. Although maritime freight is 60 per cent higher for shipments to Nouakchott compared with Dakar, the wharf is competitive because of the high inland transportation cost between Dakar and Mauritanian cities.

Mauritania's two major airports are at Nouakchott and Nouadhibou. The Nouakchott airport has a runway of 2,000 meters, sufficient for landings and takeoffs of airplanes in the medium-range category. A project to extend the runway to 4,000 meters will be financed by EDF. Other projects include the installation of an instrument landing system at a total cost of CFAF 42 million; this project will be financed by FAC.

Air Mauritanie maintains an internal service linking eight airports and airstrips throughout the country, as well as flights to the Canary Islands, southern Algeria, and western Mali. It operates six airplanes; France provides crews for the five Douglas aircraft, and the U.S.S.R. provides the crew for the sixth, a Soviet aircraft. An airplane repair hangar and a new terminal in Nouakchott, financed by the Development Bank with funds obtained from CCCE and BCEAO, each contributing CFAF 38 million, was constructed in 1968. Air Mauritanie is running at a deficit because of the low number of passengers on its external flights and on most of its internal flights, except those to and from Nouakchott. The deficit has been financed by using the company's capital of CFAF 40 million subscribed by the Government and by short-term credits. The company is endeavoring to contain expenses and to generate profits to cover past losses. It received a subsidy of CFAF 30 million from the Government in March 1968.

The cost of a project for the improvement of the telecommunication facilities in Mauritania is estimated at about CFAF 52 million, for which FAC has already granted CFAF 27 million.

In 1967 the Government reversed its policy of entrusting the operation of transportation facilities to autonomous public agencies. The independent Port Authority of Port-Etienne (Nouadhibou), established in 1964 to administer the harbor facilities, was abolished in 1967, and for a while the Government administered the facilities. In 1969, SAMMA, a private company, undertook management of the commercial section of the port of Nouadhibou, paying a rental of CFAF 9 million annually to the Mauritanian Government, which provides maintenance of the port through the Public Works Office. The National Office of Public Transport (ONTP) and the 5 per cent cargo tax levied by it were abolished in 1967. However, the Government has set up a Road Fund to subsidize transportation to the interior of the country; its resources are obtained from a gasoline tax. The Société Nationale des Transports Ferroviaires Mauritaniens, established to handle railroad traffic other than that of the Mining Company, is the only remaining independent public transportation agency.

ECONOMIC DEVELOPMENT PLANNING

EARLY DEVELOPMENT PLANNING

Before independence, modest development expenditures were financed almost exclusively by grants from the French Fonds d'Investissement pour le Développement Economique et Social (FIDES). During 1946–59 these grants amounted to CFAF 3.8 billion. About 50 per cent of the funds were spent on agriculture, 30 per cent on infrastructure, and 17 per cent on social projects.

The Government's first economic development plan extended over a period of three years (1960–62). It envisaged expenditures of CFAF 7.8 billion, of which the largest part was for infrastructure, while the traditional livestock and agricultural sector was assigned only 10 per cent of the total investment. EDF undertook to provide CFAF 3.6 billion of the required financing, FAC, CFAF 3.5 billion, and the Mauritanian Government, CFAF 0.3 billion; the remainder of the planned investment was to come from unspecified foreign sources. Details on the performance of this plan were never published, but it is known that total expenditure amounted to only 53 per cent of the funds that had been committed by EDF and FAC. The unspent portions of the funds committed as well as a number of unfinished or postponed projects were incorporated in the Development Plan, 1963–66.

PLANS SINCE 1962

Development Plan, 1963–67

The 1963–67 plan was originally scheduled to cover 1963–66. As the National Assembly did not approve the plan until July 1963, the effective dates of the plan were changed to cover the four years July 1, 1963–June 30, 1967. Preparation of a consistent and integrated plan was hampered by lack of basic statistics on the economy (e.g., reliable population survey, national income and production accounts, information on consumption patterns and foreign trade, and balance of payments data). The plan lacked an analysis of the rate of return for individual projects and had no project priorities in terms of the available financing and there was no schedule for the timing of the investments. Basically, the plan represented an effort to bring desirable objectives into focus and to catalog projects.

The plan set two basic objectives: (1) to reduce the country's dependence on foreign financing and manpower and (2) to set the stage for further economic and social development of the entire nation in a subsequent plan. The first objective was to be achieved by means of austere budgetary policies aimed at eliminating the current budget deficit. Revenues were to be increased through improvements in the fiscal system while most expenditures were to be reduced, except for infrastructure maintenance expenditure, which was to increase substantially. In order to provide better control for utilization of foreign aid, a capital budget was to be established. A study of the present and future requirement for technicians in conjunction with a program for the training and placement of Mauritanians was to be undertaken with the intention of reducing the dependence on foreign manpower. The second objective was to be achieved by an inventory of the country's human and natural resources in order to prepare a statistical foundation for the next plan, by making basic infrastructure investments in roads, ports, communications, hospitals, and schools and by encouraging small Mauritanian enterprises, particularly for servicing and distribution, which would promote the integration of the traditional and modern sectors. These investments were to be distributed so as to stimulate regional development.

The most notable accomplishment in the attempt to reduce the country's dependence on foreign financing was the elimination of the current budget deficit and hence the need for current budget subsidies from France. Over the plan period, current receipts rose by 52 per cent and current expenditures by only 17 per cent. The larger revenue stemmed mainly from higher taxes paid by the Mining Company rather than from improvements in the fiscal system as proposed by the plan. Priority given to budgetary austerity, however, was such that even some expenditures which normally would have had high priority were reduced. Maintenance expenditure did not increase at all between 1963 and 1966 and increased by only 5 per cent in 1967. In comparison, the Government's personnel expenditure went up by 17 per cent during the plan period. Although a capital budget was established, it had only a peripheral relation to the total development effort since most investment was undertaken and financed by France and EDF outside the capital budget. Only little progress was made in reducing the country's dependence on foreign personnel. The study of available manpower and its use, which was intended as the basis for an integrated program of training and placement, was never undertaken. There was little change in the number of foreigners employed in the private and public sectors during the plan period, and the shortage of qualified personnel, especially in the administration, made it difficult to implement the plan projects.

The objective of preparing a statistical foundation for the next plan by way of an inventory of the country's material and human resources was achieved only in part. Therefore, the statistical basis for the next plan is not much more extensive than for the preceding plan. A population survey was made and the program for a geological survey and mapping was implemented; certain other studies were postponed for the subsequent plan. Only part of the planned infrastructure investment in roads, communications, and schools was made, but the Nouakchott wharf and the hospital were completed as scheduled. Actual investment in agriculture and livestock was about half of the amount planned. Limited progress was made in encouraging small Mauritanian enterprises, particularly for servicing and distribution. However, a state trading enterprise, the National Import and Export Company (SONIMEX), with monopoly for the import of basic consumer goods was established.

In the public sector, actual investment amounted to CFAF 8,278 million, or 61 per cent of the planned amount of CFAF 13,563 million (Table 9). Moreover, public sector disbursements were significantly smaller than the financing available, CFAF 14,219 million, indicating delays in project implementation. There were shortfalls in all categories, except fishing and public health. Disbursements amounted to 75 per cent of the planned amount for transportation and telecommunications infrastructure. Although the targets for ports and air transportation were fulfilled, in the latter case, owing to substantial investment outside the plan, investment in roads (planned at CFAF 1,680 million) amounted to only CFAF 819 million, and that in infrastructure for river transport (planned at CFAF 200 million) amounted to only CFAF 30 million. In agriculture and livestock, only CFAF 1,176 million, or 50 per cent of the planned amount of CFAF 2,352 million, was actually invested because of both project delays and shortage of financing. The available financing of CFAF 1,758 million was only 75 per cent of the planned amount for this category. The project for the Kaédi slaughterhouse and cold storage was modified, and the construction of the Nouakchott slaughterhouse was deferred. In the mining industry, a planned CFAF 800 million water supply project for the future copper mine at Akjoujt was not undertaken. Actual public investment in the mining industry amounted to CFAF 262 million, of which CFAF 125 million represented the Government's participation in the Copper Company (SOMIMA), and CFAF 137 million part of its participation in the Mining Company (MIFERMA). Project delays also explain why investment in education and training was 43 per cent of the planned amount, and expenditure for urban infrastructure (water and electricity) was only CFAF 752 million, compared with a target of CFAF 1,912 million and an amount of available financing of CFAF 2,492 million.

In the private sector actual investment amounted to CFAF 18,429 million (compared with a plan target of CFAF 14,188 million) mainly because of the implementation of projects in the modern fishing and mining industries. In the fishing industry, the planned investment amounted to CFAF 3,110 million, greatly exceeding the planned amount

(CFAF 950 million). In the mining industry, total investment amounted to CFAF 11,293 million, compared with a target of CFAF 8,580 million, as a result of the Mining Company's development of the Fdérik mine, which had not been foreseen in the plan. Actual private investment in agriculture and livestock, services, and housing also exceeded the planned amounts. CFAF 107 million was invested in agriculture and livestock (compared with a planned CFAF 48 million), because the Kaédi tannery was completed ahead of schedule. For projects relating to oil prospecting and administrative infrastructure, however, actual private investment fell below the planned amounts.

During the plan period, 8.6 per cent of total planned public and private sector investment was to be directed to agriculture and livestock raising; however, actual disbursements were only 4.8 per cent of the total investment although more than 95 per cent of Mauritania's population is employed in the traditional sector. The shortfall by the public sector in the realization of the plan may be attributed to delays caused by the absence of trained personnel for drawing up investment projects suitable for foreign financing. Although total available financing exceeded the total funds disbursed, a shortage of financing was a problem in certain sectors, particularly in agriculture and livestock.

Annual investments of the public and private sectors are given in Table 10. Since private investments in the modern sector were predominant, changes in annual total investments closely reflect movements in the private sector investments. Private investment amounted to CFAF 4,602 million in the second half of 1963, owing mainly to the Mining Company's investment totaling CFAF 3,093 million. In 1964 the Company's investment totaled CFAF 3,200 million and in 1965, CFAF 6,410 million—investment in the Fdérik mine representing CFAF 5,000 million. In 1966, private investment declined to CFAF 3,202 million, of which CFAF 2,360 million was invested in the fishing industry. In the first half of 1967, no private investment was made in the modern sector, and total private investment was reduced to CFAF 120 million. Public investment increased progressively during the plan period, particularly in 1966, when capital budget investment rose to CFAF 761 million, compared with CFAF 291 million in 1965.

The plan relied largely on foreign sources of financing, which supplied 92 per cent of actual public sector disbursements of CFAF 8,278

TABLE 9. MAURITANIA: INVESTMENT UNDER THE DEVELOPMENT PLAN,
JULY 1, 1963–JUNE 30, 1967, BY SECTOR AND CATEGORY

(Amount in millions of CFA francs)

Category	Planned			Disbursements [1]		
	Amount	Per cent of total	Financing Available	Amount	Per cent of total	Per cent of planned
PUBLIC SECTOR						
General studies	581	4.2	475	366	4.4	63.0
Transportation and communication infrastructure	3,188	23.5	4,038	2,376	28.7	74.5
Agriculture and livestock	2,352	17.4	1,758	1,176	14.2	50.0
Mining	800	5.9	262	262	3.2	32.8
Fishing	960	7.1	1,630	970	11.7	101.0
Education and training	922	6.8	869	393	4.7	42.6
Health	770	5.7	932	804	9.8	104.4
Urban infrastructure and housing	3,043	22.4	2,924	1,072	12.9	35.2
Administrative buildings	947	7.0	989	525	6.4	55.4
Services	—	—	342	334	4.0	—
Total (or average) public sector	13,563	100.0	14,219	8,278	100.0	61.0
PRIVATE SECTOR						
General studies	1,000	7.0	...	214	1.1	21.4
Transportation and communication infrastructure	160	1.1	...	—	—	—
Agriculture and livestock	48	0.3	...	107	0.6	222.9
Mining	8,580	60.5	...	11,293	61.3	131.6
Fishing	950	6.7	...	3,110	16.9	327.4
Urban infrastructure and housing	980	6.9	...	1,290	7.0	131.6
Administrative buildings	1,200	8.5	...	650	3.5	54.2
Services	1,270	9.0	...	1,765	9.6	139.0
Total (or average) private sector	14,188	100.0	...	18,429	100.0	129.9

TOTAL INVESTMENT

General studies	1,581	5.7	580	2.1	36.7	
Transportation and communication infrastructure	3,348	12.1	2,376	8.9	71.1	
Agriculture and livestock	2,400	8.6	1,283	4.8	53.5	
Mining	9,380	33.8	11,555	43.3	123.2	
Fishing	1,910	6.9	4,080	15.3	213.6	
Education and training	922	3.3	393	1.5	42.6	
Health	770	2.8	804	3.0	104.4	
Urban infrastructure and housing	4,023	14.5	2,362	8.8	58.7	
Administrative buildings	2,147	7.7	1,175	4.4	54.7	
Services	1,270	4.6	2,099	7.9	165.3	
Total (or average)	27,751	100.0	26,707	100.0	96.2	

Source: République Islamique de Mauritanie, *Bilan d'Exécution Plan Quadriennal*, 1963–66.

[1] Total financial commitments in the private sector amounted to CFAF 19,615 million and differed from disbursements in the following categories only: general studies (CFAF 389 million) and fishing (CFAF 4,121 million).

TABLE 10.   MAURITANIA: INVESTMENTS DURING THE PLAN PERIOD 1963–67

(In millions of CFA francs)

	Public Sector	Private Sector	Total
1963 [1]	887	4,602	5,489
1964	1,447	4,095	5,542
1965	1,595	6,410	8,005
1966	2,609	3,202	5,811
1967 [2]	1,740	120	1,860

Source: Data provided by the Mauritanian authorities.

[1] June–December.

[2] January–June.

million (Table 11). Total foreign financing made available, however, amounted to CFAF 13,358 million; EDF provided CFAF 5,784 million (43 per cent) and FAC, CFAF 5,637 million (42 per cent). Private investment also was financed primarily from foreign sources, which supplied 87 per cent of total private investment; the remainder came from private domestic savings.

Planning Organization

The planning organization, once a part of the Office of the President, was moved to the Ministry of Finance in 1965. In late 1966 it was attached to the Ministry of Foreign Affairs on the grounds that the plan was financed almost completely from external sources. In 1968 a Ministry of Planning and Rural Development was established.

New Plan

In early 1970 a proposed plan, the Second Plan for Economic and Social Development, 1970–73, was put forward for consideration by the Ministry of Planning and Rural Development. The proposed second plan is rather more a catalog of necessary and desired projects than a proposal for a fixed pattern of expenditures during the four years 1970–73. While exact patterns of resource utilization have not been established, the over-all thrust of the plan is to favor agricultural and rural development. It also lays down three basic criteria to be used when considering commitment of funds for each project. These criteria are adequacy of the basic economic studies in support of each project, avail-

TABLE 11. MAURITANIA: FOREIGN AND DOMESTIC FINANCING UNDER THE DEVELOPMENT PLAN, 1963-67

(In millions of CFA francs)

	Commitments			Disbursements		
	Foreign	Domestic	Total	Foreign	Domestic	Total
Public sector						
Fonds d'Aide et de Coopération (FAC) grants [1]	5,247	—	5,247	3,934	—	3,934
European Development Fund grants	5,784	—	5,784	2,739	—	2,739
Loans	1,535 [2]	117 [3]	1,652	526	105	631
Capital budget	—	542	542	—	350	350
Other	792 [4]	202 [5]	994	446	178	624
Total public sector	13,358	861	14,219	7,645	633	8,278
Private sector	17,206	2,409	19,615	16,020	2,409	18,429
Grand Total	30,564	3,270	33,834	23,665	3,042	26,707

Sources: République Islamique de Mauritanie, *Bilan d'Exécution Plan Quadriennal, 1963-66*, and data provided by the Mauritanian authorities.

[1] Includes CFAF 2,709 million in commitments and CFAF 2,170 million in disbursements through the capital budget.

[2] Includes CFAF 1,008 million from IDA, CFAF 390 million from FAC, and CFAF 137 million from CCCE.

[3] Commitments by the Development Bank: CFAF 76 million for construction of the Nouakchott airport, CFAF 21 million for the Nouakchott slaughterhouse and cold storage, and CFAF 20 million for the construction of the Nouakchott market.

[4] Includes CFAF 428 million French aid (other than FAC), CFAF 107 million from Germany, CFAF 97 million from the U.S. Agency for International Development, CFAF 30 million from the United Kingdom, and CFAF 130 million from UN (CFAF 31 million from UNICEF, CFAF 22 million from the Freedom from Hunger Campaign, and CFAF 77 million from the Special Fund).

[5] Commitments by public and semipublic enterprises: Social Security Fund (Caisse Nationale de Prévoyance Sociale) CFAF 134 million for housing in Nouakchott and office buildings in Nouadhibou, and CFAF 5 million for the Centre de Protection Maternelle et Infantile at Nouakchott; the Development Bank's participation of CFAF 20 million in the development of the fishing industry at Nouadhibou; CFAF 25 million by the Nouakchott municipality for the construction of a city hall; and CFAF 18 million by the Société Africaine d'Electricité for high-voltage lines in Nouadhibou.

ability of personnel to run the project or the necessity of training people to do so, and careful consideration of the continuing costs which will be necessary to maintain a project after its completion.

In April 1970 the National Council of the People's Party accepted the new plan with certain modifications and called for estimates of total expenditures, and expenditures by sector, necessary to accomplish the plan's objectives.

INVESTMENT CODE

The Investment Code of 1961, the petroleum law, and the long-term investment systems for iron and copper exploration constitute the basic rules regulating private investment in Mauritania. These laws allow, within specified limits, ad hoc agreements between the Government and major foreign investors with considerable latitude regarding conditions peculiar to each industry. All such agreements require subsequent legislative approval.

The Investment Law provides for two systems (Table 12).

TABLE 12.   MAURITANIA: ENTERPRISES BENEFITING FROM THE INVESTMENT CODE

(*In millions of CFA francs*)

Nature of Fiscal Benefit and Name of Enterprise	Year of Approval	Activity	Initial Investment
Long-term fiscal system			
Société des Mines de Fer de Mauritanie (MIFERMA)	1959	Iron ore mining	45,000
Planet Oil and Mineral Corporation	1966	Petroleum exploration	...
Priority system			
Société Minière de Mauritanie (SOMIMA)	1967	Copper mining	2,000
Société Guelfi Survif (GUELFI)	1963	Fishing	750
Industrie Mauritanienne de Pêche (IMAPEC)	1966	Fishing	1,000
Société Mauritanienne de Gaz Industriel (SMGI)	1966	Liquid gas	100
Manufacture Industrielle du Cuir	1966	Leather	107
Société Mauritanienne d'Entreposage des Produits Pétroliers (SOMEPP)	1966	Petroleum storage	216
Société Mauritanienne des Industries de la Pêche (SOMIP)	1967	Fishing	120

Source: Data provided by the Mauritanian authorities.

Priority Enterprises

Fiscal benefits may be accorded to an enterprise that maintains a head office in Mauritania, invests at least CFAF 75 million in less than two years, and employs at least 20 persons. To be eligible for priority status, the enterprise must invest in mining, petroleum, food processing, power, real estate, and tourism. The fiscal benefits include complete or partial exemption from import duties and taxes on capital equipment needed for the establishment of the enterprise for three years; complete or partial exemption from import duties and taxes on raw material and spare parts for five years after the enterprise starts operating; and total exemption from the tax on commercial and industrial profits during the first five years of operation. Moreover, profits reinvested in Mauritania are subject to 50 per cent of the applicable tax.

Long-Term Fiscal System

In addition to the benefits described above, enterprises that invest at least CFAF 1 billion in less than five years and are deemed of exceptional importance to the Mauritanian economy may be granted complete or partial stabilization of fiscal charges for 25 years and a special fiscal code.

EMPLOYMENT, WAGES, AND PRICES

EMPLOYMENT, WAGES, AND SALARIES

Among the 20,000 salaried workers in Mauritania in 1968, the public sector employed about 55 per cent (Table 13) and the private sector the remainder, mainly in mining (21 per cent), building and construction (10 per cent), and commerce and services (8 per cent). Salaried employees represented only about 3 per cent of the active population (see Table 1).

The non-Mauritanian labor force in the private sector declined from 32 per cent in 1965 to 28 per cent in 1968. This decline took place mainly in the construction industry. Non-African technicians constituted about half the number of foreigners employed by the private

TABLE 13. MAURITANIA: EMPLOYMENT OF MAURITANIAN NATIONALS AND NON-MAURITANIANS, BY ACTIVITY, 1965–68

	November 30, 1965			November 30, 1966			November 30, 1967			November 30, 1968 [1]		
	Mauritanian nationals	Non-Mauritanians	Total	Mauritanian nationals	Non-Mauritanians	Total	Mauritanian nationals	Non-Mauritanians	Total	Mauritanian nationals	Non-Mauritanians	Total
Public sector [2]	...	...	11,000	...	...	12,000	...	...	10,500	...	...	10,500
Private sector												
Agriculture and fishing	397	73	470	430	59	489	518	65	583	518	65	583
Mining and quarrying	2,619	1,262	3,881	2,825	1,250	4,075	2,928	1,250	4,178	2,978	1,211	4,189
Processing industry	148	109	257	164	116	280	228	185	413	258	215	473
Commerce and other services	1,116	559	1,675	1,063	550	1,613	1,118	481	1,599	1,118	481	1,599
Building and construction	983	452	1,435	1,436	395	1,831	1,540	502	2,042	1,540	502	2,042
Total private sector	5,263	2,455	7,718	5,918	2,370	8,288	6,332	2,483	8,815	6,412	2,474	8,886
Total salaried employment	...	...	18,718	...	...	20,288	...	...	19,315	...	...	19,386

Source: République Islamique de Mauritanie, *Bulletin Statistique et Economique.*

[1] Preliminary.

[2] Estimated.

sector in 1965 and 1966. In 1964, foreigners (mostly non-Africans) occupied 90 per cent of total managerial and foreman positions, while the majority of Mauritanians were employed as unskilled workers. By 1967, however, Mauritanians had increased their representation in managerial positions to 9 per cent and in supervisory positions to 17 per cent (Table 14).

Unemployment in the cities, as well as underemployment in rural areas, remained unchanged in recent years because the population rose as fast as new job opportunities opened. The increased number of job opportunities in the private sector absorbed the increase in the number of unskilled workers. Employment in the iron ore industry is expected to remain at the present level, while the demand for manpower for fishing and agricultural infrastructure projects, as well as in the new copper mining industry, is expected to expand. Except for a special training center for fishermen in Nouadhibou and an agricultural training center in Kaédi, the training possibilites for unskilled workers are limited to the in-service training provided by the Mining Company for its employees. Provisions for the training of Mauritanians for employment in copper mining were included in the agreement with the Copper Company.

Mauritania has a quite unequal pattern of income distribution reflecting the extremes of skills available within the country. In 1963 the upper 10 per cent of wage earners in the private sector received 56 per cent of the total income from wages (Table 15). In 1967 the upper 14 per cent of wage earners received 65 per cent of wage income. The majority of wage earners in the private sector (71.5 per cent in 1963 and 66.7 per cent in 1967) were concentrated in the low-income brackets with a monthly salary of less than CFAF 20,000.

Wages are based on a guaranteed minimum hourly wage (*salaire minimum interprofessionnel garanti*, or SMIG) and salary scales applicable to various professions. SMIG applies to all salaried workers and employees. It is differentiated according to two economic sectors (industry and commerce, and agriculture) and two geographical areas: Zone I, which includes urban and industrial areas as well as some remote eastern regions, and Zone II, which encompasses the remainder of the country (Table 16).

TABLE 14. MAURITANIA: EMPLOYMENT OF MAURITANIAN NATIONALS AND NON-MAURITANIANS, BY OCCUPATIONAL CATEGORIES, 1963–67

	Management	Supervisors	Skilled Employees	Skilled Workers	Apprentices	Unskilled Workers	Total
1963							
Mauritanian nationals	3	54	200	865	1,339	2,732	5,193
Non-Mauritanians	187	911	309	1,056	370	64	2,897
Total	190	965	509	1,921	1,709	2,796	8,090
Per cent of Mauritanian nationals	2	6	40	45	79	98	65
1964							
Mauritanian nationals	12	57	242	1,110	1,470	3,063	5,954
Non-Mauritanians	184	888	295	1,117	406	128	3,018
Total	196	945	537	2,227	1,876	3,191	8,972
Per cent of Mauritanian nationals	6	6	45	50	78	96	67
1965							
Mauritanian nationals	31	102	290	986	1,267	2,587	5,263
Non-Mauritanians	211	958	261	672	279	74	2,455
Total	242	1,060	551	1,658	1,546	2,661	7,718
Per cent of Mauritanian nationals	13	10	53	60	82	97	68
1966							
Mauritanian nationals	14	135	357	1,251	1,867	2,294	5,918
Non-Mauritanians	201	1,000	327	597	206	39	2,370
Total	215	1,135	684	1,848	2,073	2,333	8,288
Per cent of Mauritanian nationals	7	12	52	68	90	98	71
1967							
Mauritanian nationals	27	212	371	1,439	1,613	2,748	6,410
Non-Mauritanians	290	993	308	633	114	115	2,453
Total	317	1,205	679	2,072	1,727	2,863	8,863
Per cent of Mauritanian nationals	9	17	53	70	93	96	72

Source: **Ministère de la Planification et du Développement Rural**, *Annuaire Statistique*, 1968.

TABLE 15. MAURITANIA: MONTHLY WAGES IN THE PRIVATE SECTOR, BY INCOME GROUPS, 1963, 1965, AND 1967

(Amount in thousands of CFA francs)

Monthly Wage (CFA francs)	1963				1965				1967			
	Wage earners		Total wages		Wage earners		Total wages		Wage earners		Total wages	
	Number	Per cent of total	Amount	Per cent of total	Number	Per cent of total	Amount	Per cent of total	Number	Per cent of total	Amount	Per cent of total
Up to 5,000	213	2.6	533	0.2	130	1.7	325	0.1	—	—	—	—
5,001–7,500	1,227	15.2	7,669	3.0	283	3.7	1,769	0.6	843	9.7	5,058	1.4
7,501–10,000	1,314	16.2	11,497	4.5	1,849	24.0	16,179	5.2	1,660	19.1	14,525	4.2
10,001–15,000	1,927	23.8	24,087	9.4	2,069	26.8	25,862	8.3	2,177	25.1	27,213	7.8
15,001–20,000	1,105	13.7	19,337	7.5	881	11.4	15,417	5.0	1,114	12.8	19,495	5.6
20,001–30,000	831	10.3	20,450	8.0	760	9.8	18,740	6.0	860	9.9	21,156	6.1
30,001–50,000	421	5.2	16,605	6.5	482	6.2	18,470	5.9	545	6.3	20,923	6.0
50,001–75,000	226	2.8	13,642	5.3	290	3.8	17,325	5.6	243	2.8	15,188	4.4
75,001 and over	826	10.2	142,974	55.6	974	12.6	196,410	63.3	1,246	14.3	225,374	64.5
Total	8,090	100.0	256,794	100.0	7,718	100.0	310,497	100.0	8,688	100.0	348,932	100.0

Source: République Islamique de Mauritanie, *Bulletin Statistique et Economique.*

TABLE 16.   MAURITANIA: MINIMUM HOURLY WAGE (SMIG)

(*In CFA francs*)

	Before January 1969		After January 1969	
	Zone I	Zone II	Zone I	Zone II
Industry and commerce	36.00	30.90	41.30	35.70
Agriculture	32.40	27.90	37.30	32.30

Source: Data provided by the Mauritanian authorities.

In January 1962 the labor union, the employers, and the Government signed a collective agreement establishing salary scales for most industrial and commercial activities. In June 1965 a government decree established salary scales for all remaining professions. The salary scales vary with the professions, except for the minimum wage, which is common and uniform for all professions. Permanently employed civil servants are paid according to the Government's own salary scale; temporary appointments are paid on the basis of the regulations applying to nonagricultural enterprises. In January 1969, the SMIG for industrial and commercial sectors was increased by approximately 15 per cent, from CFAF 36.00 to CFAF 41.30 in Zone I and from CFAF 30.90 to CFAF 35.70 in Zone II.

Average monthly per capita earnings in the private sector in 1966 (CFAF 38,000) were twice those in the public sector (CFAF 18,000). The discrepancy is due mainly to the inclusion of high-income foreign technicians in private sector statistics, while these are excluded from public sector data. In 1966 a Mauritanian worker earned about the same average monthly wages in the private sector as in the public sector. The level of the average monthly earnings in the private sector increased from CFAF 32,000 in 1963 to CFAF 40,000 in 1967, or by about 25 per cent (Table 17).

PRICES

Price control, imposed before independence, has been strengthened in recent years; the enforcement of controlled prices was made more efficient, and the scope of control enlarged so that the prices of only a few luxury items are now free. Price regulations are normally observed

TABLE 17. MAURITANIA: AVERAGE MONTHLY SALARY
IN VARIOUS SECTORS, 1963–67

(*In CFA francs*)

	1963	1964	1965	1966	1967
Agriculture and fishing	18,000	25,000	22,000	22,000	22,000
Mining and quarrying	46,000	58,000	55,000	51,000	55,000
Manufacturing	18,000	12,000	27,000	26,000	25,000
Construction and public works	20,000	16,000	26,000	24,000	25,000
Water and electric industries	28,000	44,000	27,000	33,000	36,000
Commerce and banking	35,000	31,000	37,000	35,000	42,000
Transportation and management	27,000	25,000	25,000	28,000	28,000
Services	19,000	18,000	21,000	16,000	15,000
General average	32,000	35,000	40,000	38,000	40,000

Source: Ministère de la Planification et du Développement Rural, *Annuaire Statistique*, 1968.

by wholesalers and shopkeepers in urban areas but are often evaded in the small local markets. In rural areas the enforcement of price regulations presents administrative difficulties and is not effective.

Three different kinds of controlled prices are being used: maximum price ceilings, maximum price markups, and fixed retail prices. Price ceilings are imposed on essential consumption goods, and are set for various areas by government decree following proposals from local price committees. Whenever possible, the ceilings are based on dealers' or producers' cost plus a profit margin. The prices of locally produced foodstuffs vary widely according to the region as well as the season. In order to alleviate fluctuations, the authorities attempted to establish stockpiling cooperatives which would sell food staples at constant prices, but this measure has yielded little practical result so far. The retail prices of certain imported essentials (sugar, tea, rice, and cotton fabrics) are fixed by decree. The prices of imported nonessentials are regulated by markups set by the Government on the recommendation of the Central Price Committee, composed of representatives from the Chamber of Commerce, the trade unions, and various public bodies. Markup regulations apply to wholesalers' as well as retailers' profit margins. For both, the maximum price markup ranges from 10 to 20 per cent of the import price. Only for new automobiles and spare parts are retail prices proposed by the dealers and fixed by government decree.

In order to maintain a uniform retail price for sugar throughout the country irrespective of differences in transportation cost, an equalization fund was set up, using the revenue from a consumption tax on sugar to subsidize the retail price in remote areas.

The only price index for Mauritania is a consumer price index for European families in Nouakchott, based on their expenditures. Since it does not reflect prices paid in local markets by the majority of the people, it is not representative. This index shows a rising trend during 1964–69, interrupted only by a slight decrease in 1965 (Table 18). It declined by 1 per cent in 1965 and increased by an average annual rate of 3.8 per cent in 1966–69. Factors behind the over-all increase in this index include rising freight costs and higher prices in Europe. The temporary decline in 1965 corresponded essentially to a drop in prices of food and clothing resulting from increased price competition among retailers. Devaluation of the CFA franc in August 1969 occurred too late in the year to account for all the increase of 2.9 per cent in the price index in that year. However, the devaluation is expected to have a significant effect on the price index in 1970.

PUBLIC FINANCE

BUDGET SYSTEM

Budget operations of the Central Government are recorded in the current budget (*budget ordinaire*) and the capital budget (*budget d'équipement*), both established on a calendar-year basis. Budget operations of the municipalities are financed with their own fiscal resources

TABLE 18.   MAURITANIA: CONSUMER PRICE INDEX FOR EUROPEAN
FAMILIES IN NOUAKCHOTT, ANNUAL AVERAGE, 1964–69

(*January 1961 = 100*)

	1964	1965	1966	1967	1968	1969
Food	127	123	132	137	137	136
Servants	120	120	123	130	130	139
Utilities	93	91	88	90	102	109
Clothing	108	100	104	109	122	120
Miscellaneous	142	152	156	163	169	187
General index	124	123	128	134	139	143

Sources: République Islamique de Mauritanie, *Bulletin Mensuel de Statistique,* January 1968; and data provided by the Mauritanian authorities.

and with receipts from certain taxes included in the current budget of the Central Government. Cash transactions of the Government are carried out through the Mauritanian Treasury, which also fulfills certain banking functions by accepting deposits from autonomous government agencies, municipalities, and the Postal Checking System. These functions augment the funds and the sources of short-term financing available to the Treasury to the extent that such funds are not immediately transferred. The current budget is executed over a period of 15 months (i.e., including a complementary period, January 1–March 31), and the budget accounts are closed on March 31 of the following year. Although no commitments are permitted after the close of the budget year, committed expenditures may be effected during the complementary period. Revenues and expenditures during the complementary period are recorded in the accounts of the previous year. Unspent appropriations may be transferred from one article to another within the same chapter in the budget with the authorization of the Minister of Finance, but approval by the National Assembly is required for a transfer of appropriations from one chapter to another. The capital budget is prepared in the Ministry of Planning and Rural Development and is executed on a cash basis.

AUTONOMOUS PUBLIC AGENCIES

The public sector includes several autonomous government agencies, the most important of which are the Post Office and the Social Security Fund. The autonomous agencies are subject to supervision by the Ministry of Finance, as well as the ministry to which their activities are directly related. In 1967, expenditures of the Post Office amounted to CFAF 350 million, CFAF 8 million financed through the government budget and CFAF 24 million by FAC. The Social Security Fund collects the social security taxes; in 1967, its receipts amounted to CFAF 299 million and expenditures to CFAF 236 million. Before being abolished at the end of 1967, the National Office of Public Transport subsidized the transport of goods to remote areas of the country. In 1967 this Office collected a 5 per cent transportation tax amounting to CFAF 47 million and granted subsidy payments amounting to CFAF 41 million. The Office was replaced by the Road Fund for the same purpose of subsidizing transportation of consumer goods to less accessible parts of the country. The Fund receives its revenue from a sales tax on gasoline products.

CURRENT BUDGET DEVELOPMENTS

In the five years 1964–68, current revenue increased by 62 per cent to CFAF 5.9 billion, while current expenditure rose by 30 per cent to CFAF 5.4 billion (Table 19). The current budget deficit of CFAF 0.5 billion in 1967 was followed by surpluses through 1968. Revised budget estimates for 1969, with current revenue and expenditure at a level of CFAF 6.5 billion, show a small deficit. The 1970 budget estimates provide for current revenue and expenditure balanced at nearly CFAF 7.5 billion.

Revenue

Current budget revenue increased by 10 per cent in 1967, and by 14 per cent in 1968. In 1969, this revenue was expected to increase by about 10 per cent and in 1970 by 15 per cent. Larger revenue in 1967 resulted mainly from a 10 per cent rise in receipts from indirect taxes, especially consumption and excise taxes, which almost doubled, and from larger administrative receipts. In 1968, consumption and excise taxes again rose by 53 per cent and in 1969 by an estimated 8 per cent. The 1970 budget estimates call for larger revenue from most taxes except consumption and excise taxes.

Indirect taxes.—In 1967, indirect taxes represented 74 per cent of total revenues in the current budget (import duties and taxes alone for 29 per cent, export taxes from the mining concessions for 28 per cent, and consumption and excise taxes for 16 per cent). In 1968, indirect taxes accounted for about 71 per cent of total revenue in the current budget, and in 1969 and 1970 for an estimated 69–70 per cent.

(1) Customs duties and import taxes in Mauritania reflect the association with EEC and membership in the West African Customs Union (Union Douanière des Etats de l'Afrique de l'Ouest, or UDEAO) and, until its dissolution at the end of 1969, the Customs Union with Senegal. The latter Union provided that 8.66 per cent of the customs duties and import taxes collected by the two countries under the common external tariff were to be distributed to Mauritania and 91.34 per cent to Senegal.

TABLE 19. MAURITANIA: CURRENT BUDGET, 1964–70

(In millions of CFA francs)

	1964	1965	1966	1967	1968	1969 (Revised Estimates)[1]	1970 (Budget Estimates)
Revenue							
Indirect taxes							
Customs duties and import taxes	1,405	1,292	1,310	1,499	1,484	1,442	1,935
Mining concessions	679	1,196	1,652	1,455	1,439	1,552	1,730
Consumption and excise taxes	435	745	483	818	1,251	1,346	1,248
Export taxes	11	41	62	80	51	130	303
Total indirect taxes	2,530	3,274	3,507	3,852	4,225	4,470	5,216
Direct taxes							
Income tax	749	963	808	839	954	1,086	1,436
Other	76	63	109	82	87	82	305
Total direct taxes	825	1,026	917	921	1,041	1,168	1,741
Administrative receipts and service charges	314	272	311	416	661	880	495
Total revenue	3,669	4,572	4,735	5,189	5,927	6,518	7,492
Expenditures							
Wages and salaries	...	2,401	2,500	2,725	2,908	3,577	4,116
Material and supplies	...	1,001	891	1,103	1,201	1,814	1,913
Maintenance	285	108	106	136	93	70	79
Subsidies and transfers[2]	...	440	465	561	378	542	947
Public debt service	220	214	397	301	456	470	289
Unclassified	...	—	50	139	330	67	148
Total expenditures	4,137	4,164	4,409	4,965	5,366	6,540	7,492
Current surplus, or deficit (−)	−468	408	326	224	561	−22	—

Source: Data provided by the Mauritanian authorities.

[1] IMF staff estimates based on preliminary data.
[2] Includes transfers to capital budget of CFAF 20 million in 1966, CFAF 52 million in 1967, and CFAF 195 million (estimated) in 1968.

Revenues from export taxes went to the country of origin, except that 1 per cent was withheld to cover joint administrative costs. In February 1970, products originating in UDEAO countries became subject to import taxes and fiscal duties at rates which are generally 50 per cent of the rates applicable to imports from other countries. A UDEAO member may increase this rate to 70 per cent to protect a particular domestic industry.

Except for petroleum products, which are subject to a single tax (*taxe de raffinage*), all imports are subject to several levies (Table 20): (1) a customs duty, applicable to imports from all countries except EEC and UDEAO members and ranging from 2 to 75 per cent of the c.i.f. value under the minimum tariff, on imports from those countries accorded most-favored-nation treatment (the general tariff applicable to all other countries consist of rates three times those of the minimum tariff); (2) a fiscal duty ranging from 0.5 to 50 per cent of the c.i.f. value but generally falling within the 5 to 20 per cent range, levied on all imports regardless of origin; (3) a statistical tax of 2 per cent of the c.i.f. value, applicable to all imports except some food products and most capital goods; (4) an import tax (*taxe forfaitaire à l'importation*), applicable to all imports except cereals, fresh vegetables, oranges and bananas, concentrated milk, sugar, and periodicals, and applied to the c.i.f. value including customs duties, the fiscal duty, and the statistical tax (most goods are taxed at a rate of 20 per cent, except for capital imports taxed at 2 per cent and food products—meat, butter, pasta, biscuits, canned fruits, and vegetables—as well as leather, stationery products, and furniture taxed at 30 per cent); and (5) an import turnover tax (*taxe sur le chiffre d'affaires à l'importation*), applied to the c.i.f. value, including all customs duties and import taxes payable, and ranging from 12 to 25 per cent, the higher rate applicable to luxury goods (e.g., perfumes, photographic equipment, air-conditioners, refrigerators, radios, tape recorders, musical instruments, pleasure boats, and carpets) but not applicable to staple food items and industrial raw materials.[3]

Receipts from import duties and taxes rose from CFAF 1,292 million in 1965 to CFAF 1,484 million in 1968, and were estimated at

---

[3] Before February 1968 the import turnover tax was not applied to imports originating in UDEAO countries.

TABLE 20. MAURITANIA: IMPORT DUTIES AND TAXES ON CERTAIN IMPORTS, 1970

(*In per cent of c.i.f. value*)

	Customs Duty	Fiscal Duty	Statistical Tax	Import Tax	Import Turnover Tax	Over-All Tariff Burden on Imports from	
						EEC	Countries granted the minimum tariff
Fresh vegetables	5	4	—	—	—	4.0	9.0
Fresh fruits (other than bananas and oranges)	5	4	—	20	—	24.8	30.8
Bananas	40	5	—	—	—	5.0	45.0
Oranges	15	5	—	—	—	5.0	20.0
Maize		0.5	—	—	—	0.5	0.5
Cereals	2	2	—	—	—	2.0	4.0
Flour	5	4	—	20	12	39.8	46.5
Rice						—	—
Sugar	12	2	—	20	12	14.2	27.7
Tea	7	3	—	20	12	38.4	47.8
Cement	7	10	4	20	12	53.2	62.6
Cotton textiles	20	20	4	20	12	66.7	93.6
Radios	7	20	4	20	25	86.0	96.5
Automobiles	25	20	4	20	12	66.7	100.3
Trucks	25	15	4	20	12	59.9	93.5
Construction machinery and equipment	5–30	—	—	2	12	14.2	19.9–48.5
Air-conditioners and refrigerators	5	10	4	20	25	71.0	78.5
Furniture	5	15	4	30	12	73.3	80.5
Gasoline [1]						—	—
Diesel fuel [2]						—	—

Source: Data provided by the Mauritanian authorities.

[1] Subject to a single tax of CFAF 935.29 per hectoliter.
[2] Subject to a single tax of CFAF 782.56 per hectoliter.

CFAF 1,442 million for 1969 and CFAF 1,935 million for 1970. Apart from the 1968 change in tax rates applicable to imports from UDEAO countries, the only other change in tax rates since 1966 has been the increase in January 1967 in the fiscal duty on matches (from an ad valorem tax of 1.5 per cent to CFAF 4 per box) and the increase on January 1, 1970 in the statistical tax (from 2 per cent to 4 per cent). Receipts from the Customs Union with Senegal, which amounted to CFAF 854 million in 1956, declined to CFAF 817 million in 1966, and to CFAF 574 million in 1967. The decline reflects the Mauritanian policy of diverting imports from Dakar to Mauritanian ports.

(2) Taxes on mining concessions are those collected from the Mining Company (MIFERMA) and governed by a long-term fiscal system (*régime fiscal de longue durée*), under the agreement, made in 1959, between the Mauritanian Government and the Mining Company. Originally, this agreement provided for tax payments by the Company equal to 50 per cent of profits. However, in order to ensure a flow of tax revenue before the Company's operations became profitable, the Company was to make advance payments in two stages. The first stage was to cover the period before operations began, when the Government was to receive revenue from import duties on all supplies and equipment. The duty was to be calculated at 1959 customs rates, subject to the provision that total annual payments by the Company would not exceed 5 per cent of the total value of its imports. All imports for personal consumption were to be subject to current customs rates. The second stage was to cover the period after the Company began exporting iron ore; during this period the Company's imports were still to be subject to duty but without the provision that total payments would not exceed 5 per cent of the total import value. In addition, an export duty of 5 per cent to 9 per cent on the f.o.b. value was to be levied. It was agreed that if government revenue from the export duty calculated at the end of the year turned out to be larger than the import duties actually paid during the year, the Company would pay the difference. If, however, import duties paid during the year were larger, the Company could deduct the difference from the following year's tax payments. All imports for personal consumption during this period were to be treated the same as in the investment period.

Retroactively from January 1, 1965, the Government agreed that the Company would pay a flat 9 per cent on all export earnings in lieu of the provision of the original agreement. The revenue from the export duty still constitutes advance payments on the tax corresponding to 50 per cent of profits. The new system ensures a more stable flow of revenue to Mauritania than when tax payments were based on the Company's imports.

Tax revenue from mining concessions increased from CFAF 1,196 million in 1965 to CFAF 1,652 million in 1966, owing in part to the payment in 1966 of the 9 per cent retroactive export tax, and in part to the recording in the government budget in 1966 of CFAF 192 million of tax revenue actually received from the Mining Company in 1964 and 1965. In 1967 the Company's payments declined to CFAF 1,455 million and in 1968 to CFAF 1,439 million, but were estimated at CFAF 1,552 million (24 per cent of total budgetary receipts) in 1969 and at CFAF 1,730 million (23 per cent) in 1970.

Taxation of the Copper Company (SOMIMA) is governed by a long-term fiscal system under an agreement with the Mauritanian Government made in 1967. The Copper Company was exempted from the payment of corporate income tax for five years after the first commercial shipment of 10,000 tons of ore. It was also exempted from taxes and duties on imports of supplies and equipment, except for imports of goods for personal consumption subject to tax at regular rates. Though exempt from import taxes, the Company does not have to pay the domestic turnover tax (*taxe locale sur le chiffre d'affaires*), applicable to goods and services purchased locally. It is estimated that, out of a total project cost of CFAF 14.3 billion, the Company would obtain about CFAF 6 billion worth of goods and services in Mauritania. Once ore shipments start, the Company becomes subject to an export tax equal to 1 U.S. cent per pound for copper exported or sold in Mauritania at an f.o.b. price of 40 cents or less per pound. This tax will increase to 1.25 cents per pound, if the f.o.b. price exceeds 40 cents but is less than or equal to 50 cents per pound, and to 1.50 cents per pound for an export price above 50 cents per pound.

Government revenue from the Copper Company (between 1968 and 1989) was expected to total about CFAF 15.5 billion; it is not expected, however, that the government budget will receive any substantial revenue from the Company until after 1977. About CFAF 50 million is expected annually during the construction period (1968–70) and CFAF 280 million during the beginning of the exploitation period (1971–77), CFAF 125 million from export taxes and CFAF 155 million from taxes on salaries and import taxes on goods for personal use. During 1978–88, government revenue is expected to amount to about CFAF 1,220 million annually, CFAF 610 million from the 35 per cent tax on profits and CFAF 330 million from dividends on government-owned shares in the Copper Company.

(3) Consumption and excise taxes consist of a domestic turnover tax (*taxe locale sur le chiffre d'affaires*) and several excise taxes. Mauritania levies a domestic turnover tax at an effective rate of 6.36 per cent on all sales of goods and services, except goods subject to the import turnover tax; staple food items; newspapers and periodicals; certain transactions requiring registration (e.g., insurance contracts and transfers of property); services associated with transportation, banking and finance; and the building and repair of fishing and merchant marine boats. The numerous exemptions leave the domestic turnover tax applicable mainly to construction.

Sugar is subject to an excise tax of CFAF 18,571 per ton, collected by the Chamber of Commerce. Tea is subject to a consumption tax of CFAF 100,000 per ton, and the revenue is paid into a tea fund. A tax of CFAF 250 per kilogram is levied on sales of meat, whether imported or locally slaughtered. The Government also collects excise taxes on alcoholic beverages, tobacco, and petroleum products.

Total receipts from consumption and excise taxes increased from CFAF 745 million in 1965 to CFAF 1,251 million in 1968. The increase of CFAF 335 million, compared with 1966, is due to the transfer to the 1967 budget of CFAF 270 million from the sugar fund and some increase in revenue from the domestic turnover tax and the excise tax on petroleum products; the revenue from the consumption and excise taxes rose to CFAF 818 million. In 1969, receipts were expected to increase to CFAF 1,346 million, mainly because of larger transfers to the government budget of funds from the special funds for tea and sugar taxes. Receipts from the domestic turnover tax and the excise tax on petroleum products was also expected to increase on account of the Copper Company's operations. The 1970 budget estimates, however, include only CFAF 1,248 million for total consumption and excise taxes.

(4) Export taxes include a fiscal duty levied at a variable ad valorem rate, a conditioning tax with rates of 0.25–0.5 per cent, and an export tax (*taxe forfaitaire à l'exportation*) of 5.4 per cent (Table 21). For some products there is also a so-called research tax with a maximum rate of 1 per cent, and for others a statistical tax of 2 per cent.

Receipts from export taxes increased from CFAF 11 million in 1964 to CFAF 80 million in 1967, and then declined to CFAF 51 million in 1968 (see Table 19). However, they were expected to turn upward to CFAF 130 million in 1969 and to CFAF 303 million in 1970 because of the growing exports of the fishing industry. Export taxes remain a minor source of revenue, equivalent to only 1 per cent of total revenue from indirect taxes.

Direct taxes.—Mauritania has several income and property taxes. The schedular income tax includes a tax on wages and salaries, and a tax on corporate and other profits. The tax on wages and salaries is withheld at source; rates range from 6 per cent on monthly earnings of CFAF 6,000 to 15 per cent for monthly earnings above CFAF 70,000 without allowance for family deductions. In addition, employers pay a payroll tax (*taxe d'apprentissage*) of 0.5 per cent. Corporations opera-

TABLE 21.   MAURITANIA: MAJOR EXPORT TAXES, 1970

	Tax Base	Ad Valorem Duty	Excise Tax [1]	Export Tax	Total Tax
	CFA francs per kilogram	←—————	—Per cent—	————→	*CFA francs per kilogram*
Fish (fresh and frozen) [2]	40–90	—	0.25	5.4	2.26–5.09
Fish (salted, dried, or smoked)	70	2.5	0.25	—	1.93
Lobster	500	1.0	0.5	5.4	34.5
Gum arabic	36	4.0	0.5	5.4	3.56
Meat [3]	—	1.0	0.5	5.4	6.9
Livestock [4]	—	—	—	—	—

Source: Data provided by the Mauritanian authorities.

[1] *Taxe de conditionnement.*
[2] Taxes on fish vary according to quality.
[3] F.o.b. value.
[4] There is a specific sanitary tax on exports of animals at the following rates per animal: sheep and goats, CFAF 100; cattle, CFAF 500; camels, CFAF 1,000; donkeys, CFAF 150; and horses, CFAF 600.

ting in Mauritania are subject to a 25 per cent tax on profits and a 16 per cent tax on distributed dividends. The mining companies, subject to the long-term fiscal system described under "Taxes on mining concessions," above, are excluded. Unincorporated enterprises are subject to a tax on profits, which is levied at a rate of 10 per cent on profits exceeding CFAF 100,000 and 15 per cent on profits exceeding CFAF 300,000. Those engaged in professions are taxed on the same basis as unincorporated enterprises.

The general income tax (*impôt général sur le revenu*), applicable to an individual's total taxable income, is levied at rates progressing from 2 per cent for annual incomes above CFAF 100,000 to 60 per cent for incomes above CFAF 5 million. This tax provides for family deductions.

Other direct taxes include a tax of 5 per cent on the rental value of housing (*contribution mobilière*), a real estate tax (*contribution foncière*), and a head tax (*contribution nationale*) of CFAF 100 per person for the first category and CFAF 40,000 per person for the second. The proceeds of the latter are shared between the Central Government and local authorities. In addition, there are taxes on patents, firearms, motor vehicles, and business licenses.

Total receipts from direct taxes represented about 18 per cent of the total budget revenue in 1968, or CFAF 1,041 million. Increases in 1968 of about CFAF 120 million resulted from higher wage and salary payments, larger industrial and commercial profits, and improved tax collection and recovery of arrears. In 1969, direct taxes were expected to amount to CFAF 1,168 million and in 1970 to CFAF 1,741 million.

Administrative receipts.—Among administrative receipts, revenue from public enterprises rose from CFAF 156 million in 1965 to CFAF 290 million in 1967. The increase in 1967 was due partly to the larger receipts from the Nouakchott wharf and partly to the transfer to the government budget of receipts from the Port of Nouadhibou (Port-Etienne), CFAF 18 million and the Nouakchott hospital, CFAF 27 million. In 1968, revenue from public enterprises amounted to about CFAF 287 million. Other administrative receipts include registration and stamp fees, amounting to CFAF 126 million in 1967. These receipts were higher in 1966 because of fines collected from foreign fishing boats for illegal fishing in Mauritanian territorial waters.

Expenditure

Current budget expenditure grew from CFAF 4,137 million in 1964 to CFAF 5,366 million in 1968. In 1969, expenditure was expected to increase by about 21 per cent to CFAF 6,540 million and in 1970 by 15 per cent to CFAF 7,492 million (see Table 19).

Wages and salaries rose by 13 per cent between 1965 and 1967. Wages and salaries accounted for roughly 55 per cent of total expenditures in 1967 and 1968. Although wage and salary scales have remained unchanged since 1962, the 1966 increase in personnel expenditures reflects the 5 per cent cost of living allowance granted to civil servants in Nouakchott in 1966. Expenditure for personnel increased in 1967 because the retirement age in government service was lowered from 55 to 50 (or 30 years service, whichever comes first) and upgrading of new personnel. Material and supplies accounted for 22 per cent of total expenditure in 1967 and 1968. The decline in 1966 was the result of an austerity program under which all appropriations for equipment were reduced by 10 per cent. The share of maintenance expenditures has remained about 3 per cent of total expenditure in each year since 1965. Subsidies and transfer payments accounted for 11 per cent of total expenditure in 1965; this proportion declined to 7 per cent in 1968.

CAPITAL BUDGET

While Mauritania's development plan catalogs projects that may be implemented when financing is available, the capital budget is drawn up annually on the basis of available financing and may include other projects. Expenditure in the capital budget rose from CFAF 0.3 billion in 1965 to CFAF 0.8 billion in 1966 and then declined to CFAF 0.5 billion in 1968 (Table 22). The small size of the 1965 budget reflected both a lack of financing and a shortage of personnel for project formulation and implementation. In 1966, better organization of project administration and additional available financing allowed the capital budget to increase by more than two and a half times. Most capital

TABLE 22. MAURITANIA: CAPITAL BUDGET EXPENDITURE, 1964–70

(In millions of CFA francs)

	1964	1965	1966	1967	1968	Estimated 1969	Budgeted 1970
Infrastructure	256	175	270	143	103	258	260
Administrative and residential construction	158	87	420	337	327	167	229
Purchase of supplies	—	—	32	26	19	14	71
Purchase of buildings	—	—	—	—	—	35	72
Equity participation in enterprises	14	20	39	157	67	38	62
Transfers to municipalities for projects	—	—	10	25	21	121	14
Other	—	9	—	—	1	—	57
Total	428	291	771	687	538	633	765

Source: Data provided by the Mauritanian authorities.

budget expenditures in 1966–68 were directed to building and construction, which accounted for nearly half of total capital expenditure in these years. It is estimated that the 1969 capital budget expenditure amounted to CFAF 0.6 billion, and the 1970 expenditure is budgeted at CFAF 0.8 billion. In 1969 and 1970, in contrast to earlier years, the largest item of expenditure is infrastructure.

TREASURY OPERATIONS

The over-all fiscal performance of the Central Government during 1965–68 is shown in Table 23 (which converts the budget results from a fiscal-year to a calendar-year basis) and Table 24 (which gives the Treasury's budgetary and extrabudgetary operations on a calendar-year basis).

In 1965 the Treasury had a cash surplus of CFAF 471 million, resulting from an over-all budget deficit of CFAF 217 million and a credit in its extrabudgetary operations of CFAF 688 million. This surplus and a growth in deposits with the Treasury added CFAF 679 million to the Treasury's cash balances.

In 1966 the Treasury sustained a cash deficit of CFAF 1,089 million because of an over-all budget deficit of CFAF 966 million and a debit in its extrabudgetary operations of CFAF 123 million. This cash deficit was financed mainly by a French capital budget subsidy of CFAF 600

TABLE 23.   MAURITANIA: CENTRAL GOVERNMENT BUDGET, 1965–68

(In millions of CFA francs)

	1965	1966	1967	1968
Current budget				
Revenues during fiscal year	4,572	4,735	5,189	5,927
Less complementary period	−1,855	−2,424	−2,670	−3,240 [1]
Plus preceding fiscal year's complementary period	1,641	1,855	2,424	2,670
Revenues on calendar-year basis	4,358	4,166	4,943	5,357
Expenditures during fiscal year	4,164	4,409	4,965	5,366
Less transfers to capital budget	—	−20	−52	−116
Less complementary period	−570	−589	−673	−915 [1]
Plus preceding fiscal year's complementary period	690	571	589	675 [1]
Expenditures on calendar-year basis	4,284	4,371	4,829	5,010
Current budget surplus, or deficit (−), on calendar-year basis	74	−205	114	347
Capital budget expenditures	−291	−761	−687	−538
Over-all deficit on calendar-year basis	−217	−966	−573	−191

Source: Data provided by the Mauritanian authorities.

[1] Preliminary IMF staff estimates.

TABLE 24.   MAURITANIA: BUDGETARY AND EXTRABUDGETARY
CASH OPERATIONS AND FINANCING, 1965–68

(In millions of CFA francs)

	1965	1966	1967	1968 (Estimates)
Current budget surplus, or deficit (−) [1]	74	−205	114	347
Capital budget expenditures	−291	−761	−687	−538
Extrabudgetary operations [2]	688	−123	596	−161
Treasury's over-all cash surplus, or deficit (−)	**471**	**−1,089**	**23**	**−352**
Financing				
French aid to capital budget	—	600	300	—
Changes in Treasury cash balances				
Deposits with banking system	−415	862	−497	181
Cash in till	−264	29	272	116
Net increase (−) or decrease in Treasury cash balances	−679	891	−225	297
Changes in deposits with the Treasury	220	−375	−125	75
Customs duty bills	−12	−27	27	−20

Source: Data provided by the Mauritanian authorities.

[1] Calendar-year basis.
[2] Net changes in the consolidated accounts of receipts and expenditures not yet recorded in the budget.

million and the net utilization of the Treasury's cash holdings. The Treasury's cash balances were drawn down by CFAF 891 million with a decline in deposits with the Treasury of CFAF 375 million.

A cash surplus of CFAF 23 million resulted in 1967 from the overall budget deficit of CFAF 573 million and a credit in extrabudgetary operations of CFAF 596 million. Since the French aid to the capital budget more than offset the decrease in deposits with the Treasury, its cash balances rose by CFAF 225 million.

It is estimated that the Treasury's over-all cash deficit in 1968 amounted to CFAF 352 million, reflecting an over-all budget deficit of CFAF 191 million and a debit in extrabudgetary operations of CFAF 161 million. Apparently this deficit was financed largely by net changes in the Treasury's cash balances.

MONEY AND BANKING

MONETARY SYSTEM

Mauritania is a member of the French franc area, as well as a member of the West African Monetary Union (Union Monétaire Ouest Africaine, or UMOA), along with six other African countries (Dahomey, Ivory Coast, Niger, Senegal, Togo, and Upper Volta). These countries have a common currency, the CFA franc, and a common central bank, the Banque Centrale des Etats de l'Afrique de l'Ouest (BCEAO), which is the issuing authority of UMOA and keeps its external reserves. The CFA franc is freely convertible into French francs at the rate of CFAF 1.00 = F 0.02. On August 10, 1969 the rate against the U.S. dollar became CFAF 277.710 per dollar; previously, since January 1, 1960, the rate had been CFAF 246.853. (For details of the operation of BCEAO, see Chapter 4, and for information on the change in the par value, see Chapter 6.)

STRUCTURE OF THE BANKING SYSTEM

The banking system of Mauritania includes the Central Bank (BCEAO), which it shares with the other UMOA members; two commercial banks, the Development Bank (Banque Mauritanienne de Développement, or BMD); the Postal Checking System; and since July 1969 the National Savings Fund. BCEAO operates in Mauritania, as in the other UMOA countries, through a local agency. Decisions concerning the implementation of BCEAO policies in Mauritania are taken by the National Monetary Committee. The Director of the local BCEAO agency, who sits on the National Monetary Committee in an advisory capacity, is responsible for the application of these policies.

The Treasury of Mauritania also performs certain banking operations. It accepts customs duty bills (*obligations cautionnées*), with a maturity of four months, in payment of certain indirect taxes, principally customs duties. These bills are discountable at BCEAO. The Treasury may receive deposits from public and semipublic institutions.

Besides credit extended by banks, the Caisse Centrale de Coopération Economique (CCCE), a French institution, extends medium-term and long-term credit and contributes to the financing of the Development Bank's credit operations. In addition, it acts as the authorized agent of the Fonds d'Aide et de Coopération (FAC) and the European Development Fund (EDF, or Fonds Européen de Développement, or FED) for local aid disbursements.

BANKING LEGISLATION AND REGULATIONS

Banking operations in Mauritania are regulated by Law No. 64–016 of January 18, 1964 and subsequent implementing decrees and ordinances under this law. Because of the close monetary ties with the other countries of UMOA, Mauritania's banking legislation follows closely the guidelines issued by the Board of Directors of BCEAO for its members. It consists of seven titles which define credit institutions; regulate their establishment, management, and mode of operation and control; and specify penalties for infractions. The banking legislation laid down a number of specific measures designed to strengthen the regulating powers of the monetary authorities over banks and other financial institutions. Its main features include the determination of liquidity ratios for banks; the fixation of interest rates, commissions, and service fees charged by banks; and the establishment of special requirements concerning the capital and reserves of banks and other financial institutions. The law also provides for the establishment of two institutions: the National Credit Council and the Bank and Financial Institutions Committee. The task of the first institution is to study credit policies and to advise the Minister of Finance on credit and banking regulations to be adopted. So far, however, the National Credit Council has not met. The Banks and Financial Institutions Committee, which meets at least once a year, advises the Minister of Finance on banking and credit matters and controls the implementation of banking regulations. It is composed of the Treasurer General, the Director of Planning, the Director of Commerce, and the Vice-President of the Supreme Court.

CREDIT CONTROL

Policy instruments available to the monetary authorities in the BCEAO area consist mainly of (1) ceilings on government borrowing, (2) rediscount ceilings and limits, (3) liquidity and solvency ratios, and (4) the rediscount rate.

Ceilings on Government Borrowing

BCEAO is authorized to extend to the Government short-term credit in the form of (1) direct advances; (2) rediscounting, purchasing, or making advances against Treasury bills; and (3) discounting customs duty bills. In December 1968, Article XV of BCEAO's statutes was modified so as to permit the Central Bank, by a special decision of its Board of Directors, to increase its direct advances to member governments from 10 per cent to 15 per cent of the actual fiscal receipts of the previous budget year; the limit on such direct advances is to be reduced automatically by the amount of Treasury bills held by the Central Bank and by the amount of government borrowing from banks which have rediscount facilities with the Central Bank, but not by discounted customs duty bills. In order to use this additional credit facility, the borrowing government will have to provide specific justification to BCEAO. The maximum period for such advances remains fixed at 240 days, but it can be extended by a special waiver of the Board of Directors until the first working day of the following calendar year.

Rediscount Ceilings

Rediscount ceilings and limits on short-term and medium-term credit are the principal tools of credit control in the BCEAO area. BCEAO fixes global ceilings on rediscount facilities, both short-term and medium-term, for each country, on proposals of its National Monetary Committee, for a period of six months; these ceilings can be revised only by the Board of Directors.

The global rediscount ceiling for short-term credit is based on the estimated needs of the economy for the semester under review. In arriving at this ceiling, account is taken of the commercial banks' and the Development Bank's own resources in order to ensure full use of these resources before resort to the rediscount facilities of the Central Bank. The National Monetary Committee allocates the ceiling among the banks, except for a small margin to meet unforeseen needs.

In addition to rediscount ceilings for each commercial bank and for the Development Bank, BCEAO also establishes credit limits, except on loans below CFAF 10 million, for individual enterprises on the basis of their creditworthiness. Bank loans to the private sector are rediscountable only up to the limits established for each enterprise, and interest charges on loans beyond the limits are required to be higher than on those within the limits.

Medium-term rediscount ceilings are established by BCEAO for each member country on the basis of the estimated number of investment projects likely to require medium-term credit. This ceiling is not suballocated among the commercial banks and the Development Bank. For each financial institution, however, there is a fixed limit on the extension of medium-term credit, whether rediscountable or not, during a certain period of time. Medium-term credit can be rediscounted with BCEAO only if the credit has received the prior approval of the National Monetary Committee. This approval is given on the basis of an examination of the financial situation of the enterprise applying for credit, provided that the project is in line with the general development policy of the country and would yield sufficient returns to reimburse the credit.

Liquidity and Solvency Ratios

Banks are required to maintain a prescribed minimum liquidity ratio between their liquid assets and their short-term liabilities. Liquid assets are defined as cash in hand and negotiable assets, consisting mainly of rediscountable credit and external assets, while liquid liabilities consist of deposits plus liabilities to BCEAO. This ratio was set at 70 per cent for the BCEAO accounting year 1965/66 and is to be increased by 1 percentage point each year until 1970/71, after which it will remain at 75 per cent.

In addition, the law requires the maintenance of a solvency ratio relating capital, reserves, head office funds, unappropriated provisions, and retained net profits to the total of credit extended (rediscountable or not), credit lines granted but not utilized, and guarantees and endorsements given by the institution concerned. The solvency ratio, thus defined, is 8 per cent for commercial banks, 12 per cent for the Development Bank, and 10 per cent for other financial institutions.

INTEREST RATES

Since the establishment of UMOA, BCEAO's basic discount rate has remained unchanged at 3.5 per cent. A preferential rate of 3 per cent is applied by BCEAO to the financing of operations involving exports to countries outside the BCEAO area.

Uniform regulations govern interest charges for credit extended by the banks and rates of interest paid by the banks for deposits held with them. These regulations cover the commercial banks and the Development Bank to the extent that it engages in commercial banking operations. The regulations are harmonized with those in other UMOA countries. They are intended to facilitate access to bank credit for all those willing to engage in economic activities that are productive or of general social and economic interest.

Interest rates for credit operations by the banks are calculated by applying the following basic rules: (1) a uniform basic rate (*taux de référence*), (2) an additional rate varying with the different categories of credit as specified in the regulations, and (3) a 0.25 per cent commission to BCEAO (*commission d'engagement*) on rediscountable medium-term credit; this commission, however, is waived for credits guaranteed by the Government (*aval de l'état*). At present the basic rate is equal to the rediscount rate of BCEAO of 3.5 per cent. If BCEAO's foreign assets were to decline below the level which calls for readjustment measures under the Bank's statutes, the Government could authorize BCEAO to set a basic rate different from its rediscount rate.

The range of effective annual interest rates charged on short-term credit is as follows: (1) 4.5–5.25 per cent on credits to public enterprises for the mobilization of crops and on credit to enterprises having been accorded a privileged status through enterprise agreements; (2) 5.0–6.0 per cent on advances for goods under warranty; (3) 5.5–6.5 per cent on all other credits eligible for rediscount with the Central Bank; (4) 6.0–8.0 per cent for credits granted above the global rediscount ceiling or granted beyond the individual rediscount limit set by BCEAO for each enterprise, provided the particular credit does not exceed CFAF 5 million; and (5) a uniform rate of 9.0 per cent in cases similar to (4) above, but where the particular credit exceeds CFAF 5 million.

The different types of medium-term credits are subject to the following range of annual interest rates (including the commission to BCEAO when applicable): (1) 5.5–6.0 per cent on investment credits to enterprises having been accorded a privileged status or for real estate and building projects of a recognized social character and interest; (2) 5.5–6.25 per cent on industrial or commercial credits of a recognized productive character; (3) 7.25–7.75 per cent on credit for real estate or building projects not recognized as having general social character and interest; and (4) 8.0–8.5 per cent for all medium-term credits not eligible for rediscount at the Central Bank.

Interest rates charged by the Development Bank for long-term loans cover a wide range depending on the purpose of the loan. For operations of a socially desirable character, the annual rate is 4.0–5.0 per cent; municipalities are charged 1.0–1.5 per cent in addition to the rates paid by the Development Bank on its loans from CCCE; for certain private luxury construction loans, the rate may go up as high as 9.0 per cent.

The range of interest rates on deposits with the banks are as follows: on demand deposits and time deposits of less than six months, the annual rates range from nil (for amounts up to CFAF 200,000) to 2.5 per cent (for amounts beyond CFAF 5,000,000). For time deposits, higher annual interest rates are paid on funds entrusted to the banks for a period exceeding six months and in amounts beyond CFAF 200,000 (3.5 per cent for time deposits of CFAF 200,001–CFAF 5,000,000, and 4.5 per cent for time deposits above CFAF 5,000,000). Savings deposits earn a uniform interest rate of 3.25 per cent annually; however, each account must amount to at least CFAF 10,000 and may not exceed CFAF 1,000,000.

OPERATIONS OF THE CENTRAL BANK

Operations of the Central Bank in Mauritania are reflected in Table 25.[4] The volume of operations declined during 1962–66 and rose during 1967–69 but did not regain the 1962 level.

Variations are due mainly to changes in currency outside banks and the Treasury and in government deposits (including currency held by the Treasury). It must be kept in mind, however, that the common currency for the seven UMOA countries makes it difficult to know the precise amount of currency in circulation in each particular member country, although each member country, through its local BCEAO agency, issues notes bearing its individual marking. Currency in circulation is defined in Mauritania, as in other UMOA countries, as currency issued by the local BCEAO agency less currency bearing the country's marking that has been withdrawn from circulation by the local BCEAO agency and the BCEAO agencies in the other six UMOA countries. This definition does not necessarily correspond to the actual amount of currency circulating in Mauritania. As a result of the free flow of notes and coins between UMOA member states, a portion of the notes issued by the Nouakchott agency may be circulating in the other six member countries, while a certain amount of notes issued by the other six BCEAO agencies circulates within the boundaries of Mauritania. Because of close traditional ties between Mauritania and Senegal, the flow of currency between these two countries has been especially large. Uncertainties as to the data on currency in circulation also affect the foreign assets data, which are computed as the residual or balancing item in the country's position in BCEAO after all other items have been entered in the balance sheet.

Currency held by the private sector (i.e., currency in circulation as defined above less holdings by the banks and the Treasury) declined between 1962 and 1965 with the exception of a small rise in 1964. This decline was caused mainly by a slowdown in construction activities after the Mining Company (MIFERMA) installations and the major projects in erecting the capital city of Nouakchott had been completed. Govern-

---

[4]The reader is referred to IMF's monthly statistical bulletin, *International Financial Statistics*, for up-to-date information on the Central Bank, as well as on commercial and development banks and the monetary survey.

TABLE 25. MAURITANIA: ASSETS AND LIABILITIES OF THE CENTRAL BANK, 1962–69

(In millions of CFA francs; end of period)

	1962	1963	1964	1965	1966	1967 Sept.	1967 Dec.	1968 Mar.	1968 June	1968 Sept.	1968 Dec.	1969 Mar.	1969 June	1969 Sept.
Assets														
Foreign assets														
Foreign exchange	1,518	2,319	2,054	1,605	1,652	1,788	1,724	1,703	1,732	1,722	1,559	1,662	1,502	1,091
Bilateral payments agreements	439	—	—	—	—	—	67	—	—	—	—	—	—	—
IMF gold tranche position	—	185	185	185	216	247	247	247	278	278	278	278	309	347
Claims on other BCEAO agencies	—	—	332	621	54	315	136	24	62	34	—	—	—	—
Total foreign assets	1,957	2,504	2,571	2,411	1,922	2,350	2,174	1,974	2,072	2,034	1,837	1,940	1,811	1,438
Claims on Government	—	2	1	1	1	—	1	—	—	1	1	1	1	1
Claims on banks	662	94	24	—	—	—	—	—	—	—	334	446	544	844
Assets = liabilities	2,619	2,600	2,596	2,412	1,923	2,350	2,175	1,974	2,072	2,035	2,172	2,387	2,356	2,282
Liabilities														
Reserve money	2,074	1,687	1,769	1,331	1,317	1,257	1,493	1,531	1,372	1,432	1,702	1,825	1,833	1,841
Currency outside banks	*1,978*	*1,611*	*1,701*	*1,230*	*1,246*	*1,188*	*1,425*	*1,337*	*1,279*	*1,361*	*1,561*	*1,682*	*1,726*	*1,666*
Government deposits														
Treasury deposits	—	628	469	747	92	452	305	36	213	138	217	226	128	69
Currency held by Government	544	279	285	265	392	572	362	377	409	441	246	329	344	315
Total government deposits	544	907	754	1,012	484	1,024	667	413	622	579	463	555	472	384
Foreign liabilities	1	6	73	69	122	69	15	30	78	24	7	7	51	57

Sources: IMF, *International Financial Statistics*; BCEAO, *Notes d'Information et Statistiques*; and data provided by BCEAO.

ment deposits moved exactly in the opposite direction of currency during 1962–65, rising on the whole, except in 1964; they reached their year-end peak of CFAF 1.0 billion in December 1965, when currency held by the private sector declined to its lowest level of CFAF 1.2 billion.

Foreign assets of the Central Bank increased markedly by 28 per cent to CFAF 2.5 billion in 1963, when the Mining Company started to export iron ore, and changed but little in 1964–65. At the beginning of its operations the Central Bank took over CFAF 0.7 billion of claims on the banks. However, all short-term rediscounts were repaid by the banks in 1963, and only small amounts of medium-term credit rediscounted by the Development Bank remained outstanding in 1963 and 1964. By 1965 the banks were no longer indebted to the Central Bank.

Although the volume of central bank operations rose in 1966, the reserve money and currency held by the private sector showed little change. However, the Government withdrew over CFAF 0.5 billion, or more than 50 per cent of its deposits, leading to a decline in foreign assets of almost equal size. In 1967, both foreign assets and currency expanded, and the Government added about CFAF 0.2 billion to its deposits. In 1968 and even more so in 1969, expansionary forces prevailed. In both years, in order to finance over-all deficits of the Treasury, the Government withdrew deposits which by the end of 1969, had fallen to CFAF 0.2 billion. For the first time since 1964 the banks in the last quarter of 1968 had again recourse to the Central Bank. At the end of December 1968 the latter had rediscounted CFAF 334 million, of which CFAF 175 million represented short-term and the rest medium-term paper. The effect of this increased use of resources was a rise in currency held by the private sector of CFAF 0.2 billion and a loss in foreign assets of over CFAF 0.3 billion. The year 1969 was characterized by continued large borrowing by banks from the Central Bank. Both short-term and medium-term paper were rediscounted on an increasing scale. In December 1968 the Central Bank re-established global ceilings for short-term credit and saw to it that the banks remained within these limits. The Central Bank's strong support of the banks led to an increase in currency held by the private sector of CFAF 0.1 billion by the end of September 1969 and a loss in foreign assets of CFAF 0.4 billion, or by 45 per cent, and both movements accelerated in the last quarter of 1969.

OPERATIONS OF THE COMMERCIAL BANKS AND THE
DEVELOPMENT BANK

Since late 1967, two commercial banks have been operating in Mauritania, the Banque Internationale pour l'Afrique Occidentale (BIAO) and the Société Mauritanienne de Banque (SMB). The former, with a share capital of F 60 million held mainly by French and U.S. financial groups, operates four branches in Mauritania—in Nouakchott, Nouadhibou, Zouîrât (Zouérate), and Rosso—and plans to open a fifth (in Kaédi). In early 1966 to reduce overhead costs, it made a reciprocal agreement with the French Banque Nationale pour le Commerce et l'Industrie (BNCI), which had until then maintained a branch in Nouakchott, releasing its operations and clients in Saint-Louis (Senegal) in return for the operations and clients of the second bank's branch in Nouakchott.

The Société Mauritanienne de Banque was established in 1967 with a capital of CFAF 50 million, 65 per cent subscribed by the French Société Générale, 25 per cent by other foreign banks on invitation from the Mauritanian authorities, and 10 per cent by the Mauritanian Government. The Government had supported the establishment of a second commercial bank in Mauritania in the hope that competition would make it easier for Mauritanian traders to obtain the credit needed with the change in trade flows from the port of Dakar to the wharf of Nouakchott. Actual operations started in January 1968; by December 1969 this bank held close to 20 per cent of private sector deposits in the commercial banks and the Development Bank.

The Development Bank (Banque Mauritanienne de Développement, or BMD) was established in 1961 and began operations in early 1962. Its capital, raised in 1965 from CFAF 150 million to CFAF 200 million, is subscribed by the Mauritanian Government (58 per cent), the French CCCE (34 per cent), and BCEAO (8 per cent). The paid-up capital resources are supplemented mainly by demand and time deposits, long-term borrowing from CCCE, and rediscounting with the Central Bank. The Development Bank is entitled to accept deposits from the Government, the Social Security Fund, insurance companies, and individuals or enterprises to whom it lends. Long-term loans are not rediscountable and are usually covered by CCCE loans.

Operations of the commercial banks and the Development Bank are consolidated in Table 26. Commercial banks have in the past lent primarily to traders, mainly those engaged in foreign trade, to small local enterprises, and occasionally to the Mining Company for usually very short periods. In the early sixties the combined deposits of the banks exceeded their domestic credit. Hence, in order to employ their funds profitably, they invested large portions of them outside Mauritania.

Until 1966 the Development Bank had granted all medium-term and long-term credit. The largest share of long-term loans had gone to the industrial sector, mainly the fishing industry, but an increasing proportion of long-term and, especially, medium-term loans had been allocated to private recipients for residential building projects and to local communities for the construction of market places (at Nouakchott and Kaédi) financed from resources received by the Development Bank from CCCE. Some medium-term and long-term loans had also been extended to the trading community and to the agricultural sector. Agricultural loans have been rather small so far and have been granted mainly to cooperatives (*groupements d'intérêts*) on an experimental basis and with the guarantee of the Government for the purchase of plows and other equipment. Since the Development Bank has not been able to find sufficient well-prepared development projects that would qualify for its support, its operations have recently declined.

Operations of the commercial banks, on the other hand, have steadily increased since 1967. The expansion of credit in 1967–69 was due mainly to the growing needs of traders in foreign and domestic commerce, including the National Import and Export Company (SONIMEX), the mixed company responsible for the importation of certain mass-consumption goods. Previously these goods had been imported through Senegal, where the Mauritanian traders had received trade credit. Under the new system the Mauritanian traders now needed funds from the banks, since the Company does not grant any trade credit, and the Company itself needed credit for working capital. Credit to this sector advanced rapidly in 1967–68 and exceeded CFAF 1.1 billion by the end of September 1969 (Table 27).

In 1967 and 1968 the commercial banks also granted increased credit to the fishing industry, the freezing plants connected with fishing, and the

TABLE 26. MAURITANIA: ASSETS AND LIABILITIES OF COMMERCIAL BANKS AND DEVELOPMENT BANK, 1962–69

(In millions of CFA francs; end of period)

	1962	1963	1964	1965	1966	1967		1968				1969		
						Sept.	Dec.	Mar.	June	Sept.	Dec.	Mar.	June	Sept.
Assets														
Cash	96	75	69	101	76	69	125	96	111	79	252	205	92	155
Foreign assets	1,244	936	486	694	1,340	1,151	949	1,133	398	358	398	332	263	566
Claims on private sector														
Short-term	1,084	705	866	1,136	1,025	1,660	2,101	2,295	2,904	3,311	3,466	4,020	4,381	3,967
Medium-term	214	143	142	106	106	200	262	306	313	332	343	303	328	693
Long-term	—	100	254	282	258	234	230	229	227	194	189	121	122	141
Total claims on private sector	1,298	948	1,262	1,524	1,389	2,094	2,593	2,830	3,444	3,837	3,998	4,444	4,837	4,831
Assets = liabilities	2,638	1,959	1,817	2,319	2,805	3,314	3,667	4,059	3,953	4,274	4,648	4,981	5,192	5,522
Liabilities														
Demand deposits	640	906	691	769	1,505	1,616	1,755	1,972	2,206	2,226	2,217	2,646	2,129	2,970
Time and savings deposits	68	50	50	160	200	227	386	385	385	390	397	441	439	561
Government deposits	1,270	798	520	657	450	733	734	833	561	741	668	775	846	514
Foreign liabilities	—	159	331	564	423	464	552	454	453	628	677	539	1,041	563
Credit from Central Bank	662	94	24	—	—	—	—	—	—	—	334	446	544	844
Other items (net)	−2	−48	201	169	227	274	240	414	348	288	354	134	193	70

Sources: IMF, *International Financial Statistics;* BCEAO, *Notes d'Information et Statistiques;* and data provided by BCEAO.

TABLE 27. MAURITANIA: DISTRIBUTION OF DECLARED CREDIT TO THE PRIVATE SECTOR, 1965-69

(In millions of CFA francs; end of period)

	1965	1966	1967		1968				1969		
			Sept.	Dec.	Mar.	June	Sept.	Dec.	Mar.	June	Sept.
Commerce, export, import, and retail (short-term)	150	179	250	500	528	787	736	735	1,089	1,191	1,112
Cold storage and freezing plants											
Short-term	—	214	198	233	222	196	219	227	227	242	245
Medium-term	—	20	20	10	10	10	10	10	10	10	10
Long-term	—	125	100	100	205	205	180	180	180	180	180
Total cold storage and freezing plants	—	359	318	343	437	411	409	417	417	432	435
Construction											
Short-term	136	99	209	280	468	521	689	746	815	744	427
Medium-term	—	—	—	—	—	8	8	7	7	6	23
Long-term	—	21	21	19	65	65	63	58	58	58	64
Total construction	136	120	230	299	533	594	760	811	880	808	514
Transportation											
Short-term	92	179	256	274	294	276	276	307	403	525	648
Medium-term	—	—	—	—	—	—	—	20	25	50	80
Long-term	—	—	—	—	—	—	20	35	49	49	38
Total transportation	92	179	256	274	294	276	296	362	477	624	766
Canning											
Short-term	148	174	217	190	211	296	227	247	327	379	329
Long-term	—	15	15	—	—	—	—	—	—	—	—
Total canning	148	189	232	190	211	296	227	247	327	379	329
Fishing (short-term)	—	—	183	166	218	243	323	324	219	57	57
Petroleum, import and distribution											
Short-term	148	112	120	121	161	179	132	96	117	141	113
Medium-term	—	—	25	75	95	104	104	96	96	74	74
Total petroleum	148	112	145	196	256	283	236	192	213	215	187

Mining											
Short-term	326	—	6	100	1	197	145	117	203	210	113
Medium-term	—	—	—	—	—	—	—	—	—	—	375
Total mining	326	—	6	100	1	197	145	117	203	210	488
Other declared credit											
Short-term	19	16	20	21	55	63	63	64	39	41	36
Medium-term	—	15	76	100	130	121	120	118	117	115	115
Long-term	—	49	34	31	—	—	—	—	—	—	—
Total other declared credit	19	80	130	152	185	184	183	182	156	156	151
Summation, declared credit											
Short-term	1,019	1,024	1,459	1,885	2,158	2,758	2,810	2,863	3,439	3,530	3,080
Medium-term	—	106	121	185	235	243	242	251	255	255	677
Long-term	—	258	170	150	270	270	263	273	287	287	282
Total declared credit	1,019	1,388	1,750	2,220	2,663	3,271	3,315	3,387	3,981	4,072	4,039
Other credit to private sector											
Short-term	117	51	200	215	139	148	504	604	583	860	962
Medium-term	106	71	79	77	71	70	86	92	69	93	36
Long-term	282	48	64	80	56	42	47	32	40	41	65
Total other credit	505	170	343	372	266	260	637	728	692	994	1,063
Summation, credit to private sector											
Short-term	1,136	1,024	1,659	2,100	2,297	2,906	3,314	3,467	4,022	4,390	4,042
Medium-term	106	106	200	262	306	313	328	343	324	348	713
Long-term	282	258	234	230	326	312	310	305	327	328	347
Total credit to private sector [1]	1,524	1,388	2,093	2,592	2,929	3,531	3,952	4,115	4,673	5,066	5,102

Source: Data provided by the Mauritanian authorities.

[1] Total credit shown in this table exceeds credit to private sector in Tables 26 and 28 because of the inclusion of certain long-term loans from CCCE.

petroleum industry for the importation, storage, and distribution of petroleum. During 1968 and most of 1969, credit to construction companies was at a very high level; in 1968 alone, this credit nearly trebled, reaching CFAF 811 million, most of it short-term. Many of these construction companies had been newly created in connection with the preparation of the copper mining site at Akjoujt. Since they had not yet established easily verifiable accounting procedures, they did not qualify for individual credit limits of the Central Bank; hence the banks could not rediscount their paper at the Central Bank. Most sectors, which had accounted for the largest credit expansion in 1967 and 1968, continued to maintain borrowing at a high level in 1969 through September. Heavy demands emanated from the mining and transportation sectors, again largely in connection with the construction of the mining site at Akjoujt and the Nouakchott-Akjoujt road. Credit to the mining sector in 1969 more than quadrupled to CFAF 488 million, while that to the transportation sector more than doubled to CFAF 766 million. On the other hand, credit to the fishing and petroleum sectors declined.

New credit extended by the banks to the private sector amounted to CFAF 1,204 million in 1967, CFAF 1,054 million in 1968, and CFAF 1,405 million in 1969. In 1967 and 1968 these credits were financed largely by liquidating previous foreign investments, loans from the head offices, and a small increase in deposits with the banks by the private sector. By the end of 1968 most of these sources were nearly exhausted, and in the last quarter of 1968 the banks had to turn to the Central Bank. Credit continued to expand through September 1969, and although demand deposits also gained, the banks lost CFAF 154 million in government deposits. Quasi-money on the other hand increased by CFAF 164 million while net borrowing by the banks from abroad decreased by CFAF 282 million. Since these additional resources fell far short from covering the increase in credit, the banks were obliged to raise their rediscounts at the Central Bank by CFAF 510 million.

Nevertheless, in the second half of 1969 the rate of credit expansion slowed down. In the fourth quarter, however, recourse to the Central Bank gained by CFAF 504 million, exceeding the additional amount of credit extended to the private sector (CFAF 251 million) because of the banks' deteriorating liquidity position. At the same time, net foreign borrowing increased by CFAF 508 million. The ratio of cash holdings to claims on the private sector, which had averaged between 5.5 per cent and 8 per cent during 1962–66, fell to 2.9 per cent by the end of 1969.

OVER-ALL MONETARY DEVELOPMENTS

Monetary and credit developments of the entire banking system are reflected in the monetary survey (Table 28), a consolidation of the accounts of BCEAO in Nouakchott, the two commercial banks, the Development Bank, the Postal Checking and Postal Savings Systems, and certain advances of the Treasury to the private sector in the form of customs duty bills. This table clearly distinguishes a contractionary phase (1962–65) and an expansionary phase (beginning in 1966).

In 1963, contractionary forces prevailed, since the banking system's claims on the private sector declined more than the Government's deposits. Foreign assets rose moderately while money supply declined by CFAF 31 million. Although demand deposits increased by 48 per cent to CFAF 1,078 million, this increase was offset by a decline in currency in circulation of CFAF 367 million, or about 19 per cent.

During 1964 the Government intensified its use of previously built-up deposits, and the private sector borrowed CFAF 304 million from the banking system so that total domestic credit expanded by CFAF 703 million. Most of this expansion was offset by a loss of foreign reserves, which decreased by 19 per cent to CFAF 2,653 million. Money supply declined by CFAF 174 million with all the decrease attributable to a drop in demand deposits.

In 1965, monetary developments were more complex. The Government replenished its deposits by CFAF 388 million, almost the full amount it had drawn down during the previous year. Since new borrowing by the private sector amounted to CFAF 274 million, the net impact of domestic credit extension on money supply was contractionary. This effect was reinforced by a shift from money into quasi-money at the rate of CFAF 110 million. Money supply decreased by CFAF 370 million resulting from an increase in demand deposits of CFAF 101 million, more than offset by a large decrease in currency in circulation of

TABLE 28. MAURITANIA: MONETARY SURVEY, 1962–69

(In millions of CFA francs; end of period)

						1967		1968				1969		
	1962	1963	1964	1965	1966	Sept.	Dec.	Mar.	June	Sept.	Dec.	Mar.	June	Sept.
Assets														
Foreign assets (net)	3,200	3,275	2,653	2,472	2,717	2,968	2,556	2,623	1,939	1,740	1,551	1,726	982	1,384
Domestic credit														
Claims on Government (net)	−1,712	−1,535	−1,136	−1,524	−797	−1,566	−1,125	−1,107	−958	−1,144	−942	−1,150	−1,119	−644
Bank claims on private sector	1,298	948	1,262	1,524	1,389	2,094	2,593	2,830	3,444	3,837	3,998	4,444	4,837	4,801
Treasury claims on private sector	9	14	4	16	43	10	16	17	14	38	36	46	45	38
Total domestic credit	−405	−573	130	16	635	538	1,484	1,740	2,500	2,731	3,092	3,340	3,763	4,195
Assets = liabilities	2,795	2,702	2,783	2,488	3,352	3,506	4,040	4,363	4,439	4,471	4,643	5,066	4,745	5,579
Liabilities														
Money														
Currency outside banks	1,978	1,611	1,701	1,230	1,246	1,188	1,425	1,337	1,279	1,361	1,561	1,682	1,726	1,666
Deposits with banks	640	906	691	769	1,505	1,616	1,755	1,972	2,206	2,226	2,217	2,646	2,129	2,970
Postal Checking deposits	102	172	123	146	160	190	284	149	190	205	218	213	237	288
Total money	2,720	2,689	2,515	2,145	2,911	2,994	3,464	3,458	3,675	3,792	3,996	4,541	4,092	4,924
Quasi-money	68	50	50	160	200	227	386	385	385	390	397	441	439	561
Other items (net)	7	−37	218	183	241	285	190	520	379	289	250	84	214	94

Sources: IMF, *International Financial Statistics*; BCEAO, *Notes d'Information et Statistiques*; and data provided by BCEAO.

CFAF 471 million. Net foreign assets of the banking system declined by CFAF 181 million.

The largest increase in money supply for the whole period covered was in 1966, when money supply rose by CFAF 766 million, or 36 per cent. Expansionary factors during that year emanated from the Government's drawing down its deposits by CFAF 727 million, a decrease of 44 per cent, and from an increase in net foreign assets of CFAF 245 million. Credit to the private sector decreased as sufficient liquidity became available to the economy with the balance of payments surplus.

In 1967, money supply continued to rise, but the factors in the increase reversed drastically. In contrast to the previous year, the Government rebuilt its net deposits by CFAF 328 million to CFAF 1,125 million. Credit to the private sector, on the other hand, which had decreased in 1966, rose by 82 per cent to CFAF 2,609 million, but the expansionary effect of this sharp rise was partly offset by a loss in net foreign assets of CFAF 161 million, or about 6 per cent, and an increase in quasi-money of 93 per cent to CFAF 386 million. Consequently, money supply increased by CFAF 553 million, or 19 per cent, a rate much lower than the increase in domestic credit.

The pace of domestic credit expansion accelerated in 1968, when an increase in credit to the private sector of CFAF 1,423 million was accompanied by a drawing down of the Government's deposits by CFAF 184 million. Again, the main effect was felt on net foreign assets, which decreased by CFAF 1,007 million, while money supply rose by CFAF 532 million, or somewhat over 15 per cent. Quasi-money, which had risen sharply in the previous year, increased by less than 3 per cent.

The expansionary pressures continued into 1969. Credit to the private sector was still on the upswing in the first half of the year, but decreased slightly in the third quarter. This decrease was the result of certain restrictive measures by the monetary authorities such as a lowering of the credit ceilings for certain banks and greater pressure on the banks to raise their liquidity ratios closer to the required level (73 per cent until September 1969 and 75 per cent thereafter until September 1970). The Government, after replenishing its deposits with the banking system by CFAF 208 million in the first quarter of 1969 and reducing them only moderately in the second quarter, drew heavily on the banks in the third quarter, when its net deposits fell by CFAF 475 million. Total domestic credit in the first three quarters of 1969 expanded by CFAF 1,103 million, or by almost 36 per cent. Money supply rose by CFAF 928 million, mainly in bank deposits, and quasi-money by CFAF 164 million.

Quasi-money includes deposits collected by the new National Savings Fund approved under Law No. 68-207 of July 6, 1968 and established by the implementing Decree 69-131 of February 28, 1969. By December 31, 1969 the National Savings Fund had issued 246 savings books, through which CFAF 3.4 million had been collected. The National Savings Fund pays interest at an annual rate of 3.25 per cent to its depositors. It places its excess funds with the Banque Internationale pour l'Afrique Occidentale and receives interest at an annual rate of 4.5 per cent.

In the fourth quarter of 1969, credit to the private sector continued upward by CFAF 251 million to CFAF 5,052 million because of a further increase in credit needed for imports and some medium-term credit to the mining sector. The Government continued also to draw down its deposits, though at a slower rate (by CFAF 184 million). By the end of 1969, however, the Government's net deposits with the banking system had declined to CFAF 460 million, the lowest level reached since separate statistics for Mauritania became available. Net foreign assets fell at an accelerated rate to the low amount of CFAF 321 million. Money supply receded to CFAF 4,119 million, or almost to the level of a year earlier. Demand deposits fell by an even greater amount (to CFAF 2,060 million), the difference representing mainly an increase in currency outside banks. Part of this decline in deposits, however, is due to a switch into time deposits, mainly by the foreign insurance companies, which are now required by law to keep a certain percentage of their premium receipts within Mauritania. Accordingly, quasi-money continued upward, reaching CFAF 623 million by the end of 1969.

The outlook for monetary and credit developments in 1970 is one of greater restraint. The monetary authorities will be obliged to limit the rate of further credit expansion in order to slow down the decline in net foreign assets. Since the banks are relatively illiquid and have already rediscounted most of their eligible paper, the Central Bank is in a strong position to impose its more restrictive policy.

FOREIGN TRADE, GRANTS, PAYMENTS, AND DEBT

FOREIGN TRADE

Mauritania's official foreign trade statistics, which are based on customs returns, have a limited coverage particularly for imports. They include mainly those exports and imports that pass through customs in Nouakchott and Nouadhibou. Traditionally Mauritania's foreign trade was routed through Dakar by commercial firms established in Senegal with branches and correspondents in Mauritania. A substantial part of imports, particularly consumer goods, continue to be unloaded in Dakar and transported by road to Mauritania. Under the provisions of the old Customs Union with Senegal, which was in operation until the beginning of 1970, these imports passed through customs in Dakar and were not recorded in Mauritania. In recent years, customs coverage of trade has increased. Since the completion of the port facilities in Nouadhibou, most of the trade with the northern part of Mauritania has been handled there. Similarly, the construction of the wharf at Nouakchott has resulted in a rerouting of external trade from central Mauritania. Since 1967, the operation of the National Import and Export Company (SONIMEX) has also contributed to the extension of coverage of foreign trade; this Company has a monopoly over the import of certain consumer goods (rice, tea, sugar, and two types of cotton), and all its imports are recorded. Moreover, a new customs and trade agreement with Senegal became operative in February 1970, along the lines of the trade arrangements prevailing between Mauritania and the other members of UDEAO. Under the new agreement, customs duties on imports into Mauritania, including those from third countries, are collected at the Mauritanian border; this provision should bring about a further increase in the official coverage of Mauritania's foreign trade.

Table 29 shows total recorded and estimated unrecorded trade during 1962–69. In this period, exports are estimated to have risen from CFAF 3.3 billion to CFAF 22.8 billion.[5] Estimated imports declined

---

[5] Because most data are available only for the year as a whole, it is not possible to estimate the effect of the devaluation (August 10, 1969) on trade and the balance of payments. The distortion in the 1969 CFA franc data, however, is lessened by the fact that Mauritania's transactions with France and other operations account countries in the French franc area comprise a large share of total external transactions.

TABLE 29. MAURITANIA: ESTIMATED FOREIGN TRADE, 1962–69

(In billions of CFA francs)

	1962	1963	1964	1965	1966	1967	1968	1969 (Provisional)[1]
Exports (f.o.b.)								
Recorded[2]	0.98	4.23	11.49	14.28	17.10	17.34	18.18	20.56
Unrecorded (livestock)	2.35	2.35	2.35	2.00	1.91	2.26	2.22	2.20
Total exports	3.33	6.58	13.84	16.28	19.01	19.60	20.40	22.76
Imports (c.i.f.)								
Recorded	8.81	7.42	3.88	6.14	5.68	9.10	9.34	11.70
Unrecorded								
Imports from Senegal	6.10	6.10	6.10	6.00	6.00	5.00	4.00	4.50
Imports of fishing boats	—	—	—	—	—	2.50	—	—
Purchases of fish from Canary Islands fishing fleet	0.17	0.17	0.29	0.35	0.40	0.56	0.43	0.62
Imports from Spanish Sahara	1.00	1.00	1.00	1.00	1.00	1.00	2.00	2.50
Foreign aid imports[3]	4.40	2.26	2.43	1.40	1.40	—	—	—
Total unrecorded imports	11.67	9.53	9.82	8.75	8.80	9.06	6.43	7.62
Total imports	20.48	16.95	13.70	14.89	14.48	18.16	15.77	19.32
Balance on estimated trade	−17.15	−10.37	0.14	1.39	4.53	1.44	4.63	3.44

Source: Data provided by the Mauritanian authorities.

[1] In current CFA francs; no adjustment made for the devaluation of August 10, 1969 (see text footnote 5).
[2] Includes adjustments as explained in footnotes 2 and 3, Table 30.
[3] Beginning 1967, these imports have been recorded by customs and have been included under recorded imports.

from CFAF 20.5 billion in 1962 to CFAF 19.3 billion in 1969; as a result, the estimated balance of trade changed from a deficit of CFAF 17.2 billion in 1962 to a surplus of CFAF 3.4 billion in 1969.

In 1969, estimated aggregate exports exceeded recorded exports by 10 per cent, and estimated aggregate imports by 60 per cent. Coverage of exports is better than coverage of imports because more than 80 per cent of exports consist of iron ore, all shipments of which are recorded.

Composition of Foreign Trade

Recorded trade.—Recorded exports rose from CFAF 1.0 billion in 1962 to CFAF 20.6 billion in 1969. This growth reflected almost entirely the increase in iron ore exports by the Mining Company (MIFERMA) from CFAF 2.7 billion in 1963, when production of iron ore started, to CFAF 17.6 billion in 1969, when they accounted for 85 per cent of recorded exports (Table 30). Other recorded exports consist of fish, gum arabic, and "other," including such items as scrap iron and railway material re-exported by the Mining Company. Exports of fish increased from CFAF 0.2 billion in 1962 to CFAF 1.2 billion in 1969 (Table 31), largely as a result of an increase in exports of fresh and frozen fish following the opening of several freezing plants in Nouadhibou and increases in exports of dried and salted fish, principally to the People's Republic of the Congo. In November 1967, Mauritania concluded a trade agreement with the Congo, under which the latter expected to take exports of about 4,000 tons of fish from Mauritania by 1972. The value of exports of gum arabic has been adjusted to account for the difference between the volume of total recorded production, all of which is exported, and exports as recorded by customs. Exports of gum arabic fluctuated between CFAF 0.2 billion and CFAF 0.4 billion over the period, except in 1969, when they increased to CFAF 0.9 billion. The increase reflected a larger volume harvested for export and a higher price; there was also an improvement in the recording of production.

Preliminary information indicates that recorded imports in 1969 reached a level of CFAF 11.7 billion. Activities of the Mining Company greatly influence Mauritania's recorded imports. Between 1962 and 1964, recorded imports declined from CFAF 8.8 billion to CFAF 3.9

TABLE 30. MAURITANIA: COMMODITY DISTRIBUTION OF RECORDED FOREIGN TRADE, 1962–69

(In billions of CFA francs)

	1962	1963	1964	1965	1966	1967	1968	1969 [1]
Exports								
Iron ore	—	2.71	10.65	13.09	15.59	15.37	15.28	17.51
Fish	0.22	0.32	0.37	0.59	0.66	0.99	0.98	1.25
Gum arabic [2]	0.33	0.33	0.33	0.21	0.23	0.31	0.39	0.92
Other [3]	0.43	0.87	0.14	0.39	0.62	0.67	1.53	0.88 [4]
Total recorded exports	0.98	4.23	11.49	14.28	17.10	17.34	18.18	20.56 [4]
Imports								
Foodstuffs	0.43	0.26	0.27	0.49	0.77	1.50	2.17	...
Petroleum products	0.23	0.21	0.26	0.28	0.32	0.33	0.64	...
Vehicles and spare parts	0.40	0.92	0.41	1.04	0.60	0.56	0.66	...
Capital goods	6.14	3.31	1.50	2.28	2.05	3.82	2.86	...
Other	1.61	2.72	1.44	2.05	1.94	2.89	3.01	...
Total recorded imports	8.81	7.42	3.88	6.14	5.68	9.10	9.34	11.70 [4]

Sources: Comité Monétaire de la Zone Franc, La Zone Franc, 1965; Ministère de la Planification et du Développement Rural, Annuaire Statistique, 1968; and data provided by the Mauritanian authorities.

[1] In current CFA francs; no adjustment made for the devaluation of August 10, 1969 (see text footnote 5).
[2] Adjusted to include the difference between total recorded production, all of which is exported, and exports as recorded by customs.
[3] Beginning in 1966, this item excludes value of re-exports of goods imported on a temporary basis. These do not appear in trade statistics at the time of import, but are recorded when exported.
[4] Provisional.

TABLE 31. MAURITANIA: EXPORTS OF THE FISHING INDUSTRY, 1962–69

	1962	1963	1964	1965	1966	1967	1968	1969
			VOLUME (tons)					
Fresh and frozen fish	2	1,222	1,261	2,143	2,157	5,826	5,259	6,224
Dried, smoked, and salted fish	2,681	3,034	3,306	4,322	4,891	5,093	5,474	6,108
Shell fish	—	3	21	50	82	118	50	90
Fish scrap					365	75		—
Total	2,683	4,259	4,588	6,515	7,495	11,112	10,783	12,422
			VALUE (billion CFA francs)					
Total	0.22	0.32	0.37	0.59	0.66	0.99	0.98	1.25 [1]

Source: Data provided by the Mauritanian authorities.

[1] In current CFA francs; no adjustment made for the devaluation of August 10, 1969 (see text footnote 5).

billion, largely because of the Mining Company's reduced import requirements after completion of the bulk of its installation. As a result of the Company's operational and equipment needs, however, its imports rose again in 1965, though not to the earlier high levels; since 1965 they have averaged about CFAF 5 billion annually.

The sharp increase in the value of recorded imports in 1967 can be related mainly to the extended customs coverage as a result of the rerouting of trade through Nouadhibou and Nouakchott, and the beginning of operations by the National Import and Export Company. Imports by this Company amounted to CFAF 2.6 billion in 1967, CFAF 2.1 billion in 1968, and CFAF 2.3 billion in 1969; in previous years, these imports normally were not recorded by customs. Moreover, imports for the public sector financed by foreign aid were not recorded by customs until 1967. The 25 per cent increase in recorded imports in 1969 over 1968 resulted largely from the sharp rise in imports of equipment to complete the installation of the Copper Company (SOMIMA).

Unrecorded trade.—Unrecorded exports, consisting mainly of livestock sold on the hoof to Senegal and Mali, are estimated to have averaged somewhat above CFAF 2 billion annually during 1962–69.

Unrecorded imports declined from CFAF 11.7 billion in 1962 to CFAF 7.6 billion in 1969. The rise in unrecorded imports in 1967, despite the extended customs coverage in that year, was due primarily to imports of fishing boats by the Société Mauritanienne d'Armement à la Pêche (SOMAP), financed by suppliers' credits. Excluding this special transaction, unrecorded imports declined in 1967 not only as a share in total imports, but also in absolute terms. It is estimated that unrecorded imports rose again in 1969, with improved information on imports from Spanish Sahara noted below.

Unrecorded imports include those from Senegal, mainly consumer goods produced there, and goods imported through Dakar and transported by road to Mauritania. Despite the rerouting of much of the traditional trade with central and southern Mauritania through the wharf at Nouakchott, it is estimated that the value of unrecorded imports from Senegal remains considerable. Unrecorded imports also include purchases of fish from the Canary Islands fishing fleet by the fish processing plants in Nouadhibou, estimated to have increased steadily since 1962, to CFAF 0.6 billion in 1969. Estimated imports from Spanish Sahara rose from an annual average of CFAF 1.0 billion in earlier years to CFAF 2 billion in 1968 and CFAF 2.5 billion in 1969; improved estimates of these imports have resulted from the statistical control made possible in 1969, when a free zone for goods from Spanish Sahara was in operation. Imports for the public sector financed by foreign aid were not recorded by customs before 1967; they were estimated to have declined from CFAF 4.4 billion in 1962 to CFAF 1.4 billion in 1967, on the basis that an estimated 50 per cent of public investment expenditure represented imports.

Direction of Foreign Trade

In 1967 about 44 per cent of recorded exports went to EEC countries other than France; France accounted for 19 per cent, the United Kingdom for 20 per cent, and other European countries for 4 per cent (Table 32). Exports of fish go mainly to other African countries, particularly the People's Republic of the Congo. All exports of gum arabic are shipped to France. Livestock exports go largely to Senegal and Mali and, to some extent, to Ghana and Ivory Coast.

France continues to be the predominant supplier of imports, accounting for 45 per cent of total recorded imports in 1967, most of which were capital goods for the mining industry. If the unrecorded consumer goods imported through Senegal could be classified by their origin, the French share in total imports would probably be even larger. Other suppliers of imports in 1967 were the United States (23 per cent of total imports), EEC countries other than France (11 per cent), and other European countries (2 per cent).

FOREIGN GRANTS

Foreign grants to Mauritania consist of those disbursed in Mauritania and those disbursed abroad. Disbursements in Mauritania comprise all disbursements actually transferred into Mauritania. Grants disbursed abroad consist of direct payments by the donor to the suppliers for Mauritanian imports and services (such as surveys and project appraisals and salaries paid to technical assistance personnel in Mauritania maintaining accounts in the donor country).

TABLE 32.   MAURITANIA: DIRECTION OF RECORDED TRADE, 1962–67

(*In billions of CFA francs*)

	1962	1963	1964	1965	1966	1967
Exports f.o.b.						
EEC	0.34	2.99	7.46	9.72	11.91	11.33
France	*0.33*	*1.65*	*2.31*	*2.91*	*3.52*	*3.48*
Other Europe	— [1]	0.58	3.02	3.64	3.81	4.38
United Kingdom	—	*0.54*	*2.98*	*3.53*	*3.49*	*3.55*
Africa	— [1]	0.30	0.34	0.51	0.39	0.48
Dem. Rep. of Congo	—	*0.22*	*0.29*	*0.35*	*0.29*	*0.44*
Western Hemisphere	—	0.05	0.34	0.30	0.34	0.30
United States	—	*0.05*	*0.34*	*0.30*	*0.30*	*0.11*
Other countries	0.35	0.05	0.15	0.05	0.64	0.96
Japan	—	—	*0.12*	—	*0.43*	*0.47*
Total exports [2]	0.69	3.97	11.31	14.22	17.09	17.45
Imports c.i.f.						
EEC	6.87	5.52	2.59	3.67	3.52	5.16
France	*6.39*	*5.01*	*2.09*	*2.73*	*3.02*	*4.14*
Other Europe	0.49	0.15	0.23	0.53	0.28	0.41
United Kingdom	*0.49*	*0.10*	*0.07*	*0.15*	*0.07*	*0.18*
Western Hemisphere	0.86	1.56	0.89	1.55	1.09	2.25
United States	*0.86*	*1.44*	*0.72*	*1.34*	*0.98*	*2.17*
Africa	—	—	0.03	0.06	0.23	0.27
Dem. Rep. of Congo	—	—	—	—	*0.01*	—
Other countries	0.59	0.19	0.14	0.33	0.56	1.01
Japan	—	—	—	—	—	—
Total imports	8.81	7.42	3.88	6.14	5.68	9.10

Source: Data provided by the Mauritanian authorities.

[1] No separate figure available; included in "other."
[2] Excluding adjustments made in Tables 29 and 30 for recorded exports.

The major source of foreign grants between 1960 and 1969 was France, although its share in the total declined from 92 per cent during 1960–63 to 46 per cent in 1969 (Table 33). In addition to bilateral grants, France contributes to grants administered by EDF. Bilateral aid from France consists of investment grants and technical assistance provided by FAC and budget subsidies and miscellaneous aid such as the services rendered by French research and development agencies, grants for study abroad, and technical and cultural cooperation. Investment aid from FAC, which amounted to about CFAF 5,580 million during 1960–63, declined to CFAF 418 million in 1969. The greater part of budget subsidies during 1960–63 went to finance the current budget. Since 1964, budget subsidies have been granted exclusively to finance projects in the capital budget. Such subsidies declined in every

TABLE 33. MAURITANIA: DISBURSEMENTS OF FOREIGN GRANTS, 1960–69

(In millions of CFA francs)

	1960–63	1964	1965	1966	1967	1968	1969[1]
France							
Budget subsidies	6,723	1,000	600	300	500	200	—
Technical assistance[2]	1,600	445	414	620	641	660	622
Other (mainly investment)	5,580	676	624	514	555	541	418
Total France	13,903	2,121	1,638	1,434	1,696	1,401	1,040
United States	64	195	19	24	37	10	—
Other	—	—	6	13	12	60	70
European Development Fund	1,150	628	761	563	789	1,278	1,018
United Nations	—	—	40	120	141	136	140[3]
Total	15,117	2,944	2,464	2,154	2,675	2,885	2,268

Sources: Information provided by donors, and IMF staff estimates.

[1] In current CFA francs; no adjustment made for the devaluation of August 10, 1969 (see text footnote 5).
[2] Net of contribution paid by the Mauritanian Government to the French Treasury (CFAF 30,000 for each technical assistant per month).
[3] Preliminary.

year, apart from 1967, and no subsidies were granted in 1969.

Technical assistance has been an important and increasing part of French grants to Mauritania. In 1969, French technical assistance cost CFAF 622 million, excluding the Mauritanian contribution to the French Treasury of about CFAF 105 million. Currently, there are nearly 300 French technical assistants in Mauritania, mainly in teaching, health, and other professions, including 24 specialists provided by the French air navigation security agency (ASECNA), to assist in the operation of the airports. The Mauritanian Government contributes CFAF 30,000 monthly per FAC technician, and contributes on a global basis to the cost of the airport specialists.

Under the first and second EDF programs, the EEC had committed CFAF 7.4 billion to projects in Mauritania at the end of 1969; about CFAF 6 billion of this amount had been disbursed. EEC aid has been directed toward the financing of large projects such as the hospital and the wharf at Nouakchott, a fishing harbor and the water supply system at Nouadhibou, as well as roads, schools, and rural water wells. Some technical assistance has also been provided.

Grants from the UN Development Program finance the equipment and the personnel of an agricultural training center in Kaédi. This project is to cost CFAF 233 million over a period of five years. In addition, UN has provided technical assistance, amounting to about CFAF 90 million in 1968.

Until June 1967, aid received from the U.S. Agency for International Development consisted mainly of grants for public works and for agricultural and health projects. Disbursements in 1968 represented the phasing out of U.S. aid to Mauritania, and there was no disbursement in 1969. Other bilateral aid included some equipment deliveries by Germany and the United Kingdom.

BALANCE OF PAYMENTS

Official global balance of payments data are not available for Mauritania. An attempt has been made to construct a balance of payments for 1964–69, based on various official statistics, together with other information obtained from Mauritanian and non-Mauritanian sources. The source data, however, are incomplete and the estimates are, therefore, of varying degrees of accuracy (Table 34).

During 1964–69, Mauritania's balance of payments was characterized, in most years, by a substantial trade surplus and a net inflow of official unrequited transfers and official capital; apart from 1966, these movements, however, were more than offset by a net deficit for services and private unrequited transfers and, except for 1965, a debit item under net errors and omissions. In 1967 and 1969, imports and private capital inflow were affected by large counterbalancing transactions associated with externally financed capital goods. These comprised the import of fishing boats, financed by suppliers' credits in 1967 and large imports of copper mining machinery and equipment in 1969. In each year, the associated capital inflow more than offset the outflow of private long-term capital. Apart from 1966 there was a persistent and increasing deficit in net errors and omissions, reaching nearly CFAF 4.5 billion in 1969; this amount was large enough to offset the entire net inflow of long-term capital. While there are good reasons to believe that inadequacies of coverage of many of the components of the balance of payments might generate substantial errors and omissions, it may also be presumed that the increasing net outflows during this period were largely associated with the outflow of private sector funds in the form of profits, transfers, or capital. As a result of the above movements, the net foreign assets position of the banking system deteriorated in every year, apart from 1966, the total loss of reserves in the period amounting to CFAF 3.0 billion.

Mauritania's estimated trade surplus increased from CFAF 0.1 billion in 1964 to CFAF 4.6 billion in 1968, reflecting largely the growth of iron ore exports, on the one hand, and the Mining Company's reduced import requirements, on the other. Preliminary data for 1969 indicate a decline in the trade surplus to CFAF 3.4 billion.

The item "services under aid programs" includes as a debit the cost to Mauritania of technical assistance and of other services under foreign grants, such as surveys and project appraisals, for which payments by the donor countries are made abroad; it includes as a credit item personal expenditures by technical assistants in Mauritania, estimated at 65 per cent of their remuneration. Rising interest payments on the foreign debt and payments by the mining industry for services abroad, including

TABLE 34. MAURITANIA: ESTIMATED BALANCE OF PAYMENTS, 1964–69

(In billions of CFA francs)

	1964	1965	1966	1967	1968	1969 (Provisional) [1]
A. Goods and services						
Exports f.o.b.	13.8	16.3	19.0	19.6	20.4	22.8
Imports c.i.f.	13.7	14.9	14.5	18.2	15.8	19.3
Trade balance	0.1	1.4	4.5	1.4	4.6	3.5
Services (net)	-1.7	-1.7	-1.6	-3.1	-2.4	-2.6
Investment income						
Services under aid programs (net)	-0.3	-0.3	-0.3	-0.3	-0.4	-0.4
Other services	-0.6	-2.0	-1.0	-1.7	-2.1	-2.3
Total services	-2.6	-4.0	-2.9	-5.1	-4.9	-5.3
Total goods and services	-2.5	-2.6	1.6	-3.7	-0.3	-1.8
B. Unrequited transfers (net)						
Private	-1.1	-1.0	-0.8	-0.8	-0.8	-0.9
Official	2.9	2.5	2.2	2.7	2.9	2.3
Total unrequited services	1.8	1.5	1.4	1.9	2.1	1.4
C. Capital movements (net)						
Long-term capital						
Private	0.1	-0.2	-2.8	2.0	-0.1	3.5
Official	-0.3	—	0.8	0.4	0.5	0.8
Total long-term capital	-0.2	-0.2	-2.0	2.4	0.4	4.3
Short-term capital	0.6	0.7	-0.5	0.6	-0.6	-0.7
Total capital movements	0.4	0.5	-2.5	3.0	-0.2	3.6
D. Total A + B + C	-0.3	-0.6	0.5	1.2	1.6	3.2
E. Errors and omissions (net)	-0.3	0.4	-0.3	-1.4	-2.6	-4.4
F. Over-all balance (D + E)	-0.6	-0.2	0.2	-0.2	-1.0	-1.2
G. Monetary movements (increase −), net						
Central Bank	—	0.2	0.5	-0.3	0.3	1.0
Commercial banks	0.6	—	-0.7	0.5	0.7	0.2
Total monetary movements	0.6	0.2	-0.2	0.2	1.0	1.2

Sources: Data provided by the Mauritanian authorities and the Mining Company; information supplied by main creditors; and IMF staff estimates.

[1] In current CFA francs; no adjustment made for the devaluation of August 10, 1969 (...

insurance and transportation, caused net outward payments for services to increase to CFAF 5.3 billion in 1969. Apart from 1966, the balance on goods and services was in deficit in each year between 1964 and 1969.

Net official unrequited transfers comprise all foreign official grants, including technical assistance. Grants disbursed in Mauritania are initially reflected directly in the country's reserve movements. Grants disbursed abroad, depending on the type of grant, have a counterpart debit entry in the balance of payments, either under "imports" or under "services under aid programs." Official grants averaged about CFAF 2.6 billion annually during 1964–69. Net private unrequited transfers represent the balance between inward transfers from pension payments by France to Mauritanian nationals and outward transfers, consisting mainly of estimated salary remittances of foreigners working in the mining industry and other companies in Nouakchott and Nouadhibou. Net private unrequited transfers have been a persistent debit item in recent years. However, because of official grants, net official unrequited transfers have more than offset the net outflow of private transfers.

Data on private long-term capital movements include mainly the balance between the Mining Company's repayments on its long-term debt (almost exclusively to CCCE and IBRD) and net inflows of capital in respect of the new investment by the Copper Company and the fish processing company (Industrie Mauritanienne de Pêche) in Nouadhibou. In 1967 the item also included the inflow of about CFAF 2.5 billion of suppliers' credits to finance the fishing boats. As a result of this special transaction in 1967 and the large capital inflow associated with the completion of the Copper Company's installation in 1969, the net outflows of private capital normally occurring in recent years from the Mining Company's continued heavy repayments, turned into net inflows of CFAF 2.0 billion in 1967 and CFAF 3.5 billion in 1969. Official long-term capital movements include the net utilization of foreign loans by the Central Government from CCCE, FAC, the French Treasury, and IDA (Table 35). They also cover net utilization of foreign loans by local authorities, the Development Bank, and semipublic agencies; all foreign loan transactions of these latter agencies, exclusively with CCCE, are shown in Table 36. Since 1966, there has been a net inflow of official capital into Mauritania, fluctuating between CFAF 0.5 billion and CFAF 0.8 billion annually.

TABLE 35. MAURITANIA: ESTIMATED FOREIGN DEBT OF THE CENTRAL GOVERNMENT, 1969

(In thousands of CFA francs)

Lender	Date	Interest Rate	Original Amount	Outstanding as of December 31, 1969 [1]	1969 Amortization	1969 Interest	1969 Total
Caisse Centrale de Coopération Economique	1957	2.5	60,000	30,701	3,006	824	3,830
	1960	2.2	9,907	4,085	614	100	714
	1962	1.0	{ 563,537 / 15,000	520,501	9,145	5,274	14,419
	1963	2.5	770,000	462,200	51,300	12,388	63,688
	1964	4.5	892,333	505,380	71,874	25,176	97,050
	1966	3.5	120,000	96,000	24,000	4,263	28,263
	1967	3.5	17,000	11,802	—	413	413
	1968	6.0	825,000	825,000	—	45,118	45,118
	1968	3.5	50,000	50,000	—	1,777	1,777
French Treasury	...	3.0	20,750	11,903			
	...	3.5–6.5	16,412	2,919	293	163	456
Fonds d'Aide et de Coopéra-tion	1966	3.0	140,000	140,000	—	4,258	4,258
	1966	1.0	250,000	250,000	—	2,500	2,500
	1968	1.0	31,000	29,230	—	310	310
	1968	3.0	80,000	29,983	—	912	912
	1969 [2]	0.5	75,000	46,067	—	—	—
International Development Association	1964	0.75	1,653,915	948,524	—	—	—
Total				3,964,295	160,232	103,476	263,708

Source: Data provided by the Mauritanian authorities.

[1] Foreign debt of the Central Government, excluding foreign debt of local authorities, public and semipublic bodies, and government-guaranteed suppliers' credits.

[2] SODETRAF.

TABLE 36. MAURITANIA: LOAN OPERATIONS OF THE CAISSE CENTRALE DE COOPÉRATION ECONOMIQUE, 1962–69

(In millions of CFA francs)

	Net Disbursements							
	1962	1963	1964	1965	1966	1967	1968	1969
Central Government	8	762	774	−123	−2	−127	320	274
Local authorities	1	−1	−1	−1	—	−1	−2	−2
Development Bank and semi-public enterprises	38	706	−1,097	52	−45	−59	−67	21
Private enterprises	1,400	3,850	—	−100	−113	−278	−314	−513
Total	1,447	5,317	−324	−172	−160	−465	−63	−220

Source: Data provided by Caisse Centrale de Coopération Economique.

Available data on short-term capital movements relate to the Mining Company's net transactions in respect of short-term borrowing abroad and balances maintained in foreign banks. These transactions have fluctuated between net inflows of CFAF 0.6 billion in 1964 and 1967, and a net outflow of CFAF 0.7 billion in 1969.

More than one half of the decrease in net foreign assets of the banking system of CFAF 3.0 billion during 1964–69 occurred in the Central Bank's reserves. At the end of 1969, net foreign reserves of the banking system amounted to CFAF 0.3 billion, representing net foreign assets of the Central Bank of CFAF 0.8 billion and net foreign liabilities of the commercial banks of CFAF 0.5 billion.

FOREIGN DEBT

Outstanding public external indebtedness (viz., debt of the Central Government, public and semipublic agencies, and government-guaranteed suppliers' credits) is estimated at about CFAF 8 billion (28 million [6]) at the end of 1969. About CFAF 2.3 billion of this debt resulted from guarantees by the Mauritanian Government of suppliers' credits contracted by the Société Mauritanienne d'Armement à la Pêche. When the fishing company went into liquidation, the Mauritanian Government had to assume responsibility for the repayment of the outstanding debt. Under the provisions of a moratorium agreement, repayments have been set at CFAF 250 million annually. Total public-debt service scheduled for 1970 amounts to about CFAF 1 billion, including CFAF 500 million for contractual payments under the moratorium provision, CFAF 250 million of which were due in 1969 but were not paid.

---

[6] Converted at the current rate.

CHAPTER 10

Niger

GENERAL SETTING

On August 3, 1960, Niger gained its independence. Its capital and largest city, Niamey, has a population estimated at 80,000.

Niger joined the International Monetary Fund (IMF) on April 24, 1963, current quota $10,000,000 (April 1970). On the same day it joined the International Bank for Reconstruction and Development (IBRD, or World Bank), current subscription $10,000,000, and the International Development Association (IDA), current subscription $500,000. Among other organizations, it is a member of the United Nations (UN); the Food and Agriculture Organization (FAO); the UN Educational, Scientific, and Cultural Organization (UNESCO); the General Agreement on Tariffs and Trade (GATT); the UN Economic Commission for Africa (ECA, or Commission Economique pour l'Afrique, CEA); the African Development Bank (ADB); and the Common Organization of African and Malagasy States (Organisation Commune Afrique et Malgache, or OCAM). It is also an associate member of the European Economic Community (EEC). It shares with Dahomey, Ivory Coast, Mauritania, Senegal, Togo, and Upper Volta in the West African Monetary Union (Union Monétaire Ouest Africaine, or UMOA); in a common central bank, the Banque Centrale des Etats de l'Afrique de l'Ouest (BCEAO); and in a common currency, the CFA franc, issued by that Bank. It is joined with Dahomey, Ivory Coast, Mali, Mauritania, Senegal, and Upper Volta in the West African Customs Union (Union Douanière des Etats de l'Afrique de l'Ouest, or UDEAO).

Niger, a landlocked country with an area of 1,189,000 square kilometers (459,000 square miles), is about twice the size of France. It borders Nigeria and Dahomey on the south, Upper Volta and Mali on the west, Algeria and the Libyan Arab Republic on the north, and Chad on the east. The principal port of entry, in Dahomey, is about 1,000 kilometers (620 miles) by road and rail from Niamey.

The country is a plateau, with altitudes ranging from 200 to 500 meters (650 to 1,650 feet), except for the Aïr massif and the Plateau du Djado in the north. Its highest peak (in the Aïr massif) rises to 1,900 meters (6,234 feet).

In the north the climate is Saharan and in the south sub-Saharan, with a dry season in winter and a rainy period from about June through September. Cultivation depends on the intensity of the rainfall, which diminishes progressively from south to north. The areas with annual rainfall in excess of 600 millimeters (24 inches) are suitable for groundnut cultivation. The savanna area, where precipitation ranges from 350 to 600 millimeters, lends itself to food crop and cotton cultivation. The northern part, with less than 350 millimeters of rain annually, is mostly desert and is inappropriate for permanent cultivation. Consequently, only about 25,000 square kilometers, or about 2 per cent of Niger's land area, is suitable for cultivation (see map).

Water resources are scarce and poorly developed. The Niger River traverses the extreme western part of the country for only 500 kilometers. The Komadougou Yobé (Komadugu Yobe in Nigeria), which flows into Lake Chad in the extreme east, is the only other river within Niger's boundaries. A number of depressions also provide water for limited periods after the rainy season.

Niger's population in 1968 was estimated at 3.8 million, more than half under 19 years of age; the average density was 3.2 inhabitants per square kilometer. The annual rate of population growth is estimated at 2.5 per cent. Besides Niamey, the largest towns are Zinder, Maradi, and Tahoua, each with a population of 20,000–31,000.

The economically active population, estimated at 1.7 million, is mainly engaged in agricultural and pastoral activities. Although the literacy rate is among the lowest in French-speaking Africa, it has improved in recent years. The primary school population doubled between 1962 and 1967, and the ratio of primary school pupils to all children of primary school age rose from 4 per cent in 1957 to nearly 9 per cent in 1966. Students in high schools, technical schools, and foreign institutions totaled about 3,500 in 1966.

Niger's population comprises a number of ethnic groups; the Hausa, residing mainly in south-central Niger, make up 49 per cent of the total population. Other important ethnic groups are the Djerma-Songai (22 per cent), living mainly along the Niger Valley, and the predominantly nomadic Peuhls, Touaregs, Arabs, and Bellahs (19 per cent), living mainly in the Saharan region.

Although no detailed data are available on migration, the sample survey of 1960 indicates that about 50,000 Nigeriens were living abroad, mainly as seasonal agricultural workers in Nigeria, or as workers on plantations and in industries in Ghana and Ivory Coast. African immigrants are relatively few (1,645 at the end of 1967) and consist mainly of skilled workers from Mali, Senegal, and Guinea. The estimated 6,000 Europeans in Niger are employed mostly in education, trade, and public administration.

STRUCTURE OF THE ECONOMY

GROSS DOMESTIC PRODUCT

Niger's gross domestic product (GDP) at current prices grew at an average annual rate of about 8 per cent during 1960-66, reaching CFAF 79 billion (Table 1). This increase was nearly 12 per cent in 1965 and 6 per cent in 1966. The gain in the price index relating to African consumption (see "Prices, wages, and employment," below) suggests that growth rate in GDP at constant prices was about 7 per cent in 1965, whereas in 1966 it was negative, owing to the more than 15 per cent increase in food prices. Although later official estimates of GDP at current prices are unavailable, it is likely that in 1967 GDP only

TABLE 1.   NIGER: ORIGIN AND USE OF GROSS DOMESTIC PRODUCT
AT CURRENT PRICES, 1963–66 [1]

(Value in billions of CFA francs)

	Value				Per Cent of Total	
	1963	1964	1965	1966	1963	1966
Origin						
Primary sector [2]	39.2	40.0	45.4	46.8	59.4	59.4
Secondary sector [2]	7.6	7.6	8.5	9.2	11.5	11.7
Tertiary sector [2]	14.5	14.6	16.0	18.0	22.0	22.8
Government	4.5	4.0	4.0	4.6	6.8	5.8
Households	0.2	0.2	0.2	0.2	0.3	0.3
Total GDP at market prices	66.0	66.4	74.1	78.8	100.0	100.0
Use						
Consumption						
Private	46.1	48.4	57.8	58.7	69.9	74.5
Public	8.6	8.4	8.5	9.7	13.0	12.3
Total consumption	54.7	56.8	66.3	68.4	82.9	86.8
Gross investment						
Private	8.2	7.2	5.3	7.7	12.4	9.8
Public	2.8	2.4	2.9	2.7	4.2	3.4
Total gross investment	11.0	9.6	8.2	10.4	16.7	13.2
Changes in stocks	*3.2*	*3.0*	*0.3*	*1.5*	*4.8*	*1.9*
Gross capital formation						
Private	*5.0*	*4.2*	*5.0*	*6.2*	*7.6*	*7.9*
Public	*2.8*	*2.4*	*2.9*	*2.7*	*4.2*	*3.4*
Total gross capital formation	*7.8*	*6.6*	*7.9*	*8.9*	*11.8*	*11.3*
Exports of goods and services	9.8	10.2	11.0	13.0	14.8	16.5
Less imports of goods and services	−9.5	−10.2	−11.4	−13.0	−14.4	−16.5

Sources: Commissariat Général au Plan, Service de la Statistique et de la Mécanographie, *Comptes Economiques,* and data provided by the Nigerien authorities.

[1] Because of rounding, figures do not add to all totals in this table or some of the following tables.
[2] Primary sector includes agriculture, animal husbandry, forestry, and fishing; secondary sector includes mining, manufacturing, and construction; and tertiary sector includes transport, commerce, and services.

slightly exceeded the 1966 level. Per capita GDP at current prices rose from $71 to $97 during 1960–66.

The relative importance of the economic sectors in aggregate output has not changed significantly in recent years. In 1966, agriculture (including animal husbandry, fishing, and forestry) contributed 59 per cent of total GDP at current prices. Transportation, trade, other services, and public administration comprised the next largest group with a combined share of some 29 per cent of the total; industry, mining, and construction combined accounted for the remaining 12 per cent.

Total gross domestic investment advanced from CFAF 4.6 billion in 1960 to CFAF 10.4 billion in 1966, when it was equivalent to 13 per cent of GDP. Growth, however, was uneven during the period: during 1960–63, annual investment increased rapidly to CFAF 11.0 billion, mainly as a result of large private investments, which rose from CFAF 2.6 billion to CFAF 8.2 billion. Public investment during the same period rose by 40 per cent to CFAF 2.8 billion. During 1964–66, annual gross domestic investment averaged CFAF 9.4 billion, or 15 per cent less than the level attained in 1963. In 1964 (a year of unusually low groundnut harvest, a slowdown in mining and construction, and a gain in GDP at current prices of less than 1 per cent), total gross domestic investment by both the public and private sectors declined by about 13 per cent. Although gross domestic investment continued downward in 1965, the decline was due to a decrease in stock of CFAF 2.7 billion, since gross capital formation rose from CFAF 6.6 billion in 1964 to CFAF 7.9 billion in 1965. In 1966, gross domestic investment rose to CFAF 10.4 billion as stocks were reconstituted and gross capital formation increased further. The increased investment was made mainly by the private sector in machinery and equipment, but also in vehicles and modern buildings, reflecting the establishment of a number of new enterprises during this period. In the public sector, roads and modern buildings accounted for most of the increase during these three years.

AGRICULTURE, FISHING, AND FORESTRY

Agriculture is of foremost importance in Niger; including fishing and forestry, the value of its output accounts for nearly 60 per cent of Niger's GDP and over 90 per cent of its export receipts. In the 1960's agricultural production increased only moderately. Land suitable for cultivation is limited; moreover, yields per hectare are generally low, owing to lack of irrigation, poor soils, considerable wind and water erosion, and the primitive cultivation methods used in most areas.

Crops Mainly for Food

About 90 per cent of the total cultivated area is under food crops, principally millet, beans, and sorghum (Table 2). Other important food crops are cassava, rice, onions, sugarcane, potatoes, and maize. Production of these crops is usually adequate for domestic needs. In good years, small surpluses of millet, sorghum, and beans are available for export. Small-scale exportation of onions and other vegetables is being promoted. Crop data are subject to a considerable margin of error and are not always comparable from year to year.

In the 1966/67 crop year, production of the main food staples (e.g., millet, sorghum, and rice) increased slightly, whereas production of all other major food crops declined, largely because of crop substitution. Favorable weather in 1967/68 substantially raised the over-all production of major food crops.

For the crop year 1968/69, however, preliminary official estimates indicate a considerable reduction in output of all major food crops except rice. Drought, especially in central Niger, has seriously cut production. In the Tahoua area, millet and sorghum production fell by as much as 50 per cent. Even in the more favorably situated areas, insufficient rainfall caused a decline expected to be 5 to 8 per cent. As a result, the price of millet rose to about CFAF 20–22 per kilogram, more than double the normal price. Emergency importation of sorghum was contemplated. Rice production, which had not changed much up to 1965/66, rose substantially in the following two years and was expected to increase further in 1968/69, owing to the cultivation of new improved species.

Crops Mainly for Export

Groundnuts.—By far the principal cash crop, groundnuts represent about half of the value of marketed agricultural production and about three fourths (including groundnut oil) of export earnings. They are also an important food crop; farm consumption accounts for about 18 per cent of production. Groundnuts are cultivated on a narrow strip of land in southern Niger along the border with Nigeria. Since the implementation of the EEC-sponsored agricultural program in 1964/65, the area under groundnut cultivation has expanded from 320,000 hectares to 356,000 hectares (1967/68). The crop is produced mainly on small individual farms. It is planted at the beginning of the rainy season in June–July, harvested toward the end of the year, and marketed from the beginning of December until the early months of the following year.

TABLE 2. NIGER: AREA AND PRODUCTION OF PRINCIPAL CROPS, 1965/66–1968/69

	Area Under Cultivation			Production				Yields		
	Thousand hectares →			← Thousand metric tons →				Kilograms per hectare		
	1965/66	1966/67	1967/68	1965/66	1966/67	1967/68	1968/69 [1]	1965/66	1966/67	1967/68
Food crops										
Millet	1,810	1,743	1,865	789	842	1,000	770	436	483	536
Niebe beans	468	608	689	76	68	77	62	162	112	112
Sorghum	465	546	530	266	277	342	220	572	507	645
Cassava	19	21	24	150	148	169	…	7,895	7,048	7,042
Rice	9	9	12	12	21	33	36	1,333	2,333	2,750
Maize	4	4	5	3	2	3	…	750	500	600
Sugarcane	2	1	1	41	12	21	…	20,500	12,000	21,000
Potatoes	1	—	—	20	7	12	…	20,000	6,990	10,130
Onions	2	2	2	42	36	38	…	21,000	18,000	19,000
Others	4	4	5	…	…	…	…	…	…	…
Total food crop area	2,784	2,938	3,133							
Cash crops										
Groundnuts (unshelled)	341	339	356	277	288	298	245	812	350	837
Cotton, seed (unginned)	16	14	14	7	6	8	6	438	429	571
Total cash crop area	357	353	370							
Total crop area	3,141	3,291	3,503							

Source: Ministère de l'Economie Rurale, Service de l'Agriculture, *Rapport Annuel.*

[1] Official estimates.

Production of groundnuts increased after 1965/66, reaching 298,000 tons [1] in 1967/68 (see Table 2). The increase was due not only to gradual expansion of the cultivation area but also to higher yields under the EEC aid program, which subsidized the cost of advisory personnel and the sale of selected seeds, fertilizers, and equipment. Preliminary estimates for 1968/69 indicate a smaller crop of 245,000 tons, or 18 per cent less than in the preceding year, as a result of insufficient and irregular rains.

Traditionally, shelled groundnuts and groundnut oil have been exported mainly to the French market. Under a bilateral cooperation agreement, France formerly guaranteed to purchase at support prices annual quantities fixed in relation to the size of the crop. The French support prices were higher than the world market prices, enabling Niger to sustain its cost structure, including minimum prices paid to producers and export taxes.

The Convention of Association between EEC and 18 African and Malagasy States required that beginning 1964/65 all exports of associated members should be marketed at world market prices and called for the termination of bilateral support schemes.

To facilitate the transition, EEC instituted a program of financial aid to agricultural production and diversification during 1964/65–1968/69 (Table 3). EEC aid to agricultural production included price support subsidies and subsidies for structural improvements. The latter were expected to help to improve agricultural productivity by subsidizing certain production costs such as advisory personnel, agricultural equipment, fertilizers, insecticides, and draft animals. The five-year program allocated aid by yearly installments, or tranches, for each commodity (groundnuts and cotton), and by category of aid (price subsidies and subsidies for structural improvements).

Yearly price subsidy allocations were computed on the basis of estimated exports to EEC countries and price subsidies per unit calculated from the difference between estimated world market prices and theoretical cost prices called "target cost prices" (*prix d'objectif*). "Target cost prices" were assumed to decline progressively as a result of improvements in productivity and savings in various other costs. Price subsidies

---

[1] Throughout this chapter, the word "ton" refers to a metric ton of 2,204.6 pounds.

TABLE 3. NIGER: SECOND EUROPEAN DEVELOPMENT FUND PROGRAM, AID TO AGRICULTURAL PRODUCTION, 1964/65–1968/69

(In millions of CFA francs)

	Groundnuts			Cotton			Total		
	Price support	Structural improvement	Total	Price support	Structural improvement	Total	Price support	Structural improvement	Total
First tranche (1964/65) [1]									
Original estimates	170.1	9.0	179.1	40.9	12.0	52.9	211.0	21.0	232.0
Revised estimates	163.5	15.5	179.0	40.9	10.9	51.8	204.4	26.4	230.8
Actual disbursements	2.2	15.5	17.7	18.1	10.0	28.1	20.3	25.5	45.8
Second tranche (1965/66)									
Original estimates	232.5	108.0	340.5	18.9	14.0	32.9	251.4	122.0	373.4
Revised estimates	237.5	139.2	376.7	19.8	43.1	62.9	257.3	182.3	439.6
Actual disbursements	—	66.0	66.0	33.5	23.7	57.2	33.5	89.7	123.2
Third tranche (1966/67)									
Original estimates	120.0	123.0	243.0	12.2	15.0	27.2	132.2	138.0	270.2
Revised estimates	121.4	130.2	251.6	33.8	57.6	91.4	155.2	187.8	343.0
Actual disbursements	18.4	—	18.4	33.8	...	33.8	42.2	...	42.2
Fourth tranche (1967/68)									
Original estimates	100.0	107.0	207.0	4.9	15.5	20.4	104.9	122.5	227.4
Revised estimates	504.0	118.9	622.9	2.5	59.4	61.9	506.5	178.3	684.8
Actual disbursements	317.0[2]	—	317.0[2]	—	—	—	317.0[2]	—	317.0[2]
Fifth tranche (1968/69)									
Original estimates	450.0	75.5	525.5	—	15.9	15.9	450.0	91.4	541.4
Total original estimates	1,072.6	422.5	1,495.1	76.9	72.4	149.3	1,149.5	494.9	1,644.4

Source: Data provided by the Nigerien authorities.

[1] Includes the 1963/64 aid program for cotton.
[2] Disbursements based on losses suffered with respect to groundnut production and marketing in previous years.

per unit were scheduled to decline every year, to be terminated in the last year of the program when "target cost prices" were expected to be equal to the world price (Table 4). In the course of implementation, however, the yearly tranches of aid to agricultural production were to be revised in the light of actual exports, world prices, and cost elements provided that the global limit of total funds committed under the five-year program would not be exceeded. For Niger, a cost price reduction of CFAF 6.05 per kilogram of shelled groundnuts, or 12 per cent over the five-year period, was called for.

Beginning July 1967, EEC extended to Niger for two years a supplementary price stabilization program applicable to exports of oil and oilseeds. This program aimed at alleviating the effects of major declines in world prices. Accordingly, whenever the world price of groundnuts fell short of a "reference price" set at CFAF 45.915 per kilogram, EEC undertook to pay a subsidy equivalent to 80 per cent of the difference between the "reference price" and the world price for groundnuts exported to EEC countries. Although the price stabilization scheme was separate from the price support system included in the EEC program of groundnut production, subsidy payments under the two programs do not overlap. If price subsidy payments are due under the price stabilization program as well as under the production aid program, the former is netted by an amount equivalent to 80 per cent of the overlapping amount of the latter. For example, the price subsidy payments under the production and the price stabilization programs for 1967/68 were calculated as follows:

	CFA francs per kilogram
Production aid program	
EEC "target cost price"	41.720
World market price	−38.700
Subsidy under production aid	3.020
Price stabilization program	
EEC "reference price"	45.915
World market price	−38.700
Difference	7.215
80 per cent of difference	5.772
Less 80 per cent of subsidy under production aid (CFAF 3.020)	−2.416
Subsidy under price stabilization	3.356
Total subsidy payment under both programs	6.376

Groundnut marketing involves private traders and cooperatives who are licensed by the Government to act as intermediaries in purchasing groundnuts from producers for resale to the Groundnut Marketing Company (Société Nigérienne de Commercialisation de l'Arachide, or SONARA), a mixed enterprise established in 1962 and entrusted with a monopoly in selling groundnuts to oil mills in Niger and on export markets. The price paid to producers is fixed each year by the Ministry of Economic Affairs, Trade, and Industry. In determining the producer price, the Ministry is guided by estimates of the size of the crop, world market conditions, and other factors such as the need to reduce costs under the EEC program. Before the 1967/68 season, producer prices varied from region to region. Despite the small price differential (only about CFAF 2 per kilogram), producers transported their crop to regions where the prices were higher, thereby straining the country's inadequate transportation facilities. Beginning with 1967/68 a uniform producer price was fixed for the entire country.

Apart from the producer price, other elements of cost are permissible profit margins of intermediary purchases, storage, packaging, banking, transport, insurance, and commission charges incurred by the Marketing Company and export taxes. After 1965/66, the Company's profit margin has been determined by a system of floor and ceiling prices fixed by the Price Stabilization Fund (Caisse de Stabilisation des Prix des Produits du Niger, or CSPPN) and the Marketing Company. If the Company's realized export prices exceed the ceiling, the excess accrues to the Fund. On the other hand, if the realized prices are below the floor price, the Company receives payment for the difference from the Fund. The floor price is equivalent to the Company's total cost as determined above. Therefore, in years when prices are below cost, the Company will make neither a profit nor a loss, but when prices are above the ceiling price, the Company's profit margin will be the differential between the floor and the ceiling price.

Apart from receipts from other operations, the Price Stabilization Fund receives payments of price subsidies under the EEC program of groundnut production aid. Preferential access of Niger's groundnut exports to the French market continued until 1966/67. Since guaranteed prices paid by France exceeded "target cost prices" of the EEC production aid program, EEC price subsidies were limited to small

TABLE 4.   NIGER: GROUNDNUT EXPORT PRICE STRUCTURE, MARKET SALES,
AND PRICE SUBSIDIES, 1964/65–1968/69

	1964/65	1965/66	1966/67	1967/68	1968/69
UNIT VALUE (*CFA francs per kilogram of shelled nuts*)					
Cost c.i.f.[1]					
Producer's price	22.50	22.81	22.15	18.04	18.00
Taxes [2]	5.56	3.75	3.00	2.75	2.25
Other costs [3]					
Intermediary commission	} 19.60	{ 1.60	1.60	1.60	1.60
SONARA's [4] costs		19.32	21.37	19.37	18.15
Total cost c.i.f.	47.66	47.48	48.12	41.76	40.00
French guaranteed export price c.i.f.	52.50	49.06 [5]	49.13	—	—
World market price c.i.f. European port	47.54 [6]	46.45	39.50	38.70	46.00 [7]
EEC "target cost price" c.i.f.					
Producer's price	22.15	21.25	22.45	17.63	21.25
Taxes	4.75	3.75	3.00	2.75	2.25
Other costs	23.15	21.50	22.97	21.34	20.50
Total EEC "target cost price" c.i.f.	50.05	46.50	48.42	41.72	44.00
QUANTITY (*thousand metric tons of shelled nuts*)					
Production					
SONARA purchases	106.4	156.1	191.3	181.8	150.0
On-farm consumption and stocks	15.1	26.7	−1.2	15.0	11.7
Total production	121.5	182.8	190.1	196.8	161.7
SONARA sales					
Exports					
At French guaranteed prices	77.9	100.2	150.5	—	—
At world market prices	8.8	33.0	24.6	159.0	139.7
Total exports	86.7	133.2	175.1	159.0	139.7
Sales to local refineries					
Exports of crude oil [8]	16.1	10.6	13.0	19.0	20.0
Local consumption [8]	4.2	9.3	3.4	4.0	4.0
Total sales to local refineries	20.3	19.9	16.4	23.0	24.0
Total SONARA sales	107.0	153.1	191.5	182.0	163.7
EEC PRICE SUBSIDIES (*million CFA francs*)					
EEC program estimates	163.5	237.5	121.4	504.0	...
Actual disbursements	2.2	—	18.4	317.0 [9]	...

Source: Data provided by the Nigerien authorities.

[1] Official price scale (*barème*) fixed at the beginning of each crop season.

[2] Includes export taxes and levies accruing to the Price Stabilization Fund (Caisse de Stabilisation des Prix des Produits du Niger, or CSPPN) until 1963/64 and to the Fonds de Dotations pour l'Amélioration de la Productivité Rurale until 1964/65.

[3] Includes various internal costs (e.g., handling, storage, packing, commissions paid overseas, transportation, insurance, unloading, and selling).

Footnotes continued on page 413.

amounts on account of exports at world prices to EEC countries other than France, totaling CFAF 21 million for the three years 1964/65–1966/67 (see Table 4). For 1967/68, EEC price subsidies (based on the difference between the "target cost price" of CFAF 41.72 per ton of shelled nuts and the world price of CFAF 38.70 per ton of shelled nuts) were to be paid on account of all exports to EEC countries including those to France. They were expected to total CFAF 460 million. For 1968/69, no price subsidy was expected under the EEC production aid program, since world market prices tended to be higher than the EEC's "target cost price." In addition to the above EEC price subsidies under the five-year production aid program, the Price Stabilization Fund was to receive payments on account of the EEC price stabilization program for oils and fats, applicable since mid-1967. EEC subsidies due under the price stabilization program, estimated at CFAF 450 million, have not been disbursed, pending the entry into force of the scheme anticipated in 1969.

In 1965/66 the Groundnut Marketing Company (SONARA) marketed 153,100 tons of groundnuts—19,900 tons to local oil refineries and 133,200 tons exported as shelled nuts, 100,200 tons to France and 33,000 tons to other markets (see Table 4). Stocks rose by 3,000 tons. The Company obtained a price of CFAF 49.13 per kilogram for the first 90,000 tons exported to France and CFAF 48.50 per kilogram for the remainder marketed in France; this compares with the world price of CFAF 48.50 (calculated as the average of actual realized world market prices). The unit cost was CFAF 47.48 (including the producer price of CFAF 22.81, export tax of CFAF 3.75, and other costs of CFAF 20.92). Since the price obtained on the French market exceeded the cost and only very small quantities were exported to EEC countries other than France, no payments fell due under the EEC subsidy program. Under the floor and ceiling arrangements discussed above, the

---

[4] Groundnut Marketing Company (Société Nigérienne de Commercialisation de l'Arachide).

[5] The French guaranteed price was CFAF 49.13 per kilogram for the first 90,000 tons of the quota and CFAF 48.50 per kilogram for the remainder.

[6] Shelled groundnuts from Nigeria, nearest forward shipment; beginning 1965/66, average of Niger's actual export prices realized.

[7] Estimated.

[8] Computed by the equivalent tonnage of shelled groundnuts.

[9] Disbursement based on 80 per cent of bills; total disbursement expected, CFAF 460 million.

Price Stabilization Fund (CSPPN) paid the Marketing Company CFAF 34 million on account of exports to countries other than France but received CFAF 83.2 million on account of exports to France (Table 5). The net financial results of groundnut marketing in 1965/66 were a net accrual of funds by the Fund of CFAF 49.2 million and a profit for the Company of CFAF 75.1 million.

In 1966/67 the Marketing Company sales rose to 191,500 tons of groundnuts—16,400 tons to local oil refineries and 175,100 tons exported as shelled nuts, about 150,500 tons to France and 24,600 tons to other markets. Stocks declined by 300 tons. In line with the

TABLE 5. NIGER: GROUNDNUT MARKETING AND FINANCING, 1965/66–1968/69

	1965/66	1966/67	1967/68	1968/69 [1]
UNIT VALUE (*CFA francs per kilogram*)				
Cost c.i.f. = floor price	47.48	48.12	41.76	40.00
Ceiling price	48.23	48.42	42.06	40.30
French guaranteed price	49.06	49.13	—	—
World market price	46.45	39.50	38.70	46.00
EEC "target cost price"	46.50	48.42	41.72	44.00
EEC payments to CSPPN for exports to EEC countries other than France	0.05	8.92	3.02	—
CSPPN payments to SONARA for exports to countries other than France	1.03	8.62	3.06	—
SONARA payments to CSPPN For exports to France	0.83	0.41	—	—
For exports to other countries	—	—	—	5.70
TOTAL VALUE (*million CFA francs*)				
Total EEC payments to CSPPN	—	18.40	460.00	450.00 [2]
Total CSPPN payments to SONARA	34.00	212.05	486.54	—
Total SONARA payments to CSPPN	83.17	61.71	—	741.00
Net payments to CSPPN	49.17	−131.94	−26.54	1,191.00
Net payments to SONARA	75.14	90.30	—	39.00
Receipts from domestic and foreign sales +(or −) CSPPN	6,399.48	8,516.11	6,639.84	5,239.00
Total cost c.i.f.	6,324.34	8,425.81	6,639.84	5,200.00

Source: Table 4.

[1] Estimated.

[2] Expected payments under supplementary price stabilization program applicable to exports of oil and oilseeds.

EEC program of reducing costs, the producer price was lowered in 1966/67 to CFAF 22.15 per kilogram and the export tax to CFAF 3.00. Other cost elements, however, especially transportation cost, increased, raising the total cost to CFAF 48.12 per kilogram. Nevertheless, the higher cost price for the first time fell below the "target cost price" of CFAF 48.42 per kilogram of the EEC program for that year. Actual realized world market prices declined sharply to CFAF·39.50 [2] per kilogram. The French support price, on the other hand, rose slightly to CFAF 49.13 per kilogram. Since 150,500 tons out of total exports of 175,100 tons of shelled nuts, went to France, where the price exceeded the EEC target price, EEC payments for exports at world market prices to EEC countries amounted to only CFAF 18.4 million. The subsidy payments by the Stabilization Fund to the Marketing Company increased to CFAF 212 million, while payments from the Company to the Fund, on account of the Company's exports to France, declined to CFAF 61.7 million. Consequently, the Fund had a net outflow of CFAF 131.9 million while the Company showed a profit of CFAF 90.3 million.

Marketing Company sales declined in 1967/68 to 182,000 tons. Local oil refineries took 23,000 tons, and 159,000 tons were exported as shelled nuts, all at world market prices since the French price guarantee no longer operated. The unit cost was further reduced to CFAF 41.76 by cutting the producer price to CFAF 18.04, taxes to CFAF 2.75, and other cost elements to CFAF 20.97. Although this cost was only slightly more than the EEC "target cost price," the decline in receipts, now based on world prices for total exports of 159,000 tons, raised total EEC subsidy payments to CFAF 460.0 million and the Price Stabilization Fund (CSPPN) payments to the Marketing Company even more—to CFAF 486.5 million without any offsetting payments of the Company to the Fund. Consequently, the Fund had a net outflow of CFAF 26.5 million while the Company just broke even.

In 1968/69, the Marketing Company handled 163,700 tons, selling 24,000 tons to local oil refineries and an estimated 139,700 tons as

[2] The realized price for Niger is considerably below the average world market price because the main export market other than EEC was the United Kingdom. Although sale contracts were concluded before sterling devaluation in 1967, payment was not received until after devaluation.

shelled nuts. The estimated unit cost declined to CFAF 40 per kilogram, compared with the EEC "target cost price" of CFAF 44 (as a result of slightly lower producer price, export tax, and other costs). Consequently, no EEC payments were to be due on the subsidy program. Moreover, a sharp improvement in the actual realized world market price to a record CFAF 46 per kilogram would make groundnut exports at world market prices profitable for the first time in recent years. It was estimated that CFAF 1,191 million would accrue to the Fund despite a probable decline in quantity exported. The Company expected a profit of CFAF 39 million. The improved world price in 1968/69 largely reflected the disappearance of Senegal as an exporter of shelled nuts following that country's decision to process its crop into oil.

Cotton.—Cultivation of cotton, though gaining in importance during recent years, accounted for only 3 per cent of total export earnings in 1967/68. It ranked fourth after shelled groundnuts, cattle, and groundnut oil. Cotton is produced on small farms, mainly in dried-up riverbeds in the savanna region, where the soil is best suited. Since the climate and soil are only marginally suitable for cotton, production costs are relatively high. During 1960/61–1965/66 the area in cotton more than tripled, reaching 16,000 hectares. Production increased even more markedly because yields per hectare more than doubled. During the following three years, production varied somewhat as continued improvement in yields was offset by contraction in the cultivated area.

In order to promote cotton production and marketing, the Compagnie Française pour le Développement des Fibres Textiles (CFDT), a French semipublic company, undertook the task of developing cotton cultivation in cooperation with local authorities in return for the sole right to purchase, gin, and export cotton from Niger. As the cost exceeded the market price, this Company until 1962/63 benefited from export subsidies paid by France corresponding to the difference between its cost and the actual realized export price. The subsidy was paid by the Caisse Inter-Etats de Stabilisation des Prix du Coton, a regional stabilization fund, which, in turn, is subsidized through the French budget.

Cotton is marketed in much the same way as groundnuts. In November the Government fixes the annual producer price. This price is specified for each region within a differential margin of CFAF 3.50 per kilogram. The Compagnie Française pour le Développement des Fibres Textiles purchases cotton either direct from farmers or from cooperatives. Besides the producer price, cost elements consist of ginning, storage, packaging, transport, insurance, handling charges, commissions, and export taxes.

In line with the Convention of Association with EEC calling for the marketing of all exports of associated members at world market prices and for termination of bilateral support schemes, the French subsidy ceased with the crop year 1962/63. Instead, beginning in 1963/64, EEC established an aid program similar to that for groundnuts to increase productivity and to provide price subsidies. EEC pays subsidies to Niger's Stabilization Fund (CSPPN), which, in turn, compensates the Compagnie Française pour le Développement des Fibres Textiles in full for the latter's losses on exports. Scheduled reductions in the EEC "target cost price" for the entire six years ending 1968/69 amounted to 8 per cent (or CFAF 11.5 per kilogram), and the price reached CFAF 137 per kilogram (Table 6). Annual reductions were to be achieved mainly through improvement in the yield of fiber from seed cotton (from 34.25 per cent to 36 per cent). Actually, reduction in the producer price, ginning cost, and taxes, though partly offset by an increase in other costs, did lower the cost f.o.b. to CFAF 137 per kilogram by 1968/69. The Price Stabilization Fund also paid subsidies to the Compagnie Française pour le Développement des Fibres Textiles as compensation for the supplementary cost of exporting cotton through Dahomey. This subsidy was discontinued, however, in 1965/66, when cotton export costs were reduced by routing through Nigeria.

Exporters' receipts (including subsidies) in 1963/64 totaled CFAF 277.7 million, which, minus costs, left exporters with a total net profit of CFAF 3.6 million (Table 7). Because of peak export sales in 1964/65, exporters' net profit rose to CFAF 4.6 million despite lower subsidies. In 1965/66, when export sales dropped by more than half but EEC subsidies were substantial, their net profit totaled CFAF 11.4 million. The corresponding figure was CFAF 6.4 million in 1966/67, when export sales made fair recovery, but subsidies, though still large, were reduced.

During 1967/68, rainfall was not as abundant as in 1966/67, and market sales of ginned cotton declined by 6 per cent to 2,192 tons. The

TABLE 6. NIGER: COTTON EXPORT PRICE STRUCTURE, MARKET SALES, AND PRICE SUBSIDIES, 1963/64–1968/69

	1963/64	1964/65	1965/66	1966/67	1967/68	1968/69
	UNIT VALUE (*CFA francs per kilogram*)					
Actual cost f.o.b.						
Producer price	32.60	32.60	32.60	30.00	28.50	28.50
Seed-cotton basis [1]						
Yield of ginned cotton per unit of seed cotton (*per cent*)	33.56	34.00	34.05	34.89	35.86	35.50
Ginned-cotton basis [1]	97.13	95.88	95.74	88.98	79.47	80.28
Taxes [1]	3.37	1.75	1.10	1.10	1.00	0.40
Other	51.62	50.44	52.21	53.97	54.29	56.32
Total cost f.o.b. [1]	152.12	148.07	149.05	144.05	134.76	137.00
Average export price f.o.b. (ginned-cotton basis) [2]	140.42	143.40	130.04	132.29	141.00	138.00
Exporter's profit, or loss (−), on ginned cotton	−11.70	−4.67	−19.01	−11.76	6.24	1.00
EEC "target cost price" f.o.b.						
Target producer price	32.60	32.60	32.60	30.00	28.50	31.71
Seed-cotton basis						
Target yield of ginned cotton per unit of seed cotton (*per cent*)	34.25	34.50	35.00	34.75	34.75	36.00
Ginned-cotton basis	95.20	94.20	92.90	86.33	82.01	88.10
Taxes	2.95	1.45	1.10	1.10	1.00	0.40
Other	50.35	49.35	49.00	53.95	54.81	48.50
Total "target cost price" f.o.b.	148.50	145.00	143.00 [3]	141.38	137.82	137.00

	QUANTITY (metric tons, ginned)					
Market sales of cotton	1,802	2,422	1,162	2,330	2,192	2,000 [4]
	TOTAL SUBSIDIES TO EXPORTER (million CFA francs)					
Price subsidies						
Disbursed by EEC	14.3	3.9	33.5	33.8	—	...
EEC program estimates [5]	*20.4*	*20.5*	*27.1*	*20.5*	—	—
Disbursed by CSPPN	1.7	—	—	—	—	...
Total price subsidies	16.0	3.9	33.5	33.8	—	—
Transport subsidies disbursed by CSPPN [6]	8.7	12.0	—	—	—	—

Source: Data provided by the Nigerien authorities.

[1] 1963/64–1967/68, actual; 1968/69, official price scale (*barème*).
[2] 1963/64–1967/68, actual; 1968/69, estimate.
[3] Revised by EEC and set at CFAF 144.28 per kilogram.
[4] Estimated.
[5] Estimates in the EEC five-year program of aid to agricultural production for 1964/65 and 1966/67; see also Table 3. For cotton, the first tranche of the program (CFAF 40.9 million) covered the 1963/64 and 1964/65 crops.
[6] In 1965/66, exports at lower cost through Nigeria permitted discontinuance of subsidies for cotton transportation.

TABLE 7. NIGER: COTTON MARKETING AND FINANCING, 1963/64–1968/69

	1963/64	1964/65	1965/66	1966/67	1967/68	1968/69 [1]
UNIT VALUE (*CFA francs per kilogram, ginned*)						
Cost f.o.b. World market price f.o.b. =	152.12	148.07	149.05	144.05	134.76	137.00
Niger's average realized sales price	140.42	143.40	130.04	132.29	141.00	138.00
EEC "target cost price" f.o.b.	148.50	145.00	144.28 [2]	141.38	137.82	137.00
TOTAL VALUE (*million CFA francs*)						
EEC payments to CSPPN for exporters	14.30	3.90	33.50	33.80	—	—
Additional CSPPN payments to exporters						
CSPPN subsidy	1.70	—	—	—	—	—
Transport subsidy	8.70	12.00	—	—	—	—
Total subsidy to exporters	24.70	15.90	33.50	33.80	—	—
Exporters' proceeds from exports	253.04	347.31	151.11	308.24	309.07	276.00
Total receipts of exporters from sales	277.74	363.21	184.61	342.04	309.07	276.00
Less total costs	274.12	358.63	173.20	335.64	295.39	274.00
Net profit of exporters	3.62	4.58	11.41	6.40	13.68	2.00

Source: Table 6.

[1] Official price scale and estimates.
[2] Before revision of EEC, CFAF 143.00.

decline would have been larger except for the introduction of a new variety of cotton (with a fiber content of about 37 per cent of seed cotton) which raised the country's average fiber content to 35.86 per cent in 1967/68 and accounted for 86 per cent of the reduction in cost to less than CFAF 135 per kilogram of fiber (see Table 6). Also contributing to the reduction was a lowering of the producer price and export tax, though partly offset by an increase in other costs. The reduced cost was about CFAF 3 below the EEC "target cost price" and about CFAF 7 below the world market price, which had risen slightly. Consequently no EEC subsidies were disbursed for 1967/68, and cotton exports became competitive on world markets. The net effect of these developments was a rise in exporters' net profit to a peak of CFAF 13.7 million, even without the EEC subsidies (see Table 7).

Preliminary estimates for 1968/69 indicated a fall in market sales of cotton fiber to 2,000 tons because of unfavorable rains. With an unchanged producer price, higher ginning and other costs (only partly offset by a lower export tax), the cost rose to CFAF 137 per kilogram. Nevertheless, since this cost equaled the EEC "target cost price," again no EEC subsidies were disbursed. Despite an expected lower world market price, exports should remain profitable, although exporters' net profit was forecast to total only CFAF 2.0 million.

Other crops.—Tobacco and sugarcane are minor industrial crops. Tobacco production, which usually fluctuates around 300 tons a year, decreased in 1967/68 to 241 tons. The output of sugarcane, consumed raw, averaged 30,000–40,000 tons annually between 1961/62 and 1965/66, declining to 21,000 tons in 1967/68. The development of sugarcane cultivation to supply the proposed new sugar factory is being considered. To meet the factories' requirements, present production and area would have to more than double.

Livestock and Livestock Products

Livestock represent one of the most important resources of Niger, accounting for nearly one fifth of GDP and in 1968/69 for 15 per cent of recorded exports. Cattle ownership is a status symbol and a store of wealth; consequently, owners market animals only to meet their basic needs. This attitude has hindered a large-scale commercial exploitation of livestock resources. Livestock are raised over an area of about

650,000 square kilometers, or about half of the country, where the climate discourages other agricultural pursuits. In the desert area in the north, livestock raising is a nomadic activity; in the savanna region and farther south, most herds belong to settled farmers.

EEC initiated a program in 1965 to protect the livestock population and improve the growth rate. This program includes vaccination against rinderpest, veterinary services, research on stock improvements, a cattle ranch, and well drilling. Since 1968 the Government of Niger has financed this program at an annual cost of CFAF 160,000.

Reliable data on the livestock population and its growth rate are not available. Recorded data, based on information compiled by local authorities for tax purposes, are incomplete. Official estimates take into account information from other sources, particularly vaccination reports. These estimates indicate a livestock population in 1966 of 4.1 million cattle and 8.2 million sheep and goats (Table 8). During 1968 the livestock population declined by an estimated 5 per cent because of drought. A further decline was expected in 1969, since herders, in an attempt to reduce losses through starvation, permitted overgrazing which adversely affected grass seed formation, leaving a considerable area of barren pasture in 1969. Growth of the livestock population has been hindered by insufficient watering points and pumping equipment in the dry season, improper use of pastures, and epidemics.

Recorded animal slaughter is estimated at 3 per cent of the livestock population. Although meat consumption habits have remained unchanged, controlled slaughter declined by 23 per cent in 1967 and by 2 per cent in 1968. It is estimated that the decline was accompanied by a parallel increase in uncontrolled slaughter to avoid payment of a CFAF 10 per kilogram turnover tax introduced in 1967.

Since October 1968 the Livestock Products Marketing Company (Société Nigérienne d'Exportation des Ressources d'Animaux, or SONERAN), a mixed enterprise, has had a monopoly of export meat sales and has been in charge of sales of meat from slaughterhouses.

Although the largest outlet for live animals is Nigeria, exports to Ghana and Dahomey are also considerable, and recorded exports of live animals are estimated at 3 per cent of the livestock population. It is believed that about 170,000 head are exported on the hoof, compared with only 60,000–70,000 recorded. Introduction of an export tax of 10

TABLE 8. NIGER: LIVESTOCK POPULATION, SLAUGHTER, AND PRODUCTION OF HIDES AND SKINS, 1964–68

(*In thousands*)

	Recorded Data					Official Estimates		
	1964	1965	1966	1967	1968 [1]	1964	1965	1966
Livestock population								
Cattle	2,156	2,273	2,122	2,189	...	3,900	4,000	4,100
Sheep and goats	4,463	4,636	4,319	4,707	...	7,600	7,950	8,200
Camels	257	261	217	216	...	360	360	378
Donkeys	229	227	260	258	...	315	315	331
Slaughter								
Cattle	77	77	76	65	73	145	140	...
Sheep	87	86	95	82	56	1,530	1,800	...
Goats	503	463	447	331	340			
Camels	1	2	2	1	1	3	...	...
Pigs	1	1	1	1	1	...	...	...
Production of hides and skins								
Cattle	170	149	153	164	177	...	...	...
Sheep	360	351	333	370	411	...	...	...
Goats	1,117	1,088	838	979	1,091	...	...	...

Sources: Ministère de l'Economie Rurale, Service de l'Agriculture, *Rapport Annuel*, and data provided by the Nigerien authorities.

[1] Actual data for 11 months but adjusted for full year.

per cent on the assessed value of cattle, or CFAF 1,000 per head, like
the slaughter tax, has been followed by a decline in recorded numbers
and an increase in unrecorded exports, although some of the decline is
also attributable to events in Nigeria.

Fishing and Forestry

Fresh-water fishing is a minor economic activity. The annual catch
from the Niger River and Komadougou Yobé and from Lake Chad is
believed to average 4,500 tons. More reliable figures are available for
fishing on the Niger only; about 400–600 tons of fresh fish, valued at
CFAF 20–30 million, and 300–500 tons of smoked fish, valued at
CFAF 20–40 million, are produced each year. Part of the production is
exported to neighboring countries in dried, salted, or smoked form.
Fish are taken from the Niger mainly by fishermen from Nigeria who
account for about 80 per cent of the manpower engaged in this activity.
These fishermen usually migrate to Niger early in the year to fish and
return to Nigeria toward November to sell their smoked fish, a practice
that results in much waste, since the fish have to be smoked several
times during this period to avoid spoilage. The Government of Niger
encourages the organization of fishermen's cooperatives to buy the fresh
fish, smoke it, and transport it to markets. A small-scale program
financed by UN supports this scheme.

Niger's forests are scattered in small areas over the southern part of
the country. Timber is used exclusively as firewood and in the construction of local huts. Lumber for furniture making and carpentry is
imported.

Afforestation efforts are limited in Niger. Most of the forests, on
about 600,000 hectares, are declared to be protected. Cutting and hunt-
ing in these areas is permitted only under special license. The Government has undertaken a small-scale program to plant trees exploitable
for uses such as carpentry, but it is not expected to yield results for
eight to ten years. The planting takes place mainly in the vicinity of
Niamey for the purpose of creating a green belt around the city.
Annual planting covered about 200 hectares in 1967 and 1968 at an
average cost of CFAF 120,000 per hectare. This program is supported
by the U.S. Agency for International Development (AID).

MINING

Various minerals are found in Niger. Few, however, have been exploited, and these contribute only a negligible percentage to GDP. Exploited minerals are cassiterite, gypsum, limestone, silica, and gold.

Cassiterite, a tin ore, occurs in a remote area of the Aïr massif, about 250 kilometers north of Agadez. Mining operations began in 1948 and, since 1964, have been entrusted to the Société Minière du Niger (SMDN), in which the Government is a 75 per cent shareholder. Exploitation is not mechanized; cassiterite is separated from sand in a dry process by the use of sieves. Annual production could be increased considerably if mining were converted from a handicraft to a semi-industrial operation. To this end, a study sponsored by the UN Development Program was undertaken in 1967. However, the recommendations, requiring an investment of CFAF 300 million, have not been implemented. Annual production amounts to 80–100 tons, valued at CFAF 40–50 million (Table 9). The entire output is sold to a smelting

TABLE 9. NIGER: CASSITERITE PRODUCTION, 1962–68

	Quantity	Value
	Metric tons	*Million CFA francs*
1962	59.3	22.6
1963	80.0	31.7
1964	74.6	40.9
1965	78.0	46.5
1966	83.3	42.2
1967	80.0 [1]	. . .
1968	100.0 [1]	. . .

Source: Data provided by the Nigerien authorities.
[1] Official estimates.

plant in northern Nigeria. Transportation costs are about CFAF 50,000 per ton. Two new cassiterite layers were located in the Zinder area in 1966, and experimental exploitation started in 1967. Output is expected to equal that in the Aïr massif.

Current exploitation of other minerals is of lesser importance. In 1966, about 190 tons of gypsum, 22,000 tons of limestone, and 1,900 tons of silica were mined. In the valley of the Sirba, a tributary of the Niger, annual gold production is about 2 kilograms.

Extensive explorations since 1960 indicate the existence of other minerals, which, however, are not yet exploited or economically exploitable. The leading discovery is uranium at Arhli (Arlit), in the same remote area where tin ore is mined. Deposits are estimated at 20,000 tons, with a uranium content of 2.5 pro mille. To exploit the deposits, the Société des Mines de l'Aïr (SOMAIR) was established in February 1968 with a 20 per cent participation from the Government of Niger, 40 per cent from the French Commissariat à l'Energie Atomique (CEA), and the remainder from three French companies. Total investment was estimated at CFAF 13 billion, including installation and equipment of the mines, construction of a town for 6,000 inhabitants, and an electric power station of 8,600 kilowatts. Financing was to be as follows: CFAF 3.5 billion, capital; CFAF 2.0 billion, advances from shareholders; CFAF 2.5 billion loan from the Caisse Centrale de Coopération Economique (CCCE); CFAF 0.5 billion, bank loans; CFAF 3.6 billion, suppliers' credits; and the remainder, from internally generated funds. It was expected that 900–1,000 persons would be employed, about 800 citizens of Niger. The mine is already under construction, and it is expected that experimental exploitation can start in 1970 with an output of about 200 tons, which will be increased to 750 tons in 1972. An annual production of 1,000–1,500 tons was expected at full capacity.

Turnover was estimated at CFAF 5–7 billion annually, and production costs and amortization at half this amount. The Nigerien Government will share in the profits through its 20 per cent share of capital and a 50 per cent taxation of profits.

Other minerals found, but not yet exploited, include three iron ore deposits in the Niger Valley of 100–200 million tons of ore each with an iron content of 42–55 per cent. In order to exploit these deposits on an economical basis, a cheap source of electricity, as well as navigability of the Niger River, is necessary. In an attempt to reduce transportation costs, an Austrian firm has experimented with pelletizing the ore to raise the iron content to 70 per cent and with an electrolytical method, raising this content to 90 per cent.

Coal deposits approximating 30 million tons occur in the same area as cassiterite, but exploitation seems to be unlikely because of an insufficient water supply and high transportation costs. Significant deposits of manganese have been discovered northwest of Niamey. To make exploitation possible, a railway feeder line from the Niger Valley to Ouagadougou is necessary. Deposits of lithium and molybdenum have also been found northwest of Niamey, but exploitation appears to be uneconomical because of high transportation costs. It is believed that there are oil deposits close to the Libyan border, but foreign oil companies abandoned prospecting in 1964.

Investment in prospecting for the entire period 1960–67 totaled about CFAF 7.9 billion; CFAF 4.3 billion of this amount was spent by oil companies. In 1968, investment was expected to amount to about CFAF 0.8 billion and to be financed by the UN Development Program, CEA, and the Société Minière du Dahomey-Niger. For 1969–72, prospecting was to concentrate on further search for uranium and phosphates in the Tahoua area, as well as for iron ore deposits.

MANUFACTURING

Before 1958, industrial activity was limited to a brickyard, a printing plant, a soft drink factory, and three groundnut oil mills. In the 1960's, however, industrialization accelerated. The Government's policy of encouraging industrialization, beginning with the Second Development Plan, led to the establishment of mixed enterprises. The Government, in its effort to promote private investment, extends many privileges under the Investment Code.

Even so, manufacturing contributes less than 10 per cent of GDP. Industrial growth appears to be impeded mainly by the limited size of the domestic market and competitive difficulties from imports and from newly established industries in neighboring countries.

Privately operated factories are run profitably enough for most enterprises to amortize their capital within a relatively short period. The number, types, and value of output of all manufacturing enterprises in 1966 were as follows:

	Number of Plants	Output (Billion CFA Francs)
Agricultural and food processing	7	2.18
Chemical	3	0.23
Mechanical and electrical equipment	3	0.07
Printing	4	0.05
Other	. . .	0.54
Total	. . .	3.07

At present, mixed industrial enterprises are engaged in the manufacture of cement, bricks, furniture, and pharmaceutical products, and treatment of agricultural products. These mixed enterprises represent an
investment of about CFAF 2.1 billion, of which private industry contributed about CFAF 0.7 billion. On a cumulative basis, their annual
deficits ranged between CFAF 100 million and CFAF 300 million
during 1966–68.

The most developed industry is agricultural processing including the
processing of groundnuts, cotton, and cereal; other enterprises include a
slaughterhouse, soft drink plants, and bakeries. Groundnut processing
includes three shelling plants of the Groundnut Marketing Company
(SONARA), established in 1963, 1964, and 1966, and two private
groundnut oil mills, established in 1942 and 1954. The shelling plants
have a total investment of CFAF 95 million, a total capacity of 82,000
tons of unshelled groundnuts, and a production of 38,500 tons of
shelled groundnuts in 1967/68; the mills have an investment of
CFAF 176 million, a capacity of about 30,000 tons of unshelled
groundnuts, and a total production of about 20,000 tons in 1966.
Among the cereal processing plants is a publicly owned mill established
in 1965 with an investment of CFAF 98 million and a capacity of
5,500 tons a year; it treated 5,000 tons of paddy in 1967/68. A millet
mill, established in 1967, is also a public enterprise with a total investment of CFAF 56 million and a capacity of 3,000 tons of flour per year;
it produced 1,200 tons in 1968. A rye flour mill opened in 1964 but
closed in 1967 because of lack of rye supplies. The Niamey slaughterhouse was modernized in 1967. It is a mixed enterprise with a total
investment of CFAF 165 million and a capacity of 4,000 tons of meat
a year; in 1968, production reached 3,200 tons. There is a small tannery
in Zinder. Two privately owned soft drink plants were established in
1956 and 1963, with a total capacity of 6.5 million bottles a year.
Bakeries in Niamey and Zinder have a total capacity of 600 tons a
year. Two ice plants in Niamey each produce 3 tons daily.

The textile industry consists of three cotton ginning mills operated by
the French company CFDT, with a total investment of CFAF 104 million, a capacity of 20,000 tons per annum, and a production of 7,500
tons in 1966.

Manufacture of construction materials includes the country's largest industrial enterprise, the Cement Company (Société Nigérienne de Cimenterie, or SNC), a brickyard, and a tile factory. The Cement Company is a public enterprise with shares held by the Government and semipublic enterprises; it was established in 1966 and has a total investment of CFAF 1,623 million. Although annual capacity is 30,000 tons, production has been about 20,000 tons. The price of cement is fixed at CFAF 18,000 a ton, which is CFAF 1,000–2,000 below the price of comparable imported cement. The low utilization of capacity accounts for the high fixed costs, which are about two thirds of total costs; only 75 per cent of total operating expenditures, excluding amortization, are recovered, and in 1967 the deficit was about CFAF 300 million. Production in excess of local requirements cannot be sold in neighboring countries because of high transportation costs, competition from imported cement, and competition from cement produced in some of the potential purchaser countries. In an effort to reduce financial losses, the Cement Company in 1967 began using compressed groundnut shells as fuel instead of diesel oil. Further measures which are being considered include internal reorganization to reduce general expenditures, adjustment of the depreciation scales to the real wear and tear of the equipment, increase of equity capital to reduce interest payments, reduction of staff, and a moderate increase of the sales price.

The brickyard in Niamey replaced the brickyard in Yantala (southwest of Niamey), which was the oldest industrial enterprise in the country. The new brickyard, established in 1966 with a total investment of CFAF 80 million, has a capacity of 12,000 tons of bricks a year. Like the Cement Company, the brickyard incurs losses from overcapacity. The tile factory, a private enterprise with an investment of CFAF 22 million, was established in 1965, and has a capacity of 120 square meters of tile a day.

Chemical manufacturing, only slightly developed, comprises plastics, soap, and paint factories. The plastics factory started operations in Niamey in 1965 and utilizes plastic material for the manufacture of shoes and household equipment. Total investment is CFAF 43 million, capacity is 600,000 pairs of shoes a year, and actual production was 200,000 pairs in 1966. The soap and perfume plants, belonging to a private enterprise, were founded in 1965 with an investment of

CFAF 145 million. The capacity is 3,600–4,000 tons of soap and 1,000 small bottles of perfume a year. Actual soap production in 1966 was 2,400 tons. The paint factory was established in December 1968 with a capacity of 600 tons of paint annually. Total investment was CFAF 16 million.

The metal industry includes two plants. The Société Nigérienne de Fabrications Métalliques, a public enterprise established in 1966 with a total investment of CFAF 38 million, manufactures metal furniture and agricultural tools. Production, valued at CFAF 72 million in 1968, is below capacity. A private enterprise producing about 480 tons of iron scaffoldings a year was established in 1967 with an investment of CFAF 8 million.

Other manufacturing projects under construction in 1968 involve investments of CFAF 2,538 million. They included a textile mill, a brewery, and a tannery. The textile mill, a mixed enterprise with large participation of the Trading Company (Société Nationale de Commerce et de Production, or COPRO-NIGER), will employ about 600 workmen and have a capacity of 1,600 tons of finished material a year. It was expected that operations would start by the end of 1969 and reach full capacity in 1972. The brewery was to be completed during 1969 and to have a capacity of 30,000 hectoliters annually.

Industrial projects under study include a dairy, two groundnut oil mills, a groundnut shelling plant, two tanneries, a match factory, two soft drink plants, fruit and meat processing plants, a sugar refinery, a radio assembly plant, an oxygen bottling plant, and a broom factory.

POWER AND WATER RESOURCES

Electrical power in Niger is produced by diesel generators. Distribution of electricity is provided in the urban centers of Niamey, Zinder, Maradi, Agadez, and Tahoua (Table 10). In Niamey, the Société Africaine d'Electricité (SAFELEC) formerly operated the power stations and distributed the electricity under a concession by which it received large freedom in establishing rates and in managing financial matters. Expenditures including amortization were covered by receipts. In September 1968 the Electric Power Company (Société Nigérienne d'Electricité, or NIGELEC) a mixed enterprise, was established to take

TABLE 10. NIGER: INSTALLED CAPACITY AND PRODUCTION OF ELECTRIC POWER, 1964-69

| | Installed Capacity | | | | | | Production and Consumption | | | | | |
| | Kilowatts | | | | | | Thousand kilowatt hours | | | | | |
	1964	1965	1966	1967	1968	1969 [1]	1964	1965	1966	1967	1968	1969 [1]
Niamey	6,000	6,000	9,200	9,200	10,800	10,800	14,291	15,782	19,209	21,804	24,586	27,044
Zinder	580	720	720	720	720	970	1,420	1,557	1,675	1,919	1,964	2,062
Maradi	550	550	550	550	840	1,090	1,237	1,278	1,657	1,701	2,129	2,448
Agadez	200	200	200	200	200	240	126	248	342	385	424	466
Tahoua	55	55	55	112	112	272	70 [1]	75 [1]	81 [2]	90 [1]	125 [1]	150
Total	7,385	7,525	10,725	10,782	12,672	13,372	17,144	18,940	22,964	25,899	29,228	32,170

Source: Data provided by the Nigerien authorities.

[1] Estimated.
[2] The Société Africaine d'Electricité estimated the production for 1966 on the basis of an average distribution of six hours a day.

over that company's installations and ensure production and distribution of electricity in Niger.

In Zinder, Maradi, and Agadez, the Central Government owns the producing facilities and establishes the rates, while the Electric Power Company is in charge of management under a special contract. Financial operations of the governmment-owned stations of Zinder and Maradi have improved in the past few years, and profits on these operations partly compensate for losses incurrred in Agadez. Operation of the power station in Tahoua and distribution of electricity were taken over by the Electric Power Company in August 1968, but the installations belong to the Government.

Total installed power of these five urban centers with the installation of additional generating sets, increased from 7,385 kilowatts in 1964 to 12,672 kilowatts in 1968. In addition, the Central Government operates small units in rural communities, having an approximate installed capacity of 200 kilowatts. In 1969, it was expected that installation of further generating sets would increase total capacity by some 700 kilowatts.

Although total producing capacity exceeded needs in 1969, consumption is expanding, and some facilities will become obsolete in the near future. Consumption rose from 16 million kilowatt-hours in 1963 to 29 million kilowatt-hours in 1968, as a result of the growing use of air conditioners and other electrical appliances. In 1969, consumption was expected to increase to about 32 million kilowatt-hours. No breakdown is available between industrial and household consumption. The rates charged vary according to geographical regions and the mode of consumption, with home consumption rates higher than industrial charges.

Although the hydroelectric projects south of Niamey are at an advanced stage of study, further studies with regard to seasonal variation of the water level of the Niger River are necessary. The CFAF 25–30 billion project calls for installation in three stages of 25,000, 75,000, and 100,000 kilowatts. Another hydroelectric project is contemplated on the Mékrou, on the Dahomey-Niger border.

Studies on solar energy have been undertaken with the cooperation of the French Commissariat à l'Energie Atomique (CEA). Two collector aerials devised to measure the solar energy have been operational at Niamey airport since early 1965.

Scarcity of water resources is the greatest impediment to economic development. Distribution of water in urban centers is undertaken by the Electric Power Company. The Water Supply Office (Office d'Entretien des Eaux du Sous-Sol, or OFEDES) is another public enterprise concerned with water distribution. The supply of water in the cattle-raising areas has been developed by means of small wells and drillings financed largely by Germany (DM 13 million) and EDF [3] (equivalent to $1.3 million).

TRANSPORTATION

In 1968 the road network of Niger (see map) extended for 7,468 kilometers, of which 380 kilometers were hard-surfaced roads, 2,463 kilometers all-weather roads covered with laterite, and 4,625 kilometers tracks not usable all year round.

A comprehensive road improvement program for 1967–75 was laid out by the Department of Public Works. This program includes asphalting the central east-west axis between Niamey and Zinder; expanding and improving roads linking the groundnut and cotton producing areas with their processing plants and the local markets; asphalting the road to Dahomey, a main outlet for exports; and building three bridges, one across the Niger in Niamey. Total investment under this program is expected to approach CFAF 18 billion, of which CFAF 0.8 billion is for studies and tests. Investment in 1968 was expected to be just over CFAF 2 billion, with similar annual investments until 1973; thereafter investment is expected to decline to CFAF 1 billion annually. The program will be financed on the basis of 12 per cent from the national budget, and 88 per cent from foreign grants and loans—CFAF 9.2 billion from EEC, CFAF 3.1 billion from Fonds d'Aide et de Coopération (FAC), CFAF 2.9 billion from IDA, and CFAF 0.7 billion from U.S. AID.

Niger has one vehicle for every 260 inhabitants. At the end of 1967, the number of registered vehicles was 8,450, including 2,859 passenger cars, 2,838 pickups, 318 trucks under 5 tons, and 574 trucks of 5 tons and over. The remainder comprised motorcycles, trailers, and tractors. In addition, 1,629 vehicles were registered by the dip-

---

[3] European Development Fund (Fonds Européen de Développement, or FED).

lomatic corps and people with similar privileges. The total number of
vehicles in operation increased by about 24 per cent during 1967; more
than half of this increase was on account of the diplomatic corps.

Although transportation is largely privately controlled in Niger, the
Société Nationale des Transporteurs Nigériens (SNTN), a semipublic
enterprise, has a fleet of about 150 commercial vehicles providing
transportation for practically all administrative, postal, and military
needs. Its rates, like other truck rates in Niger, depend on the distance
and type of road. The Trading Company (COPRO-NIGER) and the
Groundnut Marketing Company (SONARA) operate their own fleets.
The Société Nationale des Transports Urbains operates the city bus
lines in Niamey.

Most of Niger's foreign trade is transacted through the ports of
Cotonou in Dahomey and Lagos in Nigeria. Comprehensive traffic
figures are not available, but transportation of groundnuts, Niger's most
important export product, may be indicative of the distribution
of the foreign traffic of Niger between these two ports. During
1962/63–1965/66 about 80 per cent of the groundnut exports were
shipped via Nigeria. In 1966/67, because of the events in Nigeria,
104,000 tons of groundnuts, or 64 per cent of total exports were
shipped via Lagos and 59,000 tons via Cotonou. In 1968, more than
two thirds of the exports were transported through Nigeria. Lagos
forms the natural outlet for the trade of south-central and eastern Niger
because this route offers cheaper transport costs than shipment via
Cotonou.

The groundnut producing center at Maradi is at about the same distance from Lagos and from Cotonou, but the Nigerian route is much
cheaper as 1,150 kilometers out of a total of 1,440 kilometers are by
railroad, compared with 438 kilometers out of a total of 1,450 kilometers via Cotonou. However, the Government has paid a subsidy to
equate the costs of shipment via the two ports. Before 1959 the Government paid the subsidy direct to the Dahomey railways, which also
operated, as part of this arrangement, a truck line between Niger and
the railroad station at Parakou in Dahomey. This arrangement was generally called Opération Hirondelle. In 1959 a common venture—the
Dahomey-Niger Railway and Transport System (Organisation Commune Dahomey-Niger des Chemins de Fer et des Transports, or OCDN)

—was formed to administer the Dahomey railways, the wharf in Cotonou, and Opération Hirondelle. This venture was jointly subsidized by the two Governments. Apparently, the principal reason for attempting to redirect the trade of south-central and eastern Niger via Cotonou was a desire to maintain action independent of Nigeria and to promote economic interdependence between UMOA countries.

Opération Hirondelle was operative only from November through March, peak period for collection of groundnuts in south-central Niger and shipment to the Atlantic coast for export. This period is called "in pool" and the rest of the year "out pool." The venture had the purpose of attracting traffic, which would otherwise use the Nigerian route, by granting carriers a subsidy per ton/kilometer during the "in pool" period larger than that during the "out pool" period. During both periods, the subsidy applied to both the southbound trip, when trucks were loaded, and the northbound trip, when trucks were either partly loaded or empty. In the beginning, only licensed carriers, whether nationals from Niger or Dahomey, were entitled to the subsidy and were in fact allocated a quota. Subsequently, the system was liberalized with the subsidy payable to all carriers. In 1967/68 the subsidy paid (CFAF 5.65 per ton/kilometer in that year) was uniform for any carrier throughout the year and for both southbound and northbound traffic (Table 11).

TABLE 11. NIGER: SUBSIDIES TO ORGANISATION COMMUNE DAHOMEY-NIGER DES CHEMINS DE FER ET DES TRANSPORTS (OCDN), 1963/64–1968/69

(In CFA francs per ton/kilometer)

	"In Pool" (Nov.–Mar.)		"Out Pool" (Apr.–Oct.)	
	Loaded	Empty	Loaded	Empty
1963/64	7.60	7.60	6.00	4.00
1964/65	7.00	6.00	6.00	4.00
1965/66	6.00	6.00	6.00	4.00
1966/67	6.00	6.00	6.00	4.00
1967/68	5.65	5.65	5.65	5.65
1968/69 [1]	4.65	4.65	4.65	4.65

Source: Data provided by the Nigerien authorities.
[1] Estimated.

The volume of freight by truck to and from Niger increased substantially from 79,000 tons in 1965 to 108,000 tons in 1966 and by a further 43,000 tons in 1967 (Table 12), owing to the events in Nigeria. In 1968, this volume declined to 132,000 tons. Exports usually amounted to about 30 per cent of total truck traffic, except for 1967,

TABLE 12. NIGER: TRAFFIC, NET OPERATING INCOME, AND SUBSIDIES, ORGANISATION COMMUNE DAHOMEY-NIGER DES CHEMINS DE FER ET DES TRANSPORTS (OCDN), 1960–68

	1960	1961	1962	1963	1964	1965	1966	1967	1968
PASSENGERS (thousands)									
Passenger Wharf[1]	5	4	5	3	4	—	—	—	—
Railways	1,224	946	1,405	1,513	1,459	1,439	1,295	1,185	1,011
FREIGHT (thousand metric tons)									
Goods Wharf[1]	302	275	268	292	273	30			
Railways	174	507	894	945	252	126	164	220	197
Truck lines to and from Niger	80	89	101	95	78	79	108	151	132
Exports	...	...	...	27	24	21	31	78	63
VALUE (million CFA francs)									
Net operating income[2]									
Wharf[1]	25	32	56	83	32	−67			
Railways	−161	−80	81	77	−126	−167	−124	4	−68[3]
Operation Hirondelle	−158	−182	−157	−171	−225	−130	—[4]	—[4]	...
Readjustments[5]	29	—	−58	−10	—	—			—
Total net operating income (or deficit −)	−265	−230	−78	−21	−319	−364	−124	4	−68
Subsidies received									
Nigerien Government	133	115	58	40	70	135	—[6]	—	—
Dahomean Government	133	115	58	40	153	125	—	34	17
Total subsidies received	265	230	116	80	223	260	—	34	17
Net operating income (or deficit −) after subsidies	—	—	38	50	−96	−104	−124	38	−51

Sources: Organisation Commune Dahomey-Niger des Chemins de Fer et des Transports, *Bilans au 31 décembre 1964, 1965, 1967,* and Ministère des Travaux Publics, des Transports, des Mines et de l'Urbanisme, Direction des Transports, *Rapport Annuel.*

[1] On April 30, 1965, the activities of the wharf in Cotonou were discontinued since the port of Cotonou started operations in January 1965.

[2] After partial amortization (mainly rolling stock).

[3] Estimated.

[4] Expenditures equal receipts.

[5] Accounting readjustments made after the closing of the fiscal year.

[6] In January 1966 the Government of Niger abolished the *taxe de péréquation* on goods shipped to western Niger and increased the tariff of OCDN instead. Niger discontinued payment of subsidies to the Dahomean part of the traffic, but finances any deficit on traffic to and from Niger.

when it was over 50 per cent because of export traffic rerouted from Nigeria to Dahomey. From 80 to 90 per cent of exports hauled by the Dahomey-Niger Railway and Transport System are groundnuts. Import traffic in 1967, consisting mainly of gasoline and petroleum products, represented 60 per cent.

Net operating income of the Dahomey-Niger Railway and Transport System has fluctuated greatly since 1960. Between 1960 and 1963, its deficit declined from CFAF 265 million to CFAF 21 million, mainly reflecting increased earnings of the Dahomean railways. They operated at a high level of capacity during this period as a result of carrying, in addition to usual freight, rocks needed for the construction of the port of Cotonou. Losses of the Dahomey-Niger Railway and Transport System in these years were shared equally by the two Governments. In 1964, when the construction of Cotonou harbor was finished and because certain other problems arose, losses of the Dahomey-Niger Railway increased sharply to CFAF 319 million. According to the Dosso Agreement of 1964, operation of the new port of Cotonou was removed from the Railway. Niger was to bear 37 per cent of the Railway's deficits and Dahomey 63 per cent. Nevertheless, the deficit rose to CFAF 364 million in 1965, mainly because the activities of the old wharf of Cotonou, which had operated at a profit, were terminated. Increased traffic in 1966 reduced the total deficit to CFAF 124 million. A small operating profit of CFAF 4 million, instead of a deficit resulted in 1967 from events in Nigeria which caused much of Niger's total export-import traffic to go via Dahomey. Provisional results for 1968 indicate a deficit of about CFAF 68 million with reorientation of traffic through Nigeria and the high depreciation rate. For the next few years, it is expected that balanced operations will result from heavier traffic generated by the uranium mine being established and growing gasoline and petroleum consumption in Niger.

Niger may utilize, in addition to the traditional ports of entry Lagos and Cotonou, the ports of Abidjan and Lomé. Abidjan, with lower freight rates from and to Europe than Cotonou, more specialized port equipment, and more frequent traffic, handled 8,600 tons in 1966, and 10,100 tons in 1967 of merchandise destined for Niger. The new port of Lomé, completed in 1968, may also attract some traffic which used to go through Cotonou.

Niger's river network suitable for traffic consists of the River Niger and four of its tributaries. Only the Niger and one of its tributaries are navigable all year round by boats of up to 2 tons' loading capacity. River transport is believed to be important, but no estimates are available.

Niger's principal airports besides Niamey (class A), are Agadez, Maradi, Tahoua, and Zinder (class B); 18 minor airfields; and 69 private airstrips. The national airline, Air Niger, was established in February 1966. It is a semipublic enterprise with a capital of CFAF 10 million; 60 per cent was subscribed by the Government and 34 per cent by the Société pour le Développpement du Transport Aérien en Afrique, a French company controlled by the Union des Transporteurs Aériens. Air Niger operates aircraft on domestic routes. During the first business year from May 1966 until December 1967, Air Niger transported 10,704 passengers and 382 tons of freight and mail. The gross profit for the first business year before taxes amounted to CFAF 2.6 million. However, if CFAF 2.7 million in wages and salaries for the flying personnel, which were paid by FAC, are taken into account, Air Niger would have had a slight deficit. In 1968 it had a deficit of CFAF 11.1 million.

COMMERCE

After agriculture, commerce contributes the most to the GDP in Niger. This sector, predominantly commerce but also including transport and some other services (see Table 1), accounted for 22 per cent of GDP in 1963 and 23 per cent in 1966.

Before Niger became independent, practically all of its trade was privately controlled. The import and export trade was largely in the hands of foreign, mostly French and Lebanese, firms. Since 1962 a number of semipublic agencies have taken over part of the trading activity.

The Groundnut Marketing Company (Société Nigérienne de Commercialisation de l'Arachide, or SONARA), established in 1962, is a joint stock company, 50 per cent owned by public and semipublic bodies. It has a monopoly of groundnut exports and sales to groundnut oil mills. It deals exclusively in groundnut marketing and related activities such as shelling, transportation, and storage (see Tables 4 and 5). Its profits are determined by a system of floor and ceiling prices and commissions on groundnut shelling and transport. The Company's nominal capital is CFAF 300 million; its turnover, though fluctuating with the size and price of the groundnut crop, increased from CFAF 5.2 billion in 1964/65 to CFAF 7.2 billion in 1966/67 (Table 13). The Company's gross and operating profit more than doubled during the same period; its net profit increased at a slower rate (from CFAF 49 million in 1964/65 to CFAF 123 million in 1966/67) because of higher administrative and financial costs. Data for 1967/68, though not yet available, were expected to show a decline in net profit to about CFAF 90 million. The financial outlook for 1968/69 was favorable. The Company's assets and liabilities are shown in Table 14.

The Trading Company (Société Nationale de Commerce et de Production, or COPRO-NIGER), established in 1962, is also organized as a joint stock company with the majority of shares belonging to public

TABLE 13. NIGER: SOCIÉTÉ NIGÉRIENNE DE COMMERCIALISATION DE L'ARACHIDE, STATEMENT OF INCOME, YEARS ENDED SEPTEMBER 30, 1964/65–1966/67

(In millions of CFA francs)

	1964/65	1965/66	1966/67
Sales	5,166.1	7,321.1	7,184.0
Cost of goods sold [1]	4,810.3	6,628.0	6,408.0
Gross profit	355.8	693.1	776.0
Operating expenses			
Selling, administrative and general expenses [2]	−134.2	−372.6	−330.8
Financial costs	−98.4	−157.5	−224.3
Amortization and depreciation allowances	−48.4	−61.2	−62.4
Operating profit	74.8	101.8	158.5
Other income			
Interest and dividends	0.1	—	—
Other profits	5.3	7.3	32.4
Other deductions			
Subventions and contributions	−4.0	—	—
Exceptional and other losses	−2.1	−15.2	−0.8
Earnings before taxation on income	74.1	93.9	190.1
Taxes on income	−24.8	−33.0	−66.8
Net profit	49.3	60.9	123.3
Total cash generated [3]	*97.7*	*122.1*	*185.7*

Source: Data provided by the Nigerien authorities.

[1] Purchases, net movement in stocks, commissions to intermediaries, indirect taxes, and costs of handling, shelling, and transportation (including insurance).
[2] Personnel, travel, studies, supplies, services, fire insurance, direct taxes, and miscellaneous operating costs.
[3] Net profit, plus amortization and depreciation allowances.

TABLE 14. NIGER: SOCIÉTÉ NIGÉRIENNE DE COMMERCIALISATION DE L'ARACHIDE, ASSETS AND LIABILITIES, YEARS ENDED SEPTEMBER 30, 1965–67

(*In millions of CFA francs*)

	1965	1966	1967
Assets			
Current assets			
Cash	64.8	116.2	63.0
Receivables	570.6	488.9	478.9
Inventories	160.6	142.8	2,091.0
Total current assets	796.0	747.9	2,632.9
Fixed assets			
Organization and preoperation			
expenses	9.1	9.1	9.1
Less amortization	−2.8	−9.1	−9.1
Net	6.2	—	—
Property and equipment	177.9	263.6	304.4
Less depreciation	−69.1	−118.0	−126.6
Net	108.8	145.6	177.8
Participations, deposits, and			
guarantees	7.1	6.8	7.4
Total fixed assets	122.1	152.4	185.2
Total assets = liabilities	**918.1**	**900.3**	**2,818.1**
Liabilities			
Current liabilities			
Accounts payable	402.1	120.2	817.7
Taxes on income	24.8	31.8	66.8
Short-term bank credit	81.4	190.6	1,274.0
Total current liabilities	508.3	342.6	2,158.5
Long-term and medium-term debt	—	130.0	130.0
Shareholders' equity			
Capital	300.0	300.0	300.0
Reserves	4.7	66.8	106.3
Nonimputed profits	55.8	—	—
Net income after taxes	49.3	60.9	123.3
Total shareholders' equity	409.8	427.7	529.6

Source: Data provided by the Nigerien authorities.

or semipublic bodies (Government 33 per cent, Union Nigérienne de Crédit et de Coopération 15 per cent, and the Development Bank— Banque de Développement de la République du Niger (BDRN)—15 per cent). Its resources consist of CFAF 150 million capital and medium-term and short-term credits, mainly from the Development Bank (Table 15). Its principal function is to maintain stability of food prices in the country and to operate a system of wholesale and retail outlets. It maintains a network of about 50 shops, mainly in rural areas where cooperatives do not operate. It is also expected to stimulate diversification of agricultural production by organizing the marketing of little developed or new products.

Until 1968 the Trading Company (COPRO-NIGER) held the monopoly of meat exports, was the main distributor of food crops within the country, and controlled most of the imports of textiles. Recently, however, the Government established a cattle ranch which is expected to supply most of the meat for export as soon as the livestock population of this ranch has matured and increased sufficiently. Since October 1968 the monopoly of meat export has been transferred to the newly established Livestock Products Marketing Company (Société Nigérienne d'Exportation des Ressources d'Animaux, or SONERAN). This Company, which is in charge of the sale of meat from slaughter-houses, is a mixed enterprise with total investments of CFAF 185 million. The Trading Company's role on the domestic food crop market will also be curtailed through the promotion of the cooperative movement. Finally, the completion of the textile factory and the Trading Company's subsequent sales of its products will result in a reduction in the Company's profit margins, compared with those prevailing on imported textiles. Its net profit rose from CFAF 3 million in 1963/64 to CFAF 16 million in 1965/66, but in 1966/67 it just broke even (see Table 15). Its assets and liabilities are shown in Table 16.

TABLE 15.   NIGER: SOCIÉTÉ NATIONALE DE COMMERCE ET DE PRODUCTION,[1]
STATEMENT OF INCOME, YEARS ENDED SEPTEMBER 30, 1963/64–1966/67
(*In millions of CFA francs*)

	1963/64	1964/65	1965/66	1966/67
Sales	1,480.7	2,000.0	2,492.6	2,488.4
Cost of goods sold [2]	1,321.4	1,740.4	2,156.8	2,158.5
Gross profit	159.3	259.6	335.8	329.9
Selling, administrative, and general expenses [3]	126.4	166.9	181.0	180.8
Financial costs	38.2	75.8	97.4	100.1
Amortization and depreciation allowances	22.1	27.7	23.7	39.5
Operating profit or deficit (−)	−27.4	−10.8	33.7	9.5
Other income				
Interest and dividends	2.0	—	—	—
Commissions	8.6	—	—	—
Insurance, indemnities, and returns of amounts overpaid	9.7	8.2	—	—
Exceptional and other profits	10.5	9.5	17.2	22.6
Other deductions	—	—	−34.6	−32.1
Net profit	3.4	6.9	16.3	—
Total cash generated [4]	*25.5*	*34.6*	*40.0*	*39.5*

Source: Data provided by the Nigerien authorities.

[1] Trading Company (COPRO-NIGER).
[2] Purchases, net movement in stocks, transportation, and taxes (direct and indirect).
[3] Personnel, services, supplies, and miscellaneous operating expenditures.
[4] Net profit plus amortization and depreciation allowances.

TABLE 16. NIGER: SOCIÉTÉ NATIONALE DE COMMERCE ET DE PRODUCTION, ASSETS AND LIABILITIES, YEARS ENDED SEPTEMBER 30, 1964–67
(*In millions of CFA francs*)

	1964	1965	1966	1967
Assets				
Current assets				
Cash	16.3	91.0	58.5	18.8
Receivables	268.9	327.0	413.4	634.3
Less provision for doubtful accounts	−3.8	—	—	−39.8
Net receivables	265.1	327.0	413.4	594.5
Inventories	554.3	892.7	871.0	815.4
Less amortization	−3.5	—	—	—
Net inventories	550.8	892.7	871.0	815.4
Total current assets	832.2	1,310.7	1,342.9	1,428.7
Fixed assets				
Organization and preoperation expenses	1.4	3.1	3.1	3.1
Less amortization	−0.8	−0.7	1.3	−3.1
Net	0.6	2.4	1.8	—
Property and equipment	183.6	192.4	206.7	120.4
Less depreciation	−32.8	−36.1	59.1	54.6
Net property and equipment	150.8	156.3	147.6	65.8
Participation, deposits, and guarantees	6.8	9.7	17.7	17.4
Total fixed assets	158.2	168.4	167.1	83.2
Miscellaneous	67.2	33.5	0.4	—
Assets = liabilities	**1,057.6**	**1,512.6**	**1,510.4**	**1,511.9**
Liabilities				
Current liabilities				
Accounts payable	185.7	276.3	340.8	636.2
Short-term bank credit	624.7	906.9	784.4	661.7
Government	4.3	79.3	163.7	—
Total current liabilities	814.7	1,262.5	1,288.9	1,297.9
Medium-term debt	58.7	54.8	50.7	56.8
Shareholders' equity				
Capital	150.0	150.0	150.0	150.0
Reserves	8.2	7.3	7.3	7.2
Net income of the year	3.4	6.9	16.3	—
Less losses of previous years	—	−9.7	−2.8	—
Total shareholders' equity	161.6	154.5	170.8	157.2
Miscellaneous	22.6	40.8	—	—

Source: Data provided by the Nigerien authorities.

The Office National des Produits Pharmaceutiques et Chimiques is a public agency which enjoys a monopoly in the marketing of chemical and medical supplies and also operates its own retail outlets. Its resources consist essentially of government grants and short-term bank credit. It incurred losses in its first years of operation, but management techniques have recently been improved and former losses are now being amortized at a rapid rate.

ECONOMIC DEVELOPMENT PLANNING

DEVELOPMENT PLANS

Early Plans

Economic development is coordinated by the Planning Commission in the office of the President. The First Development Plan (1961–64), provided for investment expenditures totaling CFAF 30.1 billion; public investment outlays were to account for 63 per cent of this amount and private investments for 37 per cent. Actual disbursements during the four years, both public (CFAF 12.4 billion) and private (CFAF 12.8 billion) amounted to CFAF 25.2 billion, or 84 per cent of the original estimates. About 64 per cent of the total was financed from domestic sources and the remainder from foreign sources, largely grants and loans from FAC and EDF. Investments in basic infrastructure improvements, including roads and education and health facilities, accounted for 57 per cent, agriculture and related activities for 36 per cent, and other outlays, mainly for the preparation of projects and administrative training, for 7 per cent.

The Second Development Plan (1965–68) originally called for public investments of CFAF 33.3 billion and private investments of CFAF 9.9 billion, totaling CFAF 43.2 billion, or an amount 71 per cent higher than actual investment outlays during the first plan. The original plan estimate was subsequently revised downward to CFAF 30 billion, or to about the same level as the targets of the first plan. Though actual private investment under the second plan is not known, actual public expenditures amounted to CFAF 12.7 billion, or 38 per cent of target, compared with a 55 per cent realization rate under the previous plan. The relatively lower realization rate was due partly to the limited absorptive capacity of the economy and the shift in reliance on foreign financing (from 36 per cent during the first plan to 83 per cent in the second plan), which entailed procedural and project preparation difficulties (Table 17).

Foreign financing of the public sector development expenditures of CFAF 10.6 billion was obtained from FAC (34 per cent), EDF (30 per cent), and AID and other sources (18 per cent). The Nigerien Government's contribution of CFAF 2.1 billion was mainly from the

TABLE 17. NIGER: ACTUAL AND PLANNED PUBLIC SECTOR INVESTMENTS AND FINANCING, 1965-72

(Amount in millions of CFA francs)

| | Actual 1965-68[1] | | Planned | | | |
| | | | 1968/69-1971/72 | | 1968/69 | |
	Amount	Per cent of total	Amount	Per cent of total	Amount	Per cent of total
Expenditures						
By purpose						
Health and education	3,306	26.0	5,727	15.4	1,819	21.4
Water and mineral resources	2,810	22.1	3,772	10.2	1,351	15.9
Roads and transportation	2,518	19.8	16,810	45.3	2,508	29.6
Agriculture	1,958	15.4	7,036	19.0	1,842	21.7
Animal husbandry	572	4.5	705	1.9	232	2.7
Forestry	246	1.9	231	0.6	66	0.8
Telecommunications	140	1.1	498	1.3	112	1.3
Energy	127	1.0	59	0.2	33	0.4
Others	1,038	8.2	2,246	6.1	522	6.2
By type						
Construction	7,921	62.3	26,538	71.6	4,765	56.2
Equipment	2,162	17.0	5,220	14.1	1,695	20.0
Project preparation	1,666	13.1	2,835	7.6	1,257	14.8
Personnel	966	7.6	2,491	6.7	768	9.0
Total expenditures	**12,715**	**100.0**	**37,084**	**100.0**	**8,485**	**100.0**
Domestic financing						
Budget[2]	1,488	11.7	3,508	9.5	1,013	11.9
Road Fund	228	1.8	298	0.8	186	2.2
Local governments	420	3.3	152	0.4	51	0.6
Total domestic financing	2,136	16.8	3,958	10.7	1,250	14.7
Foreign financing						
France (FAC)	4,450[3]	35.0[3]	7,383	19.9	2,581	30.4
EDF	3,865	30.4	11,101	29.9	2,218	26.2
U.S. AID	394	3.1	889	2.4	392	4.6
Other	1,870	14.7	13,753	37.1	2,044	24.1
Total foreign financing	10,579	83.2	33,126	89.3	7,235	85.3

Source: Data provided by the Nigerien authorities.

[1] Period covered extends from January 1, 1965 through September 30, 1968.
[2] Includes expenditures through the ordinary and the capital budgets.
[3] Except for CFAF 76 million (0.6 per cent) other French aid in 1965–68.

capital budget (12 per cent), local governments (3 per cent), and the Road Fund (2 per cent). There was no net recourse to bank financing during the plan period. Actual investment outlays were for the purposes of health and education (26 per cent), water and mineral resources (22 per cent), roads and transportation (20 per cent), agriculture and animal husbandry (20 per cent), and other purposes, including tele-communications, forestry, and energy, the remainder.

Third Development Plan (1968/69–1971/72)

The Third Development Plan (October 1, 1968–September 30, 1972) for the first time attempts to assess the impact of investment expenditures on general economic activity. Moreover, expenditures are recorded on a fiscal year basis. The new plan, covering four years, provides for continuous programing, through a four-year investment program prepared each year for the public sector. Although such a program is partly based on the rhythm of expenditures in previous years, as well as the anticipated rate of disbursements on account of foreign assistance, it is also based on the assumption that project credits opened in one year may be consummated during the following year.

Under the third plan, projected public sector expenditures total CFAF 37.1 billion, or almost three times actual expenditures under the second plan. The anticipated foreign financing of 89 per cent is slightly higher than that of the second plan. So far, only 19 per cent of total expected foreign financing has been secured, mainly for first year outlays. For the entire plan period the largest share of investments is planned for improvements in roads and transportation (45 per cent); agriculture, animal husbandry, and water and mineral resources (31 per cent); health and education (15 per cent); and other purposes (9 per cent).

Planned expenditures in 1968/69 are estimated at CFAF 8.5 billion. Roads and transportation will absorb CFAF 2.5 billion (30 per cent), agriculture and animal husbandry CFAF 2.1 billion (24 per cent), health and education CFAF 1.8 billion (21 per cent), and water and mineral resources CFAF 1.4 billion (16 per cent). To finance these outlays, domestic sources, mainly budgetary contributions, are expected to provide CFAF 1.2 billion (15 per cent), and foreign sources the remainder. Although France continues to be the main source of foreign financing, its contribution has been declining in favor of multilateral assistance. By the end of the four-year plan period, the French share is expected to decline to 20 per cent, the EDF share to continue at about 30 per cent, other aid to increase to almost 40 per cent, and financing from domestic sources to furnish over 10 per cent.

INVESTMENT CODE

The first Investment Code was adopted in July 1961. It provided tax relief for newly created enterprises for periods ranging up to 20 years, but only those whose activities were of particular importance to Niger's economic and social development could be granted relief for more than 10 years. The 1961 Code was modified on February 1, 1963 to prohibit enterprises benefiting from the Investment Code to repatriate capital during the first 3 years. Moreover, repatriation of profits, salaries, and capital were made subject to the exchange regulations of the franc area; previously, conditions of such repatriation were separately formulated for each approved enterprise.

A new Investment Code was adopted on July 31, 1968. The new Code, which applies to newly established industrial enterprises or to the substantial expansion of existing ones, provides three different categories of treatment, classified as *régime de droit commun, régime d'agrément*, and *régime conventionnel*. The first category (*régime de droit commun*) applies to all investments characterized as having low priority in terms of the national development plan. It exempts for a period of 5 years all newly created enterprises from paying license fees (*patentes*), and profit and real estate taxes.

The second and third categories apply to enterprises which are likely to make a significant contribution to Niger's development effort. The second category (*régime d'agrément*) allows tax relief for 3 to 10 years, and the third category (*régime conventionnel*) for 10 to 20 years. Common provisions of the second and third categories are (1) exemptions from import taxes and fiscal duties on imported raw materials and machinery; (2) exemptions from profit, real estate, and consumption taxes and license fees; (3) reductions of up to 33 per cent in the turnover tax (for 3 years for the first category and 5 years for the second and third) in export fiscal duties, and in the standard export tax. The latter tax may also be reduced by 50–100 per cent, depending on the precise nature of the investment concerned. Further reductions in the rate of taxation, also to be determined on the basis of individual enterprises, are to be allowed for imported fuel. In order to be eligible for treatment under the third category, an enterprise must have a minimum investment of CFAF 500 million, must provide employment for 500 individuals, or must account for an expected value added by its production equal to CFAF 500 million or more a year. To ensure the special preference accorded under this category, the Government requires a formal agreement with the industrial enterprise. Included in this agreement is the stipulation that should a change in tax laws result in a higher rate of taxation, the enterprise would be exonerated from the increase. On the other hand, the enterprise would benefit from any abolition of taxes or lowering of tax rates.

PRICES, WAGES, AND EMPLOYMENT

PRICES

Consumer Price Indices

Two consumer price indices based on prices in Niamey are compiled for African and European consumers. These indices include some items, notably foodstuffs, which are subject to price controls. No wholesale price index is tabulated.

The African consumer price index is based on the consumption pattern of an unskilled worker's family. It includes 76 products, 43 of them foodstuffs and beverages. This index declined by nearly 4 per cent between 1961 and 1963, but rose by 2 per cent in 1964 and by 5 per cent in 1965 (Table 18). The increase in 1965 was due to upward movements in the cost of utilities and household goods (12 per cent), foodstuffs and beverages (4 per cent), and clothing (2 per cent). The poor food crop in 1965 resulted in a substantial rise of food prices. Apart from this temporary factor, higher prices have resulted from the 1963 change in the base for levying import taxes from c.i.f. Cotonou to c.i.f. Niger's border, and from heavier indirect taxation. The miscella-

TABLE 18. NIGER: INDEX OF CONSUMER PRICES IN NIAMEY, ANNUAL AVERAGES, 1961–68

	1961	1962	1963	1964	1965	1966	1967	1968
AFRICAN CONSUMER *(July 1962–July 1963 = 100)*								
Foodstuffs and beverages	103.2	102.0	101.0	99.7	104.0	119.8	118.5	113.8
Clothing	102.0	98.9	100.3	97.9	99.7	103.6	108.5	105.6
Utilities and households	103.0	101.4	92.4	94.2	105.9	108.6	113.3	115.3
Miscellaneous	97.0	94.5	102.2	103.5	111.7	113.5	117.9	117.7
Global index	101.7	100.7	97.8	99.8	104.9	116.0	116.6	113.6
EUROPEAN CONSUMER *(1960 = 100)*								
Foodstuffs	110.4	107.4	110.4	118.8	126.0	131.4	141.2	143.3
Clothing	110.8	107.3	105.8	115.6	122.7	128.1	139.2	146.4
Utilities and households								
Utilities	100.0	100.0	111.7	112.5	114.8	118.9	119.0	119.0
Households	—	—	—	—	125.0	125.1	135.4	136.8
Servants	105.5	100.9	99.9	112.4	112.4	112.5	141.3	155.8
Miscellaneous	104.0	103.6	105.1	106.7	106.6	112.2	127.5	137.0
Global index	107.9	105.0	108.1	115.9	120.4	125.2	137.4	143.8

Sources: Commissariat Général au Plan, Service de la Statistique et de la Mécanographie, *Bulletin de Statistiques*, and data provided by the Nigerien authorities.

neous item in the index rose in recent years, reflecting the impact of heavier taxation. Clothing, however, rose only slightly because import tariffs were reduced and larger imports of low-priced textiles came in from the Far East. In 1966 the African consumer price index increased by 11 per cent because of a 15 per cent rise in food prices following the bad 1965/66 crop of millet, sorghum, and beans, basic items in the Nigerien diet.

In 1967 the African consumer price index remained practically stable since falling food prices almost offset increases in other components. The good 1967/68 millet and sorghum crops largely explain the 4 per cent decline in food prices in 1968. Clothing prices also fell because of high stocks of textiles. Consequently, the African consumer price index declined by nearly 3 per cent in 1968. Over the period 1961–68 the African consumer price index rose by 11.7 per cent, or by 1.7 per cent a year.

The European consumer price index includes 133 articles, of which 78 are related to foodstuffs and beverages. The index is computed on the consumption pattern of a French technical assistant's family. In 1964, the index was changed from an annual basis (1960 = 100) to a monthly basis (November 15–December 15, 1964 = 100). On the earlier base, this index rose substantially during 1962–66 (by 19 per cent). From 1966 to the end of 1968 it increased by an additional 15 per cent owing to an upward movement of all its components, especially servants' wages and clothing prices. As 70 per cent of the articles included in the European consumer price index are imported, it reflects changes in import costs more than the African consumer price index. Indirect taxes, however, were also responsible for the rise in European consumer prices.

Price Control

Price controls have been gradually introduced since July 19, 1961. Legislation aims at avoiding speculation and at controlling the cost of living. The controls, however, are exercised flexibly through administrative directives to suit special conditions prevailing in different sectors of the economy. By virtue of the Decree of March 3, 1965, price controls are to be carried out by simple administrative measures taken by the Minister of Finance while previously they were enforced by government decrees.

The main features of the price control measures are as follows: (1) Regional government committees fix producer prices for locally produced essential consumption goods such as millet and sorghum; these prices changed little until 1965, except for meat, which rose because of increased sales taxes. (2) Price ceilings are determined on the basis of market conditions, for certain essential consumer goods (sugar, salt, bread, groundnut oil, fish, matches, cigarettes, and services such as hotel rooms, restaurant meals, and taxi fares). (3) Markups are fixed for imported goods, taking into account import costs and normal wholesaler profits; the markups are negotiated with representatives of the business concerned, usually at a low level for essential imported goods and at a higher level for nonessentials (imported luxuries, such as perfumes and high quality textiles, are not subject to price controls). (4) The Government establishes official prices at the wholesale level for construction materials such as cement; this system enables the Government to give formal approval to prices requested by the private sector.

Existing price controls have somewhat reduced traders' profit margins as the rise in import costs and taxation have not been wholly reflected in increases in official prices. However, the control mechanism is not very effective, especially during severe shortages, mainly because the service in charge is understaffed.

Price control regulations have not been changed since 1966. On January 4, 1969, however, the marketing of paddy and rice was liberalized. Price schedules for building materials and fuel have been changed frequently, owing to increases in shipping rates.

In June 1965 the Government established a price stabilization scheme for levying import taxes and granting subsidies from the newly created Sugar Stabilization Fund (Fonds de Soutien du Sucre) to even out internal sugar prices in different areas and to alleviate fluctuations in world market prices. Since October 1966 the Fund has operated within the OCAM Sugar Agreement. The sugar price is determined, on the one hand, by the import price of sugar from non-OCAM countries and, on the other, by the amount of taxes levied on these imports. The taxes are equal to the difference between the price of sugar imported from the OCAM area, and sugar imported from outside this area which is much lower priced. Niger must buy 70 per cent of its imported sugar from OCAM countries. Therefore, import licenses are only issued to importers who are ready to import 70 per cent of the quantity applied for from OCAM countries.

At present, the price c.i.f. Cotonou for sugar from OCAM countries amounts to CFAF 55 per kilogram, compared with a world market price of about CFAF 35 per kilogram c.i.f. Cotonou. If an importer, for example, imports 10 tons of sugar, 7 tons from OCAM countries and 3 tons from other countries, he pays an import tax of CFAF 8.5 per kilogram on the 3 tons of non-OCAM imports. If, however, he falls short of the 70 per cent from the OCAM countries, he is taxed CFAF 20 per kilogram, on the shortfall. These taxes are earmarked for the Sugar Stabilization Fund.

Owing to the price difference and the tax, uncontrolled importation of sugar is substantial, especially from Togo, Nigeria, and Dahomey, which are not participants in the OCAM agreement. Consequently, Niger's controlled imports of sugar fall short of the estimated annual requirements. When the importer cannot be reached for taxation, as in uncontrolled importing, the Nigerien Government is obliged to pay CFAF 20 per kilogram for the shortfall below the agreed 70 per cent of estimated actual imports as its contribution to the OCAM Stabilization Fund operated within the OCAM Sugar Agreement.

WAGES

Minimum wages are established in Niger by joint commissions composed of representatives of labor, management, and the Government. They are determined on the basis of the so-called "minimum vital," which is the minimum cost of living based on the consumption pattern of an unskilled laborer. The list of essential consumption goods selected for determination of the SMIG (*salaire minimum interprofessionnel garanti*) comprises 48 articles, mainly locally produced.

Two guaranteed minimum wages are enforced, one for agricultural workers (*salaire minimum agricole garanti*—SMAG) and the other for nonagricultural workers. However, since the labor force in agriculture is predominantly composed of independent farmers, the SMIG rate for nonagricultural workers is the most widely applied minimum wage. There are no wage zones in Niger because laborers are mostly concentrated in urban areas where market prices are similar so that discrepancies in the cost of living are negligible, except for Niamey, where prices are somewhat higher. Legal salary scales are established on the basis of SMIG, taking into account qualifications and total daily working hours.

Since July 1, 1962, minimum wages have remained unchanged at CFAF 27 per hour for nonagricultural workers and CFAF 24 per hour for agricultural workers.

The SMIG has been lowest in the inland countries (Niger ranks second after Chad) and highest in the coastal countries, particularly in Dahomey. Moreover, actual minimum wages were close to legal minimum wages in Niger owing to a lack of job opportunities and some unemployment, whereas they appear to be above the legal minimum wages in some coastal countries.

Social security benefits are applied to all workers as defined in the Labor Code (i.e., those working permanently either in the private or in the public sector). These benefits include (1) family allowances paid by employers, amounting to 6 per cent of monthly wages limited to CFAF 60,000 and a contribution from the national budget of CFAF 150 for each eligible child; (2) accident allowances, paid by the employers, since September 1967, at a uniform rate of 2 per cent on the same salary basis as family allowances; and (3) retirement allowances, amounting to 4 per cent of wages under or equal to CFAF 60,000 per month, the contributions for which are paid by employers (60 per cent) and by employees (40 per cent).

EMPLOYMENT

The labor market is characterized by a shortage of skilled native manpower (which has led to the employment of foreign technicians) and by widespread rural underemployment. The seasonal nature of agricultural employment leaves part of the labor force idle during a considerable time of the year.

During 1963–67, total salaried manpower increased by 53 per cent, or an average of 10.6 per cent annually, to 25,642 (Table 19). Since 1962, employment has increased by an average of about 12.5 per cent a year in the government sector, compared with 8.7 per cent in the private sector. The change in the government sector was due to the departure since 1963 of nearly 1,000 Dahomeans, who were replaced by

Table 19. Niger: Number of Wage Earners by Activity, 1963–68

	1963	1964	1965	1966	1967	1968
Government sector [1]						
Appointed civil servants	5,213	2,932	4,532	4,565	4,875	5,054
Permanent auxiliaries	3,800	5,861	6,665	7,312	8,101	8,675
Total government sector	9,013	8,793	11,197	11,877	12,976	13,729
Private sector [2]						
Construction	3,448	3,460	3,277	3,874	3,283	...
Banks	299	412	462	514	562	...
Commerce	1,216	1,339	1,558	1,432	1,547	...
Mechanical workshops	273	296	311	306	307	...
Transportation	640	818	869	1,126	1,141	...
Industries	552	741	992	1,374	1,880	...
Hotels	186	184	234	207	198	...
Consultant firms	229	265	528	612	499	...
Servants	2,500	2,500	2,500	2,500	2,500	...
Other	173	480	648	690	749	...
Total private sector	9,516	10,492	11,379	12,635	12,666	...
Total salaried manpower	18,529	19,288	22,576	24,512	25,642	...

Sources: Ministère de la Fonction Publique et du Travail, *Rapport Annuel,* 1964, 1965; R.L. Clifford, *Renseignements sur la République du Niger*, Présidence de la République du Niger, 1964; and data provided by the Nigerien authorities.

[1] Excluding army, national guard, and foreign experts.
[2] Including public and mixed enterprises.

citizens of Niger; between 1964 and 1965, employment in this sector increased by 27 per cent.

From 1966 to the end of 1967, the 4.6 per cent increase in salaried manpower was due mainly to additional employment in the government sector. From 1967 to 1968, the growth rate in this sector slowed down to 5.8 per cent. In the private sector as a whole there was no increase in employment from 1966 to 1967; sectoral increases, mainly in industry and commerce, were compensated by a large reduction in construction, after the cement factory was completed. Nevertheless, the construction industry is still employing the largest proportion of the private sector salaried manpower (26 per cent), followed by servants (20 per cent), industry (15 per cent), and commerce (12 per cent). At the end of 1967, about 18 per cent of employees in the private sector were foreigners: 13 per cent were Africans and 5 per cent were non-Africans.

General statistics on unemployment are not available; only the number of unemployed workmen who register is known. Since 1963 the number of unemployed workmen registered in Niamey has fluctuated between 1,000 and 1,300. In general it is believed that unemployment increased between 1966 and 1967.

There is a certain amount of migrant labor in Niger, though data are not available. Agricultural workers go to Nigeria, Togo, Ghana, and Ivory Coast. On the other hand, Nigerian fishermen come to Niger to fish between January and November, and Malian herdsmen work occasionally in Niger.

GOVERNMENT FINANCE

BUDGET SYSTEM AND CONTROL

In addition to the budget of the Central Government and its annexed budgets, the public sector comprises budgets of the districts (*arrondissements*) grouped in several regions (*départements*), four municipalities (Niamey, Maradi, Zinder, and Tahoua), and a number of public and semipublic enterprises.

Central government finances are reflected in an ordinary budget, which covers current revenues and expenditures; an equipment budget for capital expenditures; and several annexed budgets, especially the Road Fund, the Pension Fund, the National Lottery, the National Museum, and the Special Research Fund. Although the volume of transactions of these funds is small compared with that of the ordinary and equipment budgets, it has grown in recent years.

The ordinary budget includes receipts from taxes and public properties, as well as exceptional resources which include drawings on Reserve Funds, proceeds from the Solidarity Fund of the Conseil de l'Entente (until 1964) and from the liquidation of the former French West African Federation (Afrique Occidentale Française, or AOF) accruing to Niger (since 1964), and receipts from foreign assistance.

The fiscal year of the Nigerien Government starts on October 1 and ends on September 30. The budget is operated on a cash basis (*règle de gestion*), whereby receipts and expenditures earmarked for a particular year may be carried over into the following year for a period not exceeding two months, but within the limit of expenditures already authorized.

As a rule, expenditure authorizations (*engagement des dépenses*) are issued by each government service within the limits of its initial or revised budgetary appropriations. The authorization is then countersigned by the financial controller. Disbursements (*ordonnancement des dépenses*) are authorized by the Ministry of Finance. Beginning in 1969, all expenditures on gasoline and transportation, which previously were controlled by the Minister of Finance, are to be approved by each department concerned.

THE TREASURY

According to an agreement signed by France and Niger on October 7, 1959, management of Niger's Treasury is entrusted to the French Treasury. The Treasury's cash balances are kept with the French Treasury, under the control of the Minister of Finance of Niger. The French Treasury in turn deposits funds with the Niamey branch of BCEAO. Since 1968, however, Niger's Treasury has also kept time deposits with BCEAO (CFAF 100 million as of September 1968), earning interest at the rate of 3.5 per cent annually. This arrangement is considered provisional since lack of qualified personnel and costs of managing the Treasury's services have delayed the separation of the two Treasuries. The arrangement also permits Niger's Treasury to maintain, if necessary, short-term debit balances with the French Treasury. The debit balance at any moment, however, is subject to a limit corresponding to one fourth of the Treasury's deposits with the local agencies of the Treasury at that time. All central government transactions on both budgetary and extrabudgetary operations are centralized in the Treasury. The Treasury collects all tax revenues, including those earmarked for the equipment budget. In addition to budgetary revenue, the resources at the disposal of the Treasury include the Reserve Account, deposits of public institutions, advances from the French Treasury, and credit from BCEAO. The Treasury may also sell Treasury bills.

The Reserve Account is the aggregate of past budgetary surpluses. At the end of September 1968, it amounted to CFAF 24 million against CFAF 161 million in September 1967.

Since 1963, with the exception of the Pension Fund (Fonds National de Retraites), deposits of public and semipublic funds with the Treasury have been negligible. They are mostly deposited with the Development Bank (Banque de Développement de la République du Niger, or

BDRN), where they earn interest. Although a government decree of June 21, 1968 requires all public and semipublic institutions to hold at least 25 per cent of their deposits with the Treasury, this measure is not yet implemented. As of September 1968, such deposits were limited to CFAF 72 million from the Pension Fund and CFAF 24 million from the Social Insurance Fund (Fonds Spécial Garantie Accident du Travail).

The Treasury's recourse to BCEAO is limited to advances bearing an interest rate of 3.5 per cent annually up to the limit of 15 per cent of budgetary receipts of the previous year for 240 days, a period which may be extended to the first day of the following calendar year. The Treasury may also discount customs duty bills which represent credit extended by the Government to the private sector on account of customs duties.

The first issue of Treasury bonds was authorized in March 1968. The proceeds of the contemplated issue of CFAF 300 million will be used to liquidate payments arrears. The bonds were to have a maturity of one, two, and three years; to bear interest at 4 per cent; and to be amortized at the rate of CFAF 100 million a year.

STRUCTURE OF THE BUDGET

Revenues

The share of indirect taxes in total revenues remained relatively stable at about 55 per cent between 1964/65 and 1968/69 (Table 20). However, the share of import and export taxes after rising from 43 per cent to 56 per cent in 1965/66, fell to 32 per cent in 1968/69. During the same period, direct taxes averaged about 35 per cent of revenues. Other revenues consisted mainly of registration and stamp taxes, and receipts from government properties and services. The ratio of tax revenue to GDP was 10 per cent in 1965/66 (using the 1966 figure for GDP).

Indirect taxes.—There are four main groups of indirect taxes in Niger: import taxes, export taxes, turnover taxes, and specific excise taxes.

Import taxes comprise the major part of indirect tax receipts. They consist of (1) customs duties; (2) fiscal duties and other fees (statistical fee, examination, sealing and warehouse fees, and an earmarked

TABLE 20. NIGER: BUDGET RECEIPTS AND EXPENDITURES, 1964/65–1969/70

(Amount in billions of CFA francs)

	Amount							Per Cent of Total					
				1967/68									
	1964/65	1965/66	1966/67	Actual	Estimate	1968/69 (Estimate)	1969/70 (Estimate)	1964/65	1965/66	1966/67	1967/68	1968/69 (Estimate)	1969/70 (Estimate)
Ordinary revenues													
Tax receipts													
Direct taxes													
Income taxes	0.53	0.65	0.64	0.85	0.69	0.79	1.10	8	8	7	9	8	9
Minimum fiscal tax	1.11	1.27	1.54	1.74	1.79	1.76	2.80	16	15	17	18	18	27
Other	0.91	0.95	0.97	0.99	1.24	1.03	0.09	13	11	11	10	10	1
Total direct taxes	2.55	2.88	3.14	3.58	3.72	3.58	3.99	37	34	35	38	36	37
Indirect taxes													
Import taxes	2.43	3.05	3.20	3.10	4.07	3.63	4.11	35	37	36	33	36	38
Export taxes	0.57	0.79	0.60	0.65		0.58		8	9	7	7	6	
Other	0.65	0.97	1.08	1.24	1.12	1.47	1.72	9	11	12	13	15	15
Total indirect taxes	3.65	4.81	4.89	4.99	5.19	5.69	5.83	53	57	55	53	57	53
Other taxes	0.39	0.29	0.24	0.26	0.31	0.24	0.33	6	3	3	3	2	2
Total tax receipts	6.59	8.00	8.27	8.83	9.22	9.51	10.15	96	95	93	93	96	92
Receipts from government properties and services	0.28	0.42	0.60	0.65	0.34	0.42	0.61	4	5	7	7	4	8
Total ordinary revenues	6.87	8.42	8.87	9.48	9.56	9.93	10.76	100	100	100	100	100	100
Expenditures													
Ordinary budget													
Personnel and materials	5.53	6.19	7.14	7.42	7.08	7.33	8.08	70	70	72	72	72	66
Transfer and subsidies	1.27	1.35	1.51	1.47	1.67	1.64	2.13	16	15	15	14	16	17
Public debt [1]	0.30	0.27	0.26	0.18	0.24	0.45	0.60	4	3	3	2	4	5
Total ordinary budget	7.11	7.81	8.92	9.06	8.98	9.42	10.81	90	88	90	88	92	88
Capital budget	0.81	1.07	0.97	1.20	0.86	0.79	1.49	10	12	10	12	8	12
Total expenditures	7.92	8.89	9.89	10.26	9.84	10.21	12.30	100	100	100	100	100	100
Surplus, or deficit (—)													
Ordinary budget	−0.24	0.60	−0.04	0.42	0.58	0.51	−0.01	−23	128	−4	54	182	—
Equipment budget	−0.81	−1.07	−0.97	−1.20	−0.86	−0.79	−1.53	−76	−228	−96	−154	−282	100
Over-all deficit	−1.06	−0.47	−1.01	−0.78	−0.28	−0.28	−1.54	−100	−100	−100	−100	−100	−100

Sources: Ministère des Finances, Inspection Générale de l'Etat, *Evolution des Recettes et des Dépenses de l'Etat de 1958 à 1964*; BCEAO, *Notes d'Information et de Statistiques*; and data provided by the Nigerien authorities.

[1] Including interest payments, advances, and amortization.

surtax to the Road Fund); and (3) a standard surtax on import trans-
actions (*taxe forfaitaire représentative de la taxe sur les transactions d'importation*) levied on the total value of imported commodities inclusive of customs and fiscal duties.

Import taxes vary according to the origin of imported commodities. Imports from the franc area and EEC countries are subject to fiscal duties and fees (including the statistical fee of 1 per cent ad valorem) and to the standard surtax, ranging from 10 to 25 per cent ad valorem, depending on commodities (essentials or nonessentials). Imports from UDEAO countries are subject to the same taxes but receive a rebate of 50 per cent on their rates, except on import duties levied for protective purposes, this rebate is limited to 30 per cent. Imports from countries for which the minimum tariff is applied are subject to customs duties, in addition to fiscal and other import taxes applied to countries in the franc area and EEC countries. Imports from other areas are subject to the general tariff; the rates of the customs duties under this tariff are three times as high as those under the minimum tariff.

Export taxes include (1) fiscal duties and other fees (statistical, examination, and sealing and warehouse fees) and (2) a standard surtax on export transactions (*taxe forfaitaire représentative de la taxe sur les transactions d'exportation*) levied on the total value of exported commodities including fiscal duties. The contribution of export taxes generally represented a fifth of the amount raised from import taxes.

Turnover taxes are levied on production and services activities that are not subject to the import and export turnover tax. The rate of the tax on production is 18 per cent of the value of imports of industrial enterprises; collections of this tax are negligible, however, since these enterprises are generally exempted under the Investment Code. The rate of the tax on services was increased from 6 per cent to 9 per cent in 1963/64 and to 13 per cent in 1965/66. Since 1966/67 the turnover tax has also been imposed on the sales of cattle and since 1968/69, on the marketing of groundnuts.

Specific excise taxes are levied by the Customs Administration on alcoholic beverages, tobacco, cigarettes, and petroleum products. In the 1967/68 budget, the tax on alcoholic beverages was raised from an average of 20 per cent to 100 per cent and taxes on tobacco and cigarettes from an average of 33 per cent to 60 per cent.

Direct taxes.—The share of direct taxes in total government revenue is higher in Niger than in other BCEAO countries. Direct taxes comprise income tax (*impôts sur les revenus*), fiscal minimum tax (*impôt du minimum fiscal*), cattle tax (*taxe sur le bétail*), and other taxes such as patents and licenses.

Income tax includes (1) schedular income taxes on industrial, commercial, and noncommercial profits and on wages and salaries and (2) a general income tax on a progressive scale. The schedular income taxes consist of different standard rates on particular categories of income, such as income from dividends, interest, industrial and commercial profits, agricultural profits, noncommercial profits, and wages and salaries. Thus the tax varies with the nature of income rather than with its amount. The taxable base of the general income tax is the total net income received by the taxpayer from all sources and is imposed with progressive rates. Total income tax receipts rose by 22 per cent during 1964/65–1968/69 to CFAF 790 million (see Table 20). The Tax Administration appears to be aware that there is a larger amount of taxable income to be assessed, but it still lacks sufficient qualified personnel to improve assessment and collection.

The minimum fiscal tax is a head or poll tax. The tax rates are based on classes of taxpayers, richness of the province (*département*), and within a province, according to districts, and to residents and nonresidents within a district. In 1967/68, for example, the minimum fiscal tax was fixed at CFAF 1,240 per head in Niamey, the country's capital, for residents and CFAF 950 per head for nonresidents, compared with CFAF 300 for both residents and nonresidents in Agadez, which is one of the poorer provinces.

Within the category of direct taxes, the poll taxes provided an increasingly important source of revenue. Total receipts from this tax rose to nearly CFAF 1.8 billion in 1967/68 (from CFAF 1.1 billion in 1964/65).

Expenditures

Ordinary budget expenditures, which represented about 90 per cent of the total outlays during 1964/65–1968/69, increased by an estimated 32 per cent over this period (see Table 20). Personnel and materials alone accounted for about 70 per cent of total outlays throughout this period and, in absolute terms, for most of the rise in expenditures. They were expected to be 33 per cent higher by 1968/69 than they were in 1964/65, reflecting not only additional employment in the growing public services (especially rural affairs, education, and health) but also higher wages and salaries for civil servants. The Central Government employed about 14,000 persons in 1968, compared with 8,800 in 1964, an increase of nearly 60 per cent. Of the 14,000 persons, 5,000 were classified as civil servants; the others were in lower personnel categories (*auxiliaires et contractuels*).

Transfer payments and subsidies averaged 15 per cent of total expenditures during 1964/65–1968/69. These expenditures included mainly Niger's contributions to international institutions, expenditures on infrastructure and subsidies to local authorities, public agencies, and public and semipublic enterprises. The cost of servicing the public debt was relatively small, representing an estimated 4 per cent of total expenditures in 1968/69.

Capital expenditures, financed mainly by foreign aid and contributions from the current budget, averaged about 10 per cent of over-all expenditures during 1964/65–1968/69. These expenditures increased by 48 per cent in the first four years of this period but were expected to decrease by 34 per cent in 1968/69. The major part of these expenditures went into infrastructure and agriculture.

FISCAL DEVELOPMENTS

Actual Budget, 1964/65–1967/68

The ordinary budget was in deficit for 1964/65 and 1966/67 but was in surplus for 1965/66 and 1967/68 (see Table 20). Including capital expenditures, however, there was an over-all deficit throughout this period. These deficits exceeded CFAF 1 billion in 1964/65 and 1966/67, compared with less than CFAF 0.5 billion in 1965/66 and CFAF 0.8 billion in 1967/68.

Ordinary government revenues during this period rose by CFAF 2.6 billion to almost CFAF 9.5 billion. About half of the increase occurred in one year, 1965/66, as GDP rose by nearly 12 per cent in 1965 and by more than 6 per cent in 1966. In 1965/66, receipts from indirect taxes grew by more than 32 per cent, mainly because of the greater volume of imports and exports. Moreover, in that year, a number of tax rates were raised (e.g., minimum fiscal tax and cattle tax by 10 per cent and tax on services by 4 per cent).

In 1966/67, ordinary government revenues increased by less than CFAF 0.5 billion (5 per cent), compared with CFAF 1.6 billion in the previous year. The additional receipts arose from a higher minimum fiscal tax (CFAF 264 million), a higher head tax on livestock, and modification of the general sales tax of 2.5 per cent, which was fixed at CFAF 10 per kilogram for meat.

In 1967/68, ordinary revenues went up by CFAF 0.6 billion (7 per cent). Higher indirect tax receipts accounted for 17 per cent of this gain. The minimum fiscal tax was raised by CFAF 100 per capita for all categories and in all regions. The tax on alcoholic beverages, and fees on patents and licenses were also raised. A new tax on mixed enterprises was fixed at 0.75 per cent of the total amount of salaries and fringe benefits paid each year.

Budget Estimates, 1968/69 and 1969/70

The 1968/69 budget estimates called for a reduction in the over-all budget deficit. To this end, expansion in ordinary expenditures was limited to 4 per cent above actual outlays for the previous year and capital budget expenditures were reduced by 34 per cent to nearly CFAF 0.8 billion. Ordinary budget revenues were scheduled to rise by 5 per cent to CFAF 9.9 billion. Consequently, the ordinary budget surplus was expected to increase to CFAF 0.5 billion (actual 1967/68 CFAF 0.4 billion) and the over-all deficit of the Treasury to decline to less than CFAF 0.3 billion.

Larger government revenues were expected from economic expansion; improved tax collection; additional yields from turnover taxes (CFAF 156 million), partly because this tax was made applicable to groundnut marketing; and greater returns from import and export taxes (CFAF 457 million). Proceeds from registration and stamp duties were expected to decrease slightly because fees on licenses and patents collected in the communes are to accrue to them directly rather than be channeled through the budget as they had formerly. To improve tax collection, the Government has established a customs, fiscal, and economic police service and a system of withholding taxes due from civil servants. The rise in ordinary expenditures reflects in part increases in transfer and subsidies (CFAF 170 million) and public-debt servicing (CFAF 270 million). Capital expenditures are expected to be financed by FAC aid (CFAF 214 million) borrowing from CCCE (CFAF 45 million), and contributions from the ordinary budget (CFAF 534 million).

The 1969/70 budget estimates indicate an over-all deficit of nearly CFAF 1.6 billion, an increase of CFAF 1.3 billion over the estimated deficit for the previous year. Although total ordinary revenue is expected to rise by CFAF 0.8 billion to nearly CFAF 10.8 billion, both current and capital expenditures are budgeted at much larger amounts, totaling CFAF 12.3 billion, compared with CFAF 10.2 billion estimated for 1968/69.

OVER-ALL TREASURY OPERATIONS

Over-all operations of the Treasury, inclusive of the net position on account of annexed budgets, consistently showed a deficit during 1964/65–1967/68 (Table 21), ranging between CFAF 1.1 billion (1964/65) and CFAF 0.5 billion (1965/66). Before Niger became independent, it received substantial budgetary aid from France, either direct or through the budget of the Federation in Dakar. These French contributions declined from CFAF 400 million in 1964/65 to CFAF 192 million in 1966/67, but rose again to CFAF 327 million in 1967/68.

In financing its deficits the Treasury relied heavily on external sources and drawdowns of its deposits with the French Treasury. Consequently, deposits with the French Treasury, which had amounted to CFAF 858 million at the end of September 1964, fell to CFAF 56 million at the end of September 1968 (Table 22). The over-all liquidity position of the Treasury, inclusive of currency holdings by local agents of the Treasury, declined to CFAF 635 million by the end of 1968, compared with CFAF 1,556 million at the end of 1964. At their current level, the remaining liquid assets are regarded as minimum necessary working balances. While although use of central bank facilities had been limited before November 1968 to the rediscount of customs duty bills, the Government in November 1968 borrowed CFAF 200 million from the Central Bank. An additional CFAF 200 million was borrowed in January 1969.

TABLE 21. NIGER: OVER-ALL TREASURY OPERATIONS, 1964/65–1967/68

(In millions of CFA francs)

	1964/65	1965/66	1966/67	1967/68
Ordinary budget receipts	6,865	8,419	8,876	9,480
Ordinary budget expenditures	−7,108	−7,815	−8,919	−9,064
Ordinary budget surplus, or deficit (−)	−243	604	−43	416
Equipment budget expenditures	−813	−1,071	−966	−1,199
Annexed budgets	−32	−58	85	131
Over-all Treasury deficit	**−1,088**	**−525**	**−924**	**−652**
Domestic financing				
Domestic nonbank resources				
Change in holdings of customs duty bills	−73	−45	87	−137
Local government	65	−24	−41	10
Post Office	−35	—	—	—
Reserve funds	3	—	−158	137
Other Treasury resources	134	181	482	103
Total domestic nonbank resources	94	112	370	113
Central bank financing				
Rediscount of customs duty bills	—	—	219	4
Change in claims on Central Bank				
Deposits	—	—	—	−100
Currency holdings	54	56	−28	82
Net change in claims on Central Bank	54	56	−28	−18
Total central bank financing	54	56	191	−14
Total domestic financing	148	168	561	99
Changes in deposits with French Treasury	540	−120	163	219
External financing				
French subsidy	416	250	150	260
Contribution to equipment budget	−16	40	42	67
Proceeds of liquidating AOF [1]	—	187	8	7
Total external financing	400	477	200	334

Source: Data provided by the Nigerien authorities.

[1] Former French West African Federation (Afrique Occidentale Française).

PUBLIC ENTERPRISES

Niger's public enterprises include mainly the Price Stabilization Fund (CSPPN), the Water Supply Office (OFEDES), the Dahomey-Niger Railway and Transport System (OCDN), and the Cement Company (SNC), as well as the semipublic enterprises such as the Groundnut Marketing Company (SONARA) and the Trading Company

TABLE 22. NIGER: TREASURY LIQUIDITY POSITION,
YEARS ENDED SEPTEMBER 30, 1964–68 [1]

(In millions of CFA francs)

	1964	1965	1966	1967	1968
Deposits with French Treasury	858	318	438	275	56
Deposits with local agents	443	389	333	361	279
Customs duty bills	255	328	373	67	200
Deposits with Central Bank	—	—	—	—	100
Total Treasury liquidity	1,556	1,035	1,144	703	635
Increase, or decrease (−)	. . .	−521	109	−441	−68

Source: Data provided by the Nigerien authorities.

[1] Variations in Treasury liquidity do not coincide with Treasury financing set forth in Table 21 because of difference between payment authorizations and actual cash payments.

(COPRO-NIGER). Among these enterprises, the number of which has grown steadily in recent years, the Groundnut Marketing Company and the Trading Company play dominant roles. Because of the size of their operations, the public and semipublic enterprises in recent years have exerted considerable impact on Niger's economy. Some of these enterprises receive contributions from the budget, as well as financing from foreign sources either as loans or as subsidies. Some enterprises generate profits (e.g., Groundnut Marketing Company) or accumulate funds which they do not need for their own purposes (e.g., Price Stabilization Fund) and which they deposit with the Development Bank; others depend on government subsidies (e.g., Water Supply Office) or on borrowing from the banking system (e.g., Trading Company). In the aggregate, however, the public and semipublic enterprises have been operating at a deficit.

ANNEXED AND LOCAL BUDGETS

The annexed budgets are the Road, Retirement, and Special Research Funds; the National Lottery; the National Museum; and the National Swimming Pool. These budgets, though in deficit during 1964/65–1965/66, thereafter had a growing surplus, totaling CFAF 131 million in 1967/68 (Table 23).

Since 1963, the local authorities have administered the local budgets under the control of the Ministry of Interior. These budgets have their

TABLE 23. NIGER: ACTUAL RECEIPTS AND EXPENDITURES
OF ANNEXED BUDGETS, 1964/65–1967/68

(*In millions of CFA francs*)

	1964/65	1965/66	1966/67	1967/68
Receipts				
Road Fund	120	110	147	255
Pension Fund	69	103	115	112
National Lottery	—	28	110	239
National Museum	—	12	18	15
Special Research Fund	—	—	—	11
National Swimming Pool	—	—	—	1
Total receipts	189	253	390	633
Expenditures				
Road Fund	136	96	97	133
Pension Fund	85	189	95	122
National Lottery	—	15	97	225
National Museum	—	11	16	17
Special Research Fund	—	—	—	5
Total expenditures	221	311	305	502
Balance				
Road Fund	−16	14	50	122
Pension Fund	−16	−86	20	−10
National Lottery	—	13	13	14
National Museum	—	1	2	−2
Special Research Fund	—	—	—	6
National Swimming Pool	—	—	—	1
Total balance	−32	−58	85	131

Source: Data provided by the Nigerien authorities.

own receipts derived from local taxes and from the proceeds of taxes
levied by the Central Government (e.g., livestock and minimum fiscal
taxes). In 1963 and 1964 the Central Government transferred expenditures for primary schools and for some health services to the local
budgets, thereby increasing the share of local budgets in the proceeds
of taxes levied by the Central Government.

Although the recent changes in accounting procedures impair the
comparability of the data set forth in Table 24, the deficits became
smaller until a surplus of CFAF 8 million emerged in 1967/68. This
improvement has occurred despite a reduction in central government
subsidies beginning in 1964/65 and their elimination altogether in
1967/68.

Of the four municipalities, Niamey has the largest budget, accounting
in 1966/67 for 56 per cent of total receipts of municipalities and 57 per
cent of their over-all expenditures (Table 25). Tahoua is the newest

TABLE 24.   NIGER: REGIONAL BUDGETS, 1964/65–1967/68 [1]

(*In millions of CFA francs*)

	1964/65	1965/66	1966/67	1967/68
Receipts	715	867	904	970
Expenditures	829	966	925	962
Current expenditures	*309*	*392*	*826*	*843*
Investment expenditures	*35*	*48*	*99*	*119*
Surplus, or deficit (−)	−114	−99	−21	8
Government subsidies	9	15	10	—
Loans and drawings on reserves	105	84	11	−8

Sources: Ministère de l'Intérieur, *Etat Comparatif des Budgets des Arrondissements*, 1964–68, and data provided by the Nigerien authorities.

[1] Data for 1966/67 and 1967/68 are not comparable with those of previous years because of recent changes in accounting procedures.

TABLE 25.   NIGER: MUNICIPAL BUDGETS, 1965/66–1967/68

(*In millions of CFA francs*)

	1965/66	1966/67	1967/68
Receipts			
Niamey	159	142	219
Maradi	56	44	73
Zinder [1]	44	49	78
Tahoua	—	—	17
Total receipts	259	235	387
Expenditures			
Niamey	215	226	215
Maradi	64	47	73
Zinder [1]	50	57	73
Tahoua	—	—	16
Total expenditures	329	330	377
Balance	−70 [2]	−95 [2]	10

Source: Data provided by the Nigerien authorities.

[1] Estimates.
[2] Financed mainly by borrowing and drawing on reserves.

and smallest of the four. During its first fiscal year, 1967/68, Tahoua's budget receipts amounted to CFAF 17 million and its expenditures to CFAF 16 million.

PUBLIC DEBT

Niger's debt on December 31, 1968 consisted entirely of external debt obligations, which totaled CFAF 5.8 billion, CFAF 5.4 billion in contractual loans and the remainder in suppliers' credits (Table 26).

TABLE 26. NIGER: EXTERNAL PUBLIC DEBT ON DECEMBER 31, 1968

Lender	Repayment Period	Interest Rate	Amount		Repayments falling due (principal)		
			Original	Outstanding Dec. 31, 1968	1968	1969	1970
		Per cent	*Million CFA francs*				
Contractual loans							
CCCE	1959–2002	1.0–3.5	1,425.6	1,282.9	27.0	27.4	27.6
French Treasury	1959–87	2.5–5.1	63.2	29.0	3.2	3.2	3.2
FAC	1969–77	2.0	593.5	593.5	—	36.4	55.4
Kreditanstalt für Wiederaufbau	1971–90	2.0	812.5	812.5	—	—	—
U.S. AID	1971–2006	0.75	666.9	666.9	—	—	—
Ivory Coast	1963–67	5.0	350.0	150.0	53.0	150.0	—
International Development Association	1975–2018	0.75	1,882.1	1,882.1	—	—	—
Total		1.46 [1]	5,793.8	5,416.9	83.2	217.0	86.2
Suppliers' credits							
France	1968–71	7.5	27.1	20.3	6.8	6.8	6.8
Germany	1965–73	4.5–5.0	388.2	318.6	67.4	63.4	50.0
United States	1968–73	6.0	14.8	11.4	3.4	3.5	3.5
Tunisia	1966–69	6.5	34.2	3.1	22.8	7.4 [2]	—
Total		5.1 [1]	464.4	353.4	100.4	81.1	60.3
Grand total		**1.73** [1]	**6,258.2**	**5,770.3**	**183.6**	**298.1**	**146.5**
Government guaranteed loans							
CCCE							
Local government	1960–73	2.5	90.0	42.8	6.1	7.0	6.2
Mixed enterprises	1962–83	2.5–5.5	1,718.3	726.2	86.1	84.1	82.9
Total CCCE		2.5–5.5	1,808.3	769.0	92.2	91.1	89.1
Israel	1965–69	3.0	74.1	14.8	14.8	14.8	—
Italy	1967–70	7.5	52.7	16.9	20.7	16.9	—
Germany	1968–80	3.0	125.0	119.8	5.2	10.4	10.4
Total		4.0 [1]	2,060.1	920.5	132.9	133.2	99.5

Source: Data provided by the Nigerien authorities.

[1] Weighted average.
[2] Includes accumulated interest and fines for delayed payments.

The Nigerien Government has guaranteed payment for more than CFAF 0.9 billion of the outstanding external debt. Among the contractual loans outstanding on December 31, 1968, CFAF 1.9 billion was of French origin (mainly CCCE and FAC), and CFAF 1.9 billion came from IDA; the other lenders were Germany (Kreditanstalt für Wiederaufbau), the United States (AID), and Ivory Coast. Over 90 per cent of the suppliers' credit outstanding was German; the rest was from France, the United States, and Tunisia.

Repayments on principal due in 1968 amounted to CFAF 184 million; the amount due was to increase to CFAF 298 million in 1969 and to decrease to CFAF 146 million in 1970.

MONEY AND BANKING

MONETARY SYSTEM

Niger belongs to the franc area. It is also a member of UMOA (Union Monétaire Ouest Africaine, or West African Monetary Union) together with six other countries (Ivory Coast, Dahomey, Mauritania, Senegal, Togo, and Upper Volta). These countries have a common currency (CFA franc), and a common central bank, BCEAO (Banque Centrale des Etats de l'Afrique de l'Ouest), which is the issuing authority of UMOA and keeps its external reserves. The CFA franc is freely convertible into French francs at the rate of CFAF 1 = F 0.02. On August 10, 1969 the rate against the U.S. dollar became CFAF 277.710 per dollar; previously, since January 1, 1960, the rate had been CFAF 246.853. (For details on the operations of BCEAO, see Chapter 4, and for information on the change in the par value, see Chapter 6).

STRUCTURE OF THE BANKING SYSTEM

BCEAO operates in Niger, as in other UMOA countries, through a local agency. Decisions concerning the implementation of BCEAO policies in Niger are made by the National Monetary Committee. The director of the local BCEAO agency, who sits on the National Monetary Committee in an advisory capacity, is responsible for the application of these decisions.

Apart from BCEAO, the banking system in Niger consists of only one commercial bank, the Banque Internationale pour l'Afrique Occidentale (BIAO), the Development Bank (Banque de Développement de la République du Niger, or BDRN), and the Niger Credit Bank (Crédit du Niger).

The commercial bank, which has branches in all BCEAO countries, is a French company with a capital of CFAF 2 billion, owned mostly by Banque de l'Afrique Occidentale (51 per cent) and the International Banking Corporation (40 per cent).

The Development Bank was created in 1962; its original capital (amounting to CFAF 480 million) is owned mainly by the Nigerien Government (55 per cent), BCEAO (10 per cent), and CCCE (10 per cent); the remainder is held by various banks and private interests. The Development Bank has two local branches, at Zinder and Maradi.

The Niger Credit Bank was established in 1957 as an autonomous public institution. It has a capital of CFAF 100 million, owned by the Nigerien Government (50 per cent), CCCE (30 per cent), and other public bodies (20 per cent); its primary function is to provide loans for low-cost housing, not usually financed by other credit institutions.

The Treasury performs certain banking operations. It accepts customs duty bills (*obligations cautionnées*) with a maturity of four months in payment of taxes and duties levied on imports. These bills are freely discountable at BCEAO. Although the Treasury may receive deposits from public and semipublic institutions, such deposits in fact have been marginal and are maintained with the Development Bank.

The Caisse Centrale de Coopération Economique (CCCE), a French public institution, extends medium-term and long-term credit in Niger, and contributes to the Development Bank's financing of credit operations. In addition, it acts as the authorized agent of FAC and of EDF, for local aid disbursements.

BANKING LEGISLATION AND REGULATIONS

From 1960 to 1965, French banking laws continued to be applied in Niger, except for a small number of provisions inconsistent with independence. Interest rates and other lending procedures not governed by these laws were determined by a 1959 agreement reached by the commercial banks operating in the former French West Africa. These regulations, however, were provisional pending new legislation based on guidelines to be set by the BCEAO Executive Board for all UMOA countries. The Treaty establishing UMOA in 1962 calls for the application of uniform basic principles regulating the banking profession and the distribution and control of credit.

On May 15, 1965 the Government of Niger promulgated a law (No. 65–019) governing the banking profession and credit operations applicable to banks and financial institutions. Implementation of the general provisions of this law is governed by a series of decrees drawn up mainly during 1965.

The Minister of Finance is in charge of the over-all management of credit. Decisions are implemented through orders based on decrees taken upon his proposal. There are two advisory bodies: (1) the Economic and Social Council, which provides the monetary authorities with information and suggestions, and (2) the Professional Association of Banks and Financial Institutions, which must be consulted on all decisions concerning the banking profession.

A supervisory body, with a jurisdictional role, the Commission de Surveillance des Banques et des Etablissements Financiers, controls the application of the bank regulations. This Commission comprises a supreme court judge (Chairman), the Director of BCEAO, and an official of the Ministry of Finance. It prepares an annual report setting forth its findings. It also makes relevant proposals for over-all operation of the banking system and for the structure and organization of the banks and financial institutions.

Since these entities deal essentially with the institutional aspects of the banking profession, they do not infringe on the responsibilities assigned by the UMOA Treaty and the BCEAO statutes to BCEAO's Executive Board on monetary policy or to the Monetary Committee for the implementation of these decisions.

The law of 1965, apart from setting forth the conditions governing the operations of domestic and foreign banks and financial institutions with regard to registration, legal structure, accounting procedures, and the issue of periodic statements, introduces certain regulations concerning minimum capital and equity participation.

Any bank operating in Niger must maintain a minimum capital of CFAF 166 million. Capital is defined as the sum of paid-up equity capital, reserves, endowments, nonearmarked provisions, and net profits carried forward. The minimum capital must at least be equal to 8 per cent of credits granted (including rediscounts with BCEAO and guarantees on account of customers) on the closing date of the most recent "budget exercise." To facilitate compliance, banks received permission to increase this ratio by 1 per cent annually from 4 per cent in 1965/66 to 8 per cent in 1969/70, provided their head offices or shareholders maintained with them blocked accounts in an amount which inclusive of capital would satisfy the 8 per cent requirement. In addition to the minimum capital, banks are required to maintain an additional capital (as defined above) equal to 15 per cent of long-term credits, nonrediscountable medium-term credits, and equity participations. The latter requirement is waived if capital is equivalent to at least 12 per cent of credits granted, including rediscounts and guarantees.

At all times, financial institutions must have a minimum capital (defined as for banks) of CFAF 50 million. This capital may not be lower than 10 per cent of the credits granted by these institutions on the closing date of the last exercise.

The legislation also limits banks' participation in the equity capital of enterprises other than banks, financial institutions, and real estate companies germane to their operations and housing of their personnel. Equity participation must not exceed 25 per cent of the capital of the enterprise and 15 per cent of the banks' capital (as defined above), and the sum of all participations inclusive of subscriptions to new issues of shares or profit-sharing instruments must not exceed 75 per cent of the banks' capital. In special cases these percentages may be modified by decree.

LIQUIDITY RATIO AND RESERVE REQUIREMENTS

Pursuant to a decree of September 8, 1965, banks must permanently maintain a minimum ratio between their liquid and rediscountable assets and their short-term liabilities. This ratio, fixed at 73 per cent for the 1968/69 "exercise," is increased by 1 percentage point each year until it reaches 75 per cent, starting with the 1970/71 "exercise." Redis-

countable credits granted by a bank are included on its liquid asset
side, while rediscounted credits are included on both the liquid asset
and the current liabilities sides. This method of calculation encourages
the banks to grant rediscountable credits.

By virtue of its statutes, BCEAO may impose reserve requirements
on banks when requested by a member government, but so far this has
not been done.

INTEREST RATES

Since the establishment of UMOA, the basic discount rate of
BCEAO has been kept unchanged at 3.5 per cent. A reduced rate of 3
per cent is applied to the financing of operations involving exports to
countries other than BCEAO members. The rates charged by commercial banks are based on the BCEAO's discount rate, to which percentage points are added.

The rates for credit operations, commissions on transfers of funds,
and other service charges, as well as interest paid to creditor accounts,
are identical in all UMOA countries. Except for interest paid on private
deposits of more than six months which were increased on January 1,
1969, they have remained unchanged since 1966.

Interest rates charged by banks for short-term credits (Table 27) are
fixed in relation to the nature of the operations to be financed. Reduced
rates are applicable to credits eligible for rediscount. These preferential
rates may range up to 1 per cent according to the nature of the operations. A preferential rate is also applied to credit operations with special guarantees or considered as being in the national interest. The rate
applied by the banks for short-term credits not eligible for rediscount is
generally 9 per cent. Rates for medium-term credits range from 5.25
per cent for the most encouraged operations to 7.5 per cent for certain
nonpriority construction credits. The Development Bank applies fixed
rates determined by its by-laws.

For the 1966/67 "exercise," the average cost of short-term credit
operations, excluding commissions, was 6.15 per cent, and including
commissions 7.29 per cent. During the same period, the average rate
for medium-term credits, most of which are rediscountable, has been
lower than that for short-term operations. Including commissions, they
have been at a level close to the prescribed minimum of 5.25 per cent,

TABLE 27. NIGER: STRUCTURE OF INTEREST RATES APPLIED BY COMMERCIAL BANKS

(*In per cent per annum*)

	Within Individual Ceiling	Above Individual Ceiling
Interest charged on loans		
Short-term loans		
Rediscountable by BCEAO		
Prime customer and public agencies crop financing	4.50–5.25	9.00
Secured loans	5.00–6.00	9.00
Other credit	5.50–6.50	9.00
Not rediscountable by BCEAO		6.00–9.00
Medium-term loans		
Rediscountable by BCEAO [1]		
Prime customer and construction of social interest	5.25–5.75	
Productive industrial and commercial credit	5.25–6.00	
Other construction	7.00–7.50	
Not rediscountable by BCEAO	8.00–8.50	
	Rate	
Interest paid on private deposits		
Demand deposits	0–2.50	
Time deposits		
From CFAF 200,000 to CFAF 5 million	0–3.50	
Above CFAF 5 million	4.50	
Savings deposits	3.25	

Source: Data provided by the Nigerien authorities.

[1] In addition to the interest rates shown, a commission (0.25 per cent) is charged on medium-term credits eligible for rediscounting with BCEAO, except on those which are guaranteed by the Government.

mainly because of the large share of medium-term loans granted to enterprises eligible for preferential treatment under the Investment Code or priority status.

CENTRAL BANK OPERATIONS

Groundnut marketing produces a marked monetary cycle in Niger. The crop marketing period, late November through March, coincides with increased demands for currency with a peak in December.

Currency outside banks reached CFAF 4.2 billion in December 1968 and CFAF 2.7 billion at the end of December 1962; corresponding September lows were CFAF 2.5 billion in 1968 and CFAF 2.9 billion in 1969 (Table 28). These figures exclude notes that are circulating in Niger and that have been issued by other BCEAO agencies but include notes that are circulating in other countries and that have been issued

TABLE 28.　NIGER: ASSETS AND LIABILITIES OF THE CENTRAL BANK, 1962–69

(In millions of CFA francs; end of period)

	1962	1963	1964	1965	1966	1967		1968				1969		
						Sept.	Dec.	Mar.	June	Sept.	Dec.	Mar.	June	Sept.
Assets														
Foreign assets														
Foreign exchange	...	2,121	1,681	548	733	504	16	419	827	720	377	267	601	1,448
IMF	...	185	185	185	216	247	247	247	247	278	278	278	278	347
Total foreign assets	2,317	2,306	1,866	733	949	751	263	666	1,074	998	655	545	874	1,795
Claims on Government [1]	...[2]	...[2]	...[2]	...[2]	255	222	679	217	179	8	...[2]	...[2]	...[2]	...[2]
Claims on banks (rediscounts)														
Short-term	...	...	...	...	3,990	1,860	3,798	2,881	2,024	1,799	...	...	...	...
Medium-term	...	...	...	...	321	350	354	321	335	321	...	...	...	...
Total claims on banks	1,059	1,486	2,528	4,213	4,311	2,210	4,152	3,202	2,359	2,120	3,327	3,101	2,556	1,059
Assets = liabilities	3,376	3,792	4,394	4,946	5,515	3,183	5,094	4,085	3,612	3,118	3,982	3,646	3,430	2,854
Liabilities														
Reserve money	2,922	3,316	3,259	4,405	4,880	2,883	4,612	3,336	2,827	2,670	4,364	3,304	2,984	2,897
Currency outside banks	2,716	3,159	2,994	4,131	4,562	2,846	4,227	3,250	2,776	2,625	4,249	3,270	2,941	2,867
Treasury deposits	398	452	1,022	536	579	275	373	597	622	342	284	494	460	240
Currency held by Treasury	...	...	...	...	578	267	367	428	413	237	...	...	...	...
Foreign liabilities	9	26	116	6	6	7	109	152	162	109	74	8	124	10
Other items (net)	46	–1	–2	–1	50	18	—	—	1	–3	–740	–160	–137	–293

Sources: IMF, *International Financial Statistics*; BCEAO, *Notes d'Information et Statistiques*; and other data provided by the BCEAO.

[1] Includes customs duty bills discontinued, and the current accounts of the Treasury and the Postal Checking System.
[2] Included in other items (net).

by the Nigerien branch. It is difficult to estimate the adjustment factors necessary to tabulate the effective note circulation in Niger. It may be assumed that, on a net basis, CFA francs issued outside Niger circulate in Niger because most of Niger's unrecorded exports to neighboring countries are paid for in notes, but its imports are settled essentially through the banking system. Moreover, it can safely be assumed that considerable amounts of CFA francs issued in Niger are held in Nigeria because of the adverse effects of the events in Nigeria on the confidence in the value of the Nigerian pound.

Credit to Banks

BCEAO rediscount operations rose from CFAF 1.1 billion at the end of 1962 to CFAF 3.3 billion at the end of 1968. Most of the increase took place before September 1967. BCEAO discounts up to 80 per cent of the value of paper related to groundnuts and up to 50 per cent of that related to rice and other crops. The increase in the BCEAO's rediscounting activities arose mainly from financing the marketing of groundnuts, which reached 190,100 tons in 1966/67, against 121,500 tons in 1964/65. Moreover, through its rediscounting operations for the Development Bank, BCEAO has helped to finance the growing credit needs of mixed enterprises. The Development Bank's rediscounts at BCEAO reached CFAF 1.2 billion in September 1967 and CFAF 1.4 billion in September 1968, or 54 per cent and 66 per cent of total Central Bank's accommodations to banks.

Credit to the Government

Until November 1968, BCEAO credit to the Government was limited to the rediscounting of customs duty bills held by the Treasury. This credit, nearly insignificant during 1962–65, amounted to CFAF 255 million at the end of December 1966 and to CFAF 679 million in 1967. To mitigate its tight cash position, the Treasury had recourse to BCEAO advances in November 1968 (CFAF 200 million) and again in January 1969 for a like amount. On the basis of nonrediscounted customs duty bills (CFAF 200 million) and on the basis of the unused portion of the permissible recourse to BCEAO advances of 15 per cent of the preceding year's budgetary receipts, the Government may potentially borrow during fiscal year 1968/69 an additional CFAF 1,531 million. Since the accounts of the French and the Nigerien Treasuries have not yet been separated, the Nigerien Treasury normally has deposits with the French Treasury (see "Government finance," above) while the latter has deposits with BCEAO in Niamey. However, beginning in 1968, the Nigerien Treasury has maintained a time deposit account earning 3.5 per cent with BCEAO, amounting to CFAF 100 million at the end of September 1968.

OTHER BANK OPERATIONS AND CREDIT DEVELOPMENTS

Bank credit to the private sector more than doubled during 1962–68, reaching CFAF 10.2 billion (Table 29). About three fourths of this increase was due to (1) an expansion in short-term or seasonal credits to finance crops, mainly groundnuts, and (2) a higher level of imports. The remainder resulted from the growth in long-term credits, mainly for financing the needs of mixed enterprises which had been established without adequate capitalization.

To maintain this relatively high level of credit, banks have increasingly used BCEAO's rediscount facilities, and, to some extent, foreign borrowing. Rediscounts at BCEAO more than doubled over the three years ended September 1967. Beginning in 1968, however, rediscounting activities slowed down because of BCEAO's more restrictive monetary policy, implemented by a reduction in rediscount ceilings made available to banks and by a more rigid screening of the quality of discountable paper. The lower rediscount ceilings reflected in part a reduced level of crop financing associated with the expected decline in marketed groundnuts in 1968/69.

In addition to BCEAO's facilities, banks have access to external funds. Foreign liabilities of banks more than doubled from the end of 1962 to the end of 1966, when they exceeded CFAF 1.6 billion. After declining to CFAF 0.8 billion in September 1967, they rose again to CFAF 1.0 billion in September 1968 and to CFAF 2.2 billion in September 1969. The latter increase in foreign borrowings was encouraged by BCEAO as an alternative to the use of its facilities to improve the negative official foreign exchange position on which Niger has to pay interest.

During September 1964–68, total short-term credit advanced from CFAF 3.8 billion to CFAF 6.2 billion, although medium-term credit

TABLE 29. NIGER: ASSETS AND LIABILITIES OF THE COMMERCIAL BANKS AND THE DEVELOPMENT BANK, 1962–69

(*In millions of CFA francs; end of period*)

	1962	1963	1964	1965	1966	1967		1968				1969		
						Sept.	Dec.	Mar.	June	Sept.	Dec.	Mar.	June	Sept.
Assets														
Reserves	198	159	265	273	316	36	253	82	55	44	102	48	62	26
Foreign assets	−728	143	617	379	236	196	445	190	191	267	505	241	976	745
Claims on Government	10	147	133	165	120	101	87	70	68	48	64	46	42	9
Claims on private sector														
Financed by own resources														
Short-term	...	...	...	...	4,515	4,016	3,743	5,867	5,634	4,556	...	...	...	...
Medium-term	...	...	...	...	272	287	335	328	274	298	...	...	...	...
Long-term	...	...	...	...	426	548	588	584	690	788	...	...	...	...
Total financed by own resources	3,542	3,951	3,812	4,149	5,213	4,851	4,666	6,779	6,598	5,642	6,889	7,715	6,681	7,341
Financed by rediscounts														
Short-term	...	...	...	...	3,991	1,860	3,815	2,882	2,024	1,799	...	...	...	...
Medium-term	...	...	...	...	321	351	354	323	324	321	...	...	...	...
Total financed by discounts	1,059	1,486	2,528	4,213	4,312	2,211	4,169	3,205	2,348	2,120	3,327	3,101	2,556	1,059
Total claims on private sector	4,601	5,437	6,340	8,362	9,525	7,062	8,835	9,984	8,946	7,762	10,216	10,816	9,237	8,400
Assets = liabilities	**4,081**	**5,386**	**7,355**	**9,179**	**10,197**	**7,395**	**9,620**	**10,326**	**9,260**	**8,121**	**10,887**	**11,151**	**11,393**	**9,180**
Liabilities														
Demand deposits	1,553	2,058	2,243	2,202	2,026	1,994	2,686	2,806	2,792	2,472	2,586	3,030	2,788	2,831
Time deposits	8	43	2	2	382	471	541	455	507	452	731	657	718	719
Government deposits	1,014	1,065	892	783	928	1,052	828	821	864	761	1,045	1,111	1,180	1,034
Foreign liabilities	—	720	1,697	1,706	1,651	790	904	1,818	1,416	1,009	1,826	1,758	1,762	2,247
Credit from Central Bank	1,059	1,486	2,528	4,213	4,312	2,210	4,169	3,204	2,347	2,120	3,327	3,101	2,556	1,059
Other items (net)	448	514	−6	271	898	878	492	1,222	1,334	1,307	1,372	1,494	1,312	1,289

Sources: IMF, *International Financial Statistics*; BCEAO, *Notes d'Information et Statistiques*; and other data provided by BCEAO.

gained but little—from CFAF 0.3 billion to less than CFAF 0.5 billion
(Table 30). Until 1966 the private sector was the main user of short-
term credit. Since then, with the rapid growth of mixed enterprises, the
share of the public sector in the distribution of short-term credit has
grown rapidly. The leading share of short-term loans is extended to
retail merchants dealing in imported goods, import inventories, and the
marketing and processing of export crops (54 per cent in September
1968). Second in importance are loans to finance foreign trade (20 per
cent). Other loans include those related to construction and public
works (15 per cent), to industry (5 per cent), and to transportation
and public utilities (5 per cent). Although the share of industry in the
use of medium-term credit has increased, construction and public works
still account for the largest part (44 per cent).

TABLE 30.   NIGER: DISTRIBUTION OF SHORT-TERM AND MEDIUM-TERM CREDIT
BY MAIN SECTORS, YEARS ENDED SEPTEMBER 30, 1964–68 [1]

(In millions of CFA francs)

	1964	1965	1966	1967	1968
Short-term credit					
By economic factors					
Agriculture and fishing	10	11	12	23	60
Industry	102	134	372	443	336
Construction and public works	511	646	589	699	921
Import-export	1,173	1,258	1,621	1,355	1,237
Transportation and utilities	238	277	337	302	305
Other [2]	1,803	2,081	2,377	3,033	3,326
Total short-term credit	3,837	4,407	5,308	5,855	6,185
Public sector	*1,632*	*2,148*	*2,316*	*3,111*	*3,223*
Private sector	*2,205*	*2,259*	*2,992*	*2,744*	*2,962*
Medium-term credit					
By economic sectors					
Construction and public works	253	197	280	261	213
Transportation and utilities	—	—	15	51	48
Industry	27	71	99	92	97
Other	60	39	148	110	122
Total medium-term credit	340	307	542	514	480
Public sector	*285*	*230*	*312*	*260*	*158*
Private sector	*55*	*77*	*230*	*254*	*322*

Sources: BCEAO, *Notes d'Information et Statistiques,* and other data provided
by BCEAO.

[1] Excludes customs duty bills. Only credits registered with the Centrale des
Risques du Niger.

[2] Includes commercial activities related to the marketing and processing of export
crops, and other activities related to imports.

Government indebtedness to banks is relatively small (CFAF 48 million in September 1968) in comparison with deposits of the Postal Checking System and other public institutions with these banks (CFAF 761 million at the end of September 1968). Most of these deposits are held at the Development Bank.

Of the three banks operating in Niger, the Development Bank is by far the largest in terms of resources and lending operations. At the end of September 1968, its total outstanding credit, including loans and discounts, amounted to nearly CFAF 3.7 billion (Table 31), out of CFAF 7.8 billion of total credit extended by banks (see Table 29).

TABLE 31.   NIGER: ASSETS AND LIABILITIES OF THE DEVELOPMENT BANK, YEARS ENDED SEPTEMBER 30, 1964–68

(In millions of CFA francs)

	1964	1965	1966	1967	1968
Assets					
Current assets					
Cash	40	35	31	87	110
Banks and correspondents	205	131	109	183	259
Discounts	422	821	766	779	1,635
Receivables	51	25	88	110	68
Short-term loans	1,716	1,574	1,979	1,809	1,117
Sundry debtors	418	262	182	337	230
Medium-term and long-term advances	393	436	421	533	673
Total current assets	3,245	3,284	3,576	3,838	4,092
Fixed assets	80	133	150	166	180
Less depreciation	−16	−28	−39	−55	−70
Net fixed assets	64	105	111	113	110
Equity participation	105	218	228	268	292
Assets = liabilities	**3,414**	**3,607**	**3,915**	**4,219**	**4,494**
Liabilities					
Current liabilities					
Current accounts	1,874	1,855	1,739	2,322	2,241
Sundry creditors	516	521	812	323	312
Total current liabilities	2,390	2,376	2,551	2,645	2,555
Long-term and medium-term debt	502	654	695	729	942
Shareholders' equity					
Capital	450	450	450	450	450
Reserves	38	77	111	118	150
Net profit	34	50	30	57	51
Other accounts	—	—	78	220	348
Total shareholders' equity	522	577	669	845	999

Source: Banque de Développement de la République du Niger, *Financial Reports,* 1964–68.

During 1964–68 the Development Bank's discounting operations for financial institutions tended to increase and direct short-term loans to decrease. The major part of credits granted by the Bank were short-term accommodations to public and mixed enterprises. The agricultural sector received the largest share of credit and, within this sector, the marketing and processing of groundnuts was most important. The Bank also made loans for industry, housing, and consumption. At present, it is actively engaged in financing small industry, especially the operation of a brickyard plant, a flour mill, a textile complex, a tannery, and a millet processing plant.

In addition to its own capital, which rose from CFAF 0.5 billion in September 1964 to CFAF 1 billion in September 1968, the Bank has so far derived its resources from domestic deposits, external borrowing, a national loan (CFAF 0.5 billion), and CCCE (CFAF 0.6 billion). Its deposits (CFAF 2.6 billion at the end of September 1968) represented 76 per cent of the deposits with all banks. Until 1968, the Development Bank received deposits of almost all public and mixed enterprises. Although a law was passed in 1968 requiring public and mixed enterprises to deposit 25 per cent of their funds with the Treasury, its provisions have so far not been implemented.

OPERATIONS OF OTHER FINANCIAL INSTITUTIONS

Nonbank financial intermediaries include the Société Nigérienne de Crédit Automobile (SONICA), which operates credits for purchases of consumer goods; the Credit and Cooperative Union (Union Nigérienne de Crédit et de Coopération, or UNCC); and the National Agricultural Credit Fund (Caisse Nationale de Crédit Agricole, or CNCA).

The Credit and Cooperative Union (UNCC) was created in September 1962 following the dissolution of the Société de Prévoyance, from which it obtained CFAF 100 million. The original purposes of the Union were administrative and financial: (1) to help to develop the cooperative movement and (2) to grant agricultural credit to cooperatives and other farmers. In 1967 it was reorganized: it retained the administrative functions and the financing functions were transferred to the National Agricultural Credit Fund (CNCA). The Union is a public agency; it receives some deposits of public agencies, contributions from the national budget, deposits of cooperatives, and its own capital. The Agricultural Credit Fund operates as a private institution; its resources include the original transfer of capital from the Union of nearly CFAF 100 million, deposits from cooperatives, and a small deposit (CFAF 40 million) from the Price Stabilization Fund. In order to finance its growing operations, the Fund relies heavily on the Development Bank to obtain short-term credit. Its credit operations, mainly short-term, amounted to CFAF 357 million during 1968. Assets and liabilities of the two organizations on September 30, 1968 are shown in Table 32.

TABLE 32.   NIGER: ASSETS AND LIABILITIES OF CNCA AND UNCC,
YEARS ENDED SEPTEMBER 30, 1968 [1]

(*In millions of CFA francs*)

	CNCA	UNCC
Assets		
Current assets		
Cash	52	} 300
Short-term loans	314	
Inventories	—	42
Medium-term advances	37	—
Advances to Government	—	25
Bad debts	33	—
Total current assets	436	367
Fixed assets	—	158
Less amortization	—	−69
Equity participations	2	3
Net loss	—	3
Assets = liabilities	**438**	**462**
Liabilities		
Current liabilities		
Suppliers	1	39
Short-term bank credit [2]	205	277
Demand deposits	67	—
Total current liabilities	273	316
Medium-term debt	40	42
Subsidies	—	3
Shareholders' equity	67	101
Other capital accounts	42	—
Miscellaneous	13	—
Net profits	3	—

Source: Data provided by the Nigerien authorities.

[1] Caisse Nationale de Crédit Agricole and Union Nigérienne de Crédit et de Coopération.
[2] Mainly from the Development Bank of Niger.

In addition the Price Stabilization Fund (Caisse de Stabilisation des Prix des Produits du Niger, or CSPPN) extends loans to the Government as well as to public agencies and mixed enterprises. Operating surpluses in recent years have enabled the Stabilization Fund to make loans to the public sector and to acquire shares in various mixed enterprises. During 1966–68, loans averaged CFAF 853 million annually and equity participation CFAF 133 million.

MONETARY SURVEY

From the end of December 1962 to the end of December 1968, money supply increased by CFAF 1.1 billion, or at an average annual rate of 8 per cent (Table 33). This increase resulted largely from the expansion in credit to the private sector (CFAF 5.7 billion). During the same period, net foreign assets declined from CFAF 1.6 billion to CFAF 0.7 billion, exerting a contractionary impact on the money supply. The Government's persistent net creditor position with the banking system also exerted a slight contractionary impact on the money supply.

The movement of currency in circulation was closely related to the groundnut crop cycle. Demand for currency accelerated rapidly during the crop marketing period of November-March and gradually declined thereafter. During 1964–68 the composition of money supply also changed somewhat. The proportion of demand deposits to money supply, which averaged 46 per cent during the three years ended December 1964, declined to 34 per cent in December 1966 and averaged 41 per cent in the two years ended December 1968. In September the proportion is usually higher; it was 45 per cent in 1967, 52 per cent in 1968, and 53 per cent in 1969.

Quasi-money (time and savings deposits) remained at a low level up to the latter part of 1966. In December of that year, they rose sharply to CFAF 382 million, against CFAF 2 million in the previous June, and increased further to CFAF 719 million by the end of September 1969. The main factor behind this sudden increase was the deposits made by the Social Security Fund (Caisse de Compensation des Prestations Familiales).

TABLE 33. NIGER: MONETARY SURVEY, 1962–69

(In millions of CFA francs; end of period)

	1962	1963	1964	1965	1966	1967		1968				1969		
						Sept.	Dec.	Mar.	June	Sept.	Dec.	Mar.	June	Sept.
Assets														
Foreign assets (net)	1,579	1,703	671	−600	−472	150	−305	−1,113	−314	210	−741	−980	−35	283
Domestic credit														
Claims on private sector	4,766	5,596	6,571	8,644	9,843	7,349	9,136	10,242	9,213	7,972	10,498	11,144	9,489	8,671
Claims on Government (net)	−993	−968	−1,505	−1,046	−1,085	−937	−388	−1,046	−1,053	−877	−397	−1,308	−1,279	−821
Total domestic credit	3,774	4,628	5,066	7,598	8,758	6,412	8,748	9,196	8,160	7,095	10,101	9,836	8,209	7,850
Assets = liabilities	5,353	6,331	5,737	6,998	8,286	6,562	8,443	8,083	7,846	7,305	9,360	8,856	8,174	8,133
Liabilities														
Money supply														
Currency	2,716	3,159	2,994	4,131	4,562	2,846	4,327	3,250	2,776	2,670	4,249	3,270	2,984	2,897
Demand deposits	2,123	2,618	2,748	2,589	2,390	2,349	3,033	3,150	3,245	2,853	2,995	3,445	3,176	3,223
Total money supply	4,839	5,777	5,742	6,720	6,952	5,195	7,360	6,400	6,021	5,523	7,244	6,715	6,160	6,120
Quasi-money	8	43	2	2	382	471	541	455	507	452	731	657	718	719
Other items (net)	506	511	−7	275	952	896	542	1,228	1,318	1,320	1,384	1,484	1,295	1,294

Sources: IMF, International Financial Statistics; BCEAO, Notes d'Information et Statistiques; and other data provided by BCEAO.

FOREIGN TRADE, AID, AND PAYMENTS

FOREIGN TRADE

Data on Niger's foreign trade, compiled on the basis of customs returns and published in the Government's official *Bulletin de Statistiques,* are incomplete because of the large share of unrecorded trade with neighboring countries.

Value and Composition of Registered Trade

Exports.—Niger's principal exports are groundnuts, livestock, and related products (Table 34). Groundnuts (including oil) contributed an estimated 74 per cent of total export earnings in 1968/69 and livestock (including hides and skins) 15 per cent. The total value of Niger's exports, after rising by 21 per cent to CFAF 12.7 billion in 1966/67, declined by 24 per cent in 1967/68; a further decline was expected in 1968/69 to CFAF 8.7 billion (9 per cent). Larger exports of groundnuts explains most of the rise for 1966/67, but the declines in the following two years were due to reductions in exports of both groundnuts and livestock. In 1967/68 the value of groundnut exports (CFAF 6.2 billion) was affected by the elimination of preferential prices formerly paid by France; these prices were higher in 1965/66 by 6 per cent and in 1966/67·by 24 per cent than world market prices, which fell from CFAF 46.5 a kilogram in 1965/66 to CFAF 38.7 a kilogram in 1967/68. During 1966/67, Niger sold 150,500 tons of groundnuts to France at CFAF 49.1 a kilogram and 24,600 tons to other countries at the world market price of CFAF 39.5 a kilogram. In early 1967/68, Niger also sustained losses on its groundnut exports to the United Kingdom, when payment for 16,000 tons of groundnuts sold before devaluation of the pound sterling was received after devaluation. Despite an anticipated rise in the world market price for groundnuts to CFAF 46.0 a kilogram in 1968/69, the value of groundnut exports was expected to decline by 6 per cent to CFAF 5.8 billion, owing to the reduced volume of exports caused by drought. Exports of groundnut oil, mainly to France, declined from CFAF 0.8 billion in 1965/66 to CFAF 0.5 billion in 1966/67, but rose by 13 per cent to CFAF 0.6 billion in 1967/68. For 1968/69, exports of groundnut oil were expected

TABLE 34. NIGER: COMPOSITION OF FOREIGN TRADE, 1965/66–1968/69

(Value in millions of CFA francs)

	Value				Per Cent of Total	
	1965/66	1966/67	1967/68 [1]	1968/69 [2]	1965/66	1968/69
Exports f.o.b.						
Groundnuts	6,439	8,366	6,153	5,795	61.3	66.5
Groundnut oil	763	506	571	655	7.3	7.5
Cotton	151	308	309	275	1.4	3.2
Cattle	1,866	1,680	1,045	1,185	17.8	13.6
Hides and skins	127	120	100	100	1.2	1.1
Others	1,155	1,690	1,430	700	11.0	8.0
Total exports f.o.b.	10,501	12,670	9,608	8,710	100.0	100.0
Imports f.o.b. [3]						
Foodstuffs, beverages, and tobacco	1,200	1,041	1,034	825	13.8	9.6
Petroleum products	259	240	266	275	3.0	3.2
Raw materials	159	185	197	197	1.8	2.3
Semifinished goods	332	329	342	342	3.8	4.0
Manufactured goods						
Consumption	1,304	1,317	1,331	926	15.0	10.7
Industry	4,798	4,724	5,206	5,340	55.2	61.9
Agriculture	167	335	413	413	1.9	4.8
Total manufactured goods	6,269	6,376	6,950	6,679	72.2	77.4
Others	471	338	308	308	5.4	3.6
Total imports f.o.b.	8,690	8,509	9,097	8,626	100.0	100.0

Sources: Commissariat Général au Plan, Service de la Statistique et de la Mécanographie, *Bulletin de Statistiques*, and data provided by the Nigerien authorities.

[1] Preliminary, based on actual last quarter 1967, and first half 1968 plus equivalent third quarter 1967.

[2] Estimates.

[3] C.i.f. data in *Bulletin de Statistiques*, adjusted by 8 per cent for maritime shipping and insurance.

to rise to CFAF 0.7 billion, or by 15 per cent over the previous year's level.

Probably only half of the livestock exported are officially recorded. Exports amounted to CFAF 1.9 billion in 1965/66 but decreased by 10 per cent in 1966/67 and by 38 per cent in 1967/68, mostly because of the civil war in neighboring Nigeria, the leading importer of Niger's livestock. Based on the assumption that Nigeria's demand for Niger's products would return to a near normal level, livestock exports were forecast to rise by 13 per cent to CFAF 1.2 billion in 1968/69. The value of hide and skin exports declined by 6 per cent in 1966/67 and by 17 per cent in 1967/68 to CFAF 100 million; it was expected to remain unchanged in 1968/69. Other exports, including cotton exports, after rising substantially in 1966/67 (by 53 per cent), declined by 13 per cent in 1967/68 and were forecast to decline further (by 44 per cent), in 1968/69. The main reason for this decline was the reduction in goods normally re-exported to neighboring countries, especially textiles.

Imports.—By far the leading category among Niger's imports consists of manufactured goods, chiefly for industry; together, these goods represented 77 per cent of total imports in 1968/69 (see Table 34). Food, beverages, and tobacco combined represented nearly 10 per cent; other imports included petroleum products and raw materials. The total value of imports changed but little in 1966/67, declining by 2 per cent to CFAF 8.5 billion. As a result of producer incomes in the previous year, however, import demand was higher in 1967/68; in consequence, total value of imports rose by 7 per cent to CFAF 9.1 billion. While imports of foodstuffs, beverages, and tobacco hardly changed, reflecting Niger's increasing self-sufficiency in these products, manufactured goods, mainly destined for the agricultural and industrial sectors, increased by 9 per cent to CFAF 6.9 billion, compared with an increase of only 2 per cent in 1966/67. Imports of petroleum products, which had declined by 7 per cent in 1966/67, also increased in 1967/68 by 11 per cent to CFAF 0.3 billion. Reflecting the needs of newly created industries, imported raw materials and semifinished goods continued to increase to CFAF 0.5 billion in 1967/68. Total imports in 1968/69, however, were expected to decrease to CFAF 8.6 billion, or by 5 per cent, owing mainly to a decline in imported food products (20 per cent) and consumption goods (30 per cent). This forecast was based primarily on the assumption that the reduced agricultural production in the previous year resulted in lower incomes and hence import demand.

Direction of Trade

France remained the principal market for Niger's exports during 1965/66–1967/68, taking 54 per cent, 69 per cent, and an estimated 57 per cent of total exports in these years (Table 35). Nigeria ranked second as a market for Niger's products; its share of total exports,

TABLE 35.   NIGER: DIRECTION OF TRADE, 1965/66–1967/68 [1]

(*Value in millions of CFA francs*)

	1965/66		1966/67		1967/68	
	Value	Per cent of total	Value	Per cent of total	Value	Per cent of total
EXPORTS BY DESTINATION						
France	5,639	53.7	8,780	69.3	5,496	57.2
EEC other than France	1,113	10.6	266	2.1	855	8.9
Nigeria	1,943	18.5	2,407	19.0	2,123	22.1
UDEAO countries	546	5.2	748	5.9	355	3.7
Ivory Coast	*136*	*1.3*	...	...	...	...
Senegal	*10*	*0.1*	...	...	...	...
Dahomey	*220*	*2.1*	...	...	...	...
United Kingdom	168	1.6	—	—	—	—
United States	63	0.6	51	0.4	48	0.5
Ghana	158	1.5	215	1.7	96	1.0
Other	871	8.3	203	1.6	635	6.6
Total exports	10,501	100.0	12,670	100.0	9,608	100.0
IMPORTS BY ORIGIN						
France	4,727	54.4	4,186	49.2	4,330	47.6
EEC other than France	1,008	11.6	970	11.4	1,064	11.7
Nigeria	165	1.9	128	1.5	246	2.7
UDEAO countries	660	7.6	936	11.0	882	9.7
Ivory Coast	*252*	*2.9*	*519*	*6.1*	*500*	*5.5*
Senegal	*313*	*3.6*	*298*	*3.5*	*327*	*3.6*
Dahomey	*70*	*0.8*	*76*	*0.9*	*36*	*0.4*
United Kingdom	252	2.9	306	3.6	173	1.9
United States	209	2.4	476	5.6	600	6.6
Ghana	—	—	—	—	—	—
Other	1,669	19.2	1,306	17.7	1,802	19.8
Total imports	8,690	100.0	8,509	100.0	9,097	100.0

Sources: Commissariat Général au Plan, Service de la Statistique et de la Mécanographie, *Bulletin de Statistiques,* and data provided by the Nigerien authorities.

[1] Estimates based on customs records of controlled trade and data contained in Table 34.

based on data recorded, was 22 per cent in 1967/68 but would have been much larger if unrecorded border trade could have been taken into account. EEC countries other than France, countries which also accord special protection to Niger's products, took 9 per cent of total exports and members of UDEAO 4 per cent.

France was also the main supplier during 1965/66–1968/69. Although Niger's imports from France have declined, they still accounted for 48 per cent of total imports in 1967/68. The share of other EEC countries remained about the same; for 1967/68 it was 12 per cent. Imports from neighboring countries, including members of UDEAO and Nigeria, rose from about 10 per cent of the total in 1965/66 to 12 per cent in 1966/67 and 1967/68. U.S. imports, mainly capital goods and some food products, also increased, amounting to 7 per cent of the total in 1967/68, compared with 2 per cent in 1965/66. Imports from other countries, including members of the Council for Mutual Economic Assistance and Asian countries, accounted for approximately 20 per cent of total imports.

FOREIGN FINANCIAL ASSISTANCE

Total foreign official grants to Niger rose from CFAF 5.0 billion in 1966/67 to CFAF 5.2 billion in 1967/68, or by 4 per cent (Table 36). In 1968/69, aid disbursements are expected to rise by 80 per cent to CFAF 9.3 billion. This large increase is due partly to an expected 52 per cent rise in aid from France and a near doubling of assistance from EEC and other countries. These disbursements comprise all funds actually transferred to Niger, as well as direct payments by donor agencies on account of Niger. The latter include mainly the salaries of technical assistants which are paid into their accounts maintained abroad. The major source of foreign assistance continues to be France, followed by EEC and other sources, including the United States, Germany, the United Kingdom, and UN.

French aid, which accounted for half of the total aid disbursed in 1966/67 and 1967/68, is administered chiefly by the Fonds d'Aide et de Coopération (FAC). It includes investment grants and loans, budget subsidies, technical assistance, grants for training and scholarships abroad, technical and cultural cooperation, and various services ren-

TABLE 36.   NIGER: DISBURSEMENTS OF FOREIGN OFFICIAL GRANTS, 1966/67–1968/69

(*In millions of CFA francs*)

	1966/67	1967/68	1968/69
France [1]			
Investment aid	1,249	1,190	2,581
Budget subsidies	150	260	214
Technical assistance [2]	1,284	1,356	1,356
Reverse grants [3]	−217	−227	−227
Total France	2,466	2,579	3,924
EEC [4]			
Investment grants and technical assistance	1,266	743	2,218
Aid to production	57 [5]	303	450
Total EEC	1,323	1,046	2,668
United States	242	278	534
Other	940	1,264	2,176
Total disbursements	4,971	5,167	9,302

Sources: Data provided by the UN and by the Nigerien authorities.

[1] Excludes subsidies to French research and development agencies operating in several African countries and miscellaneous French grants which are not classified by country.

[2] Salaries paid to French technical assistants.

[3] Contribution by the Niger Government to the cost of French technical assistance.

[4] Disbursements under both the first and second EDF.

[5] Includes CFAF 39 million for structural improvements and CFAF 18 milliion for price support.

dered by French research and development agencies. Soft loans are also extended by the French Caisse Centrale de Coopération Economique (CCCE) to the public and private sectors. FAC disbursements for investment grants, which had averaged CFAF 0.9 billion a year during 1960–66, increased to CFAF 1.2 billion in 1966/67 and 1967/68 and was expected to reach CFAF 2.6 billion in 1968/69. Earlier FAC grants financed a great variety of projects with special emphasis on studies and surveys. Recently, the emphasis was changed to immediately productive crop and livestock projects. By the end of 1967/68, to CFAF 0.2 billion and in 1967/68 to CFAF 0.3 billion.

French budget subsidies averaged CFAF 0.5 billion during 1960–66 but have tended to decline in recent years. In 1966/67 they amounted to CFAF 0.2 billion and in 1967/68 to CFAF 0.3 billion.

Technical assistance is an important aspect of French aid to Niger. Its cost totaled CFAF 1.3 billion in 1966/67 and CFAF 1.4 billion in

1967/68, and was expected to total CFAF 1.4 billion in 1968/69. At the end of 1967/68, about 540 FAC technical assistants were operating in Niger, compared with 516 at the end of 1966/67 and 450 at the end of 1965/66. In addition to these assistants, who are assigned mainly to teaching functions, about 60 specialists are provided by private French agencies. The Nigerien Government contributes CFAF 40,000 a month for each FAC assistant and also contributes on a global basis to the cost of other technicians. A global estimate of such contributions by the Nigerien Government is shown in Table 36 under "Reverse grants."

EEC ranks second as a donor of aid to Niger, providing CFAF 1.3 billion in 1966/67 (27 per cent of total aid) and CFAF 1.0 billion in 1967/68 (20 per cent). Scheduled disbursements were to total nearly CFAF 2.7 billion (29 per cent of the total) in 1968/69. EEC aid has been provided within the framework of the first and second European Development Funds. Under the first EDF program, covering 1959–64, EEC committed about CFAF 7 billion on 17 investment projects relating mainly to transportation and education. At the end of 1967/68, about 87 per cent, or CFAF 6.1 billion, had been disbursed under this program.

The first Yaoundé Convention of Association between EEC and 18 African and Malagasy States, in effect since mid-1964, includes a second EDF program covering 1964–69. This program not only continued assistance for investment, but in contrast to the first program, it also included (1) technical assistance linked to EEC-financed projects and (2) aid to agricultural production and diversification. At the end of 1967/68, commitments under this program totaled CFAF 5.4 billion, 68 per cent allocated for investment, 20 per cent for aid to production, 4 per cent for aid to diversification, and 8 per cent for technical assistance related to all programs. Disbursements under the program amounted to CFAF 0.8 billion in 1967/68, 54 per cent for investments, 27 per cent for aid to production, 19 per cent for technical assistance, and none for diversification, although the Nigerien Credit and Cooperative Union was preparing a project for EEC consideration. In 1968/69, disbursements for investments were to total CFAF 2.2 billion, or 83 per cent of the EEC total. Disbursements on price support for aid to production were negligible, compared with estimates, during the first three annual tranches, while payments for structural improvements, on the whole, were higher. This shift in the rise of EEC commitments resulted from the continuation of French price support to groundnuts and from the need to increase outlays on productivity improvements in order to accelerate the adjustment of production costs in Niger to world market conditions. However, with the termination of France's preferential pricing system at the end of 1966/67, EEC aid to production, mainly for price support, was expected to amount to CFAF 303 million for 1967/68 and CFAF 450 million in 1968/69, on account of losses suffered in previous years.

Grants received from the U.S. Agency for International Development (AID) consist mainly of small-scale technical assistance in various fields, as well as some food deliveries under the Public Law 480 program. U.S. aid to Niger increased from CFAF 242 million in 1966/67 to CFAF 278 million in 1967/68 and is expected to rise to CFAF 534 million in 1968/69. Other sources of aid include agencies of various countries and the UN which provides mainly technical assistance on projects connected with education, mineral exploitation, agricultural surveys, and animal husbandry. UN aid amounted to about CFAF 390 million in both 1966/67 and 1967/68.

BALANCE OF PAYMENTS

No official over-all balance of payments data are available for Niger. Although systematic data existed until November 30, 1967 for transactions with countries outside the franc area, they are no longer recorded due to the abolition on that date of all controls on the transfer of foreign exchange to non-franc area countries. An attempt based on various official statistics and estimates has been made to construct an over-all balance of payments for Niger for 1966/67–1968/69 (Table 37).

In recent years, Niger's estimated over-all balance of payments has moved from a persistent deficit position to a slight surplus, owing mainly to increased foreign aid and grants, which offset the deteriorating balance on account of goods and services. Net foreign exchange assets—aggregate net foreign holdings of BCEAO and other banks—declined by CFAF 1.3 billion in the year ended December 30, 1965 to a negative CFAF 0.6 billion the next year, and, although the situation

TABLE 37.   NIGER: ESTIMATED BALANCE OF PAYMENTS, 1966/67–1968/69

(*In billions of CFA francs*)

	1966/67	1967/68 [1]	1968/69 [2]
A. Goods and services (net)			
Exports f.o.b.	12.67	9.61	8.71
Imports f.o.b.[3]	−8.51	−9.10	−8.63
Trade balance	4.16	0.51	0.08
Transportation and merchandise insurance (net)			
Export shipping costs	−2.50	−2.47	−1.90
Import shipping costs			
Maritime (8 per cent of c.i.f. value)	−0.87	−0.91	−0.99
Inland (12 per cent of c.i.f. value *minus* 8 per cent maritime)	−1.77	−1.80	−1.63
Total import shipping costs	−2.64	−2.71	−2.56
Total transportation and merchandise insurance (net)	−5.14	−5.18	−4.46
Investment income (net)	−0.10	−0.11	−0.12
Interest payments on official debt	−−	−0.04	−0.01
Travel (net)	0.70	0.70	0.70
Government, n.i.e.[4]			
Services under aid programs	−1.28	−1.36	−1.36
Local expenditures of foreign technical assistants	0.71	0.74	0.74
Nigerien embassies' expenses abroad	−0.16	−0.21	−0.42
Foreign embassies' expenses in Niger	1.07	1.07	1.07
Total Government, n.i.e.	0.34	0.24	−−
Total services (net)	−4.20	−4.39	−3.89
Total goods and services	−0.04	−3.88	−3.81
B. Unrequited transfers (net)			
Private (net)	−0.38	−0.38	−0.38
Official (net)	4.96	5.17	9.30
France	*2.47*	*2.58*	*3.92*
EEC	*1.32*	*1.05*	*2.67*
Total unrequited transfers	4.58	4.79	8.92
C. Nonmonetary capital (net)			
Private (net)	0.08	−0.11	−0.09
Official (net)	−0.20	−0.56	−0.14
Total nonmonetary capital	−0.12	−0.67	−0.23
D. Other nonmonetary capital and errors and omissions	−4.37	−0.18	−−
E. Over-all balance (A+B+C+D)	0.05	0.06	4.88

TABLE 37 (*concluded*). NIGER: ESTIMATED BALANCE OF
PAYMENTS, 1966/67–1968/69

(*In billions of CFA francs*)

	1966/67	1967/68[1]	1968/69 [2]
F. Monetary movements			
BCEAO			
Assets	0.76	−0.31	...
Liabilities	0.01	0.10	...
BCEAO (net)	0.77	−0.21	...
Deposit money banks			
Assets	−0.11	−0.07	...
Liabilities	−0.71	0.22	...
Deposit money banks (net)	−0.82	0.15	...
Total monetary movements	−0.05	−0.06	−4.88

Source: Data provided by the Nigerien authorities.

[1] Preliminary; based on actual last quarter 1967, and first half 1968, plus equivalent third quarter 1967.

[2] Estimated.

[3] C.i.f. data in *Bulletin de Statistiques*, adjusted by 8 per cent for maritime shipping and by 12 per cent for land shipping.

[4] Not included elsewhere.

improved somewhat in 1966 and 1967, they were a negative CFAF 0.8 billion at the end of December 1968 (see Table 33). Because of larger receipts on account of unrequited transfers and nonmonetary capital, however, the 1968/69 balance of payments was expected to show an even larger surplus (CFAF 4.9 billion) than in the year before, even with a reduction in the trade balance and a continued deficit in services. At the end of December 1968, net foreign reserves for BCEAO alone were CFAF 0.6 billion, compared with less than CFAF 0.2 billion at the end of 1967 (see Table 28).

Based on customs data, Niger's trade balance, which was CFAF 4.16 billion in 1966/67 declined to CFAF 0.51 billion in 1967/68 and to an estimated CFAF 0.08 billion in 1968/69.

Transactions on account of services in the over-all balance of payments are based on 1966 national accounts data, government finance statistics, and on estimates provided by the Nigerien authorities. Owing mainly to outlays for transportation and insurance, services have been persistently in deficit, amounting to CFAF 4.2 billion in 1966/67, CFAF 4.4 billion in 1967/68, and an estimated CFAF 3.9 billion in 1968/69. Since Niger is a landlocked country, transportation and insurance costs represent a heavy burden on the balance of payments; such expenditures, on a net basis, amounted to roughly CFAF 5 billion in both 1966/67 and 1967/68. During the same period, the outflow on account of net investment income averaged CFAF 100 million annually. For other services, including travel and government (not included elsewhere), there was a net inflow amounting to approximately CFAF 1 billion in both 1966/67 and 1967/68.

Private unrequited transfers shown in Table 37 include retirement pensions paid by the French Government to Nigerien nationals who formerly served in the French colonial administration and in the French armed forces. They also include remittances by foreign nationals (other than technical assistants) employed in Niger and Nigerien nationals working abroad. These remittances have been estimated on the basis of the 1966 national accounts. The net outflow on account of private unrequited transfers amounted to about CFAF 0.4 billion annually during 1966/67–1968/69.

Total foreign official grants to Niger rose from CFAF 5.0 billion in 1966/67 to CFAF 5.2 billion in 1967/68 and are expected to reach CFAF 9.3 billion. The latter increase is due in part to an expected 52 per cent rise in aid from France, and a near doubling in assistance from EEC and other countries.

Disbursements of foreign official grants (see Table 36) comprise all funds actually transferred to Niger, as well as direct payments by donor agencies on account of Niger. The latter include mainly the salaries of technical assistants which are paid into their accounts maintained abroad. "Official unrequited transfers" in Table 37 include the counterpart of the cost of technical assistance, shown as a debit entry under "Goods and services (net)," "Government, n.i.e.," as "Services under aid programs." The share of technical assistants' salaries transferred into Niger and spent locally is shown as a credit entry, thus balancing the corresponding increase in foreign exchange reserves.

Data shown under "Private nonmonetary capital (net)" include net receipts on account of suppliers' credit and loans granted mainly by CCCE to the private sector and mixed enterprises with a guarantee of repayment by the Nigerien Government. While in 1966/67 there were net repayments on account of private sector loans, amounting to CFAF 0.08 billion, in 1967/68 there was a net inflow of CFAF 0.11 billion due mainly to an increase (from CFAF 0.15 billion to CFAF 0.33 billion) in government guaranteed loans. Suppliers' credit in 1967/68 declined from CFAF 0.75 billion to CFAF 0.40 billion. It is expected that in 1968/69 private sector loans will rise by 3 per cent to CFAF 341 million while total repayments will decline from CFAF 262 million to CFAF 250 million, or by 5 per cent.

"Official nonmonetary capital" includes net loans to public sector by CCCE and the French Treasury, and disbursements on development loans extended by various foreign aid agencies and countries. These include (1) the German Kreditanstalt für Wiederaufbau, which disbursed CFAF 195 million in 1966/67 and CFAF 252 million in 1967/68 on a loan of CFAF 812 million for urban waterworks; (2) IDA, which disbursed CFAF 77 million in 1966/67 and CFAF 144 million in 1967/68 on a loan of CFAF 1,882 million for road construction; (3) U.S. AID, which disbursed CFAF 19 million in 1966/67 and CFAF 62 million in 1967/68 on a loan of CFAF 757 million for the construction of a bridge across the Niger River; and (4) the French FAC, which disbursed CFAF 186 million in 1967/68 on a loan of CFAF 534 million for housing and road construction.

In 1968, debt servicing amounted to CFAF 133 million or less than 2 per cent of estimated exports during that period. In 1969, the level of debt repayments is expected to remain unchanged but should decline by 25 per cent to CFAF 100 million in 1970.

Net foreign assets of the banking system fell from a high of CFAF 1.70 billion in 1963 to CFAF 0.67 billion in 1964 (see Table 33). After that year net foreign assets fluctuated but remained negative most of the time. In September 1969 they amounted to CFAF 283 million, compared with CFAF 210 million a year before. The decline in the banking system's net foreign assets in 1964 reflects both a decrease in the Central Bank's external reserves and an increase in the commercial banks' foreign liabilities.

CHAPTER 11

Senegal

GENERAL SETTING

Senegal, which attained independence from French administration as part of the Mali Federation on June 20, 1960, became a separate republic on August 20, 1960. On August 31, 1963 it joined the International Monetary Fund (IMF), current quota April 1970, $25,000,000. On the same day it joined the International Bank for Reconstruction and Development (IBRD, or World Bank), current subscription $33,300,000; the International Finance Corporation (IFC), current subscription $184,000; and the International Development Association (IDA), current subscription $1,680,000. Besides the United Nations (UN), Senegal is a member of the Food and Agriculture Organization (FAO); the UN Educational, Scientific, and Cultural Organization (UNESCO), the General Agreement on Tariffs and Trade (GATT); and the UN Economic Commission for Africa (ECA, or Commission Economique pour l'Afrique, or CEA). Other organizations of which Senegal is a member include the African Development Bank (ADB), the Common Organization of

496

African and Malagasy States (Organisation Commune Africaine et Malgache, or OCAM), and the Organization of Senegal River States (Organisation des Etats Riverains du Sénégal, or OERS). It is also an associate member of the European Economic Community (EEC).

With Dahomey, Ivory Coast, Mali, Mauritania, and Upper Volta, it participates in the West African Customs Union (Union Douanière des Etats de l'Afrique de l'Ouest, or UDEAO). It also participates with Dahomey, Ivory Coast, Mauritania, Niger, Togo, and Upper Volta in the West African Monetary Union (Union Monétaire Ouest Africaine, or UMOA); in a common central bank, the Banque Centrale des Etats de l'Afrique de l'Ouest (BCEAO); and in a common currency, the CFA franc, issued by that Bank.

The country covers an area of 197,161 square kilometers (about 76,000 square miles) on the northwestern coast of Africa. It is bounded on the north by Mauritania, on the east by Mali, on the south by Guinea and Portuguese Guinea, and on the west by the Atlantic Ocean. It surrounds The Gambia (former British territory), which occupies the lower valley of the Gambia River, in Senegal called the Gambie. Senegal is a flat country with four main rivers: besides the Gambie, these are the Sénégal (with its tributary, the Falémé), the Saloum, and the Casamance.

In the most tropical part of the country, southern Casamance, there are mangrove swamps and remnants of a high forest, including oil palms, bamboo, and African teak. Much of northwestern Senegal is semidesert, but central Senegal and most of the southern part is open savanna.

The climate is characterized by the alternation of a short wet season (three to five months) and a long dry one (seven to nine months). Annual rainfall, ranging from 250 millimeters (10 inches) in the north to 1,750 millimeters (70 inches) in the south, largely determines the type of feasible agricultural production (see map).

Senegal has an estimated population of 3.8 million (1969). The latest population census, made in 1960–61, reported a total population of 3,183,000, including 3,130,000 Africans and 63,000 non-Africans. By 1967 the African population (assuming an average annual growth rate of 2.2 per cent) had increased to 3,645,000; non-Africans (mostly French, Lebanese, and Syrians) had declined to 47,000. Density of population varies widely—from less than 3 persons per square kilometer in Sénégal Oriental to more than 1,000 persons per square kilometer in Cap Vert, including Dakar. Among the Africans, 922,000 (or one fourth) were urban, 278,000 semiurban, and the remaining two thirds rural. Migration to the cities, particularly Dakar, continues at a fairly rapid rate. The Government is attempting to maintain the rural population by distributing lands and providing facilities such as water wells.

In 1968 the estimated economically active population numbered 1,505,400, including 18,300 non-Africans (Table 1). About 84 per cent of the African labor force was employed in agriculture; 5 per cent in industry; and 11 per cent in commerce, government administration, and other sectors. Many workers migrate seasonally to urban areas and return to rural areas at the time of the groundnut harvest. There is considerable underemployment; on the average the rural population works in agriculture only three or four months a year.

Numerous ethnic groups make up the African population. Even the principal group, the Wolofs (most of whom are Muslims) number only about 800,000. Others include the Bambaras, Mandingos, Peuls, and Toucouleurs. There are also refugees from Portuguese Guinea (some 61,000 in 1966). The official language is French. Wolof is widely understood, and many dialects are spoken locally.

The capital, Dakar, has an estimated population of 600,000. In 1966, Rufisque, Saint-Louis, and Kaolack each had 50,000 or more; Thiès 40,000; and Ziguinchor 30,000.

TABLE 1.   SENEGAL: DISTRIBUTION OF ACTIVE POPULATION BY ECONOMIC SECTORS, 1968

	African Population		Non-African Population	
	Number	Per cent of total	Number	Per cent of total
Agriculture	1,247,000	83.9	300	1.6
Industry	79,700	5.4	4,300	23.5
Commerce, administration, and other	160,400	10.8	13,700	74.9
Total [1]	1,487,100	100.0	18,300	100.0

Sources: Ministère du Plan et de l'Industrie, *Situation Economique du Sénégal en 1967*, and data provided by the Senegalese authorities.

[1] Because of rounding, figures in this table and some of the following tables do not add to all totals.

STRUCTURE OF THE ECONOMY

GROSS DOMESTIC PRODUCT

National accounts in Senegal have not been calculated in detail since 1965. Estimates available for 1966, 1967, and 1968 cover agriculture and industry only, and the 1965 figures for the other sectors have been carried up to 1968 (Table 2). According to these rough data, the gross domestic product (GDP) at current market prices rose from CFAF 187.7 billion in 1964 to CFAF 200 billion in 1966, or by an average annual rate of 4.6 per cent. Although it declined in 1967, mainly because of severe drought, which reduced the groundnut crop, it rose in 1968 to CFAF 195.6 billion. Given the population growth, national income per capita rose from CFAF 47,500 (equivalent to US$192) in 1964 to CFAF 48,400 ($196) in 1966, but declined thereafter to CFAF 45,360 ($184) in 1968. During 1960–68, national income per

TABLE 2. SENEGAL: GROSS DOMESTIC PRODUCT AND NATIONAL INCOME AT CURRENT MARKET PRICES, 1964–68

	1964	1965	1966 [1]	1967 [1]	1968 [1]
TOTAL VALUE *(billion CFA francs)*					
Gross domestic production	159.67	166.22	173.56	167.38	167.41
Plus public wages [2]	26.44	24.19	25.15	25.36	26.68
Plus wages laid out of household budgets [2]	1.60	1.50	1.50	1.50	1.50
Gross domestic product	**187.71**	**191.91**	**200.21**	**194.24**	**195.59**
Less indirect taxes	−26.27	−27.02	−27.51	−25.96	−26.02
National income at factor cost	161.44	164.89	172.70	168.28	169.57
PER CAPITA VALUE *(CFA francs)*					
National income per capita [3]	47,500	47,300	48,400	45,600	45,360
GROWTH RATE *(per cent)*					
Gross domestic product (decrease −)		7.3	2.2	4.3	−3.0	0.6

Sources: Ministère du Plan et de l'Industrie, *Situation Economique du Sénégal en 1967*, and BCEAO, *Notes d'Information et Statistiques.*

[1] Estimates.

[2] Value added by these sectors based on salary payments which are not considered part of production by the national accounting system in Senegal.

[3] Based on estimated population (in thousands) of 3,400 (1964), 3,487 (1965), 3,568 (1966), 3,692 (1967), and 3,738 (1968).

capita at current prices apparently rose by an average of 3 per cent a year. Since prices are believed to have gone up 2–3 per cent a year, real per capita income apparently increased but slightly over the entire period.

The contribution of different economic sectors to domestic production changed only slightly during 1964–67 (Table 3). Agriculture's share fluctuated between a maximum of 33 per cent (1966) and a minimum of 30 per cent (1968), according to the size of the groundnut crop. The share of industry, construction, and public works, to which groundnut oil mills alone contribute about one fourth, rose from 19 per cent in 1965 to 21 per cent in 1968. Transportation and commerce, largely related to groundnut marketing, accounted for about 38 per cent of domestic production during 1964–68.

No recent estimates are available on the growth of the share of resources used for consumption and for gross investment. The latest available figures (for 1964 and 1965) indicate a stable consumption of about CFAF 149 billion annually, and a small increase in gross investment from CFAF 23 billion to CFAF 24 billion, or by 4 per cent (Table 4). Private investment seems to have decreased from slightly more than CFAF 14 billion to slightly less, while public investment rose from CFAF 9 billion to CFAF 10 billion. No data are available on net investment after deduction of amortization.

TABLE 3. SENEGAL: GROSS DOMESTIC PRODUCTION BY MAJOR SECTORS, 1964–68

(In billions of CFA francs at current market prices)

	1964	1965	1966 [1]	1967 [1]	1968 [1]
Agriculture	50.05	52.97	56.96	50.66	50.62
Mining, power, and industry	24.36	25.89	29.24	29.36	29.43
Construction and public works	5.56	5.77	5.77	5.77	5.77
Transport	10.34	10.37	10.37	10.37	10.37
Commerce	54.49	55.48	55.48	55.48	55.48
Public sector	3.59	4.41	4.41	4.41	4.41
Household production	3.57	3.71	3.71	3.71	3.71
Other services	7.71	7.62	7.62	7.62	7.62
Total	159.67	166.22	173.56	167.38	167.41

Sources: Ministère du Plan et de l'Industrie, *Situation Economique du Sénégal en 1967*, and BCEAO, *Notes d'Information et Statistiques*.

[1] Estimated.

TABLE 4. SENEGAL: SUPPLY AND USE OF RESOURCES, 1964–65 [1]

(In billions of CFA francs at current market prices)

	1964	1965
Supply of resources		
Gross domestic production	159.67	166.22
Imports [2]	44.62	40.31
Total supply = total use	**204.29**	**206.53**
Use of resources		
Total consumption	148.70	148.85
Gross investments	23.02	23.87
Exports [2]	32.57	33.81

Source: Ministère du Plan et de l'Industrie, *Situation Economique du Sénégal en 1967.*

[1] Later figures are not available.
[2] Differences in customs figure as shown in Tables 40 and 41 are unexplained.

AGRICULTURE AND FISHING

Agriculture plays an essential part in the Senegalese economy. Including forestry and fishing, it accounts for one third of GDP and employs more than four fifths of the country's working population. Groundnuts, which generate about two thirds of the money income of the rural population and almost four fifths of export proceeds, occupy nearly half of the cultivated area (Table 5). Most of the other crops (millet, rice, niebe beans, and maize) are produced for domestic use. Recently, however, cotton has been introduced. Efforts are also being made to interest farmers in growing sugarcane and to extend market gardening and fruit growing. This policy of agricultural diversification is directed both toward relieving the disadvantages of an economy based mainly on the cultivation of groundnuts and toward reducing Senegal's food deficit (food products account for 40 per cent of the value of imports).

Groundnuts

Senegal's soil and climate are especially suitable for producing groundnuts. The growth cycle coincides with the rainy season. However, the amount of rainfall and its distribution, as well as the amount of sunshine, affect the size of the crop, which fluctuates considerably. Sowing is done in June–July. Marketing usually starts in December and ends the following May.

TABLE 5. SENEGAL: AREA AND PRODUCTION OF CASH AND FOOD CROPS,
1965/66–1968/69

	1965/66	1966/67	1967/68	1968/69
AREA (*thousand hectares*)				
Crops mainly for cash				
Groundnuts	1,114.0	1,114.0	1,164.0	1,191.0
Cotton	0.4	1.0	3.0	6.7
Total	1,114.4	1,115.0	1,167.0	1,197.7
Crops mainly for food				
Millet and sorghum	1,059.0	996.0	1,135.0	1,053.0
Cassava	38.0	64.0	63.0	62.0
Rice (paddy)	82.0	88.0	101.0	64.0
Maize	54.0	54.0	71.0	35.0
Niebe beans	53.0	86.0	99.0	70.0
Vegetables	2.4	2.6	3.2	3.1
Sweet potatoes	1.2	2.1	2.7	...
Fonio [1]	13.0	13.0	...	...
Total	1,302.6	1,305.7	1,474.9	1,289.1
Total, crops listed	2,417.0	2,420.7	2,641.9	2,486.8
PRODUCTION (*thousand metric tons*)				
Crops mainly for cash				
Groundnuts	1,168.0	923.0	1,005.0	830.0
Cotton	0.3	1.2	4.1	9.8
Crops mainly for food				
Millet and sorghum	554.0	423.0	654.0	450.3
Cassava	150.0	241.0	239.0	232.0
Rice (paddy)	122.0	125.0	137.0	58.0
Maize	41.0	42.0	86.0	25.0
Niebe beans	14.0	18.0	30.0	17.0
Vegetables	32.0	35.0	41.0	41.0
Sweet potatoes	7.0	11.0	15.0	...
Fonio [1]	4.0	5.0	...	...

Sources: Ministère du Plan et de l'Industrie, *Situation Economique du Sénégal en 1967*; Ministère du Développement Rural, *Rapport Annuel, Campagne 1966/67*; *Bulletin de l'Afrique Noire* (Paris), February 4, 1970; data provided by the Senegalese authorities.

[1] Foodgrain.

Production.—Although groundnuts may be cultivated throughout the country, they are confined to the area known as the groundnuts basin. Four regions—Sine-Saloum, Thiès, Diourbel, and Casamance—alone account for 95 per cent of total production; the rest is produced in the north in the region of Fleuve (1 per cent) and in Sénégal Oriental (4 per cent). The best yields are usually obtained in Sine-Saloum, Thiès, and Casamance, where they often exceed 1 ton [1] per hectare. In Diourbel, where the soil is low in fertility, crops are highly dependent on the

[1] Throughout this chapter, the word "ton" refers to a metric ton of 2,204.6 pounds.

weather and yields vary widely (368 kilograms per hectare in 1966/67 and 920 kilograms in 1967/68).

Groundnut production has increased over the last 20 years. The cultivated area expanded from an average of 676,000 hectares, producing 565,000 tons a year, during 1949/50–1953/54 [2] to 1,164,000 hectares, producing 1,005,000 tons, in 1967/68. Peak production occurred in 1965/66, when 1,168,000 tons were harvested from 1,114,000 hectares (i.e., an average yield per hectare of 1.05 tons). Although the cultivated area was about the same in 1966/67 as in the year before, prolonged drought reduced over-all production by 21 per cent. In 1967/68 the amount and distribution of rainfall were on the whole satisfactory, but inadequate sunshine in October and November prevented the seeds from gaining weight as they ripened. This situation prevailed especially in Sine-Saloum, where yields per hectare dropped from 950 kilograms in 1966/67 to 760 kilograms in 1967/68. Unfavorable weather during the 1968/69 crop year—the third consecutive bad year—reduced the total crop to 830,000 tons, the worst crop since 1960.

In recent years the authorities have actively promoted agricultural extension services and modern farming techniques. Every year qualified technicians under the Ministry of Rural Economy prepare a program of assistance for cooperatives, which is reflected in the provision of seeds, fertilizers, fungicides, and agricultural equipment. This agricultural program is implemented by the Development Assistance Office (Office National de Coopération et d'Assistance pour le Développement, or ONCAD) and financed by the Senegal Development Bank (Banque Nationale de Développement du Sénégal, or BNDS) in the form of short-term and medium-term credits. It also covers aid from the state and EDF (European Development Fund, Fonds Européen de Développement, or FED), through the agency of the Rural Development Fund (Fonds Mutualiste de Développement Rural) in the form of subsidies and guarantees of loans granted by the Development Bank. Parallel to implementation of the agricultural program, the Government, with EDF financing, is promoting the cooperative movement and rural extension services provided under contract by the French Société d'Assistance Technique et de Coopération (SATEC).[3]

---

[2] Crop years beginning December.
[3] See "EEC aid program," below.

Disbursements under the agricultural program, amounting to CFAF 1,880 million in 1965/66 and CFAF 2,226 million in 1966/67, rose to approximately CFAF 2,500 million in 1967/68; they were estimated at CFAF 2 billion in 1968/69. Loans granted to cooperatives by the Development Bank in 1967/68 under the agricultural program totaled CFAF 1,679 million: CFAF 975 million in the form of short-term loans for the provision of fertilizers and fungicides (CFAF 807 million) and necessities to bridge the gap between crops (CFAF 168 million); CFAF 232 million in the form of two-year loans for the purchase of small individual agricultural equipment; and CFAF 472 million in the form of five-year credits for the purchase of collective farm equipment and draft animals. Short-term loans and, since the 1967/68 crop year, medium-term loans can be rediscounted at BCEAO.

Marketing.—Before Senegal became independent, farmers sold their crops to private traders at a price fixed by the Government at the beginning of the crop year. In return, these traders sold farm supplies and consumer goods to the farmers. In 1960 a decree on agricultural cooperation brought about the association of farmers in cooperatives. At the same time a public agency, the Office de Commercialisation Agricole (OCA), was created for marketing the major crops (groundnuts, millet, rice, and imported wheat) and for supplying essential goods to the farmers. Although private traders licensed by this agency continued for a while, the farm cooperatives played an increasingly important role in groundnut collection. The 695 cooperatives created when the cooperative system was established collected 22 per cent of the crop in 1960/61. By 1966/67, the cooperatives (then numbering 1,594 with a membership of 205,000) controlled 63 per cent of the crop collection, and by 1967/68 their share had grown to 98 per cent (Table 6). In July 1969 there were 1,859 cooperatives, of which 1,494 were devoted to groundnut production. Producers who do not belong to a cooperative are now obliged to deliver their crop to the cooperatives except for a few large producers, such as the Société de Développement Agro-Industrielle de la Casamance.

Under a law of June 30, 1966, the Development Assistance Office (ONCAD) was established as a public agency, with industrial and commercial functions and a capital of CFAF 2,140 million, and was entrusted with the same tasks formerly undertaken by less centralized

TABLE 6.   SENEGAL: GROUNDNUT CONSUMPTION AND MARKET SALES,
1965/66–1968/69 [1]

(*In thousands of metric tons, unshelled*)

	1965/66	1966/67	1967/68	1968/69 [2]
Total production	1,168	924	1,005	830
Less consumption on farms	−54	−50	−41	...
Less seeds kept by producers	−25	−15	−15	...
Less seeds repaid to ONCAD [3]	−89	−71	−115	84
Total sales by producers to ONCAD	1,000	787	834	623
Cooperatives				
Sales	675	452	728	561
Debt repayment in kind	64	42	91	55
Direct sales of large producers	7	11	15	7
Private traders	253	283	—	—
Loss (−)	−27	−33	−22	...
Surplus, or deficit (−), on seeds	11	−18	30	23
Total sales by ONCAD to Agricultural Marketing Board [4]	984	736	842	598
Groundnut oil mills	534	514	561	462
Shelling stations	450	222	282	136

Sources: Ministère du Plan et de l'Industrie, *Situation Economique du Sénégal en 1967*, and BCEAO, *Notes d'Information et Statistiques*.

[1] Crop year December–May.
[2] Preliminary estimates.
[3] Development Assistance Office (Office National de Coopération et d'Assistance pour le Développement).
[4] Office de Commercialisation Agricole in 1965/66 and 1966/67 and Office de Commercialisation Agricole du Sénégal in 1967/68.

regional centers. Furthermore, the new Office was given a monopoly of the marketing of some farm products (groundnuts, paddy, and millet). A law of October 12, 1967 established a new Agricultural Marketing Board (Office de Commercialisation Agricole du Sénégal, or OCAS), which has sole authority to sell both at home and abroad the farm products collected by the Development Assistance Office. The Board also holds a monopoly of the import of consumer goods of national importance (particularly rice and wheat).

Activities of the Development Assistance Office may be grouped under four heads: (1) It maintains the groundnut seed stock representing about 85,000 tons of groundnuts (worth CFAF 2 billion) distributed among 405 warehouses (*seccos*). From this stock, it advances seeds to cooperatives in May and receives reimbursement in kind at the time of the first crop deliveries in December, plus a service charge equivalent to 25 per cent of the advance. (2) It is responsible for implementing the agricultural program, which entails ordering items necessary for cultivation and installing equipment; estimates of cooperative needs are made on the spot by the Agricultural Development Company (Société de Développement et de Vulgarisation Agricole, or SODEVA) and the Regional Expansion Centers (Centres d'Expansion Régionale, or CER's). (3) It buys the groundnut, millet, and rice crops from the cooperatives and transports the output to receiving stations for sale to the Marketing Board. (4) Finally, it is responsible for the smooth running of the cooperative system.

To accomplish its tasks, the Development Assistance Office avails itself of large credits granted by local banks, particularly the Development Bank. For this purpose it benefits from the marketing and storage credit to enable it to buy crops from the cooperatives and large producers. This credit is gradually amortized by payments made by the Marketing Board on receipt of settlements from the oil mills and from exports. Since these settlements take some time, the Office bears a heavy financial burden. It also has available credits for management and preservation of seed capital and for the purchase, installation, and storage of fertilizers, farm equipment, and other cultivation needs.

Data on the recent financial position of the Development Assistance Office are not available since the latest published balance sheet is dated September 30, 1967. From the old regional centers, the Office inherited a liability of CFAF 370 million, covered by an interest-free advance from the Treasury, and had to borrow CFAF 650 million from the Development Bank to reconstitute part of the destroyed seed stock. It also has to rely heavily on repayments of its loans and advances to producers and on prompt Marketing Board payments to maintain its financial equilibrium. Before marketing operations began for the 1968/69 crop year, its claims on cooperatives included not only 86,271 tons of seeds at the beginning of the current crop year but also 45,000 tons of seeds outstanding from the preceding crop years, together amounting to approximately CFAF 2.5 billion.

The new Agricultural Marketing Board, also a public agency with industrial and commercial functions, has a capital of CFAF 363 million and is responsible for the sale of unshelled groundnuts to local oil mills under a quota fixed before each crop year in relation to mill needs and crop forecasts. The oil mills are responsible for oil sales. The Board exports the remaining crop after the groundnuts are shelled. Exports closely reflect in volume the size of the crops, the needs of the local oil mills having priority.

The Marketing Board's purchases from the Development Assistance Office are made in accordance with a scale established at the beginning of the marketing season. For making purchases the Board has a so-called prefinancing credit, which is amortized by settlements from the oil mills and exports, and by payments from the Groundnut Stabilization Fund (Caisse de Stabilisation des Prix de l'Arachide, or CSPA) intended to absorb any difference between the Office's purchase price and the Board's actual resale price (Table 7). Since the 1967/68 crop year, groundnuts have been sold at world market prices in accordance with commitments contracted under the first Yaoundé Convention. The Board's financial position shows signs of weakness affecting the Office because of delays in both settlements for sales and compensatory payments from the Stabilization Fund. On June 30, 1968 a provisional balance sheet for the Board included CFAF 2.7 billion receivable from the Stabilization Fund.

The Groundnut Stabilization Fund, created in 1958 to assist in placing the crop surplus that France could not take, is now due to absorb the Marketing Board's deficit. Its funds are constituted by EEC aid received for price support, by proceeds from trading taxes levied on oil that is exported or sold on the domestic market and levied on exported groundnuts, and by a rebate equal to one sixth of the export duty on groundnuts. During the fiscal year 1967/68, the Stabilization Fund also received the balance of the proceeds from the liquidation of the Trans-

TABLE 7. SENEGAL: GROUNDNUT EXPORT PRICES, 1964/65–1967/68

(In CFA francs per kilogram (shelled))

	Price Guaranteed by France	Average World Price
1964/65	49.50	48.93 [1]
1965/66	48.75	44.86 [1]
1966/67	48.50	44.00 [1]
1967/68	—	38.85 [2]

Sources: BCEAO, *Rapport Annuel* and *Notes d'Information et Statistiques.*

[1] Average selling price for groundnuts from Senegal during the crop year.
[2] Average up to September 30, 1968.

port Equalization Fund (Caisse de Péréquation des Transports). On June 30, 1968 the liquid assets of the Stabilization Fund amounted to CFAF 3.2 billion. Taking into account the payments to be made to the Marketing Board to absorb the deficit from the 1967/68 groundnut crop year and in anticipation of allocations from EDF for price support, the Stabilization Fund had recourse to a short-term advance provided under the Yaoundé Convention. In fact, EEC, on the basis of the EDF cash facilities, can grant advances up to an over-all ceiling of US$50 million to the 18 member states. At the end of November 1968 the Stabilization Fund had received in this way an advance of CFAF 893 million and, on account, CFAF 562 million of the CFAF 825 million granted for price support.

The Development Assistance Office took part in groundnut collection for the first time in the 1966/67 marketing season. From the crop, estimated at 924,000 tons (unshelled), producers kept about 65,000 tons for their own consumption and for seed (see Table 6), and reimbursed the Development Assistance Office more than 71,000 tons of seed in kind (i.e., a reimbursement rate of 70 per cent, or considerably lower than the usual 80 per cent rate). Over-all deliveries to the Office fell to 787,000 tons (from 1 million tons in the preceding crop year), including 452,000 tons from cooperatives and nearly 42,000 tons reimbursement for debts contracted (a reimbursement rate of 72 per cent), 283,000 tons from private traders, and 11,000 tons from large producers. With seed operations and losses, sales to the former Marketing Board totaled 736,000 tons. Local oil mills, which received 514,000 tons of this total, sold 122,000 tons of crude oil and 54,000 tons of refined oil. Shelling stations, which received 222,000 tons (unshelled), provided 158,000 tons (shelled) for export.

In the 1967/68 marketing season, the new Agricultural Marketing Board came into being, and private traders disappeared, completing the farm marketing reform begun in 1966. Improved seeds, wider use of fertilizers, expanded area under cultivation, and generally better weather than had prevailed in the preceding crop year—all contributed to the increase in the groundnut crop to 1,005,000 tons (unshelled).

Producers retained 56,000 tons for consumption and seed and made seed reimbursements of 115,000 tons (a reimbursement rate of 83 per cent, which was higher than recent previous rates). Increased sales to the Marketing Board resulted in larger allocations of 561,000 tons to the oil mills (which sold an estimated 163,000 tons of crude oil and 35,000 tons of refined oil) and 282,000 tons to the shelling stations (which supplied 194,000 tons of shelled nuts for export).

Preliminary data for the 1968/69 marketing season indicate a decline in producer sales to the Development Assistance Office (only 623,000 tons of shelled nuts, compared with 834,000 tons in 1967/68). Sales to the Marketing Board amounted to 598,000 tons (shelled), resulting in allocations of 462,000 tons (shelled) to oil mills and the remaining 136,000 tons (shelled) to shelling stations.

Price structure.—From 1960 until 1963/64, France guaranteed the purchase of Senegalese oilseeds or oil equivalent to an over-all weight of 483,000 tons (shelled) at a fixed price of F 1.05 (CFAF 52.50) per kilogram (shelled). This guarantee enabled the Senegalese Government to pay the same producer price, which was fixed at CFAF 22.75 per kilogram (unshelled) at Dakar, CFAF 22.00 at Kaolack, and CFAF 21.25 at Zinguinchor.

After 1964/65 and under the terms of the Yaoundé Convention, groundnuts were to sell at world market prices, and preferential treatment by France was to cease. To ease the impact of the reduction, EDF established a schedule of subsidies providing for gradual alignment of Senegalese prices, over a period of five years, with the world market price, estimated at CFAF 46 per kilogram (shelled) c.i.f. French port, the approximate average of world prices over the past five years.

Delay by EEC countries in drawing up a common oil price policy, however, allowed Senegal to benefit from the preferential trade agreement with France until 1966/67. The guaranteed price was based on a schedule providing gradual reduction in the price each year, but with the help of EEC subsidies, producer prices remained unchanged until 1966/67.

For 1964/65, France agreed to make purchases equal to 483,000 tons (shelled), up to 200,000 tons as shelled nuts at F 90.50 per quintal and the remaining 283,000 tons as oil at F 105 per quintal (shelled), equivalent to an average of F 99 per quintal (CFAF 49.50 per kilogram). The rest of the crop was exported, mainly to Italy and the Soviet Union, at world prices averaging CFAF 48.93 per kilogram (see Table 7).

In 1965/66 the French guarantee applied to 505,000 tons (shelled) at a reduced price of CFAF 48.75 per kilogram. The remaining crop was sold on various European markets at an average price of CFAF 44.86 per kilogram.

The French guarantee ended with the 1966/67 crop year, when it applied to 415,000 tons (shelled) at CFAF 48.50 per kilogram. Exports to countries other than France, about 15,000 tons, sold at the average world price of CFAF 44 per kilogram.

In 1967/68 the end of the French support price and the necessity of selling the entire groundnut crop at world market prices coincided with a 20 per cent drop in the latter. For the first time in seven years, the Senegalese Government lowered the producer price by about 15 per cent to CFAF 18.442 per kilogram (unshelled) at Dakar, CFAF 17.791 at Kaolack, and CFAF 16.598 at Ziguinchor (i.e., an average domestic price of CFAF 18.34). On the basis of this price, official agencies handling the marketing of groundnuts established a price structure as follows:

	CFA francs per kilogram
Average producer price	18.34
Transportation and marketing cost of the Development Assistance Office (ONCAD)	2.60
Cost to ONCAD	20.94
Transportation and marketing cost of the Agricultural Marketing Board (OCAS)	0.41
Cost to OCAS (unshelled)	21.35
Shelling cost	0.95
Shelling losses [4]	9.56
Taxation	6.29
Export cost	5.27
Cost to OCAS (shelled)	43.42
Average export price (shelled) c.i.f. European port [5]	38.85

---

[4] On an average 1 kilogram unshelled = 0.7 kilogram shelled.

[5] Up to September 30, 1968.

As the average cost of groundnuts exported during 1967/68, CFAF 43.42 per kilogram (shelled) c.i.f. European port, considerably exceeded the average selling price of exported groundnuts of CFAF 38.85, there was a loss of CFAF 4.57 per kilogram, only partly offset by the increase in EEC aid.

EEC aid program.—According to the Yaoundé Convention, EEC established a schedule of subsidies for five years from June 1, 1964, providing partial compensation for Senegal's losses after the end of the French support price. Originally, it had amounted to CFAF 8,248 million [6] as follows: CFAF 4,474 million for structural improvement projects to raise the productivity of groundnut production and CFAF 3,774 million for price support to help cover losses resulting from differences between the target cost price and the actual export sale price. This price support was intended to continue through 1966/67, when the cost was expected to approximate the world market price. However, aware that a sharp drop in the world market price for oil products could be detrimental to the associated African countries, EEC made allowance for additional compensatory aid equal to 80 per cent of the difference between a reference price of US$186 per ton (unshelled) c.i.f. (CFAF 45.915 per kilogram) and the world market price. An over-all ceiling of $13 million (CFAF 3.2 billion) was fixed for compensatory aid to the 18 associated countries. Special methods of calculation were prepared in case this aid would have to be rendered at the same time as that for price support.[7]

(1) For groundnut price support in 1964/65, to which the first segment of aid applied, EDF granted a total credit of CFAF 1,643 million, corresponding to the payment of a subsidy of CFAF 3 per kilogram on the basis of both an estimated export volume of 547,700 tons (shelled) and a target cost price of CFAF 52.50 per kilogram (Table 8). Actually, only 518,058 tons were exported, 500,253 tons to France at a guaranteed price of CFAF 49.50 per kilogram, 13,608 tons to other EEC countries at CFAF 48.07 per kilogram, and 4,197 tons to third countries at CFAF 50.56 per kilogram. The average weighted sale

---

[6] Later raised to CFAF 8,646 million subsequent to an increase in credits earmarked for structural improvements to CFAF 4,872 million.

[7] See also Chapter 10, under "Groundnuts."

TABLE 8.   SENEGAL: EEC GROUNDNUT PRICE SUPPORT PROGRAM, 1964/65–1967/68

	Shelled Groundnuts Exported	Selling Price	Target Cost Price	Differ- ence	Total Subsidy
	Metric tons	CFA francs per kilogram			Million CFA francs
1964/65					
Forecast	547,700	49.50	52.50	3.00	1,643.00
Realization	518,058	49.55 [1]	52.50	2.95	1,528.00
1965/66					
Forecast	584,750	47.50	49.50	2.00	1,170.00
Adjusted					
Exports to France	483,000	48.75	49.75	1.00	483.00
Other exports	100,000	44.00	49.75	5.75	575.00
Total	583,000	...	...	...	1,058.00
Realization					
Exports to France	517,201	48.75	49.75	1.00	517.20
Other exports	120,419	44.86	49.75	4.88	588.30
Total	637,620	...	...	...	1,105.50 [2]
1966/67					
Forecast	634,000	47.00	48.50	1.50	951.00
Adjusted	460,000	48.50	49.00	0.50	230.00
Realization					
Exports to France	442,272	48.50	49.00	0.50	221.10
Other exports	15,116	44.00	49.00	0.50	7.60
Total	457,388	...	...	...	228.70
1967/68					
Forecast	693,900	46.50	46.51	0.01	10.00
Adjusted	700,000	...	46.25	1.30	910.00
Realization	550,000	...	46.25	1.50	825.00 [3]

Source: Data provided by the Senegalese authorities.

[1] Average between French support price and other countries' prices.
[2] Of which only CFAF 1,058 million had been disbursed as forecast.
[3] Of which CFAF 562 million had been disbursed on October 22, 1968. In addition to price support subsidy, Senegal was to receive from EEC a special stabilization price subsidy, provisionally set at CFAF 1,500 million.

price was CFAF 49.55 per kilogram, and the average real support price was CFAF 2.95. The total subsidy paid was CFAF 1,528 million.

For 1965/66, with a lower target cost price of CFAF 49.75 per kilogram, EDF provided support of CFAF 1,058 million and Senegal CFAF 47 million. For 1966/67, with a lower volume of exports because of the drought and a target cost price of CFAF 49 per kilogram, actual payments for price support amounted to CFAF 229 million.

For 1967/68 it was first thought that the target cost price would correspond to the world market price and that no more than CFAF 10 million would be needed for EEC price support and the EEC compensatory aid (80 per cent of the difference between the reference price of CFAF 45.915 per kilogram and world market price) would be enough to alleviate the consequences for the Senegalese economy. In fact, as already mentioned, when France ceased purchases at a guaranteed price, world market prices dropped by about 20 per cent, and Senegal marketed most of its crop at a loss of CFAF 4.57 per kilogram. To offset part of the difference between the world market price and the adjusted target cost price, Senegal obtained a subsidy totaling CFAF 825 million (counting the remainder of previously unutilized credits). In addition, compensatory aid was given for the first time in 1967/68 to cover 80 per cent of the difference between the average world price and a reference price of CFAF 45.915 per kilogram. The total of this aid was estimated at CFAF 1,500 million.

(2) Structural improvements within the framework of aid to groundnut production and concurrent with EEC price support were intended to renovate cultivation methods and to achieve a marked increase in productivity. This program terminated on May 31, 1969, on expiration of the Yaoundé Convention, but has been continued on a wider scale with financial assistance of IBRD and IDA (see "Foreign trade, aid, payments, and reserves," below).

Originally, the credits earmarked by EDF for structural improvements amounted to CFAF 4,474 million and were to be placed by the Development Bank, which incorporated them in the public authorities' annual agricultural programs (Table 9). EEC raised the total to CFAF 4,872 million when the third segment (1966/67) was adjusted, making it possible to increase the totals for storage and for fertilizers; at the same time the amount provided for the installation of shelling machines was canceled.

In this way the program emphasized rural extension services and instruction of producers in new farming methods. Execution of the program was entrusted to a French firm, the Société d'Assistance Technique et de Coopération (SATEC), under a contract signed with the Senegalese Government in 1964, financed by the Fonds d'Aide et de Coopération (FAC) and EDF in turn. That firm was assigned the following objectives by the Government: (1) to increase groundnut productivity by 25 per cent within three years; (2) to prepare groundnut

TABLE 9.   SENEGAL: EEC PROGRAM OF STRUCTURAL IMPROVEMENTS, 1964–69

(In millions of CFA francs)

	1964/65	1965/66	1966/67	1967/68	1968/69	Total
Rural extension services	376	496.0	338	—	—	1,210
Seeds	50	40.0	45	40.0	42	217
Seed sheds	27	21.5	24	21.5	23	117
Training stations	39	38.0	35	34.0	34	180
Fertilizers	294	300.0	300	300.0	255	1,449 [1]
Shelling machines	21	176.0	180	247.0	237	861 [1]
Storage	90	—	—	—	—	90 [1]
Rural expansion centers	50	150.0	—	—	—	200
Soil preservation	—	—	29	50.0	71	150
Total	947	1,221.5	951	692.5	662	4,474 [1]

Source: European Economic Community, *Programme Quinquennal d'Aide à la Production du Sénégal*, VIII/FED/14642/64-F.

[1] Later the total for fertilizers was increased to CFAF 1,847 million, the total for storage was increased to CFAF 951 million, and the amount for shelling machines was eliminated, making the grand total CFAF 4,872 million.

areas for a more diversified economy by promoting the cultivation of millet and introducing the cultivation of new food crops; (3) to promote intensive farming in order to offset the country's food shortage and to pave the way for the integration of cattle breeding with crop farming; and (4) to train the rural instructors required to complete the work in due time. These goals were not attained by the end of the third year owing to unfavorable weather, which partly concealed the benefits that producers might have derived from the innovations. By the middle of 1969, however, the number of rural instructors totaled 672; the European staff decreased from 52 in 1965 to 42 in 1968, while the Senegalese staff rose from 1 to 49. Agricultural implements increased significantly, although the number of horses and carts remained inadequate. The use of fertilizers was hampered by several years of drought, lower groundnut prices, and higher fertilizer prices. Fertilizers were used on 12 per cent of the area under cereals and 28 per cent of the area under groundnuts. Cultivation methods have been somewhat improved.

In 1968, a Senegalese firm, the Agricultural Development Company (Société de Développement et de Vulgarisation Agricole, or SODEVA), was created to take over operations of the French firm, SATEC. The contract with the Senegalese Government, however, was extended in order to assist the establishment and management of the Agricultural Development Company. Its resources during 1968–71 amounted to CFAF 1,350 million; CFAF 580 million was provided by the Government and the remainder was extended by CCCE and by AID-UN.

At the same time the program of structural improvements stressed wider application of fertilizers, with a goal of using about 85,000 tons on 550,000 hectares in 1969. Credits were earmarked for this purpose to lower the selling price to farmers in accordance with a decreasing scale. Other measures concerned distribution and cultivation of improved seeds, construction of sheds for seeds, establishment of breeding and training centers for raising draft animals, and establishment of storage areas.

EDF was expected to finance the establishment of 16 new Regional Expansion Centers (CER's) and to complete the program of 90 others already created or being set up and financed out of the Senegalese budget and funds from the first EDF (1958–62). These centers, the first of which dates from 1958, constitute the launching pads of the agricultural program: they are responsible for implementing the plan directives and assisting the cooperatives by anticipating their needs, defining their objectives, and setting up their programs. They generally cover one district (*arrondissement*), including several villages, with about 20,000 inhabitants, and are manned by representatives of rural development technical services.

Implementation of the structural improvements program depends on the Development Assistance Office (ONCAD) for the provision of fertilizers and storage. For extension services, distribution of seeds, creation of the Regional Expansion Centers, and soil preservation, the Société d'Assistance Technique et de Coopération (SATEC) is the responsible organization, settlements being made through the Development Bank. During the first three years (1964/65–1966/67) the implementation ratio averaged 50 per cent, with nearly CFAF 2.3 billion credits used out of total commitments of over CFAF 4.5 billion (Table 10). This fairly low implementation ratio underlines the difficulties and delays encountered in executing infrastructure investment projects (e.g., seed sheds, storage areas, the Regional Expansion Centers, and training stations), for which only CFAF 0.02 billion was spent,

TABLE 10. SENEGAL: IMPLEMENTATION OF THE EEC STRUCTURAL IMPROVEMENT
PROGRAM, 1964/65–1966/67

(*Amount in millions of CFA francs*)

	Credits Granted	Credits Used	
		Amount	Per cent of total granted
1964/65	947.0	772.3	81.6
1965/66	1,346.5	621.6	46.2
1966/67	2,247.3	887.8	39.5
Total or average	4,540.8	2,281.7	50.3

Source: Contrôle Financier du Sénégal, *Les Modalités d'Intervention du Fonds Européen de Développement au Sénégal*, 1968.

whereas the extension services, seed distribution, provision of fertilizers, and soil preservation on the whole proceeded satisfactorily and represented actual expenditure of nearly CFAF 2.3 billion out of CFAF 2.4 billion of credits granted.

For the fourth year 1967/68 the amount of credits was set at nearly CFAF 2.0 billion, but no information is yet available regarding its use. It seems probable, however, that by May 1969 Senegal did not use all the remaining credits available at the end of the third year.

Cotton

During 1965/66–1968/69, production of cotton increased from 300 tons (unginned) to 9,700 tons and the area under cotton cultivation from 400 hectares to 3,000 hectares (see Table 5). The yield (1.5 tons per hectare) is one of the best in Africa. The first cotton mill was set up in Tambacounda to work the production of Casamance and Sénégal Oriental. A second cotton mill is planned in Sine-Saloum. The producer price has been fixed at CFAF 37.20 per kilogram (unginned), but after deduction of the cost of fertilizers and sanitary treatment, the producer receives only CFAF 33 per kilogram for first-quality cotton and CFAF 20 for second-quality cotton. Marketing is handled by the French Development Company (Compagnie Française pour le Développement des Fibres Textiles, or CFDT), which gins the cotton and sells the fiber to industry at CFAF 137,000–145,000 per ton, based on the world price of cotton as imported from Mali.

Crops Mainly for Food

Millet and sorghum, the basic food crops in Senegal, cover roughly 80 per cent of the total area devoted to crops grown mainly for food (see Table 5). They are cultivated in rotation with groundnuts during the same periods and are sown in June–July and harvested in September–December according to variety. Production, which had gradually increased from 392,000 tons in 1960/61 to 654,000 tons in 1967/68, dropped to 450,272 tons in 1968/69 owing to severe drought. Most of the millet grown is consumed directly by the producers; the small quantities (about 15,000 tons in 1967/68) sold are marketed by the Development Assistance Office. The producer price is established each year by the Government in close relation to groundnut prices. From 1960 to 1966, producer prices for millet remained unchanged at CFAF 20 per kilogram. They declined to CFAF 17 in 1967/68 because of the increased cost of storage. Apart from the bad 1968/69 crop the second development plan target (600,000 tons annually) was reached. The 1969–73 Development Plan calls for a further rise in production to 700,000 tons from 1.1 million hectares. Efforts will be concentrated on increasing yields per hectare.

Other food crops include cassava, maize, niebe beans, sweet potatoes, and fonio, planted by farmers mainly for their own use. Small quantities are sold on local markets. Production of cassava, niebe beans, and sweet potatoes increased considerably in 1966/67 because of the drop in groundnut and millet production.

Rice has always been a traditional subsistence food crop in Casamance, where swamp rice or upland rice is cultivated on family farms. Since most of the output is consumed directly, the rapidly rising demand for rice in the rest of the country has had to be covered by imports of 150,000–200,000 tons a year. An attempt to produce rice by mechanized methods in the Sénégal Valley (the Richard-Toll project), started in 1949, has never been profitable, and the area is to be converted to sugarcane. In 1964, another attempt was begun in the delta of the Sénégal. This project, financed by FAC, will provide, over ten years, 30,000 hectares of irrigated land available for paddy rice cultivation.

During 1965/66–1967/68, total rice production expanded from 122,000 to 137,000 tons, or by 12 per cent, and the cultivated area from 82,000 to 101,000 hectares, or by 23 per cent. Prospects for the 1968/69 crop year were not favorable because of lack of flooding in the Sénégal Valley and because of drought in the Casamance uplands. Total production dropped to 58,000 tons, or by 57 per cent from the 1967/68 level. Casamance produced only 43,000 tons (down from 101,000 tons in 1967/68) and the river area 12,000 tons (down from 31,000 tons). Only 529 tons were marketed through the official channels, against 6,500 tons in 1967/68. An over-all development scheme for rice cultivation will be implemented under the third development plan for agricultural diversification (see "Agricultural diversification program," below) in order to achieve an annual production of 250,000 tons.

Vegetables are produced mainly in Cap Vert (27,600 tons in 1968/69) and Thiès (6,200 tons in 1968/69) and around the cities. Total output rose from 32,000 tons in 1965/66 to 41,000 tons in 1967/68 and 1968/69. Most of the output is sold in urban areas. However, about 1,000 tons of green beans were exported to France by air from December 1967 to April 1968, and the quantity was expected to increase to 1,500 tons in 1968/69. A recently established plant to produce tomato concentrate closed when farmers would not accept the low tomato prices offered by the manufacturer.

Agricultural Diversification Program

In order to lessen the country's dependence on groundnut exports and on imported staple foods, the Government is considering agricultural diversification as an essential component of its agricultural policy. Under the Second Four-Year Development Plan (1965/66–1968/69), about 25 per cent of the total expenditure was allocated to agriculture, with effort concentrated on diversifying production as well as increasing productivity of groundnut and millet cultivation. This diversification program covered cotton, sugarcane, rice, vegetable, and fruit production. Significant gain in production of these crops still depends on further research, experimentation, and development of irrigation.

The cotton project, started in 1963 in the Casamance upland and in Sénégal Oriental, has been carried out by the French Development Company (Compagnie Française pour le Développement des Fibres Textiles, or CFDT) with FAC assistance and, from 1965, with EDF subsidies. The original plan called for 4,000 hectares under cotton cultivation by 1968/69. The project has been highly successful. The revised target is to reach 12,500 hectares in 1971, or production much above the 4,500 tons of cotton fiber now needed by the local textile industry. At the end of the third development plan, in 1973, the area under cotton cultivation may reach 30,000 hectares. Extension of cotton production will continue to be managed by this company. Diversion to cotton is also planned for part of lands now used for groundnuts.

The sugarcane project is less advanced than the cotton project. Since 1962, experimental tests have been made under the control of the French Institut de Recherches Agronomiques Tropicales et de Cultures Vivrières. It appears that sugarcane production is feasible on part of the land (the Richard-Toll area) where rice production proved unsuccessful. The project includes progressive cultivation of 3,200 hectares (800 hectares a year) and diversion of the Taoué River for better irrigation. Investments are estimated at about CFAF 4.6 billion, of which CFAF 0.6 billion is for the diversion of the river. Preliminary discussions for financing have been held with the Caisse Centrale de Coopération Economique (CCCE), FAC, and EDF. The output of sugar, expected to reach 30,000 tons annually, will be processed in a sugar mill and a sugar refinery to be established by French private interests (55 per cent) and the Senegalese Government (45 per cent).

Since domestic consumption of rice is growing faster than production, necessitating larger and larger imports, several projects for expanding rice cultivation are being implemented: (1) provision of extension services to farmers and the development of new land (about 2,000 hectares) in the Ziguinchor area, financed by EDF; (2) development of about 30,000 hectares in the Sénégal delta, of which about 10,500 hectares are now cultivated by small holders and cooperatives farming under the management of the Société d'Aménagement et d'Exploitation des Terres du Delta (SAED), assisted by the Société d'Assistance Technique et de Coopération (SATEC); (3) establishment of a rice mill with a capacity of processing 15,000 tons a year, so far financed by FAC; and (4) smaller rice development projects along the Sénégal. The over-all target is to reach a production of rice (paddy) of 250,000 tons at the end of the third development plan.

As part of the Sénégal delta project, an 85-kilometer embankment on the left bank of the river was completed at the end of 1969. Moreover, five new villages have been established and the population of the area is increasing steadily. Cooperatives (29 in number) and rural associations (*associations d'intérêt rural*) with a total membership of 4,500 have been set up. The rice mill at Ross Bethio has an hourly productive capacity of 4 tons of paddy rice. At the end of 1969, total investment expenditures amounted to CFAF 3 billion; the Government provided 0.9 billion and FAC extended the rest in the form of subsidies (CFAF 0.8 billion) and loans (CFAF 1.3 billion). Efforts are to be concentrated on improving management, producing tomatoes, and increasing productivity. The third plan calls for expansion of the rice area in the delta from the 10,500 hectares cultivated in 1969 to 13,500 hectares in 1973.

Expansion of market gardening depends on increased outlets, since vegetable consumption is practically limited to the urban population. Although a recent attempt to produce tomatoes for industrial processing has failed, a further attempt will be made under the third development plan, with the aim of reaching about 33,000 tons on 1,640 hectares.

Several other projects are being implemented. The most important includes the increase of confectionery production in Casamance and Sine-Saloum from about 3,000 tons of groundnuts (unshelled) to 15,000 tons in the next four years. The Sine-Saloum project, which is the larger, calls for an investment of CFAF 55 million, for which EDF financing is hoped. Attempts are also being made to develop the production of bananas, pineapples, avocados, and grafted mangoes. Experimental culture of tobacco has failed in Casamance, but encouraging results have been obtained in Sine-Saloum.

Livestock and Livestock Products

Livestock, especially cattle, plays an important role in the rural economy of Senegal. Not only is cattle raising traditionally a nomadic occupation in northern Senegal, but it is also important as a subsidiary enterprise of the sedentary farmers in the central and southern parts of the country. From 1965 to 1967, the estimated number of cattle increased from 2,219,000 to 2,476,000, or by 12 per cent, and the number of goats and sheep from 1,908,000 to 2,448,000, or by 28 per cent. These high growth rates reflect the Government's success in efforts to eradicate rinderpest and to increase livestock watering facilities by drilling wells. Nevertheless, Senegal still depends on imports to satisfy domestic meat requirements. Recorded imports in 1967 consisted of some 23,000 bovines and some 175,000 goats and sheep, mainly from Mauritania. Substantial imports and some exports, however, are not recorded. Meat consumption is estimated at 11 kilograms per person, or some 40,000 tons a year; recorded slaughter accounted for about 20,000 tons, or about half of the total.

Several projects are under way to improve livestock production and to organize and increase the marketing of meat and milk. The EDF, FAC, and other foreign assistance organizations have agreed to finance a number of these projects. The main projects actually completed are the model ranch at Doli, which can accommodate about 10,000 head of cattle on its 80,000 hectares, and the dairy complex in Saint-Louis, which began operation at the end of 1968 and has a production capacity of 5,000 liters of milk a day to be raised to 10,000 liters after one year. Dairy centers will be established in Kaolack, Thiès, and Dahra. Other projects in progress include the construction of slaughter-houses and cold storage plants. Furthermore, the Government intends to expand and improve the livestock extension service and provide better measures of sanitary control.

Fishing

Fishing provided for CFAF 4.5 billion of revenue in 1967, or about 3 per cent of national income. Moreover, fish is a major element in the diet of the population (31.4 kilograms a year per capita according to a 1964 estimate).

Two methods of fishing are used in Senegal: (1) traditional shallow water fishing, employing about 30,000 persons with trawlers and about 5,000 pirogues, half of which are equipped with outboard motors, and (2) modern deep-sea fishing, until recently undertaken by French boats unloading their tuna catch in Dakar for processing, but since 1965 by the state-owned Fishing Company (Société Sénégalaise d'Armement à la Pêche, or SOSAP) operating its own boats. A number of plants produce canned and frozen tuna in Dakar. Smaller enterprises produce frozen shrimps and canned pilchards and sardines for domestic consumption.

From 1959 to 1967, production of fish rose by 80 per cent, reaching 133,000 tons in 1967 and 70,300 tons in the first six months of 1968 (Table 11). Fish for local marketing in the form of fresh fish or dried, salted, and smoked fish totaled 124,000 tons in 1967, compared with 107,000 tons in 1966; the remainder included tuna catches for canneries and export.

Under the Second Four-Year Development Plan, the Government intended to modernize and organize the traditional fishing sector and set up a Senegalese fleet for tuna fishing and a new tuna processing plant, financed by the Soviet Union and France. At the end of 1968, the state-owned Fishing Company had five tuna boats in service and was expecting four other boats to be delivered in 1969 and ten boats in 1970/71, the latter under a Soviet Union loan. Construction of the cannery was delayed because the two existing plants in Dakar were able to process the actual tuna catch. Exports of canned tuna are directed to the French market under a guaranteed quota, which has always exceeded actual exports. Under the third plan the production target was 200,000 tons for traditional shallow-water fishing, 25,000 tons for tuna (against 10,600 tons for the first half of 1968) and 40,000 tons for sardines (against 15,600 tons in 1968). The number of tuna boats and trawlers will be increased and port infrastructure improved.

TABLE 11. SENEGAL: FISH CATCH, BY FISHING METHOD, 1965–68

	Traditional	Trawler	Tuna	Total
QUANTITY (*thousand metric tons*)				
1965	88.6	7.9	5.7	92.2
1966	96.2	10.4	8.7	115.3
1967	105.4	18.2	9.4 [1]	133.0
1968 [2]	59.7 [3]	... [3]	10.6 [1]	70.3
VALUE (*billion CFA francs*)				
1965	3.8	0.3	0.5	4.6
1966	3.4	0.2	0.7	4.3
1967 [4]	3.1	0.7	0.7	4.5

Source: Data provided by the Senegalese authorities.

[1] Of which the catch by the Société Sénégalaise d'Armement à la Pêche was 3,200 tons in 1967 and 3,000 tons in 1968.

[2] For six months only.

[3] Trawler fish catch included with traditional.

[4] Value for 1968 not available.

ENERGY AND WATER SUPPLY

Domestic consumption of firewood is roughly estimated at 3.5 million cubic meters and consumption of charcoal at 50,000 tons. In addition to firewood and charcoal consumed, about 20,000 tons of groundnut shells are burned in the oil mills to produce energy.

Domestic petroleum requirements have been covered by imports of crude oil since 1963, with the establishment at Mbao (just south of Saint-Louis) of the Oil Refinery (Société Africaine de Raffinage, or SAR), having a refining capacity of about 600,000 tons of crude oil a year. The volume of crude oil refined by the Oil Refinery rose from 272,000 tons in 1964 to 510,000 tons in 1967, responding to the increased domestic demand, particularly for gas, oil, and fuel oil, although consumption of gasoline remained practically stable (Table 12). Two foreign petroleum companies are conducting exploration on offshore concessions. Although no exploitable deposits have so far been found, there are indications of sizable deposits.

Electricity consumption doubled during 1960–68, totaling 245.3 million kilowatt-hours in 1968 and 201.5 million kilowatt-hours during the first nine months of 1969. The highest rate of growth relates to high-voltage current because of the increasing demand from the Phosphate Company (Compagnie Sénégalaise des Phosphates de Taïba, or CSPT). Electric power supply and distribution is operated by a private company. According to a concessionary agreement with the Government, the Compagnie des Eaux et d'Electricité de l'Ouest Africain (EEOA) produces 99 per cent of the total output. Total generating capacity rose to 110 million kilowatts in 1966, when a new thermal power station was built at Cap des Biches (Rufisque) with a capacity of 27.5 million kilowatts, corresponding to a CFAF 1.9 billion investment. For industry, rates range from CFAF 7 to CFAF 9 per kilowatt-hour; however, some factories received preferential prices (about CFAF 6 per kilowatt-hour and even CFAF 4.5 per kilowatt-hour for the Phosphate Company). For other customers, it amounts to CFAF 34.59 per kilowatt-hour (taxes not included). Lower rates are granted for public lighting and home appliance use. These rates are 10 per cent higher at Thiès and 20 per cent higher in other areas; this differential partly explains the concentration of industry in the Cap Vert area.

TABLE 12. SENEGAL: ENERGY PRODUCTION AND CONSUMPTION, 1964–69

	1964	1965	1966	1967	1968 [1]	1969 [1] Jan.–Sept.
Firewood (*million cubic meters*) [1]	3.5	3.5	3.5	3.5	…	…
Charcoal (*thousand metric tons*) [1]	50.0	50.0	50.0	50.0	…	…
Groundnut shells (*thousand metric tons*) [1]	20.0	20.0	20.0	20.0	…	…
Petroleum products refined from crude oil (*thousand metric tons*)	272.0	448.0	455.0	510.0	…	…
Gasoline sales (*thousand cubic meters*)	93.7	94.0	94.2	94.2	97.3	72.3
Gas oil sales (*thousand cubic meters*)	33.9	36.4	36.9	39.0	48.2	22.0
Diesel oil sales (*thousand metric tons*)	26.1	32.3	36.9	29.0	26.0	21.0
Fuel oil sales (*thousand metric tons*)	126.3	130.3	140.1	138.3	150.9	118.5
Electricity sales (*million kilowatt-hours*)						
Lighting	26.7	27.3	27.7	27.5	26.5	20.9
Household appliances	25.7	26.0	29.5	30.4	30.8	25.6
Low voltage	13.7	12.6	13.2	13.5	13.5	11.1
High voltage	130.7	138.2	152.1	168.1	174.5	143.9
Phosphate plant at Taïba	48.7	56.8	61.5	69.0	54.6	53.8
Total electricity sales	196.8	204.1	222.5	239.5	245.3	201.5

Sources: Ministère du Plan et de l'Industrie, *Situation Economique du Sénégal en 1967*, and BCEAO, *Notes d'Information et Statistiques.*

[1] Estimated.

According to a concessionary agreement with the Government, water is supplied by the Compagnie Générale des Eaux du Sénégal (CGES). In 1967, 24.7 million cubic meters of water were sold at price differentials like those for electric power. To meet increasing water needs in Dakar, EDF subsidies (CFAF 1,550 million), German loans (CFAF 2,160 million), and the Senegalese Government budget (CFAF 600 million) are providing funds to build a 250-kilometer (155-mile) water pipeline from the Lac de Guiers in northern Senegal to Dakar. About CFAF 5,700 million is to be furnished in the form of suppliers' credits, mostly from the German firm, Mannesmann.

MINING

Mining accounts for 1 or 2 per cent of GDP and for about 8 per cent of total export earnings. Its contribution to government revenue is low as a result of tax exemptions granted to the main companies under the Investment Code. Phosphates are practically the sole mineral product. However, the French Bureau de Recherches Géologiques et Minières (BRGM) and a UN Special Fund team are conducting other mineral research—excluding oil prospecting. Diamonds, gold, iron, traces of chromite, and copper have been found, but further studies are necessary. Petroleum prospecting is being carried out in offshore areas by two companies; so far without profitable results.

Two large deposits of phosphates are worked in Senegal: (1) a calcium phosphate deposit at Taïba, and (2) an aluminum phosphate deposit at Thiès (see map); each has been estimated at about 100 million tons. Production of calcium phosphate is entrusted to the internationally owned Phosphate Company (Compagnie Sénégalaise des Phosphates Taïba, or CSPT), which started operations in 1960 with an annual 600,000-ton capacity; this capacity was raised to 1,100,000 tons in 1966/67. Production of phosphate rose from 0.5 million tons in 1962 to 1.1 million in 1969 (Table 13), but phosphate exports declined from 1.1 million tons in 1966 to 0.9 million in 1969. Most of the output is exported, mainly to Japan, Germany, and the United Kingdom; however, Germany and the United Kingdom reduced their purchases in 1967 and stopped altogether in 1968. Domestic sales increased from 3,000 tons in 1966 to 35,000 tons in 1969. Prospects will depend on new investments, partly financed by the recent loan

TABLE 13. SENEGAL: PRODUCTION OF SELECTED INDUSTRIAL AND MINERAL PRODUCTS, 1960–69

(In thousands of metric tons, except as noted)

	1962	1963	1964	1965	1966	1967	1968	1969 Jan.–May
Cement	183	190	205	181	195	172	202	90
Matches[1]	11,274	10,411	9,735	13,162	14,569	8,554	9,543	...
Beer[2]	97	109	104	93	83	74	79	...
Groundnut oil (crude)	107	105	115	120	127	121	} 192	85
Groundnut oil (refined)	49	53	57	58	58	56		
Salt	48	60	56	51	61	71	84	27
Cotton yarn[3]	602	646	360	330	407	446	548	...
Cotton cloth[3]	1,124	1,178	1,213	1,131	1,346	1,426	1,083	...
Cotton blankets[3]	274	258	245	269	243	158	127	...
Processed fish	10	19	24	12	18	24	11	...
Titanium	26	16	2	—	—	—	—	—
Calcium phosphate	497	464	677	903	990	1,115	1,100	...
Aluminum phosphate	141	126	121	135	145	161	164	...
Aluminum phosphate (dehydrated)	42	18	32	18	52	52	44	...

Sources: Ministère du Plan et de l'Industrie, Bulletin Statistique et Economique Mensuel, and data provided by the Senegalese authorities.

[1] Cases of 7,200 boxes.
[2] Thousand barrels.
[3] Tons.

guaranteed by France, in order to improve productivity and cut the selling price, which now amounts to $11–13 per ton f.o.b. Dakar. The phosphate deposit at Keur Morfal (southeast of Mboro) was being abandoned in 1970 because of mining difficulties, and a new deposit at Ndomor Diop (south of Mboro) was to be in production in 1970. Then, the Company's annual productive capacity will be 1,500,000 tons.

Since 1948, the Société Sénégalaise des Phosphates de Thiès (SSPT), a branch of the French Péchiney-Saint Gobain company, has extracted the aluminum phosphate. Production increased from 145,000 tons in 1966 to 161,000 tons in 1967 and to 164,000 tons in 1969. As a result of Péchiney's advertising campaign, sales rose from 130,000 tons in 1966 to 150,000 tons in 1967. Exports go mostly to France and Spain, but some go to Ivory Coast, Cameroon, and the People's Republic of the Congo. By the end of 1968, investments amounted to CFAF 1.3 billion. No further investment is planned because of sufficient production capacity (about 250,000 tons).

Titanium has been extracted from the black sands of the beaches of Casamance by a French-owned company and from the Saloum River, but operations stopped in 1965 as a result of insufficient profits due to the decline of reserves. Another French-owned company started in 1965 to work deposits of attapulgite (used in oil drilling) in the Pout and Nianing areas. Production rose from 1,500 tons in 1966 to 2,780 tons in 1967; about 85 per cent of the output is exported. From the production of salt in Kaolack of 83,558 tons in 1968, Senegal exported 14,000 tons, mainly to Ivory Coast, Mali, and Niger. Some other mineral products used in construction, such as clayish limestone, basalt, and marble, are also being extracted in greater quantities.

MANUFACTURING

Senegal has a relatively well-developed manufacturing sector. Before World War II, Senegal imported almost all of its requirements for manufactures, and industry was limited to processing the groundnut crop; during and for about 15 years after the war, however, industrial production expanded rapidly. Because of Dakar's port facilities, its role as the administrative capital of the French West African Federation, and the Dakar-Bamako railroad, Dakar and the surrounding areas in Cap Vert provided a logical location for new industries to supply the 20 million consumers of the Federation. When the Federation broke up and the newly independent countries established competing industries in the early 1960's, Senegalese manufacturing activities began to slow down and were forced into a period of readjustment. Encouraged by new investment, fiscal incentives, and two successive good groundnut crops in 1964/65 and 1965/66 which lifted incomes in the countryside, manufacturing activity revived strongly in 1966. In 1967, the level of activity was sustained, but the growth rate was much slower than in 1966.

The industrial sector (excluding construction) contributed about 18 per cent of GDP, compared with 10 per cent in 1959 before independence. There are almost 400 industrial enterprises, employing about 30,000 workers (including seasonal wage earners). According to the official industrial index (1959 = 100, 43 enterprises), the volume of industrial production increased from 132.2 in 1962 to 160.7 in 1968 (or by 22 per cent) and to 175.6 during the first quarter of 1969 (Table 14).

For a better analysis and knowledge of this important sector of the economy, the Ministry of Planning and Industry conducted a census of industry in 1966 and 1967. The 1967 census included 133 enterprises representing 97 per cent of total turnover. According to this breakdown, the turnover of these 133 enterprises amounted to CFAF 60 billion, of which 46 per cent was exported. Food industries contributed 48 per cent of the total turnover, and oil mills 72 per cent of the food industries turnover. Wages, paid to 17,706 wage earners, amounted to CFAF 6.1 billion. Investments totaled CFAF 5.5 billion, of which CFAF 5 billion was for extension, mostly in the mining sector.

To compare 1966 and 1967, the Ministry of Planning and Industry used the 1966 census, which covered only 109 enterprises but represented 96 per cent of the turnover recorded in the 1967 census (Table 15). It appears that turnover increased by 5 per cent from 1966 to 1967, exports by nearly 7 per cent, and the number of wage earners by nearly 5 per cent. The latter figure, however, should be considered cautiously because the number of seasonal workers is not well known. The total wage bill went up by 11 per cent to CFAF 6.0 billion; investment decreased by 12 per cent, with the completion in 1966 of the Cap des Biches thermal power station at Rufisque.

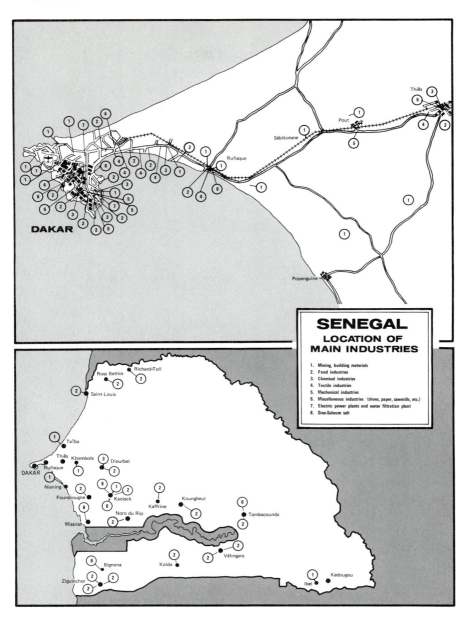

SENEGAL
LOCATION OF
MAIN INDUSTRIES

1. Mining, building materials
2. Food industries
3. Chemical industries
4. Textile industries
5. Mechanical industries
6. Miscellaneous industries (shoes, paper, sawmills, etc.)
7. Electric power plants and water filtration plant
8. Sine-Saloum salt

TABLE 14. SENEGAL: VOLUME INDEX OF INDUSTRIAL PRODUCTION AND MINING, 1962–69 [1]

(1959 = 100)

	Weight	1962	1963	1964	1965	1966	1967	1968	1969 Jan.–Mar.
Power	136	163.2	165.9	187.1	193.0	210.1	222.6	238.1	240.1
Mining	20	477.2	438.5	549.1	693.1	785.9	872.9	861.8	889.2
Building materials	56	107.0	111.5	116.6	105.5	112.0	99.4	116.7	119.3
Chemicals	45	104.2	116.4	109.0	116.2	129.2	141.8	148.9	171.9
Tobacco and matches	129	115.9	91.6	85.6	95.3	98.3	92.1	85.1	119.1
Groundnut oil	352	107.0	111.2	122.3	123.8	129.5	123.2	135.2	147.8
Grain, flour, and biscuits	62	112.0	108.4	102.4	94.3	103.6	95.1	97.6	124.7
Sugar and beverages	47	130.8	143.0	140.7	130.1	129.4	116.3	118.8	125.3
Canned goods	10	203.0	224.5	173.1	131.5	160.5	163.2	217.2	395.6
Textiles	63	122.3	134.6	134.0	151.2	189.7	216.6	197.9	234.5
Shoes	36	127.6	188.2	158.7	128.6	160.0	177.2	174.7	171.0
Others	44	223.1	148.3	184.9	158.7	299.2	256.8	152.2	132.0
General index	1,000	132.2	131.2	139.0	141.5	159.7	160.4	160.7	175.6
General index excluding mining	*...*	*125.2*	*125.0*	*130.6*	*130.3*	*146.9*	*145.9*	*...*	*...*
General index excluding mining, canneries, and groundnut oil mills	*...*	*134.3*	*131.2*	*134.6*	*133.9*	*156.6*	*158.5*	*...*	*...*

Sources: Ministère du Plan et de l'Industrie, *Bulletin Statistique et Economique Mensuel*, and *Situation Economique du Sénégal en 1967*, and data provided by the Senegalese authorities.

[1] Excluding construction.

TABLE 15. SENEGAL: INDUSTRIAL ACTIVITY CENSUS, 1966–67

| | Number of Enterprises | Turnover (Million CFA francs) | | Exports (Million CFA francs) | | Number of Wage Earners (Thousands) | | Net Wages | | Investments | | | |
| | | | | | | | | | | Extension (Million CFA francs) | | Renewal | |
		1966	1967	1966	1967	1966	1967	1966	1967	1966	1967	1966	1967
Mining	8	4,365.8	3,832.5	3,982.4	3,670.4	1,543	1,436	656.2	695.2	2,909.0	2,876.5	363.3	67.4
Food industries	29	28,190.7	28,238.6	18,073.4	19,969.9	5,057	5,290	1,515.0	1,680.1	749.0	880.4	51.1	53.2
Tobacco	5	2,521.3	2,537.6	344.4	360.0	670	600	230.7	230.8	49.5	37.2	18.3	4.9
Textiles	8	4,718.6	5,654.7	1,342.1	1,210.4	2,238	2,378	531.0	607.1	341.4	406.1	7.3	4.7
Shoes, clothing	4	1,874.5	2,076.9	594.5	754.6	1,477	1,519	470.7	468.4	61.0	100.0	26.0	45.7
Wood, furniture	6	317.0	313.0	30.3	25.0	196	212	57.1	56.0	4.5	86.4	2.6	0.7
Paper, printing	8	751.8	781.9	113.0	92.3	316	320	142.3	141.5	29.6	31.6	3.4	4.7
Chemicals and petroleum products	13	5,214.7	6,653.1	582.2	693.6	896	1,013	422.3	480.2	82.0	146.7	5.9	2.2
Building materials	7	1,153.5	1,347.6	182.0	112.0	626	611	181.8	196.5	41.8	24.7	4.2	10.4
Metal industry	18	2,539.0	2,945.8	100.2	199.4	1,172	1,042	385.0	457.4	47.5	23.1	12.5	16.2
Water, power	3	3,688.1	3,799.6	—	—	1,778	2,271	809.0	944.4	1,826.9	196.0	120.9	271.0
Total	109	55,335.0	58,181.3	25,344.5	27,087.6	15,969	16,692	5,401.1	5,957.6	6,142.2	4,808.7	615.5	481.1

Source: Ministère du Plan et de l'Industrie, Rapport Annuel de la Direction de l'Industrie Année 1967.

The largest branch of Senegalese manufacturing industry comprises the groundnut oil mills, which produced 192,000 tons of crude and refined oil in 1968, compared with 177,000 tons in 1967 (see Table 13). From 1962 to 1966, the index for volume of output rose by 21 per cent to 129.5, declined in 1967, and rose again in 1968, reaching 147.8 in the first quarter of 1969. As a priority buyer on the groundnut market, this industry is not seriously affected by fluctuations in groundnut crops and has been growing satisfactorily, increasing invested capital and production capacity. Five firms process some 500,000 tons of unshelled groundnuts a year. The largest of these enterprises, at Dakar, is a branch of a large French company. It has a crushing capacity of 225,000 tons of unshelled groundnuts (or 40 per cent of total crushing capacity in Senegal), which will be raised to 350,000 tons in 1970 through CFAF 1 billion of new investment. Production of groundnut cakes, a by-product used mainly for feeding cattle, amounted to about 200,000 tons in 1967, compared with 193,000 tons in 1966. The bulk of the oil and cake produced is exported to France, where oil sales enjoyed guaranteed prices until 1967 (see above).

Other food processing industries include mainly canneries, flour mills, sugar, and beverage factories. The canning industry operates mainly for export and depends on tuna catches. Production capacity is not fully utilized, especially since the establishment of a new plant in 1968. Although the production index for canned goods declined from 203.0 in 1962 to 131.5 in 1965, it reached 395.6 in early 1969. Expansion of the tuna catch, however, is expected to boost production in the coming years. Flour mills, which have been cut off from the export outlets of neighboring countries, work at 75 per cent of their capacity. The production index of grain, flour, and biscuits declined irregularly during 1962–67 from 112.0 to 95.1 but rose to 124.7 in the first quarter of 1969. A sugar refinery set up in 1967 has a productive capacity of 30,000 tons, which can be raised to 50,000 tons if necessary. The output of refined sugar reached 20,000 tons in 1967, compared with total domestic consumption of about 50,000 tons. Production of beer and nonalcoholic beverages declined from 238,000 hectoliters in 1966 to 188,000 hectoliters in 1967. Production of beer has been particularly affected by the loss of the market represented by the French military establishment in Senegal, and by the closing of the outlets in neighbor-

ing countries where breweries were installed after independence. The
Dakar Brewery (Brasserie de Dakar), established in 1929 with a production capacity of 150,000 hectoliters, produced only 73,800 hectoliters in 1967. The production index for sugar and beverages reached a
low point of 116.3 in 1967 but rose to 126.3 in early 1969.

The textile industry, the second largest branch of the manufacturing
sector in Senegal, has expanded considerably in recent years (see
Table 14). During 1962–67 its volume index rose by 77 per cent to
216.6, declined in 1968, then rose in the first quarter of 1969 to 234.5.
There are eight textile enterprises employing about 2,000 persons, but
the sector is dominated by two large enterprises, both foreign owned:
(1) Industrie Cotonnière Africaine (ICOTAF) with one plant at
Pikine, near Dakar (spinning, weaving, and dyeing), and another one
at Rufisque (spinning and weaving), both of which can produce
10 million meters of fabric, 250,000 blankets, and 700 tons of cotton
yarn annually, and (2) Société de Teinture, Blanchiment, Apprêt et
Impression (SOTIBA), which specializes in printing and includes, since
1967, a plant to provide the "wax" fabric. The second enterprise can
print 20 million meters of cotton fabric a year; it exports 30 per cent
of its production to Ivory Coast, Mauritania, and Niger. These two
enterprises are establishing a joint venture, a new weaving plant at
Thiès, the Société Textile Sénégalaise. Until recently Senegal had
imported cotton in bales mainly from Mali. From now on, local cotton
will furnish an increasing part of the mill supply, with the target of
fully supplying the Senegalese textile industry by 1971. In 1967, the
total turnover of the textile sector rose by almost 20 per cent compared
with 1966, and the outlook is promising for the coming years.

Shoes are produced by one factory—Bata; its output was 5.0 million
pairs of shoes in 1967, compared with 4.6 million in 1966, but did not
regain the 1963 record of 5.7 million. This industry succeeded in offsetting the loss of its outlets in the former West African Federation by
exporting to English-speaking African countries. Imports from Japan
and Hong Kong, however, continue to be smuggled through The
Gambia. The index of production, which was 127.6 in 1962, rose
sharply in 1963 to 188, but was at a lower level of 171.0 in early 1969.

The output index of the chemical industry increased by 43 per cent
during 1962–68 and by an additional 15 per cent in the first quarter of

1969, reaching 171.9 (see Table 14), mainly because of an increase in the production of refined petroleum products, soap, and fertilizers. Some other industrial production either did not advance or actually declined, but nearly all advanced in early 1969. In 1968 a new fertilizer plant at Mbao, near Dakar, was opened. It utilizes local rock phosphate and has a productive capacity of about 130,000 tons a year. It is designed mainly for the domestic market (80,000 tons were expected in 1969). Investment amounted to CFAF 3.1 billion, which was financed, inter alia, by IFC.

Other enterprises cover a wide range of activities (e.g., metalworking, battery production, wood furniture manufacturing, packing, and printing). As a whole, the index of this sector declined by 29 per cent from 1962 to 1965. In 1966, however, the index rose to 299.2 but declined thereafter to 132.0 in the first quarter of 1969, owing to difficulties in marketing batteries and metal furniture.

The building material industry appears relatively overequipped since the loss of markets in Mali and Ivory Coast for cement and the reduction of building activity in Senegal. Cement is produced by one factory, the Société Ouest Africaine des Ciments (SOCOCIM), which has a productive capacity (220,000 tons) larger than domestic needs. Output declined from 195,000 tons in 1966 to 172,000 tons in 1967. However, it reached 115,000 tons during the first half of 1968, partly because of new export contracts with the Malagasy Republic. Other plants of the industry include production of bricks and fiber-cement sheets. All generally work below their designed capacities. Although the index of output reached a low level of 99.4 in 1967, it rose in 1968, reaching 119.3 in early 1969.

Under the Second Development Plan (1965/66–1968/69), about CFAF 15.6 billion, or about 78 per cent of the total of CFAF 20 billion for industrial investment projected, was disbursed. The energy industry (with the new power plant and the petroleum refinery), the chemical industry (with the fertilizer plant), the food industry (with the oil mill extension and the sugar refinery), and the mining industry are the branches of industry reaching the highest percentages of realization.

The third plan gives priority to food processing. The main projects include three dairy plants in Kaolack, Thiès, and Dakar, two concentrated tomato plants, rice mills, cotton mills, slaughterhouses, and meat canneries. A rise in the industrial production index is projected from 100 in 1969 to 122.9 in 1978, with the highest increases in mining, textile, canneries, electricity production, chemical industries, tobacco and match production, footwear production, and oil mills. The over-all industrial turnover would rise from CFAF 69.4 billion in 1969 to CFAF 93.5 billion in 1973, of which CFAF 8.2 billion would relate to newly established industries. The value added by the industrial sector should increase from CFAF 28.2 billion in 1969 to CFAF 39.4 billion in 1973, of which CFAF 13.3 billion would be in the food processing sector and CFAF 7.8 billion in textiles. Employment in industry is planned to rise from 18,300 in 1969 to 23,750 in 1973.

The main problem for private investors remains the development of the domestic market, since exports of manufactured goods to neighboring countries are now limited by competing production in those countries. To aid private investors, the Government has recently sponsored the establishment of the Société Nationale des Etudes et Promotions Industrielles (SONEPI) with the following aims: (1) centralizing all information relating to industrial projects; (2) preparing the Government's industrial studies; (3) studying equity participation of the Government in private companies; (4) keeping in touch with investors for extension of existing industries and for creation of new industries; and (5) promoting national businessmen.

COMMERCE, HANDICRAFTS, AND TOURISM

Commercial activities in recent years have been somewhat depressed, reflecting lower purchasing power after two bad crops and the prospect of a third one in 1968/69. Apart from the reduction in the domestic market following independence, many shopkeepers complain of these matters: (1) high import duties and taxes, which encourage smuggling; (2) loss of business due to the departure of most of the French military establishment; (3) excessive numbers of shopkeepers in some cities; and (4) interference from government-owned companies. One government-owned company is the Agricultural Marketing Board (OCAS), established to purchase groundnuts and millet and to sell imported agricultural staples in the framework of the cooperative system set up in 1960 in order to prevent excessive profits by former private traders (described under "Agriculture and fishing," above). Furthermore, in 1965, the Government decided to establish the Supply and Distribution Company (Société Nouvelle pour l'Approvisionnement et la Distribution au Sénégal, or SONADIS); its equity capital is shared between the Government and two private companies in order to supply the inland country after the departure of a number of foreign shopkeepers following independence. This establishment followed a preliminary census by the Ministry of Commerce which showed weakness in the retail commerce structure, predominance of big cities, importance of the road network in supplying the country, and the level of retail prices. The targets of the Supply and Distribution Company were to set up a network of department stores throughout the country and to contribute to the training of national shopkeepers. At present, the Company controls 80 stores, and the grouping into cooperatives of national shopkeepers is progressing.

Handicraft activities, which involve about 40,000 persons (about 20,000 persons in Cap Vert alone) are in three divisions: (1) art handicrafts (i.e., gold, brass, leather, and woodworking); (2) processing handicrafts (e.g., joinery, cabinet work, weaving of clothing materials, and soldering); and (3) service handicrafts (i.e., all types of repair work). Because art handicrafts represent an expression of traditional Senegalese culture, the Government has encouraged their expansion by establishing a handicraft department at the Ministry of Commerce to promote professional training and exhibitions and to create handicraft villages in the country. The first village, set up in Dakar at Sembedioune, is also a tourist attraction.

Tourism, still relatively undeveloped, has possibilities for expansion. Senegal has many natural attractions—prime location, exceptional climate, wildlife reservations, beaches, and sport fishing—as well as a modern airport. At present there is a shortage of hotel accommodations, and the construction of two or three hotels of international class is under consideration. To expand tourism, the Government intends to develop four attractive centers: (1) in the north around Saint-Louis; (2) in the south at Ziguinchor; (3) in the east at Tambacounda, close to the national park, and (4) on the Ile de Gorée, opposite Dakar, which already has a hotel with a sport fishing club.

Under the third plan, investment expenditures in tourism should amount to CFAF 5.1 billion, compared with CFAF 0.2 billion under the second plan.

TRANSPORTATION

Dakar, one of the major African ports, has gained a considerable amount of international traffic since the closing of the Suez Canal. It is the principal port of entry not only for Senegal but also for Mali and Mauritania. The port of Dakar is adequately protected from the ocean swell by northern and southern breakwaters, both of which have been developed to provide cargo handling facilities. The entrance of the port, which is 250 meters (about 800 feet) wide and open day and night, leads into an area of water with a depth of over 10 meters (30 feet). There is no littoral sand drift in the vicinity and no river enters the harbor so that maintenance dredging is not required. Administration of the port is managed by a public agency, the Port Autonome de Dakar. In 1967, IBRD provided a $4 million loan for the extension of one mole to enable Malian traffic to be handled in a custom-free zone, and for reconstruction and dredging.

The port of Dakar handled nearly 3.8 million tons of cargo in 1968, compared with 3.7 million in 1967 (Table 16). The oil supply rose from 0.8 million tons in 1966 to 1.2 million in 1968 as a result of an increase in the number of vessels calling at Dakar (the number arriving and leaving), estimated at 11,580 in 1968, compared with 8,885 in 1966. The volume of merchandise handled reflected the decline in groundnut and phosphate exports and competition from the wharf of Nouakchott in Mauritania. Ship passenger traffic also slowed down after the departure of most of the French troops from Dakar, and the allowance of home leave every year instead of every two years for foreign technical assistants who usually travel by air. The three other ports in Senegal (Saint-Louis, Kaolack, and Ziguinchor) are used mainly for export trade.

Senegal is relatively well endowed with roads, which in 1967 included 1,923 kilometers (1,195 miles) of paved roads, 1,838 kilometers (1,140 miles) of improved earth roads, and about 10,000 kilometers (6,200 miles) of tracks. The main extension of the road network took place during the First Four-Year Development Plan.

TABLE 16. SENEGAL: PORT OF DAKAR AND TRANSPORTATION TRAFFIC, 1964–68

	1964	1965	1966	1967	1968
Port of Dakar					
Number of ships, arrivals and departures	8,453	8,518	8,885	10,926	11,580[1]
Number of passengers (*thousands*)	57	49	42	35	33
Volume of imports (*thousand metric tons*)	1,913	1,783	1,742	2,201	2,136
Petroleum	*1,005*	*873*	*828*	*1,307*	*1,206*
Rice	*186*	*177*	*180*	*156*	*192*
Volume of exports (*thousand metric tons*)	1,397	1,477	1,754	1,451	1,706
Petroleum supplies (*thousand metric tons*)	917	881	811	1,333	1,434
Railway traffic					
Number of passengers					
Total number (*thousands*)	3,219	3,335	3,720	3,663	3,574
Per kilometer (*thousands*)	285	294	288	285	277
Volume of goods transported					
Total volume (*thousand metric tons*)	1,414	1,507	1,837	1,498	1,736
Per kilometer (*million metric tons*)	257	300	333	287	292
Phosphates	*77*	*109*	*132*	*109*	...
Groundnuts	*41*	*38*	*46*	*46*	...
Dakar-Yoff airport traffic					
Number of passengers, arrivals and departures (*thousands*)	132	123	134	138	202
Merchandise loaded and unloaded (*metric tons*)	4,661	4,691	4,652	4,549	5,102

Sources: Ministère du Plan et de l'Industrie, *Situation Economique du Sénégal en 1967*, and *Bulletin Statistique et Economique Mensuel*.

[1] Estimated.

Dakar is the terminal point of the Senegal Railways, which include a main line from Dakar to Kidira on the Malian border and a major branch connecting Dakar with Saint-Louis in the north. Other branches extend to Linguère and Touba, serving groundnut production centers, to Kaolack, and to the calcium phosphate extraction works at Taïba. The main line connects with the Mali Railways, providing the principal route for Mali's export-import trade. Before independence, the two railway systems were operated under single management with headquarters and workshops in Thiès. Senegal Railways was created as a state-owned entity in 1960, taking over that part of the railway located in Senegalese territory and consisting of a total length of track of 1,032 kilometers. From September 1960 until July 1963, when all railway traffic was discontinued between Mali and Senegal, the Senegal Railways sustained considerable loss. Since the resumption of traffic in 1963, international traffic has been regulated by an agreement between the two railways providing for the handling of traffic and operations across the border, exchange of rolling stock, and common tariffs.

Despite the resumption of the traffic with Mali, the Railways' deficit has persisted. In September 1966, IDA approved a US$9 million loan to Senegal for the rehabilitation and modernization of the railways. Since 1967, the Railways' administration has taken vigorous measures to improve the Railways' finances, including dismissal of about 500 railwaymen, most of them auxiliaries or aged. Furthermore, the railroad coordination policy is being implemented through a committee grouping representatives of all types of transport. In principle, the Railways are entitled to transport the groundnut crop and fertilizers as a return cargo. Trucks transport groundnuts to the railway stations and in areas without railroads. Groundnut transportation tariffs amounted to CFAF 7 per ton/kilometer in 1967, and the Groundnut Stabilization Fund paid a subsidy of CFAF 1.85 per ton/kilometer (i.e., a total price of CFAF 8.85 per ton/kilometer) although transportation cost by truck is CFAF 8 per ton/kilometer. In 1966, total merchandise transported by the Railways reached a record of 333 million tons/kilometers because of good groundnut crops and heavy traffic with Mali. It declined to 287 million tons/kilometers in 1967, but may have picked up in 1968. Phosphates and groundnuts account for about 55 per cent of these totals. Passenger traffic declined from 294,000 passengers/kilometer in

1965 to 285,000 passengers/kilometer in 1967, with indications of a slight improvement in 1968.

Senegal has 17 airports. The main airport, Dakar-Yoff, is of international standard, with three runways, and is equipped to take all types of jet aircraft. Other airports are mainly used for domestic traffic. Activity at the Dakar-Yoff airport declined during 1962–65, and although it rose in 1966 and 1967, it did not regain the 1962 level. Transportation of freight increased from 4,122 tons in 1962 to 4,691 tons in 1965, and declined slightly thereafter.

ECONOMIC DEVELOPMENT PLANNING

METHODS AND OBJECTIVES

Development planning in Senegal is based on periods of four fiscal years. The first plan covered 1961/62–1964/65 and the second 1965/66–1968/69. A third plan for 1969/70–1973/74 is being prepared. The authorities customarily review and adjust investment projections in each plan at its midpoint, after taking into account the results achieved during the first two years and other relevant factors. The plans distinguish between sectors of the economy reserved primarily for public investment and those reserved primarily for private investment. The public investment program, elaborated in detail by sectors and projects, comprises in principle all projected public sector investments, including those to be made by the central and local governments, by public agencies, and directly by foreign assistance institutions. The public investment program, divided into annual tranches, provides a basis for formulation of the annual investment budgets of the Government and other public agencies. The program for private investment is more general and is intended to be mainly indicative.

The over-all investment targets contained in the first and second development plans were derived essentially from projections of growth in GDP. For the first plan period the projected annual growth rate at current prices was 8 per cent, for the second 6 per cent, and for the third 5.5 per cent. The first plan emphasized areas such as infrastructure and administration, considered necessary because of new needs created by independence and differences in the existing infrastructural facilities. The second plan gave priority to more directly productive investments, especially in agriculture, where the two major objectives were to increase productivity per land unit in the existing groundnut/millet growing areas and to encourage development of new crops and other productive activities in other and more fertile parts of the country. Public investment in the second plan was subdivided on a regional basis so as to bring about a more equitable distribution of benefits and reduce the concentration of investment in the Dakar area and the Cap Vert region which had emerged during the earlier period.

This approach to planning has manifested certain weaknesses. For one thing, the projections of GDP for the plan periods had generally been based on out-of-date national account estimates. For example, the projections for the second plan period starting 1965/66 were based upon estimates of actual GDP for 1959–62. Detailed project preparation has also tended to lag, leaving utilization of available foreign assistance far below expectations. A second weakness has been the procedures for following up the implementation of specific projects. The records of realized public development expenditures kept by the Ministry of Planning and Industry are figures of commitments for funds. Since 1965/66, actual disbursements of development funds through the capital budget by public agencies, and from some extrabudgetary foreign assistance sources, have been recorded in mechanized accounts kept by the Ministry of Finance (see "Government finance," below). These figures, however, cannot be fully reconciled with the projections contained in the development plans. Data on actual private investment during the plan periods have also been lacking.

Outlines for the third plan, now in progress, is putting greater emphasis on project preparation. An inventory of specific projects under way or under consideration was produced in early 1968, as the basis for selection of projects for the coming period.

SECOND FOUR-YEAR DEVELOPMENT PLAN (1965/66–1968/69)

Originally the Second Four-Year Development Plan provided for total investment over the four years of CFAF 130.1 billion, CFAF 84.2 billion for public investment and CFAF 45.9 billion for private investment. Following the midperiod review of the plan, the projected total of public investment was lowered to CFAF 72.7 billion, a figure representing expenditure commitments recorded during the first two years of the plan period plus revised projections for the remaining two years. While the commitments recorded for the first two years represented only 61 per cent of the originally projected amounts, the revised projected investment totals for the last two years were actually raised slightly above the original targets to achieve this revised total. The sectoral composition of investments and the sources of financing as originally envisaged in the plan are shown in Table 17. According to the revised plan, public investment should average about CFAF 18.2 billion a year during the plan period, compared with an average of CFAF 21.1 billion a year envisaged in the original plan. The midperiod revision to the second plan did not include any over-all revision of the projected sources of financing.

Estimates of public development expenditures actually disbursed during the first three years of the current plan, by major source of financing, are detailed in Table 18 and summarized in Table 19 (with the addition of the municipal budgets). These estimates are based on the mechanized accounts kept by the Ministry of Finance, and are not wholly comparable in coverage with projections contained in the plan in that they do not include (1) investments made on their resources by public enterprises; (2) plan investments (mainly in the agricultural sector) financed by bank loans; (3) research activities financed and carried out directly by foreign technical assistance institutions located in Senegal; and (4) foreign assistance received from certain minor donors. They also differ in timing from the plan estimates in that they include expenditures on projects carried over from the first plan. Nevertheless, these figures represent the bulk of the public investment expenditures envisaged under the plan.

These estimates indicate that actual total public investment has fallen far short of the plan expectations. In its first two years, the current plan called for public investment (including investments made on their own resources by public enterprises and bank loans) of CFAF 35.3 billion, whereas the actual figures indicate a comparable total of CFAF 13.2 billion. However, the contribution of the Central Government's budget (CFAF 8.8 billion) and municipal government budget (CFAF 0.8 billion) to these investment expenditures were almost exactly as called for in the plan; the shortfall, therefore, has occurred entirely in the foreign

TABLE 17. SENEGAL: SECOND FOUR-YEAR DEVELOPMENT PLAN (1965/66–1968/69),
OVER-ALL PROJECTED PUBLIC DEVELOPMENT EXPENDITURES AND FINANCING

(*In billions of CFA francs*)

	Plan Period, 1965/66– 1968/69	First Tranche, 1965/66– 1966/67	Second Tranche, 1967/68– 1968/69
ORIGINAL PROJECTIONS			
Expenditures			
Studies and research	3.9	2.2	1.7
Rural sector	32.7	14.4	18.3
Infrastructure, transport, and communications	17.6	9.2	8.3
Education and cultural information	8.6	3.9	4.7
Health	2.3	1.5	0.8
Housing, water supply, and drainage	14.4	7.8	6.6
Commerce, tourism, and industry	2.1	0.6	1.5
Transport	1.8	0.9	0.9
Administrative equipment	0.8	0.6	0.2
Total	**84.2**	**41.1**	**43.1**
Financing			
Government budgets (including Treasury and Caisses)	18.7	8.9	9.8
Regional budgets	1.8	0.9	0.9
Public enterprises	6.1	2.9	3.1
Bank loans			
Medium-term and long-term	3.3	1.4	1.9
Short-term	4.9	1.7	2.2
External grants	34.5	17.8	16.7
External loans	14.8	7.7	7.0
REVISED PROJECTIONS [1]			
Expenditures			
Studies and research	2.6	0.9	1.7
Rural sector	23.7	6.9	16.8
Infrastructure, transport, and communications	14.8	5.0	9.7
Education and cultural information	5.3	2.6	2.6
Health	2.2	0.8	1.4
Housing, water supply, and drainage	16.0	4.2	11.8
Commerce, tourism, and industry	6.2	3.2	3.0
Transport	0.8	0.6	0.2
Administrative equipment	1.1	0.6	0.4
Total	**72.7**	**24.9**	**47.7**

Source: Senegal, *Deuxième Plan Quadriennal de Développement et Programme d'Investissement Corrigé, July 1, 1967.*

[1] Commitments recorded for first tranche, 1965/66–1966/67.

TABLE 18. SENEGAL: ACTUAL INVESTMENT EXPENDITURES, 1965/66–1967/68 [1]

(In millions of CFA francs)

	1965/66					1966/67					1967/68				
	Investment budget and Road Fund[2]	FAC[3] assistance	EDF[4] assistance	Other assistance[5]	Total	Investment budget and Road Fund[2]	FAC[3] assistance	EDF[4] assistance	Other assistance[5]	Total	Investment budget and Road Fund[2]	FAC[3] assistance	EDF[4] assistance	Other assistance[5]	Total
Groundnut program	—	57	97	—	154	—	—	762	—	762	—	—	953	—	953
Studies	43	56	—	5	104	114	57	—	9	180	150	84	—	—	234
Water projects	64	—	—	—	64	130	85	76	—	291	114	19	317	—	451
Rural sector															
Agriculture	242	82	—	—	324	433	146	92	23	694	351	7	64	—	422
Livestock	8	—	—	27	35	141	13	—	—	154	118	—	—	—	118
Forestry	63	—	—	—	63	87	8	—	—	95	39	26	—	—	65
Fishing	4	—	—	—	4	37	—	—	—	37	16	—	—	—	16
CER's Development Assistance Office[6]	45	—	—	34	79	35	—	—	—	35	42	—	—	—	42
Total rural sector	362	82	—	61	505	732	167	92	23	1,014	568	34	64	—	667
Commerce and industry															
Industry	14	20	—	—	34	20	24[7]	—	—	44	17	69[6]	—	—	86
Commerce	18	—	—	—	18	7	—	—	—	7	12	—	—	—	12
Tourism	127	—	—	—	127	43	—	—	—	43	23	—	—	—	23
Total commerce and industry	160	20	—	—	180	70	24	—	—	94	51	69	—	—	120
Transport and telecommunications															
Routes	798	—	452	—	1,250	1,437	32	240	4	1,713	1,273	23	39	—	1,336
Postal services and telecommunications	—	—	—	—		23	—	2	—	25	19	—	—	—	19
Others	4	—	—	—	4	87	10	180	—	277	—	10	63	—	73
Total transport and telecommunications	802[2]	—	452	—	1,254[2]	1,546[2]	42	422	4	2,014[2]	1,292[2]	33	102	—	1,428[2]

Social investments														
General education	106	110	—	127	343	255	244	47	93	639	247	—	17	54	318
Technical education	22	—	—	—	22	116	—	2	—	118	68	—	3	2	73
Art, culture, youth, and sport	152	15	—	—	167	125	—	—	—	125	148	—	—	—	148
Health	32	205	—	72	309	53	44	4	5	106	109	37	—	1	147
Housing urbanization	719	16	—	—	735	961	33	—	—	994	954	20	—	—	974
Information	58	—	—	—	58	55	2	—	—	57	43	—	—	—	43
Total social investments	1,089	346	—	199	1,634	1,564	323	53	98	2,038	1,571	57	20	57	1,705
Administrative equipment	86	—	—	—	86	310	—	—	—	310	335	—	—	—	335
Participations	100	—	—	—	100	60	—	—	—	60	16	—	—	—	16
Others	694	—	—	—	694	903	—	—	—	903	415	—	—	—	415
Total	3,400[2]	561	97	716[2]	4,774[2]	5,429[2]	697	1,405	134	7,665[2]	4,514[2]	297	1,458	57	6,326[2]

Source: Mainly data provided by the Senegalese authorities.

[1] Includes investments channeled through the Treasury (i.e., those directly undertaken by the Central Government and by public enterprises financed by loans and grants, as well as technical assistance provided in cash). Excludes self-financed investments by public enterprises and foreign donations in kind.
[2] Includes Road Fund, used only for roads, in millions of CFA francs: 521 in 1965/66, 625 in 1966/67, and 633 in 1967/68.
[3] Fonds d'Aide et de Coopération.
[4] European Development Fund (Fonds Européen de Développement, or FED).
[5] U.S. and German assistance for roads, in millions of CFA francs: 452 in 1965/66 and 4 in 1966/67.
[6] Regional Expansion Centers (Centres d'Expansion Régionale) and Office National de Coopération et d'Assistance pour le Développement (ONCAD).
[7] Includes CCCE (Caisse Central de Coopération Economique) loan for a power plant in Tambacounda, in millions of CFA francs: 19 in 1966/67 and 55 in 1967/68.

TABLE 19. SENEGAL: SUMMARY OF ACTUAL PUBLIC SECTOR INVESTMENTS,
1965/66–1967/68

(In billions of CFA francs)

	1965/66	1966/67	1967/68	Total, 1965/66– 1966/67	Total, 1965/66– 1967/68
Central Government budget [1]	3.4	5.4	4.5	8.8	13.3
Municipal budgets	0.4	0.4	0.2	0.8	1.0
Loans and grants					
FAC [2]	0.6	0.7	0.3	1.3	1.6
EDF [3]	0.1	1.4	1.5	1.5	3.0
United States and Germany	0.7	0.1	0.1	0.8	0.9
Total	5.2	8.0	6.6	13.2	19.8

Sources: Tables 18 and 29 and Ministère de l'Intérieur, Direction des Affaires Municipales.

[1] Including Road Fund.
[2] Fonds d'Aide et de Coopération.
[3] European Development Fund (Fonds Européen de Développement, or FED).

grants and loans obtained and utilized. The picture is not significantly different if the third year, for which actual figures are available (1967/68), is taken into account. Over the first three years of the plan period, actual total public investment averaged CFAF 6.6 billion a year, of which CFAF 4.8 billion is provided by the Central Government and municipal governments budgets and CFAF 1.8 billion by foreign assistance.

THIRD FOUR-YEAR DEVELOPMENT PLAN (1969/70–1972/73)

Under the Third Four-Year Development Plan (1969/70–1972/73), the annual growth target remains the same (i.e., 5.5 per cent), but it includes more definite and precise projects than the two previous plans. Total planned expenditures amount to CFAF 145 billion. Agriculture's share in the new plan accounts for about 29 per cent, industry for 14 per cent, tourism for over 3 per cent, and research and studies for 10 per cent.

In the agricultural sector, efforts will be concentrated on diversification and also on three other items: increasing productivity, increasing the size of family farms, and developing new political and economic rural communities based on agricultural centers of 10,000 hectares.

Progress in the Organization of Senegal River States will permit more extensive irrigation work. Moreover, efforts will be made to increase and improve cattle raising and fishing. The total investment in agriculture will amount to CFAF 33.4 billion.

In the industrial sector, CFAF 20 billion will be invested, principally in food processing.

INVESTMENT CODE

In order to encourage economic development, Senegal adopted in 1962 an investment code granting general guarantees and tax advantages for new investments. These guarantees protect foreigners and foreign capital against discrimination in legal treatment, taxation, and social ccntributions, and allows them to transfer abroad their earnings from investments recognized as contributing to economic development. Tax advantages are given to two groups of enterprises: priority enterprises (*entreprises prioritaires*) and enterprises with a special government convention (*entreprises conventionnées*).

By decree, enterprises can qualify as priority enterprises if they plan to invest at least CFAF 40 million (equivalent to US$160,000) over a 3-year period and to create at least 40 permanent jobs (or CFAF 20 million, or 20 permanent jobs in regions other than Cap Vert). Tax benefits are substantial, including exemptions over 5 years (8 years outside Cap Vert) from the schedular income tax and from the business license tax, a deduction of reinvested capital from the schedular income tax base, and a 50 per cent reduction over 3 years in the tax rate on distributions. In addition to these benefits, the Government may grant some or all of the following tax advantages: temporary exemption from import levies on investment goods and on raw materials; exemption from export levies for up to 10 years on goods produced for export; exemption from the turnover tax on invested goods and on exported products; exemption from transfer duties on real estate; and reductions in or exemptions from property taxes on real estate up to 15 years.

Enterprises that present investment programs of at least CFAF 500 million ($2 million) over 3 years and that are considered of particular importance for the economic development of the country can conclude a convention with the Government providing for fiscal advantages in addition to those granted to priority enterprises. The exemption from property taxes on developed land can be extended from 15 years to 25 years, and the Government can guarantee that for a period of time corresponding to the planned pay-off period of the investment, but not exceeding 25 years, taxes will not be raised above the level existing at the time the agreement was signed. All fiscal levies can be maintained at this original level, including those on dividends and interest payments, and contributions to the social security system.

No information is available on the extent of investments undertaken under the Code or on the tax revenue losses resulting from the tax advantages granted.

PRICES, WAGES, AND EMPLOYMENT

PRICES

Price Control

Until 1965, price control in Senegal came under French laws dating from 1942, which established controls on certain specified consumer goods and services while leaving the prices of most goods free. In March 1965, Senegal introduced a basic regulation to unify the existing price controls. This law empowered the Government to regulate and control prices of all goods and services produced or marketed in the country. On the same date, a decree elaborated the principles of price control under this law. The following price control methods are used: (1) fixation of prices by government decision, either by direct price setting or by regulation of wholesale and retail profit margins; (2) agreement whereby prices have to be registered with the Government; and (3) control system whereby registered prices are tacitly approved after 15 days unless action is taken by the authorities. All prices which are not subject to any of these procedures are free. Furthermore, the regulation provided for partial or general freezing of prices, and established various measures in order to publicize regulated prices. It also determined the penalties applicable for violations. In fact, until July 1968, the Government had regulated mainly the prices of staple goods and services such as groundnuts, millet, rice, sugar, bread, gasoline, hotel rooms, transit trading, and transportation of persons and merchandise; other prices had remained unregulated.

On July 24, 1968, in order to prevent price increases following the increase of wages, the Government decided to freeze the prices of all goods (except Senegalese agricultural products) and services at the May 1968 level. This regulation applies to locally produced as well as imported goods, and to wholesale and retail profit margins which are determined in money value and not in percentages. However, the Minister of Trade may expressly authorize changes in markups, provided that a price increase does not result from the wage increase. By November 1968, the number of price increases submitted for official approval reached 138, most of them stemming from higher import costs.

Price Developments

In Senegal, the sole published price index is based on the consumption habits of an average European family in Dakar. This index is of limited value in assessing over-all price developments of Senegalese consumers. Furthermore, it was established in 1945 and covers only 70 items, the weights of which have most likely changed over the years.

According to this index, annual average European consumer prices in Dakar fluctuated between 1965 and May 1969 (Table 20). In general

TABLE 20.   SENEGAL: INDICES OF CONSUMER AND CONSTRUCTION MATERIAL PRICES, DAKAR, 1965–69

	1965 (Annual Average)	1966 (Annual Average)	1967 (Annual Average)	1968 (Annual Average)	1968 May	1969 (May)
Consumer prices			*(July 1945 = 100)*			
Food	671.0	703.0	694.0	685.0	672.0	691.0
Utilities	487.0	489.0	491.0	493.0	494.0	498.0
Clothing	413.0	413.0	413.0	413.0	413.0	413.0
Servants	722.0	722.0	722.0	776.0	722.0	830.0
Other	710.0	728.0	710.0	745.0	718.0	784.0
General index	633.0	652.0	648.0	653.0	635.0	668.0
Cost of construction			*(April 1951 = 100)*			
materials	223.8	227.9	231.5	237.9	231.4	245.2

Source: Ministère du Plan et de l'Industrie, *Bulletin Statistique et Economique Mensuel.*

consumer prices rose in 1966, and decreased slightly in 1967; in 1968, they rose by 0.8 per cent and decreased again by 0.5 per cent from December 1968 to May 1969. The gradual increase during 1965–68 reflects mainly the rise in servants' wages following an increase in July 1968 (15 per cent, or 7.5 per cent on an annual average), in food (2.1 per cent), and in utility prices (1.2 per cent). The upward movement of prices in 1966 seems to have been caused mainly by the increased costs of imports resulting from higher foreign prices as well as higher indirect taxation. (The turnover tax was raised from 10 per cent to 12 per cent on products and from 6 per cent to 8.5 per cent on services in 1965; the statistical tax on imports was raised from 2 per cent to 3 per cent in 1966; and excise duties were introduced on mineral water, kolanuts, and green tea in 1966.) Table 21, which shows prices of selected consumer goods in Dakar during 1965–69, indicates the rising trend in prices of imported goods (e.g., wheat flour, sardines, and detergents) and a declining trend in prices of local products (e.g., beef, lamb, chicken, and groundnut oil).

Senegal has no wholesale price index, but the statistical service compiles an index of the cost of construction materials in Dakar (see Table 20). After rising by about 1.5 per cent in 1966 and in 1967, this index rose by 2.8 per cent in 1968 and by 6.0 per cent in the first five months of 1969. During 1965–68 the principal price increases applied to imported timber, brass wire, corrugated iron, and cast pipes.

It is the opinion of the Senegalese authorities that the cost of living for the average Senegalese has been increasing by about 3 per cent a year. One factor contributing to this trend during recent years has been a change in the people's diet; during the temporary lack of staple foods in Senegal, when millet and rice had to be imported, rice became the most popular cereal. The rising trend in the world market price for rice has contributed significantly to an increase in the cost of living for the Senegalese population.

In general price controls are not very effectively enforced. In towns, competition at the retail level seems to be sufficient to prevent excessive profits; however, in the countryside, where distribution is often monopolistic and where farmers are in debt during part of the year, prices tend to be higher.

TABLE 21. SENEGAL: RETAIL PRICES OF SELECTED CONSUMER GOODS, DAKAR, 1965–69

(In CFA francs per kilogram, except as noted)

	1965 (Annual Average)	1966 (Annual Average)	1967 (Annual Average)	1968 (Annual Average)	1968 May	1969 (May)
Foodstuffs						
Wheat flour	59.00	60.00	63.00	62.00	62.00	62.00
Bread	38.00	38.00	38.00	38.00	38.00	38.00
Moroccan pasta	140.00	140.00	140.00	140.00	140.00	140.00
Potatoes	32.00	36.00	33.00	30.00	32.00	58.00
Rice, caroline (500 grams)	47.00	55.00	53.00	51.00	51.00	55.00
Beef, sirloin	467.00	387.00	400.00	387.00	423.00	387.00
Lamb, leg	422.00	364.00	364.00	370.00	365.00	379.00
Pork, rib	467.00	629.00	597.00	578.00	593.00	549.00
Chicken	383.00	380.00	367.00	375.00	381.00	364.00
French butter	633.00	523.00	477.00	408.00	416.00	377.00
Concentrated milk (can)	55.00	55.00	52.00	50.00	50.00	50.00
Local beer (66 centoliters)	59.00	63.00	63.00	63.00	63.00	62.00
Perrier water (bottle)	59.00	71.00	71.00	70.00	70.00	70.00
Chocolate (100 grams)	74.00	81.00	79.00	74.00	76.00	75.00
Refined groundnut oil (liter)	98.00	98.00	97.00	97.00	96.00	98.00
Moroccan sardines (1/4 club)	51.00	65.00	60.00	58.00	59.00	60.00
Sugar cubes	70.00	70.00	70.00	70.00	70.00	70.00
Manufactured consumer goods						
Local soap	70.00	70.00	70.00	70.00	70.00	70.00
Detergents (box)	151.00	148.00	156.00	170.00	178.00	178.00
Local cigarettes (pack)	35.00	35.00	35.00	35.00	35.00	35.00
French gauloises cigarettes (pack)	69.00	70.00	75.00	70.00	70.00	75.00
Movies (seat)	308.00	313.00	313.00	313.00	313.00	313.00
Gasoline (liter)	48.66	48.80	48.80	48.80	48.80	48.80
Utilities						
Electricity (kilowatt-hour)						
Lighting	37.52	37.53	37.53	37.88	38.12	37.86
Appliances	18.42	18.43	18.43	18.60	18.71	18.59
Water (cubic meter)	55.47	55.55	55.55	55.55	55.55	50.00
Butane gas (12 kilograms)	1,365.00	1,365.00	1,365.00	1,365.00	1,365.00	1,365.00

Source: Ministère du Plan et de l'Industrie, *Bulletin Statistique et Economique Mensuel.*

WAGES

Senegal has a legal minimum wage rate, the *salaire minimum inter-professionnel garanti* (SMIG), which differs according to categories of wage earners (agricultural or nonagricultural workers) and, until July 1968, by areas (urban or nonurban areas). SMIG serves also as a basis for minimum wage scales for various classes of salaried workers in different sectors of the economy. These scales are fixed by joint commissions, which include representatives of labor, employers, and the Government.

From August 1961 to June 1968, SMIG and associated structures of minimum guaranteed salaries remained unchanged (Table 22). There were two salary zones, one for the Cap Vert area (for 50 kilometers around Dakar) and the other for the rest of the country. On July 1, 1968 the Government approved a 15 per cent increase in the basic SMIG. The new rates of CFAF 50.60 an hour for nonagricultural workers and CFAF 43.85 an hour for agricultural workers apply uniformly throughout the country, eliminating the previous regional differences. At the same time a tripartite commission representing the Government, employers, and workers was established to determine specific increases for each category of worker. A general agreement was reached whereby (1) unskilled workers' and employees' wages were to be increased by 7 per cent, 9.5 per cent, or 15 per cent according to their respective qualifications; (2) skilled workers' salaries by 4 per

TABLE 22.   SENEGAL: HOURLY MINIMUM WAGES, 1958–68

(In CFA francs)

	Nonagricultural Workers	Agricultural Workers
December 1, 1958		
Zone I [1]	40.00	34.70
Zone II [1]	37.20	32.26
August 1, 1961		
Zone I [1]	44.00	38.15
Zone II [1]	40.90	35.50
July 1, 1968 [2]	50.60	43.85

Source: Data provided by the Senegalese authorities.

[1] Zone I comprises the Cap Vert area for 50 kilometers around Dakar; Zone II the rest of the country.

[2] The two former salary zones were unified, effective July 1, 1968.

cent or 7 per cent; and (3) professional staff salaries by 2 per cent. Following this agreement, other joint commissions (*commissions paritaires*)—each representing a specific economic sector—applied these percentages and determined in detail the minimum wages for the category of worker that they represented.

The SMIG increase affected the public sector only in the lowest categories of civil servants, temporary employees covered by collective conventions, and employees of public enterprises regulated by the Code of Labor.

In large businesses, minimum wage levels are generally observed, but in smaller businesses, particularly in commerce, wages of many workers are below the legal minimum. In addition to wages and salaries regulated by SMIG, workers in large businesses usually receive certain fringe benefits, some (e.g., family allowances and retirement) involving compulsory contributions regulated under the social security law. Additional benefits in some enterprises include a contributory medical insurance plan, which, however, is not legally required.

EMPLOYMENT

Since 1963, no statistics on employment have been compiled in Senegal. However, the Senegalese authorities estimated the total number of wage earners in 1968 at 118,000—70,000 in the private sector, 36,000 in the public sector, and 12,000 in public enterprises. During 1965–68, apparently the main increases occurred in the public enterprises and the private sector; the number in the public sector, after increasing by 25 per cent from 1961 to 1964, remained practically unchanged for budgetary reasons.

Among the 70,000 wage earners employed in the private sector, 83 per cent are Senegalese and a large proportion are unskilled. Government policy aim is to reduce the number of foreigners who hold most of the managerial jobs.

At the end of 1966, registered unemployed wage earners in the Cap Vert region totaled 37,738. In 1968, they increased by about 18 per cent to 44,420. Senegal has no unemployment compensation. The large increase in unemployment in Cap Vert during these two years resulted mostly from bad crops, which led to migratory movements from the country to the city of Dakar.

GOVERNMENT FINANCE

BUDGETARY SYSTEM

The public sector comprises the Central Government, local authorities, and public and semipublic agencies and enterprises. The Central Government has a current and an investment budget. Current budget receipts come from taxes, fees, and income from government property and services; current expenditures cover recurrent outlays and transfers to local authorities and public agencies. The investment budget covers only a part of total public sector investments, since foreign loans and grants are also channeled directly into investment projects and public agencies invest from their resources. As foreign loans have been small and domestic loans have not been available in the past four years, the current budget surplus and deposits accumulated with the Treasury have been the main sources of financing of the investment budget.

Some 50 public institutions and services operate through special accounts (*comptes spéciaux*) with the Treasury. Authorization for their operations and for deficit accounts with the Treasury is given in an appendix to the annual budget of the Central Government. The revenue is derived from earmarked resources such as social security contributions for the Pension Fund, a special gasoline tax for the Road Fund, and levies on the groundnut production for the Groundnut Stabilization Fund. Foreign and domestic loans for investments within as well as outside the investment budget and advances given by the Treasury are also carried through special accounts.

The 33 districts or large municipalities (*communes*) receive their revenue from direct taxes shared with the Central Government and from local taxes. Since 1965/66, local government finances have been reformed. The commune authorities administer their own budgets but are supervised by the Ministry of Interior and the Ministry of Finance.

Public and semipublic enterprises were brought under stricter governmental control in 1966. A state comptroller has been introduced in semipublic enterprises, and an accounting center has been set up for most of the public enterprises. In the accounting center, bookkeeping is done for 18 enterprises, which pool their liquid funds in a common cash fund kept with the Treasury. Losses incurred by some enterprises are thus offset against profits of the others.

The Treasury's accounting system and methods of expenditure control were reorganized in 1966. Use of computers added to the efficiency of tax collection and spending control. Public expenditures for each appropriation were not permitted to rise above levels predetermined for periods of the fiscal year. Within the investment budget, expenditures for all projects to be financed out of foreign loans or grants were to be open-blocked until the funds are actually received. Prefinancing of these projects through the Treasury had to be restricted because in recent years foreign contributions provided only a small part of the amounts budgeted.

Senegal's fiscal year ends on June 30, and budgetary operations are recorded on a cash basis (*principe de gestion*). At the close of the budget year, unused appropriations for current expenditures are normally revoked. Only a few balances have been transferred by the National Assembly to the following fiscal year. In the investment budget, however, unused appropriations are normally transferred, with minor amendments. In recent years, less than half of the investments planned were actually undertaken; therefore, such transfers have been substantial.

BUDGETARY DEVELOPMENTS AND PROSPECTS

Results for 1965/66–1967/68

In recent years the current budget of the Central Government has been in surplus, but the amount decreased from CFAF 4.2 billion in 1964/65 to CFAF 1.6 billion in 1967/68 (Table 23). This decrease reflected a decline in current revenues except in 1967/68, and a gradual rise in current expenditures.

In 1965/66, current revenue decreased by 2.9 per cent, mainly reflecting a drop in import tax receipts; it decreased again by 1.2 per cent in 1966/67, when the proceeds from government services and property and from taxation of groundnut exports declined. In 1967/68, higher receipts from import taxes and from direct taxes contributed to the 1.3 per cent increase in current revenue to CFAF 35.8 billion. Current revenue amounted to nearly 18 per cent of GDP in 1966/67, compared with over 19 per cent in 1964/65 (Table 24). Although this ratio has decreased in recent years, it has remained high, compared

TABLE 23.   SENEGAL: BUDGETARY OPERATIONS OF THE CENTRAL GOVERNMENT,
1964/65–1968/69

(*In billions of CFA francs*)

	Actual				Original Budget Estimates, 1968/69
	1964/65	1965/66	1966/67	1967/68	
Current revenues	36.9 [1]	35.8	35.4	35.8	36.8
Expenditures					
Current	32.5	33.1	33.3	34.2	36.8
Investment	8.5 [2]	2.9 [2]	4.8 [2]	3.9 [2]	12.7 [2]
Total expenditures	41.0	35.9	38.1	38.1	49.4
Current surplus	4.2	2.8	2.1	1.6	—
Over-all budget deficit	**4.1**	**0.1**	**2.7**	**2.3**	**12.7**
Financing					
Foreign loans	1.1	0.2	0.2	0.2	12.7 [3]
Treasury	3.0	−0.1	2.5	2.1	—

Source: Data provided by the Senegalese authorities.

[1] Of which CFAF 0.1 billion was revenue of the capital budget. In the following years revenue of the capital budget was negligible.
[2] Excludes Road Fund used only for roads.
[3] To be partly financed from an internal loan.

TABLE 24.   SENEGAL: FISCAL PERFORMANCE, 1964/65–1967/68

	1964/65	1965/66	1966/67	1967/68
INDEX (*1959 = 100*)				
Current revenues	238	233	230	233
Current expenditures	276	285	287	308
RATIO TO GDP [1] (*per cent*)				
Total revenues	19.4	18.3	17.9	...
Tax revenue	17.3	16.6	16.8	...
Total expenditures	21.6	18.3	19.3	...
Current expenditures	17.1	16.9	16.9	...
RATIO TO CURRENT REVENUE (*per cent*)				
Direct taxes	19.7	23.5	23.8	23.9
Indirect taxes	70.0	67.3	69.8	69.9
Import taxes	42.7	39.9	43.0	44.0
Export taxes	9.4	8.9	8.1	7.5
RATIO OF TAX REVENUES TO TAX BASE (*per cent*)				
Import tax proceeds to import values	37.8	35.6	37.8	...
Export tax proceeds to export value	11.2	9.4	8.1	...

Source: Mainly data provided by the Senegalese authorities.

[1] Based on estimates for July 1 to June 30, derived by taking the average of two consecutive calendar years. Basic GDP figures used for 1966 and 1967 are estimates by the Senegalese authorities (see Table 2).

with Ivory Coast (16 per cent in 1966) and Togo (11 per cent in 1965).

Current expenditures increased by 5 per cent during 1964/65–1967/68. Most of the increase came in the last year, when higher outlays were made for public wages and salaries, which account for half of total spending. Under an austerity program of the Central Government and tight expenditure control, all groups of current spending other than that for personnel were kept at or even slightly below the previous year's level.

Investment budget expenditures fell far below the estimates, amounting to CFAF 11.6 billion during 1965/66–1967/68, the first three years of the Second Four-Year Development Plan (Table 25). The current budget surplus contributed CFAF 6.5 billion to investment financing in this period. Total budgetary operations of the Central Government resulted in over-all deficits totaling CFAF 5.1 billion over the same period. Foreign loans, which had been expected to cover most of the investment outlays, actually contributed only CFAF 0.6 billion, leaving a remaining deficit of CFAF 4.5 billion in these three years that had to be financed by the Senegalese Treasury as there were no internal loans. Part of the Treasury's funds came from increases in deposits of public agencies such as the Groundnut Stabilization Fund; the remainder (CFAF 2.0 billion) came from a reduction in cash and bank funds, thus diminishing the liquid funds of the Treasury to CFAF 7.1 billion by the end of the fiscal year 1967/68.

Prospects for 1968/69

After the current and the investment budgets for 1968/69 were adopted, unforeseen expenditures became necessary and revenue estimates proved too optimistic. Corrective measures were introduced in the middle of the fiscal year, and the best that was expected was to avoid a deficit in the current budget.

Originally, the current budget was balanced at CFAF 36.8 billion, CFAF 1 billion higher than the actual revenue in the preceding fiscal year (see Table 23). The additional receipts were expected mainly from a more favorable groundnut crop. But, unfavorable rainfall conditions in the autumn of 1968 reduced the harvest, making it likely to be the third consecutive unsatisfactory crop. At first, the Government was

TABLE 25. SENEGAL: INVESTMENT BUDGET, 1961/62–1968/69

(Amount in millions of CFA francs)

	First Four-Year Development Plan						Second Four-Year Development Plan				
	1961/62[1]	1962/63	1963/64	1964/65	Four-year total	Per cent of total financing	1965/66	1966/67	1967/68[2]	Three-year total	Per cent of total financing
Expenditures											
Estimates	8,012	9,750	14,183	11,973	43,918	...	7,566	10,952	10,550	29,068	...
Actual	7,247	5,502	7,000	8,469	28,218	...	2,879[3]	4,804[3]	3,881[3]	11,564[3]	...
Revenues											
Estimates	1,391	7,140	12,270	12,046	32,847	...	6,727	10,952	10,550	28,229	...
Actual	—	715	4,000	1,282	5,997	...	224	169	222	615	...
Deficit											
Estimates	6,621	2,610	1,913	−73	11,071	...	839	—	—	839	...
Actual	7,247	4,787	3,000	7,187	22,221	...	2,655	4,636	3,658	10,949	...
Financing											
Internal											
Current budget	4,875	3,787	2,091	4,202	14,955	53	2,756	2,115	1,606	6,477	56
Reserve fund	2,372	1,000	909	2,985	7,266	25	−100	2,520	2,051	4,471	39
Loans	—	—	4,000	—	4,000	14	—	—	—	—	—
Others	—	—	—	140	140	1	—	—	1	1	—
Total, internal	7,247	4,787	7,000	7,327	26,361	93	2,655[3]	4,636[3]	3,658[3]	10,949[3]	95
External loans	—	503	—	1,142	1,645	6	224	169	222	615	5
Participation, subdivision, and other	—	212	—	—	212	1	—	—	—	—	—
Total, external	—	715	—	1,142	1,857	7	224	169	222	615	5
Total financing	7,247	5,502	7,000	8,469	28,218	100	2,879	4,804	3,881	11,564	100

Source: Data provided by the Senegalese authorities.

[1] Covers 18 months.
[2] Revised estimates instead of actual.
[3] Excludes Road Fund used only for roads.

reluctant to introduce substantial tax increases because of the possibility of further depressing economic activity. In January 1969, however, the Government adopted a package of new tax measures geared to a reform of the tax structure rather than to a short-term increase in revenues. It includes a 20 per cent surcharge on the general income tax, a 5 per cent surcharge on the tax for business licenses, and an increase of at least one third in the poll tax for those regularly employed. Some tax reliefs were also granted (e.g., the tax on houses and apartments was abolished). Although the additional levies may be offset by the tax reliefs, the revenue effect for the Central Government may be positive because the new taxes, unlike the abolished tax, will not be shared with the local authorities.

Current expenditures in 1968/69 were originally estimated at CFAF 2.5 billion above th` actual expenditures in the previous year. Most of the increase represented transfers (CFAF 1.0 billion), which were exceptionally low in the previous year; for public debt (CFAF 0.5 billion, including the first installment for the amortization of the 1964 internal loan); and for personnel (CFAF 0.4 billion).

The social unrest of May 1968, however, necessitated supplementary expenditures of more than CFAF 1 billion which were not included in the original budget for 1968/69. Expenditures for personnel were later estimated at about CFAF 0.5 billion above the amount originally budgeted. General salary rises were granted for about one third of the civil servants: (1) CFAF 0.2 billion for the 7,200 employees whose salaries are linked to those in the private sector and who received a rise on average of 5 per cent, owing to an increase of up to 15 per cent in the minimum salary scale; (2) CFAF 0.1–0.2 billion annually for salaries of about 4,800 *agents auxiliares* raised in December 1968, retroactive to July 1968; and (3) although the remuneration of the 22,650 civil servants with guaranteed status remained unchanged, about CFAF 0.2 billion for government employees living outside Dakar whose salaries were increased to equate them with those in the capital. Finally, expenditures for the University of Dakar were revised upward by CFAF 0.4 billion, part of which will be for scholarships; and indemnifications for damages caused by the social unrest were expected to total more than CFAF 0.1 billion.

In an effort to compensate for the additional expenditures, the Government blocked all nonessential appropriations as of January 1969. Even so, a balanced current budget outcome was the best that could be expected.

The estimated current budget for 1969/70 was established in balance at CFAF 37.85 billion, CFAF 1.1 billion above the 1968/69 budget estimates. Additional receipts were expected from an increase in direct taxes and in fees (CFAF 1.1 billion) and dues (CFAF 0.2 billion); indirect taxes and nontax revenues were estimated at CFAF 0.15 billion lower than in the previous year. Additional receipts resulted from upward adjustments in the rate of certain taxes following those adopted in January 1969. Moreover, a 5 per cent exceptional levy made on company reserves for the 1969/70 fiscal year was expected to yield CFAF 0.35 billion.

Investment outlays for 1968/69, originally estimated at CFAF 12.7 billion, were expected to be cut to CFAF 6.5 billion, which was still a higher amount than in the three previous years because it was the last year under the Second Four-Year Development Plan. After it became likely that there would be no surplus in current operations in 1968/69, an internal compulsory loan was introduced in February 1969 for investment financing. Other resources for investment financing included a CFAF 1.5 billion loan floated on the French market under the guarantee of the French Government, and loans under foreign aid programs. The Senegalese Treasury was expected to finance the remainder.

Investment expenditures for 1969/70 were estimated at CFAF 4.0 billion, of which CFAF 1.5 billion was allocated to balance the Second Four-Year Development Plan account. The Government planned to meet these expenditures, by borrowing only.

STRUCTURE OF CURRENT REVENUES

Receipts from direct taxes increased by 18 per cent during 1964/65–1967/68 (Table 26), owing mainly to higher tax rates and improved methods of tax collection rather than to an increase in the tax base. Their share in total current revenues of the Central Government was 24 per cent in 1967/68, and indirect taxes, which remained at about the same level, contributed 70 per cent (see Table 24). Fees and

TABLE 26. SENEGAL: CURRENT GOVERNMENT REVENUE, 1964/65–1969/70

(In millions of CFA francs)

	Actual				Estimates	
	1964/65	1965/66	1966/67	1967/68	1968/69	1969/70
Direct taxes						
Income taxes	4,954	5,839	5,749	6,119	5,570	6,740
Poll taxes	1,087	1,202	1,171	1,206	1,200	1,280
Other	1,189	1,392	1,512	1,233	1,490	1,310
Total direct taxes	7,231	8,433	8,432	8,558	8,260	9,320
Indirect taxes						
Import taxes	15,680	14,309	15,194	15,746	16,382	16,085
Export taxes	3,467	3,207	2,864	2,677	2,749	1,876
Excise duties	4,312	4,048	4,254	4,271	4,177	5,322
Turnover taxes	2,181	2,566	2,397	2,363	2,450	2,350
Other	40	5	—	5	—	—
Total indirect taxes	25,680	2⁴.135	24,709	25,062	25,758	25,633
Fees and dues	1,102	1,192	994	968	970	1,164
Nonfiscal revenue	2,723	2,066	1,244	1,252	1,762	1,733
Total current revenue	36,735	35,825	35,379	35,840	36,750	37,850

Source: Data provided by the Ministère des Finances, Direction du Trésor.

dues accounted for nearly 3 per cent, and nonfiscal revenue (including proceeds from government services, government property, and the national lottery) over 3 per cent.

Direct Taxes

Income taxes.—Income taxes contribute about two thirds of the revenue from direct taxes. However, owing to the low income level in the agricultural sector and tax exemptions, only about 100,000 taxpayers are subject to these levies.

Senegal has a system of schedular taxes on income (*impôt cédulaire sur le revenu*), with the rate varying according to the source of income. The tax on industrial and commercial profits is the most important of schedular taxes. The rate was raised in May 1966 from 25 per cent to 30 per cent and in January 1970 to 33.33 per cent. Agricultural profits are treated under the same schedule as industrial and commercial profits and the rate on noncommercial income is 20 per cent. There are lower rates for small profits, but corporations are subject to a flat minimum payment of CFAF 300,000, which is deductible from the amount due under the schedular tax. Priority enterprises enjoy an exemption from the tax on industrial and commercial profits for five or eight years (see "Investment code," above). Wages and salaries are exempted from the schedular taxes.

In addition to these levies, a general income tax (*impôt général sur le revenu*) is imposed on personal income exceeding CFAF 100,000 annually. The rates are progressive, ranging from 2 to 60 per cent. Since June 1966, private employers pay a tax on salaries at a rate of 1 per cent. Wages and salaries are also subject to a 2 per cent withholding tax earmarked for the social security system.

The annual income of individuals is also subject to a surtax (*taxe de développement*) at a rate of 3 per cent on the amount exceeding CFAF 240,000 and 8 per cent on the amount exceeding CFAF 360,000. This tax was introduced in 1962 to help to finance the development plan, and the rate was increased in 1965. In January 1969 a surcharge on the general income tax was introduced at a general rate of 20 per cent, but was limited to a payment not to exceed CFAF 500,000 for any taxpayer.

Poll and other direct taxes.—Every individual in Senegal over 14 years old is subject to a poll tax (*minimum fiscal*), ranging from CFAF 600 to CFAF 6,000 (after rises in January 1969 and January 1970). For wage and salary earners this tax is now withheld at the source. The amount due depends on the occupation, family status, and the residence of the taxpayer. This tax accounts for about 15 per cent of direct tax revenue, but the Central Government shares these proceeds with the municipalities where they are collected.

Among some ten other direct taxes, those on land and buildings are the most important, followed by a special business tax (*patentes*). The revenue from some of these taxes is also shared with the municipalities.

Indirect Taxes

Taxes on imports.—The system of import taxes in Senegal is influenced by its association with EEC and membership in two customs unions, the West African Customs Union (Union Douanière des Etats de l'Afrique de l'Ouest, or UDEAO) and the Customs Union between Senegal and Mauritania. The one with Mauritania provides that customs duties and import taxes collected by the two countries under the common external tariff be pooled and distributed on the basis of 91.34 per cent to Senegal and 8.66 per cent to Mauritania. A substantial part of the imports of the two countries enters via Dakar, and net transfers from Senegal to Mauritania were estimated at CFAF 0.9 billion in 1968/69.

Accounting for 44 per cent of total current revenue in 1967/68, customs duties and import taxes are the leading single source of revenues of the Senegalese Government. In 1965/66, receipts from import taxes dropped by almost one tenth, owing both to the suspension of customs duties on imports from EEC and to the decrease in French Government spending in Senegal after withdrawal of military personnel. Since then, however, there has been a moderate upward trend mainly because of more efficient collection after the introduction of a computerized accounting system.

Levies on imports comprise essentially six taxes: (1) Customs duties in the narrow sense (*droits de douane*), contributing only 3 per cent of total import levies in 1967/68, apply to imports from all countries except EEC and UDEAO members. Under the minimum tariff, which applies to imports from countries accorded most-favored-nation treatment, the rate ranges from 5 to 20 per cent on the c.i.f. value of most goods. Imports from other countries, including Japan, are subject to the general tariff with rates three times those of the minimum tariff. (2) Fiscal duties (*droits fiscaux*), contributing 21 per cent of total import levies in 1967/68 affect all imports irrespective of origin.[8] The rates range from 4 to 25 per cent of the c.i.f. value on most consumer goods, while most investment goods are exempt or are taxed at 5 per cent. (3) The statistical tax (*taxe de statistique*), contributing 5 per cent of the total, is levied on all imports except some food products and most capital goods. The rate was raised from 2 per cent of the c.i.f. value to 3 per cent in May 1966 and to 4 per cent for 1969/70. (4) The standard tax on transactions (*taxe forfaitaire représentative de la taxe sur les transactions*), contributing 35 per cent of the total, is applied to the

---

[8] However, goods entirely produced in Ivory Coast, Mali, and Dahomey are exempt from fiscal duties and from the other import levies, while goods from those countries but produced from imported materials and those goods originating from the other UDEAO countries are subject to half the normal rate of all import taxes.

sum of the c.i.f. value, customs duties, the fiscal duty, and the statistical tax. The tax is levied on all imports except periodicals and some basic food products, such as fresh vegetables, bananas, sugar, and concentrated milk. In June 1969 the normal rate was raised from 20.6 per cent to 22.0 per cent; however, some commodities, which are also produced domestically (e.g., oil, canned food, and leather articles), are taxed at 30.9 per cent, and most industrial investment goods have a reduced rate of 2.1 per cent. The standard tax exists separately from the turnover tax, mainly for historical reasons. (5) The general turnover tax (*taxe sur le chiffre d'affaires*), which is applied on the c.i.f. value plus all other levies mentioned above, contributed 29 per cent of total tax revenue from imports in 1967/68. On most imports the normal rate of 13.5 per cent is applied; however, some luxuries (e.g., perfume, photographic equipment, home refrigerators, and musical instruments) are subject to a 33.33 per cent rate, whereas cereals, some vegetables, and a few other items are exempted. (6) A *tax de raffinage*, contributing about 7 per cent of total import tax revenue, is applied to gasoline at a rate of 23 per cent, to diesel oil at a rate of 21 per cent, and to other mineral oil products, in addition to the other import levies. The tax is calculated on the base of standard values.

All together, these six levies on imports constitute a relatively high tax burden in Senegal. In 1966/67 the ratio of import tax receipts to the total value of imports, as reported by the customs services, was 38 per cent, compared with 19 per cent in Ivory Coast and 10 per cent in Mauritania. Furthermore, for some consumer durable goods not produced domestically (e.g., automobiles) the burden was more than 100 per cent. These circumstances have contributed to smuggling, which has become a serious problem, especially from The Gambia, where customs duties are low. Senegalese officials estimate that the loss in budgetary revenue owing to illegal imports exceeds 10 per cent of import duties paid (i.e., about CFAF 1.6 billion annually).

Taxes on exports.—Receipts from export taxes have been decreasing since 1964/65, and their share in total current revenue was 7.5 per cent in 1967/68. The decrease has been due mainly to reductions in tax rates on groundnuts and groundnut products, which are the source of some 97 per cent of total receipts from export taxes. Reductions were made in 1965 and in 1967—in connection with the alignment of the support price on the French market to the world market level—in order to buffer repercussions on the groundnut sector. Most of the remaining export taxes come from phosphates.

Senegal taxes on exports are three kinds: (1) Fiscal duties, which in 1967/68 accounted for 51 per cent of total receipts from export taxes, are levied at a rate of 12 per cent on a standard value of groundnuts and groundnut oil. Phosphates and other minerals are exempt; and the rates on raw materials (e.g., ivory and skins) used in domestic handicraft production range up to 25 per cent. (2) The standard tax on exports, representing 43 per cent of total export tax receipts, is applicable to groundnuts and groundnut oil at a rate of 5.4 per cent and to most other products at a rate of 5.68 per cent. Phosphates are temporarily exempt from this tax. (3) The remaining 6 per cent of total tax receipts from exports comes from a group of other taxes (including a *taxe de recherche* at 0.8–1.0 per cent on most products, a *taxe de conditionnement* at 0.4–0.5 per cent, and the 3 per cent *taxe de statistique*, from which groundnuts and groundnut oil are exempt).

Excise duties.—Receipts from excise duties, accounting for 12 per cent of total current receipts in 1967/68, have remained at about the same level since 1964/65. These taxes are levied on such goods as alcoholic beverages, cigarettes and cigars, certain petroleum products, soda water, kolanuts, and green tea. New taxes on coffee were introduced in 1969; and the tax rate on petroleum products and kolanuts was raised. The special gasoline tax, earmarked for the Road Fund, was also increased. Moreover the tax on edible oil was extended to include all fat products.

Turnover tax.—Proceeds from the internal turnover tax (excluding imports) have changed but little in recent years; they accounted for nearly 7 per cent of total current revenue in 1967/68. The tax is applied only once on the sale of goods produced in Senegal and on services, but exports are exempt. The rate structure, simplified in 1966, now provides a normal rate—calculated on the value excluding the tax —of 9.89 per cent. A reduced rate of 4.17 per cent applies to sugar and all goods sold by public concessionaires, and the rate on services is 9.29 per cent. The turnover tax also applies to imports and the rates are higher than the normal rate on internal transactions (see "Excise duties," above).

STRUCTURE OF CURRENT EXPENDITURES

Composition by Economic Function

During 1964/65–1967/68, expenditure for personnel rose by 15 per cent—increasing its share in total current spending from 47 per cent to 52 per cent—and the total of all expenditures other than for personnel decreased by 4 per cent (Table 27). Since expenditures were tightly controlled under the austerity program, the increase in outlays for personnel reflects mainly promotions rather than general increases in pay scales. As the cost of living rose, however, pressure for higher public salaries increased.

Purchase of materials was the second largest group of expenditures by economic functions, accounting for 18 per cent of total current spending in 1967/68. This expenditure, mainly in the Ministries of Health and Education and for military training, has decreased slightly since 1964/65.

Transfers decreased from 1964/65 to 1967/68, when they represented 15 per cent of total current spending. The amount of CFAF 5.1

TABLE 27.   SENEGAL: CURRENT GOVERNMENT EXPENDITURES, 1964/65–1969/70

(In millions of CFA francs)

	Actual				Estimates	
	1964/65	1965/66	1966/67	1967/68	1968/69	1969/70
Composition by economic functions						
Personnel	15,361	15,974	17,140	17,678	18,057	19,038
Materials	6,395	6,205	6,140	6,268	6,644	6,710
Maintenance	1,550	1,585	1,517	1,494	1,583	1,645
Transfers	5,481	5,597	5,472	5,065	6,114	5,994
Public debt	1,020	902	507	759	1,300	1,366
Miscellaneous	2,726	2,806	2,488	2,971	3,052	3,097
Total	**32,533**	**33,069**	**33,264**	**34,235**	**36,750**	**37,850**
Composition by administrative functions						
Public authorities	946	1,045	1,108	1,080	1,070	1,088
General administration	8,731	9,186	8,894	9,477	8,296	8,550
Military	3,899	3,586	3,962	4,071	4,205	4,461
Economic affairs	4,999	5,296	5,495	5,492	5,810	5,958
Social and cultural affairs	2,964	3,096	3,100	3,427	3,690	3,823
Education	5,088	5,480	6,389	6,088	6,139	6,599
General expenditures	4,886	4,478	3,808	3,841	6,240	6,005
Public debt	1,020	902	507	759	1,300	1,366

Source: Data provided by the Ministère des Finances, Direction du Trésor.

billion in 1967/68, however, was exceptionally low, mainly because transfers to Mauritania of tax receipts from imports under the customs union agreement were some CFAF 0.7 billion less than the estimated CFAF 0.94 billion. The Senegalese authorities gave three reasons for this: (1) direct imports to Mauritania have increased; (2) Mauritania had not furnished trade information before the close of the fiscal year; and (3) in the previous year, Senegal had paid in advance. Since the last two reasons are temporary, it was expected that, instead of a decrease in this expenditure—a major cause of the surplus in current budgetary operations in the previous year—a sharp increase would occur in 1968/69. Other transfers include earmarked taxes collected by the Central Government on behalf of local authorities and public agencies—such as the share of the *communes* in some of the direct taxes (some CFAF 1.2 billion annually) and the 2 per cent withholding tax on wages and salaries for the social security system (CFAF 0.5 billion) —and subsidies to the University and public and private schools (CFAF 0.9 billion), to the radio station (CFAF 0.3 billion), and to other public agencies and international organizations.

Expenditures for maintenance have been stationary in recent years, and their share of the total in 1967/68 was 4 per cent. Public debt service amounted to 2 per cent of total current spending; about two thirds of this expenditure was for interest and amortization of external loans and advances, of which debts contracted before independence formed only a minor part. The remainder was for interest on the internal loan issued in 1964 and a small amount for payments through the Pension Fund. Miscellaneous expenditures, which accounted for 9 per cent of the total in 1967/68, included the Senegalese contribution to technical assistance (CFAF 1.0 billion), rents, and equipment for administrative offices and buildings.

Composition by Administrative Function

The composition of current expenditures in 1967/68 by administrative function shows that 28 per cent of the total was for general administration, which comprises the Ministries of Foreign Affairs, Interior, Justice, Finance, and Information. Education, comprising general education and technical training, accounted for 18 per cent of the total, compared with 16 per cent in 1964/65. The increase resulted mainly from an extension in primary school facilities. Substantial funds were also allocated for education out of the investment budget. Military expenditures, which accounted for 11.9 per cent of total current spending in 1967/68, were approximately at the 1964/65 level, while outlays for social and cultural affairs increased slightly over the same period to 10.0 per cent of the total in 1967/68. Expenditures for economic affairs (comprising the expenses of the various ministries responsible for planning and industry; commerce, handicraft, and tourism; rural development; public works; and energy and water) have also expanded, accounting for 16 per cent of total current expenditures in 1967/68. A substantial part of the funds of the investment budget was also channeled into this field. General expenditures, which include transfers of earmarked taxes, have decreased since 1964/65, accounting for 11 per cent of the total in 1967/68; expenditures for public authorities were 3 per cent and for public debt 2 per cent.

INVESTMENT BUDGET

Capital Receipts

According to the estimates, the financing of the investment budget is in principle expected to come entirely from loan issues and foreign aid. But past budget results indicate that only a small share of investment outlays was actually financed from these sources. During the First Four-Year Development Plan (1961/62–1964/65), 14 per cent of total investment financing came from the issue of an internal loan of CFAF 4 billion in 1964 and 6 per cent from external loans (see Table 25). Most of the remaining financing was from current budget surpluses (53 per cent) and drawings on the reserve fund of the Treasury (26 per cent), which represented accumulated surpluses in the current budgets for previous years.

During the first three years (1965/66–1967/68) of the Second Four-Year Development Plan, revenues from loan issues contributed an even smaller share. The Government abstained from internal loans because of the limited capital market in Senegal. Although foreign loans were expected to cover most of the investment budget expenditures in this period, they actually contributed only 5 per cent of the outlays of CFAF 11.6 billion. However, the total inflow of foreign capital aid was substantially larger, since most of these funds were channeled directly into development projects undertaken outside the investment budget (see "Economic development planning," above). More than half (56 per cent) of the total investment budget financing came from surpluses in the current budget, and the remainder (39 per cent) was contributed by the Treasury. However, the Treasury's reserve fund was depleted in 1965, and the funds have come from the Treasury's general reserve.

For 1968/69, financing of the investment budget was expected from the following resources: (1) a Senegalese loan of CFAF 1.5 billion floated on the French capital market in the fall of 1968, in addition to using part of the proceeds for reimbursing the Treasury's advances, CFAF 0.5 billion was planned for use in the phosphate complex in Taïba, CFAF 0.4 billion for infrastructure investments, and the remainder for several agricultural projects (some investments have already been undertaken, mostly under interim financing by the Senegalese Treasury); (2) an internal compulsory loan launched in February 1969 (see "Public debt," below); (3) foreign loans, which were expected to contribute more than in recent years; and (4) funds from the Treasury, if necessary.

Capital Expenditures

The expenditure appropriations (*crédit de paiement*) in the investment budget are annual tranches of the total investment outlays approved in the Four-Year Development Plan (*autorisation de programme*). There are two types of appropriations: those covering projects to be financed out of general or untied loans and those for projects to be financed from foreign loans specifically tied to approved projects. In order to reduce the resort to financing from the Treasury, the latter appropriations are blocked until the credit actually has been made available.

During the first three years (1965/66–1967/68) of the Second Four-Year Development Plan, actual capital outlays were less than half the budgetary estimates. However, under the budgetary system in Senegal, unused appropriations are—with minor modifications—added to the new appropriations of the following fiscal years. Uncompleted projects may, therefore, appear in the estimates for more than one year, involving double counting if the annual appropriations are added up

over the plan period. Excluding double counting, and assuming that
investments of CFAF 6.5 billion will be undertaken in 1968/69 according to the revised estimates, total investment budget expenditures over
the second plan period should amount to about 75 per cent of the
amount originally planned.

Table 28 shows the investment program under the Second Four-Year
Development Plan for the investment budget and the actual expenditures over the first three years of the plan period. More than one third
of all investments undertaken were for social affairs, which include education and health, as well as investments in housing and urbanization.
The rate of implementation was the highest for these programs, with
almost two thirds of the authorization used. On the other hand, only
about one tenth of the amount planned for water projects has been
spent so far. But a water pipeline under construction to Dakar was
expected to require funds from the 1968/69 budget. Another important
item planned for 1968/69 was the government contribution to the
enlargement of a phosphate complex in Taïba.

TREASURY OPERATIONS

The Senegalese Treasury centralizes the financial transactions of the
public sector. Its activities fall mainly into three fields: (1) all budgetary operations of the Central Government; (2) financial operations of
public institutions, such as the Road Fund, the Pension Fund, Groundnut Stabilization Fund, and other stabilization funds, as well as some
government services channeled through special accounts with the Treasury; and (3) services as the public sector's bank in receiving deposits
of local authorities, public enterprises, and agencies. The Treasury also
makes loans and advances to local authorities and public enterprises
and extends short-term credit to importers through customs duty bills,
which can be discounted at the Central Bank (BCEAO).

Since the Treasury operates as a single unit, any cash balances may
be used to cover budgetary deficits. Additional funds have also been
obtained from the sale of Treasury bills and investment bonds. The
Treasury can also resort to the lending facilities of BCEAO (see
"Money and banking," below). The Senegalese Treasury maintains a
current account with the French Treasury, and it keeps its liquid funds
mainly with BCEAO in a current account and in a deposit account.

TABLE 28. SENEGAL: INVESTMENT BUDGET, PROGRAM UNDER THE SECOND FOUR-YEAR DEVELOPMENT PLAN (1965/66–1968/69) AND ACTUAL EXPENDITURES, 1965/66–1967/68

(*Amount in millions of CFA francs*)

	Four-Year Program 1965/66–1968/69		Actual			Three-year total, 1965/66–1967/68	
	Amount	Per cent of total	1965/66	1966/67	1967/68	Amount	Per cent of total
General studies	794	3.3	43	114	150	307	2.7
Water projects	2,732	11.3	64	130	114	308	2.7
Agriculture and fishing	5,295	21.8	362	732	568	1,662	14.4
Nonagricultural production	384	1.6	160	70	51	281	2.4
Transportation and telecommunications	2,968	12.2	281	921	659	1,861	16.1
Social affairs	6,832	28.1	1,089	1,564	1,571	4,224	36.5
Administration	1,050	4.3	86	310	335	731	6.3
Participations	1,143	4.7	100	60	16	176	1.5
Others	3,087	12.7	694	903	415	2,012	17.4
Total	24,284	100.0	2,879	4,804	3,881	11,562	100.0

Source: Data provided by the Ministère des Finances, Direction du Trésor.

LOCAL GOVERNMENT FINANCE

The local government part of the public sector comprises 33 districts and municipalities (*communes*). Dakar accounts for almost two thirds of total local revenue (Table 29). The consolidated account of the local authorities is equal to about 10 per cent of the Central Government's budget. The revenue is derived from transfers from the Central Government, from fiscal and local taxes, and from property and services. The transfers represent the returned share in certain taxes that are collected by the *communes* for the Central Government. The percentages of taxes allocated to the communal budgets were subject to annual

TABLE 29. SENEGAL: BUDGETS OF THE 33 LOCAL AUTHORITIES, 1964/65–1968/69

(*In millions of CFA francs*)

| | Actual | | | | Estimates, |
	1964/65	1965/66	1966/67	1967/68	1968/69
Revenue					
Ordinary revenues					
Transfers from Central Government	818	903	897	863	1,019
Additional levy on direct taxes	487	581	868	682	1,050
Fiscal taxes	330	564	654	439	876
Local taxes	859	647	694	830	737
Other current revenue	144	130	140	60	114
Surplus from previous year	468	531	254	672	74
Total ordinary revenue	3,106	3,355	3,506	3,546	3,871
Extraordinary revenues	499	448	249	492	60
Total revenue	3,605	3,803	3,756	4,037	3,931
Dakar	*2,049*	*2,388*	*2,477*	*2,625*	*2,479*
Expenditures					
Ordinary expenditures					
Public debt	232	85	72	...	169
Personnel	1,283	1,185	1,078	...	1,393
Material and maintenance	787	1,512	1,276	...	1,520
Social affairs	97	59	90	...	138
Investments	176	261	338	...	651
Total ordinary expenditures	2,575	3,102	2,854	...	3,871
Extraordinary expenditures (investments)	372	441	220	...	60
Total expenditures	2,947	3,542	3,074	...	3,931
Dakar	*1,844*	*2,290*	*1,844*	*2,036*	*2,479*
Over-all surplus	658	261	681	...	—
Dakar	*205*	*98*	*633*	*589*	—

Source: Ministère de l'Intérieur, Direction des Affaires Municipales.

determination before 1967, but have now been fixed by law at 85 per cent of the poll tax, business tax, and stamp duties; 70 per cent of the tax on revenue from houses and apartments (abolished in January 1969); 25 per cent of land taxes; and 50 per cent of the taxes on motor vehicles and on capital gains. The *communes* also impose a surtax (*centimes additionels*) on the total amount from all taxes mentioned above except the land tax. The rate of this surtax is 50 per cent and the revenue goes directly to the municipalities and districts which collect it. Fiscal taxes are levies on income from real estate; local taxes include levies on the number of servants employed, bills for electricity, income from cinemas and other entertainment, and licenses for serving drinks. Extraordinary revenues were derived from loans, from contributions of the Central Government for large urbanization projects and for equipment (*fonds de concours*), and from miscellaneous sources such as penalties.

The financial system of the municipalities and districts has undergone a major reform in recent years, based mainly on the Code de l'Administration Communale of June 30, 1966 and a government decree of July 4, 1966 regulating the financial operations of the local authorities. Local finances are now subject to greater supervision by the Ministry of Finance and the Ministry of Interior, which must approve both the budget and any additional expenditures. As a result, resort to supplementary appropriations during the year has been reduced. Furthermore, debts of the municipalities and districts were reviewed and consolidated, and the Treasury has extended loans and advances of about CFAF 400 million for the payment of accumulated bills.

The consolidated accounts of the *communes* have been in surplus since 1964/65, mainly because of the surplus generated by the municipality of Dakar. Surpluses are included in subsequent budgets as a revenue item. Total revenue has grown over recent years, reaching CFAF 4.0 billion in 1967/68. About one third of the expenditures were for personnel, one third for materiel and maintenance, and the rest mainly for investment.

PUBLIC ENTERPRISES

The major public enterprises with industrial, commercial, and administrative functions, except the agencies related to groundnuts—the

Development Assistance Office (ONCAD), the Agricultural Marketing
Board (OCAS), and the Development Bank—joined the Center for
Public Agencies (Centre des Etablissements Publics, or CEP) in 1966.
This Center, which is under authority of the Ministry of Finance, is in
charge of the bookkeeping of its 18 participants and of carrying out
most of their financial operations. A common computerized accounting
system has been introduced to facilitate analysis and control.

In 1967/68 the 18 enterprises shared a net loss of CFAF 0.2 billion
on consolidated account, compared with a net profit of CFAF 0.5
billion in 1966/67 (Table 30). Total receipts amounted to CFAF 11.9
billion, slightly less than in the previous year: the balance sheet showed
total assets and liabilities of CFAF 40.4 billion, 8 per cent more than

TABLE 30.   SENEGAL: SELECTED DATA FROM THE CONSOLIDATED ACCOUNTS
OF 18 PUBLIC ENTERPRISES, 1966/67–1967/68

(*In millions of CFA francs*)

	1966/67	1967/68
PROFIT AND LOSS STATEMENT		
Receipts	12,017	11,889
Current subsidies	*766*	*854*
Charges	11,712	11,836
Taxes paid	*56*	*65*
Gross profits	305	54
BALANCE SHEET		
Assets		
Fixed assets and stock	25,053	26,900
Loans and participations	3,901	4,070
Claims	2,905	3,063
Deposits with the Treasury	4,187	4,184
Cash and other liquid assets	1,379	1,879
Internal loss	—	256
Assets = liabilities	**37,425**	**40,353**
Liabilities		
Capital and reserves	25,438	26,010
Capital grants received	1,484	1,485
Treasury advances	3,270	3,167
Other liabilities	6,631	8,938
Other passive items	114	699
Gross profit	305	54
Internal profit	183	—
NET PROFIT		
Gross profit + internal profit or loss	488	−202

Source: Data provided by the accounting center for public enterprises.

in 1966/67. Current subsidies from the Central Government totaled CFAF 0.9 billion and taxes paid to the Government not quite CFAF 0.1 billion, both slightly more than in the previous year. Deposits with the Treasury were slightly reduced from the previous year to CFAF 4.2 billion and advances from the Treasury decreased by CFAF 0.1 billion, to CFAF 3.2 billion. Capital grants of CFAF 1 million were received, bringing the total to CFAF 1.5 billion. All financial transactions between the 18 enterprises and the Central Government resulted in a net contribution by the latter, amounting to CFAF 0.7 billion in 1967/68.

Within the Center for Public Agencies group, the social security scheme, the Post Office, and the Port of Dakar made large profits in 1966/67 and 1967/68, while both the railway and the Dakar bus service sustained losses, amounting to more than CFAF 300 million in 1967/68. The Central Government did not pay current subsidies to these companies, but the railway received capital grants and about half of the total amount of advances from the Treasury. Current subsidies were granted to the University of Dakar, Radio Senegal, and other enterprises, which are not expected to operate on a commercial basis. Two thirds of the total deposits with the Treasury were from the Post Office.

PUBLIC DEBT

The public debt is relatively low in Senegal, and the debt service so far does not heavily burden the budget or the balance of payments.

By June 30, 1968, total public debt outstanding, including loans contracted by public enterprises, was CFAF 20.4 billion, about 10 per cent of GDP. Three fifths of this amount (CFAF 16.4 billion) represented foreign debt. On June 30, 1969 the foreign debt was CFAF 17.6 billion; more than 91 per cent was owed to foreign governments (with France accounting for nearly four fifths) and the balance to international organizations and private sources (Table 31). Privately held foreign debt, amounting to only CFAF 56 million, is due to three loan issues in France between 1913 and 1932 for investments in West African infrastructure projects. The debts were subdivided among the West African countries in 1959, and the contribution of Senegal was set at 28.8 per cent. Remaining maturities range

TABLE 31. SENEGAL: EXTERNAL PUBLIC DEBT OUTSTANDING, 1965–69 [1]

(*In millions of CFA francs*)

	Jan. 1, 1965	Jan. 1, 1966	Jan. 1, 1967	Jan. 1, 1968	June 30, 1968	June 30, 1969
Loans from governments						
France	12,735	12,849	13,308	13,053	12,809	12,656
Germany, Federal Republic of	1,538	1,476	1,353	1,230	1,168	3,366
United Kingdom	344	345	345	295	295	—
Soviet Union	1,644	1,644	1,644	1,644	1,644	—
Total	16,261	16,314	16,650	16,222	15,916	16,022
Loans from international organizations						
IBRD	—	—	—	109	152	381
IDA	—	—	—	290	304	1,091
Total	—	—	—	399	456	1,472
Privately held debt	70	67	63	60	60	56
Total external public debt	16,332	16,381	16,713	16,681	16,432	17,550

Source: Data provided by the International Bank for Reconstruction and Development.

[1] Excluding short-term loans with a maturity of less than one year and amounts committed but not yet disbursed.

from 1 to 16 years. The total foreign debt outstanding has shown little change over the past 4 years, mainly because debt repayments nearly equaled new loan disbursements. However, most of the foreign aid received was in the form of capital grants, technical assistance, and donations in kind rather than loans (see "Balance of payments," below).

In the fall of 1968, a new Senegalese loan totaling CFAF 1.5 billion was floated on the French capital market under the guarantee of the French Government. The loan, which bears interest at 6¾ per cent and is repayable after 15 years, was subscribed mainly by French insurance companies. In January 1969, IDA approved a loan to Senegal of $6.0 million (CFAF 1.5 billion) and IBRD a loan of $3.5 million (CFAF 0.9 billion). (See "Balance of payments," below.)

The internal public debt amounted to CFAF 4.0 billion on June 30, 1968, resulting from a loan issued in January/February 1964 in the form of equipment bonds, the proceeds of which were used for capital expenditures in the investment budget. About CFAF 1.4 billion of this loan was subscribed by the commercial banks in Senegal, which had been asked to invest 15 per cent of their deposits in the bonds; insurance companies and public enterprises subscribed about CFAF 1.5 billion; and the remainder was absorbed by private subscribers. The interest rate ranges from 4 to 6.625 per cent, depending on the maturity, which runs from 5 to 10 years, with repayments beginning February 1969. In this same month, the Government introduced a new internal loan which provides for compulsory subscriptions by companies and individuals, amounting to 50 per cent of the company tax and 20 per cent of the income tax due in the previous fiscal year. The interest rate is 4 per cent, and the certificates will be redeemable in equal installments over a period of 12 years beginning on March 1, 1970.

Although no precise figures are available, the total service on the public debt in 1967/68 was estimated at some CFAF 1.1 billion, with about four fifths for amortization and interest on the foreign debt and the remainder for interest on the 1964 internal loan. Expenditures of the Central Government for the public debt totaled CFAF 0.8 billion (2 per cent of total current spending). This amount comprises payments on the internal debt and on the external debt directly

TABLE 32.   SENEGAL: FOREIGN DEBT SERVICE, 1965–70 [1]

(In millions of CFA francs)

	1965	1966	1967	1968 [2]	1969 [2]	1970 [2]
Amortization						
French Government	441	472	505	545	811	826
Other governments	62	123	123	126	130	130
International organizations and private creditors	3	3	3	3	3	32
Total amortization	506	598	631	674	945	988
Interest						
French Government	150	207	190	178	153	134
Other governments	23	76	71	62	57	53
International organizations and private creditors	4	3	4	16	37	62
Total interest	177	286	265	256	247	249
Total debt service	683	884	896	930	1,192	1,237

Source: Data provided by the International Bank for Reconstruction and Development.

[1] Excludes debt service on short-term loans with a maturity of less than one year, and on a CFAF 1,640 million U.S.S.R. loan and a CFAF 40 million French loan, for which repayment terms are not available.
[2] Estimates based on debt outstanding as of January 1, 1968.

owed by the Central Government, but excludes payments by public enterprises on their foreign liabilities. Total payments on foreign debts in the calendar year 1967, including payments by both the Central Government and the public enterprises, amounted to CFAF 0.9 billion (2 per cent of recorded exports), of which CFAF 0.6 billion was for amortization and the remainder for interest (Table 32). By 1970, this total was expected to rise to CFAF 1.2 billion, including nearly CFAF 1.0 billion for amortization.

MONEY AND BANKING

MONETARY SYSTEM

Senegal belongs to the franc area. It is also a member of the West African Monetary Union (Union Monétaire Ouest Africaine, or UMOA), together with six other countries (Dahomey, Ivory Coast, Mauritania, Niger, Togo, and Upper Volta). These countries have a common currency (CFA franc), and a common central bank, the

Banque Centrale des Etats de l'Afrique de l'Ouest (BCEAO), which is
the issuing authority of UMOA, and keeps its external reserves. The
CFA franc is freely convertible into French francs at the rate of
CFAF 1 = F 0.02. On August 10, 1969 the rate against the U.S. dollar
became CFAF 277.710 per dollar; previously, since January 1, 1960,
the rate had been CFAF 246.853. (For details on the operation of
BCEAO, see Chapter 4, and for information on the change in the par
value, see Chapter 6.)

STRUCTURE OF THE BANKING SYSTEM

Apart from BCEAO, the banking system in Senegal consists of the
Development Bank (Banque Nationale de Développement du Sénégal,
or BNDS), four commercial banks, and a financial institution. Assets
and liabilities of the Central Bank are shown in Table 33 and those of
the commercial banks and the Development Bank in Table 34.

BCEAO operates in Senegal, as in the other UMOA countries,
through a local agency.[9] Decisions concerning the implementation of
BCEAO policies in each member country are taken by the National
Monetary Committee. The director of the local BCEAO agency, who
sits on the National Monetary Committee in an advisory capacity, is
responsible for the application of these decisions.

The Development Bank was created in 1964 as the result of a
merger between the Crédit Populaire Sénégalais and the Banque
Sénégalaise de Développement. Its statutes were approved by Decree
No. 64–492 of July 3, 1964. Its capital is currently CFAF 1,360
million.

The four commercial banks are as follows: (1) Union Sénégalaise de
Banque pour le Commerce et l'Industrie (capital CFAF 690 million);
(2) Banque Internationale pour le Commerce et l'Industrie du Sénégal
(capital CFAF 500 million); (3) Société Générale de Banques au
Sénégal (capital CFAF 500 million); and (4) the Banque Internationale pour l'Afrique Occidentale, a French company (capital of CFAF 3
billion).

The Société Générale de Crédit Automobile (SOGECA) is a financial
establishment which specializes in financing the credit sales of motor
vehicles.

---

[9] There is also a subagency at Kaolack.

TABLE 33. SENEGAL: ASSETS AND LIABILITIES OF THE CENTRAL BANK, 1962–69

(In billions of CFA francs; end of September, except as noted)

	1962	1963	1964	1965	1966	1967 Sept.	1967 Dec.	1968 Mar.	1968 June	1968 Sept.	1968 Dec.	1969¹ Mar.	1969¹ June	1969¹ Sept.
Assets														
Gross foreign assets														
Foreign exchange	...	...	...	1.82	5.62	3.05	6.12	3.13	1.71	1.13	0.76	1.05	1.38	1.42
IMF	0.18	0.62	0.62	0.62	0.62	0.62	0.62	0.62	0.62	0.62	0.62	0.62	0.62	0.69
Treasury investment account	...	4.64	...	5.47	2.50	2.50	2.50	2.50	2.50	2.50	2.50	2.50	2.50	2.50
External operations of the Treasury	...	...	0.09	0.06	0.09	0.04	0.09	0.06	0.07	0.07	...	...	...	...
Intra-UMOA operations	...	...	—	-0.55	-0.25	-0.31	-0.14	-0.03	-0.01	...	...	...	...	...
Total gross foreign assets	12.75	10.02	8.70	7.42	8.58	5.90	9.19	6.28	4.89	4.32	3.95	4.10	4.53	4.26
Claims on banks (rediscount)														
Short-term	...	6.12	8.08	8.13	9.68	9.32	6.72	17.03	14.02	11.11	12.02	15.25	11.31	8.52
Medium-term	...	0.85	0.85	1.42	0.96	1.33	1.67	0.89	1.17	1.11	0.87	0.98	1.23	1.47
Total claims on banks	5.67	6.97	8.93	9.55	10.64	10.65	8.39	17.92	15.19	12.22	12.89	16.23	12.54	9.99
Assets = liabilities	18.42	16.99	17.63	16.97	19.22	16.55	17.58	24.20	20.08	16.54	16.84	20.33	17.07	14.25
Liabilities														
Reserve money²	12.09	10.77	10.35	9.92	10.77	10.57	10.21	15.54	13.44	11.70	11.92	16.43	12.17	11.02
Government deposits														
Currency held by Treasury	0.86	0.54	0.54	0.54	0.59	0.54	0.45	0.80	0.58	0.49	0.40	0.44	0.44	0.43
Investment account	2.72	4.63	4.72	4.53	2.50	2.50	2.50	2.50	2.50	2.50	2.50	2.50	2.50	2.50
Government deposits	0.24	0.45	0.54	0.38	4.45	2.42	2.88	3.29	2.76	1.32	0.72	...	0.50	...
Total government deposits	3.82	5.62	5.80	5.45	7.54	5.46	5.83	6.59	5.84	4.31	3.62	3.11	3.44	2.66
Foreign liabilities	0.96	0.02	1.01	1.12	0.28	0.03	0.75	0.21	0.20	0.02	0.31	0.01	0.47	0.09
Other items³	1.55	0.58	0.47	0.48	0.63	0.49	0.79	1.86	0.60	0.51	0.99	0.78	0.99	0.48

Sources: IMF, *International Financial Statistics*, and BCEAO, *Notes d'Information et Statistiques.*

¹ Provisional.
² Excluding currency held by Treasury and banks.
³ Includes some private deposits.

TABLE 34. SENEGAL: ASSETS AND LIABILITIES OF THE COMMERCIAL BANKS AND THE DEVELOPMENT BANK, 1962–69

(In billions of CFA francs; end of September, except as noted)

	1962	1963	1964	1965	1966	1967		1968				1969 [1]		
						Sept.	Dec.	Mar.	June	Sept.	Dec.	Mar.	June	Sept.
Assets														
Cash	1.35	0.49	0.36	0.37	0.55	0.33	0.63	1.69	0.70	0.49	1.30	0.85	0.96	0.72
Foreign assets	−0.73 [2]	3.38	3.05	1.82	1.76	2.02	1.95	1.98	2.54	1.91	1.45	2.28	3.03	1.82
Claims on Government	0.06	0.11	2.37	2.29	2.13	1.96	1.97	2.00	2.10	2.14	1.90	1.89	1.97	3.36
Claims on private sector	24.58	28.34	27.99	30.32	29.87	29.65	26.00	36.86	35.42	33.06	31.63	36.72	33.95	32.60
Assets = liabilities	**25.26**	**32.32**	**33.77**	**34.80**	**34.31**	**33.96**	**30.55**	**42.53**	**40.76**	**37.60**	**36.28**	**41.74**	**39.91**	**38.50**
Liabilities														
Demand deposits	13.74	15.78	11.53	12.38	13.21	13.93	13.04	14.89	14.94	14.76	14.48	15.78	15.97	14.92
Time deposits	1.37	0.89	0.83	1.02	0.91	1.18	0.74	0.74	0.70	0.98	1.28	1.63	1.52	1.75
Government deposits	2.71	3.28	6.18	5.07	2.23	1.71	1.66	1.67	1.69	1.67	1.65	1.71	1.71	1.89
Foreign liabilities	. . .	3.38	4.11	2.97	4.25	2.64	4.43	4.78	5.13	4.81	4.25	4.83	6.62	8.47
Credit from Central Bank	5.63	6.97	8.93	9.55	10.64	10.65	8.39	17.92	15.19	12.22	12.89	16.23	12.54	9.99
Other items (net)	1.81	2.02	2.19	3.81	3.07	3.85	2.29	2.53	3.11	3.16	1.73	1.56	1.55	1.47

Sources: IMF, *International Financial Statistics*, and data provided by BCEAO.

[1] Provisional.
[2] Net foreign assets; breakdown of assets and liabilities not available for September 1962.

The Treasury of Senegal also performs certain banking operations. It accepts customs duty bills (*obligations cautionnées*) with a maturity of four months in payment of certain indirect taxes, principally customs duties. These bills are discountable at BCEAO. The Treasury may receive deposits from public and semipublic institutions.

Besides the credit extended by banks, the Caisse Centrale de Coopération Economique (CCCE), a French public institution, extends medium-term and long-term credit and contributes to the financing of the Development Bank's credit operations. In addition, it acts as the authorized agent of the Fonds d'Aide et de Coopération (FAC) and the European Development Fund (EDF, or Fonds Européen de Développement, or FED) for local aid disbursements.

BANKING LEGISLATION AND REGULATIONS

From 1960 to 1964, except for a small number of provisions inconsistent with independence, French banking laws continued to be applied in Senegal. Interest rates and other lending procedures, not governed by these laws, were determined by a 1959 agreement reached by the commercial banks operating in the former French West Africa. However, these regulations were provisional pending new legislation based on guidelines to be set by the Board of BCEAO for the entire UMOA. The treaty establishing UMOA in 1962 calls for the application of uniform basic principles regulating the banking profession and the distribution and control of credit.

On July 10, 1964, the Government of Senegal promulgated a law (No. 64–49) governing the banking profession and credit operations applicable to banks and financial institutions. Implementation of the general provisions of this law are governed by a series of decrees drawn up mainly during 1965.

The Minister of Finance is in charge of the over-all management of credit. Decisions are implemented through orders based on decrees taken upon his proposal. There are two advisory bodies: (1) the Economic and Social Council, which provides the monetary authorities with information and suggestions, and (2) the Professional Association of Banks and Financial Institutions, which must be consulted on all decisions concerning the banking profession.

BCEAO is charged with the implementation of the bank regulations and with the control of credit.

A supervisory body, with a jurisdictional role, the Commission de Surveillance des Banques et des Etablissements Financiers, controls the application of the bank regulations. This Commission comprises a Supreme Court Judge (Chairman), the Director of BCEAO, and an official of the Ministry of Finance. It prepares an annual report setting forth its findings. It also makes relevant proposals as to the operation and over-all results of the banking system and the structure and organization of the banks and financial institutions.

Since these entities deal essentially with the institutional aspects of the banking profession, they do not infringe upon the responsibilities assigned by the UMOA treaty and the BCEAO statutes to BCEAO's Board of Directors on monetary policy, and to the Monetary Committee for the implementation of these decisions.

The law of 1964, apart from setting forth the conditions governing the operations of domestic and foreign banks and financial institutions with regard to registration, legal structure, accounting procedures, and the issue of periodic statements, introduces certain regulations concerning minimum capital and equity participation.

Any bank operating in Senegal must maintain a minimum capital of CFAF 250 million. Capital is defined as the sum of paid-up equity capital, reserves, endowments, nonearmarked provisions, and net profits carried forward. The minimum capital must at least be equal to 8 per cent of credits granted (inclusive of rediscounts with BCEAO and guarantees on account of customers) on the closing date of the most recent accounting year. To facilitate compliance, banks were permitted to increase by 1 per cent annually this ratio from 4 per cent in 1965/66 to 8 per cent in 1969/70, provided that their head offices or shareholders maintained with them blocked accounts in an amount which, inclusive of capital, would satisfy the 8 per cent requirements. In addition to the minimum capital, banks are required to maintain an additional capital (as defined above) equal to 15 per cent of long-term credits, nonrediscountable medium-term credits, and equity participations. The latter requirement is waived if capital is equivalent to at least 12 per cent of credits granted, inclusive of rediscounts and guarantees.

Any financial institutions must maintain a minimum capital (defined as for banks) of CFAF 50 million. This capital may not be lower than 10 per cent of the credits granted by these institutions on the closing date of the last accounting year.

The legislation also fixes limits to banks' participation in the equity capital of enterprises other than banks, financial institutions, and real estate companies germane to their operations and housing of their personnel. Equity participation must not exceed 25 per cent of the capital of the enterprise and 15 per cent of the banks' capital (as defined above). The sum of all participations inclusive of subscriptions to new issues of shares or profit-sharing instruments must not exceed 75 per cent of the banks' capital. In special circumstances, these percentages may be modified by decree.

LIQUIDITY RATIO AND RESERVE REQUIREMENTS

Pursuant to a decree of September 8, 1965, banks must permanently maintain a minimum ratio between their liquid and rediscountable assets and their short-term liabilities. This ratio was fixed at 74 per cent for the fiscal year 1969/70 and will be increased by 1 percentage point to 75 per cent, starting with 1970/71. Rediscountable credits granted by a bank are included on its liquid asset side, while rediscounted credits are included on both the liquid asset and the current liabilities sides. This method of calculation induces the banks to grant rediscountable credits.

INTEREST RATES

Since the establishment of UMOA, the basic discount rate of BCEAO has remained unchanged at 3.5 per cent. A reduced rate of 3 per cent is applied to the financing of operations involving exports to countries outside the BCEAO area. The rates charged by commercial banks are based on BCEAO's discount rate, to which percentage points are added.

The rates for credit operations, commissions on transfers of funds, as well as interest paid to creditor accounts, are identical in all UMOA countries. These rates were fixed in Senegal by an order of December 28, 1965, which took effect from February 5, 1966. Except for the rates of interest paid on private deposits of more than six months, which were increased on January 1, 1969, the rates have remained unchanged since 1966. The scale applicable to the other services rendered by banks was fixed by an order of August 17, 1966. However, this scale, based on principles common to the UMOA countries, was adapted to the needs of Senegal.

Interest rates charged by banks for short-term credits (Table 35) are fixed in relation to the nature of the operations to be financed. Reduced rates are applicable to credits eligible for rediscount. These preferential rates may vary up to 1 per cent according to the nature of the operations. Thus a minimum rate of 5.5 per cent and a maximum rate of 6.5 per cent are applied to overdrafts, the form of credit most frequently used in Senegal. A preferential rate is also applied to credit operations with special guarantees or considered as being in the national interest. The rate applied by the banks for short-term credits not eligible for rediscount is generally 8 per cent. Rates for rediscounted medium-term credits range from 5.25 per cent for the most encouraged operations to 7.5 per cent for other operations. Interest rates for non-rediscountable medium-term credits range between 8 per cent and 8.5 per cent. The Development Bank applies fixed rates determined by its by-laws.

For the fiscal year 1966/67, the average cost of short-term credit operations was 6.15 per cent excluding commissions and 7.29 per cent including commissions. During the same period, the average rate for medium-term credits, most of which are rediscountable, was lower than that for short-term operations. Including commissions, these medium-term credit rates have been at a level close to the prescribed minimum of 5.50 per cent. This circumstance resulted from the importance within total medium-term credits of loans granted to enterprises eligible for preferential treatment under the Investment Code.

MONETARY AND CREDIT DEVELOPMENTS

Over-All Developments

Monetary and credit developments in Senegal are subject to a marked seasonality because of groundnut crop marketing and processing requirements. Credit usually starts to expand quickly in December, reaches a peak in March, and then falls rapidly until September–November.

TABLE 35. SENEGAL: STRUCTURE OF INTEREST RATES APPLIED
BY THE COMMERCIAL BANKS

(*In per cent per annum*)

	A. Within Individual Limits; B. Rates	A. In Excess of Individual Limits
A. Interest paid on credit		
Short-term		
Crop financing for public agencies		
Credits granted to productive enterprises entitled to a founding agreement or an approval agreement or to preferential treatment	BR [1] +1.00 min. +1.75 max.	BR +4.50 (fixed rate)
Advance on commodities properly guaranteed	+1.50 min. +2.50 max.	+4.50 (fixed rate)
Other credits or advances rediscountable by BCEAO	+2.00 min. +3.00 max.	
Other credits or advances not rediscountable by BCEAO in an amount of less than CFAF 1,000,000	. . .	+2.50 min. +4.50 max.
Other credits or advances in an amount exceeding CFAF 1,000,000 not rediscountable by BCEAO	. . .	+4.50 (fixed rate)
Medium-term		
Credits rediscountable by BCEAO [2]		
Construction credits not declared of social content, or not meeting the criteria for housing of social interest as defined by the Government	. . .	+3.50 min. +4.00 max.
Industrial or commercial credits of a productive nature	. . .	+1.75 min. +2.50 max.
Investment credits to enterprises having a founding agreement or credits for construction of social interest	. . .	+1.75 min. +2.25 max.
Credits not rediscountable by BCEAO	. . .	+4.50 min. +5.00 max.
B. Interest paid on deposits		
Government or quasi-government deposits	Free	. . .
Accounts of less than 6 months		
CFAF 0–200,000	—	. . .
CFAF 200,001–500,000	1.00	. . .
CFAF 500,001–1,000,000	1.50	. . .
CFAF 1,000,001–5,000,000	2.00	. . .
More than CFAF 5,000,000	2.50	. . .
Accounts of more than 6 months		
CFAF 0–200,000	—	. . .
CFAF 200,001–5,000,000	3.50	. . .
More than CFAF 5,000,000	4.50	. . .
Savings accounts	3.25	. . .

Source: Data provided by the Senegalese authorities.

[1] BR = BCEAO's rediscount rate (currently 3.5 per cent).

[2] In addition to the interest rates indicated, two commissions, of 0.25 per cent and of 0.15 per cent, are applied to medium-term credits rediscountable by BCEAO, with the exception of credits granted with government backing.

Money supply on a September–September basis rose by 14 per cent during 1965–69 (Table 36). However, the rate of increase varied from one year to the other. After rising to 6 per cent in 1965/66, it dropped to 2 per cent in 1966/67, rose above 6 per cent in 1967/68, and dropped again in 1968/69 by 1.3 per cent. At the end of September 1969, money supply amounted to CFAF 27.9 billion, or CFAF 3.4 billion above the September 1965 level.

In the year ended September 1966, money supply had risen by CFAF 1.5 billion. There was an increase in net foreign assets of nearly CFAF 0.7 billion. The net creditor position of the Government and claims on the private sector each declined by CFAF 0.9 billion.

In 1966/67, money supply rose by CFAF 0.5 billion as a result of an increased use by the Treasury of its deposits with the banking system, while net foreign assets declined slightly by nearly CFAF 0.6 billion and claims on the private sector by CFAF 0.3 billion.

In the year ended September 1968, the CFAF 1.7 billion increase in money supply reflected a rise in claims on the private sector by CFAF 3.4 billion accompanied by the Government's drawing down its banking deposits further by CFAF 1.2 billion. These expansionary trends were partly offset by a decrease in net foreign assets (CFAF 3.8 billion). At the end of September 1968, net foreign assets amounted to CFAF 1.4 billion. However, in September 1968, about CFAF 2.5 billion was expected to be disbursed by EDF on account of groundnut price support subsidy.

In 1968/69 the decline in money supply reflected a sharp decrease in net foreign assets, which dropped from CFAF 1.4 billion in September 1968 to a negative figure of CFAF 2.4 billion in September 1969. Claims on the private sector declined somewhat—by CFAF 0.5 billion, or by 1.4 per cent. These contractionary trends were partly offset by the Government's drawing down its banking deposits by CFAF 1.4 billion.

Other components in the money supply varied only slightly during the three years ended September 1968. Time deposits with the banks, which had declined from CFAF 1.0 billion at the end of September 1965 to CFAF 0.9 billion one year later, rose to CFAF 1.2 billion during the next year and amounted to CFAF 1.0 billion at the end of

TABLE 36. SENEGAL: MONETARY SURVEY, 1962–69

(In billions of CFA francs; end of September, except as noted)

	1962	1963	1964	1965	1966	1967		1968				1969 [1]		
						Sept.	Dec.	Mar.	June	Sept.	Dec.	Mar.	June	Sept.
Assets														
Foreign assets (net)	11.06	10.02	7.56	5.74	5.81	5.24	5.96	3.27	2.11	1.40	0.84	1.53	0.47	-2.48
Claims on Government (net)	-5.61	-7.44	-7.73	-6.65	-6.60	-4.06	-4.51	-5.40	-4.30	-2.89	-2.40	-1.96	-2.04	-0.11
Government deposits	*8.02*	*10.51*	*12.97*	*11.96*	*10.75*	*8.04*	*8.57*	*9.44*	*8.47*	*6.85*	*6.27*	*5.75*	*6.08*	*5.44*
Claims on private sector														
Bank credit	24.58	28.34	27.99	33.41	29.87	29.65	26.00	36.86	35.42	33.06	31.63	36.73	33.95	32.60
Customs duty bills	1.49	1.61	0.99	1.13	0.97	0.87	1.07	1.18	0.94	0.86	1.00	1.11	0.93	0.89
Total claims on private sector	26.07	29.95	28.98	34.54	30.84	30.52	27.07	38.04	36.36	33.92	32.63	37.84	34.88	33.49
Assets = liabilities	**31.52**	**32.53**	**28.81**	**33.63**	**30.05**	**31.70**	**28.52**	**35.91**	**34.17**	**32.43**	**31.07**	**37.41**	**33.31**	**30.90**
Liabilities														
Money														
Currency	12.09	10.77	10.48	14.72	10.77	10.57	10.21	15.54	13.44	11.70	11.92	16.43	12.17	11.02
Demand deposits [2]	13.74	15.78	11.53	12.02	13.23	13.96	13.05	14.90	14.96	14.75	14.48	15.78	15.97	14.92
Postal checking deposits	2.36	2.96	2.86	2.25	2.01	2.02	2.06	2.04	2.03	1.82	1.97	2.08	2.08	1.96
Total money	28.19	29.51	24.87	28.99	26.01	26.55	25.32	32.48	30.43	28.27	28.37	34.29	30.22	27.90
Quasi-money	1.37	0.89	0.83	1.04	0.91	1.18	0.74	0.74	0.70	0.98	1.28	1.63	1.52	1.76
Other items (net)	1.96	2.13	3.11	3.60	3.13	3.97	2.46	2.69	3.04	3.18	1.42	1.49	1.57	1.24

SOURCES: IMF, *International Financial Statistics*, and data provided by BCEAO.

[1] Provisional.

[2] Including some private deposits with BCEAO.

September 1968. They increased to CFAF 1.8 billion by the end of September 1969.

Nor was there much change in the composition of the money supply over this three-year period. Currency in circulation represented almost 41 per cent of the money supply at the end of September 1965 and slightly more than 41 per cent three years later; the corresponding proportions of demand deposits changed only from 51 to 52 per cent. Deposits with the Postal Checking System declined from 9 per cent to 6 per cent. In 1968/69, however, currency in circulation represented 39 per cent of the money supply, demand deposits 54 per cent, and deposits with the Postal System 7 per cent.

Because the Government drew down its banking deposits by substantial amounts, its net creditor position declined from CFAF 6.5 billion to CFAF 0.1 billion over the period 1965–69. At the end of September 1969, government deposits amounted to CFAF 5.4 billion, compared with CFAF 12.0 billion four years earlier.

Commercial Bank and Development Bank Credit to the Economy

Outstanding short-term credit during 1965–68 varied seasonally according to the financing needs of the groundnut crop marketing and processing, which reach their peak in March. In the 1965/66 crop year a record quantity was harvested, and short-term credit rose to CFAF 35.0 billion on March 31, 1966 (Table 37). It declined to CFAF 32.1 billion one year later with the shortfall in the groundnut crop and amounted to CFAF 32.2 billion on March 31, 1968. In September, usually the low point for this credit, it remained at CFAF 25–26 billion in the first two years. In September 1968, however, it amounted to CFAF 28.5 billion, partly because of delays in the cooperatives' repayments to the Development Assistance Office and in the Groundnut Stabilization Fund's reimbursement of the Marketing Board.

Credit for groundnut crop financing is provided by a consortium of five banks headed by the Development Bank, which grants 58 per cent of the total extended to the Development Assistance Office for marketing and 20 per cent of the total extended to the Marketing Board for export or processing. At its peak (March 1966), the credit for groundnuts represented 47 per cent of all declared short-term credit, but the proportion declined to 27 per cent in September 1968 (Table 38).

TABLE 37. SENEGAL: DOMESTIC CREDIT, 1965–68

(In billions of CFA francs)

	1965 (Sept.)	1965/66 Dec.	1965/66 Mar.	1965/66 June	1965/66 Sept.	1966/67 Dec.	1966/67 Mar.	1966/67 June	1966/67 Sept.	1967/68 Dec.	1967/68 Mar.	1967/68 June	1967/68 Sept. [1]
BCEAO													
Claims on banks													
Short-term	8.13	12.38	18.06	12.77	9.68	10.19	15.65	13.00	9.32	6.72	17.03	14.02	11.11
Groundnut financing	...	*3.60*	*13.10*	*7.23*	*2.32*	*2.47*	*9.59*	*5.85*	*1.88*	*0.14*	*9.04*	*4.92*	...
Medium-term	1.42	1.64	1.07	1.30	0.96	1.60	1.54	1.10	1.33	1.67	0.89	1.17	1.11
Total	9.55	14.02	19.13	14.07	10.64	11.79	17.19	14.10	10.65	8.39	17.92	15.19	12.22
Commercial and development banks													
Short-term	16.57	15.28	16.69	16.70	15.27	14.80	16.43	15.56	16.23	13.04	14.67	16.17	16.93
Medium-term	2.66	2.36	2.71	2.06	2.28	1.48	1.24	1.60	1.39	2.17	1.82	1.60	1.63
Long-term	1.07	1.45	1.47	1.49	1.50	1.50	1.46	1.57	1.65	1.86	1.93	1.95	1.91
Unclassified loans	0.47	0.21	0.23	0.24	0.23	0.36	0.58	0.53	0.49	0.53	0.52	0.55	0.46
Total	20.77	19.30	21.10	20.49	19.28	18.14	19.71	19.26	19.76	17.60	18.94	20.27	20.93
Foreign banks	0.18	0.15	0.20	0.22	—	—	—	—	—	0.01	—	—	—
Total domestic credit (all private sector)	30.50	33.47	40.43	34.78	29.92	29.93	36.90	33.36	30.41	26.00	36.86	35.46	33.15
Less mobilization bills to be paid [2]	−0.18	−0.06	−0.14	—	−0.05	−0.08	−0.06	−0.05	−0.76	—	—	−0.04	−0.09
Total, adjusted	30.32	33.41	40.29	34.78	29.87	29.85	36.84	33.31	29.65	26.00	36.86	35.42	33.06

Sources: IMF, *International Financial Statistics*, and data provided by BCEAO.

[1] Provisional.
[2] For adjustment with Table 34.

TABLE 38. SENEGAL: UTILIZATION OF SHORT-TERM CREDIT, BY MAJOR ECONOMIC SECTORS, 1965-68 [1]

(Amount in millions of CFA francs)

	Sept. 1965		Mar. 1966		Sept. 1966		Mar. 1967		Sept. 1967		Mar. 1968		Sept. 1968	
	Amount	Per cent	Amount	Per cent	Amount	Per cent	Amount	Per cent	Amount	Per cent	Amount	Per cent	Amount	Per cent
Seasonal credit (groundnuts)														
Marketing and storage	0.6	2.3	12.5	35.3	3.6	14.0	9.8	30.2	2.0	8.2	10.1	31.1	5.1	18.1
Exports	0.4	1.5	0.6	1.7	—	—	0.4	1.2	—	—	0.7	2.2	0.2	0.7
Oil mills	4.5	17.0	3.4	9.6	4.6	17.9	3.5	10.8	4.7	19.2	1.9	5.8	2.2	7.8
Total seasonal credit	5.5	20.8	16.5	46.6	8.2	31.9	13.7	42.3	6.7	27.3	12.7	39.1	7.5	26.6
Various credit to cooperatives														
Development Assistance Office [2] and Agricultural Marketing Board [3]	4.4	16.7	2.6	7.4	3.6	14.0	3.7	11.4	4.4	18.0	3.2	9.8	5.2	18.4
Rice	—	—	—	—	—	—	—	—	—	—	*1.1*	—	*2.2*	—
Other credit														
Agriculture [4]	0.2	0.8	0.1	0.3	0.1	0.4	0.2	0.6	0.1	0.4	—	—	0.1	0.4
Industry [5]	3.2	12.1	2.9	8.2	2.6	10.1	3.0	9.3	2.8	11.4	3.3	10.2	3.2	11.3
Construction and public works	1.3	4.9	1.0	2.8	0.7	2.7	0.9	2.8	0.7	2.9	1.0	3.1	0.9	3.2
Transportation and transit	0.9	3.4	0.9	2.5	0.8	3.1	0.7	2.2	0.6	2.4	1.0	3.1	0.7	2.5
Commerce [6]	8.9	33.7	7.8	22.0	7.4	28.8	7.5	23.1	6.7	27.3	7.8	24.0	7.9	28.0
Other	0.4	1.5	0.4	1.1	0.4	1.6	0.6	1.9	0.6	2.4	0.8	2.5	0.7	2.5
Total other credit	14.9	56.4	13.1	37.0	12.0	46.7	12.9	39.8	11.5	46.9	13.9	42.8	13.5	47.9
Credit of less than CFAF 10 million nondeclared individually	1.6	6.1	3.2	9.0	1.9	7.4	2.1	6.5	1.9	7.8	2.7	8.3	2.0	7.1
Total declared credit	26.4	100.0	35.4	100.0	25.7	100.0	32.4	100.0	24.5	100.0	32.5	100.0	28.2	100.0

Source: Data provided by BCEAO.

[1] Based on declarations to the Centrale des Risques.
[2] Office National de Coopération et d'Assistance pour le Développement (ONCAD).
[3] Office de Commercialisation Agricole du Sénégal (OCAS).
[4] Other than groundnuts.
[5] Other than oil mills.
[6] Excluding the Agricultural Marketing Board.

Other credits granted to the Office and Board (for the agricultural program or for rice purchases) declined from CFAF 4.4 billion to CFAF 3.6 billion in the first year but rose to CFAF 5.2 billion in September 1968, or to 18 per cent of all declared short-term credit. This expansion reflects in part the Government's efforts to provide fertilizers, insecticides, seeds, and small equipment to farmers through the Development Bank, which supplies agricultural credit.

Short-term credit for other activities declined slightly in 1966/67 from CFAF 14.9 billion in September 1965 during the next year. Although it rose to CFAF 13.5 billion in September 1968 (when it represented 48 per cent of total short-term credit), it remained below the 1965 level. Trade credit, mainly for imports, fluctuated between CFAF 8.9 billion in September 1965 and CFAF 7.9 billion in September 1968, usually reaching a peak in November just before the beginning of the groundnut crop, which determines the purchasing power of the population. Credit to industry (excluding oil mills) remained practically unchanged throughout the period, amounting to CFAF 3.2 billion in September 1968. Credit to construction and public works declined slightly from CFAF 1.3 billion in September 1965 to CFAF 0.9 billion in September 1968. In addition, short-term credit to the private sector is provided by the Treasury in the form of customs duty bills (*obligations cautionnées*), which amounted to about CFAF 1 billion during this period.

Outstanding medium-term credit, which accounted for less than 10 per cent of total credit to the economy, declined from CFAF 4.1 billion in September 1965 to CFAF 2.7 billion in September 1968 (see Table 37). This decrease reflected the cessation in 1964 of the financing of a large housing program and a shortage of productive commercial and industrial projects while amortization of former loans followed its course. Moreover, some large enterprises used to get medium-term credit from foreign banks abroad. Medium-term credit granted by the commercial banks generally decreased over these three years, while the share of the Development Bank increased because this Bank finances the agricultural program. At the end of September 1968, Senegal's ceiling for total medium-term credit was CFAF 4.4 billion; outstanding credits initiated by the Development Bank amounted to CFAF 1.6 billion and those extended by the commercial banks to CFAF 1.2 billion.

Most of the loans were to the agriculture, mining, and construction sectors.

Long-term loans are granted by the Development Bank either from its own resources or from special CCCE advances and largely to mining, industry, and construction. These loans rose from CFAF 1.1 billion at the end of September 1965 to CFAF 1.9 billion at the end of September 1968.

Rediscount Operations of the Central Bank

Short-term credit rediscounted reaches a high level in March, the peak of· groundnut crop financing. It declined from CFAF 18.1 billion in March 1966 to CFAF 15.7 billion in March 1967, rose to CFAF 17.0 billion in March 1968, and declined to CFAF 15.3 billion in March 1969, averaging roughly one half of total short-term credit.

During 1965–68, short-term credit granted to the private sector by the commercial banks and the Development Bank increased by CFAF 3.3 billion, of which nearly CFAF 3.0 billion was rediscounted at BCEAO (see Tables 33 and 37). Bank resources remained relatively stable, as a CFAF 1 billion increase in their own resources was offset by a decrease of the same amount in bank deposits.[10] Short-term rediscount maximums are usually utilized up to 95.97 per cent.

In this period, medium-term credit rediscounted at BCEAO fluctuated between a maximum of 53 per cent of the total and a minimum of 30 per cent. These variations, however, are not significant since the banks are free to decide what type of credit they prefer to mobilize according to their liquidity position.

So far, the Government has not used BCEAO's facilities for short-term advances or for rediscount of customs duty bills.

Operations of Other Financial Institutions

Besides the four commercial banks and the Development Bank, other financial institutions are the Postal Savings Bank, the Société Générale de Crédit Automobile (SOGECA), and CCCE.

---

[10] Include demand, time, and government deposits.

The Post Office receives savings deposits through a National Savings Bank. The amount of savings deposits increased from CFAF 345 million in September 1965 to CFAF 442 million in September 1968.

During the fiscal year 1966/67, the Société Générale de Crédit Automobile, a financial institution specializing in consumer credit mainly for car purchases, granted credits of CFAF 594 million, or 33 per cent more than during 1965/66. Unpaid bills totaled CFAF 22 million at the end of September 1967, and outstanding credit CFAF 352 million, of which CFAF 245 million has been discounted with other banks.

CCCE acts as executive agent for FAC and EDF. In addition, it extends medium-term and long-term advances to the Government, the Development Bank, and private concerns. It may participate in the capital of public and private enterprises. CCCE loans are in the form of global advances for investments of small amounts, and special advances for specific projects. In Senegal, no global advances have been granted since 1964. Total CCCE disbursed advances amounted to CFAF 21.3 million in 1965, CFAF 478.4 million in 1966, and CFAF 733.7 million in 1967. Net outstanding advances totaled CFAF 14.6 billion on December 31, 1967. Of the outstanding net claims (CFAF 14.6 billion), CFAF 8.2 billion was on the Government, CFAF 0.1 billion on local governments, CFAF 3.4 billion on semipublic institutions (which covered mainly the Development Bank), and CFAF 2.9 billion on private enterprises.

FOREIGN TRADE, AID, PAYMENTS, AND RESERVES

FOREIGN TRADE

Senegal's foreign trade statistics, based on customs records, have a limited coverage for several reasons: (1) Because the price of certain import or export commodities is not known at the time of shipment, these imports or exports are valued, for customs purposes, at standard values fixed each year by the Government (*valeurs mercuriales*). The standard values are usually lower than market prices, and certain transactions on goods tend to be undervalued in customs statistics. (2)

Trade with UDEAO member countries [11] is not submitted to customs duties and there is no systematic recording of these trade flows. Moreover, large differences exist between recorded exports to other UDEAO countries and recorded imports into Senegal from those countries. Adjustments have been made accordingly in Table 39. (3) Mauritania

TABLE 39. SENEGAL: FOREIGN TRADE (ADJUSTED), 1965–67

(*In billions of CFA francs*)

	1965		1966		1967	
	Imports	Exports	Imports	Exports	Imports	Exports
Customs statistics	40.6	31.7	39.7	36.8	40.4	33.9
Adjusted for petroleum products	−0.3	...	−0.3	...	0.5	...
Unrecorded trade with UDEAO countries [1]						
Dahomey	—	0.2	—	0.2	—	0.2
Ivory Coast	0.1	1.0	0.1	1.0	0.1	1.1
Mauritania	2.0	3.5	2.0	3.0	2.0	2.5
Niger	—	0.4	—	0.4	—	0.4
Upper Volta	—	0.3	—	0.3	—	0.3
Unrecorded trade with other neighboring countries: The Gambia [2]	2.6	...	2.8	...	3.8	0.7
Total	45.0	37.1	44.3	41.7	46.8	39.1
Trade balance	−7.9		−2.6		−7.7	

Sources: Ministère du Plan et de l'Industrie, *Situation Economique du Sénégal en 1967, Bulletin Statistique et Economique Mensuel*; BCEAO, *Notes d'Information et Statistiques;* Ministry of Finance, Statistics Office, Bathurst, *Statistical Summary, 1966/67;* and data provided by the Senegalese authorities.

[1] Union Douanière dès Etats de l'Afrique de l'Ouest; the 1966 figures for Dahomey, Ivory Coast, Niger, and Upper Volta resulted from the difference between Senegalese recorded trade with these countries and national statistics of these countries; however, 1965 and 1967 figures have been estimated to be the same as in 1966.

[2] Approximately 70 per cent of certain imports into The Gambia are estimated to be re-exported to Senegal, while about 50,000 tons of unshelled groundnuts were sold to The Gambia in 1967 at about CFAF 13 per kilogram.

and Senegal form a single territory for customs purposes and only merchandise imported into Mauritania via Dakar is recorded; border trade in either direction is not recorded. Estimates of unrecorded trade with Mauritania have been attempted on the basis of data provided by the Senegalese authorities. (4) Substantial imports of goods are smuggled

[11] Apart from Senegal, the West African Customs Union (Union Douanière des Etats de l'Afrique de l'Ouest, or UDEAO) includes Dahomey, Ivory Coast, Mali, Mauritania, Niger, and Upper Volta.

into Senegal from The Gambia, and some Senegalese livestock and groundnuts are sold to The Gambia without being recorded. Considering the amount of certain imports into The Gambia compared with that country's population and per capita income, it has been estimated that 70 per cent of certain goods imported into The Gambia (e.g., foodstuffs, tobacco, sugar, beverages, and fabrics) were later smuggled into Senegal. (5) Finally, customs figures include errors in the registration of petroleum product imports. Corrections have been made, according to real imports, by the oil refinery (SAR), the sole importer of crude oil in Senegal.

The foreign trade figures used in the balance of payments estimates have been adjusted according to these various factors. These adjustments raised the value of imports and exports, as recorded by customs, by 11 per cent and 17 per cent in 1965, by 12 per cent and 13 per cent in 1966, and by 16 per cent and 15 per cent in 1967. However, the foreign trade movements examined in the following section are based on customs statistics (after adjustment for petroleum products), since these alone provide a detailed breakdown of recent trade developments.

Composition of Trade

Exports.—Recorded exports (Table 40), which amounted to CFAF 31.7 billion in 1965, rose to CFAF 37.4 billion in 1968. Since groundnut exports account for nearly 80 per cent of total export earnings, these totals depend heavily on both the size of the groundnut harvest and the price in overseas markets. After deliveries to oil mills, the remainder goes to shelling centers for export as shelled groundnuts. Because oil mills have a priority on supply and because domestic consumption of refined oil remains practically unchanged, exports of crude and refined oil continued to gain from 142,000 tons in 1965 to 198,000 tons in 1968.[12] About 98 per cent of groundnut oil exports go to France, where, until 1967, they sold at guaranteed prices higher than the world market prices. According to customs records, groundnut

---

[12] Annual exports of groundnut oil do not correspond exactly to quantities of groundnuts crushed during the corresponding year because of differences of timing in production and sales.

TABLE 40. SENEGAL: COMPOSITION OF EXPORTS, 1965-68 [1]

(Value in billions of CFA francs)

	1965		1966		1967		1968	
	Value	Per cent of total	Value	Per cent of total	Value	Per cent of total	Value	Per cent of total
Groundnut products								
Shelled groundnuts	9.2	29.0	12.9	35.1	7.7	22.7	8.2	21.9
Groundnut crude oil	10.7	33.8	10.8	29.3	11.9	35.1	11.2	29.9
Groundnut refined oil	2.4	7.6	2.4	6.5	2.5	7.4	2.1	5.6
Groundnut cakes	2.6	8.2	2.5	6.8	4.1	12.1	5.4	14.4
Total groundnut products	24.9	78.5	28.6	77.8	26.2	77.3	26.9	71.8
Phosphates	2.7	8.5	2.6	7.1	2.6	7.7	2.6	7.0
Canned fish	1.1	3.5	1.3	3.5	1.5	4.4	1.6	4.3
Other	3.0	9.5	4.3	11.6	3.6	10.6	6.3	16.9
Total exports	31.7	100.0	36.8	100.0	33.9	100.0	37.4	100.0

Sources: Ministère du Plan et de l'Industrie, *Situation Economique du Sénégal en 1966, en 1967* and *Bulletin Statistique et Economique Mensuel*, and data provided by the Senegalese authorities.

[1] Based on customs statistics.

oil export receipts amounted to CFAF 13.1 billion in 1965 and to CFAF 14.4 billion in 1967, but declined to CFAF 13.3 billion in 1968. By 1968, the export price had been aligned with the world market price, which, in October 1968, was about 20 per cent below the 1967 guaranteed French price.

Exports of shelled groundnuts reflect the size of the crop more closely than oil production does. From 217,000 tons in 1965, they rose sharply in 1966, fell in 1967, and reached 243,000 tons in 1968. Receipts from shelled groundnut exports advanced from CFAF 9.2 billion in 1965 to CFAF 12.9 billion in 1966, decreased sharply in 1967, and amounted to CFAF 8.2 billion in 1968. Exports to France sold at guaranteed prices accounted for CFAF 8.5 billion in 1965, CFAF 9.5 billion in 1966, and CFAF 6.5 billion in 1967. The remainder, sold to other countries at world market prices, totaled about 200,000 tons; the world market price averaged CFAF 38.85 per kilogram, or about 20 per cent below the 1967 French guaranteed price.

Exports of groundnut cake, a by-product of the oil mills, which brought CFAF 2.6 billion in 1965, rose substantially in 1967 and still further to CFAF 5.4 billion in 1968. This product, used for feeding cattle, is sold mainly to France, which buys about 75 per cent of total groundnut cake in terms of export value.

Phosphate exports rose until 1965, when they reached 867,000 tons, valued at CFAF 2.7 billion. The quantity declined in 1966 and 1967 because of marketing difficulties, but export proceeds remained fairly stable at CFAF 2.6 billion. The volume recovered somewhat (810,000 tons) in 1968, when the value was CFAF 2.6 billion. The share of phosphates in total export earnings was 7 per cent in 1968.

Canned fish exports rose progressively from CFAF 1.1 billion in 1965 to CFAF 1.6 billion in 1968, and their share in aggregate export value rose from 3.5 per cent in 1965 to 4.3 per cent in 1968. Other exports include fresh fish and vegetables, salt, raw materials, and manufactured goods such as paints, soap, fabrics, shoes, and metal containers. They accounted for about 10 per cent of total export value in 1965–67 but for 17 per cent in 1968, with increased exports of wheat flour and fabric and shoes.

Imports.—Total recorded imports during 1965–67 remained virtually unchanged, averaging CFAF 40 billion a year and accounting for about

20 per cent of GDP. In 1968, however, they rose to CFAF 44.5 billion (Table 41). Imports of foodstuffs represent about 40 per cent of total imports by value.

Because of bad weather, which reduced millet production, and changes in the diet of the population, Senegal has imported increasingly larger quantities of rice, valued at CFAF 7.0 billion in 1968, compared with CFAF 4.5 billion in 1965, and representing 43 per cent of foodstuff imports and 16 per cent of total import value. A small part of the imported rice is smuggled into certain neighboring countries, where domestic prices are higher than in Senegal. The other main foodstuffs imported are sugar, which declined from CFAF 3.1 billion in 1965 to CFAF 2 billion in 1968; dairy products; vegetables; fruits; kolanuts; tomato concentrate; beverages; and green tea. Foodstuff imports from neighboring countries (e.g., livestock from Mauritania, kolanuts from Guinea, and sugar and beverages from The Gambia) are usually not recorded.

Textiles rank second to foodstuffs as an import group. Their share in total import value, after a slight rise from 16 per cent in 1965, decreased to 11 per cent in 1968. Imports of textiles, mainly cotton in bales and raw and printed fabrics, amounted to CFAF 5.9 billion in 1967; they decreased to CFAF 4.8 billion in 1968 since Senegal has stepped up cotton production and has established a new weaving plant at Thiès. Large quantities of fabrics are said to be smuggled into Senegal from The Gambia, and cotton imports from Mali and Upper Volta are not systematically recorded.

The three import categories of metal and metal goods, machines, and vehicles rose from CFAF 8.6 billion in 1965 to CFAF 11.0 billion in 1968, when they accounted for 25 per cent of total import value.

Imports of petroleum products, accounting for 3 to 6 per cent of total import value, have consisted mainly of crude oil since the Mbao refinery was set up in 1964.

The value of the chemical products imported rose from CFAF 2.3 billion in 1965 to CFAF 4.0 billion in 1968, with larger purchases of dyes and detergents for use in the textile industry and of fertilizers for use in agriculture. Moreover, the Government's efforts in public health led to greater use of pharmaceuticals; imports of pharmaceuticals rose by 50 per cent during 1965–68. Fertilizer imports increased by 75 per

TABLE 41. SENEGAL: COMPOSITION OF IMPORTS, 1965–68

(*Value in billions of CFA francs*)

	1965 [1]		1966 [1]		1967 [1]		1968 [2]	
	Value	Per cent of total	Value	Per cent of total	Value	Per cent of total	Value	Per cent of total
Foodstuffs, beverages, and tobacco	16.2	40.2	15.7	39.8	16.0	39.1	16.2	36.4
Rice	*4.5*	*11.2*	*4.3*	*10.9*	*5.5*	*13.4*	*7.0*	*15.7*
Sugar	*3.1*	*7.7*	*2.4*	*6.1*	*2.2*	*5.4*	*2.0*	*4.5*
Kolanuts	*1.0*	*2.5*	*1.0*	*2.5*	*1.0*	*2.4*	*...*	*...*
Dairy products	*1.1*	*2.7*	*1.3*	*3.3*	*1.2*	*2.9*	*1.4*	*3.1*
Vegetables and fruits	*1.1*	*2.7*	*1.2*	*3.0*	*1.1*	*2.7*	*2.1*	*4.7*
Petroleum products	2.2	5.4	2.2	5.6	2.3	5.6	1.4	3.1
Crude oil	*1.8*	*4.5*	*1.8*	*4.6*	*2.1*	*5.1*	*...*	*...*
Chemical products	2.3	5.7	2.7	6.9	2.9	7.1	4.0	9.0
Fertilizers	*0.4*	*1.0*	*0.5*	*1.3*	*0.7*	*1.7*	*0.4*	*0.9*
Pharmaceutical products	*0.6*	*1.5*	*0.7*	*1.8*	*0.7*	*1.7*	*0.9*	*2.0*
Textiles	6.4	15.9	6.6	16.7	5.9	14.4	4.8	10.8
Cotton	*3.6*	*8.9*	*3.4*	*8.6*	*3.2*	*7.8*	*2.5*	*5.6*
Artificial fibers	*1.3*	*3.2*	*1.3*	*3.3*	*0.8*	*2.0*	*0.5*	*1.1*
Metal and metal goods	2.9	7.2	2.2	5.6	2.4	5.9	3.0	6.7
Machines	3.5	8.7	3.5	8.9	4.1	10.0	4.6	10.3
Electrical	*1.4*	*3.5*	*1.2*	*3.0*	*1.5*	*3.7*	*1.7*	*3.8*
Vehicles and spare parts	2.2	5.5	2.4	6.1	2.7	6.6	3.4	7.6
Buses	*—*		*0.4*	*1.0*	}	}		
Private cars	*0.7*	*1.7*	*0.8*	*2.0*	*1.0*	*2.4*	*1.3*	*2.9*
Other	4.6	11.4	4.1	10.4	4.6	11.2	7.1	16.1
Grand Total	40.3	100.0	39.4	100.0	40.9	100.0	44.5	100.0

Sources: Ministère du Plan et de l'Industrie, *Situation Economique du Sénégal en 1966*, en *1967* and *Bulletin Statistique et Economique Mensuel*, and data provided by the Senegalese authorities.

[1] Based on customs statistics after adjustment for petroleum products and including partial trade recorded with other UDEAO countries.

[2] Based on customs statistics only as reported in *Bulletin Statistique et Economique Mensuel*.

cent from 1965 to 1967 but decreased in 1968, when a new fertilizer plant using local rock phosphate was opened; since then imports have been limited to sulphur, chlorate of potash, and ammonia, needed for fertilizer production.

Direction of Trade

In 1968, franc area countries accounted for about 79 per cent of total export value and for 62 per cent of total import expenditures (Table 42). Among the franc area countries, France remains by far the major market for Senegalese exports, taking not only the bulk of groundnut products exported but also a major part of canned fish. Exports to France declined from CFAF 25.6 billion in 1965 to CFAF 24.8 billion in 1968 as a result of the elimination of the preferential French price for groundnut oil and shelled groundnuts. Recorded exports to franc area countries other than France are relatively small, partly as a result of the development of competing industries in neighboring countries. They amounted to only CFAF 1.4 billion in 1965, but increased to CFAF 4.9 billion in 1968. A relatively large part of unrecorded exports go to the other UDEAO countries and consist of livestock, rice, fabrics, and other goods processed in Senegal. They are estimated at 15–20 per cent of the total recorded export value.

Exports to EEC countries other than France, which amounted to CFAF 1.6 billion in 1965, went up in 1966, when they consisted mainly of groundnut shipments to Italy and phosphate shipments to Germany. They decreased in 1967 and rose in 1968 to CFAF 3.5 billion, reflecting larger exports to the Netherlands, Belgium, and Italy.

Exports to the United Kingdom, almost exclusively phosphates, remained practically unchanged during 1965–67, totaling CFAF 0.7 billion in 1968. Exports to the United States are very small. Those to other countries rose from CFAF 2.6 billion in 1965 to CFAF 3.4 billion in 1968. Among these countries, Senegal's main customers are Japan, Norway, and Sweden.

Geographically, Senegal's import trade is somewhat more diversified than its export trade. Imports from franc area countries declined from CFAF 29.7 billion, or 74 per cent of total imports, in 1965 to CFAF 27.4 billion, or 62 per cent, in 1968. This decline resulted mainly from the decreasing share of France in Senegal's supplies. The decrease

TABLE 42. SENEGAL: DIRECTION OF RECORDED FOREIGN TRADE, 1965–68 [1]

(*Value in billions of CFA francs*)

	1965 Value	1965 Per cent of total	1966 Value	1966 Per cent of total	1967 Value	1967 Per cent of total	1968 Value	1968 Per cent of total
IMPORTS BY ORIGIN								
Franc area countries								
France	21.6	53.6	20.3	51.5	18.7	45.7	19.7	44.3
Other franc area countries	8.1	20.1	6.5	16.5	8.7	21.3	7.7	17.3
Total franc area countries	29.7	73.7	26.8	68.0	27.4	67.0	27.4	61.6
EEC countries other than France	4.9	12.2	5.5	14.0	5.4	13.2	6.7	15.0
United Kingdom	0.5	1.2	0.4	1.0	0.4	1.0	0.5	1.1
United States	1.7	4.2	1.8	4.6	1.2	2.9	1.6	3.6
Other countries	3.5	8.7	4.9	12.4	6.5	15.9	8.3	18.7
Total imports	40.3	100.0	39.4	100.0	40.9	100.0	44.5	100.0
EXPORTS BY DESTINATION								
Franc area countries								
France	25.6	80.8	27.1	73.6	27.1	80.0	24.8	66.3
Other franc area countries	1.4	4.4	2.3	6.2	1.7	5.0	4.9	13.1
Total franc area countries	27.0	85.2	29.4	79.8	28.8	85.0	29.7	79.4
EEC countries other than France	1.6	5.0	2.9	7.9	1.2	3.5	3.5	9.4
United Kingdom	0.4	1.3	0.4	1.1	0.5	1.5	0.7	1.9
United States	0.1	0.3	—		—		0.1	0.3
Other countries	2.6	8.2	4.1	11.2	3.4	10.0	3.4	9.0
Total exports	31.7	100.0	36.8	100.0	33.9	100.0	37.4	100.0

Sources: Ministère du Plan et de l'Industrie, *Bulletin Statistique et Economique Mensuel* and *Situation Economique du Sénégal en 1967*; BCEAO, *Notes d'Information et Statistiques*; and data provided by the Senegalese authorities.

[1] Including adjustment for petroleum products and trade recorded with other UDEAO countries.

in imports from France (from CFAF 21.6 billion in 1965 to CFAF 19.7 billion in 1968) affected mainly sugar, textiles, and metal goods. The Senegalese balance of trade with France was positive during 1965–67, rising from CFAF 4.0 billion in 1965 to CFAF 5.1 billion in 1967. Recorded imports from other franc area countries, after increasing from the CFAF 8.1 billion recorded in 1965 to CFAF 8.7 billion in 1967, declined to CFAF 7.7 billion in 1968. These imports consisted mainly of crude petroleum from Gabon and Algeria, rice from Cambodia, sugar from the Malagasy Republic, fruit from Morocco and Ivory Coast, and fabrics from Dahomey. In 1968, imports from franc area countries other than France accounted for 17.3 per cent of total imports, and the Senegalese balance of trade with these countries showed a deficit, which narrowed from CFAF 6.7 billion in 1965 to CFAF 4.2 billion in 1966, but widened to CFAF 7.0 billion in 1967. It was reduced to CFAF 2.8 billion in 1968. Unrecorded imports from other UDEAO countries include mainly cotton from Mali and Upper Volta, and livestock from Mauritania. The latter has been estimated at about CFAF 2 billion a year. Imports smuggled from The Gambia to Senegal were estimated to rise from CFAF 2.6 billion in 1965 to CFAF 3.8 billion in 1967. Although some exports of cattle and groundnuts are smuggled from Senegal to The Gambia, the balance of trade with this country is believed to be substantially in deficit.

Imports from EEC countries other than France rose from CFAF 4.9 billion in 1965 to CFAF 6.7 billion in 1968, representing 15 per cent of total import value. The deficit in trade with EEC countries other than France narrowed slightly from CFAF 3.3 billion in 1965 to CFAF 3.2 billion in 1968.

Imports from the United Kingdom averaged CFAF 0.5 billion during 1965–68. Imports from the United States declined slightly, from CFAF 1.7 billion in 1965 to CFAF 1.6 billion in 1968. Imports from other countries increased substantially from CFAF 3.5 billion in 1965 to CFAF 8.3 billion in 1968, when their share in total imports amounted to about 19 per cent. This trend was due to increasing imports, largely of rice, from mainland China, Brazil, and Venezuela.

INTERNATIONAL FINANCIAL ASSISTANCE

Gross disbursements of foreign aid rose from CFAF 10.3 billion in

1965 to CFAF 12.5 billion in 1967 (Table 43). During these three years France provided on average about 60 per cent and EDF 26 per cent; the remaining 14 per cent came mainly from the United States, Germany, and IBRD and its affiliates.

Aid from France

French aid took the form of (1) FAC grants and soft-currency loans, (2) technical assistance, (3) subsidies for the University of Dakar (staff and other expenditures) and scholarships, (4) CCCE soft-currency loans, and (5) financial advantages in the form of a guaranteed price for groundnut product exports.

Total disbursements of French assistance increased from CFAF 6.1 billion in 1965 to CFAF 7.5 billion in 1967, mostly in the form of grants (CFAF 6.6 billion in 1967). FAC grants declined from CFAF 1.2 billion in 1965 to CFAF 0.8 billion in 1967. In 1968, however, they increased to CFAF 1.5 billion by the end of September. During 1959–67, FAC disbursements of financial grants totaled CFAF 6.7 billion, of which CFAF 0.5 billion was disbursed in France for project study purposes. They covered productive investments (essentially for agriculture, infrastructure, and social equipment) and general expenditures. FAC also provided some soft-currency loans for specific projects amounting to CFAF 0.2 billion in 1965, CFAF 0.3 billion in 1966, and CFAF 0.1 billion in 1967; during the first nine months of 1968, they reached CFAF 0.4 billion.

Technical assistance is a major aspect of French aid to Senegal. At the end of 1967, there were 1,511 French experts and technical advisors in Senegal as part of the Mission Française d'Aide et de Coopération. The cost of the French technical assistance program totaled about CFAF 4 billion a year, including the Senegalese Government contribution at the rate of CFAF 55,000 a month for each technical assistant. Apart from this technical assistance, France provides about 210 professors to the University of Dakar, as well as scholarships to Senegalese and other African students at this University, and contributes up to 83 per cent of the running expenditures of the University. This total assistance rose from CFAF 1.7 billion in 1965 to CFAF 2.0 billion in 1967. Various agencies of the French Government have continued to allocate funds for scientific research, the running of the Institut Pasteur and the Weather Bureau, and other purposes. Apart from this recorded financial and technical assistance, France also provided indirect aid through employment offered to Senegalese workers with the running of its military establishment in Dakar and through its public expenditures for military purposes.

Furthermore, CCCE extends medium-term and long-term loans to the Government, to public and semipublic institutions, and to private enterprises. Total drawings on these loans amounted to CFAF 1.23 billion during 1965–67.

Aid from EEC

Since 1960, EEC has extended financial grants under the first and second programs of the EDF. Under the first EDF program, CFAF 10.8 billion was committed to Senegal and CFAF 6.6 billion had been disbursed at the end of 1967. During the first nine months of 1968, funds disbursed under this program amounted to CFAF 0.3 billion. This aid has been directed mainly to the preparation and realization of projects for infrastructure (51 per cent), social equipment (33 per cent), production (10 per cent), and project studies (6 per cent). In 1964 the first Yaoundé Convention with 18 African States provided that under a second EDF program, covering 1964–69, a global sum of CFAF 10.9 billion was to be granted to Senegal in order to compensate for the elimination of the French preferential treatment of Senegalese groundnut exports and to increase and diversify agricultural production. At the end of 1967, disbursements amounted to CFAF 5.1 billion, including CFAF 2.8 billion for price subsidies. Disbursements during the first nine months of 1968 totaled CFAF 0.83 billion. Furthermore, in 1966 the European Investment Bank granted a loan of CFAF 0.6 billion to establish the Société Industrielle d'Engrais du Sénégal (SIES); from this loan CFAF 0.3 billion was disbursed in 1967.

Aid from Other Sources

Apart from France and EEC, Senegal receives financial and technical assistance from other countries and international organizations. Because of the difficulties in the valuation of all forms of this assistance, only part of the aid from these other sources has been taken into account.

U.S. aid includes development grants, donations from voluntary relief agencies, and technical assistance, including Peace Corps volunteers. Table 43 does not include the counterpart funds generated in local currency by the sale of rice in 1964 and earmarked for development loans.

In 1962, Germany granted a loan of DM 25 million (about CFAF 1.5 billion) to finance road construction. Most of this amount was disbursed during 1962–64 and only CFAF 0.4 billion remained for disbursement in 1965. Other disbursements shown in Table 43 cover mainly technical assistance. Another loan of DM 35 million (about CFAF 2.2 billion) was granted in 1968 for the construction of a water supply line from Lac de Guiers to Dakar.

The United Nations and several specialized agencies are working in Senegal in various fields. In Table 43 this assistance is covered by the other technical assistance items but is likely to have been undervalued.

TABLE 43.   SENEGAL: DISBURSEMENTS OF FOREIGN AID, 1965–68

(*In billions of CFA francs*)

	1965	1966	1967	1968[1]
France				
FAC[2] grants	1.23	0.86	0.80	0.35
FAC[2] loans	0.02	0.27	0.13	0.52
CCCE[3] loans	0.02	0.48	0.73	...
Dakar University (investment)	0.13	0.20	—	...
Dakar University (professors and scholarships)	1.70	1.79	2.00	...
Technical assistance (other than teachers)	3.00	3.00	3.00	...
Other[4]	...	0.67	0.84	...
Total France	6.10	7.27	7.50	...
EEC				
EDF[5] grants	2.71	2.88	2.14	1.90
European Investment Bank loans	—	—	0.30	0.47
Total EEC	2.71	2.88	2.44	2.37
United States	0.20	0.32	1.23	0.05
Germany, Federal Republic of	0.70	0.20	—	—
IBRD	—	—	0.11	0.14
IDA	—	—	0.30	0.11
IFC	—	0.20	0.30	0.68
Technical assistance[6]	0.60	0.60	0.60	...
Total foreign aid disbursements	10.31	11.47	12.48	...

Sources: BCEAO, *Rapport Annuel 1967*, and data provided by CCCE, U.S. Agency for International Development, and the Senegalese authorities.

[1] All disbursements not available for 1968.
[2] Fonds d'Aide et de Coopération.
[3] Caisse Centrale de Coopération Economique.
[4] Scientific research, scholarships, and training in France.
[5] European Development Fund (Fonds Européen de Développement, or FED).
[6] Including UN experts.

In 1967, IBRD granted a $4 million loan (about CFAF 1 billion) to finance extension of the port of Dakar. In 1967, IDA granted a $9 million loan (about CFAF 2.2 billion) to finance the modernization of Senegalese railways, and in 1966 IFC participated in the equity capital of the Société Industrielle d'Engrais du Sénégal for CFAF 0.2 billion and granted a CFAF 0.6 billion loan to the same company. Disbursements from IBRD and IDA began in 1967 and amounted to CFAF 0.11 billion for the former and CFAF 0.30 billion for the latter. IFC disbursed CFAF 0.20 billion in 1966 and CFAF 0.30 billion in 1967. On January 14, 1969, an IBRD loan of $3.5 billion (about CFAF 0.86 billion) and IDA credits for $6.0 million (about CFAF 1.5 billion) were granted to Senegal. These loans and credits were to continue a program, started in 1964 with EEC financing, to improve groundnut production, mainly through provision of credit for small farm implements and technical assistance.

In addition to the assistance already described, Senegal received technical assistance and financial commitments from some other countries (Belgium, Canada, the Republic of China, Israel, and the Soviet Union). The value in money terms of such assistance could not be estimated. Disbursements were expected to start in 1969.

BALANCE OF PAYMENTS

Official balance of payments data are not available for Senegal. So far, data are available only for transactions with countries outside the French franc area. Liberalization of the exchange control system in July 1967 provided for registration of all foreign transactions with a view to the preparation of comprehensive balance of payments statistics, but these data are not yet available in a usable form. On the basis of what information is available, Table 44 estimates the over-all balance of payments for 1965–67. Complete foreign trade statistics for 1968 are not yet available. According to these estimates, there was a deficit in the over-all balance of payments of CFAF 2.5 billion in 1965. Although there was a surplus of CFAF 2.3 billion in 1966, a deficit (CFAF 2.1 billion) occurred again in 1967.

The trade balance—including freight and insurance on merchandise —showed a large deficit in 1965, amounting to CFAF 7.9 billion. In 1966 this deficit became smaller (CFAF 2.6 billion) because of

TABLE 44.   SENEGAL: ESTIMATED BALANCE OF PAYMENTS, 1965–67

(In billions of CFA francs)

	1965	1966	1967
A. Goods and services			
Merchandise			
Exports f.o.b.	37.10	41.70	39.10
Imports c.i.f.	−45.00	−44.30	−46.80
Trade balance	−7.90	−2.60	−7.70
Services			
Transportation	3.09	3.20	4.39
Travel	−2.90	−2.57	−2.62
Investment income (Government) [1]	−0.07	−0.17	−0.17
Government			
Services under aid program	−5.20	−5.20	−5.20
Senegalese embassies	−0.50	−0.50	−0.50
Local expenditures of foreign, civil, and military personnel	4.96	4.96	4.96
Total services	−0.62	−0.28	0.86
Total goods and services	−8.52	−2.88	−6.84
B. Unrequited transfers			
Private sector			
Pensions received from France	1.50	1.50	1.50
Foreign workers' remittances	−2.50	−3.00	−3.50
Senegalese workers' remittances	1.20	1.20	1.20
Foreign government grants [2]	0.50	0.74	1.75
Government			
Foreign government grants	10.17	10.64	9.71
Senegalese contribution to technical assistance cost	−1.00	−1.00	−1.00
Contributions to international organizations	−0.14	−0.16	−0.16
Total unrequited transfers	9.73	9.92	9.50
C. Nonmonetary capital			
Private long-term capital (international organizations)	—	0.20	0.60
Central Government			
Loans received			
Drawings	0.54	0.75	1.27
Repayments	−0.51	−0.60	−0.63
Total nonmonetary capital	0.03	0.35	1.24
D. Net errors and omissions	−3.71	−5.09	−5.98
E. Estimated over-all balance of payments (A + B + C + D)	−2.47	2.30	−2.08
F. Monetary movements (increase −)			
Commercial banks			
Liabilities	1.89	0.41	−0.77
Assets	0.42	0.31	0.02
Central Bank			
Liabilities	−0.02	−0.98	0.61
Assets	0.18	−2.04	2.22
Total monetary movements	2.47	−2.30	2.08

Sources: IMF, *International Financial Statistics*, data provided by the Senegalese authorities, and Fund staff estimates.

[1] Of which interest paid on foreign loans represented CFAF 0.18 billion in 1965, CFAF 0.29 billion in 1966, and CFAF 0.26 billion in 1967.

[2] Includes scholarships, U.S. grants, and United States P.L. No. 480, Title II.

increased groundnut export receipts. In 1967, however, groundnut export receipts declined while imports increased, resulting in a large trade deficit (CFAF 7.7 billion). Although detailed 1968 figures are not yet available, indications are that a large trade deficit recurred with the continued decline in groundnut export prices and decreased phosphate exports. Imports were estimated to have remained at the 1967 level because of continued large imports of staple goods. As imports have not varied significantly in recent years, the trade balance depends largely on the level of exports. Groundnuts account for about 80 per cent of total export receipts, and this share is determined by both the rise of the crop and the world market price.

Other current transactions are estimated to have improved somewhat during 1965–67: receipts increased from CFAF 8.8 billion in 1965 to CFAF 10.5 billion in 1967, while payments rose only from CFAF 9.4 billion to CFAF 9.6 billion, resulting in a surplus of nearly CFAF 0.9 billion in 1967, following small deficits (CFAF 0.6 billion in 1965 and CFAF 0.3 billion in 1966). However, since these estimates have a certain margin of error and do not cover all transactions, the above figures should be considered with caution.

The surplus on transportation (excluding charges related to imports), which include services rendered to Mali through the railway and the port of Dakar, and to ships berthing at the port, rose from CFAF 3.1 billion in 1965 to CFAF 4.4 billion in 1967 with the improvement of trade relations with Mali and heavier traffic at Dakar, subsequent to the closure of the Suez Canal. Foreign travel during 1965–67 involved a net deficit which decreased (from CFAF 2.9 billion to CFAF 2.6 billion) according to rough estimates of residents' expenditures abroad. Tourist receipts in Senegal apparently improved somewhat. Investment income represents only the interest paid on the external public debt, whereas transfers of private profits and dividends are not available. Government services cover the total cost of technical assistance programs provided to Senegal, estimated at CFAF 5.2 billion a year. It is assumed that technical assistants spend about 60 per cent of this amount in Senegal and that the remainder is retained outside the country. For military personnel in Senegal, it is estimated that all the pay is spent locally.

The surplus on unrequited transfers went up from CFAF 9.7 billion in 1965 to CFAF 9.9 billion in 1966, and then down slightly to CFAF 9.5 billion in 1967. After declining from CFAF 0.7 billion in 1965 to CFAF 0.4 billion in 1966, the surplus on private transfers rose to nearly CFAF 1.0 billion in 1967, owing to an increase in scholarships granted by France and donations by U.S. voluntary relief agencies, which more than offset the increase in estimated foreign workers' remittances.

The bulk of private unrequited transfer items consists of pension payments by France to Senegalese nationals (about CFAF 1.5 billion a year) and of the balance of remittances by foreigners employed in Senegal and by Senegalese workers established mainly in France. The latter has been estimated at CFAF 1.2 billion a year while foreign workers' transfers were estimated to rise from CFAF 2.5 billion in 1965 to CFAF 3.5 billion in 1967. Some scholarships and training costs in France and grants from U.S. voluntary relief agencies are included in these transfer items.

For net official transfers, substantial surpluses occurred because of technical and financial assistance granted by foreign countries; they amounted to CFAF 9.0 billion in 1965, CFAF 9.5 billion in 1966, and CFAF 8.5 billion in 1967.

Data on private short-term and long-term capital movements are not available apart from equity investment in 1966 by IFC (CFAF 0.2 billion) in the establishment of Société Industrielle d'Engrais du Sénégal, and drawings (CFAF 0.6 billion) on loans granted by the European Investment Bank and IFC to the same company. Official long-term capital movements refer to drawings on loans granted by FAC, CCCE, IBRD, IDA, and Germany. These drawings totaled more than CFAF 0.5 billion in 1965, CFAF 0.7 billion in 1966, and CFAF 1.3 billion in 1967. Repayments on external public debt include amortization of loans from international organizations, France, and Germany. They accounted for CFAF 0.5 billion in 1965 and CFAF 0.6 billion in 1966 and 1967, leaving an estimated net nonmonetary capital rising from less than CFAF 0.1 billion in 1965 to CFAF 1.2 billion in 1967. These figures include movements and long-term loans granted by international organizations. No information is available concerning private capital movements, and their net balance is included in the residual item "errors and omissions." The net outflow on account of this item rose from CFAF 3.7 billion in 1965 to nearly CFAF 6.0 billion in 1967.

FOREIGN RESERVES

Gross foreign assets of BCEAO, which had remained unchanged between 1964 and 1965, increased from $38 million at the end of 1965 to $46 million at the end of 1966 (Table 45). Thereafter, they declined, amounting to $15 million by the end of September 1969. The foreign liabilities of BCEAO declined from $5 million at the end of 1965 to $1 million at the end of 1966. After a small rise in 1967, they became negligible at the end of September 1968 and 1969. External reserves of BCEAO in Senegal consist of Senegal's imputed share in the common pool of reserves of UMOA and of funds invested abroad for the account of the Treasury (in its investment account). They are held in French francs with the French Treasury.

During 1964–69 the foreign reserve position of the commercial banks and the Development Bank was consistently negative as their liabilities substantially exceeded their assets. These assets declined from

TABLE 45. SENEGAL: FOREIGN ASSETS AND LIABILITIES OF THE BANKING SYSTEM, 1964–69

(*In millions of U.S. dollars*; *end of period*)

	1964	1965	1966	1967	1968 (Sept.)	1969 (Sept.)
BCEAO						
Assets: Convertible exchange [1]	38 [2]	38 [2]	46	37	17	15
Liabilities	5	5	1	3	—	—
Net total, BCEAO	33	33	45	34	17	15
Other banks						
Assets	11	9	8	8	8	7
Liabilities	12	19	21	18	19	−31
Net total, other banks	−1	−10	−13	−10	−11	−24
Net foreign assets or liabilities (−) of the banking system	32	23	32	24	6	−9

Sources: IMF, *International Financial Statistics,* and data provided by the Senegalese authorities.

[1] Includes the IMF gold tranche position.

[2] The 1964 and 1965 figures differ from those in the *International Financial Statistics* because of different coverage.

$9 million in 1965 to $7 million by the end of September 1969, compared with foreign liabilities averaging $19 million in 1965–68 and totaling $31 million at the end of September 1969.

The decline in foreign assets of BCEAO and the rise in foreign liabilities of other banks changed the foreign reserve position of Senegal's banking system from a positive $32 million in 1966 to a negative $9 million by the end of September 1969.

CHAPTER 12

Togo

GENERAL SETTING

The Republic of Togo became independent on April 27, 1960. It comprises that part of former Togoland which was made a French mandated territory after World War I and in 1956 an autonomous republic within the French community. Lomé, the capital, with a population of about 93,000, is the largest city and port in the country.

On August 1, 1962, Togo became a member of the International Monetary Fund (IMF); its current quota (April 1970) is $11.25 million. On the same day it joined the International Bank for Reconstruction and Development (IBRD or World Bank), current subscription $15 million; soon after, on August 21, 1962, it joined the International Development Association (IDA), current subscription $760,000, and on September 4, 1962, the International Finance Corporation (IFC), current subscription $83,000. It is also a member of the United Nations (UN); Food and Agriculture Organization (FAO); the UN Educational, Scientific, and Cultural Organization (UNESCO); the General Agreement on Tariffs and Trade (GATT); the UN Economic Commission for Africa (ECA, or Commission Economique pour l'Afrique, CEA); the African Development Bank (ADB); and the Common Organization of African and Malagasy States (Organisation Commune Africaine et Malgache, or OCAM), among others. It is also an associate member of the European Economic Community (EEC). It participates with Dahomey, Ivory Coast, Mauritania, Niger, Senegal, and Upper Volta in the West African Monetary Union (Union Monétaire Ouest Africaine, or UMOA); in a common central bank, the Banque Centrale des Etats de l'Afrique de l'Ouest (BCEAO); and in a common currency, the CFA franc issued by that Bank.

Predominantly agricultural, Togo grows a variety of crops. Although the industrial and especially the mining sectors have expanded markedly in recent years, they still contribute less than one fifth of the country's gross domestic product (GDP).

In Ewe, the language of the south, Togo means "at the water's edge." From the Gulf of Guinea on the south, Togo reaches northward, between Ghana on the west and Dahomey on the east, about 510 kilometers (320 miles) to its boundary with Upper Volta. Its greatest width from east to west is only about 225 kilometers, but along the coast, the country is just about 50 kilometers wide. The total area is 56,600 square kilometers (21,850 square miles). A mountain chain, ranging from 600 to 1,000 meters in elevation, crosses Togo from northeast to southwest, forming the watershed for the Volta River basin on the west and the Mono River basin on the east. The country's highest point is Pic Baumann (Mont Agou), 1,035 meters (3,400 feet) high, near the town of Agou in the southwest.

There are four geographical regions: the sandy coastal plains containing the Ouatchi Plateau and stretching about 60 kilometers inland, the fertile Mono Tableland, the mountain range (Chaîne du Togo and Chaîne de l'Atakora), and the sandstone Oti Plateau in the north. Togo has a humid, tropical climate, but the humidity decreases toward the north, except in the mountainous areas.

The population of Togo in 1969 was estimated at 1.8 million (Table 1), including about 2,500 foreigners, mainly French. This estimate is based on the last population census made in 1959 and 1960, a sample survey of the population carried out in 1961, and an average

TABLE 1. TOGO: ESTIMATES OF POPULATION, 1959–60, 1968, AND 1969

Region [1]	Census 1959–60	Population Estimates 1968	Population Estimates 1969	Average Annual Growth Rate
	←	*Thousands*	→	*Per cent*
Coastal	489	594	610	2.7
Plateau	366	476	492	3.4
Central	363	413	420	1.7
Savanna	222	263	269	2.3
Total or average	1,440	1,746	1,791	.2.6

Source: Ministère du Commerce, de l'Industrie, du Tourisme et du Plan, *Population Active et Emploi au Togo, 1967*, and BCEAO, *Indicateurs Economiques Togolais*, December 1969.

[1] These regions comprise the following *circonscriptions*: Coastal—Lomé, Anécho, Tsévié, and Tabligho; Plateau—Akposso, Atakpamé, Klouto, and Nuatja; Central—Bassari, Lama-Kara, Niamtougou, Pagouda, Baflio, Sokodé, and Soutoboua; and Savanna—Dapango, Kandé, and Mango (see map).

annual growth rate of 2.6 per cent. The rate of population growth ranges from 1.7 per cent in the central region to 3.4 per cent in the plateau region. Density of population averages 30 persons per square kilometer but is only about 25 per square kilometer in the savanna region of the extreme north, compared with 200 or more in some coastal areas.

The indigenous population comprises 18 major ethnic groups, with a variety of languages and customs. The Ewe of the coastal region, though not a majority, form one of the leading groups. They also live in Ghana. Other important groups are the Adja-Ouatchi (who extend into Dahomey from southern Togo), and the Kabrai-Losso in the north. Many dialects are spoken: besides Ewe in the south, Twi is common in the north and Hausa is spoken in many places throughout the country. French is the language of commerce, the Government, and the schools. There are about 400,000 Christians and 150,000 Muslims; the latter live mainly in the north.

Togo's population is comparatively young; 56 per cent of the total are under 20 years of age. The economically active population, estimated at 647,700 in 1967, against 565,300 in 1961, is expected to increase to 699,300 by 1971, or at about the same rate of growth as the total population. About 78 per cent of the economically active population is estimated to be engaged in agriculture, mainly as self-employed workers.

School-age children (6–13 years) numbered an estimated 408,000 in 1968; 171,000, or 42 per cent, were in schools, compared with 39 per cent in 1965. The number of pupils in secondary schools has risen rapidly, reaching about 12,000 in 1968. The Institut du Bénin in Lomé, Togo's school for higher education, was established in 1965 and has a liberal arts faculty with about 100 students. In addition, about 550 Togolese nationals are pursuing their education and training abroad.

STRUCTURE OF THE ECONOMY

GROSS DOMESTIC PRODUCT

Togo's gross domestic product (GDP) at current prices rose from CFAF 33.0 billion in 1963 to CFAF 64.5 billion in 1969 (Table 2). After taking account of the improvements in coverage, which explain part of the large increase during 1963–66, the annual growth rate of GDP at constant prices was estimated at 5–7 per cent. Per capita income, which has also risen, was equivalent to $130 in 1969. GDP figures for 1967–69 are estimates prepared by the staff, as official estimates for this period are not available. During this period the economy continued to grow at about the same rate as in the earlier years.

Agriculture still contributes more than any other sector to GDP; however, its share (including animal husbandry, fishing, and forestry) declined from 53 per cent in 1963 to 43 per cent in 1969. The greatest relative increases during this period were for manufacturing, mining, public utilities, and commerce; the combined share of these sectors rose from 24 per cent of GDP in 1963 to 39 per cent in 1969, reflecting mainly the rapid development of phosphate production and of manufacturing of consumer goods.

Estimates of the use of GDP indicate growth in both exports and gross fixed capital formation during 1963–69 (see Table 2). Exports more than tripled in this period, representing 27 per cent of GDP in 1969, compared with 17 per cent in 1963. The greatest advance was in phosphate exports, although the principal agricultural exports (coffee, cocoa, and palm products) also expanded.

TABLE 2. TOGO: ORIGIN AND USE OF GROSS DOMESTIC PRODUCT AT CURRENT PRICES, 1963–69

(Value in billions of CFA francs)

	Value							Per Cent of Total						
	1963	1964	1965	1966	1967	1968	1969	1963	1964	1965	1966	1967	1968	1969
Origin														
Agriculture (including animal husbandry, fishing, and forestry)	17.7	18.9	20.1	23.3	24.1	25.8	27.7	53.4	49.3	46.3	43.9	43.9	44.5	42.9
Mining	} 2.6	2.0	2.6	3.4	2.7	2.9	3.1	} 7.9	5.2	6.0	6.4	4.9	5.0	4.8
Manufacturing		1.5	2.4	5.3	5.7	6.1	6.5		3.9	5.6	10.0	10.4	10.5	10.1
Public utilities		0.8	1.0	1.4	2.1	2.3	2.5		2.1	2.3	2.6	3.8	4.0	3.9
Construction	0.9	1.3	1.6	1.6	1.5	1.7	1.9	2.7	3.5	3.7	3.0	2.7	2.9	2.9
Commerce	5.5	7.1	8.1	9.7	10.2	10.3	12.9	16.6	18.3	18.6	18.3	18.6	17.8	20.0
Government	2.2	2.9	3.1	3.5	3.6	3.6	3.8	6.7	7.6	7.1	6.6	6.6	6.2	5.9
Households	} 4.2	1.0	1.0	1.1				} 12.7	2.6	2.3	2.1			
Transportation		2.2	2.4	2.8	5.0	5.3	6.1		5.7	5.6	} 5.2	9.1	9.1	9.5
Other services		0.7	1.1	1.0					1.8	2.5	} 1.9			
Total GDP at current prices [1]	**33.0**	**38.4**	**43.5**	**53.1**	**54.9**	**58.0**	**64.5**	**100.0**	**100.0**	**100.0**	**100.0**	**100.0**	**100.0**	**100.0**
Use														
Consumption														
Private	28.7	29.9	32.4	41.4	43.6	47.3	51.9	86.9	77.8	74.5	78.0	79.4	81.5	80.4
Public	2.9	3.4	3.5	3.9	4.0	4.0	4.2	8.8	8.9	8.0	7.3	7.3	6.9	6.6
Total consumption	31.6	33.3	35.9	45.3	47.6	51.3	56.1	95.7	86.7	82.5	85.3	86.7	88.4	87.0
Gross investment														
Gross fixed capital formation	3.2	5.8	8.2	7.3	} 7.9	} 7.4	} 8.7	9.7	15.1	18.8	13.7	} 14.4	} 12.8	} 13.5
Inventory accumulation	1.3	2.4	2.1	1.4				3.9	6.2	4.9	2.7			
Total gross investment	4.5	8.2	10.3	8.7	7.9	7.4	8.7	13.6	21.3	23.7	16.4	14.4	12.8	13.5
Exports of goods and services	5.5	8.8	9.1	11.9	13.6	14.6	17.5	16.7	22.9	20.9	22.4	24.8	25.2	27.1
Less imports of goods and services	−8.6	−11.9	−11.8	−12.8	−14.2	−15.3	−17.8	−26.0	−30.9	−27.1	−24.1	−25.9	−26.4	−27.6

Sources: For 1963–66: Ministère du Commerce, de l'Industrie, du Tourisme et du Plan, Direction du Plan, *Comptes Nationaux*. For 1967–69: staff estimates, which should be considered as an indication only.

[1] Because of rounding, figures do not add to all totals in this table and some of the following tables.

Gross fixed capital formation rose from CFAF 3.2 billion in 1963 to CFAF 7.3 billion in 1966. Much of this increase resulted from investment in the private sector, especially in phosphate mining, industry (brewery and textile mill), and transportation. Capital formation in the public sector, on the other hand, was mainly infrastructure. Construction of the port of Lomé absorbed most of the public sector investments, which were financed largely from foreign aid. Gross capital formation in the private sector probably declined with the completion of certain projects by 1967. No new major industrial investments have since been made in this sector.

Estimates of the use of GDP also indicate the rising proportion of gross investment financed from domestic sources. Gross domestic savings represented 13 per cent of GDP in 1969, against 4 per cent in 1963 (Table 3). The ratio of the excess of imports over exports to gross investment declined continuously from 69 per cent in 1963 to 3 per cent in 1969. During 1963–65, consumption apparently advanced at a slower rate than gross investments or GDP. During 1966–69, however, this trend appears to have been reversed; consumption increased by 24 per cent, compared with no increase in gross investment and an increase in GDP of only 21 per cent.

AGRICULTURE, FISHING, AND FORESTRY

Agriculture is of foremost importance in Togo; the value of agricultural production (including the output from animal husbandry, fishing, and forestry) accounted for more than two fifths of Togo's GDP in 1969 and for two thirds of its exports, although its percentage share of

TABLE 3. TOGO: DOMESTIC SAVINGS AND GROSS INVESTMENT, 1963–69

(In billions of CFA francs)

	1963	1964	1965	1966	1967	1968	1969
GDP at market prices	33.0	38.4	43.5	53.1	54.9	58.0	64.5
Consumption	31.6	33.3	35.9	45.3	47.6	51.3	56.1
Domestic savings	1.4	5.1	7.6	7.8	7.3	6.7	8.4
Excess of imports over exports	3.1	3.1	2.7	0.9	0.6	0.7	0.3
Gross investment	4.5	8.2	10.3	8.7	7.9	7.4	8.7

Source: Table 2.

GDP has gradually decreased in recent years. It employs about three fourths of the economically active population. Roughly one fifth of the land area in Togo is cultivated, and one fifth is left fallow. Food crops, mainly millet and corn, take up approximately 85 per cent of the cultivated land; the rest is devoted to industrial or export crops—cotton, groundnuts, coffee, and cocoa.

Based on national income data, the absolute value of agricultural production has risen in recent years. The output of most food and cash crops has increased, especially since 1967/68, by the adoption of improved cultivation methods and the use of mineral fertilizers. Still greater production could be obtained by extension of the cultivated area, more widespread adoption of improved methods of cultivation and animal husbandry, and expansion of investment in the rural sector.

Crops Mainly for Food

According to official estimates, production of the leading food crops— cassava (manioc), rice, maize, beans, millet, and sorghum—has risen in recent years, while that of yams and voandzou (Bambara groundnuts) has remained at a standstill or has declined (Table 4). Over-all production of food crops generally satisfies domestic consumption and provides some surplus of maize, cassava, yams and sorghum for export— mainly to neighboring Ghana, Dahomey, and Upper Volta. Until recently, rice had been an outstanding exception; for some years, production had remained low and substantial quantities had been imported. In 1967/68, however, production swelled, enabling the country to cut rice imports sharply. The output of cassava increased considerably after the introduction of seedlings of a higher yielding variety, with assistance from the French Bureau pour le Développement de la Production Agricole (BDPA). The Government is relying on foreign technical assistance to help in expanding the production of millet and sorghum.

Crops Mainly for Export

Coffee, cocoa, and palm kernels are the principal export crops. Other crops include groundnuts and cotton; production of these crops has increased in recent years (see Table 4). On the other hand, production of copra, castor beans, sheanuts, and kapok has leveled off or declined;

TABLE 4. TOGO: AREA AND PRODUCTION OF PRINCIPAL CROPS, AND DOMESTIC SALES AND EXPORTS OF EXPORT CROPS, 1960/61–1968/69

	1960/61	1961/62[1]	1962/63	1963/64	1964/65	1965/66	1966/67	1967/68	1968/69
AREA (*thousand hectares*)									
Food crops									
Cassava (manioc)	85	95	136	128	133	134	134	146	143
Yams	83	71	90	104	108	124	123	124	99
Maize	154	143	139	175	184	192	192	188	199
Millet and sorghum	221	242	244	224	287	394	393	460	261
Rice	15	16	25	27	27	31	30	27	29
Beans	36	104	43	53	57	56	56	95	45
Voandzou (Bambara groundnuts)	16	10	15	18	16	12	12	16	7
Export crops									
Coffee	17	20	20	23	26	36	36	36	36
Cocoa	12	13	15	16	16	16	16	16	18
Coconut palms	6	4	5	4	4	4	4	4	4
Cotton	53	46	43	61	57	62	62	67	54
Groundnuts (peanuts)	25	48	40	40	39	43	45	39	21
QUANTITY (*thousand metric tons*)									
Food crops (production)									
Cassava (manioc)	564	690	987	1,088	1,012	982	1,017	1,075	1,186
Yams	800	385	857	1,001	989	895	1,040	1,076	850
Maize	81	101	84	66	78	87	101	93	115
Millet and sorghum	99	151	74	119	116	136	178	195	111
Rice	11	8	18	16	17	16	18	28	18
Beans	9	26	13	14	12	16	16	16	29
Voandzou (Bambara groundnuts)	7	5	7	9	9	8	6	7	5
Export crops									
Coffee									
Total production	7	14	9	11	9	12	6	13	15
Domestic sales	10	12	7	19	9	14	6	11	17
Exports	10	12	6	16	11	14	6	11	10

Cocoa									
Total production	..	..	..	..	15	12	15	15	16
Domestic sales	13	11	11	14	18	15	16	18	20
Exports	11	11	10	13	17	16	17	15	21
Palm kernels									
Total production	13	10	10	10	17	14	18	15	17
Domestic sales	..	..	12	15	15	17	13	14	19
Exports	11	10	13	14	15	17	12	15	16
Copra									
Total production	3	4	3	3	3	3	3	3	..
Domestic sales	..	..	3	3	1	1	1	1	1
Exports	5	2	3	4	1	1	1	1	1
Cotton									
Total production [2]	9	8	8	6	8	8	10	11	7
Domestic sales [2]	7	6	9	4	6	8	10	11	16
Exports (fiber)	2	2	3	1	1	3	3	3	2
Exports (cottonseed)	3	2	4	1	2	2	5	4	..
Groundnuts (peanuts)									
Total production [3]	12	20	22	17	18	20	13	16	9
Domestic sales (shelled)	..	..	3	3	2	3	4	6	5
Exports (shelled)	3	2	3	3	2	3	4	6	5

Sources: Ministère des Finances, de l'Economie et du Plan, *Inventaire Economique du Togo*, 1964 and 1966, and data provided by the Togolese authorities.

[1] According to agricultural sample testing at the end of 1961/62.
[2] Seed (unginned) cotton.
[3] Unshelled.

these crops, as well as cotton and groundnuts, are subsidized. Marketing of export crops is entrusted to the Office of Agricultural Products (Office des Produits Agricoles du Togo, or OPAT), a public agency formed in 1964 to incorporate the various commodity stabilization funds previously maintained.

Coffee.—Robusta, the predominant type of coffee produced in Togo, is grown mainly on small farms in the southwestern part of the country, within the Palimé-Atakpamé-Badou triangle and in the vicinity of Tsévié. Production has fluctuated widely and has averaged 14,000 tons[1] since 1967/68. During the last three years, the area under coffee has doubled from that reported in the early 1960's.

There is more than the expected divergence between reported domestic production figures and domestic sales recorded by the Office of Agricultural Products (see Table 4). Although the latter are generally regarded as more exact, in some years they do include coffee originating from neighboring countries. Exports have ranged from 6,000 tons to 16,000 tons annually; the higher level was in 1963/64 when the weather was exceptionally favorable and fertilizers were used; the lower level was in 1962/63 and 1966/67 when rainfall was inadequate and irregular, and did not coincide with the blossoming of the coffee trees.

In 1968/69, domestic production of coffee exceeded the export quota of 10,266 tons allocated to Togo under the International Coffee Agreement (ICA), and the Office of Agricultural Products accumulated large stocks of coffee. For 1969/70, Togo's quota was 10,193 tons, while production of coffee is estimated to have reached 15,000 tons.

In 1964/65 the Office of Agricultural Products realized only a modest profit per kilogram (CFAF 11.73) on its coffee transactions after paying the producer price, export taxes, and various handling charges (Table 5). With the volume of exports at 11,000 tons, its total gross profit was also modest—CFAF 72 million (Table 6). In the following year it lowered the producer price from CFAF 75 to CFAF 70 per kilogram. As world prices advanced, its profit per kilogram almost tripled in 1965/66, and with a larger volume of exports, total gross profit

---

[1] Throughout this chapter, the word "ton" refers to a metric ton of 2,204.6 pounds.

TABLE 5. TOGO: UNIT COST, EXPORT PRICE, AND PROFIT (OR LOSS) ON MARKETED EXPORT CROPS, 1964/65–1968/69

(Amount in CFA francs per kilogram)

	Cost				Actual Export Price[2]	Gross Profit, or Loss (−)		EEC Subsidy	Net Profit, or Loss (−)	
	Producer price	Export taxes	Other	Total[1]		Amount	Per cent of cost		Amount	Per cent of cost
Coffee[2]										
1964/65	75.00	21.96	21.07	118.03	129.76	11.73	9.9	—	11.73	9.9
1965/66	70.00	22.85	20.76	113.61	145.51	31.90	28.1	—	31.90	28.1
1966/67	70.00	22.85	20.76	113.61	155.70	42.09	37.0	—	42.09	37.0
1967/68	75.00	23.22	21.04	119.26	156.76	37.50	31.4	—	37.50	31.4
1968/69	75.00	23.91	20.32	119.23	158.30	39.07	32.8	—	39.07	32.8
Cocoa[2]										
1964/65	70.00	17.92	15.38	103.30	107.57	4.27	4.1	—	4.27	4.1
1965/66	40.00	10.37	13.23	63.60	85.69	22.09	34.7	—	22.09	34.7
1966/67	55.00	11.49	14.34	80.82	98.34	17.51	21.7	—	17.51	21.7
1967/68	70.00	16.87	15.14	102.01	148.00	45.99	45.1	—	45.99	45.1
1968/69	80.00	18.13	15.20	113.33	203.40	90.07	79.5	—	90.07	79.5
Groundnuts (shelled)[2]										
1964/65	30.00[3]	...	...	47.06	41.19	−5.87	−12.5	5.25	−0.62	−1.3
1965/66	27.00[3]	...	...	44.30	38.79	−5.51	−12.4	4.50	−1.01	−2.3
1966/67	27.00[3]	...	...	44.30	37.73	−6.57	−14.8	3.50	−3.07	−6.9
1967/68	27.00[3]	...	...	44.30	29.92	−14.38	−32.5	3.00	−11.38	−25.7
1968/69	27.00[3]	...	...	43.88	44.10	0.22	0.5	—	0.22	0.5
Cotton fiber[2]										
1964/65	30.00[4]	...	...	144.77	123.28	−21.49	−14.8	7.22	−14.27	−9.9
1965/66	27.00[4]	...	...	136.29	115.12	−21.17	−15.5	9.50	−11.67	−8.6
1966/67	27.00[4]	...	...	136.29	110.09	−26.20	−19.2	6.80	−19.60	−14.4
1967/68	27.00[4]	...	...	136.29	112.37	−23.02	−17.6	5.20	−18.72	−13.7
1968/69	30.00[4]	...	...	133.34	115.60	−17.74	−13.3	2.20	−15.54	−11.7
Palm oil[5]										
1964/65	...	—	...	50.34	53.36	3.02	6.0	—	3.02	6.0
1965/66	...	—	...	50.62	45.06	−5.56	−11.0	—	−5.56	−11.0
1966/67	...	—	...	...	30.69	...	...	—	...	...

Source: Data provided by the Togolese authorities.

[1] F.o.b. Lomé.
[2] Marketed by the Office of Agricultural Products (Office des Produits Agricoles du Togo, or OPAT).
[3] For unshelled groundnuts.
[4] For seed (unginned) cotton.
[5] Marketed by Société Togolaise d'Extraction de l'Huile de Palme (SOTEHPA).

TABLE 6. TOGO: TOTAL PROFIT (OR LOSS) ON MARKETED CROPS, 1964/65–1968/69 [1]

(In millions of CFA francs)

	1964/65			1965/66			1966/67			1967/68			1968/69		
	Pur-chases	Sales	Profit, or loss (–)	Pur-chases	Sales	Profit, or loss (–)	Pur-chases	Sales	Profit, or loss (–)	Pur-chases	Sales	Profit, or loss (–)	Pur-chases	Sales	Profit, or loss (–)
Coffee	746	818	72	1,627	2,110	483	698	934	236	1,243	1,646	403	1,366	1,512	146
Cocoa	1,560	1,602	42	1,091	1,394	303	1,470	2,227	757	1,631	2,226	595	2,991	4,202	1,211
Groundnuts	98	85	–13	152	131	–21	173	143	–30	254	171	–83	249	205	–44
Copra	20	24	4	45	44	–1	39	34	–5	21	23	2	44	35	–9
Palm kernels	315	374	59	676	691	15	404	380	–24	537	661	124	591	495	–96
Cotton [2]	—	—	—	344	281	–63	589	518	–71	422	411	–11	353	271	–82
Castor beans	3	3	—	11	8	–3	8	6	–2	9	10	1	4	3	–1
Sheanuts	7	8	1	47	31	–16	4	8	4	39	57	18	17	29	12
Kapok	—	—	—	14	16	2	24	20	–4	23	16	–7	12	9	–3
Total	2,745	2,914	165	4,007	4,706	699	3,409	4,270	861	4,179	5,221	1,042	5,627	6,761	1,134

Source: Data provided by the Togolese authorities.

[1] All marketed by the Office of Agricultural Products (Office des Produits Agricoles du Togo, or OPAT).
[2] The 1964/65 cotton crop was exported in 1965/66.

reached CFAF 483 million. The upward trend continued in world prices through 1968/69 and in unit profit through 1966/67, but the sharp contraction in export volume cut the total profit by nearly half in 1966/67. Despite a lower unit profit in 1967/68 (when the higher producer price was restored), the total gross profit again exceeded CFAF 400 million because of considerable recovery in export volume. In 1968/69, total gross profit on coffee declined to CFAF 146 million because the Office was unable to sell all the coffee it bought, owing to Togo's quota under ICA.

Cocoa.—Domestic cocoa comes from small farms, mainly in the same region that produces coffee (the Palimé-Atakpamé-Badou triangle). During 1963/64–1967/68 the area utilized for cocoa remained stable and production increased only slightly. In the last few years, cocoa trees have been attacked by a disease that growers can control only by cutting out the affected trees and replanting. In 1968/69, however, both the area under cultivation and the production of cocoa increased.

Domestic sales and exports of cocoa have consistently exceeded domestic production by the quantities of Ghanaian cocoa purchased. From 1965/66 to 1968/69, domestic production rose by one third to 16,000 tons and domestic sales by the same proportion to 20,000 tons (see Table 4). Exports rose to 21,100 tons in 1968/69, compared with 16,000 tons in 1965/66.

Rising world prices after 1965/66, accompanied by a larger export volume, provided growing total profits from cocoa for the Office of Agricultural Products. In 1966/67, total gross profits reached CFAF 757 million (see Table 6).

In 1967/68 a 50 per cent rise in world prices more than doubled the unit profit even with a higher producer price of CFAF 70 per kilogram. However, in July 1967, Ghana devalued its new cedi and raised its producer price by 30 per cent. These developments narrowed the difference between the producer prices for cocoa in the two countries, which has been the principal reason for re-export of Ghanaian cocoa through Togo. With less cocoa marketed and exported, the Office realized a smaller total gross profit on cocoa in 1967/68 (CFAF 595 million).

World cocoa prices rose further in 1968/69, and even though Togo's producer prices and export taxes also went up, the unit profit per kilogram doubled over the previous year and the total gross profit on cocoa reached CFAF 1,211 million.

Palm and coconut products.—Palm kernels are collected from wild palm groves, which cover an area of about 4,000 hectares in southern Togo. Production of palm kernels fluctuates considerably but averaged about 16,000 tons a year during 1965/66–1968/69. The producer price for palm kernels remained at CFAF 21 per kilogram over this entire period. To expand production of palm kernels and to reduce the cost of production, the EEC European Development Fund (EDF) is financing a project to develop plantations on some 3,000 hectares. In 1966/67 and 1968/69, export prices for palm kernels fell, and the Office of Agricultural Products incurred losses on its sales.

Palm oil is processed and exported by the Société Togolaise d'Extraction de l'Huile de Palme (SOTEHPA). On exports of 485 tons of palm oil in 1964/65, the palm oil agency made a profit of CFAF 3.02 per kilogram (see Table 5). In 1965/66, exports rose to 711 tons; however, the export price declined to CFAF 45.06 per kilogram from CFAF 53.36 in the previous year, while the cost price rose slightly. As a result, the palm oil agency incurred a loss of CFAF 5.56 per kilogram, or 11 per cent of the cost.

Coconut palms covered an area of about 6,000 hectares in 1960. This area, however, became infected with the kaincopé disease, which reduced the area to about 4,000 hectares in 1967/68 and cut the production of copra (see Table 4). Exports declined to a greater degree (from about 5,000 tons in 1960/61 to about 1,000 tons in 1968/69) because of rising domestic demand for coconut oil.

Cotton.—Production of cotton (largely the Mono variety) has expanded in recent years. It is grown mainly in east-central Togo near the Dahomey border. The Compagnie Française pour le Développement des Fibres Textiles (CFDT) is helping Togo to extend the area under the high-yielding Allen variety by 4,000 hectares. From 1964/65 to 1968/69, domestic sales of seed (unginned) cotton rose from 6,000 tons to 16,000 tons and exports of the fiber from 800 tons to 2,000 tons (see Table 4). In some years, domestic sales exceed domestic production because they include some Dahomey cotton.

Cotton is exported at world market prices. Domestic production costs, however, are high and losses have been partly covered by EEC subsidies. In 1964/65 the cost of cotton fiber was CFAF 144.77 and its f.o.b. export price CFAF 123.28 per kilogram, resulting in a loss of CFAF 21.49 per kilogram, or 15 per cent of the cost (see Table 5). EEC paid a subsidy of CFAF 7.22 per kilogram, computed as the difference between the export price and the EEC target price of CFAF 130.50 per kilogram for 1964/65. The remaining deficit of CFAF 14.27 per kilogram, or 10 per cent of the cost, was covered by the Office of Agricultural Products. In 1965/66 the cost declined to CFAF 136.29 per kilogram with a reduction of the producer price and some economies in handling costs. The EEC subsidy of CFAF 9.50 per kilogram, the maximum allowed, left the Office with a net loss of CFAF 11.67 per kilogram, or 9 per cent of the cost. During the next two years, the cost of cotton did not change; however, lower world market prices and decreasing EEC price support during the fourth and fifth years of the support program, resulted in greater unit losses for the Office. In 1968/69, even with some reduction in cost, some gain in the world market price, and the remaining EEC subsidy, the Office will sustain a net loss of CFAF 15.54 per kilogram, or 12 per cent of cost.

Groundnuts.—Most of the groundnuts are grown in east-central and northern Togo. The area in groundnuts expanded considerably in 1961/62; thereafter it remained more or less stable at about 40,000 hectares. According to official estimates, total domestic production (unshelled) reached a record of 22,000 tons in 1962/63 but did not exceed 20,000 tons thereafter (see Table 4). Fluctuations reflect favorable or unfavorable weather. The bulk of the crop is consumed locally. The ratio of local consumption to the total crop of groundnuts changes reciprocally with the supply and price of rice in the country. Exports of shelled groundnuts, though still small, rose from 2,000 tons in 1964/65 to 6,000 tons in 1967/68. Irregular rainfall in 1968/69 reduced sharply both the area under cultivation and production; exports also declined, to 5,000 tons.

Under a program, renewed each year, France had agreed to take up Togo's entire exportable surplus of groundnuts at a guaranteed price, fixed at CFAF 49.50 per kilogram (shelled) c.i.f. in 1964/65 and at CFAF 48.50 in 1965/66 and 1966/67; thereafter the French price guarantee was discontinued. However, Togo actually received less than the guaranteed price from France in these years, mainly because the quality of exports did not measure up to the specification in the agreement. The export price actually received averaged CFAF 46.25 per kilogram c.i.f. in 1964/65 and CFAF 43.71 in 1965/66. In addition to the French guaranteed price, Togo is entitled to an EEC subsidy under the provisions of the first Yaoundé Convention of Association.

The Convention of Association between EEC and 18 African and Malagasy States required that all exports of associated members should be marketed at world market prices and called for the termination of bilateral support schemes. To facilitate the alignment of costs to world market prices, EEC agreed to provide aid during a five-year transitional period, from 1964/65 to 1968/69. EEC assistance is aimed at increasing productivity and providing price subsidies. Under the EEC plan, price subsidies for groundnuts are computed on the basis of differences between the actual export prices and a target cost. Target costs were scheduled to decline annually until they equaled the expected world market price in the fifth year of the program, when the price subsidy was to terminate. Computed on this basis, the amount of the EEC subsidy in 1964/65 was equivalent to CFAF 5.25 per kilogram of shelled groundnuts, for which full compensation has been received. The cost of shelled groundnuts f.o.b. Lomé was reduced from CFAF 47.06 per kilogram in 1964/65 to CFAF 43.88 during 1965/66–1968/69 (see Table 5). This result reflects mainly a reduction in the producer price in 1965/66; other costs, including export taxes and various handling charges, scarcely changed. The actual export price f.o.b. of shelled groundnuts declined from CFAF 41.19 per kilogram in 1964/65 to CFAF 29.92 in 1967/68 but rose to CFAF 41.10 in 1968/69.

Consequently, net losses on groundnuts increased from about 1 per cent of the cost in 1964/65 to 26 per cent in 1967/68. In 1968/69, however, a 37 per cent rise in world market prices resulted in a small profit (0.5 per cent).

Marketing of Agricultural Products

The Office of Agricultural Products (Office des Produits Agricoles du Togo, or OPAT), though a public agency established to market cash crops, operates through private traders who, directly or by means of intermediaries, handle the crops from time of purchase from the producers to the time of delivery to the Office at the port. The Office compensates these traders for their expenses and pays a commission, according to a scale decreed by the Government annually for each product. This scale also specifies the producer price, handling charges, and the export taxes to be paid by the Office on each product. Until 1970, however, the Office was exempt from payment of the profit tax. Export sales are made by local firms in Paris and London, acting as agents of the Office.

Profits of the Office of Agricultural Products rose substantially during 1964/65–1968/69, mainly from its coffee and cocoa operations (see Table 6). Palm kernels also usually yield good profits. On almost all other crops, however, the Office sustained losses.

On September 30, 1969 the Office had noninterest-bearing deposits with the Treasury amounting to CFAF 1.7 billion and an additional CFAF 1.9 billion on deposit with the commercial banks. Its outstanding loans to the Government and various public agencies totaled CFAF 1.9 billion. In 1967 the Office provided a grant of CFAF 50 million to the Regional Development Administration and contributed CFAF 100 million to the capital of the National Agricultural Credit Fund (Caisse Nationale du Crédit Agricole).

Livestock and Livestock Products

Climatic and ethnic factors have favored the concentration of cattle raising in the savanna region of northern Togo, but other livestock are kept more or less throughout the country. Official estimates for 1961–68 indicate an increase in cattle from about 144,000 to 200,000; sheep and goats from 702,000 to 1,575,000, pigs from 177,000 to 350,000, and poultry from 1,091,000 to 1,787,000. The capacity of government-controlled slaughterhouses has increased with new additions in Niamtougou, Tsévié, and Anécho at a total cost of CFAF 6.0 million, financed by the French FAC (Fonds d'Aide et de Coopération); a new slaughterhouse in the Lomé area has been built with FAC financing at a cost of CFAF 325 million. Controlled cattle slaughter is about 8 per cent of the cattle population, but the rate for controlled sheep and goat slaughter is just about 2 per cent. The cattle rate is similar to that prevailing in many other West African countries. Local meat production satisfies only two thirds of domestic consumption, necessitating imports of meat as well as live cattle (more than 15,000 head in 1966).

Fishing and Forestry

Coastal, lagoon, and river fishing produced a total catch of about 10,500 tons in 1969, compared with 3,200 tons in 1954. Even so, some 8,000 tons of fish were imported in 1969 to meet domestic requirements.

Fishing is conducted mainly under traditional methods by an increasing number of local fishermen—some 12,000 in 1969, compared with 10,500 in 1954. This increase was largely due to the need for other sources of income because of the declining profitability of coconut groves infected by the kaincopé disease (see "Palm and coconut products," above). In 1967, about 600 boats were engaged in fishing, 400 of them motorized.

Industrial fishing has been in the experimental stage, mainly because of the lack of natural shelter or harbors along Togo's coast. On completion of the new port in 1968, however, two fishing trawlers with a total capacity of 700 tons of fish a year, were provided by Germany. To expand the local fish catch, the Government has initiated a program, assisted by FAO and Germany, to set up fishing cooperatives, modernize equipment, facilitate the purchase of motor barges, and install refrigerated storage in Lomé, Palimé, and Sokodé.

Forests cover about 10 per cent of Togo's total area. Production of firewood satisfies domestic needs but the output of timber, estimated at 6,000 cubic meters in 1969, is apparently insufficient and is supplemented by imports. The total value of forest products in 1969 was estimated at CFAF 40 million.

MINING AND QUARRYING

The relative importance of mining has increased since the exploitation of phosphate began in 1961. Mining contributed more than 6 per cent to GDP in 1969.

The phosphate deposits in Kpémé, northeast of Lomé, are estimated at 100 million tons, or the equivalent of 50 million tons of ore with a tricalcium phosphate content of at least 81 per cent. The Togo Mining Company (Compagnie Togolaise des Mines du Bénin, or CTMB), Togo's most important enterprise in mining and industry, has a share capital of CFAF 3.0 billion, which was raised from CFAF 2.4 billion in January 1966; the Togolese Government holds 20 per cent of the share capital. Other principal shareholders are the Grace Company of the United States (47 per cent of the shares), the French Compagnie Financière pour les Pays d'Outre-Mer and the Société des Produits Chimiques Péchiney-Saint Gobain. From its establishment until 1969, the Mining Company's investment totaled about CFAF 11 billion, including the cost of mining equipment, a 25-kilometer railroad linking the mine with the Company's processing plant, a diesel electric station, and port facilities. In 1966, gross investment amounted to CFAF 1.6 billion; the Mining Company employed more than 1,000 workers and technicians and paid CFAF 244 million in export taxes. Benefiting from the provisions of Togo's Investment Code, the Mining Company did not pay tax on its profits until the end of 1966.

Between 1962 and 1968, extraction of raw phosphates rose from 248,000 tons to 2.6 million tons, and the output of processed phosphates from 197,000 tons to 1.4 million tons (Table 7). Phosphate exports increased in value from less than CFAF 0.2 billion in 1961 to CFAF 3.9 billion in 1968, when they represented more than a third of

TABLE 7. TOGO: PRODUCTION AND EXPORTS OF PHOSPHATE, 1961–68

	Production of Phosphate		Exports	
	Raw	Processed	Volume	Value
	←———— Thousand metric tons ————→			Million CFA francs
1961	. . .	79	57	155
1962	248	197	197	489
1963	1,068	476	470	1,068
1964	1,549	776	778	1,948
1965	1,963	982	982	2,198
1966	2,210	1,152	1,111	3,415
1967	2,049	1,300	1,123	3,350
1968	2,632	1,375	1,357	3,862
1969 (9 months)	1,777	1,045	1,063	2,687

Sources: Ministère des Finances, de l'Economie et du Plan, *Inventaire Economique du Togo*, 1964; Compagnie Togolaise des Mines du Bénin, *Rapport Annuel*, *1966*; and data provided by the Togolese authorities.

total exports. According to provisional data, exports reached 1.45 million tons in 1969, compared with 1.36 million tons in 1968. Togolese phosphates are marketed by a Paris trading firm, the Union Phosphatière Africaine, which also handles sales for Tunisia and Senegal. In 1967, exports went to 11 countries, mainly EEC members, and 70 per cent of the sales were made outside the franc area. The Mining Company's profits in 1966, the last year of profit tax exemptions under the Investment Code, amounted to CFAF 1.9 billion. In 1967 and 1968, profits declined to about CFAF 1.0 billion, reflecting also falling world market prices. It is intended to expand the capacity of the processing plant to reach about 1.8 million tons in 1971. Under the aegis of the UN Industrial Development Organization (UNIDO), the Mining Company has a project to construct a fertilizer plant with a capacity of 120,000 tons at an estimated cost of CFAF 1.5 billion. The plant will probably be completed in the early 1970's.

Togo also has deposits of iron ore and limestone. The iron ore deposits, estimated at 50 million tons, contain low-grade ore, and there are no definite plans for exploiting them. However, there is a project for using limestone for producing cement and clinker; the latter would be exported to Ivory Coast, Ghana, Upper Volta, and Dahomey. The Government intends to launch a second program of mineral prospecting with the assistance of the UN Development Program; the first program, also assisted by the UN (Special Fund), was carried out in 1963. There are also two quarries, and a marble plant is being established near Lomé.

MANUFACTURING

In 1969, manufacturing contributed 10 per cent of the GDP, compared with 4 per cent in 1964 (see Table 2). This rise was due largely to the addition of a textile plant and a brewery. More rapid industrial growth in Togo appears to be impeded mainly by the limited size of the domestic market and the difficulty of selling in neighboring markets because of competition from imported goods and from newly established industries in those countries. After Togo's independence, the Government encouraged foreign and domestic private investment in Togo and promulgated a liberal Investment Code in 1965 (see "Economic development planning," below).

Manufacturing in Togo comprises a small number and variety of enterprises. So far the most developed are the processing of food and other agricultural products, and the manufacture of beverages (including plants producing tapioca, starch, and palm oil; four modern bakeries; and a brewery). The tapioca and starch mill (S.A. Compagnie du Bénin), established in 1950 in Ganavé near Anécho, employs about 100 persons and has a capacity of 6,500 tons of cassava starch a year. It is a mixed enterprise in which the Office of Agricultural Products participates. Extreme fluctuations in annual production (1,000–6,500 tons) in the past, depending largely on the supply of cassava, have created financial difficulties for the enterprise. Cassava production in Togo usually exceeds domestic consumption, and the excess was either exported to neighboring countries, or sold to the Compagnie du Bénin, depending on the export price and the price paid by the mill. In order to improve the profitability of the mill, the following measures have been taken: technical assistance has been given to cassava growers through regional development organizations, and producer prices have been fixed to guarantee the regular supply of cassava to the mill, which is being extended since its size was judged to be suboptimal. Investments amounted to CFAF 11 million in 1966 and CFAF 45 million in 1967. The enterprise also enjoys fiscal privileges to ensure its profitability.

The palm oil mill (Société Togolaise d'Extraction de l'Huile de Palme, or SOTEHPA), a state enterprise established in 1953 in Alokoégbé (near Tsévié), has an annual capacity of 1,000 tons of palm oil. It employs about 25 persons. Oil production has fluctuated, but in general it has increased in recent years. In 1966, however, it remained at 694 tons, still well below capacity. The mill has obsolete equipment and has encountered marketing problems in recent years, mainly because of competition from Ivory Coast. However, the mill is in the process of reorganization, assisted by an EEC subsidy of CFAF 41 million, but its future will depend on the success of the oil palm plantation now being envisaged and the resulting regular supply of raw material.

One of the most important industrial enterprises at present in Togo is the brewery (Brasserie du Bénin). The brewery, a mixed enterprise, with a share capital of CFAF 189 million, of which the Government holds 25 per cent, is in Lomé. It had a capacity of 30,000 hectoliters of beer and 10,000 hectoliters of soda water, which was fully utilized; in 1968 the capacity was expanded to 60,000 hectoliters. About 175 persons are now employed. Total investment is estimated at CFAF 500 million, and the brewery is operating at a profit. Besides the brewery, there are two soft drink factories: the larger one, in Lomé, has a capacity of 15,000 hectoliters and employs about 45 people.

The textile industry includes a textile mill, three cotton ginning mills, and one kapok ginning mill. The textile mill (Industrie Textile Togolaise, or ITT), established in 1966 in Dadja, employs about 650 persons and has an annual spinning capacity of 9 million yards of printed cloth. Its share capital is CFAF 120 million, of which the Government owns 25 per cent; the rest is held by foreign interests, mainly German. Total investment amounted to CFAF 1.2 billion in 1966. The textile mill faces serious financial and marketing difficulties because of Japanese competition. Since Japanese yard goods can be imported at a price only slightly above the mill's cost, sale prices of domestic goods cannot be raised significantly. On the other hand, an imposition of a protective tariff on imported textiles would favor unregistered imports. Therefore, the Government has granted the textile mill other tax privileges under the Investment Code, mainly related to imports of raw materials and machinery. The Government also restricts imports of textiles corresponding to the variety produced by the mill through a scheme which requires local merchants to purchase one yard of domestic textiles for every two yards that they import. Through these measures, the textile mill was able to operate without loss in 1968. Export opportunities for Togo-made textiles will be limited in the future as a large textile mill is being established in Ivory Coast. The three cotton ginning mills process 8,000 to 9,000 tons of seed cotton annually.

The chemical industry includes only a plastics factory and a soap factory. The Société Togolaise de Plastiques, founded in 1966, is a mixed enterprise and mainly produces household articles. Total investment amounts to CFAF 35 million and its staff consists of 25 people. The plant started operations in December 1967. The Société Chimique et Industrielle Africaine, a soap and perfume factory established in the Lomé area in 1953, employs about 40 people. The annual production capacity is 1,500 tons of soap and 1,000 hectoliters of perfume; in 1966, the factory produced 500 tons of soap and 500 hectoliters of perfume. Other industrial and semi-industrial enterprises include two quarries, the government printing press, furniture factories, and building and road construction enterprises.

Several industrial projects are expected to be realized in the near future. The most important of them is the construction of a cement and clinker factory, a plant producing fertilizers from phosphates, a match factory, a salt factory, and a plant producing oxygen and acetylene.

POWER

The major supplier of electric power is the National Electric Power Company (Compagnie de l'Energie Electrique du Togo, or CEET). In addition, a number of municipal authorities and certain private companies (the Mining Company and the textile mill) operate power-generating plants to meet their own requirements. The National Electric Power Company, a state enterprise, was established in 1963 with a capital of CFAF 431 million to operate Togo's only hydroelectric plant at Palimé. On January 1, 1965, it took over the Lomé power plant, which was owned by a French private company, the Union Electrique d'Outre-Mer (UNELCO). The purchase of the Lomé plant was financed partly by the Government and partly from the proceeds of a loan from the Office of Agricultural Products. Its capacity was substantially expanded in 1966. With this increase, the power production capacity is sufficient to meet current domestic requirements, and the Togolese authorities reduced electricity rates by 10 per cent. This reduction, which brought the Togolese rates in line with those in Dahomey, was offset by an increase in sales with no loss in the Electric Power Company's over-all income. The Company had a surplus every year since 1965; its policy is to use the surplus from current operations to finance its expansion program.

Total production of electricity in Togo more than doubled during 1963–68, reaching 53.7 million kilowatt-hours (Table 8) mainly because of the rapid increase in power production in the industrial sector, particularly the phosphate mine.

Although the electric power capacity of 21.02 megawatts is adequate at present, the demand for electricity is expected to rise in the next five years requiring an estimated increase in capacity of 15 megawatts. To meet these increased needs and the requirements of Dahomey, an

TABLE 8. TOGO: INSTALLED ELECTRIC POWER CAPACITY AND
ANNUAL PRODUCTION, 1963–69

	CEET		Mining Company Plant (Kpémé) [2]	Textile Mill Plant (Dadja) [3]	Other [4]	Total
	Thermoelectric plant (Lomé) [1]	Hydroelectric plant (Palimé) [2]				
INSTALLED CAPACITY (*kilowatts*)						
1963	2,100	1,600	6,300	—	500	10,500
1964	2,100	1,600	6,300	—	500	10,500
1965	3,000	1,600	6,200	2,000	500	15,300
1966	6,050	1,600	8,200	2,000	168	18,018
1967	6,225	1,600	7,500	2,000	168	17,493
1968	9,750	1,600	7,500	2,000	168	21,018
1969	9,750	1,600	7,500	2,000	168	21,018
ANNUAL PRODUCTION (*thousand kilowatt-hours*)						
1963	9,872	20	11,098	—	1,000	21,990
1964	7,559	3,269	15,403	—	1,000	27,231
1965	8,913	3,583	21,144	—	1,000	33,582
1966	10,911	4,194	24,673	1,304	170	41,252
1967	12,178	4,696	27,428	2,890	200	47,392
1968	13,382	5,694	29,578	4,830	200	53,744
1969	18,855	5,124 [5]	24,072 [6]	3,307	200	. . .

Sources: Ministère du Commerce, de l'Industrie, du Tourisme et du Plan, *Inventaire Economique du Togo*, 1962–63, 1964, and 1966, and data provided by the Togolese authorities.

[1] Until 1963, Union Electrique d'Outre-Mer; thereafter Compagnie de l'Energie Electrique du Togo (CEET).

[2] Compagnie Togolaise des Mines du Bénin; 6,000 kilowatts of installed capacity are utilized.

[3] Industrie Textile Togolaise.

[4] Estimated.

[5] Eleven months.

[6] Nine months.

agreement to build a linkup with the power system in Ghana was reached among the three countries. The power will be transmitted by a high-tension line of 350 kilometers from the Akosombo (Volta) Dam in Ghana to Togo (Lomé) and Dahomey (Cotonou). The power line will be exploited by a joint Togo-Dahomey electric company, the Communauté Energie du Bénin. The estimated cost of the project is $6 million, to be financed by a soft loan from Canada. The project is expected to be completed in 1971. In addition, four smaller thermoelectric plants, financed by the Government of Togo at an estimated cost of CFAF 145 million, are presently under construction with a total capacity of 700 kilowatts. They are all expected to start operating in 1970.

TRANSPORTATION

Togo's road network covers 7,173 kilometers, of which 206 kilometers are hard-surfaced roads and 1,068 kilometers are all-weather roads for vehicles up to a maximum weight of 6.5 tons. There are three main road systems: (1) the coastal road betwen Ghana and Dahomey; (2) the road northward from Lomé through the center of the country to Upper Volta; and (3) roads serving the cocoa and coffee producing area. The coastal road and, to some extent, the north-south road are important internationally; the former carries a significant amount of traffic between Nigeria and Ghana. Road projects under way include the paving of the Lomé-Palimé and the Tsévié-Tabligbo roads with EDF financing. EDF also provided financing for a preinvestment study of the Atakpamé-Palimé-Badou road. A future project is the construction of a road from Sokodé to Upper Volta; this road probably would add to the activity of the port of Lomé.

About 5,000 vehicles are operating in Togo; roughly half are trucks owned chiefly by specialized transportation firms or directly by trading firms.

The government-owned National Railway (Chemins de Fer du Togo) has a network of 489 kilometers, with three main lines: Lomé to Anécho, Lomé to Palimé, and Lomé to Blitta, all of meter gauge. Built at the beginning of the century the Railway has obsolete equipment and faces increased competition from road transportation. Passenger traffic has progressively declined from more than 2.2 million in 1960 to about 1.6 million in 1968 (Table 9). Freight tonnage rose steadily between 1961 and 1964 to over 100,000 tons, declined sharply to 80,000 tons in 1965 but increased again to over 100,000 tons in 1967 and 1968. Losses from operating the railroad were slightly offset by the profits from operating the wharf. In 1968, with the completion of the new port, which is administered by a separate authority, the wharf was abandoned. Complete abandonment of railroad operations has been considered, but recently it was decided to deactivate only the Lomé-Palimé line; this measure is expected to reduce the railroad's operating losses. There is a project to build a 19-kilometer railroad line to link Avéta (northeast of Lomé and the site of the planned cement factory) with the Lomé-Blitta line.

TABLE 9. TOGO: WHARF AND RAILROAD TRAFFIC, 1960–69

	1960	1961	1962	1963	1964	1965	1966	1967	1968	1969
WHARF TRAFFIC [1]										
Ships arriving and leaving										
Number	360	364	469	477	486	362	389	447	444	490
Net tonnage (*thousand tons*)	1,143	1,204	1,469	1,501	1,398	1,087	1,121	1,298	1,296	…
Number of passengers embarking and disembarking	4,137	4,355	4,886	5,448	6,547	3,984	3,795	1,856	701	6,703
Volume of imports (*thousand metric tons*)	86	86	106	104	109	117	140	126	190	235
Volume of exports (*thousand metric tons*)	48	57	46	53	65	57	60	54	63	80
RAILROAD TRAFFIC										
Number of passengers (*thousands*)	2,287	2,342	1,827	1,835	1,831	1,689	1,734	1,722	1,644	845 [2]
Goods and baggage carried (*thousand metric tons*)	96	60	74	78	105	80	82	104	121	63 [2]
Number of engines	22	20	18	18	20	23	22	22	23	23
Distance covered (*thousand kilometers*)	987	937	999	942	934	1,246	1,264	1,329	972	1,002

Sources: Ministère des Finances, de l'Economie et du Plan, *Inventaire Economique du Togo* and *Bulletin Mensuel de Statistique;* Ministère des Travaux Publics, Mines, Transports, et Postes et Télécommunications, *Rapport Annuel sur les Activités du Port et du Chemin de Fer,* 1966; and data supplied by the Togolese authorities.

[1] In 1968, when the new port of Lomé started operations, wharf operations ceased.
[2] Six months only.

Furthermore, there is a 25-kilometer private railroad system (belonging to the phosphate mine) which links the mine in Kpémé with the processing plant, the powerhouse, and port facilities.

Lomé is Togo's principal port; a second port at Kpémé is used exclusively to handle phosphate shipments. Until 1968, Togo's overseas foreign trade, 190,000 tons of imports and 63,000 tons of exports in that year, was handled by the wharf in Lomé (see Table 9). The new port, a man-made harbor, built a few kilometers east of Lomé, has an annual capacity of 500,000 tons; this volume should be reached in some 20 years. The port started operating in 1968. Total investment is CFAF 5.4 billion, of which CFAF 4.5 billion was furnished by the German Kreditanstalt für Wiederaufbau at an annual interest rate of 2 per cent. Port revenues are expected to exceed the operating expenditures. As traffic increases in later years, it is expected that the debt service, which starts in 1970, can be increasingly met from port income. A German loan of CFAF 62 million for a harbor tug was extended in 1968.

The principal airport of the country, in Lomé, was recently opened to jet traffic. From 1960 to 1968 the number of passengers embarking and disembarking almost tripled, reaching 16,000, and freight and mail handled doubled, reaching 410 tons annually during the same period. Togo has other airports in Atakpamé, Sokodé, Sansanné-Mango, and Dapango. The national airline is Air Togo, which operates within the country and to neighboring countries.

COMMERCE

After agriculture, commerce contributes most to GDP in Togo. Its share in the total GDP rose from 17 per cent in 1963 to about 20 per cent in 1969 (see Table 2). The relative importance of trade in Togo's economy is attributable to (1) Togo's geographical situation and ethnic ties with neighboring countries, (2) the comparatively large percentage of domestic foodstuffs sold rather than consumed by the producer, and (3) the liberal trade and commercial policy of the Government.

A number of large foreign firms are engaged in export-import activities. Their import trade has become dominant since the Office of Agricultural Products handles the export of the main agricultural products.

In addition to the foreign firms, numerous local traders with relatively small operations transact most of the transit trade with the neighboring countries. These traders also form the main link for distribution between towns and rural areas.

In 1962 the Government established the State Export-Import Company (Société Togolaise d'Exportation et d'Importation, or SOTEXIM) as a distributing agency for essential consumer goods to rural areas, where private trade did not give adequate service and prices of essential consumer goods were excessively high. This agency was provided with a capital of CFAF 45 million. However, it failed to live up to the Government's expectations. In order to cover the high costs of its operations, it has undertaken the marketing of luxuries and certain nonessentials, which were relatively more remunerative (see also "Public enterprises' budgets," below).

ECONOMIC DEVELOPMENT PLANNING

FIVE-YEAR PLAN (1966–70)

Objectives and Administration

Togo's first Five-Year Plan (1966–70) was approved by the National Assembly in July 1965. It calls for a total gross fixed investment of CFAF 28.6 billion, or CFAF 5.7 billion annually (Table 10). The average annual investment is, therefore, approximately equal to 11 per cent of Togo's 1966 GDP. The plan lays down the over-all objectives to be pursued and the different priorities to be placed on different economic sectors.

The three general objectives of the plan are "to ensure national independence, to establish the structural basis for development, and to take both immediate and long-term actions which will eliminate disequilibria and promote expansion." For 1966–70 the following specific aims are to be pursued:

(1) balance the budget, which is to become a real planning budget, and earmark a minimum of CFAF 3.4 billion for public investments during the five-year period;

TABLE 10. TOGO: PLANNED INVESTMENT UNDER THE FIVE-YEAR
DEVELOPMENT PLAN (1966–70)

(*Amount in millions of CFA francs*)

	Amount			Per Cent of Total
	Public	Private	Total	
Infrastructure and communications	8,206	2,100	10,306	36
Rural development	5,141	800	5,941	21
Housing and town planning	1,734	2,800	4,534	16
Trade and industry	1,416	2,400	3,816	13
Education	1,336	300	1,636	6
Health	1,195	140	1,335	4
Administration	840	—	840	3
Social welfare	184	—	184	1
Total	20,052	8,540	28,592	100

Source: Haut Commissariat au Plan, *Plan de Développement Economique et Social, 1966–70.*

(2) strengthen the balance of payments and raise the percentage of imports covered by exports from 72 per cent in 1964 to 85 per cent in 1970;

(3) establish an inventory of all natural resources and implement a program of applied research and agricultural experimentation; and

(4) provide adequate transportation infrastructure and start a program of rural development throughout the country by increasing productivity of "men and soil."

In order to facilitate the implementation of the plan, the Government has reorganized its planning administration: The National Commission for Planning, which was set up in July 1965, has become a part of the Ministry of Commerce, Industry, Tourism, and Planning. This Commission, in addition to being in charge of drawing up the plan, controls its execution and, where required, assists with project preparation. Beginning in December 1965, public regional development agencies (Sociétés Régionales d'Aménagement et de Développement, or SORAD's) were established in five regions of the country. The role of each SORAD is mainly to organize and centralize the execution of regional development programs in the rural sector.

Structure and Financing of Investment

With a total investment of CFAF 28.6 billion, the plan aims at an average annual growth rate in GDP of about 5 per cent during the plan period. If this rate is achieved and Togo's population increases at an annual rate of 2.6 per cent, per capita national income would grow by an annual rate of 2.4 per cent.

Public investment is expected to be concentrated on the development of infrastructure and rural development, while a substantial part of private investment is to be devoted to housing, town planning, trade, and industry. Of the total planned outlay, 36 per cent is to be invested in infrastructure and communications, 21 per cent in rural development, 16 per cent in housing and town planning, and 13 per cent in trade and industry (see Table 10). The largest investment in infrastructure is for the construction of new roads, including the surfacing of about 300 kilometers of existing roads (CFAF 3 billion). A substantial amount of investment in rural development is used to finance the expansion of production of export and subsistence crops and the modernization of agriculture through the creation of pilot villages and the construction of dams for land irrigation. According to the new revision of the plan, public investments were reclassified in five main sectors instead of eight sectors as originally presented.

It is expected that 64 per cent of the total financing of the plan will by provided by external resources, and the rest domestically (Table 11). About 70 per cent of the foreign financing is to consist of grants, 25 per cent of loans, and 5 per cent of private foreign capital and supplier credits.

Actual investment during the plan period is expected to exceed the original target. Revised estimates put the total amount of investment under the plan at CFAF 40.7 billion, or 42 per cent above the planned target (Table 12); as of June 1969 an amount of CFAF 29.5 billion was already committed. About two thirds of the increase in total investment is on account of the cost overruns of which about 80 per cent is expected to occur in infrastructure, particularly for the construction of the port of Lomé. The balance of the increase in total investment represents the net addition as a result of the implementation of projects not originally included in the plan and the abandonment or postponement of others envisaged in the plan.

TABLE 11. TOGO: PLANNED FINANCING OF THE FIVE-YEAR DEVELOPMENT
PLAN (1966–70)

(*Amount in millions of CFA francs*)

	Amount			Per Cent of Total
	Public	Private	Total	
Internal				
Budget	3,409	—	3,409	12
Private savings	—	6,730	6,730	24
Total internal	3,409	6,730	10,139	36
External				
Official loans	4,540	—	4,540	16
Official grants	12,103	800	12,903	45
Private capital	—	400	400	1
Suppliers' credits	—	610	610	2
Total external	16,643	1,810	18,453	64
Total financing	20,052	8,540	28,592	100

Source: Haut Commissariat au Plan, *Plan de Développement Economique et Social, 1966–70.*

TABLE 12. TOGO: REVISED INVESTMENTS UNDER THE FIVE-YEAR
DEVELOPMENT PLAN (1966–70)

(*Amount in millions of CFA francs*)

		Committed Financing [1]	
	Revised Plan Estimates	Amount	Per Cent of Revised Estimates
Infrastructure	25,256	18,834	75
Rural development	5,643	4,557	81
Education, health, social welfare	3,821	1,934	51
Trade and industry	4,595	3,287	72
Administration	1,393	847	61
Total or average	40,708	29,459	72

Source: Data supplied by the Togolese authorities.

[1] As of June 30, 1969.

Most of the additional investment is being financed from foreign aid related to the projects concerned. However, domestic financing has also increased. The amount of public investment financed from domestic resources is to reach CFAF 7.2 billion, compared with the planned target of CFAF 3.4 billion; of this amount CFAF 4.4 billion is to come from the government budget and CFAF 1.8 billion from direct investment by the Office of Agricultural Products. Private investment has also exceeded the targets, particularly in the areas of housing and transportation.

A second five-year plan, to cover the period 1971–75, is currently under preparation. While its objectives have not yet been quantified, priority will be given to the rural sector, where the emphasis will be put on increasing production. Infrastructure will still absorb the largest part of investment mostly owing to the execution of ongoing projects. A new department has been created in the Bureau of Planning charged with the responsibility of preparing new projects.

INVESTMENT CODE

In order to encourage foreign and domestic private investment, an Investment Code was promulgated on July 21, 1965. The Code guarantees foreign investors the right of freely transferring abroad all capital invested in Togo and all investment income originating from this capital, provided that the foreign exchange regulations are respected.

The Code also provides for certain tax benefits to apply to newly established or expanding enterprises, after these are approved by government decree as "priority enterprises" because of their importance for the economic development of the country. Under the Code, these enterprises are exonerated from payment of import duties and turnover taxes on imports for a period of 10 years, and furthermore are granted for this period a reduction of up to 50 per cent on export taxes and turnover taxes on exports. In addition, for a period of 5 years after beginning operations, the approved enterprises are exonerated from payment of tax on industrial and commercial profits, and for a period of 6 years from the payment of business fees (*droits de patente*); they are also granted a reduction of up to 50 per cent of the registration fee.

Enterprises of particular importance for the economy of Togo may be granted a "regime of long fiscal duration" according to which they are guaranteed stable rates of taxation for the following maximum periods:

(1) 15 years for enterprises with investments from CFAF 20 million to CFAF 100 million.

(2) 20 years for enterprises with investments from CFAF 100 million to CFAF 500 million.

(3) 25 years for enterprises with investments amounting to more than CFAF 500 million.

The above limits may be extended for periods up to 5 years to cover the period of installation of the enterprise.

An enterprise desiring to be granted the "regime of long fiscal duration" has to conclude with the Government a founding agreement setting out the obligations of the enterprise and the guarantees given by the Government; the agreement also establishes the time during which it will be in force. As a general rule, the Government grants such enterprises for the duration of the agreement, exoneration from payment of import duties and turnover taxes on imports as for "priority enterprises." In addition, it guarantees that the following taxes will remain stable for the period specified in the agreement: import and export duties, turnover taxes on imports and exports, statistical tax, tax on industrial and commercial profits, payroll tax, turnover tax, and business and registration fees.

PRICES, WAGES, AND EMPLOYMENT

PRICES

Data on Togo prices are fragmentary. The only available consumer price index is constructed according to the consumption pattern of Europeans living in Togo and is used mainly as a basis for determining the cost of living for foreign technical assistants. As such, it has limited value for tracing the effect of price developments on the Togolese consumer. Besides this index, only data on retail prices of selected commodities are published.

The European consumer price index (May 1961 = 100) rose from 115.0 in September 1964 to 127.6 in September 1969 (Table 13), or by 11 per cent, mainly reflecting upward movements in household goods (26 per cent) and foodstuffs (16 per cent). The annual increase ranged between −0.5 per cent (1969) and 5.8 per cent (1967) but averaged 2.1 per cent over the period.

During 1964–68, retail prices remained stable or declined for most of the major domestic products (Table 14). Between 1964 and 1967 the price of coconut oil rose by 12 per cent as demand for this com-

TABLE 13. TOGO: EUROPEAN CONSUMER PRICE INDEX IN SEPTEMBER, 1964–69

(*May 1961 = 100*)

	1964	1965	1966	1967	1968	1969	Per Cent of Change, 1964–69
Foodstuffs	102.7	106.0	109.0	110.8	118.9	118.6	15.5
Beverages	121.8	126.6	134.4	137.7	127.6	127.5	4.7
Household goods	115.0	115.3	115.1	147.5	144.9	144.4	25.6
Transportation	120.8	121.0	122.8	122.6	122.6	121.5	0.6
Health facilities	121.3	124.5	128.8	130.3	132.2	125.7	3.6
Clothing	131.7	127.9	136.2	132.4	124.6	129.1	−2.0
Miscellaneous	117.5	113.5	124.0	119.8	129.6	129.2	10.0
Global index	115.0	116.6	120.6	127.6	128.2	127.6	11.0

Source: Ministère du Commerce, de l'Industrie, du Tourisme et du Plan, *Bulletin de Statistique.*

TABLE 14. TOGO: AVERAGE RETAIL PRICES OF MAJOR DOMESTIC AND IMPORTED PRODUCTS, 1964–68

(*In CFA francs per kilogram, except as noted*)

	1964	1965	1966	1967	1968
DOMESTIC PRODUCTS					
Maize	21	20	23	17	17
Maize flour	28	29	20	16	39
Potatoes	52	52	59	59	52
Yams	21	21	27	25	21
Greens	58	49	58	41	47
Palm oil (*liter*)	71	75	97	83	70
Coconut oil (*liter*)	91	97	103	102	95
Red peppers	171	83	118	101	75
Green peppers	143	79	89	86	65
Beef meat	225	238	225	225	225
Pork meat	175	215	225	225	225
Live chickens	195	190	192	188	191
Smoked fish	218	231	195	191	156
Bricks (*thousand*)	1,200	1,200	1,200	1,200	1,200
IMPORTED PRODUCTS					
Groundnut oil (*liter*)	138	136	135	134	113
Salt	18	17	17	18	18
Red wine (*66 centiliters*)	85	80	86	92	87
Pails (*each*)	240	239	243	262	262
Pagne cloth (*12-yard piece*)	2,523	2,530	2,533	2,400	2,526
Cement (*ton*)	9,142	9,049	8,797	8,217	7,674
Corrugated iron (*sheet*)	326	312	273	270	254
Sugar	80	72	60	47	47
Metal basins (*each*)	442	402	442	465	450

Source: Ministère du Commerce, de l'Industrie, du Tourisme et du Plan, *Bulletin de Statistique.*

modity increased partly because of changing taste but also because the supply fell with the reduction in output from the kaincopé disease. Reported prices also decreased for major imported products, except wine and some household goods.

Price controls were introduced in Togo in 1965. A decree of January 6, 1965 gave the authorities power to regulate prices when necessary. In January 1966, when the Government raised the rates of certain import taxes, prices of those goods were frozen at their December 1965 level in order to keep dealers from immediately raising prices of their stocks. Price controls were imposed on foodstuffs, cotton textiles, footwear, cigarettes, tobacco, alcoholic beverages, electrical appliances, petroleum products, and cement. Later, controls on some of these goods were lifted, but those on foodstuffs, footwear, and petroleum products remained.

The decree and ordinance of April 22, 1967, replacing the 1965 regulations, are more elaborate. They stipulate that price controls for specified products are to be established by ministerial order and that the regional authorities are responsible for establishing price controls for all other products. Three principal types of controls are envisaged in this decree: profit margins, official prices (*homologation des prix*), and price ceilings; but the last one has not been applied so far. Profit margins are fixed for wholesale and retail traders of imported products on the basis of the "free warehouse" cost of the product. Excessive prices have not occurred so far because of keen competition in the market. The official price for a product is established on the proposal of the dealer in concurrence with the authorities. The 1967 price control regulations have recently been somewhat modified as to the prices of petroleum products (after the closing of the Suez Canal) and shoes. In 1969, price control was expanded over the whole country, and price control officers have been appointed for three regions. Generally no profit margins are fixed for domestic products. If necessary, the Government will try to influence the market price of such products by restricting or facilitating imports or exports.

The aim of price controls is primarily to deter merchants from speculative action and overcharging. The large number of small dealers makes supervision of controls by the authorities difficult, and, therefore, public enlightenment is a key to effective controls. Every two weeks the

Government broadcasts the lowest prices obtainable in the market for the main consumer articles in order to widen public information on the market and promote free competition. Excessive prices are not publicized by radio, but action is taken against them.

Price control·officers also check the stocks of major consumer articles and urge wholesale merchants to keep adequate supplies in order to avoid shortages which could cause temporary price increases.

Another measure to avoid excessive prices and large price discrepancies among the various regions and to provide a permanent supply of basic consumer goods and equipment in remote rural areas was the creation· of the State Export-Import Company (SOTEXIM). As a state enterprise, this Company maintains shops in areas where only a few private traders usually operate and where lack of competition could cause excessive prices (see also "Commerce," above, and "Public enterprises' budgets," below).

WAGES

Available wage statistics in Togo relate only to the guaranteed minimum wage rates (Table 15). As in many other French-speaking Afri-

TABLE 15. TOGO: GUARANTEED MINIMUM WAGE RATES FOR NONAGRICULTURAL AND AGRICULTURAL WORKERS IN URBAN AND RURAL AREAS, 1960, 1963, AND 1970

(In CFA francs per hour)

Category and Zone [1]	1960	1963 [2]	1970 [3]	Per Cent of Change, 1960–70
Nonagricultural workers				
Zone I (urban)	27.50	29.70		30
Zone II	. . .	22.30	} 35.64	. . .
Zone III	15.50	19.33		130
Agricultural workers				
Zone I (urban)	23.85	25.75		30
Zone II	. . .	19.33	} 30.90	. . .
Zone III	15.50	16.74		99

Source: Ministère des Finances, de l'Economie et du Plan, *Inventaire Economique du Togo.*

[1] Zone I—Municipalities of Lomé, Anécho, Palimé, Tsévié, and Atakpamé; Zone II—Coastal and Plateau regions excluding the five municipalities in Zone I; and Zone III—Central and Savanna regions. For *circonscriptions* comprising these regions, see fn. 1, Table 1.
[2] As of November 1, 1963.
[3] As of January 1, 1970.

can countries, there exist in Togo minimum wage rates by urban and rural areas decreed by the Government for unskilled nonagricultural (*salaire minimum interprofessionnel garanti,* or SMIG) and agricultural (*salaire minimum agricole garanti,* or SMAG) workers. Minimum wages for nonagricultural workers are higher than those for agricultural workers. For each category, minimum wages were highest in urban areas. The differences reflected allowances made for the lower cost of living outside Lomé. Since these allowances were more or less arbitrary, the authorities decided to abolish in January 1970 the wage differences between the urban and rural areas. At the same time guaranteed hourly minimum wage rates (based on the so-called "minimum vital," the minimum cost of living derived from the budget of a low-income family in Lomé) were raised 20 per cent above those previously prevailing in the urban zones implying therefore a higher increase in rural salaries than in urban salaries. In practice, SMIG and SMAG are applied by the public sector and the larger private enterprises.

Wages and salaries for each important category of workers or employees are fixed through collective bargaining (*conventions collectives*) on the basis of SMIG and SMAG. For example, in the building and public works enterprises, wages are fixed through collective bargaining, but a distinction is made between different skills and categories of wage earners, such as building workers, quarry workers, and other industrial workers and drivers.

In the public sector, wages and salaries are fixed according to scales determined by the Government. Data on salaries, however, are not published, and there are no centrally kept wage and salary records. For the period 1966–68, government wages and salaries were frozen and promotions were limited.

EMPLOYMENT AND LABOR ORGANIZATIONS

Togo's economically active population in 1969 was estimated at 600,000, or about one third of the total population. About 78 per cent of the economically active population were working in the agricultural sector, 17 per cent were nonsalaried workers, and 5 per cent were salaried workers in the nonagricultural sector. About 55 per cent of the salaried workers were employed in the private sector, mainly in industry, commerce, and construction; about 45 per cent were employed in the public sector.

Unemployment has not been a serious problem in the cities in recent years, but some 6,000 persons were registered in Lomé as searching for jobs in 1969. Some decline in employment was expected in Lomé after the completion of the port and the dismissal of workers engaged on the wharf. The 1966–70 Development Plan calls for employment to increase by 9,000 in the private sector and by 3,000 in the public sector.

The larger of two trade unions in Togo is the Union Nationale des Travailleurs Togolais (UNTT) with a membership comprising most government workers and employees, and a large number of workers in private trade and industry. The second and much smaller union is the Confédération Syndicale des Travailleurs Togolais (CSTT). Labor unions are not important in the agricultural sector. In the nonagricultural sector they participate in discussions with the Government and employers concerning possible increases in SMIG. Although there is freedom to strike in Togo, there has not been any strike since independence.

GOVERNMENT FINANCE

STRUCTURE OF THE PUBLIC SECTOR

The public sector in Togo comprises the Central Government, 7 municipalities, 19 regions, and 19 public enterprises. Budget operations of the Central Government are recorded in an ordinary budget (*budget général*), which also includes certain investment expenditures, and an investment budget (*budget d'investissement*). Most development expenditures financed by foreign aid and foreign public capital, however, are outside the central government budget.

The municipalities and regions derive most of their resources from special levies, and their budgets are controlled by the Ministry of Interior and the Ministry of Finance. All the public enterprises except the National Railway Company have separate budgets. These enterprises are subject to a dual control: by the ministry to which their activities are directly related and by the Ministry of Finance. The Railway Company, which is not accorded financial autonomy, has no separate budget; its operations are recorded as part of the central government ordinary budget as an annex, subject to the same controls as the ordinary budget.

The principles governing the budgetary operations of the Central Government are set out each year in a Finance Law (*Loi de Finances*). Preparation of the budget commences in April, when only the final results of the budget of two years earlier are known. Expenditure estimates for wages and materials are prepared separately by each government service and submitted to the Ministry of Finance, while all other expenditure estimates are compiled within the Ministry of Finance. Receipts are estimated on the basis of the latest available actual data, also taking into account the expected development of economic activity and possible new revenue measures. A preliminary draft budget is prepared after consultations between the various departments concerned and the Ministry of Finance, which is then reviewed and, if necessary, modified by the Council of Ministers before it is submitted for presidential approval.

BUDGET CONTROL

The current system of government accounting in Togo is the budget year or commitment system (*règle de l'exercice*). Although Togo's government budgets are established on a calendar-year basis, the execution of the current budget is extended over a period of 15 months as the budget accounts are not closed until March 31 of the following calendar year. The first three months of the following calendar year, January–March, is called the complementary period of the "exercise."

Under Togo's budget system, in contrast to other budget systems, new commitments on the basis of appropriations of the old budget can also be made during the complementary period. Usually even the 15-month period is not strictly applied, but the entire budget period is stretched over 24 months. Consequently, two budgets are carried out at all times. However, in order to comply with the regulations, all receipts and disbursements made after the end of the fifteenth month are dated back to March 31. This commitment system developed historically in Togo, based on the principle that all revenues and expenditures which originate in a particular fiscal year, as laid down in the budget, should be registered under that year even if actual receipts, commitments, and disbursements are made afterward. Naturally, few arrears are carried over into the next budget, but it does cause a delay of at least 12 months until the books for a particular fiscal year can be closed. Therefore, the preparation of any new budget can be based only on the actual results of the budget before the last one.

Another feature of Togo's budget system is that after the end of the calendar year only a relatively small amount of government receipts is still outstanding, compared with payments to be made. This delay in expenditure, compared with revenue, also results in an easier liquidity position for the Treasury. Therefore, current accounts at the end of the calendar year also show a more substantial surplus than after the accounts are finally closed at the end of the complementary period.

Like the current budget, annexed budgets and budgets of regional authorities are kept on a commitment basis (*règle de l'exercice*), whereas the investment budget is operated on a cash basis (*règle de gestion*).

In Togo, the Treasury manages the budgetary and other financial operations of the public sector. The Treasury acts as a cashier—collecting revenues and making payments on account of the central government budgets, the annexed budgets, operations of a budgetary nature which are kept outside the budget in special accounts, and the local budgets. It also performs the function of a banker; it collects deposits from the public agencies, gives advances and loans to them, and extends credit in the form of overdrafts for financing the central government deficit. Moreover, the Treasury grants short-term credit to the private sector through the acceptance of customs duty bills in payment of indirect taxes and has short-term liabilities vis-à-vis the private sector (*consignations*), as well as outstanding bills and payment vouchers. It can obtain additional liquid funds through advances from, and discounting of customs duty bills with BCEAO, loans from the French Treasury with which it maintains a current account, and recourse to liquid funds of public agencies which are kept on deposit with the local banking system and abroad.

STRUCTURE OF THE GOVERNMENT BUDGET

Revenues

In 1969, government revenues amounted to roughly 11 per cent of

GDP. Actual receipts (direct taxes, taxes on imports and exports, and other revenues) and actual expenditures (ordinary and investment budget, together with earmarked finance) for 1960–69 are shown in Table 16. The following description of the structure of government revenues, however, is based on Table 17 which includes estimates of revenues and expenditures during 1966–70, because of the greater detail for revenues. Ordinary budget revenues consist mainly of indirect taxes, almost entirely taxes on imports and exports; in 1970 direct taxes account for only about 19 per cent of total revenues, and receipts from government properties and other receipts for about 13 per cent.

Besides customs duties on imports and exports, indirect taxes include a turnover tax, which applies only to sales of manufactured products (10 per cent) and services rendered (8 per cent). There is also a quarterly tax on vehicles, ranging from CFAF 125 for a bicycle to CFAF 18,000 for a bus. Import duties are levied without discrimination between countries or currency areas. They have yielded increasing revenues in recent years because of the expansion in volume and value of imports, while the rates have remained more or less unchanged. Actually, import duties are low compared with those in neighboring countries. Export duties yield a much smaller revenue than import duties; few exports are taxed and then generally at a lower rate than imports.

In addition to the normal import and export duties, there is a standard surtax on imports and a standard surtax on export transactions (*taxe forfaitaire représentative de la taxe sur les transactions d'importation et d'exportation*); these taxes are fixed at 18 per cent on imports and 6.5 per cent on exports. A number of other fees are collected on the goods at the time of entry or exit including a customs stamp duty, a statistical fee of 3 per cent on the proceeds of import and export taxes, an earmarked surtax levied for the benefit of the Road Fund (*taxes au profit du Fonds Routier*), and a surtax on alcoholic beverages.

Direct taxation in Togo has been modeled after the French system. The main direct taxes are the income tax, the progressive tax on all profits, a tax on wages paid by employers, a tax on rental values (*droit de patente et licence*), a land tax, and a capitation tax. Income tax is levied on industrial and commercial profits at 25 per cent for individu-

TABLE 16. TOGO: ACTUAL BUDGET RECEIPTS AND EXPENDITURES AND EARMARKED FINANCING, 1960–69 [1]

(In millions of CFA francs)

	1960	1961	1962	1963	1964	1965	1966	1967	1968	1969
Ordinary budget										
Revenue										
Direct taxes	186	...	...	...	...	402	496	601	603	740
Taxes on imports and exports	2,128	...	...	...	...	3,421	4,065	4,600	4,483	4,826
Other revenue	657	...	...	...	...	958	863	372	913	1,534
Total revenue	2,972	3,242	3,528	3,520	4,794	4,781	5,424	5,573	5,999	7,100
Expenditures										
General services	881	...	...	...	...	1,396	1,557	1,647	1,323	1,408
Defense	—	...	...	...	...	651	610	584	622	676
Economic services	498	...	...	...	...	811	791	605	957	1,055
Social services	800	...	...	...	...	1,106	1,212	1,269	1,422	1,540
Contributions and subsidies[2]	389	...	...	...	...	559	547	739	573	778
Debt service	68	...	...	...	...	114	122	252	514	400
Other	26	...	...	...	...	89	104	300	45	103
Total expenditures	2,662	2,964	3,546	3,924	4,855	4,726	4,944	5,396	5,456	5,960
Balance on ordinary budget	310	278	−18	−404	−61	54	480	177	543	1,140
Investment budget expenditure	520	176	197	217	217	608	1,254	1,081	116	530
Over-all balance on ordinary and investment budget	**−210**	**102**	**−215**	**−622**	**−278**	**−554**	**−774**	**−904**	**427**	**610**
Earmarked financing										
French subsidy	136	31	—	—	111	139	150	—	—	—
Borrowing from OPAT[3]	214	80	—	3	—	—	701	550	—	—
Borrowing from other sources[4]	144	130	13	90	—	—	50	18	12	12
Total earmarked financing	495	240	13	93	111	139	901	568	12	12
Other Treasury resources (deficit −)	285	342	−202	−529	−167	−414	127	−336	439	622

Source: Data provided by the Togolese authorities.

[1] On a calendar year basis; detailed breakdown on tax receipts for different categories is not available.
[2] Net of transfer to investment budgets of CFAF 609 million in 1967 and CFAF 420 million in 1968.
[3] Office of Agricultural Products (Office des Produits Agricoles du Togo).
[4] Including mainly CCCE.

TABLE 17. TOGO: BUDGET ESTIMATES OF RECEIPTS AND EXPENDITURES, 1966–70

(In millions of CFA francs)

	1966	1967	1968	1969	1970
Ordinary budget					
Receipts					
Direct taxes	434	500	603	714	1,499
Taxes on imports	3,035	3,232	3,125	3,310	4,075
Taxes on exports	713	719	700	650	825
Domestic indirect taxes	149	140	183	199	305
Other taxes	82	100	279	294	260
Total tax revenue	4,413	4,691	4,890	5,167	6,964
Income from public property and service fees	387	409	699	807	547
Miscellaneous receipts	167	174	482	559	469
Total receipts	4,967	5,274	6,071	6,533	7,980
Expenditures					
General services	1,164	1,306	1,318	1,404	1,701
Defense	693	620	622	676	809
Economic services	941	977	800	885	789
Social services	1,111	1,237	1,495	1,614	1,835
Public debt	181	316	514	452	627
Interventions, contributions, and subsidies [1]	924	864	902	1,067	1,439
Total expenditures	5,015	5,320	5,651	6,098	7,200
Wages and salaries	*3,267*	*3,376*	*3,388*	*3,613*	*4,211*
Materials	*639*	*762*	*742*	*856*	*1,118*
Other	*1,109*	*1,182*	*1,521*	*1,629*	*1,871*
Balance ordinary budget	−47	−46	420	435	780
Investment budget expenditures	812	569	432	450	795
Over-all balance	−859	−615	−12	−15	−15

Source: Data provided by the Togolese authorities.

[1] Net of transfer to the investment budget.

als and 37 per cent for companies. The rate of tax on other profits is 25 per cent. A general tax on wages and salaries is levied at the source on employees' earnings in excess of CFAF 8,000 a month; the rate ranges between 2 and 45 per cent. In addition, there is a surtax on wages and salaries, originally fixed at 1 per cent and increased to 3 per cent in 1966 and to 4 per cent in 1969; the surtax applies to total wage bills of the employers. The tax on rental values, imposed on all commercial and industrial enterprises, consists partly of a fixed amount and partly of a proportion (10 per cent) of the rental value. The land tax is applied only in certain urban areas; its rate ranges between 10 and 20 per cent, and the proceeds accrue to local authorities. A capitation tax on men, amounting to about CFAF 1,200 a year, also accrues to local authorities.

Before Togo became independent, it relied heavily on French aid for ordinary budget support. This aid was gradually reduced after 1960 and was discontinued altogether in 1966.

Expenditures

Actual expenditures in the ordinary budget rose by 124 per cent during 1960–69. Rapid growth in government expenditures reflected the expansion in the social sector and in government functions after independence. The outlay for general services, the major item in the ordinary budget, almost doubled during 1960–67; however, its share of total actual expenditures declined from 33 per cent to 24 per cent between 1960 and 1969. Expenditure on social services (i.e., health, education, and welfare) went up more than 90 per cent, but its share of the total decreased from 30 per cent in 1960 to 27 per cent in 1969. Other items of expenditure, in order of their importance in 1969, were economic services, contributions and subsidies, defense, and service on the public debt; the last item was less than 8 per cent of the total in 1969.

When government ordinary expenditures are divided into wages and salaries, materials, and other expenses, the first category accounted for well over half of the estimates for 1969–70 (see Table 17). The number of employees paid by the central government budget rose from 4,956 in 1960 to 7,700 in 1966, including the military. A recent study by the Togolese statistical service estimates the average net monthly salary at CFAF 36,000 (about $146) for a high-grade civil servant and at CFAF 13,500 for the lower levels. These estimates indicate that wages in the public sector in Togo are considerably below those in other UMOA countries.

Expenditures in the investment budget include direct investment, subsidies, and participations. Actual outlays dropped by about one third from CFAF 520 million in 1960 to CFAF 176 million in 1961, remained fairly low through 1964, and rose to a peak of CFAF 1,254 million in 1966 (see Table 16). The high level of investment expenditure in 1960 reflected mainly the government contribution to the construction cost of the Hotel du Bénin (CFAF 300 million). The Government's acquisition of the hitherto private electricity company (CFAF 275 million) was mainly responsible for the increase in investment budget expenditure to CFAF 608 million in 1965. In 1966, the first year of the plan, these expenditures reached CFAF 1,254 million because they included the Government's participation of CFAF 576 million in the capital of the Mining Company (Compagnie Togolaise de Mines du Bénin). Outlays for administrative construction and economic infrastructure also increased in 1966. Since 1966, however, the investment expenditures have tended to decrease, reflecting the cut in investments for the railway and for participation, in the light of the completion of major industrial and infrastructure projects.

FINANCING BUDGET DEFICITS, 1960–69

During 1960–69 the combined ordinary and investment budget was in deficit except for 1961, 1968, and 1969 (see Table 16). Mounting over-all deficits of CFAF 774 million in 1966 and CFAF 904 million in 1967 reflected active government participation in mixed enterprises. In most recent years, however, the ordinary budget yielded a surplus to help finance the investment budget. During 1960–63, ordinary expenditures outpaced revenues in growth, leaving the ordinary budget with a deficit of CFAF 404 million in 1963. In the following year the deficit was reduced substantially; thereafter the ordinary budget has been constantly in surplus, reaching CFAF 1,140 million in 1969.

Most of the cumulative deficit in the over-all budget was financed through loans from the Office of Agricultural Products, French subsidies, and Treasury resources (see Table 16). In 1960 and 1966, earmarked funds exceeded the over-all deficit, the difference being added to the Treasury resources. The Office was the major source of financing, with loans totaling CFAF 1.5 billion, used exclusively to finance government participation in the capital of public and semipublic enterprises. Subsidies from France for the ordinary and capital budgets amounted to CFAF 567 million in 1960–66 but were terminated in 1966. Borrowing from other sources totaled CFAF 469 million; CCCE was the major creditor (see "Treasury operations, 1964–69," below).

ANNEXED BUDGETS, 1964–69

In addition to executing the central government budget, the Treasury administers the accounts of the annexed budgets. Before 1967, the financial operations of several public enterprises were annexed to the Government's ordinary budget. Since 1967, only the operations of the National Railway Company are annexed to the Government's budget as the other public enterprises have become autonomous agencies. As shown in Table 18, except for 1966, the operations of the annexed budgets have resulted in small surpluses averaging CFAF 27 million a year. In 1966, the deficit was CFAF 23 million and resulted from the operations of the State Pharmacy (Togopharma).

TREASURY OPERATIONS, 1964–69

A net deficit resulted from the combined operations of the central government and annexed budgets from 1964 until 1967 (Table 19). This deficit reached a maximum of CFAF 892 million in 1967. In the subsequent two years there was a surplus, amounting to CFAF 819 million in 1968 and to CFAF 617 million in 1969. In 1967, earmarked funds exceeded the over-all deficit, and the net Treasury operations showed a surplus.

Table 20, based on data supplied by the Treasury, summarizes its financial position for 1964–69. These data include, in addition to the Treasury's transactions with the Central Government, already discussed, balances with various independent public agencies and with the private sector.

In the Treasury's liquid assets, the major component is its savings deposits with BCEAO. After a slight decline in 1965, these deposits increased sharply to CFAF 2.3 billion at the end of October 1969 (Table 20). Until 1967 this increase reflected the substantial rise in the public agencies' deposits with the Treasury, especially the pension fund, the City of Lomé, and the Post Office; thereafter it reflects the surpluses realized on the Government's budgetary operations. Other Treasury deposits include a small demand deposit with BCEAO, working balances at the local agencies, and a small balance at embassies abroad. In addition, the Treasury holds an average of CFAF 460 million worth of customs duty bills, as a form of credit granted to the private sector.

Under liabilities, the deposit of the Office of Agricultural Products is the most important source of Treasury working funds. During 1964–69 the Office maintained a balance averaging CFAF 1.6 billion at the Treasury. Other depositors among the public entities include the Post

TABLE 18. TOGO: ACTUAL RECEIPTS AND EXPENDITURES OF ANNEXED BUDGETS, 1964–69

(In millions of CFA francs)

	1964		1965		1966		1967		1968		1969	
	Debit	Credit	Debit	Credit	Debit	Credit	Debit	Credit	Debit	Credit	Debit	Credit
Annexed budgets												
National Railway Company	586	621	550	550	543	567	511	523	452	520	367	374
National Water Authority[1]	35	30	45	40	—	—						
State Pharmacy[2]	119	100	148	191	393	346						
Total annexed budgets	740	751	743	781	936	913	511	523	452	520	367	374
Surplus or deficit (credit)	11	—	38	—	—	23	12	—	68	—	7	—

Source: Data provided by the Togolese authorities.

[1] Since 1966 the National Water Authority has become an autonomous agency.
[2] Since 1967 the State Pharmacy has become an autonomous agency.

TABLE 19. TOGO: FINANCING OF TRANSACTIONS OF THE
CENTRAL GOVERNMENT, 1964–69

(In millions of CFA francs)

	1964	1965	1966	1967	1968	1969
Surplus, or deficit (−), of the Central Government						
Ordinary and investment budget [1]	−278	−554	−774	−904	427	610
Annexed budgets [2]	11	38	−23	12	68	7
Total surplus, or deficit (−)	**−267**	**−516**	**−797**	**−892**	**819**	**617**
Financed by						
Earmarked funds for the ordinary and investment budget [1]	111	139	901	568	12	12
Net Treasury operations	−156	−377	104	−324	831	629

Source: Data provided by the Togolese authorities.

[1] From Table 16.
[2] From Table 18.

Office, local authorities, and the Social Security Fund. The deposits of these entities have increased in recent years, raising total public sector deposits from CFAF‘2.6 billion at the end of 1964 to CFAF 3.4 billion at the end of October 1969.

THE 1970 BUDGET

For 1970, current revenues are slated at nearly CFAF 8.0 billion, or 22 per cent above the 1969 budget estimates, and current expenditures at CFAF 7.2 billion, or 18 per cent above the budget estimates for 1969 (see Table 17). The resulting current surplus is CFAF 780 million, which is CFAF 345 million more than the budgeted 1969 surplus. In keeping with the practice introduced in 1968 of limiting appropriations under the investment budget to the surplus generated on the current budget and other minor capital receipts, investment expenditures are budgeted at CFAF 795 million, leaving the over-all budget virtually in balance.

Compared with the 1969 budget estimates, the CFAF 1,447 million increase in current receipts in 1970 will occur mainly under receipts from direct taxes following new tax measures. The most important of

TABLE 20. TOGO: ASSETS AND LIABILITIES OF THE TREASURY, 1964–69

(*In millions of CFA francs; end of period*)

	1964	1965	1966	1967	1968	1969 [1]
Assets						
Liquid assets						
Cash	22	36	27	37	59	77
Demand deposits at BCEAO	44	44	70	117	10	3
Savings deposits at BCEAO	1,575	1,300	1,435	2,040	2,075	2,320
Deposits at Postal Checking System	24	47	105	69	301	547
Deposits at local agents	232	352	283	263	320	299
Deposits at embassies abroad	52	104	183	85	123	230
Short-term credit to private sector	468	444	515	460	359	523
Assets = liabilities	**2,416**	**2,327**	**2,618**	**3,071**	**3,247**	**3,999**
Liabilities						
Deposits						
Public sector deposits						
Local authorities	141	158	74	101	211	222
OPAT [2]	1,548	1,648	1,603	1,434	1,685	1,685
Post Office	121	86	90	289	470	720
Other	537	537	646	1,228	837	804
Total public sector deposits	2,347	2,429	2,413	3,052	3,203	3,431
Private sector deposits	126	72	75	7	—	—
Earmarked foreign aid funds and international organizations	90	−14	42	−28	—	—
Total deposits	2,563	2,487	2,530	3,031	3,203	3,431
Other items (net)	147	−160	88	40	44	568

Source: Data provided by the Togolese authorities.

[1] As of October 31, 1969.

[2] Office of Agricultural Products (Office des Produits Agricoles du Togo).

these measures is the decision of the Government to subject the Office of Agricultural Products to the payment of the corporate profit tax from which it was previously exempted, yielding the Government about CFAF 600 million in 1970. Some income tax rates were also raised and are expected to produce additional revenues of CFAF 120 million. The Government also announced increases in some export taxes: on coffee from 12 per cent to 20 per cent, on cocoa from 7.5 per cent to 10 per cent, on copra from 2 per cent to 4 per cent, and on palm kernels from 4 per cent to 6 per cent. These measures, plus the anticipated growth in exports, are to increase revenues from export taxes by about 27 per cent over the 1969 estimates. Receipts from import taxes are budgeted at CFAF 765 million above the level of the 1969 estimates on account of an anticipated rise in imports.

On the expenditure side, the budget reflects the impact of the 1969 decision to unblock the government salaries, the devaluation of the CFA franc, and the revaluation of the deutsche mark. Over two thirds of the growth in current expenditures will come from a 17 per cent increase in outlays for wages and salaries, most of which results from the increase in the salaries of government employees; the remainder comes from the creation of new administrative services. Outlays on materials and supplies are estimated to increase by about CFAF 262 million over the 1969 budget estimates. Public debt charges will rise by CFAF 175 million, mainly because of the commencement of servicing on loans from the Office of Agricultural Products during 1966–67.

The 1970 budget is the first budget after the devaluation of the CFA franc and includes the effects of this measure on government revenues and expenditures. It is estimated that the devaluation will have a net beneficial effect of approximately CFAF 250 million on the fiscal position of the Government: revenues, mostly from import duties, will increase by some CFAF 350 million; and expenditures, mostly on purchases of imported materials and supplies, contributions to international organizations, and servicing of external debt, will rise by about CFAF 100 million.

REGIONAL AUTHORITIES' BUDGETS

The budgets of the regional authorities follow the "exercise" system. These are shown in Table 21 for 1963–69. Total receipts and expenditures recorded for such budgets, estimated at CFAF 630 million in "exercise" 1969, equaled about 10 per cent of total estimated budget expenditures of the Central Government in the same year.

While expenditures of the regions rose by 43 per cent during 1963–69, those of the municipalities doubled, reaching CFAF 305 million in 1969. The budget of the municipality of Lomé, the largest among the local budgets, accounted for some 70 per cent of over-all municipalities' expenditure. Construction of a market hall in Lomé was chiefly responsible for the rapid increase in expenditures of the municipalities in recent years. In the aggregate, the operations of the regional authorities' budgets have shown a slight surplus since 1963, averaging CFAF 45 million a year.

TABLE 21. TOGO: BUDGET RECEIPTS AND EXPENDITURE OF THE
REGIONAL AUTHORITIES AND MUNICIPALITIES, 1963–69

(*In millions of CFA francs*)

	Actual						Estimates
	1963	1964	1965	1966	1967	1968	1969
"Exercise" data							
Receipts							
Municipalities	173	198	200	261	255	219	305
Regions	244	248	245	249	255	283	325
Total receipts	417	446	445	510	510	502	630
Expenditures							
Municipalities	154	167	175	219	222	191	305
Regions	227	232	230	238	243	263	325
Total expenditures	381	399	405	457	465	454	630
Surplus, or deficit (−), by "exercise"	36	47	40	53	45	48	—

Source: Data provided by the Togolese authorities.

PUBLIC ENTERPRISES' BUDGETS

In addition to the National Railway Company administered through an annexed budget, 18 other public enterprises have autonomous budgets. The most important one in this category is the Office of Agricultural Products. This agency's annual turnover fluctuates widely depending on crops and world market prices (see "Marketing of agricultural products," above). Its net income is of a parafiscal nature because most of the cost of produce sold is annually determined by government decree while sales are made at world market prices. Its operations have always yielded considerable net profits, amounting to about CFAF 1.1 billion in 1968/69, against CFAF 0.2 billion in 1964/65 (see Table 6). In recent years, the Office has maintained a balance of about CFAF 1.6 billion with the Treasury (see Table 20) and about an equal amount with the commercial banks.

The Social Security Fund (Caisse de Compensation des Prestations Familiales et des Accidents du Travail) has a total income of about CFAF 300 million a year; deficits in family allowances were more than offset by the surplus of the labor accidents division of the fund. The State Export-Import Company (Société Togolaise d'Exportation et d'Importation, or SOTEXIM) was created in 1962 to supply basic consumer goods and equipment in remote rural areas; in recent years, however, it has extended its activities to the urban areas and to the sale of luxury items. The company has permanent resources of CFAF 196 million, including a capital of CFAF 45 million and a permanent loan from the Government of CFAF 50 million. Although its total sales have risen rapidly in recent years to a level of about CFAF 800 million, its losses have increased. Other public enterprises with financial autonomy include the National Electric Power Company (Compagnie de l'Energie Electrique du Togo), discussed elsewhere (see "Power," above), and a number of smaller enterprises. Most of these enterprises have received financial assistance from the Central Government.

PUBLIC DEBT

As of December 31, 1969, Togo's total outstanding public debt, including the undisbursed portion of aid committed, amounted to CFAF 10.5 billion at the new exchange rate following the devaluation of the CFA franc in August 1969, of which 85 per cent represented debts repayable in foreign currencies (Table 22). In 1969, debt-service payments totaled CFAF 400 million, or about 6 per cent of the Government's current receipts, and are estimated to reach CFAF 590 million by 1971.

Internal public debt outstanding at the end of 1969 amounted to CFAF 1.6 billion, which is owed entirely to the Office of Agricultural Products. In 1969, payments of these debts totaled CFAF 125 million and will increase to CFAF 227 million in 1970; they are estimated to decline thereafter.

External public debt outstanding at the end of 1969 amounted to CFAF 8.9 billion. The largest amount (70 per cent) was owed to the Federal Republic of Germany, most of it representing two loans extended by the Kreditanstalt für Wiederaufbau. The second largest creditor was France, which accounted for 14 per cent of the total outstanding foreign debt. Canada extended a loan of CFAF 720 million in 1969 in connection with the supply of electricity from Ghana, but this loan is as yet undisbursed. Outstanding suppliers' credit, originating mainly from the Netherlands, amounted to CFAF 151 million. Annual external debt-service payments (which amounted to CFAF 275 million in 1969, or less than 3 per cent of the 1969 estimated receipts from

TABLE 22. TOGO: PUBLIC DEBT ON DECEMBER 31, 1969 AND ESTIMATED DEBT SERVICE, 1969–72

(*In millions of CFA francs*)

	Initial Amount	Outstanding on December 31, 1969	Service Payments												
			1969			1970			1971			1972		
			Interest payments	Amortization	Total	Interest payments	Amortization	Total	Interest payments	Amortization	Total	Interest payments	Amortization	Total
Internal (OPAT)[1]	2,161	1,599	22	103	125	39	188	227	33	154	187	30	167	197
External[2]														
Loans from Governments														
France	1,494	1,263	16	48	64	16	47	63	14	48	62	14	49	63
Federal Republic of Germany	6,258	6,258	92	—	92	—	119	119	125	111	236	95	132	227
Yugoslavia	390	207	7	52	59	6	71	77	4	59	63	5	63	68
Canada	720	—	—	—	—	—	—	—	—	—	—	—	—	—
Total loans from Governments	8,862	7,728	115	100	215	22	237	259	143	218	364	114	244	358
Loans from IDA	1,029	1,029	—	—	—	—	—	—	—	—	—	—	—	—
Privately held debt	394	173	9	51	60	10	42	52	6	36	42	6	29	35
Suppliers' credit	*324*	*151*	*8*	*49*	*57*	*9*	*40*	*49*	*5*	*34*	*39*	*5*	*27*	*32*
Total external	10,285	8,930	124	151	275	32	279	311	149	254	403	120	273	393
Total public debt	12,446	10,529	146	254	400	71	467	538	182	408	590	150	440	590

Source: Data provided by the Togolese authorities.

[1] Including small debts owed to the former Cocoa Price Stabilization Fund.
[2] Repayable in foreign currencies and adjusted for the devaluation of the CFA franc in August 1969 and the revaluation of the deutsche mark in October 1969. Includes the undisbursed portion of the committed aid.

recorded exports) were to rise by about CFAF 100 million in the subsequent three years.

MONEY AND BANKING

MONETARY SYSTEM

Togo belongs to the franc area. With Dahomey, Ivory Coast, Mauritania, Niger, Senegal, and Upper Volta it is also a member of the West African Monetary Union (Union Monétaire Ouest Africaine, or UMOA). These countries share a common currency, the CFA franc, and a common central bank, the Banque Centrale des Etats de l'Afrique de l'Ouest (BCEAO), which is the issuing authority of UMOA and keeps its reserves. The CFA franc is freely convertible into French francs at the rate of CFAF 1 = F 0.02. On August 10, 1969 the rate against the U.S. dollar became CFAF 277.710 per dollar; previously, since January 1, 1960, the rate had been CFAF 246.853. (For details on the operations of BCEAO, see Chapter 4, and for information on the change in par value, see Chapter 6.)

STRUCTURE OF THE BANKING SYSTEM

The banking system of Togo includes the Central Bank (BCEAO), which it shares with the other UMOA members; three commercial banks; and the Development Bank (Banque Togolaise de Développement, or BTD). BCEAO operates in Togo, as in the other UMOA countries, through a local agency. Decisions concerning the implementation of BCEAO policies in Togo are taken by the National Monetary Committee. The Director of the local BCEAO agency, who serves on the National Monetary Committee in an advisory capacity, is responsible for the application of these policies. The Central Bank's assets and liabilities in Togo are shown in Table 23.

The Treasury of Togo also performs certain banking operations. It accepts customs duty bills (*obligations cautionnées*) with a maturity of four months in payment of taxes and duties levied on imports, principally customs duties. These bills are discountable at BCEAO. The Treasury also receives deposits from certain public agencies and makes advances to them.

TABLE 23. TOGO: ASSETS AND LIABILITIES OF THE CENTRAL BANK, 1962–69
(In millions of CFA francs; end of period)

	1962	1963	1964	1965	1966	1967		1968				1969		
						Sept.	Dec.	Mar.	June	Sept.	Dec.	Mar.	June	Sept.
Assets														
Foreign assets														
Foreign exchange	705	...	992	2,743	2,869	2,808	3,190	4,042	3,718	3,437	3,950	4,242	4,154	3,983
Treasury investment account	1,262	...	1,575	1,300	1,435	2,300	2,040	1,650	2,000	1,950	2,075	1,940	1,930	2,100
IMF	278	...	278	278	278	278	278	278	278	278	278	278	278	278
Total foreign assets	2,245	2,226	2,845	4,320	4,582	5,386	5,508	5,970	5,996	5,665	6,303	6,460	6,362	6,361
Claims on banks (rediscounts)														
Short-term	792	974	1,016	25	—	—	—	—	—	—	—	—	—	—
Medium-term	500	430	330	49	77	91	71	94	68	45	—	58	—	—
Total claims on banks	1,292	1,404	1,346	74	77	91	71	94	68	45	—	58	—	—
Claims on Government														
Rediscount of customs duty bills	—	—	—	—	—	—	—	—	—	—	—	—	—	—
Advances	—	—	6	—	—	—	—	—	—	—	—	—	—	—
Postal checking deposits	1	3		1	—	—	8	—	—	—	—	—	—	—
Total claims on Government	1	3	6	1	—	—	8	—	—	—	—	—	—	—
Assets = liabilities	3,538	3,630	4,197	4,395	4,659	5,477	5,587	6,064	6,064	5,710	6,303	6,518	6,362	6,361
Liabilities														
Currency and bankers' deposits	2,273	2,361	2,477	2,912	3,011	3,024	3,262	4,092	3,767	3,565	3,899	4,245	4,036	4,031
Currency outside banks	*2,254*	*2,325*	*2,433*	*2,798*	*2,877*	*2,962*	*3,174*	*3,971*	*3,619*	*3,449*	*3,765*	*4,126*	*3,920*	*3,935*
Government deposits														
Treasury deposits	40	51	35	44	78	20	98	29	35	19	57	15	55	29
Treasury investment account	1,262	1,393	1,575	1,300	1,435	2,300	2,040	1,650	2,000	1,950	2,075	1,940	1,930	2,100
Currency held by Treasury	117	101	96	134	127	130	143	236	204	154	187	308	264	163
Total government deposits	1,419	1,545	1,706	1,478	1,640	2,450	2,281	1,915	2,239	2,122	2,318	2,262	2,248	2,291
Foreign liabilities	125	5	14	5	7	3	44	57	58	20	86	10	74	39
Other items	−280	−281	—											

Sources: BCEAO, *Notes d'Information et Statistiques*; IMF, *International Financial Statistics* (monthly); and data supplied by the Togolese authorities.

Besides the credit extended by banks, the Caisse Centrale de Coopération Economique (CCCE), a French public institution, extends
medium-term and long-term credit and contributes to the financing of
the Development Bank's credit operation. In addition, it acts as the
authorized agent of the Fonds d'Aide et de Coopération (FAC) and
the European Development Fund (EDF) for local aid disbursements.

BANKING LEGISLATION

Until 1965, banks in Togo were basically governed by French banking laws, which, under a decree of 1955, were made applicable also to
the French overseas territories. These laws remained in force after
Togo's independence with modifications of only a few provisions incom-
patible with the country's new status. Interest rates and certain other
banking operations, though not covered by these laws, continued to be
governed by an agreement concluded in 1959 among the commercial
banks operating in former French West Africa. Since 1965, operations
of banks in Togo are governed by the Banking and Credit Law,
enacted on July 21, 1965, which applies to all banks and other financial institutions with the exception of BCEAO, National Savings Bank
(Caisse Nationale d'Epargne, or CNE), CCCE, notaries, and insurance
companies. Implementation of the general provisions of this law are
governed by a series of decrees drawn up during 1965. Togo's Banking
Law of 1965 is the result of a joint decision, taken by the UMOA
countries in May 1962, which calls for the application of uniform basic
principles regulating the banking profession and the control of credit.

According to the new regulations, banks must permanently maintain
a minimum liquidity ratio between certain assets and liabilities. The
minimum liquidity ratio is derived by relating cash and negotiable
assets of banks (consisting largely of rediscounted assets and credit eligible for rediscounting) to their short-term liabilities, including
BCEAO's rediscounts. Starting at 70 per cent, this ratio is to be raised
by 1 percentage point a year for a period of five years, after which a
ratio of 75 per cent must be maintained. For the 1969/70 "exercise,"
the ratio was 74 per cent.

The new banking and credit legislation also provides for a schedule
of interest rates to be applied by the deposit money banks. Before the
new regulations, the deposit money banks charged virtually uniform

interest rates, graduated according to the customer's creditworthiness. As a result, small customers were usually charged fairly high interest rates. The new interest rate schedule is not based on creditworthiness alone as a criterion, but is designed to favor the financing of operations which aid the country's economic development and to penalize credit for nonproductive purposes. This approach is in line with the BCEAO policy, which determines the eligibility of a customer for rediscounting on the basis of his use of credit for productive purposes, and hence reinforces the effectiveness of rediscounting as a tool of monetary policy. Under the new regulation, the interest rate for short-term credit ranges from 4.5 per cent on rediscountable credit for certain types of productive enterprises to 9 per cent on nonrediscountable credit. For medium-term credit, the rates range from 5.25 per cent to 8.50 per cent. Deposit rates are 0–2.5 per cent on demand deposits and up to 4.5 per cent for time deposits.

A third set of regulations under the new law concerns the observance of certain solvency requirements by banks: each bank must have a minimum statutory capital of CFAF 50 million. Moreover, all commercial banks must maintain a minimum solvency ratio of 8 per cent between shareholders' equity and credit commitments; for development banks, the ratio is 12 per cent.

OPERATIONS OF THE COMMERCIAL BANKS AND THE DEVELOPMENT BANK

The three commercial banks operating in Togo are the Banque Internationale pour l'Afrique Occidentale (BIAO), the Banque Nationale de Paris (BNP), and the Union Togolaise de Banque (UTB). The first bank, which has French and U.S. shareholders, and the French bank operate in several other UMOA countries. The third bank, the only Togolese bank, has a capital of CFAF 100 million; 35 per cent was subscribed by the Togolese Government and the remainder by French, German, and Italian commercial banks.

Operations of the commercial banks and the Togolese Development Bank, during 1962–69 are presented in Table 24. After an increase to CFAF 3.9 billion in 1964, bank credit to the private sector declined sharply in 1965. This reduction, mainly in short-term credit, was due to the extremely poor coffee crop and less financing required for coffee

TABLE 24. TOGO: ASSETS AND LIABILITIES OF COMMERCIAL BANKS, THE DEVELOPMENT BANK, AND THE POSTAL CHECKING SYSTEM, 1962–69

(In millions of CFA francs; end of period)

	1962	1963	1964	1965	1966	1967		1968				1969		
						Sept.	Dec.	Mar.	June	Sept.	Dec.	Mar.	June	Sept.
COMMERCIAL BANKS AND DEVELOPMENT BANK														
Assets														
Cash and balances with														
Central Bank	33	33	60	128	88	79	81	68	128	111	112	76	81	77
Foreign assets	−508¹	64	574	1,108	1,614	1,630	1,478	1,576	2,240	2,178	1,577	2,681	3,927	3,977
Claims on private sector														
Short-term	...	2,599	2,911	1,933	2,205	1,998	2,694	3,456	2,531	3,075	4,347	4,484	3,920	3,766
Medium-term	...	582	468	166	272	311	359	287	413	215	306	327	392	429
Long-term	...	426	558	603	691	805	804	827	816	1,005	955	989	1,012	1,010
Total claims on private sector	3,201	3,607	3,937	2,702	3,168	3,114	3,857	4,570	3,760	4,295	5,608	5,800	5,324	5,205
Assets = liabilities	**2,726**	**3,704**	**4,571**	**3,938**	**4,870**	**4,823**	**5,416**	**6,214**	**6,128**	**6,584**	**7,297**	**8,557**	**9,332**	**9,259**
Liabilities														
Demand deposits	1,248	1,369	1,854	2,256	2,693	2,850	3,291	3,950	3,567	4,087	3,639	4,248	5,254	4,731
Time deposits	47	96	114	169	152	252	299	270	279	287	1,014	1,160	1,492	1,723
Foreign liabilities	—	795	958	1,190	1,460	949	1,105	1,160	1,172	1,267	1,549	1,468	1,482	1,667
Credit from Central Bank	1,292	1,404	1,346	74	77	90	71	94	68	45	—	58	—	—
Other items (net)	137	40	298	247	488	681	650	741	1,041	899	1,095	1,622	1,105	1,138
POSTAL CHECKING SYSTEM														
Deposits²	110	112	142	161	166	173	213	209	210	202	145	240	229	231

Sources: IMF, *International Financial Statistics* (monthly), and data provided by BCEAO.

¹ Before September 1963 separate figures for foreign liabilities were not available.
² These deposits are included with "Money" in Table 27.

stocks. In 1966, as the amount of marketed coffee recovered, bank credit rose but only by 17 per cent, influenced somewhat by a small reduction of coffee producers' price; on the other hand, the decrease in both marketed cocoa and cocoa producers' price in 1966 also lessened the credit demand. Bank credit to the private sector continued upward during 1967 but did not surpass the 1964 level; however, by the end of September 1968, it had reached CFAF 4.3 billion and by the end of September 1969, CFAF 5.2 billion. The rapid expansion of credit in 1968–69 was associated with the demand for financing a sharp increase in the cocoa producer price from CFAF 40 to CFAF 80 per kilogram and the rise in marketed coffee to 10,520 tons in 1967/68 and further to 17,210 tons in 1968/69. Other factors were the financing requirements of the regional development agencies (SORAD's) and large increases in imports.

Until 1965, slightly over one third of bank short-term credit was rediscounted with the BCEAO. Since then, this rediscounting has virtually disappeared. Reduction of BCEAO's short-term rediscounting resulted partly from a rise in demand deposits and partly from an increase in the use of banks' own resources. During September 1967-September 1969, demand deposits rose by 66 per cent to CFAF 4.7 billion. Until 1967 some banks increasingly employed locally raised funds in their own operations instead of investing them abroad. This development was achieved through moral suasion by the monetary authorities, as well as through compliance with the various regulations under the new Banking and Credit Law. By its provision on solvency, the Law led also to an augmentation of the commercial banks' capital. In 1968 and 1969, however, this trend was reversed owing mainly to the emergence of attractive investment conditions abroad. With rising liquidity of the banks, BCEAO's rediscount ceiling on short-term credit was repeatedly reduced and was finally eliminated for all banks in September 1967.

The Development Bank was established in July 1967, when the Crédit du Togo, a public credit institution, was transformed into a development bank. The new Development Bank assumed all the assets and liabilities of the Crédit du Togo, but the capital was raised to CFAF 300 million from CFAF 112.5 million. The Government holds a majority interest of 60 per cent in the capital of the Development

Bank, CCCE 20 per cent, BCEAO 10 per cent, and the Social Security Fund and commercial banks the remaining 10 per cent.

In addition to its capital and the government contributions to the bank's agricultural projects, the Development Bank resources include loans from CCCE and other domestic institutions, a credit line with BCEAO for rediscounting, and some deposits. The institution has relied mainly on CCCE loans to supplement its own resources. CCCE makes loans to the Development Bank in two forms: (1) global advances, which are extended to finance operations of a general character but are subject to CCCE's approval concerning each project to be financed, and (2) special advances, which are tied to specific projects. Global advances mature in ten years and carry an annual interest rate which was raised in 1966 from 2.5 per cent to 3.5 per cent. In February 1969, the Development Bank also obtained from the Office of Agricultural Products, an advance of CFAF 200 million, of which half would mature in five years and the other half in ten years.

The Development Bank has made little use of the existing rediscounting facilities of BCEAO. Apart from the relatively higher cost of BCEAO loans in the past (3.5 per cent against 2.5 per cent charged by CCCE) and their shorter maturity, credit from BCEAO has been limited mainly because of the high liquidity position of the Development Bank.

The purpose of the Development Bank is to use its resources to further any project designed to expand agriculture, handicrafts, commerce, and fishing, as well as to promote housing construction and to participate in the capital of private and public enterprises. In addition, the Bank also manages the portfolio of the Government's participation in the capital of several companies and advises the Government on investment problems.

Total credit of the Development Bank rose steadily from CFAF 0.7 billion at the end of 1963 to CFAF 1.4 billion in September 1969 (Table 25). The increase was almost entirely in long-term credit (mostly housing); its share in total credit extended by the Bank increased from 64 per cent in 1963 to 77 per cent in September 1969.

Although the Development Bank has extended the major part of its credit to finance real estate enterprises, it has progressively expanded its

TABLE 25. TOGO: CREDIT OPERATIONS OF THE DEVELOPMENT BANK,[1] 1963–69

(In millions of CFA francs; end of period)

	1963	1964	1965	1966	1967		1968				1969		
					Sept.	Dec.	Mar.	June	Sept.	Dec.	Mar.	June	Sept.
Credit by duration													
Short-term	86	70	88	77	84	86	127	106	121	115	113	108	140
Medium-term	157	138	114	166	158	167	141	133	136	162	165	169	184
Long-term	426	558	603	691	805	804	827	816	1,005	1,019	1,054	1,075	1,086
Total credit	**669**	**766**	**805**	**934**	**1,047**	**1,057**	**1,095**	**1,055**	**1,262**	**1,296**	**1,332**	**1,352**	**1,408**
Credit financing													
Demand deposits	36	24	41	101	43	34	29	24	223	6	6	6	7
Time deposits	24	16	12	2	3	—	1	1	1	2	2	2	30
Foreign assets (net)	509	569	591	683	771	759	759	743	743	815	815	842	842
Credit rediscounted with BCEAO[2]													
Short-term	35	29	25	—	—	1	—	—	—	—	—	—	—
Medium-term	5	—	8	4	3	2	45	—	45	—	22	—	—
Total rediscount	40	29	33	4	3	3	45	—	45	—	22	—	—
Government deposits (net)	2	1	—	—	10	10	10	10	7	—	112	78	78
Other items (net)	58	126	129	144	217	251	251	277	243	473	375	424	451

Source: Data provided by the BCEAO.

[1] Until 1967, Crédit du Togo.

[2] Rediscounts with BCEAO may differ from those shown in the statement of BCEAO's operations (Table 23) because the latter are based on BCEAO's balance sheets, while data shown here are based on the balance sheets of the Development Bank.

credit to established rural organizations, including farmers' cooperatives and rural development agencies. The Bank is expected to promote industrial projects and to expand its industrial credit operations, although the real estate sector will probably remain its main field of operations.

OPERATIONS OF OTHER FINANCIAL INSTITUTIONS

As a source of short-term credit to the private sector, the Treasury ranks after the commercial banks in Togo, accounting for 19 per cent of the total in September 1969 (Table 26). Private sector credit is extended by the Togolese Treasury through its acceptance of customs duty bills, which mature in four months and earn interest at a rate of 3 per cent a year. The low rate of interest (0.5 per cent below BCEAO's discount rate) largely explains the Treasury's outstanding credit to the private sector ranging between CFAF 363 million in 1963 and CFAF 499 million in 1966.

Through its many branches, the Postal Checking System acts as the main depository for the private sector in the interior of Togo. It also keeps its funds on deposit with the Treasury. Short-term deposit liabilities of the Postal Checking System to the private sector amounted to CFAF 231 million in September 1969 compared with deposit liabilities of CFAF 4,500 million for the commercial banks and CFAF 7 million for the Development Bank. The facilities of the Post Office are also used by the National Savings Bank, which has collected a steadily increasing amount of savings, from CFAF 212 million at the end of 1962 to CFAF 463 million in December 1967 and CFAF 611 million in September 1969. The bulk of the funds collected by the National Savings Bank is invested in France with the Caisse des Dépôts et de Consignations, earning annual interest at a current rate of 6.25 per cent.

Though its operations declined from CFAF 2.6 billion at the end of 1963 to CFAF 1.4 billion in September 1969, or by 46 per cent, the French CCCE continues to be the major lender of long-term credit to the private sector in Togo (see Table 26). CCCE is the major source of funds for the Togolese Development Bank, while it acts also as the local disbursement agent for aid from FAC and EEC.

TABLE 26. TOGO: CREDIT TO THE PRIVATE SECTOR, EXTENDED BY THE COMMERCIAL BANKS, THE DEVELOPMENT BANK, AND THE TREASURY, 1963–69

(In millions of CFA francs; end of period)

	1963	1964	1965	1966	1967		1968				1969		
					Sept.	Dec.	Mar.	June	Sept.	Dec.	Mar.	June	Sept.
Short-term credit extended													
By banks	2,599	2,911	1,933	2,205	1,998	2,694	3,456	2,531	3,075	4,347	4,484	3,920	3,766
By the Treasury	363	468	444	499	479	449	381	462	394	359	391	385	447
Total short-term	2,962	3,379	2,377	2,704	2,477	3,143	3,837	2,993	3,469	4,706	4,875	4,305	4,213
Medium-term and long-term credit extended													
By banks	1,008	1,026	769	963	1,136	1,181	1,096	1,089	1,279	1,261	1,316	1,404	1,439
By CCCE	2,567	2,462	2,359	1,778	1,778	1,778	1,708	1,630	1,630	1,421	1,421	1,421	1,421
Total medium-term and long-term	3,575	3,488	3,128	2,741	2,914	2,959	2,804	2,719	2,909	2,682	2,737	2,825	2,860
Total credit	6,537	6,867	5,505	5,445	5,391	6,102	6,641	5,712	6,378	7,388	7,612	7,130	7,073
Total credit excluding CCCE	3,970	4,405	3,146	3,667	3,613	4,324	4,933	4,082	4,748	5,967	6,191	5,709	5,652

Sources: BCEAO, *Notes d'Information et Statistiques*, and data provided by the Togolese authorities.

MONETARY DEVELOPMENTS

During 1962–67, money supply rose by 85 per cent to CFAF 6.7 billion (Table 27). The increase was almost entirely due to a rise in the country's net foreign assets position. At the end of 1967, foreign assets totaled CFAF 5.8 billion, compared with CFAF 1.9 billion in 1962 and CFAF 1.5 billion in 1963; that is, they tripled in five years. The increase occurred mainly in BCEAO's net foreign asset holdings, which rose by CFAF 3.3 billion, owing to rising export proceeds. The public sector, on the other hand, exercised a net deflationary effect throughout this period except in 1965 as the Government maintained a more and more important net creditor position vis-à-vis the banking system. Movements of domestic credit, capital, and unclassified items during this period also exerted a contractionary effect on money supply. The banking system's total domestic credit at the end of 1967 was CFAF 1.8 billion, against CFAF 1.9 billion in 1962 and CFAF 2.4 billion in 1964. The reduction over 1962–67 was due to the increase of CFAF 829 million in public sector's net credit position with the banking system; this increase more than offset the increase (CFAF 724 million) in bank credit to the private sector.

Money supply continued to expand during 1968, reaching CFAF 7.7 billion in September, against CFAF 6.0 billion in September 1967. This expansion reflects both the sharp increase in the banking system credit to the economy (CFAF 1.6 billion) and the rise in its foreign exchange reserves (CFAF 0.5 billion); quasi-money, though still a small amount, increased also from CFAF 96 million in 1963 to CFAF 287 million in September 1968, when it was equal to 4 per cent of money supply, compared with 3 per cent in 1963.

In 1969, money supply rose by 15 per cent to CFAF 8.9 billion at the end of September, reflecting the steep rise in net foreign assets (CFAF 2.2 billion) and a substantial increase in claims on private sector (CFAF 959 million). A large part of the increase in money supply occurred in demand deposits which as a percentage of money supply rose from 49 per cent in 1967 to 56 per cent in 1969. Quasi-money rose by CFAF 1.4 billion in response to higher interest rates on time deposits of public entities granted by banks in November 1968. In September 1969 total deposits of the public sector (including the Government) amounted to CFAF 3.1 billion, against CFAF 1.1 billion

TABLE 27. TOGO: MONETARY SURVEY, 1962–69

(*In millions of CFA francs; end of period*)

	1962	1963	1964	1965	1966	1967		1968				1969		
						Sept.	Dec.	Mar.	June	Sept.	Dec.	Mar.	June	Sept.
Assets														
Foreign assets (net)	1,890	1,490	2,447	4,233	4,729	6,064	5,837	6,329	7,006	6,556	6,246	7,664	8,734	8,723
Domestic credit														
Claims on Government (net)[1]	−1,698	−1,794	−2,030	−1,758	−1,997	−2,798	−2,527	−2,123	−2,509	−2,334	−2,642	−2,517	−2,479	−2,578
Claims on private sector	3,593	3,970	4,405	3,146	3,683	3,616	4,317	4,971	4,228	4,693	5,967	6,191	5,710	5,652
Total domestic credit	1,895	2,176	2,374	1,388	1,686	818	1,790	2,847	1,719	2,359	3,325	3,674	3,230	3,074
Assets = liabilities	**3,785**	**3,666**	**4,821**	**5,621**	**6,415**	**6,881**	**7,627**	**9,176**	**8,725**	**8,915**	**9,571**	**11,338**	**11,964**	**11,797**
Liabilities														
Money[2]	3,612	3,807	4,429	5,216	5,736	5,985	6,678	8,130	7,396	7,738	7,550	8,614	9,402	8,954
Quasi-money[3]	49	96	114	169	152	252	299	270	279	287	1,014	1,160	1,492	1,723
Other items (net)	124	−237	278	236	527	644	650	776	1,050	890	1,007	1,563	1,070	1,120

SOURCE: IMF, *International Financial Statistics* (monthly), and data supplied by the BCEAO.

[1] Represents the total of claims on Government by the Central Bank, the commercial banks, and the Development Bank, and of the counterpart of the Postal Checking System deposits *minus* the total of deposits by the Treasury with the Central Bank, the commercial banks, and the Development Bank.

[2] Includes currency in circulation, deposit money (sight deposits) with the commercial banks and the Development Bank, and Postal Checking System.

[3] Represents time and saving deposits with the commercial banks and the Development Bank, but excludes deposits with the Savings Bank.

in September 1966. Time deposits of the public sector amounted to CFAF 1.2 billion in September 1969, representing about a third of total public sector deposits. Other items (net) rose to CFAF 1.1 billion in September 1969 from CFAF 0.9 billion in September 1968.

FOREIGN TRADE, AID, AND PAYMENTS

FOREIGN TRADE

Value and Composition of Trade

The foreign trade accounts of Togo, based on customs data, have shown an annual deficit of about CFAF 2–3 billion in recorded trade for many years (Tables 28 and 29). In 1968 the deficit of recorded trade declined to about CFAF 2.0 billion because of substantially increased exports and somewhat lower imports. Besides the recorded trade, there is a fair amount of border trade, particularly with Ghana but also with Dahomey. The Togolese authorities and BCEAO have made the necessary adjustments in the customs data; the results are shown in the balance of payments below. According to the adjusted data, the trade deficit has significantly declined from CFAF 2.5 billion in 1965 to less than CFAF 0.9 billion in 1966. Togo's trade position moved into surplus in 1967–69; this surplus is estimated to have reached CFAF 1.1 billion in 1969.

Exports.—Recorded exports more than doubled in value between 1962 and 1968, partly on account of the exceedingly rapid expansion of phosphate exports, which contributed to 34 per cent of the total value in 1968 (see Table 28). With the expansion of the phosphate mine, the volume of phosphate exports rose from 57,000 tons in 1961 to 1.3 million tons in 1968 (see Table 7). Coffee and cocoa are the leading agricultural export crops. Exports of coffee reached their peak value in 1964; their value has fluctuated widely from year to year because of variations in the volume of the crop, as well as in the price of coffee. The value of cocoa exports grew steadily between 1962 and 1967, reflecting a favorable combination of volume and world market prices. In 1968, coffee and cocoa together represented 43 per cent of the value of recorded exports. Other exports in 1968 included palm

TABLE 28. TOGO: RECORDED EXPORTS, 1962–69 [1]

(Customs data)

	1962	1963	1964	1965	1966	1967	1968	1969 [1]
	VALUE F.O.B. (billion CFA francs)							
Coffee	1.43	0.80	2.53	1.37	1.95	0.84	1.60	1.30
Cocoa	1.18	1.18	1.63	1.69	1.69	2.35	2.31	2.93
Phosphates	0.49	1.07	1.95	2.15	3.77	3.03	3.23	3.03
Palm products	0.30	0.40	0.45	0.58	0.54	0.43	0.57	0.40
Cotton (fiber and seed)	0.27	0.39	0.18	0.29	0.28	0.36	0.38	0.01
Cassava products	0.12	0.17	0.16	0.12	0.03	0.07	0.11	0.06
Groundnuts (shelled)	0.08	0.12	0.11	0.08	0.13	0.14	0.16	0.18
Copra	0.07	0.12	0.15	0.05	0.04	0.03	0.02	0.02
Other	0.30	0.26	0.29	0.35	0.44	0.64	1.17	1.25
Total	4.24	4.51	7.45	6.68	8.87	7.89	9.55	9.18
	PER CENT OF TOTAL							
Coffee	34	18	34	20	22	11	17	14
Cocoa	28	26	22	25	19	30	26	32
Phosphates	12	24	26	32	43	38	34	33
Palm products	7	9	6	9	6	5	4	4
Cotton (fiber and seed)	6	8	2	5	3	5	4	—
Cassava products	3	3	2	2	—	1	1	1
Groundnuts (shelled)	2	3	2	1	1	2	2	2
Copra	2	3						
Other	7	7	4	5	5	8	12	14
Total	100	100	100	100	100	100	100	100

Sources: Ministère des Finances, de l'Economie et du Plan, *Inventaire Economique du Togo* and *Bulletin Mensuel Statistique*; and data supplied by the Togolese authorities.

[1] Ten months only.

TABLE 29. TOGO: RECORDED IMPORTS BY MAJOR CATEGORIES, 1962–69

(Customs data)

	1962	1963	1964	1965	1966	1967	1968	1969 [1]
	VALUE C.I.F. (million CFA francs)							
Consumer goods								
Foodstuffs, beverages, and tobacco	1,869	1,743	2,232	1,920	2,645	2,538	2,189	2,577
Manufactured goods	2,263	2,499	3,882	3,765	4,261	4,327	4,562	4,315
Total consumer goods	4,132	4,242	6,114	5,685	6,906	6,865	6,751	6,892
Raw materials and intermediate products	965	1,056	1,313	1,649	1,866	1,778	1,988	2,091
Energy	418	428	463	389	483	505	536	627
Capital goods	1,210	1,440	2,397	3,376	2,413	1,985	2,348	2,449
Total	6,724	7,167	10,286	11,100	11,668	11,133	11,623	11,929
	PER CENT OF TOTAL							
Consumer goods								
Foodstuffs, beverages, and tobacco	28	24	22	17	23	23	19	22
Manufactured goods	34	35	38	34	37	39	40	36
Total consumer goods	61	59	59	51	59	62	59	58
Raw materials and intermediate products	14	15	13	15	16	16	17	18
Energy	6	6	5	4	4	4	4	4
Capital goods	18	20	23	30	21	18	20	20
Total	100	100	100	100	100	100	100	100

Sources: Haut Commissariat au Plan, *Comptes Nationaux du Togo, Année 1964,* and *Bulletin Mensuel de Statistique.*
[1] Provisional; 10 months only; does not add to all totals.

products (6 per cent of the total export value), cotton fiber and seed (4 per cent), and shelled groundnuts (2 per cent).

During the first ten months of 1969, Togo's export performance continued to be satisfactory. Total recorded exports reached CFAF 9.2 billion and the average monthly exports were some CFAF 100 million higher than in 1968.

Imports.—During 1962–65, recorded imports rapidly increased from CFAF 6.7 billion to CFAF 11.1 billion (see Table 29); thereafter they advanced at a slower rate and amounted to CFAF 11.6 billion in 1968. The shift to a higher level of imports after 1963 is explained primarily by the higher level of investment and the increasing proceeds from exports beginning in that year. The composition of imports fails to indicate a clear trend over the period 1962–68.

Imports of foodstuffs, beverages, and tobacco fluctuated around 20 per cent of total imports. The rapid rise in imports of capital goods until the end of 1965 reflected increasing investments up to this year; but thereafter these imports declined to a level of about 20 per cent of total imports. The share of raw materials and intermediate products rose from 14 per cent to 18 per cent of total imports in this period; the share of manufactured consumer goods in general showed an upward movement. Energy requirements were roughly constant in absolute amounts, and, consequently, diminished slightly in relative terms.

During the first ten months of 1969, Togo's imports continued to rise. The share of foodstuffs and beverages rose to 22 per cent from 19 per cent in 1968 and that of raw materials and other production goods to 42 per cent, reflecting both an increase in re-exports and a further growth in domestic demand.

Direction of Trade

The EEC countries, including the franc area, are Togo's principal customers, taking a total of CFAF 8.3 billion, or 87 per cent of the registered exports, in 1968 and CFAF 6.2 billion, or 54 per cent of its registered imports (Table 30). France is still the most important single customer of Togo; it buys most of the country's coffee and also a large share of the other agricultural exports and of the phosphate production. However, primarily as a result of the increasing importance of phosphate sales, France's previously predominant position among Togo's

TABLE 30. TOGO: DIRECTION OF TRADE, 1962–69

(Customs data; value in millions of CFA francs)

	Value								Per cent of total		
	1962	1963	1964	1965	1966	1967	1968	1969 [1]	1962	1968	1969 [1]
EXPORTS BY DESTINATION											
Franc area	2,529	2,514	3,477	3,099	3,811	3,355	4,120	3,316	60	43	36
France	*2,214*	*2,397*	*3,283*	*2,900*	*3,574*	*2,995*	*3,678*	*3,016*	*52*	*39*	*34*
Dahomey	*81*	*121*	*120*	*131*	*144*	*139*	*152*	*150*	*2*	*2*	*2*
EEC other than France											
Netherlands	246	278	557	831	1,491	1,372	2,233	2,209	6	23	24
Germany	102	117	430	604	517	837	1,000	1,401	2	11	15
Belgium-Luxembourg	253	262	470	429	618	540	634	869	6	7	9
Italy	183	370	591	597	666	426	310	355	4	3	4
Total	784	1,027	2,048	2,461	3,292	3,175	4,177	4,834	18	44	52
United Kingdom	53	70	87	133	166	240	459	234	1	5	3
Ghana	68	44	26	17	97	41	37	21	2	1	1
United States	427	355	743	44	188	72	2	15	10	—	—
Japan	118	144	294	292	378	342	422	397	3	4	4
All others	260	375	773	633	895	669	332	365	6	3	4
Total exports f.o.b.	4,239	4,529	7,448	6,679	8,827	7,894	9,549	9,182	100	100	100

Imports by Origin

Franc area	2,801	2,944	3,590	4,051	4,134	3,753	4,139	4,468	*42*	*35*	*38*
France	*2,232*	*2,397*	*2,896*	*3,470*	*3,596*	*3,268*	*3,666*	*3,975*	*33*	*32*	*33*
Dahomey	*124*	*150*	*225*	*238*	*204*	*162*	*141*	*114*	*1*	*1*	*1*
EEC other than France											
Germany	393	397	1,372	2,161	1,435	1,170	831	813	6	7	7
Italy	90	132	145	144	226	257	557	546	1	5	5
Netherlands	389	372	629	351	500	446	521	601	6	5	5
Belgium-Luxembourg	115	169	97	81	173	143	207	174	2	2	1
Total	987	1,070	2,243	2,737	2,334	2,016	2,116	2,134	15	19	18
United Kingdom	866	715	982	651	949	902	1,040	1,397	13	9	12
Ghana	246	340	272	252	428	533	371	333	4	3	2
United States	324	302	324	365	352	451	516	662	5	4	5
Japan	344	641	1,455	1,548	1,602	1,400	1,316	854	5	11	7
CMEA countries [2]	173	180	262	302	313	346	246	580	3	3	5
Mainland China	51	66	159	150	328	563	553	345	1	5	3
All others	932	909	999	1,044	1,228	1,169	1,326	1,156	13	11	10
Total imports c.i.f.	6,724	7,167	10,286	11,100	11,668	11,133	11,623	11,929	100	100	100

Sources: Ministère des Finances, de l'Economie et du Plan, *Inventaire Economique du Togo, 1962–63*, and *Bulletin Mensuel de Statistique*.

[1] Provisional; 10 months only.
[2] Albania, Bulgaria, Czechoslovakia, East Germany, Hungary, Mongolia, Poland, Rumania, and U.S.S.R.

customers declined from 52 per cent of total exports in 1962 to 39 per cent in 1968; the relative position of the other EEC countries is rising and reached 44 per cent in 1968. In 1968 the Netherlands had a 23 per cent share in Togo's exports since it took large quantities of phosphate and most of Togo's cocoa crop. In the same year, Germany absorbed about 10 per cent and Belgium-Luxembourg 7 per cent of Togo's exports. Exports to the United States dwindled during the period, whereas those to Japan (phosphates) and the United Kingdom (cotton and starch) increased.

On the basis of registered trade, exports to franc area countries other than France have represented only 3–5 per cent of the total in recent years; however, if the sizable nonrecorded trade with Dahomey were taken into account, total exports to these countries might exceed 10 per cent. Recorded exports to Ghana are of minor importance. Apparently, a substantial part of exports to Ghana, mostly consumer goods like textiles and tobacco, also is not reflected in the trade statistics.

France continues to be Togo's leading supplier, accounting for about 32 per cent of total registered imports in 1968. The French share has declined from 33 per cent in 1962. Imports from other EEC countries, chiefly Germany, rose steadily from 15 per cent in 1962 to 25 per cent in 1965; thereafter this share declined and was 18 per cent in 1968. The United Kingdom also decreased in importance as a supplier during 1962–68; its share declined from about 13 per cent to 9 per cent. The declining trend in imports from other EEC members and the United Kingdom contrasted with the rising trend in imports from Japan; its share of imports rose from 5 per cent in 1962 to 14 per cent in 1964–66, although they declined to 11 per cent in 1968. Imports from Ghana, largely cocoa, are only partly reflected in registered imports.

During the first ten months of 1969, France's share in Togo's exports declined to 34 per cent, while that of the other EEC countries rose to 52 per cent. However, France's share in imports rose to 33 per cent, whereas that of the EEC declined to 18 per cent.

FOREIGN FINANCIAL ASSISTANCE

During 1962–69, actual disbursements of foreign financial assistance to Togo in the form of grants averaged about CFAF 2.4 billion a year (Table 31). The major donors were France and EEC. French assist-

TABLE 31. TOGO: DISBURSEMENTS OF FOREIGN OFFICIAL GRANTS, EXCLUDING MILITARY AID, 1962–69

(In millions of CFA francs)

	1962	1963	1964	1965	1966	1967	1968	1969
France								
Investment grants	307	289	598	622	476	535	670	700
Technical assistance	177	162	169	237	382	190	301	380
Scholarships and trainee program	40	63	133	134	95	65 }	—	—
Budget subsidies	—	—	111	139	175	—	—	—
Other	—	—	—	—	21	75	—	—
Total French aid	524	514	1,011	1,132	1,149	865	971	1,080
Federal Republic of Germany	114	282	269	329	330	250	230	554
United States								
Public Law 480, Titles II and III	318	51	148	46	87	48	…	…
Other	75	248	217	179	180	106	…	…
Total U.S. aid	393	299	365	225	267	154	215	249
EEC	326	558	424	595	527	594	353	968
United Nations	240	235	277	278	232	258	501	720
Nonclassified	10	5	32	128	100	139	49	64
Total	1,607	1,893	2,378	2,687	2,605	2,260	2,319	3,635

Sources: Mainly from OECD, *Geographical Distribution of Financial Flows to Less Developed Countries*, 1960–64, and 1965 (preliminary version); and data provided by BCEAO, CCCE, and U.S. Agency for International Development.

ance, amounted to CFAF 1.1 billion in 1965 and 1966; after some decline in 1967, it rose in 1968 and further in 1969, when it again amounted to CFAF 1.1 billion. EEC aid increased from CFAF 0.3 billion in 1962 to nearly CFAF 1.0 billion in 1969. French aid consisted mainly of investment grants, technical assistance, and budget aid; however, since the beginning of 1967, Togo has no longer received budget aid. EEC aid was used mainly for agricultural development and diversification, education, and road construction.

German grants, totaling CFAF 2.4 billion for the eight years 1962–69, were used for various training and social investment programs. The United States has provided varying amounts of commodity support under its Public Law 480 program in recent years, in addition to grants under the U.S. Agency for International Development. Total grants from the United States amounted to CFAF 2.1 billion over the entire period 1962–69. UN aid, amounting to about CFAF 2.7 billion, covered largely the cost of the experts provided under the UN Technical Assistance Program.

BALANCE OF PAYMENTS

The balance of payments of Togo with the rest of the world for 1965–69 is shown in Table 32. Because of improvements in the method of compilation from year to year, the figures for some items are not fully comparable throughout the period covered.

The over-all balance, which had a surplus of CFAF 1.7 billion in 1965, declined in 1966. During the next three years, however, it improved, showing a cumulative surplus of CFAF 5.0 billion according to preliminary data and estimates for 1969. Togo's foreign trade balance, in deficit by CFAF 2.5 billion in 1965, improved in the following year and during 1967–69 had a growing surplus. Since imports are recorded on a c.i.f. basis in these balances of payments, the negative service balances resulted mainly from net debit entries for passenger fares, remitted earnings, and dividends and undistributed profits. The major share of the dividends and undistributed profits was from the phosphate mine.

In all the years covered by these balances of payments, there was a large net inflow of foreign capital. Most of the credit entries on official unrequited transfers represented disbursements of foreign aid which

TABLE 32.   TOGO: SUMMARY OF BALANCE OF PAYMENTS, 1965–69

(*In billions of CFA francs*)

	1965	1966	1967	1968 [1]	1969 [2]
A. Goods and services					
Exports f.o.b.[3]	8.7	11.9	12.4	14.1	17.0
Imports c.i.f.[3]	−11.2	−12.8	−12.2	−13.4	−15.9
Trade balance [3]	−2.5	−0.9	0.2	0.7	1.1
Investment income	−1.4	−0.4	−0.8	−1.3	−1.2
Government, n.i.e.	−0.4	−0.2	−0.1	−0.2	−0.2
Other services	−0.5	−1.0	−0.9	−1.2	−1.3
Total goods and services (net)	−4.8	−2.5	−1.4	−2.0	−1.6
B. Unrequited transfers (net)					
Private	0.4	0.4	0.3	0.3	0.3
Government	2.8	2.0	2.1	2.4	3.6
Total unrequited transfers	3.2	2.4	2.4	2.7	3.9
C. Nonmonetary capital (net)					
Private	0.8	−0.1	−0.5	0.2	0.2
Official	0.6	1.3	1.5	0.1	−0.2
Total nonmonetary capital	1.4	1.2	1.0	0.3	—
D. Basic balance (A + B + C)	−0.2	1.1	2.0	1.0	2.3
E. Net errors and omissions	1.9	−0.5	0.2	−0.1	—
F. Over-all balance (D + E)	1.7	0.6	1.8	0.9	2.3
G. Monetary movements (net)					
Central Bank	−1.5	−0.3	−0.9	−0.8	—
Commercial banks and other institutions	−0.2	−0.3	−0.9	−0.1	—
Total monetary movements	−1.7	−0.6	−1.8	−0.9	—

Source: Data supplied by the Togolese authorities.

[1] Provisional estimates.
[2] IMF estimates based on partial data for the first nine months.
[3] Based on adjusted trade figures.

were estimated to amount to CFAF 3.6 billion in 1969. Debit entries include Togo's contributions toward the administrative expenses of international organizations. Private unrequited transfers, represented an inflow of capital of about CFAF 0.3 billion throughout the period. Credit entries include scholarship grants from foreign governments, EEC, and pension payments by the French Government. Debit entries are mainly workers' remittances.

Nonmonetary capital, which, on a net basis, showed a large capital inflow of CFAF 1.4 billion in 1965, decreased to CFAF 0.3 billion in 1968, with the decline in private capital inflow. Private direct investment was highest in 1965 (CFAF 1.1 billion) but declined thereafter to CFAF 0.1 billion in 1967. Other private long-term liabilities increased from CFAF 0.3 billion in 1965 to CFAF 0.8 billion in 1967, mainly because of repayments on loans from the French CCCE and repayments on private loans.

The Central Government received substantial long-term loans throughout the period; they amounted to CFAF 0.9 billion in 1967.

Most of the loans were disbursed by Germany, chiefly for construction of the port of Lomé and the water supply system in Sokodé. However, no major loans were made to the Government in 1968 and 1969. In the latter year, owing mainly to an increase in public short term investment abroad, there was an outflow in net official capital movements estimated at about CFAF 200 million.

In 1963, Togo's net foreign assets amounted to CFAF 1.5 billion; since that time its net foreign assets have improved continuously, reaching CFAF 8.7 billion in September 1969 (see Table 27). Two thirds of this increase was accounted for by commercial banks, whose net foreign assets rose to CFAF 2.3 billion in September 1969. Togo's share in the BCEAO's net foreign assets amounted to CFAF 6.4 billion or equal to estimated imports for five months of 1969.

CHAPTER 13

Upper Volta

GENERAL SETTING

Upper Volta became independent on August 5, 1960. It joined the International Monetary Fund (IMF) on May 2, 1963; its current quota (April 1970) is $10,000,000. Also on May 2, 1963, Upper Volta became a member of the International Bank for Reconstruction and Development (IBRD, or World Bank), with a current subscription of $10,000,000, and the International Development Association (IDA), with a current subscription of $500,000. Other international and regional organizations of which Upper Volta is a member include the United Nations (UN); Food and Agriculture Organization (FAO); UN Educational, Scientific, and Cultural Organization (UNESCO); General Agreement on Tariffs and Trade (GATT); West African Monetary Union (Union Monétaire Ouest Africaine, or UMOA); Common Organization of African and Malagasy States (Organisation Commune Africaine et Malgache, or OCAM); and African Development Bank (ADB).

The country covers an area of about 274,200 square kilometers (106,000 square

miles), roughly equal to half the size of France, lying between the
Sahara Desert and the coastal lowlands of West Africa. On the south
it is bordered by Ivory Coast, Ghana, and Togo; on the southeast
by Dahomey; on the northeast by Mali; and on the north and west by
Niger (see map). Upper Volta is completely landlocked; its shortest
distance to the sea is about 800 kilometers (500 miles) through Ivory
Coast. The land is generally flat except for the range of hills—the
Falaise de Banfora—in the southwest. The southwest is drained by
branches of the Komoé; the central part by three branches of the Volta
(Volta Noire, Volta Rouge, and Volta Blanche); and the northeast
by branches of the Niger. These rivers reach the sea in countries to the
south, but none is navigable to the sea.

There are two seasons: the shorter, rainy season usually lasts from
July to October and the longer, dry season from November to June.
Annual rainfall averages 1,400 millimeters (56 inches) in the extreme
southwest, dwindling northeastward to less than 250 millimeters.

In most places the soil is poor and has been subjected to erosion by
heavy downpours in the rainy season, aggravated, in populated areas,
by destruction of the natural vegetation. The most fertile areas are in
the southwest and along the rivers. Semidesert conditions prevail in the
northeast. Shortage of water limits agriculture over much of the country, and rivers and wells often run dry several months before the annual
rains begin.

The total population in 1969 was estimated at 5.3 million, including
temporary migrants working abroad. The relatively small urban population is concentrated in Ouagadougou, the capital (about 100,000);
Bobo Dioulasso (70,000); and Banfora, Kaya, Koudougou, and Ouahigouya. Roughly half of the total population belong to the Mossi; the
other half comprise a number of smaller ethnic groups and some 3,500
resident foreigners.

Population density (19 persons per square kilometer) is high
compared with that of neighboring countries (e.g., 3 in Niger and 12 in
Ivory Coast). It ranges from only 4 per square kilometer in the eastern
and northern regions to some 35 persons in the central plateau area,
peopled mostly by the Mossi. Geographical distribution of the population does not generally correspond with the distribution of natural
resources; the less productive central plateau, occupying about one

fourth of the land area, supports nearly half of the total population, and other regions—especially the fertile southwestern corner—are relatively underpopulated. This distribution has persisted, despite considerable demographic pressure for migration, mainly because of the cohesion of the Mossi group but also because of the high incidence, until recently, of epidemic diseases such as sleeping sickness in the areas with more nearly adequate rainfall and water supply.

A fairly large part of the population migrates to neighboring countries in search of employment. In recent years, about three fourths of the migrants are believed to have gone to Ivory Coast and one fourth to Ghana, where most find work as plantation laborers. Some migrants go for less than six months and return for the crop season; others stay longer. A few have settled abroad permanently. Migrants' earnings returned to Upper Volta represent an important element in the country's balance of payments.

Some internal migration also occurs, mostly from the densely populated rural Mossi area to the cities or to less populated agricultural areas.

In 1967/68, elementary schools had 129,400 pupils, secondary schools 10,150, and public technical schools 2,160. Upper Volta has no institutions of higher education, but several hundred students attend universities abroad. The National School of Administration, opened in Ouagadougou in 1960, offers training for government positions. The technical college in Ouagadougou has about 300 students; smaller technical schools include an agricultural training center at Sarya (Saria), near Koudougou.

STRUCTURE OF THE ECONOMY

GROSS DOMESTIC PRODUCT

National income data, on a comparable basis, are available only for 1965 and 1966. These data indicate that gross domestic product (GDP) at current prices increased by 3.2 per cent in 1966 to CFAF 58.2 billion (Table 1). National income rose by 5.6 per cent to CFAF 50.8 billion. Per capita GDP in 1966 was estimated at about US$50, which is among the lowest in Africa.

TABLE 1. UPPER VOLTA: GROSS DOMESTIC PRODUCT AT CURRENT PRICES,
BY ORIGIN, 1965 AND 1966

(*Value in billions of CFA francs*)

	1965	1966 Value	1966 Per cent of total
Agriculture (including livestock, fishing, and forestry)	26.9	28.4	48.8
Mining	0.2	0.2	0.3
Manufacturing (including artisan work)	3.0	3.2	5.5
Construction and public works	2.3	2.3	4.0
Transport	2.0	1.9	3.3
Commerce	12.0	11.7	20.1
Government administration	4.8	4.8	8.2
Other services	5.2	5.7	9.8
Total	56.4	58.2	100.0

Source: Ministère du Plan et des Travaux Publics, *Comptes Economiques de la Haute-Volta, 1965–66.*

The rural sector (agriculture, livestock, fishing, and forestry) contributed nearly 50 per cent to GDP in 1966, commerce 20 per cent, and government and other services nearly 20 per cent. Accordingly, the role of all other sectors (i.e., mining, industry, construction, and transportation) in Upper Volta's economy was very small.

Private and public consumption represented about 94 per cent of GDP in 1966 and investments 12 per cent, the additional resources coming from the excess of imports over exports (Table 2). Private sector investment declined slightly on account of a drop in housing construction, while private consumption rose, accounting for about 84 per cent of GDP. The government sector in Upper Volta is small; in 1966, the public sector's consumption and investment together absorbed about 17 per cent of GDP.

AGRICULTURE, FISHING, AND FORESTRY

Crop Production

Crop production generates more than one third of GDP, a significant part of this contribution representing subsistence farming. Frequent shortages of basic foodstuffs have induced agricultural producers in Upper Volta to emphasize the growing of food crops. Consequently,

TABLE 2.   UPPER VOLTA: USE OF RESOURCES, AT CURRENT PRICES, 1965 AND 1966

(*Value in billions of CFA francs*)

	1965	1966 Amount	1966 Per cent of total GDP
Consumption			
Private	46.8	48.9	84.0
Public	6.3	6.0	10.3
Total consumption	53.1	54.9	94.3
Gross fixed capital formation			
Private	4.2	3.4	5.8
Public	2.8	3.6	6.2
Total gross fixed capital formation	7.0	7.0	12.0
Net addition to stocks	1.6	1.5	2.6
Exports of goods and services	6.0	6.7	11.5
Less imports of goods and services	−11.3	−11.9	−20.4
Total	56.5	58.2	100.0

Source: Ministère du Plan et des Travaux Publics, *Comptes Economiques de la Haute-Volta, 1965–66.*

the output of export crops is relatively small even with recent expansion.

Aside from annual fluctuations due to weather, production of the principal food crops (sorghum, millet, and maize) has been rising slowly in recent years (Table 3). However, production of rice, a staple food for middle-income groups, has been increasing steadily in recent years; in 1968 it totaled 59,000 tons,[1] compared with 45,000 tons in 1962. Domestic consumption even of exported crops, mainly groundnuts, sheanuts, and sesame seed, is considerable and must be satisfied before the surplus can be exported. For instance, from the 1968/69 crop of groundnuts, only 9,000 tons, about 7 per cent of total production, were exported. Similarly, exports of sesame seed and sheanuts constitute a small share of total production.

Cotton production has progressed remarkably. During 1960–68 the cultivated area expanded from 23,000 hectares to 75,000 hectares and production from 1,000 tons to 32,000 tons (unginned). It is hoped that production will reach 150,000 tons by 1980. This rapid increase is

---

[1] Throughout this chapter, the word "ton" refers to a metric ton of 2,204.6 pounds.

TABLE 3.   UPPER VOLTA: AGRICULTURAL PRODUCTION, 1962–68

(In thousands of metric tons)

	1962	1963	1964	1965	1966	1967	1968
Food crops							
Sorghum	508	719	878	779	797	. . .	. . .
Millet	261	316	377	410	379	. . .	. . .
Maize	78	109	126	171	137	137	139
Rice	45	25	33	38	52	57	59
Peas and beans	158	177	108	. . .	. . .	....	. . .
Export crops							
Groundnuts (unshelled)	113	129	135	131	129	130	133
Sesame seed	6	4	6	12	13	14	16
Sheanuts [1]	. . .	15	2	19	—	21	15
Cotton (unginned)	13	10	11	10	19	20	32

Source: Ministère des Finances et du Commerce, *Situation Economique de la Haute-Volta et Perspectives d'Avenir.*

[1] Marketed production of crop season ended in year indicated; no data on actual production available.

largely attributed to the efforts of the Compagnie Française pour le Développement des Fibres Textiles (CFDT), a French semipublic institution engaged in promoting cotton production in several developing countries.

Several other agricultural extension services, mainly French, operate in Upper Volta under bilateral foreign assistance programs covering specific products. For instance, the Institut de Recherches pour les Huiles et Oléagineux Tropicaux (IRHO) is mainly concerned with groundnut production, and the Société d'Etude Sucrière de Haute-Volta (SESU) conducts experiments on sugar production. Others, such as the Société d'Assistance Technique et de Crédit Social Outre-Mer (SATEC), provide general technical assistance and training to small farmers. Most of these institutions have achieved limited success in their operations.

The Government has approached rural development and expansion of agricultural production on a regional basis. It has divided the country into ten regions; rural development in each region has been entrusted to a specialized agency—Office Régional de Développement (ORD). It is the responsibility of each Regional Development Office to study, formulate, and implement development projects within the region; to teach farmers modern techniques; and to assist in increasing production. These activities are carried out in cooperation with the above-mentioned agricultural extension services. So far, eight Regional Offices have been established.

Agricultural Marketing

Since the Compagnie Française pour le Développement des Fibres Textiles began operations in Upper Volta, it has had a monopoly on the marketing and export of cotton. In principle, the marketing of other agricultural commodities has been left in the hands of private traders. However, to ensure adequate marketing facilities, particularly in remote areas of the country, the Government has established several marketing institutions throughout the years.

Starting with the 1967/68 crop season, the marketing of export products other than cotton was assigned to the Office of Commercial Crops (Société Voltaïque de Commercialisation, or SOVOLCOM), created in early 1967. In addition, the Office was given the function of purchasing and selling, at wholesale or retail, food crops and imported foodstuffs in order to avert shortages and price increases. Ordinarily, the Office does not subsidize the commodities it markets, limiting itself to buying during the harvest season, maintaining stocks, and selling during the off season. However, because of substantial losses and management difficulties, its activities, beginning in the 1968/69 crop season, were limited to the marketing of domestic food crops and imported foodstuffs. The monopoly of marketing export crops other than cotton was given to the Regional Development Offices within their respective regions; private traders were authorized to market those crops in other areas. When the Regional Offices were unable to market the whole crop by the end of the regular marketing season, the Government extended the 1968/69 marketing season and authorized private traders to market the remaining crop.

At the beginning of each crop season, the Government fixes a minimum producer price for each export product. Producer prices for groundnuts, sheanuts, and sesame seed differ according to delivery, whether in Ouagadougou or in Bobo Dioulasso; the price for cotton differs according to quality, regardless of the locality where it is delivered.

Minimum producer prices are supported by the Price Stabilization Fund (Caisse de Stabilisation des Prix de la Haute-Volta, or CSPHV) through a program under which actual export prices are compared with a predetermined "statistical price" for each commodity, and differences within a certain range are either reimbursed or collected by the Fund. Fluctuations beyond this range result in a windfall profit or a loss to the exporter. The "statistical price" is determined after considering the Government's announced producer price and other charges incurred by traders and exporters such as transportation and handling, as well as a certain profit margin.

Producer prices for each of four export commodities remained stable during 1961/62–1969/70 in spite of fluctuations in world market prices (Table 4). However, the Price Stabilization Fund had to pay large subsidies on groundnuts and cotton exports, amounting to about CFAF 130 million in 1967/68. In the following season, producer prices for groundnuts and cotton were reduced by about 3 per cent and subsidy payments to less than CFAF 30 million. In the same season the producer price for sesame seed was raised by about 1 per cent. As a result of the price support policy followed in recent years, the Stabilization Fund is in a fairly comfortable financial position. At the end of the 1967/68 season its assets amounted to about CFAF 180 million with the expectation of a further increase in the 1968/69 season.

Livestock and Livestock Products

Although livestock accounts for only about 10 per cent of GDP, it is the leading source of money income in the rural sector and constitutes the principal economic activity in the eastern and northern parts of the country, where rainfall is usually scarce and crop production most difficult. In other parts of the country, livestock is raised in conjunction with other agricultural activities, but large-scale mixed farming is still uncommon.

The estimated livestock population consists of about 2.3 million head of cattle, 1.5 million sheep, and 2.3 million goats. In the last few years, herds have been increasing at an average annual rate of 2.3 per cent, and this growth rate is not expected to exceed 3 per cent in the coming 15 years. The annual rate of increase in domestic and foreign demand exceeds 5 per cent.

In spite of the potential for livestock development in Upper Volta and the high return that could be derived from investments in livestock

TABLE 4. UPPER VOLTA: CASH CROP MARKET SALES, EXPORTS, PRODUCER PRICES, AND PRICE STABILIZATION FUND OPERATIONS, 1961/62–1969/70

	Market Sales	Exports [1]	Producer Prices	Price Stabilization Fund Operations	
				Subsidy payments	Reimbursement receipts
	Thousand metric tons		*CFA francs per kilogram*	*Million CFA francs*	
Groundnuts, shelled					
1961/62	3.3	0.9	27.50	. . .	—
1962/63	4.3	3.5	27.50	. . .	—
1963/64	5.5	3.6	27.50	17.9	—
1964/65	5.6	4.3	26.75	—	—
1965/66	8.4	5.8	26.75	7.7	—
1966/67	10.9	7.4	26.75	. . . [2]	—
1967/68	10.3	8.8	26.75	65.9	—
1968/69	10.4	8.9	25.75	15.0 [3]	—
1969/70	12.0	. . .	25.75	. . .	—
Cotton					
1961/62	2.3 [4]	0.7 [5]	34.00 [6]	. . .	—
1962/63	6.6 [4]	2.2 [5]	34.00 [6]	. . .	—
1963/64	8.0 [4]	2.7 [5]	34.00 [6]	23.9	—
1964/65	8.8 [4]	3.0 [5]	34.00 [6]	36.3	—
1965/66	7.5 [4]	2.5 [5]	34.00 [6]	54.7	—
1966/67	16.3 [4]	5.7 [5]	34.00 [6]	91.2	—
1967/68	17.3 [4]	6.2 [5]	34.00 [6]	63.7	—
1968/69	32.0 [4]	11.5 [5]	32.00 [6]	14.0 [3]	—
1969/70	40.0 [4]	. . .	32.00 [6]	. . .	—
Sheanuts					
1961/62	14.2	2.4	9.75	. . .	—
1962/63	0.5	0.5	9.75	. . .	—
1963/64	15.2	3.8	7.00	23.4	—
1964/65	1.5	1.0	7.00	. . .	—
1965/66	18.7	3.1	7.00	38.8	—
1966/67	—	—	7.00	—	—
1967/68	20.8	14.5	7.00	—	65.9
1968/69	15.3	12.2	7.00	—	80.0 [3]
1969/70	19.0	. . .	7.00	—	. . .
Sesame seed					
1961/62	0.7	0.7	26.50	—	—
1962/63	2.0	2.0	26.50	—	—
1963/64	2.3	2.1	26.50	—	—
1964/65	2.4	2.1	26.50	—	—
1965/66	1.7	1.7	26.50	—	—
1966/67	2.6	2.6	26.50	—	3.0
1967/68	2.9	2.9	26.50	—	6.2
1968/69	3.5	3.5	26.75	—	4.9 [3]
1969/70	3.5	3.5	26.75	—	. . .

Sources: BCEAO, *Indicateurs Economiques*, October 1969, and data provided by the Upper Volta authorities.

[1] Data refer to exports during the indicated crop season and may differ from foreign trade data.

[2] Most of the required subsidies were paid by France; the Price Stabilization Fund disbursed only CFAF 3.6 million.

[3] Estimated.

[4] Unginned cotton.

[5] Ginned cotton.

[6] For first-quality unginned cotton; producer prices for second quality are CFAF 4.0 per kilogram lower.

raising, only about 3 per cent of total investments was allocated for this sector in the 1967–70 Development Plan. In addition, little of this investment was directed toward solving the basic problems facing that sector, among them an inadequate water supply and deficiencies in pasture and sanitary conditions. Furthermore, animal husbandry methods, which have improved very little in recent years, lag behind those in many other countries.

The activities of a number of recently established companies will foster the development and export of livestock. These companies include two cattle raising farms, one plant for the treatment and tanning of hides, and a slaughterhouse in Ouagadougou with an annual capacity for processing 7,500–10,000 tons of meat. The slaughterhouse may also refrigerate about 3,500 tons of meat a year.

Fishing and Forestry

Rivers, pools, and artificial lakes created by dams are fished by traditional methods, and the catch provides a small supplement to food requirements. Total production in 1964, estimated at 2,500 tons, was all consumed within Upper Volta. The maximum potential production, based on presently available water resources, is estimated at 6,000 tons annually if modern methods of seeding and fishing were employed.

Upper Volta has little high forest, and most of its natural trees are relatively small and not suitable for commercial exploitation. Some 8 per cent of the total land area is set aside as "classified forest" under protection of the Bureau of Waters and Forests, which regulates cutting, undertakes fire control measures, and attempts to promote reforestation. Production of timber is virtually nonexistent, while firewood and other domestic requirements are satisfied locally by collection in the "bush." This practice has led to stripping even the smaller trees near densely populated areas, with adverse consequences for cultivation of crops.

MINING

Upper Volta is not rich in mineral resources. Apart from manganese deposits, which have been discovered in relatively large quantities, only traces of other minerals have been found. These include gold at Gangaol (near Dori in the northeastern part of the country), copper at

Gaoua (in the southwestern part), bauxite, and lead. Studies financed by the UN Development Program and by the French Fonds d'Aide et de Coopération (FAC) are currently under way in order to determine whether these minerals exist in commercially exploitable quantities.

The manganese deposits at Tambao in the northeastern part of the country consist of some 8 million tons of manganese oxide and a large, but undetermined, quantity of carbonate ore. Upper Volta's manganese is of high quality with a metal content ranging from 45 per cent in the carbonate ore to more than 50 per cent in the manganese oxide. Preliminary estimates indicate a possible annual production of 400,000–500,000 tons; on that basis, oxide deposits could be exploited for about 20 years. Development of this resource would raise the value of Upper Volta's exports by some CFAF 3.3 billion annually, or about 60 per cent above the present level. It would also represent a large contribution to the country's GDP and to government revenue.

A U.S. company, Union Carbide Corporation, has expressed interest in exploiting these deposits provided the present railway linking Abidjan (Ivory Coast) with Ouagadougou would be extended to Tambao so as to facilitate the shipment of the mineral. However, since manganese deposits are relatively small and the construction of the required railway link would entail considerable costs, this project is still under consideration and may not be undertaken in the near future, unless other minerals in relatively large quantities are discovered in the same area.

MANUFACTURING

The manufacturing sector in Upper Volta accounts for only about 5 per cent of GDP. In 1966 there were 36 industrial plants, located in Ouagadougou, Bobo Dioulasso, and Koudougou. Most of them were engaged in processing domestic agricultural commodities and in producing import substitutes. In that year their total production was estimated at about CFAF 3 billion.

The leading industries are cotton ginning, vegetable oil processing, tanning of hides, manufacture of leather products, assembling of bicycles and motorcycles, and production of beer and soft drinks. In several plants established to serve a market larger than that of Upper Volta, production has fallen below capacity since neighboring countries have established similar industries. Industrial activity in Upper Volta has also been affected by the limitations of natural resources and skilled labor, as well as by high transportation costs.

The 1967–70 Development Plan allocates CFAF 4.0 billion, or about 15 per cent of total projected investments, for the development of the manufacturing sector. It estimates that, as a result, the value of manufacturing production would increase to about CFAF 6.0 billion, that is, double the value in 1966. The plants that have already been established and started operations since the beginning of the plan period include those for producing cigarettes, matches, and bricks.

Among the factories under construction, the most important is a large textile mill in Koudougou, which was expected to begin operations in late 1969. Total investments in this plant are estimated at CFAF 5 billion over a period of 10 years. Investment during the first stage, already completed, amounted to CFAF 1.2 billion, about one half financed by the Kreditanstalt für Wiederaufbau and the remainder by FAC, CCCE, and the firm's capital. Initially, the factory will employ 500 persons; this number will increase to 2,500 in 1978 when full production capacity is reached. A sugar refinery, with an annual capacity of 15,000 tons, is under construction in Banfora; it was expected to begin operations in early 1970. Total investments are to amount to about CFAF 300 million, and production is to be sufficient to meet domestic consumption. Initially, this factory will process and refine raw sugar imported from the People's Republic of the Congo (Brazzaville); later, the plant will be vertically integrated with sugarcane plantations in the same area. Other industrial projects under consideration include a new vegetable oil mill, a bicycle tire plant, and a pasteurizing plant for dairy products.

TRANSPORTATION

Upper Volta has a fairly extensive road network, about 16,000 kilometers in length; about one fourth consists of all-weather roads (national roads). In the last few years the road network has deteriorated owing to inadequate maintenance, leaving parts of the national roads impassable during the rainy season. About CFAF 5 billion has been allocated in the Four-Year Development Plan for the rehabilitation and improvement of the road system.

Road transportation for freight and passengers is provided by a large company, Transafricaine, which handles about half of the traffic, and by individual truck owners. In order to reorganize the transport sector and to extend the services to remote areas, the Government is considering the creation of a new semipublic company, which will have the monopoly for all domestic transport. The Transafricaine and the syndicate of individual transporters will participate in this new company.

The most important link with the exporting points on the Atlantic Ocean is the railway which connects Ouagadougou and Bobo Dioulasso with Abidjan (Ivory Coast). This railroad is owned and operated by the Governments of Ivory Coast and Upper Volta through a joint company, the Régie du Chemin de Fer Abidjan-Niger (RAN). It handles about 90 per cent of Upper Volta's foreign trade as well as a significant share of that of Niger and Mali. In 1968 it carried about 345 million tons per kilometer (compared with 325 million in 1967 and 318 million in 1966), and it is operating at about full capacity. For this reason, the Goverment is considering the opening of a new access route to the Atlantic Ocean through an all-weather road, linking Ouagadougou to Lomé in Togo. The length of this projected road, to be completed in eight to ten years, is about 980 kilometers (some 200 kilometers shorter than the railway), and construction was expected to begin shortly.

Transportation by air within Upper Volta is limited to nonscheduled traffic in light aircraft. The major airports at Ouagadougo and Bobo Dioulasso handle international traffic, and several small airstrips are located in other parts of the country. Upper Volta has a small share in Air Afrique, which is the common airline of a number of French-speaking African countries and is financially self-supporting. The major towns are linked by telephone or radio.

POWER AND WATER

Electric power is supplied in three major cities (Ouagadougou, Bobo Dioulasso, and Ouahigouya) by a private company, the Société Africaine d'Electricité (SAFELEC), which operates in several West African countries. Total production of electricity has expanded rapidly, from 9.6 million kilowatt-hours in 1961 to 20.5 million kilowatt-hours in 1965. All electrical power is thermally generated and, because of high fuel costs, is expensive (CFAF 24 per kilowatt-hour), compared with neighboring countries.

SAFELEC also supplies water in these three cities and, since early 1965, in Koudougou and Kaya. In 1965 it supplied a total of 3.17 million cubic meters, at a cost of CFAF 50 per cubic meter.

In the rural areas, water is supplied by wells or barrages. The Fonds d'Aide et de Coopération (FAC) and the European Development Fund (EDF) of the European Economic Community have made extensive studies of water requirements in the different areas in 1959–64 at a total expenditure of CFAF 3.7 billion (CFAF 1.1 billion, FAC, and CFAF 2.6 billion, EDF). Actual construction completed up to 1966 included approximately 30 barrages and 100 wells, financed with FAC and EDF credits totaling about CFAF 1.2 billion; an additional 23 barrages and 60 wells, costing CFAF 0.8 billion, were in progress. These projects usually provide only for human and animal requirements; the area under irrigation is small (1,200 hectares in 1966).

ECONOMIC DEVELOPMENT PLANNING

EARLY DEVELOPMENT EFFORTS

Before August 1967, Upper Volta had an intermediate plan (1963–64) and a five-year development plan (1963–67), which, however, were not systematically implemented. These two plans were confined to a number of public sector projects, which were to be financed by foreign grants, mainly from FAC and EDF. Although disbursements of foreign resources during 1963–67 lagged behind commitments, total investments ranged between CFAF 2.5 billion and CFAF 3.0 billion annually.

More than one half of investment expenditure undertaken before August 1967 was directed toward the rural projects sector aimed at (1) increasing water supply, (2) soil preservation, and (3) introduction of modern techniques through the agricultural extension services. Emphasis was also given to rehabilitation of the road network. While EDF financed a few relatively large projects, FAC financed mainly a large number of small projects.

1967–70 DEVELOPMENT PLAN

In August 1967 the Government of Upper Volta launched its first development plan, based on a total investment expenditure of CFAF 33.0 billion. This figure includes expenditures of CFAF 5.5 billion, which the authorities considered optional and for which no financing was available. The plan was the outcome of a thorough study of the problems confronting each sector, its potentials, and the projects needed for its development. More than 55 per cent of this optional tranche represented infrastructure projects, including the first stage of the railway linking Ouagadougou with Tambao, a project classified as optional mainly because of the uncertainties as to negotiations with foreign investors interested in exploiting the manganese deposits (see "Mining," above).

Several hypothetical GDP growth rates were envisaged in the Plan ranging from 3.2 per cent to 4.5 per cent; it was the Government's belief, however, that a rate of about 4 per cent could be realized.

Distribution of Investment Expenditure

Of total investment valued at CFAF 27.5 billion, about 60 per cent was allocated, in almost equal parts, to infrastructure and to rural development and 18 per cent to the social sector (Table 5). This allocation reflects the Government's desire to encourage the productive sectors in the economy and to keep to a minimum the expansion in the current budget expenditure that would result from enlarged social services.

Infrastructure investments totaled CFAF 8.3 billion, of which CFAF 6.1 billion, or about 73 per cent, were for roads. Less than 20 per cent of this amount was earmarked for the construction of about 1,100 kilometers of new secondary roads. Most of the remainder was allocated for rehabilitating and paving existing roads, such as the road from Bobo Dioulasso to Faramana (118 kilometers), the road from Ouagadougou to Pô (163 kilometers), and the road from Ouagadougou to Koupéla (145 kilometers).

The plan allocated CFAF 7.9 billion to the rural sector, CFAF 6.1 billion to Regional Offices for crop production, and only CFAF 0.9 billion for livestock raising. Encouraged by the Regional Offices in cooperation with foreign agriculture extension agencies, cotton production was expected to reach 49,000 tons by 1970, about double the output in

TABLE 5. UPPER VOLTA: 1967–70 DEVELOPMENT PLAN AND ITS FINANCING[1]

(Value in billions of CFA francs)

	Projected Investments				Total		Financing	
	1967	1968	1969	1970	Value	Per cent	Domestic	Foreign
Infrastructure	0.5	2.6	2.5	2.7	8.3	30	1.2	7.1
Roads	*0.5*	*1.2*	*2.0*	*2.4*	*6.1*	*22*	*—*	*6.1*
Rural sector	1.3	2.2	2.6	1.8	7.9	29	1.7	6.2
Regional Offices	*1.1*	*1.5*	*2.1*	*1.4*	*6.1*	*22*	*1.6*	*4.5*
Livestock	*0.1*	*0.4*	*0.3*	*0.1*	*0.9*	*3*	*—*	*0.9*
Nonrural sector	0.7	2.3	1.6	1.0	5.6	20	1.1	4.5
Manufacturing	*0.4*	*1.7*	*1.3*	*0.7*	*4.1*	*15*	*0.1*	*4.0*
Social sector	1.3	1.1	1.2	1.2	4.8	18	0.3	4.5
Education	*0.5*	*0.5*	*1.1*	*1.0*	*3.1*	*11*	*—*	
Other	0.3	0.1	0.2	0.3	0.9	3	0.1	0.8
Total	4.1	8.3	8.1	7.0	27.5	100	4.4	23.1

Source: République de Haute-Volta, *Plan Cadre, 1967–1970.*

[1] Because of rounding, figures in this table and some of the following tables in this chapter do not add to all totals.

1967, and other crops were expected to increase from 10 per cent to 50 per cent. Investments under the plan for construction of dams and projects for combating the disease of river blindness are expected to contribute considerable additional benefits to the rural sector.

Manufacturing investments under the plan covered the establishment of factories for producing import substitutes and for the processing of domestic agricultural commodities. Apart from those that have already been established since 1967 and those currently under way (see "Manufacturing," above), the plan calls for the establishment of factories for producing bicycle tires, paints, and shoes; cotton gins; and vegetable oil processing plants. Some CFAF 1.9 billion of the CFAF 4.1 billion originally estimated for manufacturing was expected to be financed by the private sector.

Financing of the Plan

The 1967–70 Development Plan is basically a program for investments by the public sector, mostly through foreign financial assistance. Domestic and foreign private financing accounted for only about 11 per cent of total projected investments.

Foreign resources were expected to finance investment expenditures amounting to CFAF 23.1 billion, or 84 per cent of the total, about CFAF 20.0 billion in the form of grants and the remainder in loans from international organizations and foreign private investments. About 70 per cent of the total was expected from EDF (CFAF 9.2 billion) and FAC (CFAF 7.1 billion). More than 50 per cent of FAC's financial assistance was to be directed to rural development, and about the same share of EDF resources to infrastructure projects. Other sources of financing included the United States, the Federal Republic of Germany, and the Republic of China. The plan called for a contribution of CFAF 2.5 billion from the central and local governments, or more than one half of the total of CFAF 4.4 billion estimated to be financed by domestic resources. The Development Bank was expected to finance CFAF 0.8 billion of investment expenditure and the domestic private sector about CFAF 1.1 billion.

When the plan was published in August 1967, resources of about CFAF 10.3 billion, or 37 per cent of the total, were already assured.

Since then, additional resources have been committed; by mid-1969 an estimated 80 per cent of the total envisaged foreign financing had already been secured.

Implementation of the Plan

Data available on the implementation of the plan during 1967 and 1968 indicate that actual investments, about CFAF 6.7 billion, have been considerably less than originally anticipated. Compared with original targets, the rate of implementation declined from 69 per cent in 1967 to 46 per cent in 1968. Actual investments, however, increased to CFAF 2.8 billion in 1967 and to CFAF 3.8 billion in 1968. Although investments in 1968 represented less than one half those envisaged, they were much larger than average investments before the adoption of the plan.

In relation to projected investments, the rate of implementation was above the over-all average in the productive sectors, in social services, and in research, but was below the average in infrastructure projects. This situation is attributed in part to delays in disbursements due to difficulties encountered in fulfilling formalities required by EDF, which is expected to finance about 60 per cent of all infrastructure projects under the plan. No detailed data are available on the implementation of the plan in 1969, but until the middle of the year total investments lagged behind the original target of CFAF 8.1 billion.

INVESTMENT CODE

In order to promote investment and the inflow of foreign private capital, the Government adopted an Investment Code in June 1962. The Code outlines the broad framework of the benefits and advantages that the authorities may grant to prospective foreign investors. Originally, only the representatives of the Customs and Direct Taxation Departments were responsible for conducting these negotiations. More recently, representatives from the Departments of Planning, Industry, and Finance and Commerce have also participated in the discussions, allowing evaluation of proposed investments on a broader perspective.

The Code specifies the activities in which new investments may be accorded preferential treatment, which may be of the two following types:

Regime A—a guarantee is given that rates of taxation prevailing at the time the investment takes place will remain unchanged for a specific period, up to 30 years, regardless of any subsequent modification in tax legislation.

Regime B—special fiscal arrangements and concessions may be granted, in addition to those of Regime A, to investments of particular importance to the economic and social development of the country. These benefits include exemptions or reductions in income, customs, and other specified taxes for a certain period, usually not to exceed 25 years, and are negotiated separately for each proposed investment.

Since the implementation of the Investment Code, the Government has negotiated 19 agreements with foreign investors, of which 14 were in force in 1969.

PRICES AND WAGES

PRICES

Data on price developments in Upper Volta are confined to two indices, covering the consumption pattern in the Ouagadougou area for unmarried African workers and for European families (Table 6). Neither index is considered wholly representative on account of deficiencies in coverage. No data are available on price developments outside the capital, but prices in remote areas are much influenced by relatively high transportation costs and limited competition among traders. The consumer price index for African workers indicates a decline of about 5 per cent in prices between December 1965 and December 1968, followed by a sharp increase during the first two quarters of 1969. On the other hand, the index for European families indicates an increase throughout the whole period. Because of the difference in the consumption pattern between these two indices and their deficient coverage, it is not possible to ascertain the reasons for the apparent discrepancy in price developments between December 1965 and December 1968. However, in view of recent increases in the prices for imported goods and in domestic taxes, the over-all level of prices might have risen at an average annual rate of 2–3 per cent during the last few years.

TABLE 6. UPPER VOLTA: CONSUMER PRICE INDICES, OUAGADOUGOU, 1962–69

	Weights	1962	1963	1964	1965	1966	1967	1968				1969		
								Mar.	June	Sept.	Dec.	Mar.	June	Sept.
UNMARRIED AFRICAN WORKERS (1958 = 100)														
Foodstuffs	41.3	126.9	124.9	121.9	119.0	128.2	118.9	112.0	117.8	119.2	98.7	132.0	147.5	145.9
Rent	17.1	100.0	133.3	133.3	133.3	133.3	133.3	133.3	133.3	133.3	133.3	133.3	133.3	133.3
Clothing	10.9	214.5	243.9	246.4	244.3	235.7	238.4	241.9	241.9	241.9	241.9	245.3	245.3	245.3
Global index		138.9	148.9	149.7	148.4	151.9	145.1	145.9	148.8	148.5	140.3	157.5	162.3	162.8
EUROPEAN FAMILIES (1964 = 100)														
Foodstuffs	43.5	⋯	⋯	100.0	103.0	110.7	109.1	107.4	112.3	113.5	111.1	116.4	127.4	123.8
Clothing	10.0	⋯	⋯	100.0	112.3	109.0	124.8	125.0	112.1	112.1	128.0	133.8	⋮	⋮
Global index		⋯	⋯	100.0	102.4	109.8	112.7	112.7	113.4	114.8	114.1	117.6	123.8	122.2

Sources: Ministère du Plan et des Travaux Publics, *Bulletin Mensuel d'Informations Statistiques et Economiques*, and BCEAO, *Indicateurs Economiques*.

Food prices in Upper Volta are subject to sharp fluctuations mainly on account of seasonal factors. Most of the changes in over-all prices reflected in the price index for African unmarried workers are related to such fluctuations. In order to reduce the impact of seasonal variations on the supply and prices of food, the Office of Commercial Crops established a chain of retail stores throughout the country (see "Agricultural marketing," above). However, in view of the lack of appropriate storage facilities and managerial difficulties which resulted in substantial operational losses, the agency's activities have been reduced and stores where the turnover was below certain minimum levels were closed.

To limit profits of wholesalers and retailers the Government has established price controls on both imported and locally produced goods. The controls take the form of a determined maximum retail price for essential commodities (e.g., foodstuffs and pharmaceutical products) and of a maximum margin of profit for wholesalers and retailers for most other goods. Despite periodic checks on market prices by government inspectors and the liability of violators to fines, suspension of their licenses, or terms in prison, these price controls have not been fully effective.

WAGES

A fixed schedule of minimum wage rates for private sector employees and temporary employees in government service is determined by law and has been in effect in Upper Volta since 1953. Minimum wage rates differ according to the type of activity and whether it is performed in the urban centers or in the rural areas. The minimum hourly wage rate for agricultural workers is CFAF 25.13 around Ouagadougou, Bobo Dioulasso, and Banfora or their adjacent areas, and CFAF 21.36 elsewhere, that is, in the rural areas. In all other economic activities, the corresponding minimum hourly wage rates are CFAF 29.00 and CFAF 24.65. These rates had not been changed since January 1960 until important changes were introduced in December 1969. The system of wage zones has been abolished. There are now two minimum hourly wage rates, regardless of location; one for agricultural workers and the other for nonagricultural workers. At the same time, the minimum hourly wage rate for agricultural workers was raised to CFAF 26.88, and that for nonagricultural workers to CFAF 31.00. The effect of these measures was to raise the minimum wage rate in rural areas by some 26 per cent and in urban areas by about 7 per cent. In addition to these minimum rates, the wage legislation determines basic levels of remuneration for most occupations and several for almost all grades and skills within each occupation. Furthermore, regular increases in the minimum wage rates and in the basic levels of remuneration are provided for years of uninterrupted service with the same enterprise. These increases amount to 3 per cent after the third year, and 1 per cent annually thereafter, up to a maximum of 15 per cent of the minimum wage rate or basic remuneration.

Actual wages of unskilled laborers in the private sector tend to be the same as the minimum wage rate, but salaries of skilled and white collar workers are usually much higher than their basic minimum rate on account of the greater demand for the services of these particular groups. The number of wage earners in the private sector in 1967 was estimated at about 11,000, of which only about 1,000 were engaged in agriculture. Unification of the two wage zones, which is being considered, will represent an increase of almost 18 per cent for those workers in the rural zone, receiving the minimum wage rates. No detailed data are available to permit an estimate of the over-all impact of such unification; however, the average wage level in the rural area may increase by about 10 per cent.

The salary scale for the permanent employees in government service has changed somewhat in recent years. In January 1967, the Government reduced the salaries of this group by 10 per cent across the board as part of the program to reduce expenditures. With the improvement in the fiscal situation, the salary scale was restored in January 1969 to its previous level, and a general salary increase of 2.6 per cent was granted beginning December 1969. In 1967 there were about 10,000 persons in the government service, some 6,500 classified as permanent employees. In addition, about 3,500 persons were employed in public enterprises.

In addition to minimum wage rates, workers and laborers, in both the private and the public sectors, are entitled to receive a family allowance. Before January 1967, this allowance amounted to CFAF 1,500 per month per child, up to the sixth child; but since then it has been reduced to its present level of only CFAF 700.

Although the cost of living appears to have remained reasonably stable during the last two years, the purchasing power of wage earners declined considerably during 1967 and 1968 because of the 10 per cent reduction in wages of permanent government employees, the sharp reduction in family allowances, and the relatively high increase in the average tax burden, mainly on account of the "patriotic contribution" (see under "Other direct taxes," below).

MIGRATION

Large numbers of Upper Voltans emigrate to neighboring countries in search of work. It is estimated that migrants may number as many as a million, mostly working in the coffee and cocoa plantations of Ivory Coast. This migration is regulated by a convention concluded in 1960; under this convention, migrant workers receive a monthly salary of CFAF 2,500, which was then the prevailing minimum wage rate in Ivory Coast.

This large flow of migrants has been advantageous to Upper Volta. Not only has it reduced considerably the unemployment problem, but it has also contributed to the favorable balance of payments in recent years because of the remittances by the migrants to relatives in Upper Volta.

GOVERNMENT FINANCE

STRUCTURE OF THE PUBLIC SECTOR

The public sector of Upper Volta comprises the Central Government, a number of municipalities and rural communities, and some public and semipublic entities. The most important of these entities are the Social Security Fund, the Price Stabilization Fund (Caisse de Stabilisation des Prix de Haute-Volta), the Office of Commercial Crops (Société Voltaïque de Commercialisation), and, since January 1969, the Post Office. These entities are financially autonomous, deriving most of their resources from service charges and specific levies, and to a lesser extent, from government subsidies.

Ordinary and investment expenditure are provided for in a single budget. However, expenditure on road maintenance (financed by a special Road Fund) and capital expenditure (financed by foreign resources) are not included in the budget except for some equipment expenditure financed by a subsidy from the French Government.

All cash transactions of the Government are made through the Treasury. In addition, the Treasury maintains deposits of public and semipublic entities and extends short-term credit to the private sector through customs duty bills received in lieu of cash payments.

BUDGET SYSTEM AND CONTROLS

The fiscal year in Upper Volta is the calendar year. Revenues are entered into the accounts of the year in which they are collected. Payments relating to a given year made before the end of January of the following year in Ouagadougou, or before the end of February elsewhere, are recorded in the accounts of the given year.

Control over government expenditure is effected at different stages. Ten per cent of appropriations for materials expenditure is blocked at the beginning of each financial year and can be used only on authorization of the Minister of Finance and the President of the Republic. At the beginning of each quarter, the Ministry of Finance allocates to each ministry an amount to cover expenditures during the following three months. These amounts are determined on the basis of expenditure appropriations and estimated revenue collections. Expenditure authorizations are issued by each service within the limits of the allocated appropriations and are approved by the Director of the Budget and the Financial Controller. Disbursements are made by the Treasury after authorization by the Financial Controller and the Director of Accounts. Unused appropriations during any fiscal year are automatically canceled, except for some investment appropriations which can be carried forward. Transfers of appropriations from one section of the budget to another require the approval of the Minister of Finance, while transfers from one chapter to another can be made only by the Council of Ministers. Transfers of appropriations from one title to another require a Presidential Ordinance. The Inspector General of Finance is responsible for the postauditing of expenditure and revenue which are reported quarterly by each ministry or specialized service. The establishment of an Audit Court to postaudit accounts is contemplated.

The basic rules governing the preparation of the budget and its execution, as well as financial controls and the accounting system, were established by a decree issued in 1912. The Ministry of Finance, through the Budget Bureau, has the responsibility for preparing the budget. Annual budget expenditures and receipts must be balanced. Budgetary forecasts have improved considerably in recent years. A reform of present regulations to give, inter alia, broad responsibilities to the special agencies of the Treasury located in rural areas is under consideration. This reform is expected to improve controls over expenditure and to increase tax collection.

FISCAL DEVELOPMENTS, 1962–69

Since independence, Upper Volta has had persistent deficits in the government budgets, and by the end of 1965, the accumulated deficit amounted to CFAF 2.7 billion. In addition, payment arrears totaling about CFAF 1.4 billion had been ascertained. The accumulated deficit was financed by foreign resources, mainly grants and loans from France, and by domestic resources at the disposal of the Treasury. Contributions from France to Upper Volta's current budget continued until 1964, but since then, annual subsidies have been allocated exclusively to the financing of capital expenditure. Financing was also obtained from Ghana and from the Solidarity Fund (Fonds de Solidarité du Conseil de l'Entente). Domestic resources used to finance the deficit included deposits of public entities such as the Social Security Fund and the Price Stabilization Fund, as well as the funds of the Postal Checking System and of the National Savings Bank.

The present Government, which assumed office in January 1966, took a number of measures to restore equilibrium in the public finance and to repay outstanding arrears. In 1966 and 1967 these measures were directed toward reducing expenditure and increasing government receipts. An effort was made to reduce expenditure for almost all purposes. In 1966 the allowances of high-ranking government officials were reduced, and in 1967 wages and salaries for all permanent employees in government service were cut by 10 per cent and family allowances were reduced. In addition, subsidies to local governments, as well as allocations to investment expenditure, were scaled down. No major

changes in taxation were made in 1966; in 1967, however, the base
and rates of certain taxes were changed and new taxes were introduced.
These new taxes included a temporary income tax ("patriotic contribution") and a small payroll tax. Few changes were made in the indirect
taxation. Rates of import taxes on a number of essential commodities
(e.g., some foodstuffs, medicine and medical equipment, and certain
industrial products) were reduced. In spite of these efforts, actual
receipts and expenditure under the 1966 budget still resulted in a
deficit, which, however, did not exceed CFAF 160 million (Table 7),
compared with CFAF 308 million in 1965.

Ordinary revenue increased somewhat in 1967 over 1966 while total
expenditure declined by 8 per cent. Although extraordinary receipts fell
by about 37 per cent, actual receipts and expenditure under the 1967
budget resulted, for the first time in recent years, in a surplus (CFAF 232
million, or some 3 per cent of total receipts). Deducting from total
receipts the French subsidy of CFAF 450 million earmarked for the
financing of equipment expenditure and excluding public debt amortization payments from total expenditure, the Treasury had a net over-all
deficit of CFAF 39 million in 1967, compared with CFAF 558 million
in 1966 (Table 8). This greatly improved performance permitted the
Treasury to substantially reduce its outstanding utilization of domestic
financing resources. Net indebtedness to the banks and other financial
institutions was reduced by CFAF 472 million.

In 1968, the Government's fiscal policy followed the broad lines
adopted in the previous year with only minor changes introduced on
tax rates and on the level of expenditure. Ordinary revenue was almost
CFAF 0.7 billion higher than in 1967, a gain of about 9 per cent,
while expenditure increased by CFAF 0.4 billion, a gain of less than 5
per cent. A surplus of CFAF 363 million, or about 4 per cent of total
receipts, was realized. Adjustment of this figure for the subsidy received
and for the amortization of public debt left a net over-all surplus of
CFAF 18 million in 1968, allowing the Treasury to further reduce its
net use of domestic financing resources. Net indebtedness to the banks
and other financial institutions declined by CFAF 484 million.

Considerable progress was also made in the liquidation of the ascertained payments arrears. Besides receipts from the "patriotic contribution," the Government allocated considerable funds for this purpose,

reducing outstanding arrears from CFAF 1.4 billion at the end of 1965 to CFAF 0.2 billion by December 31, 1968. Furthermore, these remaining arrears reportedly have not yet been repaid because most claimants had not been able to properly substantiate their claims.

Application of strict fiscal policies during 1966–68 had a dampening impact on domestic demand. In the 1969 budget, the Government took certain measures to expand the disposable income of wage earners. The salary scale of the permanent employees in government service was adjusted upward to its pre-1967 level, and more investment expenditure was budgeted. Schedular taxes on wages and salaries were reduced and their structure was modified. Loss of revenue resulting from these reductions was partly compensated by higher taxes on commercial and industrial profits and a higher turnover tax. In addition, a tax on imported goods at the rate of 3 per cent was introduced.

The government budget for 1969 has been approved with receipts and expenditure balanced at CFAF 9.5 billion. Compared with actual performance in 1968, this budget represented an 8 per cent increase in receipts (CFAF 0.7 billion) and a 12 per cent increase in expenditure (CFAF 1.0 billion). Actual receipts and expenditures under the 1969 budget, however, were expected to result in a surplus about equal to that attained in the previous year; receipts during the first three months of 1969 were running in line with budget estimates, while expenditures were being kept a little below appropriations. During that period the Government's over-all position vis-à-vis the banks and other financial institutions sector improved by more than CFAF 0.6 billion, compared with CFAF 0.4 billion during the first three months of 1968.

1970 BUDGET

The 1970 budget estimates provided for total receipts (not including foreign aid) and expenditures balanced at CFAF 9.76 billion (see Table 7). These receipts represented an increase of CFAF 0.28 billion, or about 3 per cent, over the 1969 budget estimates, which included CFAF 0.45 billion from foreign aid. Hence, the increase in revenues expected to be derived from Upper Volta's own resources amounted to CFAF 0.73 billion, most of which was to come from indirect taxes. Receipts from import duties were expected to rise by CFAF 0.43 billion

TABLE 7. UPPER VOLTA: GOVERNMENT BUDGET, 1962–70

(In millions of CFA francs)

	1962	1963	1964	1965	1966	1967	1968	1969 (Original Estimates)	1970 (Original Estimates)
Receipts									
Ordinary revenue									
Taxes									
Direct taxes	1,426	1,949	2,002	1,983	2,112	2,096	2,102	2,127	...
Indirect taxes	3,312	4,676	4,962	5,130	4,692	4,356	5,038	5,753	...
Registration and stamp fees	140	152	146	133	137	136	194	152	...
Unclassified taxes	38	—	—	—	10	9	7	...	...
Total taxes	4,916	6,777	7,110	7,245	6,951	6,597	7,341	8,032	8,861
Nontax revenue									
Income from property	42	29	53	35	35	34	46	34	...
Service charges and arrears	379	467	555	543	443	935	873	861	...
Total nontax revenue	421	496	608	578	478	969	919	895	784
Total ordinary revenue	5,337	7,273	7,718	7,823	7,429	7,566	8,260	8,927	9,645
Extraordinary receipts									
Foreign									
French aid	500	1,150	930	671	523	450	450	450	...
Solidarity Fund	237	125	—	—	92	—	—	—	...
Total foreign	737	1,275	930	671	615	450	450	450	...
Domestic									
Reimbursement for claims on Neighboring countries	32	—	1	45	8	4	6	5	...
Former French West Africa					179	14	—	7	...
Former French-held retirement funds					200	169		—	
Reimbursement on loans	15	7	19	9	51	5	1	23	...
BCEAO profits	—	6	16	68	68	69	90	70	···
Total domestic receipts	47	13	36	122	506	261	97	105	112
Total extraordinary receipts	784	1,288	966	793	1,121	711	547	555	112
Total receipts	6,121	8,561	8,684	8,616	8,550	8,277	8,807	9,482	9,757

Expenditures									
Public debt									
Amortization and interest	108	264	198	230	411	341	296	430	...
Pensions	80	107	168	164	146	171	186	244	...
Total public debt	188	371	366	394	557	512	482	674	710
Personnel and material [1]									
Personnel	3,764	4,142	4,379	4,495	4,606	4,020	4,218	4,776	...
Material	2,307	1,891	2,079	1,602	1,358	1,420	1,526	1,583	...
Total personnel and material	6,071	6,033	6,458	6,097	5,964	5,440	5,744	6,359	7,078
Transfers [2]	1,317	1,712	1,866	1,816	1,405	1,056	1,062	1,191	1,065
Capital expenditure [3]	793	833	631	617	784	1,037	1,156	1,258	904
Total expenditures	8,369	8,949	9,321	8,924	8,710	8,045	8,444	9,482	9,757
Surplus or deficit (−)	−2,248	−388	−637	−308	−160	232	363	—	—

Sources: Upper Volta, *Budget de l'Etat* and *Compte Définitif du Budget de l'Etat.*

[1] Includes carry-over from previous years, 1966–69.
[2] Includes carry-over from previous years, 1963–65.
[3] Includes carry-over financed by French aid.

TABLE 8.   UPPER VOLTA: FINANCING OF BUDGET OPERATIONS,   1966–68

(*In millions of CFA francs*)

	1966	1967	1968
Budget surplus, or deficit (−)	−160	232	363
Adjustment for			
Subsidy receipts	−523	−450	−450
Amortization of public debt	125	179	105
Total adjustment	−398	−271	−345
Net over-all surplus, or deficit (−)	−558	−39	18
Financing			
Investment expenditure subsidy	523	450	450
External resources			
French Treasury	−130	—	—
Net foreign borrowing	−125	−179	−105
Other	−46	166	−3
Total external resources	−301	−13	−108
Domestic resources			
Official entities	11	49	128
Banks and other financial institutions	110	−472	−484
Private sector	150	−1	−71
Total domestic resources	271	−424	−427
Other Treasury operations including statistical discrepancies	65	26	67

Sources: Table 7; Ministère des Finances et du Commerce, *Situation de la Trésorerie*; and BCEAO, *République de Haute-Volta—Execution du Budget de l'Etat, Mouvements des Opérations du Trésor Public Voltaïque*, and *Situation Résumée des Opérations de la Trésorerie de Haute-Volta.*

to CFAF 4.23 billion, mainly as a result of a rise in the value of imported goods following the devaluation of the CFA franc. In addition, the yield of the turnover tax was expected to increase by CFAF 0.30 billion as a result of the tax reform measures introduced at the beginning of January 1970. Receipts from direct taxes were expected to increase in 1970 by CFAF 0.09 billion to CFAF 2.21 billion. The direct taxation reforms, which took effect with the 1970 budget, were not expected to result in an appreciable increase in revenue, since they were to be largely offset by an increase in the minimum income exempted from the tax.

Ordinary expenditure was budgeted at CFAF 8.85 billion for 1970, against CFAF 8.22 billion for 1969. The rise in ordinary expenditure was due partly to an increase in the salaries of government employees. Government expenditure on wages and salaries was budgeted at CFAF 5.48 billion for 1970, or about 56 per cent of total expenditure, against 53 per cent for 1969. In order to stabilize this type of expenditure in the future, the Government was considering various measures such as limiting the increase in the number of government personnel, restricting promotions and salary increases, and encouraging early retirement for older employees.

STRUCTURE OF GOVERNMENT REVENUE

Between 1961 and 1967, fiscal revenue increased at an average annual rate of about 8 per cent. Nevertheless, over-all government receipts declined, owing to a sharp reduction in other receipts, mostly foreign budget grants. In 1968, however, total receipts (CFAF 8.8 billion) were about 3 per cent higher than in 1966 in spite of a drop in receipts other than revenue of CFAF 0.5 billion, or less than half of those in 1966.

Direct and indirect taxes contribute four fifths of government revenue in Upper Volta. Until 1968 the Government had placed greater emphasis on direct taxation. Indirect taxation had been modified only in order to minimize its impact on domestic prices or to reduce incentives for smuggling. In 1968 this over-all tax policy was changed; in 1969, direct taxes were somewhat reduced in order to provide tax relief to those in the lower income brackets, and, with some recovery in economic activity, turnover taxes were increased.

Direct Taxes

Since independence there has been no structural reform in direct taxation, which follows the system that prevailed in the Federation of French West Africa. Direct taxes contributed 24 per cent of total budget revenue in 1968 (Table 9). The minimum income tax, the head tax on livestock, and the schedular income tax on wages and salaries are the leading direct taxes in Upper Volta; in 1969 they were expected to account for about 90 per cent of direct tax revenue. The burden of direct taxation has increased substantially since 1966, although this fact is not reflected in budget figures because personal incomes have been reduced; the extraordinary income tax ("patriotic contribution") has not been allocated to the budget, and since 1968 receipts from some taxes have been transferred to local governments.

SURVEYS OF AFRICAN ECONOMIES, VOL. 3

TABLE 9. UPPER VOLTA: GOVERNMENT RECEIPTS FROM DIRECT TAXES, 1963–69

	1963	1964	1965	1966	1967	1968	1969 [1]
VALUE (million CFA francs)							
Income taxes							
Minimum personal income tax	1,011	1,152	1,055	1,057	1,065	975	1,125
Tax on livestock	—	—	—	—	—	80	115
Schedular income tax on wages and salaries	739	664	729	532	831	866	623
Commercial, agricultural, industrial, and noncommercial profit tax	—	—	—	170	154	159	177
General income tax	—	—	—	49	58	44	60
Total income taxes	1,750	1,816	1,784	1,808	2,108	2,124	2,100 [3]
Property taxes [2]	71	74	74	71	9 [3]	[3]	[3]
Business and unclassified taxes							
Business fees and licenses	...	...	...	101	2 [4]	[4]	[4]
Unclassified	...	...	...	131	—	—	27
Total business and unclassified taxes	128	112	124	232	2	—	27
Adjustment [5]	—	—	—	—	−23	−22	—
Total direct taxes	1,949	2,002	1,983	2,112	2,096	2,102	2,127
PER CENT OF TOTAL RECEIPTS							
Income taxes	20.4	20.9	20.7	21.1	25.5	24.1	22.1
Property taxes	...	0.9	0.9	0.8	—	—	—
Business and unclassified taxes	...	1.3	1.4	2.8	2	—	0.3
Adjustment [5]	...	—	—	—	−0.2	−0.2	—
Total direct taxes	22.8	23.1	23.1	24.7	25.3	23.9	22.4

Source: Data supplied by the Ministry of Finance and Commerce, Tax Office and Office of Miscellaneous Contributions.

[1] Estimated.
[2] Includes tax on household occupation 1963–65.
[3] Partly suppressed and partly transferred to local authorities.
[4] Transferred to local authorities.
[5] Due to need for reclassification of certain items, mainly interest and penalties.

720

The most important direct tax is the poll tax, called the minimum income tax, which with the head tax on livestock, contributes about one half of direct tax revenue.

Minimum income tax.—The minimum income tax is a slightly progressive tax on every resident over 14 years of age. Before 1967, rates ranged from CFAF 410 to CFAF 8,000 according to income and the relative prosperity of the region of residence. In 1967 the three lower rates of CFAF 410, CFAF 460, and CFAF 540 were increased by CFAF 40, and the tax was extended to retired civil and military personnel who had previously been exonerated. In 1968, retired persons were no longer taxed at the highest rate, and since 1969 they have once again become exonerated. To improve collection of this tax, which is difficult to assess, partly because of the mobility of the population, the Government appointed 10 census agents in 1968, and this number was to increase to 28 in 1969. Except for 1968, separate data on the yield of this tax are not available. A 15 per cent increase in receipts was expected for 1969 from improved collection and higher personal income.

Head tax on livestock.—The head tax on livestock, which had been unified at CFAF 200 in 1966, was reduced to CFAF 175 in 1969, when a CFAF 50 compulsory inoculation tax, earmarked for the livestock services, was introduced. The head tax is shared by local governments but since 1968 has accrued mostly to the Central Government. Larger receipts were expected for 1969 on account of a better livestock census. The inoculation program may be difficult to implement, and it is feared that rather than improve registration procedure, the tax may result in a larger number of animals remaining without vaccination.

Schedular income tax on wages and salaries.—Collection of the schedular income tax on wages and salaries represented about 40 per cent of direct tax revenue in 1968. Fluctuations in actual receipts from this tax, which is levied on all wage earners and withheld at the source, reflect the substantial changes in rates made since 1966. In 1967 the rate for salaries above CFAF 10,000 per month was raised from 10 per cent to 15 per cent and salaries below this level, previously exempted, were at the rate of 3 per cent. In spite of the general 10 per cent reduction in the salaries of the public sector, which substantially reduced personal incomes, receipts from the schedular income tax on wages and salaries rose from CFAF 532 million in 1966 to CFAF 866 million in 1968, or by about 63 per cent. Effective in January 1969, the Government adopted a new rate structure to make the tax more progressive. Wages and salaries of less than CFAF 10,000 per month were once again exempted from the schedular tax of 3 per cent; the rates were reduced from 15 per cent to 10 per cent for monthly salaries of CFAF 10,000–30,000 and from 15 per cent to 12 per cent for salaries above CFAF 30,000. These reductions were expected to reduce the yield of this tax by some CFAF 243 million in 1969.

Profit tax.—The commercial, agricultural, industrial, and noncommercial profit tax represents only 8 per cent of direct tax revenue. In 1969, the rate was increased from 32 per cent to 35 per cent for corporations and from 25 per cent to 28 per cent for individual firms. In addition, the minimum tax based on the estimated turnover introduced in 1966 was extended to all corporations and individuals. Receipts from this tax decreased slightly in 1967 and 1968. Assessments in early 1969 were higher than in previous years, and the ratio of actual collections to assessments apparently remained the same; therefore, the budgeted rise in revenues from this tax probably materialized in 1969.

General income tax.—The progressive general income tax levied in addition to the schedular tax contributes less than 3 per cent of direct tax revenue. The applicable rates have not been changed since 1966, and the proceeds declined in 1968. A withholding system for the collection of this tax in 1969 was introduced and higher receipts were expected as a result of the greater economic activity.

Other direct taxes.—Among other direct taxes is the payroll tax (2.5 per cent per year paid by private employers), which yields about CFAF 50 million per year.

Other developments in direct taxation between 1966 and 1969 were the transfer to local governments of some minor business and property taxes and imposition of the "patriotic contribution," an extraordinary income tax levied on Upper Volta citizens regardless of residence, which was collected between March 1967 and March 1968. The proceeds of this tax were allocated to a special Treasury account for repayment of arrears. For wage earners, the tax was set at one half of one month's salary; for business, at one half of the value of the business license; and for all others, at a fixed amount of either CFAF 100 or CFAF 200, according to residence of the taxpayer. Some CFAF 460 million was collected, equivalent to about 22 per cent of direct tax revenue in 1967.

Indirect Taxes

Indirect taxes contributed 57 per cent of total budget revenue in 1968 (Table 10). About 7 per cent higher indirect taxes were collected in 1968 than in 1966, and the estimate for 1969 (CFAF 5.8 billion) represented an increase of 14 per cent over actual receipts in 1968. Collections during the first three months of 1969 were in line with budget estimates.

More than two thirds of indirect tax proceeds come from fiscal and customs duties, mainly those applicable to imports.

Fiscal duties.—Fiscal duties on imports ranging from 1 to 30 per cent apply to all imports except those originating from the countries forming the Union Douanière de l'Afrique de l'Ouest (UDEAO). Those imports are subject to a *taxe unique*, which amounts in principle to half the amount of the minimum import tax applicable to imports from third countries. Most capital goods are exempted from fiscal duties.

Customs duties.—Upper Volta does not levy customs duties on imports from counrties of either the EEC or the French franc area. Imports from countries with which Upper Volta maintains a trade agreement and those which have such agreements with France (e.g., Brazil, Denmark, the U.S.S.R., the United Kingdom, and the United States) are subject to a minimum tariff with rates ranging from 1 to 25 per cent of the actual value of imports.[2]

Other indirect taxes.—Imports are also subject to a surtax, which generally amounts to 25 per cent of the actual value regardless of the origin of the goods. Basic consumption goods and capital goods are either taxed at a lower rate or exempted.

Exports are subject to a fiscal duty of 0.5–15 per cent, to a 1 per cent service tax, to a 5.4 per cent surtax, and to the temporary subsidization tax. A special tax is also levied on cattle exports.

---

[2] For certain consumption and capital goods a statistical value, usually lower than the actual value, is used for the computation of duties.

TABLE 10. UPPER VOLTA: GOVERNMENT RECEIPTS FROM INDIRECT TAXES, 1963–69

VALUE (million CFA francs)

	1963	1964	1965	1966	1967	1968	1969 [1]
Import duties and taxes							
Customs duties	741	671	616	839	878	1,072	1,043
Fiscal duties	933	891	934	559	589	678	807
Total import duties and taxes	1,674	1,562	1,550	1,398	1,467	1,750	1,850
Consumption taxes and tobacco monopoly							
Consumption taxes on							
Petroleum	...	...	...	233	235	231	267
Imported beverages	...	...	...	137	108	108	120
Meat	...	...	...	—	—	—	60
Local beverages	...	...	...	49	50	55	54
Grazing rights	...	...	...	17	19	16	16
Kolanuts	...	...	...	15	11	10	10
Ammunition	...	...	...	7	9	10	9
Tobacco	...	...	...			1	—
Tobacco monopoly	...	...	...	423	388	409	470
Total consumption taxes and tobacco monopoly	970	871	876	881	820	840	1,006
Turnover taxes							
Compensatory turnover tax on imports [2]	1,507	1,934	2,099	1,121	1,000	1,130	1,170
Taxe unique	...	...	...	777	626	708	781
Turnover taxes	...	...	...	414	399	305	610
Fiscal duties on exports	11	38	38	87	123	159	152
Licenses	...	...	...	7	5	7	6
Total turnover taxes	1,864	2,357	2,534	2,406	2,153	2,309	2,719
Export duties	...	...	...	42	31	54	47
Import and export service taxes	...	...	...	9	2	4	10
Miscellaneous taxes							
Statistical tax on imports	...	...	...	103	79	86	92
Statistical tax on exports	...	...	...		23	31	27
Documents	...	...	...	1	1	1	—
Warehouse	...	...	...	2	1	1	2
Total miscellaneous taxes	168	172	168	106	104	119	121
Adjustment [3]	—	—	—	-150	-221	-38	—
Total indirect taxes	4,675	4,962	5,130	4,692	4,356	5,038	5,753

PER CENT OF TOTAL BUDGET RECEIPTS

Import duties and taxes	19.6	18.0	18.0	16.3	17.7	19.9	19.5
Consumption taxes and tobacco monopoly	11.3	10.0	10.2	10.3	9.9	9.5	10.6
Turnover taxes	21.8	27.1	29.4	28.1	26.0	26.2	28.7
Export duties	...	...	...	0.5	0.4	0.6	0.5
Import and export service taxes	...	...	...	0.1	—	—	0.1
Miscellaneous taxes	1.8	2.0	2.0	1.2	1.3	1.3	1.3
Adjustment [3]	—	—	—	-1.7	-2.7	-0.3	—
Total indirect taxes	54.6	57.1	59.6	54.9	52.6	57.2	60.7

Source: Data supplied by the Ministry of Finance and Commerce, Tax Office and Office of Miscellaneous Contributions.

[1] Estimated.
[2] Includes development tax on imports 1963–65.
[3] Due to need for reclassification of certain items, mainly interest and penalties.

In order to help economic recovery, and to avoid increases in the domestic price level, the Government reduced customs and fiscal duties in 1967 for some major consumption products (e.g., medical supplies, cotton fabrics, tobacco, and bicycle tires). In October 1967, however, the specific tax on gasoline and gas oil was increased by some 30 per cent. At the same time, 59 per cent of all taxes levied on petroleum products was allocated to a special Treasury account earmarked for road maintenance and improvement. Effective January 1968, fiscal and customs duties on imports and exports were regrouped, and border control was improved through an administrative reorganization. Duty rates, both fiscal and customs, on imports of telecommunications parts, pesticides, fertilizers, farm equipment, construction materials, vehicles, school books, and newspapers were reduced by 10 to 20 per cent. With the 1969 budget, several rates of the turnover taxes have increased, and a tax on foreign-produced goods was introduced at rates of 2.5 per cent when imported by small retailers and 3 per cent when imported by registered importers. Furthermore, the special tax on sugar imports was increased by CFAF 5 per kilogram.

Consumption taxes (*droits de consommation*) [3] and the turnover tax with rates of 4–14 per cent represent some 18 per cent of indirect tax revenue. The substantial increase in revenue from these taxes estimated for 1969 should result from the higher turnover tax and from the expected recovery in economic activity.

A special tax commission on which the private sector is represented was established in 1967 to study and recommend measures aimed at simplifying and rationalizing the tax system. At the request of the authorities, an expert from the IMF staff provided technical assistance in this study at the end of 1968. The main recommendations contained in his report were to improve the progressiveness of the minimum income tax, to replace the present income-splitting system by one with standard deductions, to reduce the various rates of the turnover taxes, and to simplify the import duty structure. Some steps, such as the regrouping of customs and fiscal duties, have already been taken along the broad lines of those recommendations, and the authorities have indicated their intention to further improve the tax system.

---

[3] On tobacco, petroleum products, ammunition, imported and locally produced beverages, kolanuts, and grazing rights for cattle in transit.

STRUCTURE OF GOVERNMENT EXPENDITURE

Current expenditure accounts for most government budget appropriations. Although the share of capital expenditure has increased in recent years, it still amounted to less than 14 per cent of total expenditures in 1968 (Table 11).

Wages and salaries, including family allowances, represent the largest expenditure category, accounting for 50 per cent of total expenditures in 1968. Maintenance and materials accounted for about 18 per cent, transfers for nearly 13 per cent, public debt service for less than 4 per cent, and pensions for 2 per cent.

Steps taken in 1966 to reduce current expenditure were confined to a number of day-to-day decisions affecting mainly personnel, such as the reduction in expenditure of representations abroad and in special allowances to higher government officials. Expenditure for materials was slightly reduced.

In preparing the 1967 budget, however, the Government made a more comprehensive review of expenditures. Salaries and wages of all permanent government employees were reduced by 10 per cent, and family allowances were reduced from CFAF 1,500 per month per child to CFAF 700 up to the sixth child. As a result actual expenditure for personnel declined by CFAF 584 million, or almost 13 per cent. Expenditure for materials remained practically unchanged, but transfer payments, mainly subsidies to public entities and grants to schools, were cut by CFAF 348 million. Actual current expenditure in 1967 was CFAF 918 million lower than in 1966. The 1968 budget followed the broad lines adopted in the previous year, and only a slight increase in expenditure for materials was permitted. With the improvement in the over-all fiscal position, some increases were permitted in the 1969 budget appropriations. The salary scale of government employees was adjusted upward to its 1966 level, and expenditures for health, education, rural development, and public works were increased.

Between 1966 and 1968, capital expenditure rose by about 47 per cent, and a further increase was budgeted for 1969. Disbursement under the general title "Equipment financed by French aid" is the most

TABLE 11.   UPPER VOLTA: GOVERNMENT EXPENDITURES, 1966–69

	1966	1967	1968	1969 [1]
VALUE *(million CFA francs)*				
Current expenditure				
By function				
General administration				
Institutions	145	170	89	106
Unclassified ministries and common				
expenditures	1,444	1,397	1,624	1,689
Pensions	146	170	186	244
Total general administration	1,735	1,737	1,899	2,039
Foreign affairs				
Ministry	150	89	105	128
Contributions	179	188	218	265
Total foreign affairs	329	277	323	393
Defense and justice				
Army	976	909	931	1,045
Interior and security	816	669	678	787
Justice	53	44	51	62
Total defense and justice	1,845	1,622	1,660	1,894
Social services				
Public health	796	690	712	812
Veterans	5	3	5	7
Total social services	801	693	717	819
Cultural services				
Education and sports	1,049	906	971	1,152
Scholarships and grants to schools	455	450	370	482
Total cultural services	1,504	1,356	1,341	1,634
Economy				
Finance and trade	534 [2]	364	390	435
National development and agriculture	456	383	483	576
Public works	101	73	— [3]	— [3]
Post Office	210	162	180	4
Total economy	1,301	982	1,053	1,015
Debt service	411	341	295	430
Total current expenditure	7,926	7,008	7,288	8,224
By economic category				
Personnel	4,559	3,965	4,219 [4]	4,736
Pensions	146	170	186	244
Materials	1,004	1,005	1,491 [4]	1,338
Maintenance	27	29	35	85
Transfers (including subsidies, contribu-				
tions, and loans)	1,404	1,056	1,062	1,191
Carry-over from previous years	375	442	—	200
Debt service	411	341	295	430
Capital expenditure				
Road maintenance	. . .	151	326	379
Housing and building	. . .	33	102	8
Equipment materials	. . .	—	20	8
Investment and studies	. . .	302	204	343
Shares in official entities	. . .	101	54	69
Equipment financed by French aid	523	450	450	450
Total capital expenditure [5]	784	1,037	1,156	1,257
Total expenditures	8,710	8,045	8,444	9,481

TABLE 11 (*concluded*). UPPER VOLTA: GOVERNMENT EXPENDITURES, 1966–69

	1966	1967	1968	1969 [1]
PER CENT OF TOTAL EXPENDITURES				
Public debt				
Amortization and interest	4.7	4.2	3.5	4.5
Pensions	1.7	2.1	2.2	2.6
Total public debt	6.4	6.4	5.7	7.1
Personnel and materials [4]				
Personnel	52.9	50.0	50.0	50.4
Materials	15.6	17.6	18.1	16.7
Total personnel and materials	68.5	67.6	68.0	67.1
Transfers	16.1	13.1	12.6	12.6
Capital expenditure [5]	9.0	12.9	13.7	13.3
Total expenditures	100.0	100.0	100.0	100.0

Source: Upper Volta, *Compte Définitif du Budget de l'Etat.*

[1] Estimated.
[2] Including CFAF 93 million shares subscriptions in official entities.
[3] Since 1968 public works expenditures are budgeted under the Ministry of National Development.
[4] Includes carry-over from previous years and maintenance.
[5] Includes equipment financed by French aid (CFAF 523 million in 1966 and CFAF 450 million in following years) not included in the government budget.

important single category of capital expenditure.[4] The relative proportion of this disbursement to total budgeted investment expenditure, however, declined from 67 per cent in 1966 to an estimated 36 per cent in 1969. This decline was due to a reduction in the subsidy by CFAF 73 million in 1967 and to no change since then, while over-all budgetary allocations to capital expenditure more than tripled between 1966 and 1969. Most of the increase in capital expenditure was allocated to disbursements for road maintenance, which more than doubled between 1967 and 1968 and was expected to increase further in 1969.

MONEY AND BANKING

MONETARY SYSTEM

Upper Volta belongs to the franc area. Together with Dahomey, Ivory Coast, Mauritania, Niger, Senegal, and Togo, it is also linked in

---

[4] Investment expenditures financed by the European Development Fund (EDF) and the French Fonds d'Aide et de Coopération (FAC) are not included in the government budget.

the West African Monetary Union (Union Monétaire Ouest Africaine, or UMOA). These countries share a common currency, the CFA franc, and a common central bank, the Banque Centrale des Etats de l'Afrique de l'Ouest (BCEAO), which is the issuing authority of UMOA and keeps its external reserves. The CFA franc is freely convertible into French francs at the rate of CFAF 1.00 = F 0.02. On August 10, 1969, the rate against the U.S. dollar became CFAF 277.710 per dollar; previously, since January 1, 1960, the rate had been CFAF 246.853. (For details on the operation of BCEAO, see Chapter 4, and for information on the change in the par value, see Chapter 6.)

STRUCTURE OF THE BANKING SYSTEM

The banking system of Upper Volta includes the Central Bank (BCEAO), which it shares with the other UMOA members, two commercial banks, and the Development Bank (Banque Nationale de Développement, or BND). BCEAO operates in Upper Volta, as in other UMOA countries, through a local agency. Decisions concerning the implementation of BCEAO policies in Upper Volta are taken by the National Monetary Committee. The Director of the local BCEAO agency, who sits on the National Monetary Committee in an advisory capacity, is responsible for the application of these policies. Operations of the Central Bank in Upper Volta are summarized in Table 12.

Assets and liabilities of the commercial banks, the Development Bank, and other financial institutions are given in Table 13. The two commercial banks are the Banque Internationale pour l'Afrique Occidentale (BIAO) and the Banque Nationale de Paris (BNP). The first bank, which operates in all UMOA countries, maintains a branch office in Bobo Dioulasso, besides the main office in the capital.

The major source for medium-term and long-term credit is the Development Bank, established in 1961 with a capital of CFAF 355 million, of which the Government subscribed CFAF 225 million. The other shareholders are the French Caisse Centrale de Coopération Economique (CCCE) with CFAF 100 million and BCEAO with CFAF 30 million.

Other financial intermediaries that perform some banking operations are the Treasury and the Postal Checking System (see Table 13), as

TABLE 12. UPPER VOLTA: ASSETS AND LIABILITIES OF THE CENTRAL BANK, 1962–69

(In billions of CFA francs; end of period)

	1962	1963	1964	1965	1966	1967 Sept.	1967 Dec.	1968 Mar.	1968 June	1968 Sept.	1968 Dec.	1969 Mar.	1969 June	1969 Sept.
Assets														
Foreign assets	3.48	3.60	3.34	3.45	4.02	4.69	4.55	4.98	5.28	5.22	5.78	5.92	6.57	6.96
Claims on Government	0.03	0.20	0.21	0.20	0.37	0.01	0.15	0.06	—	—	—	—	—	—
Claims on banks														
Short-term	0.10	0.35	0.82	0.91	0.47	0.24	0.58	0.64	—	—	0.28	0.64	0.31	...
Medium-term	0.02	0.07	0.18	0.14	0.08	0.07	0.08	0.07	0.06	0.04	0.06	0.07	0.07	...
Total claims on banks	0.12	0.42	1.00	1.05	0.55	0.31	0.66	0.71	0.06	0.04	0.34	0.71	0.38	0.39
Assets = liabilities	**3.63**	**4.22**	**4.55**	**4.70**	**4.94**	**5.01**	**5.36**	**5.75**	**5.34**	**5.26**	**6.12**	**6.63**	**6.95**	**7.35**
Liabilities														
Currency and bankers' deposits	3.10	3.94	4.31	4.48	4.72	4.23	4.68	4.34	4.05	4.17	4.88	4.80	4.37	4.72
Currency outside banks	*3.05*	*3.90*	*4.26*	*4.43*	*4.69*	*4.15*	*4.60*	*4.28*	*3.99*	*4.08*	*4.77*	*4.74*	*4.32*	*4.60*
Foreign liabilities	0.10	0.08	0.04	0.01	0.01	0.01	0.05	0.34	0.15	0.01	0.20	0.01	0.06	0.01
Government deposits	0.40	0.39	0.20	0.20	0.21	0.77	0.63	1.07	1.14	1.08	1.04	1.82	2.50	2.62
Other items (net)	0.03	−0.19	—	0.01	—	—	—	—	—	—	—	—	0.02	—

Sources: IMF, *International Financial Statistics*, and BCEAO, *Indicateurs Economiques (Haute-Volta)*.

TABLE 13. UPPER VOLTA: ASSETS AND LIABILITIES OF COMMERCIAL BANKS, DEVELOPMENT BANK, AND OTHER FINANCIAL INSTITUTIONS, 1962–69

(In billions of CFA francs; end of period)

	1962	1963	1964	1965	1966	1967 Sept.	1967 Dec.	1968 Mar.	1968 June	1968 Sept.	1968 Dec.	1969 Mar.	1969 June	1969 Sept.
COMMERCIAL BANKS AND DEVELOPMENT BANK														
Assets														
Cash and balances with Central Bank	0.08	0.05	0.04	0.04	0.04	0.06	0.08	0.06	0.04	0.09	0.20	0.05	0.05	0.12
Foreign assets	0.25	0.37	0.16	0.25	0.17	0.26	0.19	0.25	0.86	0.68	0.61	0.48	0.33	0.37
Claims on private sector														
Short-term	1.74	2.47	2.88	3.03	2.53	2.22	2.66	3.01	2.34	2.33	3.12	3.63	3.53	3.66
Medium-term	0.26	0.37	0.48	0.45	0.38	0.42	0.39	0.29	0.28	0.30	0.32	0.33	0.32	0.36
Long-term	0.14	0.18	0.25	0.37	0.45	0.47	0.48	0.46	0.47	0.47	0.48	0.53	0.55	0.57
Total claims on private sector	2.14	3.02	3.61	3.85	3.36	3.11	3.53	3.76	3.09	3.10	3.92	4.49	4.40	4.59
Assets = liabilities	2.47	3.44	3.81	4.14	3.57	3.43	3.80	4.07	3.99	3.87	4.73	5.02	4.78	5.08
Liabilities														
Demand deposits	1.85	1.58	1.41	1.46	1.44	1.61	1.65	1.89	2.22	2.27	2.33	2.37	2.44	2.39
Time deposits	0.19	0.15	0.21	0.14	0.09	0.08	0.06	0.09	0.14	0.17	0.14	0.15	0.17	0.23
Foreign liabilities	...	1.00	0.91	1.08	0.78	0.76	0.90	0.89	1.03	0.81	1.22	1.17	1.09	1.25
Credit from Central Bank	0.12	0.42	1.00	1.05	0.55	0.31	0.65	0.71	0.06	0.04	0.34	0.71	0.38	0.39
Other items (net)	0.31	0.29	0.28	0.41	0.71	0.67	0.54	0.49	0.54	0.58	0.70	0.62	0.70	0.82
OTHER FINANCIAL INSTITUTIONS														
Treasury: claims on private sector	0.15	0.29	0.40	0.23	0.26	0.19	0.21	0.41	0.07	...	0.14	0.15	0.10	0.12
Postal Checking System: deposits	0.43	0.48	0.39	0.38	0.40	0.39	0.34	0.47	0.45		0.36	0.47	0.50	0.44

Sources: IMF, International Financial Statistics, and BCEAO, Indicateurs Economiques (Haute-Volta).

well as the National Savings Bank. The Treasury extends credit to the private sector by accepting customs duty bills (*obligations cautionnées*) with a maturity of four months in lieu of immediate payment of certain indirect taxes, mainly customs duties. These bills are discountable at BCEAO. In addition the Treasury receives deposits from public and semipublic institutions, as well as from the private sector under special circumstances. The Postal Checking System receives deposits from the private sector and keeps most of its resources with the Treasury.

The National Savings Bank, an autonomous public institution, receives savings deposits through the Postal Checking System but does not engage in credit operations. Most of its resources are kept with the Treasury.

In addition to credit extended by banks, CCCE extends medium-term and long-term credit and contributes to the financing of the Development Bank's credit operations. It also acts as the authorized agent of the Fonds d'Aide et de Coopération (FAC) and the European Development Fund (EDF, or Fonds Européen de Développement, or FED) for local aid disbursements.

BANKING LEGISLATION

With the treaty establishing UMOA in 1962, the governments of the member countries undertook to adopt basically uniform banking legislation. In Upper Volta, new banking legislation was introduced on July 29, 1964. This legislation specifies the basic conditions and regulations governing banks and other financial institutions. In accordance with this legislation the Minister of Finance, in consultation with a Comité des Banques et des Etablissements Financiers, is responsible for the management of the over-all credit policy; and the Central Bank has certain regulatory powers over banks and other financial institutions. The National Credit Council—composed of government officials and representatives from the trade, agricultural, industrial, and banking sectors and the Professional Association of Banks—advises the Minister of Finance on all matters concerning the banking profession and credit regulations.

The banking legislation of 1964 and a subsequent decree of 1965 stipulate a minimum capital requirement of CFAF 50 million for each bank and CFAF 10 million for each other financial institution operating in Upper Volta. Furthermore, commercial banks' capital must represent at least 8 per cent of total outstanding credit inclusive of rediscounts with the Central Bank and contingent liabilities on account of guarantees. For the Development Bank, this minimum capital ratio is set at 12 per cent and for other financial institutions at 10 per cent. Banks and financial institutions are also required to allocate 15 per cent of net profits to a Reserve Fund.

The legislation also regulates the banks' participation in the capital of nonbank enterprises and financial institutions. Participation in any given enterprise should not exceed 15 per cent of the banks' capital and aggregate participations should not exceed such capital.

Banks are required to maintain a minimum ratio between their liquid and rediscountable assets and their short-term liabilities. This ratio was fixed at 70 per cent for 1965/66 and was to increase by 1 percentage point each year until it reaches 75 per cent in 1970/71. In view of its composition, this ratio encourages banks to grant rediscountable credits.

BCEAO is empowered by virtue of its statute to impose reserve requirements on deposit liabilities of banks and credit institutions when so instructed by the Government. Thus far, this has not been done.

OVER-ALL MONETARY AND CREDIT DEVELOPMENTS

Between December 1962 and September 1969, money supply rose by about 40 per cent to CFAF 7.43 billion (Table 14), an average annual increase of about 5 per cent. Before 1967 the gain in money supply primarily represented a rise in total domestic credit both to the Government and to the private sector; since then it has stemmed mainly from expansion in the net foreign assets of the banking system.

Between December 1962 and December 1966, money supply rose by CFAF 1.19 billion, or by 22 per cent, to CFAF 6.53 billion; the increase was reflected solely in a rise in currency in circulation outside banks by CFAF 1.64 billion, as demand deposits with banks and with the Post Office declined during the period by CFAF 0.45 billion. The increase in money supply was due mainly to a rise in total domestic credit by CFAF 1.59 billion, as net foreign assets declined by CFAF 0.22 billion. The banking system's net credit to the Government, which had a negative balance of CFAF 0.6 billion in 1962, rose steadily in the following years, and by December 1966 the Government was a net

TABLE 14. UPPER VOLTA: MONETARY SURVEY, 1962–69

(In billions of CFA francs; end of period)

	1962	1963	1964	1965	1966	1967		1968				1969		
						Sept.	Dec.	Mar.	June	Sept.	Dec.	Mar.	June	Sept.
Assets														
Foreign assets (net)	3.63	2.89	2.54	2.60	3.41	4.18	3.79	4.00	4.97	5.09	4.97	5.22	5.75	6.08
Domestic credit														
Claims on Government (net)	−0.06	0.01	0.01	0.13	0.20	−0.58	−0.41	−0.73	−0.83	−0.88	−0.92	−1.57	−2.15	−2.41
Claims on private sector	2.29	3.31	4.01	4.08	3.62	3.30	3.74	3.90	3.16	3.21	4.06	4.63	4.50	4.70
Total domestic credit	2.23	3.33	4.02	4.21	3.82	2.72	3.33	3.17	2.33	2.33	3.14	3.06	2.35	2.29
Assets = liabilities	**5.86**	**6.22**	**6.56**	**6.81**	**7.23**	**6.90**	**7.12**	**7.17**	**7.30**	**7.42**	**8.11**	**8.28**	**8.10**	**8.37**
Liabilities														
Money	5.34	5.96	6.06	6.27	6.53	6.15	6.60	6.64	6.66	6.75	7.45	7.59	7.27	7.43
Quasi-money	0.19	0.15	0.21	0.14	0.09	0.08	0.06	0.09	0.14	0.17	0.14	0.15	0.17	0.23
Other items (net)	0.33	0.11	0.29	0.40	0.61	0.67	0.46	0.44	0.50	0.50	0.52	0.54	0.66	0.71

Sources: IMF, *International Financial Statistics*, and data provided by BCEAO.

borrower of CFAF 0.20 billion. Credit to the private sector rose between December 1962 and December 1966 by CFAF 1.33 billion, or by 58 per cent, to CFAF 3.62 billion; most of the increase occurred during 1963–65 and was financed, to a large extent, by credit from BCEAO, and by foreign borrowings. Between 1965 and 1966, credit to the private sector declined by CFAF 0.46 billion.

After 1966, money supply continued to grow mainly because of rising demand deposits, since the currency in circulation outside banks remained stable. In the two years ended September 1969, money supply rose by CFAF 1.28 billion, or by 21 per cent, to CFAF 7.43 billion. During this period, the increase stemmed from a gain in the net foreign assets of the banking system by CFAF 1.90 billion to CFAF 6.08 billion, as total domestic credit declined by CFAF 0.43 billion. Most of the gain in the net foreign assets took place in the last year and reflected the favorable balance of payments. Credit to the private sector rose in the two years ended September 1969 by CFAF 1.40 billion, or by 42 per cent; all the increase was in the last year and was due to a revival in economic activity following the austerity measures adopted in the previous two years. The increase in credit to the private sector was more than offset by a sharp decline in the net credit to the Government, reflecting the continued improvement in public finance.

Quasi-money remained small; between December 1962 and September 1969 it rose by CFAF 0.04 billion, or by about 21 per cent, to CFAF 0.23 billion. In September 1969, quasi-money represented about 3 per cent of total money supply.

CENTRAL BANK OPERATIONS

Assets and liabilities data of the Central Bank in Upper Volta indicate that currency in circulation rose rapidly in the four years ended December 1966 but has since remained relatively stable (see Table 12). During this period, currency in circulation outside banks rose by CFAF 1.64 billion, or by 54 per cent, to CFAF 4.69 billion; in the following years, it fluctuated rather sharply and by September 1969, currency outside banks was CFAF 0.09 billion below the level of December 1966. The increase in the currency in circulation during the years ended 1962–66 resulted chiefly from the rapid expansion in credit to the Government and to banks.

The Central Bank's credit to the Government rose rapidly between 1962 and 1963 and again between 1965 and 1966; later it declined sharply, and by mid-1968 the Government had no credit from the Bank. Government deposits with the Bank rose substantially after 1966, and by September 1969 they were more than 12 times as much as they were in December 1966. Credit to banks fluctuated widely from year to year in response to the banks' needs in financing seasonal crops. Total credit granted by the Central Bank to the Government and to banks rose from CFAF 0.15 billion in December 1962 to CFAF 1.25 billion in December 1965 but declined after that, and in September 1969 it amounted to CFAF 0.39 billion.

The Central Bank's foreign assets doubled between December 1962 and September 1969, reaching CFAF 6.96 billion; all the increase took place after 1965, with a particular increase of CFAF 1.7 billion in the year ended September 1969.

OPERATIONS OF OTHER BANKS

Between December 1962 and September 1969, bank credit to the private sector rose by CFAF 2.45 billion, or by an average annual rate of about 11 per cent, to CFAF 4.59 billion. About 60 per cent of the increase took place in the two years ended September 1969. During 1962–66, short-term, medium-term, and, especially, long-term credit expanded considerably. On the other hand, during the two years ended September 1969, short-term and long-term credit rose, but medium-term credit declined.

In the distribution of short-term credit by economic sectors, the financing of commercial activities—mainly those related to import and export—continued to dominate, although its share in total short-term credit declined from more than 60 per cent in December 1965 to about 45 per cent in December 1968 (Table 15). On the other hand, larger amounts of short-term credit are being directed toward the financing of export crops; in December 1968 this credit represented almost 25 per cent of the total. With more long-term credit becoming available in recent years, short-term credit for building construction has declined; in December 1968, credit for construction and public works represented about 7 per cent of total outstanding short-term credit, compared with almost 12 per cent in December 1965.

TABLE 15. UPPER VOLTA: DISTRIBUTION OF SHORT-TERM CREDIT
BY MAIN ECONOMIC SECTORS, 1965–MARCH 1969

(In percentages; at end of period)

	1965	1966	1967	1968	March 1968	1969
Commerce	60.4	59.0	51.9	44.7	46.7	41.6
Import and distribution [1]	*28.7*	*31.3*	*28.5*	*22.3*	*25.6*	*21.4*
Production of export crops	4.5	9.2	17.0	24.6	26.8	32.4
Transportation	5.9	8.4	8.1	7.1	7.5	6.7
Construction and public works	11.6	11.3	5.9	6.8	4.9	5.9
Industry	4.1	1.0	2.3	2.2	1.4	2.1
Other	13.5	11.1	14.8	14.6	12.7	11.3
Total	100.0	100.0	100.0	100.0	100.0	100.0

Source: Mainly from BCEAO, *Indicateurs Economiques (Haute-Volta)*.
[1] Includes petroleum products imports.

Banks have been able to finance the expansion in credit to the private sector from the increase in their demand and time deposits and from long-term foreign borrowing, mainly from CCCE. Credit from the Central Bank also rose during the period; in September 1969, it represented 8.5 per cent of credit to the private sector extended by banks, compared with 5.6 per cent in December 1962.

FOREIGN TRADE, AID, DEBT, AND PAYMENTS

RECORDED FOREIGN TRADE

Foreign trade data, derived from customs statistics, are incomplete because a portion of Upper Volta's trade escapes recording. Unrecorded trade consists largely of livestock exported on the hoof to neighboring countries, which is usually exchanged for food products and other consumer items that are then imported clandestinely. Lack of information on those unrecorded transactions does not permit adjustments in trade statistics to be made.

Composition of Exports

Cattle, other livestock, and refrigerated meat are Upper Volta's main exports (Table 16). In 1968 these commodities accounted for 53 per cent of recorded exports, compared with 55 per cent in 1962. Exports

TABLE 16. UPPER VOLTA: COMPOSITION OF RECORDED EXPORTS, 1962–68

(Value in millions of CFA francs)

	Value							Per Cent of Total	
	1962	1963	1964	1965	1966	1967	1968	1962	1968
Cattle	699	752	1,257	1,441	1,498	1,501	1,589	35.9	30.0
Other livestock	283	368	583	702	709	770	936	14.5	17.7
Cotton (ginned)	50[1]	113[1]	249[1]	257	304	842	913	2.6[1]	17.3
Sheanut products									
Sheanuts	77	8	118	63	155	68	311	4.0	5.9
Shea butter and oil	42	21	37	62	51	12	54	2.1	1.0
Total sheanut products	119	29	155	125	206	90	365	6.1	6.9
Groundnuts (shelled)	15	101	119	162	204	283	302	0.8	5.7
Refrigerated meat	90[2]	83[2]	132[2]	66	200	259	280	4.6[2]	5.3
Sesame seed	13	60	61	88	64	118	118	0.7	2.2
Cottonseed	8	20	69	48	32	98	123	0.4	2.3
Hides and skins	17	121	204	110	204	85	77	0.9	1.5
Gold	290	287	228	248	116	—	—	14.9	—
Other	361	366	257	433	448	393	585	18.6	11.1
Total	1,945	2,300	3,314	3,680	3,985	4,429	5,288	100.0	100.0

Sources: Ministère du Développement et du Tourisme, *Bulletin Mensuel de Statistiques* and *Rapport Economique*, 1965, and Ministère des Finances et du Commerce, *Situation Economique de la Haute-Volta*, 1969.

[1] Includes some cloth.
[2] Includes some fish.

of cattle and other livestock rose from CFAF 1.0 billion in 1962 to CFAF 2.5 billion in 1968, while refrigerated meat exports rose from less than CFAF 0.1 billion to almost CFAF 0.3 billion.

Expansion in cotton and cottonseed exports in recent years has contributed greatly to Upper Volta's improved trade position. Ginned cotton exports rose from less than CFAF 0.1 billion in 1962 to about CFAF 0.9 billion in 1968, and those of cottonseed also increased markedly, together accounting for 20 per cent of the total export value in 1968. Other exports that increased substantially include sheanut products (7 per cent of total export value in 1968), groundnuts (6 per cent), and sesame seed. Gold exports, which accounted for about 15 per cent of total exports in 1962, ceased in 1967, when existing mine deposits were exhausted.

Composition of Imports

Recorded imports, after having declined slightly in 1967, resumed their upward trend in 1968 (Table 17), partly because stocks of imported goods were replenished or enlarged in anticipation of higher customs duties imposed on January 1, 1969. In general, consumer goods account for about half of total imports and raw materials and semiprocessed goods for one fourth. In 1968, however, a significant increase in imports of equipment goods and a reduction by one third in imports of raw materials and semiprocessed goods changed the pattern of import composition. Imports of foodstuffs, which rose in 1966, declined thereafter. Imports of fuels and lubricants consistently increased, though at a moderate rate, throughout the period.

Direction of Foreign Trade

The French franc area countries are the principal trade partners of Upper Volta, and their relative importance, especially in the country's export trade, rose during 1962–68 (Tables 18 and 19). In 1968, Upper Volta's exports to that area contributed about 74 per cent of the total export value, and imports from that area represented some 77 per cent of the total import value.

Ivory Coast is the leading single export market for Upper Volta's products, taking about 53 per cent of total exports in 1968. Exports to

TABLE 17. UPPER VOLTA: COMPOSITION OF RECORDED IMPORTS, 1962–68

(*Value in millions of CFA francs*)

	Value							Per Cent of Total	
	1962	1963	1964	1965	1966	1967	1968	1962	1968
Consumer goods	5,286	5,409	6,645	5,299	5,506	4,218	5,653	61.7	55.9
Foodstuffs	*1,745*	*2,336*	*3,146*	*2,238*	*2,500*	*2,112*	*1,901*	*20.4*	*18.8*
Textiles	*...*	*...*	*...*	*982*	*780*	*749*	*1,057*	*...*	*10.4*
Equipment goods	1,283	1,039	1,163	1,185	1,142	1,506	2,001	15.0	19.8
Trucks	*...*	*...*	*...*	*225*	*260*	*220*	*336*	*...*	*3.3*
Other vehicles	*...*	*...*	*...*	*213*	*210*	*129*	*270*	*...*	*2.7*
Raw materials and semiprocessed goods	1,727	2,388	1,331	2,349	2,102	2,659	1,785	20.1	17.6
Parts for assembling cycles and motorcycles	*...*	*...*	*...*	*241*	*180*	*298*	*239*	*...*	*2.4*
Cement	*...*	*...*	*...*	*280*	*220*	*214*	*237*	*...*	*2.3*
Fuels and lubricants	274	316	345	336	544	587	681	3.2	6.7
Total	8,569	9,152	9,484	9,169	9,294	8,970	10,120	100.0	100.0

Sources: Same as Table 16.

TABLE 18. UPPER VOLTA: RECORDED EXPORTS BY COUNTRY OF DESTINATION, 1962–68

(Value in millions of CFA francs)

	Value							Per Cent of Total	
	1962	1963	1964	1965	1966	1967	1968	1962	1968
Ivory Coast	435	592	1,000	1,795	2,010	2,185	2,806	22.4	53.1
France	352	610	671	521	717	600	749	18.1	14.2
Ghana	831	758	985	649	598	601	532	42.7	10.0
Japan	19	7	116	48	89	120	359	1.0	6.8
Mali	22	110	177	155	152	106	134	1.1	2.5
United Kingdom	6	15	45	47	46	52	110	0.3	2.1
Belgium	28	6	—	—	3	69	97	1.4	1.8
Italy	9	22	39	105	54	140	90	0.5	1.7
Germany	1	1	—	—	2	—	57	0.1	1.1
Senegal	26	16	6	10	1	7	8	1.3	0.2
Netherlands	7	2	4	—	—	15	3	0.4	—
Other	209	161	271	350	313	534	343	10.7	6.5
Total	1,945	2,300	3,314	3,680	3,985	4,429	5,288	100.0	100.0
French franc area	909	1,422	2,010	2,583	3,045	3,351	3,909	46.6	73.9
UMOA	535	684	1,050	1,899	2,167	2,330	2,923	27.4	55.3
EEC	397	641	714	626	776	824	996	20.4	18.8

Sources: Same as Table 16.

TABLE 19. UPPER VOLTA: RECORDED IMPORTS BY COUNTRY OF ORIGIN, 1962–68

(Value in millions of CFA francs)

	Value							Per Cent of Total	
	1962	1963	1964	1965	1966	1967	1968	1962	1968
France	4,386	4,449	5,095	4,909	4,048	4,029	4,424	51.2	43.7
Ivory Coast	853	1,708	1,470	1,505	1,630	1,374	1,623	10.0	16.0
Germany	144	151	167	223	247	291	449	1.7	4.4
Mali	134	387	483	543	711	575	424	1.6	4.2
United States	324	163	222	191	346	217	419	3.8	4.1
Belgium	37	69	98	170	472	168	326	0.4	3.2
Senegal	504	421	308	270	330	316	299	5.9	3.0
Netherlands	179	207	234	190	176	179	250	2.1	2.5
Italy	62	61	79	144	106	242	134	0.7	1.3
United Kingdom	319	238	126	119	136	85	123	3.7	1.2
Ghana	447	352	323	212	118	143	108	5.2	1.1
Japan	199	100	75	12	11	46	32	2.2	0.3
Other	981	846	804	681	963	1,305	1,509	11.4	15.0
Total	8,569	9,152	9,484	9,169	9,294	8,970	10,120	100.0	100.0
French franc area	6,177	6,280	7,726	7,467	7,390	7,218	7,819	72.1	77.3
UMOA	1,402	2,335	2,007	1,849	2,015	1,725	1,958	16.4	19.3
EEC	4,808	4,937	5,673	5,636	5,049	4,909	5,583	56.1	55.2

Sources: Same as Table 16.

France, representing about 14 per cent of the total, have remained fairly stable in recent years. Exports to Ghana declined considerably during 1962–68 but still represented some 10 per cent of Upper Volta's recorded exports in 1968. Japan is becoming an important outlet for Upper Volta's products; in 1968 it absorbed about 7 per cent of total exports.

France is by far the largest supplier of Upper Volta's imports, but its share in these imports went down from 51 per cent in 1962 and 54 per cent in 1965 to 44 per cent in 1968. Although Ivory Coast ranks second as a supplier in the import trade, its share of the total imports in 1968 was only 16 per cent. Mainly reflecting an increase in imports from Germany and the Netherlands, the share of EEC countries other than France rose from 5 per cent in 1962 to almost 12 per cent in 1968.

FOREIGN FINANCIAL ASSISTANCE

Practically all official foreign assistance received by Upper Volta is in the form of grants. Disbursements of foreign aid rose from CFAF 4.3 billion in 1965 to CFAF 5.5 billion in 1968 (Table 20). During those years, France provided on an average about 58 per cent of total aid received and EEC 25 per cent. French aid, channeled mainly through FAC, increased from CFAF 2.5 billion in 1965 to CFAF 3.6 billion in 1967 but declined to CFAF 3.2 billion in 1968. Development aid and technical assistance represented the bulk of those disbursements. Almost two thirds of total assistance to Upper Volta during 1966–68 was primarily directed toward the productive sectors, particularly toward agricultural projects (Table 21). EDF, through which EEC aid is distributed, provided financing for a small number of relatively large projects, primarily infrastructure. Though representing a small share of total aid disbursements, assistance from UN and its specialized agencies increased substantially between 1965 and 1968.

EXTERNAL PUBLIC DEBT

About 59 per cent of the total public external debt outstanding on December 31, 1968 (US$20.1 million) represented loans from the French Government (Table 22), mostly incurred when Upper Volta

TABLE 20. UPPER VOLTA: FOREIGN AID RECEIPTS, BY MAJOR DONORS, 1965–68

(*In millions of CFA francs*)

	1965	1966	1967	1968
France				
Development aid	967	1,190	1,678	1,343
Technical assistance [1]	760	753	970	1,037
Direct aid to equipment budget	448	523 [2]	450	450
Scholarships and trainee-ships	190	135	126	140
Military aid	50	86	76	126
Other	100	154	298	115
Total France	2,515	2,841	3,598	3,211
EEC	1,345	1,362	577	1,198
UN and specialized agencies	170	277	209	444
Federal Republic of Germany	110	126	105 [1]	164
United States	91	189	166	...
Republic of China	27	67	51	78
Israel	25	13	7	5
Other [3]	...	156	187	411
Total	4,283	5,031	4,900	5,511

Sources: Ministry of Planning and Public Works.

[1] Net of Upper Volta's contribution, which amounted to CFAF 210 million in 1965, CFAF 227 million in 1966, CFAF 167 million in 1967, and CFAF 121 million in 1968.

[2] Includes CFAF 223 million of aid granted in 1965 and utilized in 1966.

[3] Including both official and private grants.

TABLE 21. UPPER VOLTA: DISTRIBUTION OF TOTAL FOREIGN AID COMMITMENTS OF MAJOR DONORS, BY CATEGORY OF PROJECTS, 1966–68

(*Amount in billions of CFA francs*)

	FAC		EDF		Total	
	Amount	Per cent of total	Amount	Per cent of total	Amount	Per cent of total
Productive sectors						
Agriculture	1.80	50.4	0.62	13.1	2.42	29.2
Livestock raising	0.15	4.2	—	—	0.15	1.8
Other	0.31	8.7	—	—	0.31	3.7
Total productive sectors	2.26	63.3	0.62	13.1	2.88	34.7
Infrastructure	0.60	16.8	3.88	82.2	4.48	54.1
Social services	0.59	16.5	0.20	4.3	0.79	9.5
Research	0.12	3.4	0.02	0.4	0.14	1.7
Total commitments	3.57	100.0	4.72	100.0	8.29	100.0

Source: Ministry of Planning and Public Works, Department of Planning.

TABLE 22. UPPER VOLTA: EXTERNAL PUBLIC DEBT, 1968

(In thousands of U.S. dollars)

	Outstanding Balance December 31, 1967	Operations During 1968			Outstanding Balance December 31, 1968
		Drawings	Amortization	Interest	
Debt to governments					
Disbursed					
France	11,303	1,265	712	167	11,856
Germany	—	832	—	11	832
Ghana	4,560	—	182	115	4,378
Total disbursed	15,863	2,096	894	293	17,065
Undisbursed	3,927	527[1]	2,096[2]	—	2,357
Total debt to governments	19,790	2,623	2,990	293	19,422
Other debt					
Disbursed					
Publicly held debt					
Banque Internationale pour l'Afrique Occidentale	41	—	3	3	37
Suppliers' credit	243	537	134	49	646
Undisbursed	26	—	26	2	—
Total disbursed	310	537	163	54	684
Undisbursed	537	—	537[2]	—	—
Total other debts	847	537	700	54	684
Total public external debt	20,637	3,160	3,690	347	20,106
Disbursed	*16,173*	*2,633*	*1,057*	*347*	*17,749*
Undisbursed	*4,463*	*527[1]*	*2,633[2]*	—	*2,357*

Source: Data supplied by the International Bank for Reconstruction and Development.

[1] Represents loan authorizations.
[2] Represents loan disbursements.

was still part of the former French West African Federation. Since then, except for a FAC advance of CFAF 146 million in 1968, the French Government has made no direct loans to the Government of Upper Volta. Most disbursements received have been advances made by the Caisse Centrale de Coopération Economique (CCCE) to finance operations of the Development Bank (Table 23). In 1968, however, CCCE disbursed about CFAF 249 million in long-term advances to official entities. Also in 1968, Upper Volta received US$832,000 (about CFAF 205 million) from the German Kreditanstalt für Wiederaufbau, representing about one third of a loan which is intended to finance the establishment of a textile factory. Other debts denominated in foreign currency include a loan from the Government of Ghana received in 1961, of which US$4.4 million (about CFAF 1.1 billion) was outstanding at the end of December 1968.

Estimated future service payments on Upper Volta's external public debt outstanding on December 31, 1968, including undisbursed amounts, total nearly US$1.2 million (about CFAF 0.3 billion) annually, representing roughly 6 per cent of the country's registered export earnings in 1968 (Table 24).

BALANCE OF PAYMENTS

Comprehensive balance of payments estimates are not available for Upper Volta. Data presented in Table 25 for 1966–68 are tentative estimates prepared on the basis of fragmentary information.

Much of Upper Volta's foreign trade is not recorded, and insufficient information is available for making adjustments of data provided by the customs statistics. No data are available on most service transactions. The available data indicate, however, that Upper Volta had a large negative trade balance during 1966–68 and a large deficit on goods and services combined, estimated at CFAF 5.4 billion in 1968. This deficit, however, was more than offset by a net inflow of unrequited public and private transfers, and official capital movements were in approximate balance. The over-all balance, therefore, though slightly under CFAF 1 billion in 1966, exceeded that amount in 1968.

Nontrade transactions with franc area countries are free from control and registration; hence estimates of private and official transfers, as well

TABLE 23. UPPER VOLTA: FOREIGN DEBT TO CAISSE CENTRALE DE COOPÉRATION ECONOMIQUE AND FONDS D'AIDE DE COOPÉRATION, 1966–68

(In millions of CFA francs)

	Outstanding Balance Dec. 31, 1965	Operations During 1966			Outstanding Balance Dec. 31, 1966	Operations During 1967			Outstanding Balance Dec. 31, 1967	Operations During 1968			Outstanding Balance Dec. 31, 1968
		Drawings	Amortization	Interest		Drawings	Amortization	Interest		Drawings	Amortization	Interest	
Debt to CCCE													
Long-term advances													
Government	2,397.5	—	45.3	26.4	2,352.1	—	56.0	25.5	2,296.2	—	59.3	24.5	2,236.9
Development Bank [1]	261.7	52.6	35.9	7.1	278.4	64.9	58.5	8.7	284.8	154.6	54.4	10.9	385.0
Official entities	73.6	—	8.0	1.8	65.6	—	8.1	1.6	57.5	249.0	8.1	1.4	298.4
Total long-term advances	2,732.8	52.6	89.2	35.3	2,696.1	64.9	122.6	35.8	2,638.5	403.6	121.8	36.8	2,920.3
Medium-term advances													
Development Bank [1]	89.4	41.7	20.0	2.7	111.1	17.2	35.0	3.2	93.3	45.4	42.5	3.5	96.2
Official entities	7.8	—	3.9	0.2	3.9	—	3.9	0.1	—	—	—	—	—
Total medium-term advances	97.2	41.7	23.9	2.9	115.0	17.2	38.9	3.3	93.3	45.4	42.5	3.5	96.2
Total debt to CCCE	2,830.0	94.3	113.1	38.2	2,811.2	82.1	161.5	39.1	2,731.8	449.0	164.3	40.3	3,016.5
Debt to FAC	—	—	—	0.1	—	9.6	—	0.3	9.6	146.2	—	0.3	155.8
Total debt to CCCE and FAC	2,830.0	94.3	113.1	38.3	2,811.2	91.7	161.5	39.4	2,741.4	595.2	164.3	40.6	3,172.3

Source: Data supplied by the Caisse Centrale de Coopération Economique.

[1] Data may differ from outstanding debt reported for the Development Bank because the Bank separately accounts for advances made to some official entities no longer in existence but for which the Bank is responsible for debt-service payments.

TABLE 24. UPPER VOLTA: ESTIMATED FUTURE SERVICE PAYMENTS ON EXTERNAL
PUBLIC DEBT, 1969–75 [1]

(*In thousands of U.S. dollars*)

	1969	1970	1971	1972	1973	1974	1975
Loans from governments							
France	747	681	556	608	785	737	626
Germany	2	3	3	4	4	72	139
Ghana	292	287	283	278	456	447	438
Total loans from governments	1,041	970	841	889	1,245	1,256	1,203
Privately held debt							
Publicly issued bonds	7	7	7	6	4	4	3
Banque Internationale pour l'Afrique Occidentale	285	267	75	70	34	—	—
Total privately held debt	291	273	82	77	38	4	3
Total service payments	1,332	1,244	923	966	1,282	1,260	1,207
Amortization	1,100	1,046	759	782	1,065	1,058	1,029
Interest	232	196	164	184	217	202	178

Source: Data supplied by the International Bank for Reconstruction and
Development.

[1] Including undisbursed amounts on December 31, 1968 but excluding a
$602,000 loan from France for which repayment terms are not available.

as capital movements, are subject to a large margin of error. The net
inflow of unrequited transfers apparently decreased after 1967 to
CFAF 6.8 billion in 1968, even with large official transfers resulting
from increased disbursements of foreign aid. The bulk of private sector
unrequited transfer receipts consists of remittances by emigrant workers
from Upper Volta (mainly in Ivory Coast). These remittances are estimated at CFAF 4.0 billion annually. In addition, pension payments
made by the French Government to Upper Voltans average about
CFAF 1.8 billion annually and miscellaneous receipts total about
CFAF 0.2 billion. Most unrequited transfers abroad represent remittances by foreign nationals working in Upper Volta; these remittances
are estimated at about CFAF 0.3 billion. Accordingly, it is estimated
that the net inflow of unrequited transfers to the private sector
amounted to CFAF 5.7 billion annually during 1966–67 and to
CFAF 2.2 billion in 1968. Estimated net receipts from official transfers
increased from CFAF 3.5 billion in 1966 to CFAF 4.6 billion in 1968.
This increase reflected large disbursements of foreign government
grants to Upper Volta. Upper Volta's contributions to international

TABLE 25.   UPPER VOLTA: BALANCE OF PAYMENTS ESTIMATES, 1966–68

(*In billions of CFA francs*)

	1966	1967	1968
A. Goods and services			
Exports f.o.b.	3.99	4.43	6.96
Imports c.i.f.	−9.29	−8.97	−12.24
Trade balance	−5.30	−4.54	−5.28
Other transportation and travel	...	...	−1.22
Interest on public debt	...	...	−0.07
Other interest	...	...	0.07
Investment income	...	...	−0.39
Government, n.i.e.[1]			
Services under aid programs	...	−0.67	−2.17
Diplomatic personnel expenditures	...	0.42	0.93
Other	...	...	0.09
Total Government, n.i.e.	...	−0.25	−1.15
Other services	...	...	2.60
Total goods and services	−5.30	−4.79	−5.44
B. Unrequited transfers			
Private	5.70	5.70	2.21
Central Government	3.47	3.52	4.62
Total unrequited transfers	9.17	9.17	6.83
C. Nonmonetary capital			
Private	...	...	0.75
Central Government			
Drawings on loans	0.09	0.09	0.60
Amortization payments	−0.15	−0.20	−0.27
Capital participations	...	...	−0.10
Total Central Government	0.06	−0.11	0.23
Total nonmonetary capital	0.06	−0.11	0.97
D. Total A + B + C	3.81	4.32	2.36
E. Net errors and omissions	−2.97	−3.85	−1.13
F. Over-all balance (D + E)	0.84	0.47	1.23
G. Monetary movements			
Central Bank			
Assets (increase −)	−0.58	−0.53	−1.23
Liabilities	...	0.04	0.15
Total Central Bank	−0.58	−0.49	−1.08
Commercial banks and Development Bank			
Assets (increase −)	0.08	−0.01	−0.43
Liabilities	−0.34	0.03	0.26
Total commercial banks and Development Bank	−0.26	0.02	−0.17
Other institutions	...	...	0.02
Total monetary movements	−0.84	−0.47	−1.23

Sources: Tables 12–19 for 1966 and 1967; for 1968, data provided by BCEAO, including adjustments for unrecorded trade.

[1] Not included elsewhere.

organizations were estimated to have remained at about the same level throughout the period.

Little information is available on private capital movements, but it is estimated that there was a net inflow of over CFAF 0.7 billion in 1968. Data on public debt operations indicate that in both 1966 and 1967, amortization payments exceeded drawings on loans and that in 1968 the net inflow of official nonmonetary capital amounted to CFAF 0.2 billion, or a total inflow of nearly CFAF 1.0 billion.

Net errors and omissions were negative throughout 1966–68. Although this entry was fairly large, year-to-year changes have been relatively small.

The over-all balance of payments, which was CFAF 0.8 billion in 1966, rose to CFAF 1.2 billion in 1968.

During the three years ended 1968, net foreign assets of the Central Bank, consisting of Upper Volta's imputed share in the common pool of foreign reserves of UMOA, rose by more than 60 per cent to CFAF 5.6 billion (see Table 12). This upward trend continued in 1969. Although the commercial banks and the Development Bank improved their foreign assets position during this period, their position remained negative, and in early 1969 became increasingly negative (see Table 13). The combined net foreign assets of the banking system rose by more than 90 per cent during the three years ended 1968 to nearly CFAF 5.0 billion (see Table 14), and to CFAF 6.1 billion by the end of September 1969 (equivalent to more than 7½ months of the average recorded imports during 1966–68).

MAPS

These maps were designed by the Graphics Section of the International Monetary Fund as an aid to the reader in locating features mentioned in this book. Although every effort has been made to make them accurate, they are not intended to take the place of more formal maps. The boundaries shown are not necessarily authoritative. Moreover, no attempt has been made to distinguish between improved and unimproved roads.

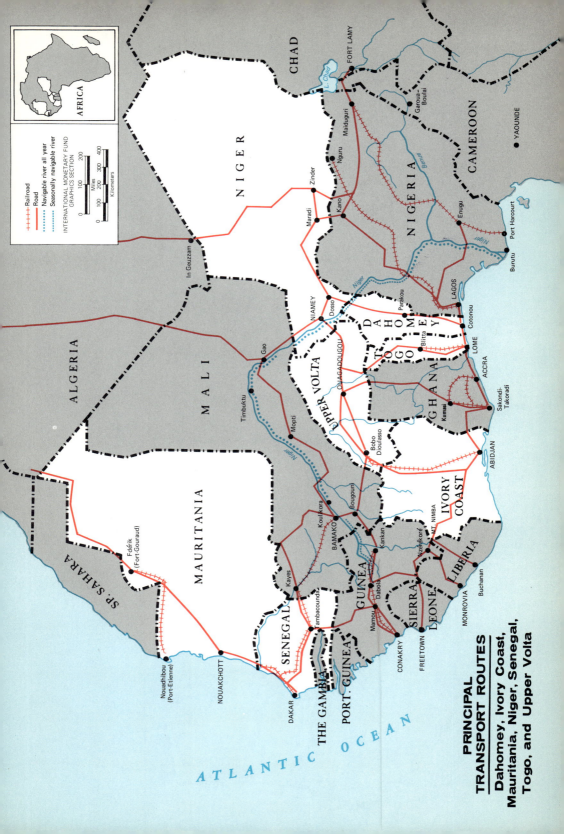

AFRICA

Railroad
Road
Navigable river all year
Seasonally navigable river
INTERNATIONAL MONETARY FUND
GRAPHICS SECTION

Miles
0   100   200   300   400
Kilometers
0   100   200

CHAD

FORT LAMY
L. Chad

Garoua-
Boulai

CAMEROON

YAOUNDE

NIGER

In Geuzzam

Zinder

Nguru
Maiduguri

Maradi
Kano

NIGERIA

Enugu

Port Harcourt

Benue

Burutu

ALGERIA

NIAMEY
Dosso

Parakou

Niger

LAGOS
Cotonou
LOME
ACCRA

MALI

Gao

UPPER VOLTA

OUAGADOUGOU

D
A
H
O
M
E
Y

Blitta

T
O
G
O

GHANA

Timbuktu

Mopti

Bobo
Dioulasso

Kumasi

Sakondi-
Takoradi

SP. SAHARA

Fdérik
(Fort-Gouraud)

MAURITANIA

Koulikoro
BAMAKO

Bougouni

Kankan

ABIDJAN

IVORY
COAST

Nouadhibou
(Port-Etienne)

NOUAKCHOTT

Kayes

Tambacounda

GUINEA

Dabola
Mamou

Nzérékoré

MT. NIMBA

LIBERIA

Buchanan

DAKAR

SENEGAL

THE GAMBIA

PORT. GUINEA

CONAKRY

FREETOWN

SIERRA
LEONE

MONROVIA

ATLANTIC OCEAN

**PRINCIPAL
TRANSPORT ROUTES
Dahomey, Ivory Coast,
Mauritania, Niger, Senegal,
Togo, and Upper Volta**

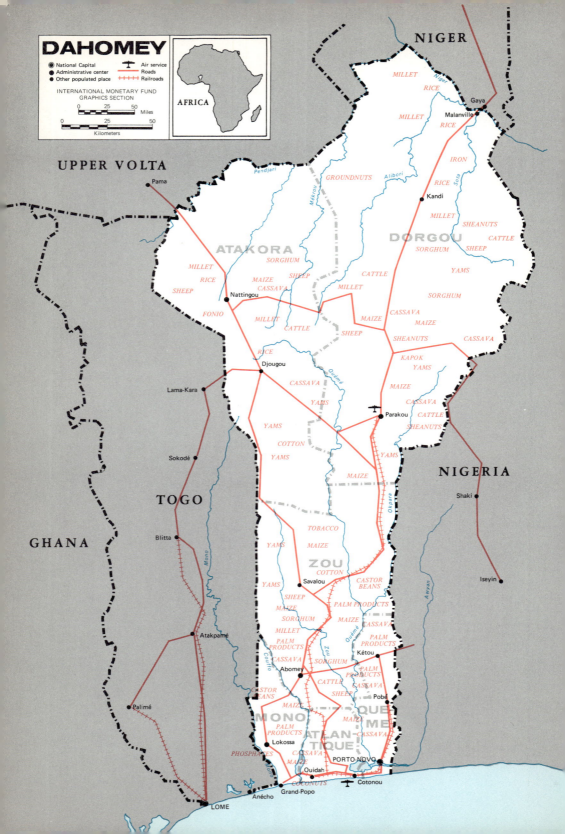

DAHOMEY

- ◉ National Capital
- ● Administrative center
- ● Other populated place
- ╫ Air service
- — Roads
- ╫╫╫ Railroads

INTERNATIONAL MONETARY FUND
GRAPHICS SECTION

Miles
0   25   50

Kilometers
0   25   50

AFRICA

NIGER

UPPER VOLTA

GHANA

TOGO

NIGERIA

MILLET
RICE

Gaya
Malanville

MILLET
RICE

Niger

IRON
RICE

Kandi

GROUNDNUTS

Pendjari
Mékrou
Alibori
Sota

Pama

MILLET
SHEANUTS
CATTLE
SHEEP

ATAKORA

DORGOU

SORGHUM
SHEEP
CATTLE
MILLET
MAIZE
CASSAVA

YAMS
SORGHUM

MILLET
RICE
SHEEP

Nattingou

FONIO
CATTLE
MILLET

MAIZE
SHEEP
CASSAVA
MAIZE
SHEANUTS

KAPOK
YAMS

CASSAVA

RICE
Djougou

Ouémé

CASSAVA
YAMS

MAIZE

CASSAVA
CATTLE
SHEANUTS

Lama-Kara

Parakou

Sokodé

YAMS

COTTON
YAMS

YAMS

Shaki

MAIZE

NIGERIA

TOBACCO

Blitta

YAMS
MAIZE

Mono

Okpara

Iseyin

ZOU

COTTON

Savalou

CASTOR
BEANS

Anyan

YAMS

SHEEP
MAIZE
SORGHUM
MILLET
PALM
PRODUCTS
CASSAVA

Atakpamé

PALM PRODUCTS
MAIZE

CASSAVA

PALM
PRODUCTS

Kétou

Ouémé
Zou

SORGHUM
CATTLE

PALM
PRODUCTS
CASSAVA

Abomey

Palimé

CASTOR
BEANS

SHEEP

Pobé

MAIZE

Couffo

MONO

MAIZE

QUE
ME

PALM
PRODUCTS

ATLAN
TIQUE

CASSAVA

Lokossa

PHOSPHATES

CASSAVA
MAIZE

PORTO-NOVO

Grand-Popo

COCONUTS

Ouidah

Cotonou

Anécho

LOME

MALI

UPPER VOLTA

GUINEA

LIBERIA

GHANA

Nzérékoré

Odienné

Touba

Danané

Toulepleu

Guiglo

Tabou

San-Pédro

Sassandra

Soubré

Lakota

Gagnoa

Duékoué

Daloa

Issia

Oumé

Divo

Man

Bouaflé

Séguéla

Mankano

Béoumi

Bouaké

Boundiali

Korhogo

Wangolodougou

Ferkéssédougou

Bouna

Dabakala

Katiola

Mbahiakro

Dimbokro

Toumodi

Tiassalé

Agboville

Akebéfia

ABIDJAN

Grand-Lahou

Grand-Bassam

Adzopé

Aboisso

Bonoua

Assini

Mafèrè

Abengourou

Agnibilékrou

Bondoukou

Berekum

CASSAVA · YAMS · MAIZE · PLANTAINS · COCOA · RICE · BANANAS

GULF OF GUINEA

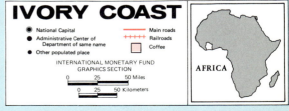

IVORY COAST

◎ National Capital
● Administrative Center of
Department of same name
• Other populated place

— Main roads
+++++ Railroads
▨ Coffee

INTERNATIONAL MONETARY FUND
GRAPHICS SECTION

0   25   50 Miles

0   25   50 Kilometers

AFRICA

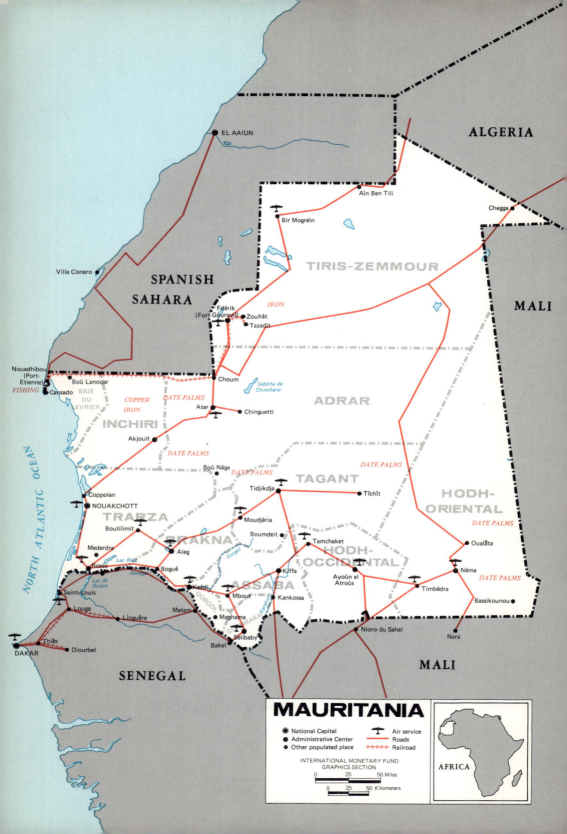

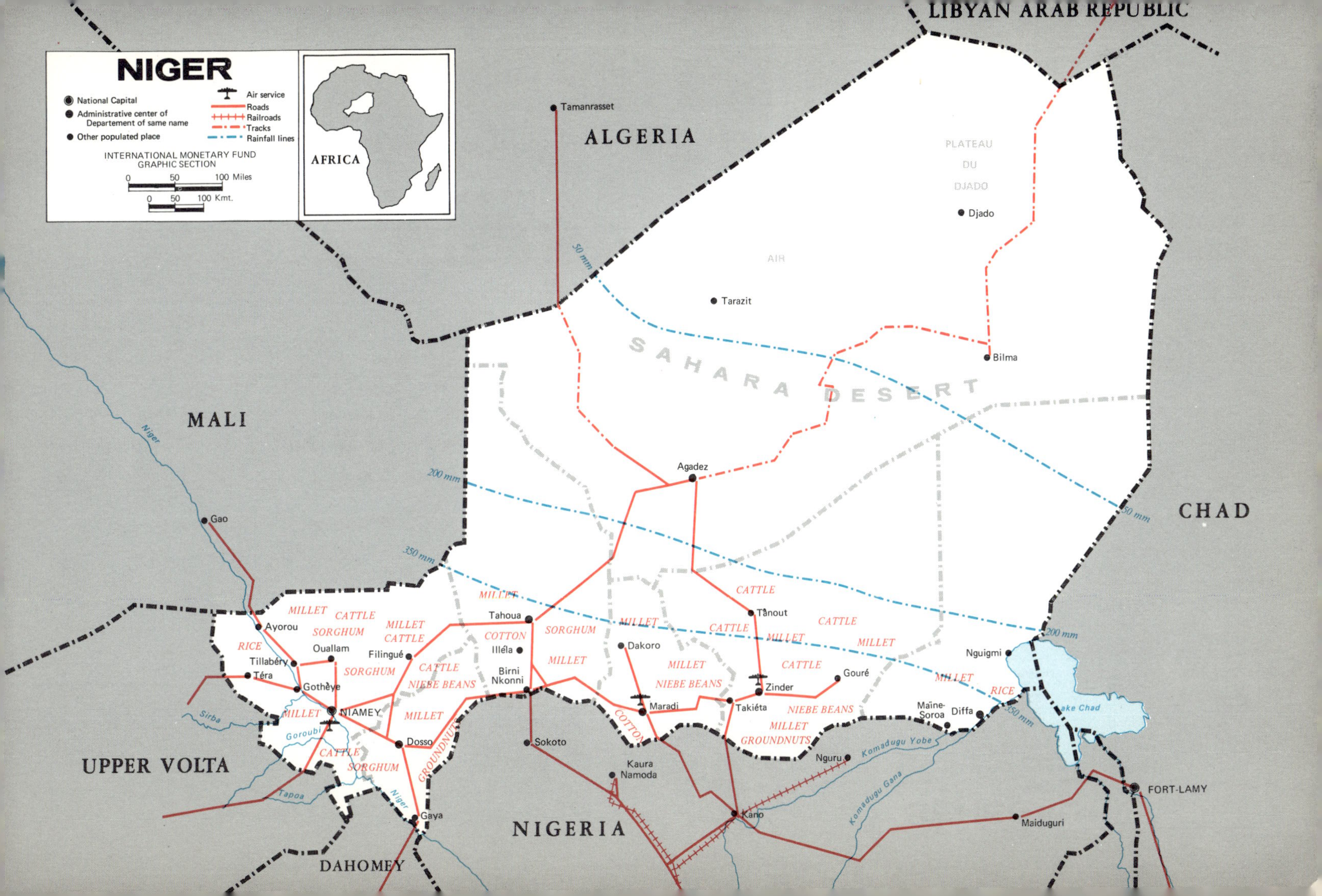

NIGER

LIBYAN ARAB REPUBLIC

CHAD

ALGERIA

NIGERIA

MALI

UPPER VOLTA

DAHOMEY

AFRICA

SAHARA DESERT

PLATEAU DU DJADO

AÏR

Lake Chad

FORT-LAMY

Maiduguri

Djado

Bilma

Tarazit

Tamanrasset

Agadez

Tahoua

Dakoro

Tanout

Gouré

Zinder

Takiéta

Maradi

Maïné Soroa

Diffa

Nguigmi

Kano

Nguru

Kaura Namoda

Sokoto

Birni Nkonni

Illéla

Madaoua

Filingué

Dosso

Gaya

Ouallam

Niamey

Gothèye

Tillabéry

Téra

Ayorou

Gao

Komadugu Yobe

Komadugu Gana

Niger

Goroubi

Sirba

Dargol

Taboa

CATTLE

MILLET

NIEBE BEANS

GROUNDNUTS

RICE

SORGHUM

COTTON

Legend

- ● National Capital
- ◉ Administrative center of Departement of same name
- ● Other populated place

Air service
Roads
Railroads
Tracks
Rainfall lines

50 mm
100 mm
150 mm
200 mm
350 mm

100 Miles
50
0

100 Kmt.
50
0

INTERNATIONAL MONETARY FUND
GRAPHIC SECTION

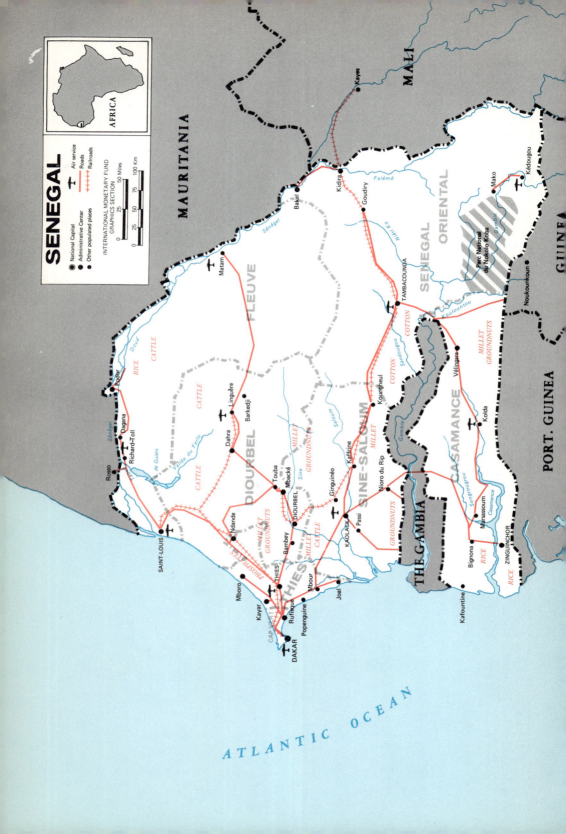

SENEGAL

- ● National Capital
- ● Administrative Center
- ○ Other populated places

- ✈ Air service
- ‐‐ Roads
- +++ Railroads

INTERNATIONAL MONETARY FUND
GRAPHICS SECTION

50 Miles
0   25   50   75   100 Km

AFRICA

MAURITANIA

MALI

SENEGAL ORIENTAL

GUINEA

PORT. GUINEA

THE GAMBIA

CASAMANCE

SINE-SALOUM

DIOURBEL

THIES

FLEUVE

ATLANTIC OCEAN

Kayes
Kidira
Goudiry
Bakel
Mako
Kédougou
Noukounkoun
Parc National
du Nokolo Koba
TAMBACOUNDA
Matam
Podor
Ogana
Richard-Toll
Rosso
Linguère
Barkedji
Dahra
SAINT-LOUIS
Mboro
Kayar
Ndande
Bambey
Touba
Mbacké
DIOURBEL
Ginguinéo
Kaffrine
Koungheul
Vélingara
Kolda
Marsassoum
ZINGUINCHOR
Bignona
Kafountine
Popenguine
Rufisque
Mbour
Joal
THIES
DAKAR
KAOLACK
Passi
Nioro du Rip

RICE
CATTLE
CATTLE
CATTLE
CATTLE
MILLET
GROUNDNUTS
PHOSPHATES
MILLET
GROUNDNUTS
MILLET
CATTLE
MILLET
GROUNDNUTS
COTTON
COTTON
COTTON
MILLET
GROUNDNUTS
RICE
RICE
RICE

Sénégal
Doué
Vallée du Ferlo
Lac de Guiers
Sine
Saloum
Gambie
Falémé
Niéri Ko
Sandougou
Koulountou
Songrougrou
Casamance

CAP VERT

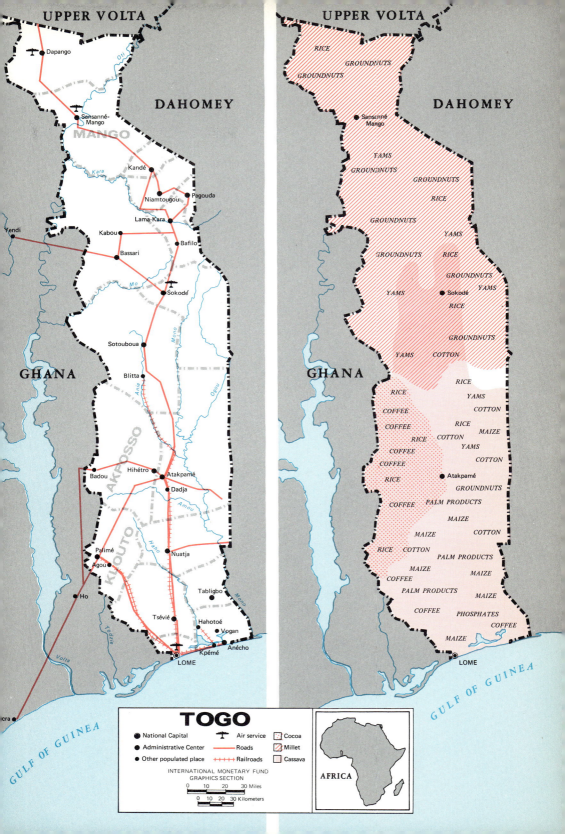

UPPER VOLTA

DAHOMEY

GHANA

Dapango

Sansanné-Mango

MANGO

Kandé

Niamtougou Pagouda

Lama-Kara

Kabou

Bassari Bafilo

Sokodé

Sotouboua

Blitta

Yendi

AKPOSSO

Badou Hihétro

Atakpamé

Dadja

KLOUTO

Palimé

Agou Nuatja

Ho

Tabligbo

Tsévié

Hahotoé

Vogan

Kpémé Anécho

LOME

GULF OF GUINEA

TOGO

● National Capital   ✈ Air service   ▨ Cocoa
● Administrative Center   ━ Roads   ▨ Millet
• Other populated place   ┿ Railroads   ☐ Cassava

INTERNATIONAL MONETARY FUND
GRAPHICS SECTION

0   10   20   30 Miles
0   10   20   30 Kilometers

AFRICA

UPPER VOLTA

DAHOMEY

GHANA

RICE

GROUNDNUTS

GROUNDNUTS

Sansanné Mango

YAMS

GROUNDNUTS

GROUNDNUTS

RICE

GROUNDNUTS

YAMS

GROUNDNUTS

RICE

GROUNDNUTS

YAMS

YAMS

Sokodé

RICE

GROUNDNUTS

YAMS COTTON

RICE

RICE

YAMS

COFFEE

COTTON

COFFEE

RICE

RICE

MAIZE

RICE

COTTON

COFFEE

YAMS

COFFEE

COTTON

RICE

Atakpamé

COFFEE

GROUNDNUTS

PALM PRODUCTS

MAIZE

MAIZE

COTTON

RICE

COTTON

PALM PRODUCTS

MAIZE

COFFEE

MAIZE

PALM PRODUCTS

MAIZE

COFFEE

PHOSPHATES

COFFEE

MAIZE

LOME

GULF OF GUINEA

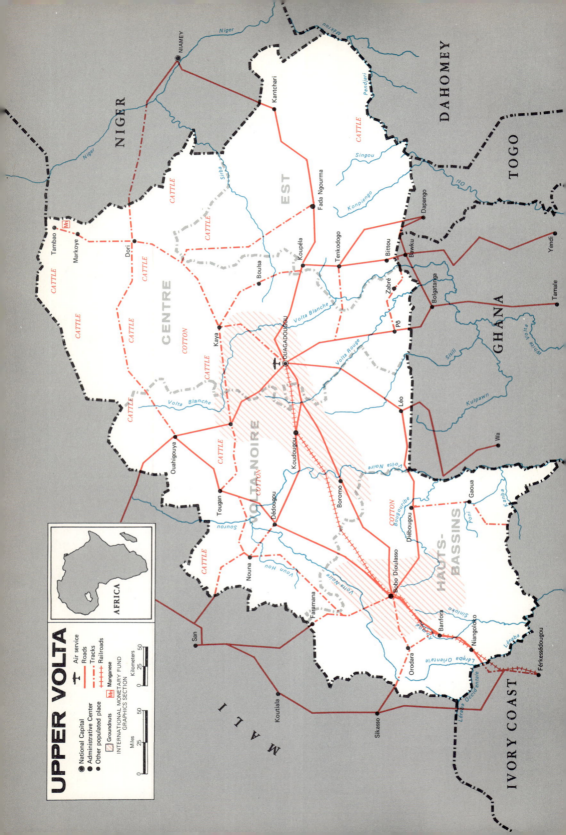

UPPER VOLTA

Air service
● National Capital
● Administrative Center
• Other populated place
▣ Groundnuts

Roads
Tracks
Railroads
M̲ Manganese

INTERNATIONAL MONETARY FUND
GRAPHICS SECTION

Kilometers
0   25   50

Miles
0   25   50

AFRICA

NIGER

DAHOMEY

TOGO

GHANA

IVORY COAST

MALI

EST

CENTRE

VOLTA NOIRE

HAUTS-
BASSINS

NIAMEY

Niger

Niger

Niger

Kantchari

CATTLE

Singou

Pendjari

Dapango

Tambao
Markoye
Dori

CATTLE

CATTLE

CATTLE

CATTLE

CATTLE

CATTLE

CATTLE

CATTLE

CATTLE

CATTLE

Sirba

Méhou

Fada Ngourma

Konpienga

Boulsa

Koupéla

Tenkodogo

Bittou

Bawku

Yendi

Tamale

Bolgatanga

Zabré

Pô

Léo

Wa

Sissili

Kulpawn

White Volta

Kaya

COTTON

OUAGADOUGOU

Volta Blanche

Volta Rouge

Volta Blanche

Ouahigouya

CATTLE

COTTON

Tougan

Koudougou

Dédougou

Boromo

Diébougou

COTTON
Bougouriba

Gaoua

Volta Noire

Poni

Kamba

Nouna

CATTLE

Voun Hou

Volta Noire

Bobo Dioulasso

Sinloko

Banfora

Niangoloko

Ferkessédougou

San

Fatamana

Orodara

Léraba Orientale

Léraba Occidentale

Léraba

Koutiala

Sikasso

Sourou

INDEX

INDEX

References (page numbers) in the index are to the text, footnotes to the text (*n*), and tables (*t*); the maps are not included. References to individual countries in the first six chapters and in the following seven country chapters are indicated by a symbol in bold face type preceding the page number or numbers, as follows: **da** for Dahomey, **iv** for Ivory Coast, **ma** for Mauritania, **ni** for Niger, **se** for Senegal, **to** for Togo, and **up** for Upper Volta. General references to the first six chapters are indicated by page number only; that is, no symbol precedes the page numbers.

French West African Federation (Afri-
que Occidentale Française, or
AOF), 2; **ni** 454; **up** 719
aid disbursed, **up** 716*t*
budgetary aid, **ni** 462–63
economic cooperation, 12–13
membership, 2, 13*n*; 46*n*
French West African States, *see* French
West African Federation
FSSPPE (Fonds de Stabilisation et de
Soutien des Prix des Produits à l'Ex-
portation), *see* Stabilization Fund for
Agricultural Exports
FSTTOM, *see* Fonds de Soutien des
Textiles des Territoires d'Outre-Mer

Gambie (Gambia) River, **se** 497
Ganavé, tapioca and starch mill, **to** 633
Gangaol, gold, **up** 698
Gaoua, copper, **up** 699
Gas, industrial, **ma** 326–27
GDP, *see* Gross domestic product
General Agreement on Tariffs and
Trade (GATT), membership, **da** 144;
iv 220; **ma** 309; **se** 496; **ni** 401;
to 614; **up** 689
Germany, Federal Republic of, finan-
cial aid, **iv** 303; **ma** 343*t*; **se** 576*t*,
606; **to** 685*t*–86; **up** 745*t*
Government finance, *see* Budgets
Gross domestic product (GDP),
da 145–50; **iv** 222–27; **ma** 312–13;
ni 403–405; **se** 499–501; **to** 616–18;
up 691–92
by sector of origin, **da** 146–47;
iv 226–27; **ma** 312–13, 500;
to 616–17; **up** 692
growth rates, 3, 63–67; **da** 146;
iv 222–24; **ma** 312–13; **ni** 403;
se 499; **to** 616; **up** 691
use, **da** 146, 148–50; **iv** 224–26;
ni 404–405; **se** 500–501;
to 616–17; **up** 692–93*t*
Groundnut Marketing Company (Société Nigérienne de Commercialisation
de l'Arachide, or SONARA),
ni 411–16, 428, 434, 438–40, 463–64
Groundnut Stabilization Fund (Caisse
de Stabilisation des Prix de l'Arachide, or CSPA), **se** 507–508, 539,
554, 556–57, 570, 589
Groundnuts, **da** 155–56, 157–59;
iv 228*t*; **ma** 314*t*; **ni** 406–16;
se 501–16; **to** 619–24, 627–28;
up 693–96
export prices, **da** 158; **ni** 411–16;
se 507, 510, 512; **to** 623*t*, 628;
up 696

exports, 3; **da** 155, 209–11; **ni** 406,
408, 412–16; **se** 512; **to** 621*t*, 627;
up 697*t*
export taxes, **to** 623*t*, 628
French support price, **se** 509–13;
to 627–28
marketing, **ni** 411–16; **se** 504–509;
to 622; **up** 695
market sales, **da** 155; **ni** 412*t*; **se** 505;
to 624*t*; **up** 697*t*
price support subsidies, **da** 155,
157–59; **ni** 408–10, 411–16;
se 509–13; **to** 622–23, 628; **up** 697*t*
processing, **da** 156, 163; **ni** 428;
se 508–509, 528, 532
producer prices, **da** 155–56; **ni** 411–16;
se 509–11; **to** 623*t*, 628; **up** 695–97
production, **to** 619, 621*t*; **up** 693–94
production program, **da** 155;
ni 406–407; **se** 503–504
supplementary price stabilization
program, **ni** 410; **se** 511, 513
support for structural improvement,
da 157–59; **ni** 408–16; **se** 513–16;
to 628
world market prices, **da** 155; **ni** 408,
412–16; **se** 507, 509–11, 513;
to 628
Guarantee Fund (Fonds d'Entraide et
de Garantie des Emprunts du Conseil de l'Entente), 24–26, 68–69;
da 163
GUELFI, *see* Société Guelfi Survif
Gum arabic, **ma** 313–14
Gypsum, **ma** 325

Handicrafts, **ma** 312–13; **se** 536
Hausa, **ni** 403
Hides and skins, *see* Livestock and
products
Hotel du Bénin, **to** 656

IBRD, *see* World Bank
ICA, *see* International Coffee Agree-
ment
ICODA, *see* Industries Cotonnières du
Dahomey
ICOTAF, *see* Industrie Cotonnière
Africaine
IDA, *see* International Development
Association
IFAC, *see* Institut Français de Recher-
ches Fruitières Outre-Mer
IFC, *see* International Finance Corpo-
ration
Ile de Gorée, tourism project, **se** 536
IMF, *see* International Monetary Fund

Koua, **iv** 222
Koudougou, **up** 690–91
  industrial plants, **up** 699
  textile mill, **up** 700
  water supply, **up** 702
Koupéla, road, **up** 703
Kreditanstalt für Wiederaufbau, **da** 162;
  ni 467–68; **to** 664–65; **up** 700
Kpémé
  electric power plant, **to** 636*t*
  phosphate deposits, **to** 631
  port, **to** 639
  railway, **to** 639
Kroumen, **iv** 222

Labor Codes, **da** 174; **ni** 452
Labor unions, **da** 175; **to** 650
Lac des Guiers, water pipeline, **se** 525
Lagos, port, **ni** 433
Lake Chad, **ni** 402, 424
Lengué, **iv** 244
Linguère, railway, **se** 539
Livelihood, **iv** 242
Livestock and products, **da** 160; **iv** 242;
  ma 312*t*, 316–17; **ni** 421–24;
  se 520–21; **to** 629–30; **up** 696, 698
  economically active population in
    livestock raising, **ma** 316; **se** 520
  dairying, **ma** 312; **se** 521
  export tax, **ni** 422, 424
  exports, **ma** 317; **ni** 421–22, 424,
    485*t*–86
  growth rates, **da** 160, **ma** 316–17;
    ni 422–23; **se** 520–21; **to** 629;
    up 696
  imports, **da** 160; **iv** 242; **se** 521;
    to 629–30
  meat consumption, **ma** 316; **ni** 422;
    se 521; **to** 630
  numbers, **da** 160; **ma** 316; **ni** 422–23;
    se 520; **to** 629; **up** 696
  projects, **da** 160; **iv** 242; **se** 521;
    up 698
  slaughter, **ni** 422–23; **se** 521; **to** 629
  slaughter tax, **ni** 422
  share of GDP, **ma** 312*t*; **ni** 421;
    up 696
Livestock Products Marketing Company
  (Société Nigérienne d'Exportation
  des Ressources d'Animaux, or
  SONERAN), **ni** 422, 441
*Loi Plan de Développement Econo-
  mique, Social et Culturel, 1967–70,*
  iv 251
Lomé
  airport, **to** 639
  brewery, **to** 633
  capital, **to** 613

  cost of living, **to** 649
  employment, **to** 650
  Institut du Bénin, **to** 616
  market hall, **to** 662
  municipality, **to** 662
  port, **ni** 437; **to** 637, 639, 688
  refrigerated storage, **to** 630
  road, **to** 637; **up** 701
  slaughterhouse, **to** 629
  soap and perfume factory, **to** 634
  thermoelectric plant, **to** 636*t*

Machinery Unit (Arrondissement d'Ou-
  tillage Mécanique), **iv** 262
Mahogany, **iv** 244
Maize, **da** 151–52; **iv** 228; **ma** 313–14;
  ni 407*t*; **se** 501–502, 517; **to** 619–20;
  up 693–94
Mali, 13*n*, 24, 72
Mali Federation, **se** 496
Mandé, **iv** 222
Mandingos, **se** 498
Manganese, **iv** 246
  deposits, **up** 699
  exports, 3; **iv** 297*t*
Mangoes, **iv** 241
Manioc, *see* Cassava
Manufacture Industrielle du Cuir,
  ma 344
Manufacturing, *see* Industry: manufac-
  turing; Secondary sector
Maradi
  airport, **ni** 438
  branch of Development Bank, **ni** 469
  electric power, **ni** 430
  groundnuts, **ni** 434
  municipality, **ni** 454
  population, **ni** 403
MAURELEC, *see* Société Mauritanienne d'Electricité
Mbao
  fertilizer plant, **se** 534
  oil refinery, **se** 523
Mbout, road, **ma** 332
Meat, *see* Livestock and products
Mékrou, hydroelectric project, **ni** 432
MIFERMA (Société des Mines de Fer
  de Mauritanie), *see* Mining Company
Millet, **da** 151; **iv** 228*t*; **ma** 313–14;
  ni 405–407; **se** 501–502, 517;
  to 619–20; **up** 693–94
  imports, **ma** 313–14
  marketing, **se** 504–505
  producer cooperatives, **ma** 316
  producer price, **se** 517
  retail price, **ni** 406
Minerals
  exports, 3
  see also specific minerals

Wages, 7; **da** 173–75; **iv** 258–59; **ma** 347, 349–50, 351*t*; **ni** 451–52; **se** 552; **to** 648–49; **up** 709–11
minimum (SMIG), **da** 172–75; **iv** 258–59; **ma** 347, 350; **ni** 451–52; **se** 552; **to** 648–49; **up** 709–11
Water resources, **ni** 402
Water supply, **ma** 330; **se** 525; **up** 702
Water Supply Office (Office d'Entretien des Eaux du Sous-Sol, or OFEDES), **ni** 433, 463–64
West African Customs Union (Union Douanière des Etats de l'Afrique de l'Ouest), *see* UDEAO
West African Customs Union (Union Douanière entre les Etats de l'Afrique Occidentale, or UDAO), 13–18
convention, 14–16
establishment and membership, 13
harmonization of fiscal system, 15
problems of implementation, 16–18
revenue distribution, 16–17
tariff structure, 13–14
West African Economic Community
membership, 26
projects, 27
West African Monetary Union (Union Monétaire Ouest Africaine), *see* UMOA
Wheat, **ma** 314*t*
imports, **se** 505
Wolofs, **se** 498

World Bank
loans, **da** 153; **iv** 274; **ma** 320–21; **se** 576–77, 606*t*–607
membership and subscription, **da** 143; **iv** 220; **ma** 309; **ni** 401; **se** 496; **to** 603; **up** 689

Yams, **da** 151; **iv** 228; **to** 619–20
Yantala, brickyard, **ni** 429
Yaoundé Convention of Association of African and Malagasy States with the EEC, *see* EEC (European Economic Community): association conventions
Yttrium, **ma** 325–26
Yugoslavia, loans, **to** 665*t*

Ziguinchor
port, **se** 510, 537
tourism project, **se** 536
Ziguinchor area, rice project, **se** 519
Zinder, **ni** 469
airport, **ni** 438
bakery, **ni** 428
branch of Development Bank, **ni** 469
cassiterite, **ni** 425
electric power, **ni** 430
municipality, **ni** 454
population, **ni** 403
road, **ni** 433
tannery, **ni** 428
Zouîrât (Zouérate), **ma** 375